The Psychosocial Development of Minority Group Children

Editor

Gloria Johnson Powell, M.D.

Associate Editors

Joe Yamamoto, M.D.
Annelisa Romero
Armando Morales, D.S.W.

BRUNNER/MAZEL, *Publishers* • New York

Library of Congress Cataloging in Publication Data
Main entry under title:

The Psychosocial development of minority group children.

  Includes bibliographies and index.
  1. Children of minorities—Mental health—United States.
2. Children of minorities—Mental health services—United
States. 3. Child mental health services—United States.
4. Children of minorities—United States. I. Powell,
Gloria J. [DNLM: 1. Minority groups—Psychology.
2. Family characteristics. 3. Child development. WA 305
P974]
RJ507.M54P79 1983   155.4'57   82-22677
ISBN 0-87630-277-0

SECOND PRINTING

Published by
BRUNNER/MAZEL, INC.
19 Union Square West
New York, New York 10003

MANUFACTURED IN THE UNITED STATES OF AMERICA

This book is dedicated to George Tarjan, M.D., past President of the American Academy of Child Psychiatry, one of the Commissioners on the President's Commission on Mental Health, and Director of the Mental Retardation/Child Psychiatry Program at the Neuropsychiatric Institute at the U.C.L.A. Center for the Health Sciences.

More than anyone else in American child psychiatry today, Dr. Tarjan has dedicated his career to providing mental health services to the underserved. In so doing, he has created institutions where there were none, and services for the mentally retarded, the underserved and minority group children who once were the invisible clients in the mental health care and human services delivery system. His quiet, competent wisdom has been admired by all who know him. His compassion for the needy and his deep sense of humanitarianism has been a beacon of light inspiring us all to persist in pursuing the goal of expanding quality mental health services for all America's children.

He has been a knowledgeable teacher, a wise and inspiring mentor, and a caring friend to so many of his younger colleagues. He has been a visionary leader in his field and in this country when there were so few with such a quality. Most truly, in the words of the poet, Longfellow, it can be said of George Tarjan:

"In quietness and confidence
Have been his strength."

Foreword

As a Japanese American, I have long been aware of the severe and persistent problems faced by non-whites in America. For too long, however, the majority of studies on these people have concentrated on Afro-Americans and Hispanics. This focus is understandable and justified, but as a result, the word "minority" has become synonymous with the terms "Black" and "Chicano." Unfortunately, our many other sociocultural groups with similar, if not greater, problems have been neglected.

Majority and minority people alike should avoid the common conceptual mistake of unthinkingly lumping America's non-whites under an "umbrella identity." Very real and profound cultural, historical and linguistic differences separate Afro-Americans, Japanese-Americans, Indian-Americans, Filipino-Americans and other hyphenated nationalities. The unique traits of these people have been labeled as weaknesses or inabilities to cope because of both the paucity of research by investigators who are members of minority groups themselves and questionable interpretations of some prior studies. However, awareness of and appreciation for minority potential can transcend present levels and be recognized and acknowledged as strengths through which American culture can be greatly enhanced.

For these reasons, I welcome the addition of this volume to the ongoing national minority debate. I am especially pleased that the editors and many of the contributors to this work are themselves members of minority groups. While the research herein is just a beginning, I sincerely hope this volume will serve as an incentive for other ethnic group professionals to conduct further research on all aspects of America's subcultures. If attempted, cooperative efforts by both majority and minority group members will hasten or bring to fruition the constructive contribution of our collective skills and abilities to the mainstream of American life.

DANIEL K. INOUYE
UNITED STATES SENATOR FROM HAWAII

Preface

This book had its conception, as it were, several years ago when the senior editor was at the Institute for Child Development at the University of Minnesota. Harold Stevenson, then the Director of the Institute, asked me to give a seminar on the growth and development of minority group children. At the time I was also the Director of Mental Health Services at the University of Minnesota's Children and Youth Project, the Community-University Clinic for Children, dubbed "CUCC" or "CUCK" by the children who attended.

The Clinic's population consisted of 65% American Indian children, 20% Caucasian, and 15% Afro-American, all of whom met the Office of Educational Opportunity criteria for poverty. Having worked with Hispanic children in the Los Angeles Head Start Programs, with Afro-American children throughout the United States, and with African children in Ethiopia and East Africa, I was ready to try the seminar for I believed that "it was an idea whose time had come." I busily began to prepare the course—the reading lists, the course content, the lecture schedule, student presentations of their special projects, and the visits to community agencies such as Head Start Programs, Mother-Child Centers, and, of course, the "CUCK" Clinic. There was a method to my madness, and I was hoping that many of the graduate students from the Institute would become involved in some of the programs at the Clinic which was desperately understaffed in terms of mental health professionals as well as psychological and educational services. The planners of the Clinic had thought about the physical health needs of these children but not about their minds or psyches or the vast numbers of social problems which interfered with their health maintenance, both physically and emotionally. In short, I needed help and I saw a potential source of manpower.

The idea worked. Many of the students from the Institute did become involved in the Clinic as their special project for the course and they told their friends in social welfare, anthropology, and nursing who took the same course I was teaching at the Clinic for the staff and received Inde-

ix

pendent Study Credit.

As for the Institute course, it grew. Whereas, Harold Stevenson and I had at first envisioned a small seminar of twelve Ph.D. candidates, the requests to enroll were in the 40's and 50's. I expanded the seminar to 20 participants and gave a "brown bag lunch seminar" on selected topics and issues on minority group children. There was standing room only.

What became clear to this then young assistant professor, teaching in graduate school for the first time, was that these students in child development and clinical psychology were hungry for knowledge about the psychosocial development of minority group children and that they, as well as the students in the course at the Clinic, were going to be part of the mental health manpower of the future.

During that year at the University of Minnesota, I also gave lectures about minority group children in the Department of Sociology, in the School of Social Welfare, for the Lutheran Social Services who were involved in interracial adoptions, for the Washburn Child Guidance Clinic, and for the staff at many Headstart Programs and public schools.

At the end of the year, I truly understood the need for a basic textbook on the psychosocial development of minority group children and their families. Those involved in providing human services to minority group children needed to know what I had had to learn as I worked in Africa with sick children and their families—cultural nuances, family life patterns and their ways of thinking and believing about the world. It was then that I decided to write a book. But then there were two years in Uganda and Tanzania (1971–1973) setting up child psychiatry clinics, teaching in the medical schools, and helping to set up a network of Maternal-Child Centers throughout Tanzania. And then there was another year trying to help a new Department of Psychiatry at the new Martin Luther King, Jr. Hospital in Watts. And, finally, back to U.C.L.A. as a faculty member to teach, to do research, and to write. There I discovered my co-editors who had had similar experiences and felt as I did that mental health professionals need to understand the psychosocial development of minority group children in order to deliver the kinds of services that would be receptive to their needs and comprehensible within their cultural context, their beliefs and norms, and the social network of their families and communities.

As I look up from my writing, excited that the book is finally ready for press after so many roadblocks and difficulties, I notice that it is January 15th, the birthdate of Martin Luther King, Jr. How prophetic! As a young medical student standing in, sitting in, and riding the freedom buses, I can remember my moment of confrontation with him when I had decided to drop out of medical school for a few years and work full time for the Civil Rights Movement. All our students were in jail in Alabama and Mississippi; there was a press blackout; and we needed more students to keep the Freedom Rides going. I had decided to leave medical school and recruit and train more students. But, Dr. King banged his fist on the table and said emphatically, "You will stay in school, because when all of this is over, we will need your skills for the nation's children." He knew how much I wanted to be a child psychiatrist. I have never ever forgotten those wise words.

So although the idea for this book was conceptualized in 1970, the seeds were planted in Nashville, Tennessee, in 1961. This book, however, is just a beginning, for it will take more than this textbook to meet manpower and program needs for a mental health delivery service system that will expand to include appropriate and culturally suitable services for minority group children.

GLORIA JOHNSON POWELL
Los Angeles

Contents

PART II: *Psychosocial Development*

PART III: *Family Life Patterns*

PART IV: *Mental Health Issues for Minority Group Children*

PART V: *Educational Issues Regarding Minority Group Children*

PART VI: *Research and Social Policy Issues*

Contributors

GEORGE ANDERSON, M.S.W.
Private Practice
Mental Health Consultant
Los Angeles County Department of
  Mental Health
Los Angeles, California

VICTOR BERNAL Y DEL RIO, M.D.
Executive Director
Puerto Rico Institute of Psychiatry
San Juan, Puerto Rico

IRVING H. BERKOVITZ, M.D.
Senior Psychiatric Consultant for
  Schools
Los Angeles County Department of
  Mental Health
Clinical Professor in Psychiatry
University of California , Los Angeles
Los Angeles, California

**EVELYN LANCE BLANCHARD,
  M.S.W.**
Community Development Specialist
Indian Health Service
Portland, Oregon

ANTHONY D. BROWN, Ph.D.
Assistant Director
American Indian Studies Center
University of California, Los Angeles
Los Angeles, California

ELIZABETH CARR, R.N., M.N.
Adjunct Assistant Professor
Department of Education
George Washington University
Washington, D.C.

JANICE H. CARTER, M.D., M.P.H.
Fellow, Child Development/Child Abuse
  Division
Martin Luther King, Jr. County
  Hospital
Los Angeles, California

ROBERT CHIN, Ph.D.
Professor
Department of Psychology
Boston University
Boston, Massachusetts

YVONNE FERGUSON, M.D.
Assistant Professor
Mental Retardation/Child Psychiatry
  Division
Department of Psychiatry
Neuropsychiatric Institute
U.C.L.A. Center for Health Sciences

ROSSLYN GAINES, Ph.D.
Professor
Mental Retardation/Child Psychiatry
  Division
Department of Psychiatry
Neuropsychiatric Institute
U.C.L.A. Center for Health Sciences

KENNETH W. HERNASY, M.A.
Research Assistant
American Indian Study Center
University of California, Los Angeles
Los Angeles, California

RICHARD L. HOUGH, Ph.D.
Chief, Health Services Research
  Affiliation
Veterans Administration, Brentwood
  and
Associate Research Sociologist
Neuropsychiatric Institute
U.C.L.A. Center for Health Sciences

MAMORU IGA, Ph.D.
Professor
Department of Sociology
California State University at
  Northridge
Northridge, California

LUKE I.C. KIM, M.D., Ph.D.
Assistant Clinical Professor
Department of Psychiatry
University of California, Davis
Davis, California

LEWIS M. KING, Ph.D.
Director
Fanon Research and Development
  Center
Charles Drew Postgraduate Medical
  School
Los Angeles, California

MITSURU KUBOTA, Ph.D.
Associate Professor
University Counseling and Guidance
California State University at Los
  Angeles
Los Angeles, California

DANIEL D. LE, D.Th., M.S.W.
Director of Indochinese Mental Health
  Clinic
Assistant Clinical Professor
Department of Psychology
University of Southern California
Los Angeles, California

DANIEL MEJIA, Ph.D.
Assistant Professor
Department of Psychology
Immaculate Heart College
Los Angeles, California

**NANCY BROWN MILLER, M.S.W.,
  Ph.D.**
Assistant Professor
Department of Pediatrics
University of California, Los Angeles
Los Angeles, California

EMELICIA MIZIO, M.S.W.
Account Executive
Management Recruiters
Forest Hills, New York

ARMANDO MORALES, D.S.W.
Professor, Director, Spanish Speaking
  Psychosocial Clinic
  and
Chief of Clinical Social Work Services
Department of Psychiatry
U.C.L.A. Center for Health Sciences

PAUL R. MUNFORD, Ph.D.
Adjunct Associate Professor
Mental Retardation/Child Psychiatry
  Division
Department of Psychiatry
U.C.L.A. Center for Health Sciences

**FAYE UNTALAN MUÑOZ, M.P.H.,
  D.S.W.**
Division of Mental Health and Human
  Services
Western Interstate Commission for
  Higher Education
Boulder, Colorado

HECTOR F. MYERS, Ph.D.
Associate Professor
Department of Psychology
University of California, Los Angeles
Los Angeles, California

DOLORES G. NORTON, Ph.D.
Associate Professor and Associate Dean
School of Social Service Administration
University of Chicago
Chicago, Illinois

ELIGIO R. PADILLA, Ph.D.
Assistant Professor
Department of Psychology
University of New Mexico
Albuquerque, New Mexico

GLORIA JOHNSON POWELL, M.D.
Associate Professor
Mental Retardation/Child Psychiatry
  Division
Department of Psychiatry
U.C.L.A. Center for Health Sciences

RODNEY N. POWELL, M.D., M.P.H.
Professor and Deputy Director
International Medex
School of Medicine
University of Hawaii
Honolulu, Hawaii

JOHN RED HORSE, Ph.D.
Associate Professor
School of Social Work
Arizona State University
Tempe, Arizona

ARMANDO RODRIQUEZ, Ph.D.
Commissioner
Equal Employment Opportunity
  Commission
Washington, D.C.

ENRIQUE RIVERA ROMERO, M.D.
Director
Child Psychiatry Division
Puerto Rico Institute of Psychiatry
San Juan, Puerto Rico

ANNELISA ROMERO
Senior Editor
Neuropsychiatric Institute
U.C.L.A. Center for Health Sciences

ARTURO ROMERO, Ph.D.
Department of Psychology
University of California, Riverside
Riverside, California

ROLANDO A. SANTOS, Ph.D.
Professor
Department of Educational Foundations
California State University at Los
  Angeles
Los Angeles, California

LINDBERGH S. SATA, M.D.
Professor and Chairman
Department Of Psychiatry
D.P. Wohl Memorial Mental Health
  Institute
St. Louis, Missouri

ESTHER SINCLAIR, Ph.D.
Assistant Professor
Mental Retardation/Child Psychiatry
  Division
Department of Psychiatry
U.C.L.A. Center for Health Sciences

FAUSTINA SOLIS, M.S.W.
Division of Health Protection
State of California
Department of Health
Sacramento, California

DAVID SUE, Ph.D.
Associate Professor
Department of Psychology
University of Michigan
Dearborn, Michigan

DERALD W. SUE, Ph.D.
Professor
Department of Educational Psychology
California State University at Hayward
Hayward, California

DIANE M. SUE, Ed.S.
School of Education
University of Michigan
Ann Arbor, Michigan

STANLEY SUE, Ph.D.
Professor
Department of Psychology
University of California, Los Angeles
Los Angeles, California

FRANK J. TRANKINA, Ph.D.
Director
Hispanic Outreach Clinic
Child Psychiatry Outpatient
    Department
Neuropsychiatric Institute
U.C.L.A. Center for Health Sciences

WILLIAM A. VEGA, Ph.D.
Professor
Mexican-American Studies in Public
    Health
San Diego State University
San Diego, California

FRED WISE, Ph.D.
Research Associate
Department of Psychology
Michigan State
East Lansing, Michigan

GAIL E. WYATT, Ph.D.
Associate Professor
Mental Retardation/Child Psychiatry
    Division
Department of Psychiatry
U.C.L.A. Center for Health Sciences

JOE YAMAMOTO, M.D.
Professor and Chief
Adult Ambulatory Care Services
Department of Psychiatry
U.C.L.A. Center for Health Sciences

KEUN H. YU, M.D.
Director of Child and Adolescent
    Psychiatry
Northwestern Community Mental
    Health Center
Baltimore, Maryland

The Psychosocial
Development of
Minority Group
Children

Prologue:

America's Minority Group Children: The Underserved

Gloria Johnson Powell, M.D.

INTRODUCTION

Many of America's children have little or no access to mental health or physical health care except on an episodic emergency or crisis intervention basis. The Report of the Joint Commission on Mental Health of Children in 1970 noted that children of minority groups were at special mental health risk, and frequently received prejudicial treatment by social, educational, health, and mental health institutions. The Commission's Committee on Children of Minority Groups noted that for some minority groups admission rates to state institutions exceeded those for the general population and that large proportions of minority group children were among the 75 to 80% of the retarded population that demonstrated no obvious brain damage or organic defects but many of whom come from impoverished backgrounds.

Again, in 1978 the Task Panel Report on Infants, Children, and Adolescents of the President's Commission on Mental Health noted:

Traditionally, minority and low-income children have not been offered services suitable to their background and needs. It is a well-documented national scandal that whereas mid-

3

dle-class, non-minority children with behavior problems receive appropriate mental health services in voluntary clinical settings, minority children are likely to receive the attention of the police and juvenile courts for the very same behavioral problems (P.C.M.H., Volume III, Appendix, 1978, p. 646).

The frequency of mental health disorders in children will fluctuate depending on age, sex, and social circumstances. Robbins' (1978) review of epidemiology studies revealed that the general prevalence of serious mental health problems among children between 3 to 15 years of age is approximately 5 to 15%. However, it is well known that emotional disorders are more common in boys than in girls, somewhat more frequent in adolescence, and more frequent among inner-city children (Robbins, 1978).

There has been an increase in psychiatric disorders for children under age 18 years. The reasons for such increases are not readily determinable and are probably multicausal. However, what is important about the increase in psychiatric services for children is the significant differences in rate of institutionalization and severity of diagnoses by race (Myers, 1980). Non-white males are institutionalized more than twice as often as white males and non-white females are institutionalized about one and a half times as frequently as white females (NIMH, 1977). The NIMH Report shows that more and more urban children who perform poorly in school are being diagnosed as emotionally disturbed and mentally retarded. Clearly, there is a relationship between academic under-achievement and emotional disorders.

Among the recommendations emanating from the President's Commission on Mental Health (Vol. II, 1978) regarding mental disorders in children, particular reference was made regarding factors influencing psychosocial development. This book is intended to highlight those psychosocial factors which impinge upon the development and mental health of minority group children.

DEFINITION AND DISTRIBUTION OF MINORITY GROUP POPULATIONS

The definition and classification of race and ethnicity have been complicated by the diversity of definitions of the various groups. In the past, the various population-based surveys of the National Center for Health Statistics as well as the Census Bureau relied on interviewer observation to determine race. Respondents were assigned to one of three racial groups—white, black, or other—and often all members of the household were assigned the same racial category as the respondent. There was a great need for a standard classification for collection and presentation of data on race and ethnicity. Consequently, the Office of Management and Budget established standard categories to be used by all federal surveys. Respondents can now classify themselves into one of five racial ethnic groups: American Indian or Native Alaskan, Asian or Pacific Islander, black (not of Hispanic origin), Hispanic, and white (not of Hispanic origin). The U.S. Department of Health, Education and Welfare's Report, *Health United States, 1979*, noted that population size, age, sex structure, socioeconomic composition and other characteristics differentiate minority groups from the white population and these characteristics influence health—both physical health and mental health, as we shall see.

The 1977 Health Interview Survey lists Afro-Americans (not of Hispanic origin) as the largest minority group, with an estimated population of 23 million (USDHEW, 1979). The largest percentage of Afro-Americans live in the South (54%) but 18%, 20%, and 4% of the Afro-American population live in the Northeast, North Central, and Western geographic regions respectively. Within the Standard Metropolitan Statistical Areas (SMSAs), the percentage of Afro-Americans is 76%, with 57% residing in the central city and 19% residing outside the central city. Twenty-four percent reside outside the

SMSAs. Most important, however, 35% of Afro-Americans are under 17 years of age.

While Afro-Americans represent 11% of the population, the Hispanics (excluding Puerto Ricans, but not Puerto Ricans residing on the U.S. mainland) represent 5.6% of the population, totaling an estimated 12 million. The Mexican-Americans (7 million) are the most numerous of the Hispanic population. The Puerto Ricans are second with 1.7 million and the Cubans third with 774,000. All three Hispanic groups are more urbanized than the white population (not of Hispanic origin).

Among the Mexican-Americans, only 1% live in the Northeast and 7% in the North Central areas. The greatest population density of the Mexican-American population is in the South and West, with percent distributions of 36% and 56% respectively. Among the Hispanic population, 79% of the Mexican-American population, 95% of the Puerto Rican population and 98% of the Cuban population reside in metropolitan areas (SMSAs), with 42%, 74%, and 44% respectively living in the central city areas (USDHEW, 1979).

It is important to note, however, that by the most moderate estimates the Hispanic population is the fastest growing population in the United States and will be the largest minority group in less than 25 years. The impact of this population increase will have many ramifications in terms of the allocations of health and mental health resources and manpower. In Los Angeles, 70% of all children in Head Start Programs are Hispanic. Recent Ethnic Surveys of the Los Angeles Unified School District show 44% Hispanic total enrollment, but in grades K through 6 the enrollment is more than 50% (Los Angeles Unified School District, 1978).

As of 1975, American Indians and Alaskan Natives had a population of 827,000, a figure which represents a 51% increase over the 1960 census. This increase cannot be explained by underenumeration or overenumeration or by changes in birth or death rates between the census years. Rather, the explanation probably lies in the shifts in racial identification which have become an important social factor among American Indians (Passel, 1976).

Although American Indians live in every state of the union, they are heavily concentrated in the states of Oklahoma, Arizona, California, New Mexico, and North Carolina. Since 1975, there has been a major shift of the American Indian population to California. In fact, within the past 10 years the American Indian population in California has tripled (USDHEW, 1979). American Indians, like other minority groups, are becoming urban dwellers, with Los Angeles, San Francisco, Oklahoma City, Tulsa, Phoenix, Minneapolis, Chicago, Seattle, Buffalo, New York City and Dallas having the largest concentrations.

There are an estimated 3 million people of Asian or Pacific Island origin, most of whom live in the West and highly urbanized areas. This ethnic and racial minority group represents a population diverse in cultural norms, historic origins, and social and economic status. Previous government surveys have subsumed the diverse group of people now classified under Pacific/Asian as "other" and it has been difficult to collect consistent data because of this factor. Some surveys have included data only on Japanese or Chinese, but not in a consistent fashion. Since 1969, the public-use mortality tapes have contained the following racial identifications: white, black, American Indian, Chinese, Japanese, Filipino, Hawaiian, other Asian or Pacific Islander, and other races. The vital statistics from Hawaii are somewhat more specific in designating the various groups within the Pacific/Asian ethnic group and list, in addition to the specific groups above, Korean, Samoan, and Vietnamese (Hawaii State Department of Health, 1979). The Subpanel on Mental Health of Pacific/Asian Americans of the President's Commission on Mental Health indicated that there are some change processes within the Pacific/Asian American group:

This nearly chaotic change process is being stimulated by the immigration from several Asian and Pacific countries, the arrival of Indo-Chinese "refugees" and a variety of other factors and forces at local, state, and national levels (P.C.M.H., Vol. III, 1978, p. 739).

These changes will be alluded to in the chapters on Pacific/Asians. In respect to Pacific/Asian children, 32% are under 17 years of age. Indeed, it should be noted that the percentages of children under 17 years of age is greater for each minority group than the 27% figure for whites (Afro-Americans 35%; Hispanic, 41%).

The President's Commission on Mental Health paid special attention to special populations, which included minorities, women, and the physically handicapped. The task panel focused especially on eight groups, of which four were the Pacific/Asian Americans, the Afro-Americans, the Hispanic Americans, and American Indians and Alaskan Natives. This is not to deny the urgency for services and the needs of the other four groups—American women, Americans of European ethnic origin, the hearing impaired, and the handicapped, but it is important to note that the ethnic minority groups are special populations at risk because of their non-white status.

The special populations are American who are characterized (1) by uniqueness and diversity in terms of race, ethnic origin, sex and physical status and (2) by de facto second class status in American society.

. . . . The special populations are those groups who are both overrepresented in the statistics on mental health, and on the basis of the studies prepared by subpanels, are already underserved or inappropriately served by the current mental health system in this country (P.C.M.H., Vol. III, 1978, p. 731).

The Task Panel on Infants, Children and Adolescents of the P.C.M.H. has noted that "children have been seriously underserved" and recommends "categorical

funding for a full range of mental health services to children and adolescents" (P.C.M.H., Vol. III, 1978, p. 612). The Subpanels on Asian/Pacific Americans, Afro-Americans, Hispanic Americans, and American Indians and Alaskan Natives have all emphasized the lack of appropriate mental health services. Minority group children, then, are the most invisible to the mental health delivery system and the most underserved—which is the reason this book is needed and being written.

THE NATURE AND SCOPE OF THE BOOK

This book is not complete, and it is just a beginning—a beginning process in the education of mental health professionals about the mental health needs of minority group children. It is hoped that a textbook devoted to the psychosocial development of minority group children will make apparent the gaps in knowledge and research and encourage others to fill in the missing pieces. It is hoped that this first textbook in child psychiatry devoted to the social and emotional needs of minority group children will serve as an impetus to require all training programs in child psychiatry, social work, and psychology to include this area as one of the requirements in their curriculum. There will never be enough minority group mental health professionals to meet the mental health needs of the growing numbers of minority group children in need of services. White mental health professional are needed to fill the manpower shortage in this area. This is not to deny the fact that many white mental health professionals have provided dedicated services to minority group children or to impugn the efforts and attempts of many national, state, and local organizations which have tried to provide such services. We hope this book will add impetus to their noble efforts.

The authors of the various chapters are

mostly minority group professionals. The editors felt that it was particularly important that the cultural perspective be maintained. All too often, others have spoken for us or about us, sometimes with clarity and understanding and sensitivity to the cultural nuances and norms. However, ofttimes because of ethnocentric attitudes, myths and stereotypes have been perpetuated. The authors come from various ethnic and racial groups as well as from a wide range of disciplines and experiences. What is common to all the contributors is that they have all worked on the front lines. They have all been part of the cutting edge of change in providing human services to minority group families and children. In short, they can really "tell it like it is."

Although, in many respects, it would have been more convenient to divide the book into four sections, each representing one of the four minority groups, it was decided, instead, to integrate the various minority groups into a conceptual framework which illustrates some of the commonalities inherent in each group. This process is not to deny the uniqueness and cultural diversity of each group but to help the reader integrate the mass of data into a framework that would help summarize the essential data. Secondly, the book is organized conceptually in a way that will assist mental health professionals to think about the problems and needs of children in a comprehensive way. It is a method of collecting data and information in order to get a comprehensive picture of the child, his family, his community, his culture, and his interaction with social institutions which impinge upon his life in various ways.

HEALTH AND NUTRITION

In Silver's (1978) book on *Child Health: America's Future*, he forthrightly states that "the future of social policy is embedded in child health."

Since the health of children is the eventual health of adults, and the health of children is therefore the health of the nation, why aren't we more concerned about it? Why aren't we doing more? (p. 3)

Silver notes, as have others (Harvard Child Health Project Task Force, 1977), that poverty and minority group status impose a special disadvantage. Nutritional deficiency is three times more common among minority group children and infant mortality is twice as high among minority group children as among white children in general. Minority group children receive fewer medical services. These facts will be documented in the chapters on the health status of Afro-Americans, Hispanic, and American Indian children. Although there are problems similar to all three groups, there are some unique differences that should be noted in reading the three chapters.

The omission of a chapter on the health status of Pacific/Asian children is not to deny that problems exist, although they have been considered "the model minorities." Indeed, the Statistical Report of the Department of Health of Hawaii (1979) details some of the health problems there exist among Pacific/Asian children that are similar to health problems of minority group children on the mainland. There is no special report on Alaska or Puerto Rico, but the data are implied from the chapters by Rivera Romero and Bernal y del Rio on the mental health of Puerto Rican children.

A child who is in poor health status is at greater risk for psychosocial problems. Hence the book would be incomplete without considerable attention paid to the health status of minority group children.

PSYCHOSOCIAL DEVELOPMENT

Not every section contains a chapter on every racial and/or ethnic group. This section is fairly comprehensive, however, in that there are chapters on Afro-American children, Mexican-American children, American Indian and Alasken Native children, Filipino-American children, Korean-American children, Chinese-American children and Japanese-American children. The style of each of the chapters differs purposely to allow the uniqueness, cultural diversity, and special issues for each group to emerge. The reader will note similarities and differences in psychosocial development among each of the minority groups of children.

FAMILY LIFE PATTERNS

In order to understand a child, one needs to understand his or her family. This section is crucial to an understanding of the growth and development, mental health needs, and interactions with the education system of minority group children. The editors are especially pleased that this volume includes chapters on the the family life patterns of Pacific Island families and American Indian families since so little has been written about these groups, especially by indigenous mental health professionals. So often, the uninitiated mental health practitioners presume that all minority group families are the same, or else they hold stereotypic views of family life patterns of various minority groups. Such ignorance and insensitivity are among the many deterrents to access to care for minority group children and their families.

MENTAL HEALTH NEEDS
AND PROBLEMS

This section of the text is, of course, the core of the volume. Although not inclusive of all the Pacific/Asian groups, it presents chapters on Japanese-American children, American-Indian children, Afro-American and Vietnamese children. For those Pacific/Asian groups that have not been included—e.g. Koreans, Filipinos, Pacific Islanders—the reader is referred to the chapters on the psychosocial development and family life patterns of those groups.

The chapter on the mental health needs and problems of Hispanic children covers Mexican-American, Puerto Rican, Cuban and other Hispanic children. We feel fortunate, indeed, to have a chapter about mental health services in Puerto Rico, for this is useful in comparing what has been done on the U.S. mainland with what needs to be done not only in Puerto Rico but in Hawaii and Alaska.

THE IMPACT OF SCHOOLS

More than 65% of all the children in EMR classrooms in the United States are minority group children (Jones, 1973). Are such failures due to the children or the schools? Satz (1977) without equivocation states that "the present educational policies and practices operate with negative conquences for the mental health of more than eight million children" (quoted in P.C.M.H., Vol. III, 1978, p. 672). Others maintain that more than 90% of the learning problems are teaching problems (Durrell, 1964). Likewise, Bloom (1976) is convinced of the similarity in learning ability as well as rate of learning and motivation for all students when there are favorable learning conditions. The school failure among minority group children is iatrogenic due to schools that provide unfavorable learning environments, especially for minority group children. The consequences can be measured in terms of maladaptive emotional and social development, low self-esteem, and diminished educational and occupational attainment.

One of the major issues facing schools today is school desegregation. Two chapters have been devoted to this issue, one in terms of the consequences for Afro-American children and the other in terms of the role of the mental health consultant. Although the chapter on the implications and consequences of school desegregation focuses on Afro-American children, the omission of the other minority group children is not meant to imply that there are no consequences for these children also. Sinclair and Mejia in their chapters allude to the effects of school desegregation on Hispanic children and two of the chapters on American Indian children refer to the effects of school on these children.

IQ testing and academic achievement tests have been a focus of controversy for some time, as has bilingualism and "Black English" or Ebonics. These three issues are reviewed in this section.

The section is further broadened by Dr. Gaines' chapter reviewing 21 federal preschool programs.

This section on schools would be incomplete without Dr. Rodriquez's chapter on "Educational Policy and Cultural Plurality" which presents and examines educational philosophy vis-à-vis the minority group child.

RESEARCH AND SOCIAL ISSUES

The concluding section includes a comprehensive chapter on the juvenile justice system and its effects on minority group children. It will provide many insights to the reader who is unfamiliar with the problems and inconsistencies within the system.

Mr. Romero's chapter presents a model of how mental health research should be done on Mexican-American children but the principles he elucidates are pertinent to research on other minority group children as well.

And, finally, the Epilogue deals with the second major problem (after racism) faced by American minority group children—poverty. Its debilitating physical, psychosocial, and spiritual effects will be elaborated. The data presented clearly indicate what Walter Mondale so passionately stated on December 9, 1970:

For we are failing our children. . . . The most obvious victims of course are the 10 million children living in poverty and the untold millions maimed by racism (quoted by George Silver in *Child Health: America's Future*, 1978, p. ix).

REFERENCES

Bloom, S. *Human Characteristics and School Learning*. New York: McGraw Hill, 1976.

Durrell, D. Learning factors in beginning to read. In: W.G. Cutts (Ed.), *Teaching Young Children to Read*. Washington D.C.: U.S. Government Printing Office, 1964.

Harvard Child Health Project Task Force (H.C.H.P.T.F.). *Developing a Better Health Care System for Children, Vol III*. Cambridge, MA: Ballinger, 1977.

Hawaii State, Department of Health, Statistical Report, 1979.

Joint Commission on Mental Health of Children (J.C.M.H.C.) *Crisis in Child Mental Health: Challenge for the 1970's*. New York: Harper and Row, 1970.

Jones, R. Racism and mental health in the schools. In: C.V. Willie, B. Kramer & B. Brown (Eds.), *Racism and Mental Health*. Pittsburgh: University of Pittsburgh Press, 1973.

Los Angeles Unified School District, Los Angeles City Board of Education. *Integrated Educational Excellence Through Choice: Response to Court Order of February 7, 1978*. Submitted to the Los Angeles Superior Court, March 12, 1979.

Meyers, H.F. & King, L.M. Youth of the Black underclass: Urban stress and mental health. *Fanon Center Journal*, May 1980, *1* (1), 1–29.

National Institute of Mental Health. *Psychiatric Services and the Changing Institutional Scene, 1950–1985*. DHEW Publication No. (ADM) 717–433, Series B, 12, 27, 1977.

Passel, J.S. Provisional evaluation of the 1970 Census count of American Indians. *Demography* 1976, *13*, 397–409.

President's Commission on Mental Health (P.C.M.H.). *Mental Health in America: 1978. Volumes I, II & III*. Stock No. 040–000–00390. Washington, D.C.: U.S. Government Printing Office, 1978.

Robbins, L.N. Mental disorders in childhood. Working Paper prepared for the President's Commission on Mental Health, February 1978.

Satz, P. Specific learning disabilities: A brief state of the art. Monograph prepared for the Working Group on Learning Failure and Unused Learning Potential, 1977.

Silver, G.A. *Child Health: America's Future*. Germantown, MD: Aspen Systems Corporation, 1978.

U.S. Department of Health, Education and Welfare; Office of Health Research, Statistics, and Technology. *Health United States: 1979*. DHEW Publication No. (PHS) 80–1232, Washington, D.C.: U.S. Government Printing Office, 1979.

PART I

The Health Status of Minority Group Children

CHAPTER 1

Vision or Sight: Health Concerns for Afro-American Children

Janice H. Carter, M.D., M.P.H.

If you close your eyes, you will see me. Your hands may know me, for myself.
—Carter, 1980

In the Year of the Child, 1979, children were seen in varied and startling views, like butterflies flexing in the spring sunlight. The media enlarged the voice and visual imagery surrounding the child, simultaneously making visible the needs and promises unrealized for this immature majority. Repeated unveilings bared complex issues—immunizations, disease, mortality, morbidity, disabilities, racism, abuse. They made strange bedfellows of the healer and the adjudicator. Within this disturbing climate, the child—once a minority in economic and political forecasting—grew to new regard as a barometer for social change. In the Year of the Child, children were reclassified as a majority whose needs could not be ironed away. This wrinkle poses significant challenges for all involved in fulfilling the international declarations of children's rights.

As is true for all children, the Afro-American child is subsumed within a myriad of fascinating categories and fits imperfectly into many. Historically conceptualized as miniature adults, children today are seen as fledglings subject to rapidly changing theories and projections. Numerous imputations fall to the child—ethnocentric, sexual, social, psycho-medical—but rarely is the child seen beneath these indicators. It is of increasing importance to see the child aside from color and to attend to the ethnic correlates of pathology. As a modern concept of the child emerges, this reciprocal vision will increase the odds for a comprehensive psychosocial development of which medical care is a part.

The role of caretakers is part of the medical care parcel. This function increases in importance as large numbers of minority children enter the ambit of health care. Stereotypically, parents and pediatricians shared the concern of child welfare. This burden now falls onto a larger pair of shoulders. Today the role of therapist is expanding to include the function of liaison and case coordinator. Ideally, the psychotherapist stands in both the position of interpreter and arbitrator of comprehensive health care. We can bridge the gap between health and ignorance by facilitating trust and knowledgeable compliance between caretakers and child.

The archetype of healer has always included an educational aspect. Today, this aspect of the healer is assuming a greater significance. Early suspicions and questioning can turn a supposition of obvious behavioral problems into a discovery of iron deficiency anemia, plumbism (lead poisoning), hearing defects, or learning disability. Conversely, the spindly adolescent with sickle cell disease may be masking suicidal ideation with a surprisingly avid attention to oral contraception. The full assumption of a healing role by a psychotherapist can allow an Afro-American child to become visible in an often overburdened and overwhelming medical system. A deliberate investigation into the health needs of our darker children will bring these needs to the fore and will represent a commitment to medicine and the rights of all children.

HEALTH INDICES

And the Scoundrel whose nickel won him a Vicious Beast and Little Ten from the Nickelodeon remarked, "They have sight but they cannot see. The blind man sees more without eyes."

—Carter, 1980

Exploration of the health problems of America's offspring reveals disquieting data for the investigating sociologist. Recent decades bear witness to remarkable gains in access to medical services, but America's children have not shared fully in these gains. Statistics support the discontent aimed at a health care system that is unresponsive to, and perhaps uncaring about people's needs. The discrepancy between concern for the health care of all children and its provision is disturbing.

Data which characterize childhood mortality, morbidity, and disability are compiled nationally. The figures presented represent an aggregate of divergent regions, life styles, socioeconomic status and variable access to health care services. The amalgamated data are not indicative of individual segments, racial minorities, or age group pathology. Fitting data into existing definitions of morbidity may obscure new morbidities, and soften the impact of events outside the accepted medical model. Despite this softening limitation, the national rates for child health problems are arresting. In 1979, 10 million American children—one out of seven—were without regular medical care; 20 million children below 17 years of age—one out of three—had never seen a dentist; 13% of all in-school 17-year-olds were functionally illiterate; 5.3 million adolescents were diagnosed as problem drinkers; in the 30 years since 1950, the adolescent suicide rate more than tripled (Young, 1980). Given America's affluence, this list of ills is not in keeping with expressions of concern for the well-being of our children. The prospects for Afro-American children are significantly poorer.

Despite a younger and more fertile population, Afro-Americans experience a death rate almost twice that reported for their white counterparts. In 1976, neonatal morbidities placed black infants at a 92% higher rate of risk for demise in the first year of life. In the first seven days, black infants succumbed 87% more frequently than white infants (U.S. Health, 1978). The infant mortality rate for blacks in 1979 was 21.5 deaths per 1,000 live births, versus 14.4 recorded for white infants (Bureau of the Census, Population Estimates and Projections, 1980). Had the mortality differential been eliminated in 1976, of the 13,120 black infant deaths, 6,280 would not have occurred (U.S. Health, 1978). Differences in mortality at birth, and in the ensuing first year of life, combine with a fourfold higher maternal mortality rate to curtail black survival.

Perhaps even more devastating is the realization that mortality rates for black infants lag 10 to 15 years behind white infant survival. (Moreover, morbidity and disabilities also reflect a pattern delay of similar magnitude.) However, it is not beyond the capacity of health services to dramatically reduce infant losses. Evidence from Bronfenbrenner's 1976 survey of several federally funded five-year, maternal and infant care programs revealed the possibility of such a reduction (Bronfenbrenner, 1976). Denver lowered the target area mortality from 34.2 to 21.5; corresponding decreases were quoted for Birmingham (from 25.4 to 14.3) and duplicated in Omaha, with a reduction from 33.4 to 13.4 deaths per 1,000 live births (Bronfenbrenner, 1976). Sadly, the 1979 Bureau of the Census Report revealed that nonwhites, 85% of whom were black, continued to show a disproportionately high mortality rate (Bureau of the Census, 1979).

The association between adequate, early prenatal care and the prevention of infant mortality is well documented. Other correlations also exist; premature and low-birth-weight infants—babies born at or below 2,500 grams—suffer a substantially higher rate of hypoglycemia, pulmonary hemorrhage, fetal infection, and handicapping conditions (Schaffer and Avery, 1977). Prematurity, often associated with low birth weight, has been long recognized as a factor in increased infant morbidity—convulsive disorders, spastic diplegia, mental retardation, and higher risks of deafness and blindness. In 1976, one out of five deliveries (570,000) were by mothers below 20 years of age, and two of every five babies were delivered to unwed adolescents (U.S. Health, 1978). The mothers facing the greatest risk of infant deliveries of low-birth-weight babies—black adolescent mothers—were least likely to have received care; 14% received no prenatal care in the first two trimesters. During this same year (1976), the proportion of low-birth-weight infants born to black adolescent mothers was 15%, twice the reported national proportion of 7%.

Medical care can be a crucial factor in child survival. The critical issue is access to and allocation of prenatal and intensive neonatal special care resources. Given prompt attention, low-birth-weight infants can survive the crucial first seven days with only half the mortality rate of unattended low-birth-weight infants. Kleinman et al. (in press) report that this reduction in early neonatal mortality is significant. Early medical intervention not only postpones neonatal death but also results in a reduction of overall neonatal mortality (U.S. Health, 1978). Still, 46% of black women have had no early prenatal care, and as of 1976, a black baby remained five times more likely to be born outside a hospital and unattended by a physician.

Children are notoriously hardy once they survive infancy. This natural propensity to recuperation, with and without professional intervention, tends to obscure the actual rate of childhood illnesses. Before the boon of antibiotic therapies, infectious and parasitic diseases were the major barriers to childhood survival. Accidents, homicide, and poisonings now outdistance infection as the leading killers of children (Williams, 1975). By 1974, accidents represented 40% of all deaths in preschoolers, and homicide ranked fifth. Suicide and homicide ranked among the top five causes of death in school-aged children (Harvard Child Health Project Task Force, 1977). Despite this turn of events, nonwhite children suffered higher death rates and succumbed to illnesses which in 1974 no longer ranked as concerns for their white schoolmates.

In 1976, black children were more likely than white children to die from accidents, poisonings, and violence—5.4 and 2.9 deaths per 10,000 preschool children respectively; 2.4 and 1.4, respectively, for elementary school children (U.S. Health,

1978). At each age, boys outdistance girls in rates of accidents, violence, and other causes of death.

Immunization provides a further buffer against childhood mortality and morbidity. Despite the unequivocal evidence that polio immunization is effective, nearly 5 million American children—one third between ages one and four years—were not fully immunized against polio in 1974. By 1976, 34% of children one to four years of age were not protected against measles, almost 4% had not received a single DPT immunization, and nearly 10% had not received a dose of polio vaccine (U.S. Health, 1978). Less than half of younger children were immunized against mumps. As expected from previous records of health care, 30.5% of nonwhites under one year of age had had no doses of DPT and 42.7% had not received polio vaccine—a rate unchanged since 1975.

NUTRITION AND THE ENVIRONMENT

Winnie the Pooh could have easily explained the difference between himself and Piglet. Obviously Winnie had the size of a bear, whereas Piglet though small had much the larger brain. Piglet would never have admitted it, but secretly he felt that Pooh had the advantage. "After all, Pooh has the love of a boy!"
—Carter, 1980

The Afro-American child stands roughly in the same circumstance as Piglet. Compared to his white playmate, the black child has fared poorly because of his lack of affection from the powerful providers of health services. Several ethnic differences prevail, which concerned caretakers should take note of when evaluating the health resources and status of the black child.

Nutritional assessment of the black child is stymied by dimensional, hematological, and biochemical differences, apart from disparities in socioeconomic status. Although nutritional surveys conducted outside the United States have suc-

cessfully employed North American standards, recalibration of the investigated norms may be needed in evaluating the status of black children (Garn and Clark, 1976).

Dimensional proportions typically reflect nutritional status during periods of growth. Historically, black fetuses demonstrate greater weight gains in the first two trimesters of pregnancy than comparable gestational-aged white fetuses (Bergner and Susser, 1970). Unfortunately, the third trimester—typically a period of maximal weight augmentation for white fetuses—accounts for such significant decrement in poundage as to lose the gains made by the black fetus in the first six months. When socioeconomic status and length of gestation are well accounted for, black neonates remain diminutive. Reversal of this state occurs within the next year of life. This trend continues from the second to the fourteenth year and results in black boys and girls attaining their adult stature earlier than their white peers. Extrapolation of growth potential from sparsely collected growth points, however, misinterprets this growth differential and results in an overcalculation of adult proportions. The risk inherent in these stature assessments is well stated by Garn and Clark (1976):

If the white norms are alone employed, then the proportion of black neonates adjudged small for term will be unduly large. But from the second year on, if white standards are exclusively used, then some proportion of black children actually at nutritional risk will be improperly judged satisfactory or normal, to their long-term disadvantage.

Reports of developmental precocity in black neonates have been bandied about and often reproduced since 1940. It is now accepted that this advanced development is not transient but continues into adolescence. Individual differences in rate of milestone acquisition cross racial lines, yet motor precocity remains a feature germane to adequate counseling, and anticipatory guidance, for those involved in the care of black neonates and adolescents. Misrepresentation of this neurologic advantage creates undue stress, stigmatizes families, and can place at risk otherwise normal infants.

Black children remain advanced with regard to skeletal maturation. The black child evidences earlier postnatal ossification centers in the hand and consistently advanced dental eruptions, even with controls for socioeconomic level and per capita income (Garn et al., 1972). Radiogrammetric measures of skeletal mass, obtained from hand radiographs of 26,000 children enrolled in the Ten State Nutrition and Pre-School Nutrition Surveys, confirm higher bone density, larger mineral mass, and greater skeletal mass in individuals of largely African ancestry (Garn, 1972). This mass relationship is apparent from the fetal period onward. Significant attention to this finding is well directed; dimunition of bony mineral mass is one of the clinical manifestations of protein-calorie malnutrition, osteodystrophies of renal origin, lactose deficiencies, hemoglobinopathies and other bone loss situations. In all reported instances of osteomalacia, black patients assessed by white standards demonstrate greater bone persistence. Thus, the black patient who is at risk for osteomalacia, and its complications of bony trauma, is prone to hidden morbidities and inadequate treatment. Restated more dramatically, comparisons of our black offspring with age-matched white peers can obfuscate essential malnutrition and morbidities to their long-term detriment.

Environmental factors bear heavily upon all members of a community. The reality of this statement resounds when analysis of certain urban centers is displayed in correlation to human responses. The air above Los Angeles Basin supports pollution averages comparable to ambient carbon monoxide levels produced by smoking one pack of cigarettes daily (Stewart et al.,1973). Carboxyhemoglobin levels of

6%-10% obtained from women who smoke one pack of cigarettes per day are thought to be a primary causal component in the observed weight reduction of infants born to these women (Longo, 1976; Younoszai et al., 1968). Studies in 1972 correlated cigarette smoking with weight decrements of 100 to 300 grams in offspring (Rush and Kass, 1972). Stewart et al. (1973) recorded ambient carbon monoxide levels of 300 parts per million as a frequent occurrence in Los Angeles, whereas other investigators have demonstrated impaired reproductive success in experimental animals under simulated levels of ambient Los Angeles Basin carbon monoxide, nitrous oxide, and ozone content (Hueter et al., 1966; Lewis et al., 1967). Concern for low-birth-weight infants born to mothers living in highly polluted urban environments has now become more than a minor suspicion in the life cycle of poor minorities and adjacent population segments (Williams et al., 1977). While the poor urban black may bear the brunt of environmental harassment, all groups are exposed to such pollution.

Plumbism is another uniquely man-made hazard with environmental consequences for all children, with a preponderance of affected black children. Affecting over 400,000 American children under the age of six years, it still accounts for some 150 to 200 childhood deaths per year (Harvard Child Health Project Task Force, 1977). The incidence of mortality has steadily decreased in the past 27 years, but a recent review of cases seen in 1955–56 and 1975–76 reported 1.6% mortality of affected children in the 20 years between reviews (Cohen, 1980). Usually, this loss occurred within one day of hospital admission, and brain lead levels measured 0.16 to 0.26 mg per hundred grams—two to four times normal.

Lead is a highly toxic substance without known function in normal human physiology. Its demonstrated deleterious effects on renal function, central nervous system metabolism, and hemoglobin synthesis result in chronic debilitating sequelae—severe life-threatening encephalopathy, anemia, renal failure, seizures, cerebral palsy, psychosocial behavioral deficits, mental retardation, and long-term disabilities. Authorities have revised levels of lead serum defined as poisonous downward from 40 µg/dl to 30/µg/dl, and greater when associated with erythrocyte protoporphyrin levels of 110 µg/dl or higher. It is still likely that existing lead in our environment—whether in air, water, dust, peeling paint or on surfaces or utensils —will remain hazardous to our children. The child playing out-of-doors is also at risk from lead in auto exhaust, which is inhaled or swallowed from the air and/or licked from the surfaces of dirty toys. Thus, at this late date:

We know now that children cannot be considered out of danger merely because they do not live in old, dilapidated housing in so-called lead-belts of inner cities (Cohen, 1980).

The lead belt affects all children, especially Afro-American, unlucky in the choice of residential setting.

Anemias

Hemoglobin and hematocrit indices have long been useful guides to health assessment. Standards of normal red blood cell volume are crucial to determinations of anemia and estimates of recovery from states of malnutrition. In true form, the black child again demonstrates a difference in cellular volume, which calls for support of population-specific norms. The Ten State Nutrition and Pre-School Nutrition Surveys referred to above, together with data obtained from Kaiser Permanente, National Health Examinations, and a variety of other regional surveys, concur that a general difference of 1.0 grams/100 ml in hemoglobin concentration and 3% lower values in hematocrit exist in all ages through the seventh decade (Garn et al., 1975). Explanations for

this difference based upon income, socioeconomic data, or pregnancy status during the first two trimesters of pregnancy are not borne out. Even infants receiving feeding supplementation for the first 18 months demonstrate similar lowered blood indices. Whether this difference represents nutritional effects or genetic coding remains a question for further research.

Iron deficiency anemia

The true prevalence of iron deficiency anemia within the entire child population is not known. However, large scale surveys indicate that 14% of all children are anemic and a majority of them have hematocrits indicative of iron deficiency (Harvard Child Health Project, 1977). Herbert (1980) quoted a study which concluded that, in the United States, iron deficiency anemia resulting from inadequate iron intake accounted for anemia in 25% of infants, up to 6% of children, 15% of menstruating females, and 30% of pregnant women. Within the past decade, the U.S. Survey reports iron deficiency anemias among 3–24% of infants aged 6 to 24 months (Smith and Rios, 1974). Of this age group, 29–68% suffer effects of iron deficiency without the later manifestations of anemia (Oski and Stockman, 1980). The greatest incidence of iron deficiency without overt anemia is in children of the lower socioeconomic groups, among which Afro-Americans predominate.

Socioeconomic class is inversely correlated with incidence of iron deficiency anemia. A 20% incidence of anemia was noted in children from lower income families in Owen et al.'s study of 5,000 randomly selected preschoolers (Owen et al., 1974). Danneker reproduced this income denominator in his Pennsylvania survey of children aged 3 months to 6 years living in Allegheny County (Harvard Child Health Project, 1977). Black families reviewed had a 19% incidence of anemia, compared to 41.2% in black families receiving public assistance. Reorganization of Danneker's data, according to a crude social class index based on the father's occupation and degree of education, expressed this social disparity as between the two lowest social ranks: 23.8% of the lowest class black children had low hemoglobins compared to 7.5% of age peers in the next lowest class (Harvard Child Health Project, 1977).

The incidence of iron deficiency anemia is biphasic. An initial peak occurs in children six months to two years of age. The second rise is generated in early adolescence by increased metabolic requirements and poor nutritional practices during the growth spurt that deplete existing iron stores. Childhood anemia is felt to result from negative or low iron stores at birth that are further compromised by consumption of low-absorbable iron from cow's milk, and the gastrointestinal irritation and blood loss caused by this foreign animal protein (Wilson and Lahey, 1971).

Low iron stores have been correlated with increased illnesses, feeding difficulties, fatigue, listlessness, anorexia, impaired weight gain, decreased attentiveness, impaired cardiorespiratory function, and impaired muscular activity during exercise (Werkman et al., 1964; Webb and Oski, 1974). Scores of iron deficient adolescents record impaired performance on intellectual tests, and decrements in latency and associative reaction time. Webb and Oski (1974) reported complaints of irritability, restlessness, and impaired attentiveness leveled against iron-deficient adolescents in the academic milieu. Symptoms of shortness of breath, palpitations, dizziness, and poor psychological function mimic cardiovascular and psychiatric disorders, and must be distinguished from anemia-related illnesses. These disturbances result from deficiencies felt by systems dependent upon iron and ferrous ions normally incorporated into or used as cofactors to facilitate the tricarboxylic acid cycle, the respiratory chain, and other mitochondrial enzyme systems.

Behavioral aberrations in iron-deficient infants remit within several days of iron replacement therapy—well before there are significant or measurable levels of increased hemoglobin. Thus, while controversy continues regarding association of iron therapy with reported increased susceptibility to infection, studies are insufficient to preclude use of iron where needed (Oski and Stockman, 1980). Certainly, reports of increased disruptive, irritable, and restless behaviors in adolescents and infants warrant concern for subsequent risks of misdiagnosis and/or inappropriate retributions for these symptomatic behaviors.

Sickle cell disease

Anemias are physiologic handicaps. Reduction in red blood cell volume, survival, or metabolism cripples successful respiratory transport, cellular nutrition, and host immune defenses. Simultaneously, anemias of chronic duration stress the cardiac reserves and result in reduced circulatory capacity. The anemias of sickle cell disease demonstrate the human capacity for compensation when confronted with chronic, immutable anemia.

Inherited, debilitating, and incurable, the anemias of sickle cell disease cause morbidity and mortality characterized by sporadic and unexpected major medical complications. Despite diagnostic advances in the field of molecular genetics, human services are limited for children born with sickle cell disease. Patient ignorance and medical disinterest retard the appropriate rendering of services. Misdiagnosis, inappropriate and painful therapies, premature deaths, and unwarranted psychosocial disturbances accompany this apathetic attitude. Lack of medical assertiveness wastes human resources that could be used to help the black American child affected by this disorder (Whitten et al., 1974). Efforts to expand clinical interests and generate more compassionate, effective treatments may not alter the genetic endpoint for the black child with sickle cell disease, but such efforts can positively enhance the affective life experience of the black child as pulmonary advances have shaped the struggle of white peers with cystic fibrosis.

Sickle cell disease covers a range of clinically significant hemoglobinopathies. Sickle cell anemia (homozygous SS hemoglobin disease), sickle cell C hemoglobin disease, and sickle cell thalassemia are among the best known of these anemias. In the United States screening for sickle cell disease has detected an incidence of sickle cell trait in American blacks of one in 12 and sickle cell disease of one in 600 (Pudd, 1977). Primarily a black-related anemia in America, this gene is not restricted to those of African descent. Widespread international incidence is reported in areas where malaria is endemic—Sicily, Greece, Turkey, southern Arab states, and southern India (Williams, 1975). Associations between malaria and sickle gene frequencies have generated the teleologic rationale that sickle cell heterozygotes derive a selective advantage over the ravaging complications of malaria. Similar arguments have been proposed regarding the increased fertility of whites with cystic fibrosis trait. Increased cognizance of the multi-racial frequency of sickle cell disease is a critical issue in non-stigmatizing discussions of genetic screening, counseling, and appropriate therapies.

Pathophysiologic consequences of sickle cell disease stem from cellular injuries—by-products of repetitive vascular occlusive events and chronic hemolytic anemia. The sickled erythrocyte is fragile, inflexible, and prematurely destroyed. Its death throes create circulatory impairments that lead to tissue hypoxia, increased anemia, organ infarction, and a cascade of intravascular sickling in susceptible erythrocytes. Pain is widespread and migratory. Temporary blood stasis, pooling, and/or dramatic shifts in blood flow impede normal cellular function and critically wound sensitive areas via rapid reduction in oxygen pressure and respiration. Suffocating tissues crumble and leak caustic enzymes and tissue substances. Usually, consequences of vascular occlusion are mild, but repeated episodes create a marked alteration in psychosocial behavior and progressive organ damage. A combination of acute and massive tissue destruction in the lung, brain, retina, spleen, kidney, and femoral head eventually results in permanent, progressive loss of function (Vichinsky and Lubin, 1980).

Anemias secondary to sickle cell disease are chronic, partially compensated for by overproduction of blood components. The ongoing demand for increased red cell production is a direct response to chronic intravascular cellular deformation and hemolysis. Episodes of red cell destruction, traditionally referred to as "crises," are repeated. Three forms of anemic crises are most commonly encountered: sequestration crises, aplastic crises, and the most frequently seen variety, painful or vaso-occlusive crises. Hyperhemolytic crisis is also noted, but is generally restricted to sickle cell disease homozygotes with glucose 6-phosphate dehydrogenase (G-6-P-D) deficiency exposed to oxidant drugs. Cognizance of these crises variants and their manifestations can prevent rapid life-threatening reduction in circulating hemoglobin and death.

Splenic sequestration crisis may occur in a child under five years whose splenic tissue has not yet been hardened and shrunk by repeated infarctions. Typically, the child presents during a viral infection, appearing weak, pale and acutely discomforted by a rapidly enlarging abdomen. Massive pooling of blood into the spleen can effectively starve the remaining circulation and within hours lead to death (Seeler and Shwiaki, 1972).

Less frequent are anemias due to transient red cell aplasia or hyperhemolysis. Whether hemoglobin concentration is reduced by cessation of bone marrow production, or by the sudden acceleration of red cell death, the child presents as weak, pallid and irritable. Folic acid replacement may reduce the number of aplastic crises. Hemolytic episodes, however, are unusual and self-limited. (Lindenbaum and Klipstein, 1963; Smith et al., 1969).

Painful crises are exceedingly variable. One-third of affected children report one episode every year; another third suffer episodes monthly or weekly (Vichinsky and Lubin, 1980); the remainder experience a variable frequency of episodes. Vaso-occlusive crises are not associated with the pronounced changes in hematologic status seen in the aforementioned crisis varieties, yet produce significant functional restraints upon the human system.

In the Afro-American neonate, fetal hemoglobin resists sickling and protects against painful crises during the first three months of life. The physiologic fall in fetal hemoglobin exposes 30% of sickle cell anemia infants to their first musculoskeletal, vaso-occlusive crises within the first year of life. Classically, infants develop polydactylitis, or painful hand-foot syndrome. A child so affected appears feverish, with tense, tender symmetrical swellings of the metacarpals and metatarsals. Attacks may be confused with juvenile rheumatoid arthritis or acute rheumatic fever. Where redness occurs, salmonella osteomyelitis needs to be considered. Duration may vary from several days to weeks, and the attacks may resolve slowly. Repeated episodes endanger bone construction, and recurrent infection is not uncommon.

During the first two years of life, acute hemolytic crises appear with infection and other stressful insults. Serious, sometimes fatal, complications ensue following minor infections or vaccinations. Encapsulated organisms—streptococcus, salmonella, pneumococcus—extract a tremendous toll from sickle cell victims. Respiratory infections and, according to recent studies, mycoplasma infections have augmented the ranks of commonly encountered

infant illnesses. Functional loss of the spleen by infarction and tissue destruction prevent adequate immune responses in these children, although some host defenses can be mounted without splenic assistance (Pegelow et al., 1980).

From the third year onward, hand-foot syndrome and hemolytic crises are replaced by painful vaso-occlusive crises and infrequent aplastic episodes. By this time, chronic anemia with hemoglobin of 7 grams and hematocrits of 20% is common. The bone marrow reflects its chronic overtime by skeletal enlargement. Weakness, fatigue, cardiac enlargement, and cor pulmonale have imprinted their effects (Ng et al., 1967). Typically, the child with sickle cell will appear diminutive, slender, younger in appearance than chronologic age suggests, and barrel-chested, with retarded puberty, protruberant abdomen and thin extremities. Often appearing fragile, these children may seem infantilized or sullen.

The side effects and medical complications of sickle disease are myriad. Basically, they involve all areas supplied by the circulation and reflect damage due to circulatory wastage. Neurologic complications have been reported in 26% of all patients. Cerebral vascular accidents occur in 4-17% of all patients (mean age of onset by 10 years) and are responsible for 16% of the deaths in these children (Portnoy and Herion, 1972). Strokes tend to recur in over 50% of cases and lead to progressive neurologic deterioration. Warning may be as mild as dizzy spells, fainting, or recurrent headache.

Ocular damage may develop in as many as 90% of all patients. Frequent ophthalmologic examination is critical, since patients are asymptomatic and suffer progressive retinal vascular occlusion and neo-vascular proliferation, acute retinal vessel rupture with glaucoma, retinal detachment and loss of vision, with few warnings. Severe retinal damage has been reported in children younger than 10 years (Armaly, 1974; Goldberg, 1972).

Adolescents suffer repeated hardship when affected by sickle hemoglobinopathies. Biologically prone to iron deficiency anemia, affected black adolescents face dual hemoglobin reductions from sickled cells' reduced longevity and reduction in cell volume via repeated crises. Each severe episode means days and weeks of missed classroom activities, and may result in loss of academic competence. Immature appearance, delayed puberty, and altered psychosocial function are handicapping factors. Reduction of pain during crises may also impair intellectual function, as analgesics decrease the level of cerebral acuity.

Obstetrical complications in childbearing-aged females increase mortality and morbidity risks for infants and mothers. Severity and frequency of vaso-occlusive crises, and risk of pulmonary infarction, eclampsia, and infection rise during pregnancy. Fetal wastage has been reported as high as 40% of all pregnancies (Morrison and Wister, 1976). Recommendations for contraception need to incorporate complications of increased infection, compliance, and estrogen effects on vascular stasis. Recent research into effectiveness of non-pharmacologic agents—diaphragm and cervical cap, condom and foam—suggests use of effective contraceptive methods involving mutual responsibility and reduced major and minor costs.

Adolescent Hypertension

Currently, the concept of adolescent and childhood hypertension is in a state of flux. Prior to 1950, studies on childhood hypertension were rare. Lack of clear, reproducible definition of the problem in this age group has been a major deterrent to estimation and detection (Dube et al., 1975; Kilcoyne, 1978). While an exact definition remains the subject of some debate, Kilcoyne et al. (1974) reported preliminary data suggesting that high cardiac output in adolescence could be a predominant developmental antecedent to adult hypertension. Surveys of Afro-American adults repeatedly have tabulated high vulnerability to development and sequelae of hypertensive cardiac disease in this population. Emergence of arterial hypertension during adolescence is also dramatic in this group. The number of black adolescents with elevated blood pressures is greatest between ages 17 and 18 years, with onset of elevated pressures appearing two years earlier than generally reported in white age-mates (Kilcoyne et al., 1974).

Some of the longitudinal studies in this age group demonstrate marked morbidity and surprising mortality from chronic elevation of blood pressure. In 1958, Perera published findings of a diagnostic hypertensive survey among youths with a mean age of 20 years at the time of the initial observation. Preliminary recordings revealed 8 of 30 dead from hypertension after a mean survival of 21 years following detection. Among the 22 survivors, a majority had cardiac enlargement and suffered effects of advanced target organ dysfunction. Similar unpleasant findings have been documented in other studies (Heyden, et al., 1969).

Kilcoyne (1978) points to Loggie's astute commentary in regard to this problem. Loggie concluded that the range of problem incidence varied from 0.6% to 20.5%, thus reflecting a lack of comprehension and problem definition. For susceptible Afro-American, Latin, and undetected white children, the need for adequate questioning and detection is pressing (Loggie, 1977).

The extent of health concerns for the Afro-American child has been barely touched upon in this section. The range of needs is deeper than one chapter can hope to assess. Problems with detection of dermatologic exanthema, subtle immunologic differences and diverse signs associated with infections are better given over to extensive textbooks of medicine and ancillary health service references.

However, it is clear that the category of what we have labeled as Afro-American health is vast and easily assumes proportions as great as one's imagination.

PSYCHIATRIC CONSIDERATIONS

While the elephant paraded about the carpet, the dragon slid under the couch.
"Did you really see the animals performing?" asked the therapist."I cannot see anything, but my hands followed them until I stopped to eat."
"Strange," whispered the therapist, "I thought I'd put my lenses in backwards."

—Carter, 1980

Few data have been produced that segregate the varied presentations of children for psychiatric intervention. Behavioral problems, including non-compliance, inattention, acting-out, or hyperactivity, represent common concerns regarding children. The more severe psychopathologies—autism, schizophrenia, psychosis, characterological disorders — tend to be packaged with queries of organic etiologies as precipitating events or confounding interfaces. A racial division of presenting pathologies has not been clearly outlined, but a literature scan implies that black children suffer much the same morbidity as whites, but incline toward greater involvement and chronicity. Delayed access to mental health services plays a significant function in this regard.

The Afro-American child who enters for psychiatric counseling may puzzle the conscientious clinician. In what manner is this youthful client best served? How does this child's ethnic background alter the tone of the interview, confuse the medical issues, or cloud the psychiatric presentation of disease? The private practitioner, long weaned from academic ties, may wince at the prospect of confusing ethnicity with uncomplicated behavioral disorders. The academician frowns when disposed to ferret out more than a

pure psychosis or depressed reaction to chronic disease. Each client entering offers opportunities for multiple diagnostic alternatives. One might hope that the physique has been well examined before the psyche, but in actuality, this is not often the case.

The following profiles are offered to engage the curious and to illustrate the ongoing power of mind and body—age, sex, and race notwithstanding.

Seventeen-year-old Dadise, wearing beaded braids and generic T-shirt, lies propped in a county hospital bed. Dadise complains bitterly about his medically imposed rest and he is unconcerned that movement will prevent proper knitting of bone to ligament. History reveals that his athletic career has been ended by a trochanteric ligamentous tear, while recurrent headaches during the preceding three months have warped his otherwise cheery humor. Admission blood-pressure was 110/95 and physical examination was essentially unremarkable.

Tamika is a 14-year-old, single black female who carries into clinic her frenetic six-month-old baby boy, Quenislyn. She reports that her child-caring difficulties have resulted in referral by her primary nurse practitioner for services in a high-risk clinic. While Tamika recounts her trials, Quenislyn sits easily upon the carpet, chortling and investigating objects resting in front of him. As the interview winds down, this solid six-month old promptly rocks backwards, emitting laughter and sustaining a crashing bump to his occiput. Head trauma is minimal.

Marilyn, a spindly, immature-appearing girl, has been hanging around the medical center emergency room. The admitting medical resident and pediatric intern try to estimate this child's exact age while her entering complaint is registered by the triage desk nurse. Her request for morphine or pain medication produces distressful glares as she seems barely old enough to smoke, let alone to ingest class-one narcotics. Perusal of her six-volume medical record reveals her age to be 23 and her major health complaint to be sickle cell crises and pain management. When examined by the medical resident, Marilyn concedes that codeine is an appropriate pain substitute but that she is concerned about pregnancy and would like a suitable oral contraceptive.

Tammy is a big-boned 18-year-old black female who presents with complaint of coughing nightly, increased difficulty seeing, and progressive weight loss. Despite maternal premonitions that Tammy is ill, Tammy feels fairly well and is troubled primarily by her fatigue. Questioned about her decreasing exercise tolerance, Tammy volunteers, "If a person was pregnant, would an abortion be bad?" Further immunologic assessment reveals that Tammy is suffering the effects of sarcodiosis. In view of this finding, is pregnancy a benign state?

These are short histories of adolescents seen at community hospitals and clinics in California. They represent a small sample of ways in which ethnicity and black-related diseases alter the alternatives for patients in a psychiatric milieu. Simple attention to the organic patterns of disease may uncover more extensive problems which also require care. And the challenge of coping with the problems of all of one's patients is rewarding, even if somewhat taxing.

CONCLUSION

Establishing a firm handle upon the health care status of the Afro-American child, or any segment of child welfare, demands concerted and patient effort.

Despite our attention, we must ask ourselves if we have ascertained correctly the precise needs of the black child, or barely scratched the surface with gentle questionings. It will remain for the future to determine how effectively our estimates have answered the base set of health concerns posed by our children—black and other hued. However, so long as poverty and racial distinctions couple as the chief cripplers of our youth, the random misallocation and maldistribution of our national resources cannot be tolerated. The weight of national statistics, studies, and case histories speaks convincingly for our efforts to alter the conditions which now handicap our children and prevent the Afro-American child from receiving his just consideration as a unique creature.

REFERENCES

Armaly, M. Ocular manifestations in sickle cell disease. *Archives of Internal Medicine*, 1974, *133*, 670.

Bergner, L. and Susser, M. Low birth weight and prenatal nutrition: An interpretative review. *Pediatrics*, 1970, *46*, 946.

Bronfenbrenner, U. The state of American families and children. *Toward a National Policy for Children and Families*. Washington, D.C.: National Academy of Sciences, 1976.

Bureau of the Census, U.S. Department of Commerce, P-24, No. 869. Population estimates and projections. *Current Population Reports*, January 1979.

Bureau of the Census, U.S. Department of Commerce, P-25, No. 870. Population estimates and projections. *Current Population Reports*, January 1980.

Carter, J. *Images*. Unpublished work, 1980.

Cohen, G.J. Lead poisoning. *Clinical Pediatrics*, 1980, *19(4)*, 245.

Decastro, F.J., Biesbroeck, R., Erikson, C., Farrell, P., Leong, W., Murphy, D., and Green, R. Hypertension in adolescents. *Clinical Pediatrics*, 1976, *15*, 24.

Dube, S.K., Kapoor, S., Ratner, H., and Tunick, F. Blood pressure studies in black children. *American Journal of Diseases of Children*, 1975, *129*, 1177.

Garn, S.M. The course of bone gain and the phases of bone loss. *Orthopedic Clinics of North America*, 1972, *3*, 503.

Garn, S.M. and Clark, D.C. Problems in the nutritional assessment of black individuals. *American Journal of Public Health*, 1976, *66(3)*, 262.

Garn, S.M., Sandusky, S.T., Nagy, J.M., and McCann, M.B. Advanced skeletal development in low-income negro children. *Pediatrics*, 1972, *80*, 965.

Garn, S.M., Smith, N.J., and Clark, D.C. Lifelong differences in hemoglobin levels between blacks and whites. *Journal of National Medical Association*, 1975, *67*, 91.

Goldberg, M.F. Treatment of proliferative sickle retinopathy. *Transamerican Academy of Ophthalmology and Otolaryngology*, 1972, *75*, 537.

Harvard Child Health Project Task Force: Vol. I: Toward a Primary Medical Care System Responsive to Children's Needs. Cambridge, MA: Ballinger Publishing, 1977.

Herbert, V. Megaloblastic anemias. In: P.B. Beeson, W. McDermott, J.B. Wyngaarden (Eds.), *Cecil Textbook of Medicine.* Philadelphia: W.B. Saunders, 1979, 1719-29.

Herbert, V. The nutritional anemias. *Hospital Practice,* 1980, *15(3),* 86.

Heyden, S., Bartel, A.G., and Hames, L.G. Elevated blood pressure levels in adolescents: Evans County, Georgia, seven-year follow-up of 30 patients and 30 controls. *JAMA,* 1969, *205,* 1683.

Hueter, F.G., Contner, G.L., Busch, K.A., and Hinners, R.G. Biological effects of atmosphere contaminated by auto exhaust. *Archives of Environmental Health,* 1966, *12,* 553.

Kilcoyne, M.M. Natural history of hypertension in adolescence. *Pediatric Clinics of North America,* 1978, *25,* 47.

Kilcoyne, M.M., Richter, R.W., and Alsop, P.A. Adolescent hypertension: Detection and prevention. *Circulation,* 1974, *50,* 758.

Kleinman, J.C., Kovar, M.G., Feldman, J.J., and Young, C.A. A comparison of 1960 and 1973-74 early neo-natal mortality in selected states. *American Journal of Epidemiology,* in press.

Lewis, T.R., Hucter, F.G., and Busch, K.A. Irradiated automobile exhaust: Its effects on the reproduction of mice. *Archives of Environmental Health,* 1967, *15,* 26.

Lindenbaum, J. and Klipstein, F.A. Folic acid deficiency in sickle cell anemia. *New England Journal of Medicine,* 1963, *269,* 875.

Loggie, J.M.H.: Prevalence of hypertension and distribution of causes. In: M.I. New and L.S. Levine, (Eds.), *Juvenile Hypertension.* New York: Raven Press, 1977, p. 2.

Longo, L.D. Carbon monoxide: Effects on oxygenation of the fetus in utero. *Science,* 1976, *194,* 523.

Morrison, J.C. and Wister, W.L. The use of prophylactic partial exchange transfusion in pregnancies associated with sickle cell hemoglobinopathies. *Obstetrics and Gynecology,* 1976, *78,* 516.

Myerson, R.M., Harrison, E., and Lohmuller, H.W. Incidence of significance of abnormal hemoglobin: Report of a series of 1000 hospitalized negro veterans. *American Journal of Medicine,* 1959, *26,* 543.

Ng., M.L. Cardiovascular findings in children with sickle cell anemia. *Diseases of the Chest,* 1967, *52,* 788.

Oski, F.A. and Stockman, J.A. Anemia due to inadequate iron sources or poor iron utilization. *Pediatric Clinics of North America,* 1980, *27,* 237.

Owen, G.M., Kram, K.M., Garry, P.J., Lowe, J.E., and Lubin, A.H. A study of nutritional status of pre-school children in the United States, 1968-1970. *Pediatrics,* 1974, *53,* part 2, supplement.

Pegelow, C.H., Wilson, B., Overturf, G.D., Tigner-Weekes, L., and Powers, D. Infection in splenectomized sickle cell disease patients. *Clinical Pediatrics,* 1980, *19(2),* 102.

Perera, G.A. The course of primary hypertension in the young. *Annals of Internal Medicine,* 1958, *49,* 1348.

Portnoy, B.A. and Herion, J.C. Neurological manifestations of sickle cell disease. *Annals of Internal Medicine,* 1972, *76,* 643.

Pudd, Abraham M. (Ed.) *Pediatrics,* 16th Edition. New York: Appleton-Century-Crofts, 1977. pp. 1149-1155.

Rush, P. and Kass, E.H. Maternal smoking: A reassessment of the association with perinatal mortality. *American Journal of Epidemiology,* 1972, *96,* 183.

Schaffer, A., and Avery, M. *Diseases of the Newborn.* Philadelphia: W.B. Saunders Co., 1977.

Seeler, R.A. and Shwiaki, M.Z. Acute splenic sequestration crisis (ASSC) in young children with sickle cell anemia. *Clinical Pediatrics,* 1972, *11,* 701.

Smith, H.L., Oski, F.A., and Brody, J.I. The hemolytic crisis in sickle cell disease: The role of glucose 6-phosphate dehydrogenase deficiency. *Journal of Pediatrics,* 1969, *74,* 549.

Smith, N.J. and Rios, E. Iron metabolism and iron deficiency in infancy and childhood. *Advances in Pediatrics,* 1974, *21,* 239.

The social and economic status of the black population in the U.S.: An historical view 1790-1978. *Current Population Reports.* Bureau of the Census, U.S. Department of Commerce, P-23, No. 80, 1973.

Stewart, R.P., Baretta, E.D., Platte, L.R., Stewart, E.B., Kalbfleisch, J.G., Yserloo, B.V., and Rimm, A.A. Carboxyhemoglobin in concentrations in blood from donors in Chicago, Milwaukee, New York and Los Angeles. *Science,* 1973, *182,* 1362.

U.S. Health. USDHEW #(CPHS)78-1232, December 1978.

Vichinsky, E.P. and Lubin, B.H. Sickle cell anemia and related hemoglobinopathies. *Pediatric Clinics of North America,* 1980, *27,* 429.

Webb, T.E. and Oski, F.A. Behavioral status of young adolescents with iron deficiency anemia. *Journal of Special Education,* 1974, *8,* 153.

Werkman, S.L., Shifman, L., and Skelly, T. Psychosocial correlates of iron deficiency anemia in early childhood. *Psychosomatic Medicine,* 1964, *26,* 125.

Whitten, C.F., Waugh, D., and Moor, A. Unmet needs of parents of children with sickle cell anemia. Bethesda, MD: National Institute of Health. DHEW #(NIH)275-77, 1974.

Williams, L., Spence, M.A., and Tideman, S.C. Implications of the observed effect of air pollution on birth weight. *Social Biology,* 1977, 24, 97-102.

Williams, R.A. (Ed.) *Textbook of Black Related Diseases.* New York: McGraw-Hill, 1975.

Wilson, J.F. and Lahey, M.E. Studies on iron metabolism: Further observations on cow's milk-induced gastrointestinal bleeding in infants with iron deficiency anemia. *Journal of Pediatrics,* 1971, *84,* 335.

Young, J. (Ed.) National commission on the international year of the child. *Los Angeles Times,* April 21, 1980.

Younoszai, M.K., Kacic, A., and Haworth, J.C. Cigarette smoking during pregnancy: The effect upon the hematocrit and acid-base balance of the newborn infant. *Canadian Medical Association Journal,* 1968, *99,* 197.

CHAPTER 2

Factors Relating to
the Health Status of
Mexican-American Children

Faustina Solis, M.S.W.

This chapter will provide an overview of major child health problems and health issues that confront Hispanic populations, especially those living in the Southwest. Although persons of Mexican descent comprise the largest number of Hispanics (approximately 14,500,000 nationally), increasing numbers of Central and South Americans, Cubans, and Puerto Ricans are migrating to the Southwest. Though there may be similarities among all these groups, there is also a range of marked differences, particularly in socioeconomic-educational status. Some newer immigrants have left their homeland for political rather than economic reasons. Many represent a strong middle-class group with ability to compete advantageously in the labor market due to their technical and professional preparation. This chapter will be concerned generally with those persons of low or marginal income. This is not meant to imply that health needs are ap-propriately met for those in the middle class, but that preventive and primary care availability does not generally pose the problem for them that it does for families of limited resources. Middle-class families express as major concerns services for the chronically ill, the developmentally disabled child, or for the child displaying atypical behavior. These latter categories merit specialized attention which cannot be addressed justly in this overview.

There exists a paucity of health data and health statistics on Hispanic populations. Only white and black populations seem to be significantly represented in general health statistics. This major lack has been identified repeatedly (Cervantes, 1972). Recently there have been increased efforts to conduct research on several aspects of health problems and issues related to Hispanics. The most prominent studies address the nutritional status of

26

Mexican-American children, treatment modalities to meet mental health needs of Latino populations, concepts of health and healing in the Southwest (Farge, 1975), substance abuse in adolescents, and attitudinal approaches to health care services in Puerto Rican and Mexican-American families. Glaringly lacking are epidemiologic or baseline data on the health status of children from the Spanish-speaking population. Availability of this information could serve as one of the most important tools in the determination of priorities for planning and subsequently in the allocation of health care resources. In this outline of health problems of Hispanic children, references of studies will be based on data available, whether in reference to Spanish surnamed or to Mexican-American children. The principal focus will be on issues intricately bound to general health problems of these children.

The broad issues of health problems of ethnic minorities in this country cannot and should not be separated from health issues affecting the general population. A reference to health should not center on the absence of disease or dysfunction, but must encompass those factors that impinge on health, such as heredity, nutrition, housing, emotional and physical stress, poverty, and environmental hazards. Lack of understanding and improper assessment of these complexities in determining major health problems will be more apparent as in-depth evaluations of health status are conducted. Cultural values, socioeconomic status, environmental influences, health care practices, and utilization of health services are factors that also bear significantly on health maintenance.

IMMIGRANT PERSPECTIVES

Early Hispanic immigrants included persons with a broad range of economic standing, skills, and training. Profession-als, technicians, skilled craftsmen, and unskilled laborers ventured forth with no assurance of economic opportunity in a new country. As with most immigrants, cultural heritage and customs were zealously guarded, particularly because the new immigrants felt economically disadvantaged and alienated in their search for social stability. In their minds, the return to their country of origin was a sustaining hope. For the Mexican immigrant in particular, this hope was not unrealistic, since the homeland was relatively close. The thought of a possible return, plus ongoing strong relationships with relatives and friends from Mexico, made it increasingly difficult and from their perception, unnecessary, to embrace another culture, other modes of behavior, or another language. The perceived alienation from the dominant culture reinforced the strong grasp of their heritage. The Mexican immigrants brought with them values centering around Mexican concepts of family life, relationship with the community, and governmental authorities. It was difficult for them to seek and respond to the programs of American public agencies. Only a serious emergency would motivate them to seek assistance, and even in that situation, solutions offered by public or private agencies might not be entirely trusted. It is conceivable that inculcation of distrust was as much a part of the first generation immigrants' conditioning as were other protective defenses.

Earlier immigrants applied these same characteristics in their approach to health care services and utilization of facilities. Specifically, the Mexican perspective stressed:

1) The importance of organization, structure, sense of responsibility, and interdependence within the family. Since priority activities were centered on seeking economic security, heads of households and older children were required to be involved in the search for full or part-time employment. Usu-

ally the mother, or older nonemployed siblings, undertook the total care of the family, including that of older dependent adults and younger children. Should a need have existed for services not provided by the family, it was their responsibility to negotiate these services.

2) Hispanic women brought with them generations of experience in nursing care and treatment of common illnesses and diseases, which was taught in varying degrees to most female members of the family. Not infrequently, pre-adolescent and adolescent youth served as interpreters and liaisons with the incomprehensible world of public services.

Frequently health care providers cannot understand why Hispanic patients appear to understand and to agree to a prescribed preventive and/or treatment plan and yet never initiate or comply with the plan successfully. This action may have nothing to do with the provider or the appropriateness or inappropriateness of the recommended plan. Decisions about health care and treatment procedures required are not made by the patient alone; they must also be supported by the human network providing the patient's social supports. That network, to a great extent, begins with the immediate family. The effective utilization of health services depends heavily on personnel understanding the value systems that are the legacy of generations of Hispanics. In spite of the many diversities among Hispanics (degrees of differences in value systems between social classes and within them), there are culturally determined health related components which must be considered—health beliefs and health care practices of the individual or the family, and determination of individuals who truly are the decision-makers for the family.

MAJOR HEALTH PROBLEMS

Birth and Mortality Data

Though there continue to be deficiencies with respect to health and welfare services for children and families, data indicate that there have been some major achievements in reducing the mortality rates of infants. From 1964 to 1974, deaths per 1,000 live births declined from 24.8 to 16.5. This demonstrates a significant improvement in the welfare of families. Nonetheless, infant mortality for nonwhites in the United States is nearly twice that of whites. For example, in California total infant mortality rate per 1,000 live births in 1965 was 19.0. The Spanish surnamed rate was 18.4 and the black 28.6. In 1974 the overall infant mortality rate was 12.5, the Spanish surnamed 11.6, white 11.6, and black 19.9. Spanish-speaking perinatal and infant mortality rates among total births were somewhat lower. In 1974, of total children born, all races showed a perinatal death rate of 24.9 and an infant death rate of 16.1. The Spanish surnamed showed a perinatal death rate of 23.1 and an infant death rate of 13.6. Table I indicates perinatal and infant mortality rates among total births by type of hospital and race of child.

The data reflect possible greater utilization of Title XIX benefits for delivery service in private hospitals. The number of county hospitals has been reduced. There has been a steady increase in the number of women who seek care during the first and second trimesters. In the 1974 birth cohort in California, of 50,786 total births, 57.8% of the women sought care during the first trimester of their pregnancy, 27.5% of the women had prenatal care during the second trimester, and 3% sought no care (these births showed a perinatal death rate of 50.3%). Early and continuous prenatal care is a public health measure that needs to be vigorously promoted in the Hispanic population group.

TABLE 1

Observed and Age-adjusted[a] Perinatal and Infant Mortality Rates
Among Total Births by Type of Hospital of Birth and Race of Child
1974 and 1970 California Birth Cohorts

Type of Hospital and Race	Total Births	Live Births	Mortality Rate[c] Perinatal	Infant
		1974 Birth Cohort[b]		
County Hospital	34,070	33,639	24.9	18.4
Spanish Surnamed	19,628	19,435	19.5	14.2
White	9,005	8,872	28.6	21.8
Black	4,341	4,246	41.2	29.0
Private Hospital	228,193	226,088	18.2	13.0
Spanish Surnamed	56,659	56,123	17.2	12.1
White	135,249	134,071	17.4	12.2
Black	23,938	23,635	26.1	20.6
Other Hospital	50,002	49,473	19.6	12.6
Spanish Surnamed	10,694	10,562	21.4	11.8
White	33,151	32,824	18.5	12.2
Black	2,925	2,878	28.4	18.4
		1970 Birth Cohort[b]		
County Hospital	37,496	36,939	32.2	22.6
Spanish Surnamed	16,833	16,601	28.0	19.6
White	12,895	12,713	32.5	22.2
Black	6,482	6,355	44.9	31.1
Private Hospital	272,994	270,231	22.3	16.0
Spanish Surnamed	52,554	51,986	22.0	14.8
White	183,474	181,765	21.0	15.1
Black	25,641	25,246	34.3	24.7
Other Hospital	54,332	53,794	23.2	16.4
Spanish Surnamed	8,000	7,904	26.0	18.7
White	40,230	39,853	21.7	15.2
Black	3,367	3,320	36.8	25.9

[a] 1970 rates adjusted by direct method to 1960 California total births by age of mother, excluding age unknown.
[b] Unadjusted rates.
[c] Perinatal death rates are per 1,000 total births; infant death rates are per 1,000 live births.
Source: Adapted from State of California, Department of Health, Division of Public Health, Maternal and Child Health, Birth Cohort Records 3/15/77.

Although these figures indicate a 10% increase in earlier care from the 1960 figures, there is still need for improvement (State of California Department of Health, 1975.).

A special study of reproductive health care among the poor in San Antonio, Texas (Gibbs et al., 1974) revealed significant maternal and perinatal mortality, with an infant mortality rate of 42 per 1,000 births. Careful study of underutilization of obstetrical and prenatal resources resulted in modification of services

to diminish deterrents and obstacles which added to patients' reluctance to seek care.

Through appropriate counseling, education, and promotion, particularly in community clinics, maternal and infant care projects, and public health maternal services, Hispanic women have accepted the importance of early prenatal care. They may tend to be shy and still self-conscious about physical examinations, but the assurance and understanding of staff have allayed many of their fears.

Significant factors that have contributed to the decline of perinatal and infant mortality rates suggest: 1) improvement in the standard of living of many families; 2) improvement in nutrition; 3) establishment and location of maternal and infant projects in high risk areas of urban centers; 4) greater availability of primary care in both urban and sparsely populated areas; 5) greater availability of public health education and outreach programs with individualized services to mothers and children; 6) efforts of parents to assume increasing responsibility for care of themselves and their children; 7) demonstrated progress in the family's knowledge of prevention and treatment of childhood ailments and diseases.

The five leading causes of death in children (ages 1–4) in the United States general population have been accidents, malignant neoplasms, congenital anomalies, influenza and pneumonia, and homicide. These are also leading causes of death in the four border states of the Southwest—California, Arizona, New Mexico, and Texas—which have a high concentration of Hispanic populations. In New Mexico, however, heart diseases and diarrheal diseases replace congenital anomalies and homicide as two of the five leading causes of death (Alvarez, 1975).

Acute and Chronic Health Problems

Respiratory conditions, infective and parasitic diseases, and injuries are acute conditions prevalent in children 16 years of age and younger. Chronic problems that concern parents, schools, and the community in general are the high rate of dental disease and learning disabilities (Brother, 1976). The concern centers not only on the existence of these conditions, but also on the lack of facilities and services to correct them.

In low-income areas, nutritionally related conditions are also major health problems. Preliminary reports from the California Child Health Disability Pre-vention Program (1976) were reviewed (State of California Department of Health, 1976). Of 45,000 screening reports in these data, 14,500 were those of Mexican-American children. The predominant nutritionally related problem of all California children screened was obesity. The mean incidence of Mexican-American children who were above the 95th percentile of height and weight was 13.77%; this same analysis shows 8.62% of white children as being above the 95th percentile of height and weight. The problem of overweight in Mexican children appears to be greatest from 1 through 9 years. Overweight was seen in 15.4% of Mexican-American children at 1 through 9 years and in 9.8% of white children in the same age group. In all age groups, Mexican-American children were shorter than white children.

In those youngsters found to be below the 5th percentile of height for age, increase occurred in the groups from 4 to 6 years, 7 to 8 years, and 13 to 15 years. About 10% of Mexican-American babies were above the 95th percentile of weight for age.

During the past eight years, iron deficiency anemia has been identified as a major public health problem in American children. In incidence of anemia in these results, however, Mexican-American children are below or almost comparable to white children in California. The mean for the aggregate group of children screened was 6.89% (hemoglobin of 10 grams or below). The Mexican-American children in this group found to have a hemoglobin of 10 grams or below was 6.68%. The nutritional data for the screening consisted of anthropometric measurements of height and weight, hemoglobin and/or hematocrit indicators of iron status of the child.

In the Ten State Nutrition Survey (Carter, 1974), the standard used for low hemoglobin was 11 grams per 100 milliliters. Measuring against this standard, 10% of the Spanish-American preschool children in low income states were anemic in contrast to 14% of white children and 24.9% of black children. In a special study for determining vitamin A status of Mexican-American four-year-olds, neither iron deficiency anemia nor protein deficiency was found; however, of all serum vitamin A determinations done, 48% fell within the low category (Fry, et al., 1975). Another study revealed that vitamin A deficiency seemed to be the dominant nutritional problem among young Mexican-American children. Mean nutrient intake was low in the 6- to 8-year-old children, but not in those from other age groups (Larson, et al., 1974).

The rejection of more healthful foods in the cultural diet and the adoption of less healthful foods in the American diet have created nutritional imbalances in Hispanic children.

It is important to realize that existing patterns for sustaining certain feeding practices consist of a complexity of factors. In addition to cultural reference factors, feeding patterns develop and are maintained for economic, social, and psychological reasons.

Parents who have known hunger as children and who consider the provision of food an important demonstration of parental affection will experience difficulty in understanding the concept of dieting in children, i.e., limiting or withdrawing foods the child finds pleasurable. The provision of certain foods, particularly sweets, may be the parents' only possible expression of affectionate indulgence. Thus, shaming parents by suggesting a lack of love for their children because they permit overeating may merely intensify the parents' sense of inadequacy in caring for their family and their increasing distrust of a dominant culture that attempts to destroy their family values—their strongest social inheritance. Young Hispanic children may interpret being placed on a limiting diet as severe punishment, since they are rarely disciplined by being deprived of food.

Plump, robust babies may be perceived as healthy. Frail-looking children or youngsters who pick at their food or eat very little are often considered sickly. In Hispanic families where there are a number of older children and adults, younger children may be fed between meals by many members of the household.

Television programs, neighborhood salesmen, and candy vending machines present an additional dilemma to parents who understand the importance of reducing consumption of unhealthful foods such as sweets and carbonated drinks. These influences are particularly evident in closely knit neighborhoods in the low income sectors of urban areas, in sparsely populated areas, or in farm labor centers in rural regions. Itinerant tradesmen selling candy, pop, or ice cream are daily visitors during certain seasons of the year. Parents have difficulty resisting the pleadings of children who parents feel have so little gratification from their daily existence, even though they know that there is little money for necessary table foods.

It is unlikely that educational methods (distribution of pamphlets or diet sheets indicating the importance of specific foods) will be very productive in changing nutritional behavior in socially and economically disadvantaged populations. Factors affecting food practices and the potential for modifying their influence need to be assessed. Prominent among these are: established food patterns, limited incomes, availability and cost of food within neighborhoods, influence of advertisements, and importance of conforming to dominant social patterns. Also, some urban and rural families may not have appropriate refrigeration or proper cooking utensils and facilities. This will dictate the kinds of foods they consume.

Nutritionists have enlarged their promotional efforts to incorporate a number of effective approaches to encourage greater participation of parents in determining how nutrition may be improved. Diet lists containing unliked and unfamiliar foods may not be received enthusiastically by children or parents. Parents who help children to have a positive approach to unfamiliar foods and alter methods of preparation of familiar foods will find beneficial nutritional change less painful. Parents can be challenged to be creative and can be given recognition for their own special knowledge and resources.

In school district preventive dental programs, the importance of nutrition has been stressed. The objectives of these programs are not only to identify dental health needs in school-age children, but also to establish ongoing educational programs on proper dental hygiene and nutrition for maintenance of good dental health. These programs are most successful when school personnel are able to participate actively in the educational program. Parents should also be included and their support enlisted to help their children maintain newly learned dental hygiene and nutritional practices.

Providers of prenatal care, whether private physicians, public health departments, community health centers, or other sources of health care, have been cognizant of the need to emphasize nutritional surveillance, particularly to mothers who tend to disregard their own special nutritional needs in order to assure more and better quality food for other family members.

Severe Chronic Conditions and Disabilities

Coping with severe chronic illness or physical and mental developmental disabilities in children has been particularly frustrating for the Hispanic family. Though parents tend to identify acute conditions of illness in infants and toddlers, they may be less aware of physical and motor development abnormalities during the child's early life (Lei, 1972). They may not compare their child's growth and development with that of siblings or other children in the neighborhood. As the child grows,

however, social behavior is carefully observed. Aggressive and hyperactive conduct, uncontrolled, emotional outbursts, or marked withdrawal are viewed with concern, no matter how young the child may be. Once convinced that the child has a serious and possibly uncorrectable condition, the parents make an effort to meet the child's special needs.

The Hispanic family will usually assume the care of a child with gross disabilities without seeking outside sources of help until the family's physical and economic resources are drained. This is understood as an obligation of parenthood. Parents consider that primary caring responsibility rests with them and not elsewhere. Even when supportive assistance is available, they may prefer to provide care by themselves to the extent possible.

Diagnostic and rehabilitative care for the chronically ill child is often fragmented and inadequate. These services may be unresponsive to the values of ethnic minority families. In meeting with a group of parents of disabled children, the author learned that most of their children were seen in diagnostic centers, and most parents had participated in counseling services. Nonetheless, in time, they realized that what they knew about their children's conditions was minimal. They wanted to know more about disabilities in general, and how best to help other parents coping with the same concerns. They felt that frequently medical information was not disclosed to them because they were considered intellectually incapable of understanding, or because knowledge of the severity of the condition would be unnecessarily stressful to them. Their question was: Who has the right to make these assumptions?

It was apparent to them that most of the professional staff felt proper services had been rendered and saw no reason why any of the parents should have any question about the condition of their children. What was particularly impressive was that these parents seemed to have a strong desire to know more, not for the purpose of becoming technically sophisticated, but because gaining sufficient knowledge about their child's level and patterns of development would provide them with a sense of security in helping their children achieve their optimal potential for growth and development.

The whole spectrum of congenital abnormalities, developmental disabilities, and neurological disorders is prevalent in this ethnic group population. Parents strive to have the disabled child be as much a part of the family as the other children. Hispanic families have probably been less aggressive in securing needed services for the education and supervision of children with multiple needs. Some of this is due to lack of knowledge of sources of care and proper utilization of these resources. In the absence of alternatives, Hispanic parents have had to develop resources to cope with the supervision, training, and support of their children. Institutional placement—even family care arrangements — would be considered a last resort and not a satisfactory alternative to ambulatory care or day schooling, particularly for educable children and young people.

SOURCES OF CARE

Assumptions are frequently made that the type of health care providers utilized by Hispanic populations is determined by their socioeconomic status. This is not the case in many instances. As in the general population, Hispanic families will seek health resources they consider to be most appropriate for their children wherever these may be available, regardless of the cost. For practical reasons, for those illnesses not considered to be an emergency, the family more likely will first approach known trusted available sources nearby (primarily family resources, friends, or a known "successful" folkhealer). Private care may be sought by those families having even the most meager income if the illness of the child, in their assessment, warrants it. Low income families believe the very best of care is provided by a private physician. Clinic care or ambulatory care provided by a non-physician may be considered initially inferior. As families become more informed about health resources, they learn to differentiate between specialized services and generalized clinic care. Some neighborhood health center personnel in both urban and rural areas experienced difficulty in getting the enrolled population to accept non-physician providers since it was assumed that they provided an inferior level of care. Some low income patients felt resentful that middle-class families were always provided with physicians, even in the clinics, and yet they were expected to accept professionals with less education as continuous providers. Subsequently, many of these patients have learned to appreciate and value the special roles of physician's assistants and nurse practitioners. Another reason for the initial resistance to non-physician providers was the feeling that "innovative ideas" are always tested out on the poor.

Families may also adopt a dual system of health care, consulting simultaneously various health resources—sometimes even for the same illness. Health providers in Mexican border counties are alert to the fact that some of their patients use physicians on both sides of the border for various members of the family, adults or children. This procedure may not continue for a very long time since it can be expensive.

Some of the problems which prompt the dual system of health resources can be attributed to lack of comprehensive care, inappropriateness of care, and private and public services that are psychologically alien to Hispanic families. Those in most pressing need of services are not those who have selected a source of care, but those who continue to be without care either because they are not informed about the availability of resources or because they distrust the system, only venturing to seek care in times of urgency in emergency rooms of county and community hospitals.

The increased number of undocumented and illegal aliens has posed a major crisis for many public primary care resources. It is difficult to deal with the demands to provide much needed care in the face of policies which limit or prohibit primary care to the illegal alien. Thus, a great deal of responsibility for meeting the needs of this group falls on voluntary community health facilities.

Public health service demands have risen markedly, but resources are not adequate to meet the needs required in the high-risk urban and rural areas. Reducing public health nursing visits to homes and community agencies, as has occurred in some counties, will inevitably reduce early detection of disease and health problems that need rapid and appropriate intervention. The trend towards converting preventive health services into primary care centers deemphasizes the preventive role of public health facilities, particularly early case finding, community disease control, prenatal care, and child health services.

Hispanic families in rural areas have traditionally had little if any access to comprehensive health care. Those families engaged in agricultural work have been particularly at risk during peak harvest months as well as during periods of unemployment when they have returned to their home base. Since the enactment of the California Seasonal Agricultural Worker's Health and Federal Migratory legislation, migratory families (especially mothers and children) have had better access to sources of health care. During the decade from 1960 to 1970, most of the services to the rural areas, and specifically to agricultural workers, were provided through migrant health clinics offering limited primary care services and preventive health care (Fuentes, 1974).

Public health departments were asked to include migratory populations in their preventive programs. However, outreach efforts or intensive services of a preventive nature were not always possible with the resources available, even within public health jurisdictions.

Substandard working and living conditions have contributed and continue to contribute to the health problems of agricultural populations. Inadequate supervision of children exposes them to toxic pesticides, injuries in the field, accidents in the farm labor centers or in their living quarters. In addition, physical care may be inappropriate and nutrition improper when both parents have to work in the fields. The provision of day care facilities in farm labor areas allowed comprehensive care, including full-day supervision for school age children, and in some centers, for infants from 6 weeks of age. However, the demands for day care could not be met within the farm labor centers or for those families who did not live nearby. Consequently, children were supervised and cared for by other children not too much older than themselves; these older children then could not take advantage of the opportunities for special schooling and other social activities provided for migratory children. Sporadic family day care was also provided, but sometimes children were supervised by adults who were already taking care of numerous other children. Appropriate opportunities for social growth were not prominently visible for these agricultural migrant children.

Although agricultural migratory families, whether interstate or intrastate, have special problems of housing and working conditions, the lack of health resources is not unique to the agricultural worker. The rural poor, and even rural residents who have a better means of livelihood, face very much the same problems of paucity of health resources and unavailability of transportation in times of need. Organization and operation of emergency medical care services continue to be a critical lack in rural areas.

In an effort to meet some of the needs of the rural population, several comprehensive health centers were developed in the Southwest—in California, Colorado, Arizona, New Mexico, and Texas—under the auspices of HEW. The rural community health centers were patterned after urban comprehensive health centers and included many basic service components common to the urban centers. The provision of transportation was a major program component, since care is usually inaccessible because of the enormous distances separating remote areas from sources of care. Even though, at this time, satellite clinics have been organized, the program consists essentially of mini-community centers.

Innovative health educational components have not always been well integrated in primary care delivery. Preventive programs are by and large traditional in nature—immunization clinics, health education devoted to prevention of specific diseases, disease orientation, and selective nutritional projects. There is less emphasis on providing educational tools for families and communities to assist in mutual assistance in such matters as early identification of common childhood illnesses and understanding preventive measures in early pregnancy, early infancy, and childhood. Rural families do not have the opportunity to attend special education sessions in health centers. Nonetheless, given the requirements for reporting of public services, the measurement of success of service appears centered in summing up the number of patient encounters in health care facilities, rather than on the optimal utilization of the professional staff for health restoration and maintenance.

PUBLIC HEALTH CARE RESOURCES

The debate continues on how to establish priorities on behalf of children in this country. The lack of a coordinated approach to children's services, and specifically children's health services, seems to indicate an absence of public policy and has hindered progress towards equity and quality in children's services for all population groups. The disjointed programming for children must in some way express conflicting attitudes. As presently organized, health care services for mothers and children characterize the inconsistencies and complexities of general health care in this country.

The earliest examples of tentative public policy relating to children's welfare were the organization and development of the Children's Bureau in 1912 and the enactment of the Social Security Act of 1935. Title XIX, enacted in 1965, with all of its benefits for AFDC eligible children, can be considered primarily a payment mechanism for specific services. Even basic services of Early Periodic Screening Diagnosis and Treatment Services which must be assured by states for eligible children through age 21 are not uniformly provided. Preventive services in Title XIX are not specifically fostered or promoted. Low income Hispanic populations, like other ethnic group populations, have utilized the Social Security Title V benefits selectively. These are benefits which are concerned with Maternal and Child Health Services and Crippled Children's Services. Maternal and Child Health Services, to be most effective, must be comprehensive in nature, including preventive diagnostic, treatment, and rehabilitative services. Children and Youth projects and Maternal and Infant care projects, initially demonstration programs, have continued to operate for specific target areas. Though the services provided through these special projects are extensive, comprehensive, and observe quality standards, the population reached through these programs is limited in relation to the needs of low income groups. The rural areas have been virtually excluded from these special demonstration Title V projects.

This is not to say that maternal and child health funds are not available for other preventive programs in prenatal care and in child health services, but these are limited in number, inadequate, and usually limited to those projects which can link existing resources to provide a broader approach to maternal and child health services. New programs, innovative programs, cannot be sustained on limited allocations.

The reluctance of public and private health care resources to alter traditional modalities of providing service is made manifest in that voluntary and community based clinics have multiplied significantly all over the country in the last five years. Many of these clinics provide special obstetrical and pediatric services, and family health clinics offer both primary and preventive services. When these clinics were established, the intent was to support them on a voluntary basis. It quickly became obvious, however, that services could not be provided without a funding source. County resources as well as state funds have been supporting part of the community health clinic services. Funds are spread through a wider variety of modalities of care, but it is questionable whether the needs of ethnic minorities are being met or will continue to be met except on an episodic basis. Health promotion and health maintenance continue to be a low priority.

A national or state strategy for child health has not yet been developed. Whatever partial policies and services have been established on behalf of children in recent years have been more a political accident than a studied approach. Considering the governmental and the community's interest in children, it is unsettling that minimal standards of health services for *all* children have not been established.

The express needs of children and families for maintenance of health must be addressed, though service priorities cannot be established on equal levels for all groups. For example, demands for continuous care for the chronically ill poor will merit greater allocation of resources than demands for the middle-class chronically ill who have had the advantages of continuous preventive intervention. Services for poor and low income minority children must be more complex. In addition to health care, they must encompass full utilization of non-health resources such as schools, day care, and recreation centers, and home supervision of children whose parents must work.

The following selected groups of children have special service needs which are generally ignored:

—Pre-adolescent and adolescent youths, whose problems are identified only when they become so severe as to be considered social or medical liabilities by the youth, his or her family, or society.
—Alien infants or children who may at times be dependent on public resources for emergency or continued health care.
—Children who are unfortunate in not having a family, and therefore are considered for out-of-home placement either in foster homes, juvenile detention homes, or other institutional settings. Though providing basic life supports, these may not include remedial and supportive resources to enhance optimal development.
—Very young children who are disabled or become homicide victims because they cannot defend themselves against conscious or misplaced aggression from adults.

In addition to the child-focused array of important public and community services, attention must be given to the educational preparation of professionals and technical personnel who will be working with populations of bicultural background and limited means. Technical skills are not sufficient when one is working in urban and rural areas; a professional must know about health hazards and health practices in these communities which need to be altered.

The concept of prevention is not demonstrated in the allocation of resources or in professional education. It is usually by chance that professionals become interested in integrating preventive measures and health education as a part of total treatment and patient surveillance.

Though in the early 1970s there seemed to be a concerted effort to recruit ethnic minority students into the health professions, the numbers graduated are not significant in the face of this rapidly growing population. In addition, there is little evidence that medical, nursing or public health schools consistently offer courses in the curriculum to prepare health professional students to understand the cross-cultural components in health and illness. Occasionally there may be a lecture or two in the core curriculum which alludes to cross-cultural factors, or there may be elective course offerings, but in the main professionals will learn about health values in actual practice. These professionals will increasingly be faced with providing care to a multi-cultural population. Though this review has tended to highlight the problem areas in the provision of health care, recognition must be given to the progress that has been achieved by both Hispanic and non-Hispanic providers of care, administrators and planners who have contributed to the modification of health care delivery patterns to meet the special needs of this group.

Another area which merits special attention is the necessity for recognizing the potential for self-care in individuals, families, and community groups. Promotion of inappropriate dependence on physicians or other health professionals denies the abilities of individuals and families to undertake responsibility for early detection of common health problems, surveillance of proper growth and development in children, and maintenance of good health. Preventive care is so institutionalized that it is perhaps ineffective for individuals and families with greatest need for this type of care. Schools capable of influencing children's behavior have not initiated public health education for young school-age children as an integral part of education. To expect health services to be totally responsible for preventive care is unrealistic. By making such an assumption, one avoids considering other options. Child development is not only a process of physical development; it is an experience of learning that starts from the day a child is born. Yet we restrict a child's learning of self-maintenance, assuming that only parents, friends, relatives, or health care professionals can take this responsibility. Consequently, teenage youths have little knowledge of human sexuality, the significance of responsible parenthood, and children's growth and development. Yet these young persons become parents at very early ages.

There is no simple answer to the health needs of minority children and youth.

REFERENCES

Alvarez, H.R. The border: Health without boundaries. In Report of U.S.-Mexico Border Public Health Association, Mexico, 1975 (unpublished).

Brother, S.R. *Nutrition in California.* Assembly Office of Research, Sacramento, California, November 1976, 13–15.

Carter, J. *The Ten-State Nutrition Survey: An Analysis.* Southern Regional Council, Atlanta, Georgia, October 1974.

Cervantes, R.A. The failure of comprehensive health services to serve the urban Chicano. *Health Services Reports*, December 1972, *87*(10), 932–939.

Farge, E.J. *La Vida Chicana: Health Care Attitudes and Behaviors of Houston Chicanos.* San Francisco: R and E Research Associates, 1975.

Fry, P.C., Eithelman, J.D., and Kelly, K. Vitamin A status of Mexican-American four year olds from non-migrant families, *Nutrition Reports International*, January 1975, *11*(1), 71-78.

Fuentes,J.A. The need for effective and comprehensive planning for migrant workers. *American Journal of Public Health*, January 1974, *64*(1), 2-10.

Gibbs, C.E., Martin, H.W., and Gutierrez, M. Patterns of reproductive health care among the poor of San Antonio, Texas. *American Journal of Public Health*, January 1974, *64*(1), 37-40.

Larson, L.B., Dodds, J.M., Massotii, D.M., and Chase, H.P. Nutritional status of children of Mexican-American migrant families. *Research, Journal of the American Dietetic Association*, January 1974, *64*, 29-35.

Lei, T-J. Family socio-cultural background and the behavioral retardation of children. *Journal of Health & Social Behavior*, Pacific State Hospital, California Department of Mental Hygiene, September 1972, *13*, 47-50.

State of California Department of Health, California Child Health Disability Prevention Program's Preliminary Report, Oct.-Dec. 1976 (Unpublished).

State of California Department of Health, Maternal Child Health, Birth Cohort Records. Sacramento: Family Health Services, 1975.

CHAPTER 3

The Impact of Culture on the Health of American Indian Children

Anthony D. Brown, Ph.D.

and Kenneth W. Hernasy, M.A.

Until recently, the American health care estbablishment has made few attempts to consider the traditional ways in which Indians have maintained good health and treated their ill. When Indian culture has been considered at all by health care professionals, it has usually been in terms of how the culture has served as a barrier to the effective utilization of health services (Coulehan, unpublished manuscript, 1976). The reluctance by health personnel to consider positive aspects of Indian culture is a major failure of a health delivery system that in most communities appears otherwise adequate in terms of quantity and quality of services* (Coulehan). It is an unfortunate irony that the nation's rural Indians have available to them a free, comprehensive health care system, yet rank lowest

in the country on many indictators of personal health. The 1976 American Indian Policy Review Commission (AIPRC) reported, for instance, a death rate from influenza and pneumonia twice that of the general population; a death rate from tuberculosis five times as high; and a rate for cirrhosis of the liver four times as high. The AIPRC also reported that the death rate for Indians in the 5–24 year age group was two to three times that of the total United States population (Kemberling, 1973). Wallace (1973) reported that 20%

---

*The Indian Health Service of DHHS has the responsibility for providing health services to American Indians who live on or near reservations. These services include hospital care, dental care, convalescence, and community outreach. Where facilities are not available, or where specialists are needed, services are contracted out to local hospitals.

of all American Indian deaths occur in infants and children, in contrast to only 5.9% among the U.S. population as a whole. Finally, the major illnesses that affect Indians are largely illnesses of childhood.

The health of American Indian youth is of central concern because American Indians comprise an especially young population. Studies have found that the median age for Indians is 17.3. This age compares with 29.5 for the United States as a whole. In addition, the birth rate for Indians is approximately twice that of the general U.S. population (Wallace, 1973).

In this chapter, the authors would like to make and support the contention that Indian culture need not serve as a barrier preventing Indian youth from receiving proper health care. Furthermore, to the extent that there is a barrier, it is one that has been unnecessarily created by the prejudice or indifference of Anglo health care professionals toward traditional Indian medicine. This belief is based on evidence found in the ethnographic literature on Indians, and on the authors' experiences as Indian professionals involved in health care delivery systems for Indians.

INDIAN MEDICINE: SUPERSTITIOUS OR EFFECTIVE?

Even though Anglo health personnel are generally sympathetic to Indian culture, their basic attitude seems to be that Indian medicine and medicine men are nothing more than holdovers from a superstitious past (Guidotti, 1973). Their attitude implies that there is little of value in Indian herbal theory, Indian curing ceremonies, and traditional Indian healers. This belief fails to take note of the fact that, at the time of the first European contact, the two forms of medicine were similar in effectiveness, with each containing its own irrational elements (Vogel, 1970). Indian medicine did, at times, rely on supernatural intervention.

But this appeal to the supernatural is no different from having a Catholic priest bless an ill person with holy water, or join the family in saying a rosary.

In the treatment of illness for which the cause was obvious (e.g., poisoning, fractures, wounds, snake bites, and skin irritations), Indian medicine was both rational and effective. What Vogel (1970) has called the irrational element of Indian medicine appears when there was no apparent cause for an illness, and when rational methods brought no relief. In these cases Indians resorted to such shamanistic practices as incantations, dances, and the beating of drums. So much has been made of this ritualistic approach to healing that it has come to characterize the totality of traditional Indian medicine.

Perhaps beliefs about Indian medicine held by Anglo health professionals are understandable. Vogel has pointed out that Western writers have consistently denigrated the accomplishments of American Indians. He gives as an example the statement of Dr. Benjamin Rush in an address before the American Philosophical Association in 1774 that: "We have no discoveries in material medicine to hope for from the Indians of North America" (Vogel, 1977, p. 2). In a more recent example of the same sentiment, Kraus (1954) noted that the use of traditional medicine among the Apache and Papago contributed to their health problems.

Guidotti (1973) has noted, however, that the "indiscriminate denial of an important part of Indian culture [Indian medicine] erodes confidence in Western practitioners (p. 6)." As a result, Anglo health care professionals have created a situation where it is often difficult for them to obtain the cooperation of the Indian community. Western medical practitioners might have followed the historical example of the Catholic Church. In order to promote conversions of Indians to Catholicism, the Church was active in incorporating Indian rituals and beliefs into its liturgy. Instead, the health profession has chosen to ridicule or disdain Indian medicine with a resulting alienation of many members of the Indian community.

In some ways, the ethnocentricity of health professionals stands in the way of all segments of American society receiving comprehensive health care. Warner (1977) has pointed out how the inadequate description of illness in Western thought is detrimental to good medical treatment. He listed four areas of belief about illness in Western thought that are so narrow that they constitute misconceptions. The four areas are: rigid categories of illness; single cause for an illness; static view of illness; and sharp distinction between diseases of mind and body. Warner reports, for instance, that these limited views of illness may have led to an overuse of surgery. He notes that "if we conceive of an illness as an intrusive, well defined, static object, we are more likely to want to cut it out." He also points out that Western constraints on the conception of illness make it difficult for patient and doctor alike to perceive the relevance that personality and social factors have on the cause and prevention of an illness. The conception of illness by American Indians, on the other hand, is generally less narrow. Although there are variations between tribes, most tribes emphasize treating the whole person (Primeaux, 1977).

While many Indian people today believe that modern health care is effective in treating the physical symptoms of an illness (Kniep-Hardy and Burkhardt, 1977), they feel that Western health care neglects what can be thought of as the psychological state of the individual. In addition, the sick person's entire family is usually left out of the therapeutic process.

Recent findings have given support to the Indian belief that self-perceptions of the ill person are of great importance to successful treatment. A review of placebo studies indicated that about 35% of pa-tients benefited from placebo treatment (Benson and Epstein, 1975). Indian healers have long known that encouraging a patient to have faith in a cure greatly increases the probability of a cure; hence, great emphasis was placed on the elaborate ritual that might accompany diagnostic and herbal therapy and on bringing family and clan members into the treatment process for support and comfort. Many Indians are not encouraged by what they see as the typical Western approach of a quick examination by a doctor, a supply of pills, followed by a request to call again in three days if improvement is not noted.

The authors' experiences while working on Indian health programs have given them ample opportunity to observe Anglo health professionals' attitudes toward Indian medicine and toward treating Indians. One of the most frequent comments heard from health personnel was that Indians are reluctant to seek medical assistance until it is possibly too late for effective treatment. This was repeated often enough to indicate some truth to the belief. Health personnel usually attributed this reluctance to the absence in Indian culture of a future orientation and of a tradition of preventive medicine. In addition, it was posited that Indians were fatalistic about coming down with an illness, or held such an immature conception of causal agents in disease that they would not have been expected to be concerned about such things as sanitation, isolation of the ill person, and overexposure to the elements. In effect, health personnel believed that Indian culture acted as a barrier that prevented Indians from receiving needed medical attention.

However, a review of the ethnographic literature indicates that Anglo health personnel are mistaken in their beliefs about Indian culture. The following is a brief review of ethnographic literature pertaining to traditional Indian health care practices. Corlett (1935) noted:

The Indian possessed a large measure of common sense. He knew that many natural conditions would or might affect him adversely. For example, he realized that extreme exposures to heat or cold were injurious, that man needed food and water in order to live, and that certain plants and animals, as well as other men, could easily make him suffer and even cause him to die. Sickness that arose from such causes often was understood and regarded in a sensible manner (p. 69).

The ubiquity of the medicine man was central to the health care system of pre-Columbian Indians. When an Indian had a health problem, a medicine man was called in to perform the necessary ceremonies to eradicate the health problem. However, the medicine man was also summoned to perform certain ceremonies that were preventive in nature since their purpose was to ensure a healthful future. The Navajo tribe, for instance, observes the cradleboard, first laugh, and female puberty rite as special forms of preventive medicine called "Blessingway." As part of the Navajo puberty rite called "Kinaalda," certain taboos are observed in order to ensure a healthful future for the child (Brandt, 1978). Lewis (1974) reports participating in a "yuiupa," or sing, among the Teton Dakota, performed by a medicine man to insure continued good health for a patient.

Among a number of tribes, herbs were taken as a form of contraception. Recent evidence indicates that the herbs proved quite effective in reducing the possibility of pregnancy (Vogel, 1977). Medicine bags, in use among many tribes, were a form of preventive medicine. The contents of these bags served as charms to ward off evil, which could be in the form of an illness. One of the most common cultural traits among North American Indians was the use of the sweatbath. Although it served many purposes, nearly every tribe looked upon the sweatbath as a way to either improve or maintain good health. As an interesting aside, note the current popularity of saunas in the U.S.

A historical example indicates that Indians were aware of the part that nutrition plays in the maintenance of good health. In the sixteenth century, it was reported that a European colonial vessel was stranded in the ice on one of the Great Lakes. The crew came down with the vitamin deficiency disease, scurvy. The local Iroquois successfully treated the colonial crew with special leaves and bark boiled in water. Through the ages, the Iroquois had become aware of the properties of this herb to prevent scurvy (Fenton, 1941).

In summary, many historical examples support the belief that Indians practice preventive medicine. Indians also demonstrate a sophistication in their understanding of the causes of illness and in many of their treatments. Finally, the evidence indicates that the healing practices of Indians are based on an elaborate, internally consistent world view that places human beings in harmony with their natural surroundings. An illness is the physical and spiritual manifestation of disharmony with these natural processes. Thus, *both* processes require treatment.

INDIAN AND ANGLO MEDICINE: A COLLABORATIVE APPROACH

Anglo health personnel are now starting to work with Indian culture, instead of trying to work around it. In some hospitals, Indian medicine men are being welcomed for the comfort and aid they can bring to child patients. The authors would like to encourage this trend by making the following observations on Indian behavior and values that need to be considered by Anglo health professionals working with Indians. An effort was made to include only observations on behavior typical of many American Indian tribes.

1) Health personnel should consider the family of a child who is ill. This consideration can consist of permitting them

every opportunity to be with and comfort the sick child. It could also mean that other members of the family could be treated for sympathetic symptoms. As the other members of the family start to feel better, the sick child may also start to improve.

2) "Permissive" childrearing is common among many tribes. As a consequence, health personnel have expressed the concern that Indian parents will not force their children to take Anglo medicine, to undergo therapy, and to come into the hospital. The problem probably once again is between the Anglo health personnel and the parents. If the health personnel explain clearly to the parents the need for the child to undertake some action, then the parents usually have no trouble gaining the cooperation of the child. In most cases of this kind, the parents have not been convinced of the effectiveness of the recommended treatment, and thus are unenthusiastic about having their children undergo treatment.

3) In treating Indian alcoholics, the therapeutic approach of Alcoholics Anonymous and Synanon or other group procedures that entail public confessions of guilt should be avoided. Cathartic releases or emotional displays are not part of Indian culture and might do the Indian alcoholic more harm than good.

4) Public Health Service hospitals that treat Indians are often very crowded during periods when new patients are admitted. As a result, there is a tendency to avoid preventive medical check-ups. However, health personnel should be aware that when Indians come to them seeking medical advice, or expressing desire for physical exams, they should not treat these events lightly. A thorough check-up is usually warranted in these cases.

5) It has commonly been reported that Indians are reluctant to permit health workers making visits to enter their homes. Usually, conversation with the visiting health workers takes place outside the home in the yard. It is our belief that this practice is not a matter of Indians being inhospitable. The resistance from Indians may be attributed to the unexpected nature of most home visits by health workers. Where possible, health workers making home visits should let the Indian family know in advance when to expect them. This advance notice for the Indian family would be consonant with a common Indian cultural practice of a waiting period before beginning a social interaction.

6) Most Indian people have a tradition of personal modesty. This is especially true for women. Health personnel should attempt to respect this cultural view, or risk alienating their clients.

7) Hospitals that serve large numbers of Indians should make an attempt to serve patients traditional Indian food. It is the authors' understanding that this is rarely done, even when there are no special dietary considerations. Hospital administrators should find that, in return for a small change in their kitchen operation, they can gain substantial rapport with the Indian community.

8) The personal space in which interpersonal communication takes place is larger in the Indian community than it is in the Anglo community. Consequently, Anglo health personnel should avoid standing too close to their clients, or touching them unnecessarily.

9) There are three areas of Indian behavior that have come to represent barriers to Indian people receiving effective health care. The behaviors are: lack of concern and attention to the passage of time; noninterference with the affairs of others; and delay in seeking medical attention. All of these behaviors have been mentioned many times, both in the literature and by health personnel working with Indians.

From a Western framework, perceived unconcern with time can be a problem because Indians may be vague in relating to doctors how long they have had the symptoms of an illness. It also may present a problem if fixed time schedules are not followed in taking prescription drugs. Social noninterference presents a problem because it is thought that many times a sick child or family member will not be encouraged by other family members to seek needed medical attention. The third behavior, delay in seeking needed medical attention, presents obvious problems to effective health care.

These traditional behaviors can be effectively neutralized, and possibly be made to work to the advantage of Indian people, by the implementation of a health education program that attempts to validate modern day optimal health care practices in terms of traditional behavior. A basic approach would be the use of health paraprofessionals from the Indian community to reinterpret traditional Indian behavior to their communities. The Indian paraprofessionals would explain to their communities that parallels exist between traditional forms of behavior and present behavior that are useful in today's society. As an example, in the past as well as now, Indian people had to be concerned with the passage of time in order to conform to the rigid time demands found in many tribal rituals. In addition, in many tribes there were situations (taboos, ceremonies) in which it was permissible to coerce other individuals, or interfere in their behavior.

It is hoped that by pointing out such possible parallels between modern and traditional cultures, an accommodation can be reached which makes good health care meaningful to Indians in terms of traditional values. The Indian paraprofessional will be teaching that, like all viable cultures, Indian culture is not static, but an alive and enduring body of beliefs, values and attitudes capable of integrating new ideas and accommodating new realities.

Preliminary work with Indian health paraprofessionals by one of the authors indicates that both the health aides and the Indian community were receptive to efforts to build a bridge between tradi-

tional beliefs and modern Western health care practices. Here the underlying rationale is that most Indians want to live by their culture and will resist behavior that seems to lead to assimilation, even when that behavior might prove personally beneficial.

SUMMARY AND CONCLUSIONS

The values and attitudes of Indian culture have been accused of being the cause of low school achievement, high unemployment, and poor health among Indian people. Western society has always implicitly looked down on Indian culture and sought to force assimilation on Indian families. Assimilation was thought to be needed in order to remove Indian children from a culture that was considered to be empty, meager, and nonadaptive to the modern world. Nevertheless, most Indian people have not fully assimilated, except in terms of material culture. A more realistic approach is to look for all that is positive in Indian culture, and then work to encourage these cultural strengths. In this way, it is hoped that there will be an end to the irony of Indian children having a free, comprehensive health care system available to them at the same time that they possess low general levels of health.

REFERENCES

American Indian Policy Review Commission. *Report on Indian Health.* Washington, D.C.: Government Printing Office, 1976.

Benson, A. and Epstein, S. The placebo effect: A neglected asset in the care of patients. *JAMA,* June 23, 1975, *232,* 12.

Brandt, P. Two different worlds ... the Navajo child's interactions within the health care system. In: M. Leminger (Ed.), *Transcultural Nursing: Concepts, Theories and Practices.* New York: Wiley, 1978, Chapter 14.

Corlett, W.T. *The Medicine Man of the American Indian and His Cultural Background.* Springfield, IL: Charles C Thomas, 1935.

Coulehan, J.L. Health and social needs of Navajo Indian children. Department of Community Medicine, University of Pittsburgh School of Medicine. Unpublished manuscript, 1976.

Fenton, W.N. Contacts between Indians and colonial medicine. Washington, D.C.: Smithsonian Institute, 1941.

Guidotti, T.L. Health care for a rural minority; Lessons from the Modoc Indian country in California. *California Medicine*, April 1973, *118*, 4.

Harvard Child Health Project Task Force, Vol. II: Children's Medical Care Needs and Treatment. Cambridge, MA: Ballinger, 1977.

Kemberling, S.R. The Indian health service: Commentary on a commentary. *Pediatrics,* June, 1973, *51*, 6.

Kniep-Hardy, M. and Burkhardt, M.A. Nursing the Navajo. *American Journal of Nursing*, January, 1977, *77*, 1.

Kraus, B.S. Indian health in Arizona. Bureau of Ethnic Research, University of Arizona, 1954.

Lewis, T.H. An Indian healer's preventive medicine procedure. *Hospital & Community Psychiatry*, February, 1974, *25*, 2.

Primeaux, M.H. American Indian health care practices—A cross-cultural perspective. *Nursing Clinics of North America*, March, 1977, *12*, 1.

Vogel, V.J. American Indian medicine. Norman: University of Oklahoma Press, 1970, p. 265 or p. 813.

Vogel, V.J. American Indian influence on the American pharmacopeia. *American Indian Culture and Research Journal*, 1977, *2*, 2.

Wallace, H.M. The health of American Indian children. *American Journal of Diseases of Children*, March, 1973, *125*.

Warner, R. The relationship between language and disease concepts. *International Journal of Psychiatry in Medicine*, 1977, 7, 1.

PART II

Psychosocial

Development

CHAPTER 4

Coping with Adversity:
The Psychosocial Development
of Afro-American Children

Gloria Johnson Powell, M.D.

How maddening it was to have been born black in a cottonfield with aspirations
of grandeur. . . . From the beginning unwarranted mores and social boundaries
designed to stifle and oppress my hopes and dreams, compounded and intensified the realities of being black and poor. Blackness meant subordination
and suppressed pride. Poverty meant an insufficient amount of fuel to feed my
roaring fires of fantasy. Frustrated and confused as to the reasons for the
conspiracy against me, questions arose concerning the society around me. As
the cloud of innocence lifted and cleared my vision, I fell fast and hard before
a crude stone wall of racism. The pagans who guarded the wall allowed peeks
through tempting loopholes to what lay beyond. There thrived the world of
my dreams—a beautiful world with white-washed houses, green lawns and
enclosed by dainty picket fences. The citizens stood proud and tall. It was a
world of wealth, love and equality. It was the white world. Why did hatred
separate us? To perceive the hatred as a personal insult was to drink the venom
of self-destruction. I became a crazed dog running in circles snapping after my
tail. When the futility of my actions set in, I discovered self-worth and found
the most important riches of all—happiness, love, and pride.

by a Tenth-grade Afro-American student after reading Maya Angelu's
I Know Why the Caged Bird Sings

49

INTRODUCTION: CRIPPLES AND DEFICITS

In 1950 at the White House Conference on Children, the eminent psychologist Kenneth Clark paid particular attention to the issue of the psychological well-being of Afro-American children when he presented data on the effects of discrimination on the emotional development of Afro-American children (Witmer and Kotinsky, 1952). This information was eventually used as part of the social science testimony in the NAACP brief in the 1954 U.S. Supreme Court case on school desegregation, which is reviewed in Chapter 31 in this volume (Clark, 1939, 1947, 1952).

Previous to Clark's report, Deutscher and Chein (1948) had presented similar data on the psychological effects of discrimination, based upon their survey of social scientists. Even earlier, Dollard (1937) had written about the socialization process of Afro-American children and adolescents, and as far back as the late 1930s and early 1940s, the American Educational Council had funded studies throughout various regions of the U.S. to understand "the degree of character torsion (which) systematic oppression exerts upon human personality." These studies of Afro-American children served as a catalyst for subsequent studies. All this research identified the malignant effects of discrimination on the psychosocial development of Afro-American children.

In 1970 the *Report of the Joint Commission on the Mental Health of Children* noted that "only rarely does the child of an ethnic minority escape the damaging effects of racism" which combined with poverty "cripples the minority-group child in body, mind, and spirit" (p. 215). In 1978 the President's Commission on Mental Health paid particular attention to the problems of minority-group persons, and noted the special needs and problems of their children. What emerged from all this concern and research was the image of the Afro-American child as a psychological cripple. In our urgency to right the wrongs of racism and put our humanistic values into practice, we had unwittingly produced yet another negative stereotype of Afro-American children.

I call attention to this situation neither to impugn the dignity and humane intentions of our national committees nor to deny the existence of many urgent mental health problems among Afro-American children, but rather to focus professional attention on the mentally healthy as well as the mentally ill. An important goal for mental-health practitioners must be to identify Afro-American children who overcome the vicissitudes of racism and poverty. By examining the degree of psychological well-being that these children experience, and by studying the coping strategies that make them so strong, we will be able to design effective programs to prevent and treat the damage that racism and poverty do to others.

A major stumbling block to focusing on health rather than illness has been the supposition by some that it is doubtful that any Afro-American child can grow up psychologically unscathed in this racist, negrophobic, white-dominated culture — that no matter what the parameters of psychological well-being might be, they cannot be or are rarely achieved by Afro-American children. Much of the discussion and research on ego development in Afro-American children appears to support this view.

Simpkins et al. (1975) have summarized succinctly the theoretical perspectives on which most research on Afro-Americans has been based—e.g., a deficit model which defines the white middle-class culture as the acceptable norm. Valentine (1971) presented an alternative with his conceptualization of a bicultural model composed of standardized Afro-American group behavior as well as behavioral patterns from the mainstream of the Euro-American cultural system. Nobles (1980) warns that the self-hatred literature "should be accepted as valid information only with considerable doubt and caution" (p. 20). Still others caution that the overemphasis on pathology "even when motivated by sympathy results in dehumanization" (Thomas and Sillen, 1972, p. 46). What has been overlooked in the fervent search for the pathology, according to Gurin and Epps (1975), is the minimization of the role of the oppressor and, more especially, of the adaptive strengths of Afro-Americans. All too often the coping strategies and strengths of Afro-Americans have been ignored. Part of the task of this chapter is to help identify those coping strengths.

The second task of this chapter is to sort out the theories and data and identify what is plausible and realistic about the psychologic development of the Afro-American child. Hopefully, what will emerge are some baseline data about the psychosocial development, minus the stereotypes and the psychological cripple and deficit models. First, some of the theories will be reviewed and their validity examined. Then, the literature on the psychosocial development of Afro-American children will be reviewed, particularly in the areas of self-concept development, sex role development and socialization, and the effects of father's absence.

Self-concept studies comparing Afro-Americans and whites during the period 1943-1958 showed that self-concept was less adequate among Afro-Americans (Dreger and Miller, 1960). These findings correspond to the conclusions reached by Kardiner and Ovesey (1968), Mosby (1972), and other social scientists. From an historical perspective, it should be noted that such studies reviewed by Dreger and Miller (1960) were done during the pre-civil rights era and just shortly after the 1954 Supreme Court desegregation decision whose full impact was not felt until the 1964 Civil Rights Act. Indeed, studies on self-concept done between 1959 and 1965 did not indicate any changes in self-concept among Afro-Americans (Dreger and Miller, 1968). A careful critique of the Dreger and Miller (1968) review for those

studies related to children revealed a hodgepodge of theoretical concepts on self-esteem and serious problems in measurement and sample selection (Powell, 1973).

In a review of the theoretical perspectives on self-concept, Barnes (1972) attempts to make some projections about the possibilities of the Afro-American child developing positive self-concept in this society. He concludes that the possibilities are nil. He takes note of the fact that the Afro-American child's family has been socialized to believe they are substandard human beings and that the child learns the undesirability of his black skin color and hair texture, attributes which belong to one of the three categories of stigma outlined by Goffman (1963). Barnes lists the following findings and references regarding self-concept in Afro-American children (p. 168):

(a) incomplete self-image;
(b) negative self-image and preference for white;
(c) rejection of and expressed hostility toward his own group.

Such self-hatred and low self-esteem have been thought to have negative effects on the child's cognitive and affective status and achievement orientation, with the following reported consequences (p. 169):

(a) high anxiety level;
(b) high level of maladjustment;
(c) neuroticism and rejection of other Afro-Americans;
(d) inability to delay gratification;
(e) low-level orientation toward achievement;
(f) proneness toward delinquency;
(g) confusion of sexual identity or sex role adoption;
(h) sense of little personal control over the environment;
(i) low achievement motivation;
(j) unrealistically high aspirations.

It should be noted that none of these studies cited by Barnes (1972) was comprehensively critiqued in terms of methodology, sampling, etc. Herzog and Sudia (1973) have suggested caution in generalizing from "limited, qualified, or shakily based research findings . . . to a population for which these findings are not clearly applicable" (p. 213).

There were two psychiatric studies done during the mid to late 1960s which reached different conclusions; both are worth reviewing briefly. Hauser's study (1971, 1972) in New Haven junior and senior high schools was an attempt to clarify the relationship between patterns of identity formation and sociocultural context through a longitudinal study on non-middle-class white and Afro-American young males. Hauser concluded that rather than manifesting change with further experience and education, the patterns among the Afro-American youth showed fixed self-images, unchanging in their content or integration with one another. The patterns were consistent with the definition of identity foreclosure and a disruption in ego identity development. However, the patterns of whites revealed progressive identity formation and not the diminished psychological growth demonstrated by the Afro-American youth.

Another study was reported by Coles (1967) who described Afro-American children undergoing school desegregation in the South. His conclusions about the damaged psyche and mental status of the children he studied varied significantly from Hauser's:

So it is not all disorder and terror for these children. As they grow older, go to school, think of a life for themselves, they can envision a life which is quiet, pleasant and uneventful for long stretches of time, or at least as much so as for any "other" children. That is, the Negro child will play and frolic, eat and sleep like all other children; and, though this may seem no great discovery, it is essential that it be mentioned in a discussion which necessarily singles out special pains or hazards for analysis (p. 340).

Barnes (1972) has noted that the self-hatred of the Afro-American child has negative effects on cognitive and affective development as well as on academic achievement. Meanwhile, empirical data on positive self-concept among Afro-American children began to be reported (Soares and Soares, 1969, 1972; Powell and Fuller, 1970, 1972; Powell 1973; Rosenberg and Simmons, 1972). The details of those studies will be reported later in this chapter. Let us begin by examining the theory of self-concept as a psychological entity.

AN OVERVIEW OF SELF-CONCEPT THEORIES

It cannot be denied that self-concept is the growing child's most basic structure of who he is. It is the foundation on which he bases his actions, thought, and sets directions to his life. Because of the psychological and human essence of the self-concept, any theory about its etiology, significance, and growth becomes central to the psychology of the self. Self-concept is a diverse phenomenon and Rosenberg (1979) is to be congratulated for having abstracted the essence of the four major principles advanced regarding self-concept formation to "bring an impressive level of coherence to a diversity of empirical data" (p. 62).

For Harry Stack Sullivan (1947), who represents one of the major theories, the self is made up of a collection of self-appraisals. The reflected appraisal principle includes *direct reflections* (how particular others view us), *perceived self* (how we believe they view us), and the *generalized other* (attitudes of the community as a whole). These principles are internalized in the "me" and serve as a perspective for viewing the self. It stands to reason that some consistency is needed between how others view us and how we view ourselves, for "considerable discordance between our self-view and the view others hold of us may generate considerable difficulty" (Rosenberg, 1979, p. 63).

The second theory of self-concept principles reviewed by Rosenberg (1979) is that of the principle of social comparison—à la Pettigrew (1967) and his social evaluation theory. People learn about themselves by comparing themselves to others, but such a process may result in positive, negative, or neutral self-perceptions, depending on the standards employed for comparison.

The self-attribution theory of Bem (1967) is yet another perspective on self-concept development theory. The definition of attribution includes the process of inferring or perceiving the dispositional properties of "entities in the environment" (Kelley, 1967). Rosenberg's (1979) interpretation of these concepts is that the attribution theorist would be interested in understanding the bases from which people draw conclusions about their own motives or underlying characteristics and how they go about verifying their tentative conclusions.

The fourth principle advanced about self-concept is the theory of psychological centrality. This theory views the self-concept as an organization of components which are hierarchically interrelated in complex ways:

What the principle of psychological centrality calls to attention, however, is that to the extent that individuals focus their sense of worth on different self-components, the success of one person is not necessarily achieved at the expense of the other. (Rosenberg, 1979, p. 21)

These four principles suggest the complexity, social component, and individual variation in self-concept.

However, the people who stimulate the child most significantly are those in his immediate world with whom he constantly interacts. For G.H. Mead (1934), the original sense of self is composed of the attitudes, words, gestures of the significant others whom the child encoun-

ters, perceives and mimics, and with whom he interacts.

The child's first period of self-image is created by his parents. Through his interactions with his parents he comes to know what is expected of him, and he compares his expectations with his own behavior. However, part of the expectation of Afro-American parents for their children is that they conform to a standard of behavior that will protect them from the dangers of racism. The self-image developed during this period will play a major role in their personality development. Racism impinges on this necessary process for minority-group children, the consequences of which extend into every aspect of their lives.

In summary, all theories indicate to some extent the social interaction and social cognition of self-concept. For children, then, what they perceive about themselves in their immediate environment begins to fashion their self-concept. The wider the world expands for children, the greater the array of self-pictures perceived.

A REVIEW OF THE LITERATURE ON THE POSITIVE SELF-CONCEPT OF AFRO-AMERICAN CHILDREN

In 1969, a pilot study on the psychological effects of school desegregation on 7th, 8th, and 9th graders was carried out in a southern city using the Tennessee Self-Concept Scale and a Socio-Familial Questionnaire given to 614 white and Afro-American students (Powell and Fuller, 1970). Although previous research had focused on the damaged self-percept of Afro-American students, the data from this study showed that there was a self-concept gap between Afro-American and white students, with Afro-American students having significantly higher (or more positive) scores than white students. Those Afro-American students having the highest self-concept scores were those in segregated or predominantly Afro-American schools. The hypothesis of the study which eventually involved 1,754 southern junior high school students from three Southeastern schools was that the changing social, cultural, and political milieu in the South was affecting self-concept development of both white and Afro-American children, and that the amount and degree of self-concept change would be dependent not only on the degree of family stability and economic status, but also on the amount, degree, and kind of social, cultural, and political changes within the community. The data from the 279 Afro-American students in Nashville, the setting of the pilot study, indicated that the Afro-American student, regardless of sex, type of school attended, socioeconomic status, educational or occupational level of parents, IQ, or academic achievement, scored higher than white students compared on similar variables.

The Afro-American students had particularly significantly higher (more positive) scores than white students on (a) identity (Who am I?), (b) self-satisfaction (How do I feel about myself?), (c) moral-ethical self, and (d) certainty about the self.

The family background data in the pilot study were significant in that they did not show the pattern of family instability among Afro-American families so widely reported in other studies. It should be noted, too, that family stability, SES, educational and occupational status of parents were not the most significant variables mediating high self-concept among the Afro-American students. The most significant variables were race and type of school (Powell and Fuller, 1970, 1972; Powell, 1973).

In considering the variables for positive self-concept among the young southern Afro-American adolescents studied in Nashville, Powell and Fuller (1972) noted some significant historical and social changes. From 1949 to 1969 the majority of comparative studies of self-concept studies showed Afro-American children having lower scores on such scales than whites. However, the milieu to which a child is exposed influences his emotional and cognitive development; changes in that milieu are likely also to cause changes in that development.

Between 1949 and 1969 major sociopolitical changes occurred in American society, the most noteworthy of which was the 1954 U.S. Supreme Court School Desegregation decision and subsequent legal litigation around Civil Rights issues. Major social changes in Afro-American communities occurred as a result of such litigation, as well as the non-violent movement of Martin Luther King, Jr., the student sit-in movement, the rise of the Black Muslim movement with its emphasis on "black supremacy," the increase of "black consciousness" with the recurrent theme of "Black is Beautiful," the riots in the 1960s in all of the major American cities demanding "Black Power," and the concurrent increase of Afro-American Studies on college campuses, along with pride in Afro-American culture and a reexamination of African ancestral roots. Such major social, cultural, and political changes in Afro-American life could not have occurred without concomitant psychological changes.

Soares and Soares (1969) studied the self-perceptions of 229 disadvantaged 4th to 8th grade children of whom two-thirds were Afro-American and Puerto Rican, and one-third white, and 285 advantaged students who were 90 percent white and 10 percent from various minority groups. The self-perceptions studied included (a) the self-concept (how the individual believes himself to be at the moment), (b) the ideal concept (how he wishes he were or hopes to become), and (c) reflected selves (how he believes others view him) which included perceptions of (1) classmates, (2) teachers, and (3) parents. Thus, five measures of self-perception were studied.

The children in the disadvantaged area

school with the two-thirds Afro-American and Puerto Rican students had higher mean self-concept scores and greater variability in their self-perceptions. Although there were no sex differences on any of the five measures, the school and sex combination showed significant differences on self-concept, reflected self-parent, and reflected self-classmates. In addition, the school and grade interaction showed significant differences between boys and girls on self-concept, reflected self-classmates, and reflected self-teachers. Thus, the interaction of school, sex, and grade indicated a trend towards lower scores for boys as they go from fourth to eighth grade, but a tendency for girls to obtain higher scores as they progress from fourth to eighth grade. Advantaged girls tended to have higher scores than advantaged boys, but disadvantaged and/or minority-group boys tended to have higher self-perceptions than disadvantaged and/or minority-group girls. These findings are in direct contrast to Hauser's (1972) study of disadvantaged white and Afro-American boys.

Baughman and Dahlstrom (1968) in their study of southern rural white and Afro-American children noted that a comparison of self-attitudes of eighth-grade students contradicted the pervasive assertion of the damaged self-attitudes of Afro-American children. Indeed, the Afro-American children in this study more frequently reported themselves as being popular with peers, satisfied with being the kind of person they were, and having a happier home life than did the white children.

Similarly, a study of Afro-American students in three southern cities (Powell, 1973) showed that Afro-American students in each of the cities scored significantly higher on the Tennessee Self-Concept Scale than white students.

In addition, the Afro-American students scored significantly higher than the white students on identity, moral-ethical self, self-satisfaction, and family self. These data are particularly interesting in view of the stereotypic view of Afro-American children as being delinquent and antisocial and of the Afro-American family as being chaotic and destructive to the self-percept of the Afro-American child.

The conclusion that the concept of low self-esteem among Afro-American children must be discarded is supported by the exhaustive recent literature reviews by Wylie (1978), Christmas (1973), Rosenberg (1979), and Weinberg (1977). Such reviews indicate that the vast majority of the studies reveal: (1) either that there is little or no difference in self-concept between white and Afro-American children or, (2) that Afro-American children have higher self-esteem than white children. In addition, studies with large sample sizes, i.e., those by Hunt and Hardt (1969), Powell (1973), Rosenberg and Simmons (1972), do not find that the self-percept of Afro-American children is damaged. According to Wylie (1978), whose review of the literature included 53 studies on racial/ethnic status and self-esteem, those who still adhere to the theory of the damaged self-percept of the Afro-American child arising from the disadvantaged social position of Afro-Americans in the United States must now carry the burden of proof of this viewpoint.

Noting the differences in results of self-concept studies of Afro-American children prior to the early 1960s from those done in the late 1960s and in the 1970s, the most obvious question to be asked is whether these differences are due to differences in methods of measuring self-concept or whether they reflect actual changes in self-concepts of Afro-American children. The response should be that the differences are due to both. Wylie's (1978) review of the methodology of self-concept studies is supportive of the measurement differences. The studies of Hall et al. (1972) and Rosenberg (1979), as well as the most recent studies done in the 1970s, are supportive of the view that actual changes in the self-perception of Afro-

Americans have occurred over time. Considering the compelling lack of evidence for the damaged self-percept of the Afro-American child, Rosenberg (1979) concludes that the theory of reflected appraisals—that people who evolved in a society will internalize that society's negative view of them—is not at fault. He proposes that the conversion of society's attitude toward the individual's group into the individual's attitude toward the self is "logically compelling" only if one assumes individual awareness and agreement as well as personal relevance and significance for the individual.

One of the most thorough studies to date testing the various theories of self-concept is the Rosenberg and Simmons (1972) study of Baltimore school children in grades 3–12. It is interesting to note that among the Baltimore students 12 percent of the Afro-American children went to desegregated schools and only 30 percent lived in desegregated neighborhoods. The authors pointed out that the children tended to interact primarily with members of their own group. In a consonant segregated environment where the child is surrounded by others like him, he may have very limited day-to-day interpersonal experience with discrimination. His world is one of home and school. If both the home neighborhood and the school are Afro-American, the child is less likely to be exposed to the negative attitudes about his racial group and more likely to hear positive statements about people of his own racial group. The Powell (1973) study in three southern cities confirms this finding.

The assumption of agreement regarding reflected appraisals presupposes that a person agrees with what society thinks of his group. Many studies now show that Afro-Americans do not believe the negative stereotypes about themselves or that they are inferior to whites (Brigham, 1974; Campbell, 1976; Lawrence, 1975; Middleton, 1972). In regard to the assumption of agreement, Rosenberg (1979) concludes that even if the Afro-American child knows that his group is held in low esteem, that information does not mean that he will agree with that assumption. In fact, he may rightly assume that "he lives in a bigoted, irrational society composed of bigoted irrational whites" (Rosenberg 1979). He may also come to understand that the bigotry and irrationality are not his fault nor the fault of his racial group. In addition, he may assume that the contradiction of the bigotry juxtaposed with the concept of equality in the American creed which is taught in school is the white man's problem to resolve.

The assumption of personal relevance can also be seriously questioned, for the Afro-American child's perceptions of society's evaluation of his group may not coincide with his own personal feelings about himself, irrespective of his age. In addition, the conclusions regarding the assumption of significance can also be questioned. One of the major misconceptions in assuming that societal racism will directly influence global self-esteem arises from the lack of understanding about the centrality of interpersonal relationships of the primary significant others such as mother, father, siblings, teachers and classmates. The significant others in the Afro-American child's life are not the majority group or society as a whole. Norton makes a special issue of these factors in her chapter (11) in this volume. The misconception regarding the assumption of significance is illustrated by data from the Baltimore study (Rosenberg and Simmons, 1972) in which 70 percent of the Afro-American children who perceived the attitudes of their significant others still had high self-esteem. However, among the white children only 43 percent with favorable perceptions of attitudes about them from significant others and 12 percent with unfavorable attitude-perceptions of significant others had high self-esteem.

Rosenberg (1979) offers another reason—that of social comparison—for the

expectation that self-esteem among minority-group members should be lower
than that of majority-group people, e.g.,
the issues of income, academic performance, family structure, and skin color. In
all four respects, according to the general
value system of this society, the Afro-
American child is placed in a decidedly
inferior position compared to the white
child. The Afro-American child is much
more likely to be poor; his academic performance is more likely to be below the
white; he is substantially more likely to
stem from a stigmatized family structure;
and he is characterized by physical features which in the view of both Afro-
Americans and whites are less estheti-
cally pleasing than the caucasoid model.
However, even given the soundness of the
principle of social comparison, the major
defect in this kind of rationale is the assumption that Afro-American children
use whites as their comparison reference
group. Although social comparisons do
affect self-esteem, for whites as well as for
Afro-Americans, the Afro-American child
compares himself with other Afro-Americans and not with whites. However, it is
important to remember that the Afro-
American child's comparisons are done on
the basis of the actual structure of the environment in which he predominantly
lives.

Be this as it may, this thesis presupposes that most Afro-American children
are poor and live in predominantly Afro-
American neighborhoods. It ignores the
issue that with the upward mobility of
Afro-Americans, many Afro-American
children are growing up outside of the
ghetto and in desegregated or integrated
environments. Indeed, the problem of the
Afro-American underclass is directly related to the desertion of the ghetto by the
middle- and upper-class Afro-Americans.
In this regard, Wilson (1980) addresses
the issue of the growing division between
the Afro-American underclass and the
middle class. Thus, any discussion and
elucidation of self-concept development of

Afro-American children cannot fail to consider the emerging middle class among
the Afro-American population and their
self-concept vis-à-vis their social-class status and other variables such as life-style
and the particular environmental and social circumstances in which they find
themselves. Indeed, the issue of the middle-class Afro-American child is a significant one that is rarely noted.

The question still remains, however,
given the vicissitudes of discrimination
and prejudice in this country, how it is
possible that the self-esteem of Afro-
American children is not lower than that
of white children? Social comparison remains a fundamentally basic principle in
determining self-concept effects. Once
again, however, the differences in the
comparisons that result reflect the consonance or dissonance of the environment
for the individual. A review of dissonant
context in self-esteem in the areas of religion, race, and social class reveals some
interesting results. Rosenberg's (1962)
New York study found that Catholics
raised in non-Catholic neighborhoods had
lower self-esteem than Catholics raised in
Catholic or mixed neighborhoods and that
Jews raised in non-Jewish neighborhoods
had lower self-esteem than Jews raised in
Jewish or mixed neighborhoods. And finally, Protestants raised in non-Protes-
tant neighborhoods had lower self-esteem
than Protestants raised in Protestant or
mixed neighborhoods. The 1972 Baltimore study by Rosenberg and Simmons
showed that at the junior high school level
Afro-American children attending white
schools had somewhat lower self-esteem
than Afro-Americans attending predominantly Afro-American schools, and the
difference was even greater at the senior
high school level. Powell's (1973) study
also reported lower self-esteem among
Afro-American students attending predominantly white schools in the South.

Social class does not always produce a
dissonant socioeconomic environment detrimental to self-esteem for Afro-American

children. However, for both upper- and lower-class white children, dissonant socioeconomic environments appear inimical to self-esteem. Although there are some studies showing that an increase in SES among Afro-American students leads to an increase in self-esteem, there are other studies which indicate just the opposite (Powell, 1982; Coleman et al., 1966; Kaplan, 1971). Indeed, self-esteem among lower socioeconomic Afro-American children may be considerably higher than that among middle- and upper-SES Afro-American students (Soares and Soares, 1969, 1972).

Attitudes, values, or competency levels may also affect the contextual environment which will influence the way in which a child is evaluated and thus affect his self-esteem. One factor which was found to have particular significance in the Rosenberg and Simmons (1972) Baltimore study was family structure, with 30 percent of the Afro-American children coming from separated or never-married families compared to 6 percent of the white children. The most desirable family structure in American society, as Rosenberg (1979) points out, is the intact nuclear family. The least desirable is the unmarried or abandoned mother and child family. It would seem reasonable to infer, then, that children from these stigmatized family structures would have lower self-esteem. However, the Baltimore study showed that these consequences depended on the racial context in which the family structure occurred. A comparison of Afro-American children from separated or never-married families with Afro-American children from other family structures revealed that in the predominantly Afro-American schools there was no difference in self-esteem levels. However, Afro-American children from separated or never-married families attending predominantly white schools, when compared with other Afro-American children in these same schools, had lower self-esteem. Forty-two percent of the Afro-American children

from separated or never-married families had low self-esteem compared with 19 percent of the other Afro-American children who came from intact families in the mixed or white school.

The Baltimore research paradigm was replicated in a midwestern city by Simmons et al. (1977) using the same self-esteem measures. The results were similar, which is to say that the impact of the separated or never-married family structure on the Afro-American adolescent's self-esteem was dependent on the school context.

The Baltimore study also showed that the instability of the self-concept in group misidentification was related to the dissonant communication within the dissonant environment. Among the junior and senior high school Afro-American students, the more racially dissonant the student's neighborhood or school, the greater the chances that he had been teased, laughed at, or left out of things because of his race (Rosenberg and Simmons, 1972; Powell, 1973; Simmons et al., 1977). The greater self-concept instability of Afro-American children in dissonant school settings may be due to the fact that the white children and teachers in these settings do not provide sufficient confirmation for the Afro-American child's self-concept. In such school environments the minority child is likely to hear more depreciatory and fewer laudatory things about his group and about himself as a group member. One could understand how such communications could contribute to the decreased self-esteem and the increased awareness of the low esteem in which one's group is generally held in the society. This kind of awareness often brings weakening of group pride and identification. However, it is important to note that in regard to the Baltimore study Rosenberg and Simmons (1972) stress that in spite of the dissonant settings:

Only in the rarest of instances do we find the kind of strong racial disidentification implied by Kardiner and Ovesey, 1951; Erikson, 1966;

Lewen, 1948; and others. (p. 111)

Indeed, there is little evidence of real Afro-American self-hatred or flat racial misidentification. Rather, the effect of the dissonant context appears to be to make racial identification slightly more equivocal or uncertain than would otherwise be the case, but not to produce strong group rejection or shame of oneself as an Afro-American (Rosenberg and Simmons, 1972; Rosenberg, 1979).

THE SOCIALIZATION PROCESS OF THE AFRO-AMERICAN CHILD

Clausen (1968) defines socialization as the process by which the child learns the way of life in his family and of "the larger social groups in which he must relate and perform adequately" to qualify for adult status (p. 4). Clausen outlines (p. 5) the general tasks to be accomplished in this lengthy process as the following:

1. initial provision of nurturance and protection to insure survival of the infant;
2. a stable relationship with a loving person or persons and enough attention to develop responsive accommodations to others;
3. establishment of a degree of trust with the primary caretaker needs;
4. socially appropriate ways of meeting the gratification of physical needs;
5. acceptable control of aggressive and expressive impulses;
6. acquisition of physical, cognitive and social competence;
7. achievement of familiarity with the physical and social environment and learning appropriate behaviors for given situations and people;
8. incorporation of values and moral norms and development of goals that will prepare the child for the future;
9. achievement of autonomy without disruption of family ties;
10. ability to relate to other adults for

effectiveness in the pursuit of gratifying individual and group goals.

It is important to remember that socialization is a cumulative process which must be programmed according to the growing abilities of the child.

In regard to the Afro-American child, according to Wilson (1978), there are two major forces which influence the socialization process: (a) a caste-class interaction process which mediates how he will define himself, and (b) particular sociocultural group norms.

Wilson's (1978) review of the importance of culture in determining the socialization process includes the four important functions of culture, namely: (1) that culture defines situations; (2) that culture defines attitudes, values, and goals; (3) that culture defines myths, legends, and the supernatural, and (4) that culture provides behavior patterns. It is to the family, however, that the society assigns the primary task of managing the socialization process as outlined by Clausen (1968). Norton's chapter will discuss the family as the socializing unit in terms of self-concept development and cognitive competence which is expounded upon in greater detail in this volume in the chapters on testing (Padilla and Wyatt), ebonics (Sinclair), and school desegregation (Powell). Norton takes note of the socialization tasks which are accomplished by the Afro-American family, most of which fall within the realm of those defined by Clausen.

In order for the Afro-American family to prepare the child to function, in Wilson's (1978) view, the expectations of the child's class and culture must be translated into practices, and "the parents' view of the expectations of the larger culture must fit the social realities" (p. 164). In short, the socialization process utilized by the family is "affected by the geophysical, economic, and psychosocial resources of the family and community" (p. 165). Wilson contends that the caste-class status of many Afro-American families makes it difficult for Afro-American parents to meet socialization goals for their children and to provide for their physical or psychosocial needs. The caste-class system with its origins in racism and negrophobia defines the person and the group as one and the same. The caste-race system provides a restrictive socialization process which ultimately determines how the child perceives himself and thinks about himself, but most especially how he is viewed by the larger society in which he lives. The socialization process by its racist caste system shapes the conceptualization of the self which is basic to the very core of the individual's psychological well-being. Wilson's view, then, of the socialization process of the Afro-American child is that it is still determined by the caste-system of racism and economic deprivation.

Review of the most recent studies on self-concept development indicate that the Afro-American child's socialization and conceptualization of the self do not necessarily have to be impaired by racism. Norton has focused in Chapter 11 on the coping strategies of Afro-American families that help detoxify the caste-race system for the growing Afro-American child and insure the accomplishment of the 10 tasks outlined by Clausen (1968) for the socialization process of childhood which leads to adult competency.

Barnes (1972) concurs with Norton (Chapter 11) in stressing the importance of the family in mediating an adequate self-esteem for the Afro-American child in spite of the vicissitudes of racism and denigration of self which can occur. Barnes' systems approach to the development of self-concept in Afro-American children utilizes Billingsley's (1968) conceptualization of the Afro-American family as a social system (p. 173):

The (Afro-American) family is embedded in a matrix of mutually interdependent relationships with the Afro-American community and the wider society. And there are subsystems within the family: husband-wife; mother-son; father-daughter; grandmother-mother-daughter, and so forth. The (Afro-American) community includes schools, churches, lodges, social clubs, funeral societies, organized systems of hustling, and other institutions.

Lewis and Weinraub (1976) also stress the social network system as a way of understanding the developmental process of the child. In developing his systems approach to self-concept development in Afro-American children, Barnes (1972) takes particular note of (1) the mutual interdependence of the Afro-American community, and (2) the development of group solidarity and a sense of peoplehood with the development of Afro-American norms and goals by which Afro-Americans can redefine themselves. The emergence of these two processes is reflected in "the natural" hair style, the African dress and names among Afro-Americans (p. 178):

... It is possible for a (Afro-American) child to have or develop a positive, actualizing self-concept in this society under certain conditions. These conditions are that the Afro-American community containing the child and family be characterized by a sense of peoplehood, group identification or (Afro-American) consciousness or pride, and that the family be identified with or experience a sense of belonging to the community. It is postulated that when these conditions prevail, the (Afro-American) community interposed between the family and white community, serves as a filter against the harmful inputs from the latter.

Barnes is not alone in this point of view which includes support from Carmichael and Hamilton (1967), Sizemore (1969), and Erikson (1968), who all affirm that self-determination is an integral part of ego identity. Likewise, these social scientists espouse the point of view that institutions in the Black community have been founded based on the ideology of self-determinism.

To test these hypotheses, Barnes (1972) studied group identification and self-concept among Afro-American children in four Model Cities elementary schools. The data showed that regardless of SES, the ethnic identity and self-concept scores of children whose parents have a high level of political and community activity such as participating in Model Cities Citizens Activities, voting for Afro-American candidates, and attending school meetings were higher than those whose parents were uninvolved in the Afro-American community activities. In addition, children whose parents tended to blame the caste-class system for the inequities among Afro-Americans and who believed in collective and militant action as the solution to the problems of Afro-Americans had higher group identification and self-concept scores.

Lewis and Weinraub (1976) take particular note that the young child's social, affective, and intellectual development are not solely determined by the mother-infant relationship and have conceptualized the social network system as a way of understanding child development. The Goodall (1971) and Harlow and Harlow (1969) primate studies and the Rheingold and Eckerman (1975), and Lewis et al. (1975) human studies clearly indicate that the child's peer relationships occur at the same time as its maternal relationship. Needless to say, the infant's relationships with father, grandparents, and siblings begin early in life and do not operate in complete isolation from the child's relationship to the mother.

It should be recognized, argue Lewis and Weinraub (1976), that man is by nature a social animal and "part of a large social network from the very beginning of life" (p. 160). From their viewpoint, the attachment literature emphasized the mother-infant relationship very strongly and ignored other social and non-social relationships. The results have been that the conceptualization of attachment has retarded a conceptual framework that investigates other social interactions which influence the child's early development.

The social network theory can be useful in examining the world of the Afro-Amer-

ican child and how he acquires knowledge about himself, his family, and his environment and his coping strategies which help him overcome the vicissitudes of racism. Such a model can account for how the child develops that repertoire of behaviors that are distributed within the social network according to the object, function, and the situation of the specific interaction.

An understanding of the kinship network is particularly important for the Afro-American child if there is to be any understanding of his psychosocial development and his coping mechanism. The omission has led to many misconceptions and the perpetuation of defunct and psychopathological models of the development of Afro-American children.

Carol Stack's (1974) *All Our Kin* is an attempt to study the social network of Afro-American children growing up in a poor urban area. Her study is important because it takes note of the fact that the absent Afro-American father is not always so absent. Direct and indirect modes of influence are noted and have been discussed in Stack's (1974) and Ladner's (1971) studies. The former study is particularly important in that it examined a domestic network of northern urban ghetto diffused over several kin-based households with an extended cluster of kinspeople related chiefly through children but also through marriage and friendship. The life-history material collected indicated the positive role that Afro-American men play in family life not only as a parent and a contributor to their own family network of children and spouse but also as a valuable resource to the network of their own kin. Indeed, households had shifting memberships of three generations of kin. The study highlights, however, the cooperation between male and female siblings who live in or near the same household. Stack (1974) emphasizes the fact that the pattern of close cooperation of adult siblings has gone unnoticed in the analysis of the lower-SES Afro-American family. The omission of such data underestimates the constant and close contact of children with male relatives. Stack also pays particular attention to the fact that household boundaries are elastic but continuous and no one model prevails.

The work of Lewis et al. (1975) has stressed the need for alternative modes of influences rather than the direct effects of social objects. Lewis and Weinraub (1976) suggest that "members of the social network may affect the child directly or indirectly" and that "the modes of influence affect and are affected by cognitive as well as socio-emotional development."

Sex Role Development and Socialization

Kagan (1964) has suggested that the acquisition of sex role behavior is the single most important and long-term aspect of the socialization process. Most theorists focus upon the effects of direct reinforcement, particularly by parents, which begins early in childhood and infancy and continues throughout the childhood period. The reinforcement mechanism, however, may be too simplistic an approach to account for the differential behavior between boys and girls. The importance of the modeling process in sex role acquisition has been stressed in most studies on sex role development. The modeling process theory proposes that the acquisition of the variety of behaviors which are involved in gender role patterning is accomplished by years of observing parents and imitating characteristic behavior of the same parent. Now many studies suggest, however, that there are many other factors involved in the modeling process, including the availability of the parental model, the similarity of the parental model to the child as perceived by the child, the powerfulness of the parental model as perceived by the child, and the nurturant qualities of the parental model (Maccoby and Jacklin, 1974).

In most of the theories regarding sex role development, the behavior of the parents is considered to be the primary process in the acquisition of gender identity. Kohlberg (1966), however, is a proponent of the cognitive developmental view which suggests that the beginning process in the gender role acquisition stage is the child's recognition of being a boy or a girl. After that, the self-labeling process occurs; a positive value comes to be placed on all activities and behaviors which seem to be related to boyness or girlness. Although parents have considerable input into this process, Kohlberg also considers that the cognitive view allows for the possibility of other important sources of influence in sex role development.

In a review of sex typing and role modeling, Maccoby and Jacklin (1974) question the theory that boys and girls make sex type choices based upon sex models. They note that most theories on sex typing and role modeling emphasize the role of imitation and identification in the acquisition of the child's sex type behavior. The reviewers enumerate several major themes that emerge from their critique of literature but conclude that (1) children will imitate the more dominant, powerful figure when more than one model is available, and (2) all things being equal, children will choose to imitate the most nurturant model. Thus, although children are clearly sex typed, their degree of sex typing is unrelated to that of the same sex parent. When children have choices of models, they do not consistently select same sex models. Consequently, it cannot be concluded that sex typing originates through the role of modeling. These conclusions are vital to the understanding of the complexities of the varieties in family life styles among Afro-American children. From these studies of sex type and the role of modeling, a review of the literature of the effect of father absence on Afro-American boys becomes clearer in terms of its consequences for Afro-American children, as well as providing suggestions for alternative models of sex role acquisition that may be available and more significant.

There have been a number of studies which have investigated sex role preference in Afro-American pre-school children. Using the IT scale for children, Dill et al. (1975) measured the sex role preferences of 46 male and 47 female Afro-American subjects and the original normative white male sample. Indeed, Afro-American subjects seemed to manifest sex role preference similar to their white peers, although female scores were more variable. They suggest that previous assumptions concerning the socialization of sex role behavior of Afro-American children are challengeable and must be reinvestigated.

McNabb (1973) replicated a study on delinquent acting out and the task of sexual identification among Afro-American male adolescents. The hypothesis of the study was that the acting-out behavior among Afro-American male adolescents is associated with high levels of unconscious femininity and conscious masculinity. The subjects in the replication study were 14- and 16-year-old boys who were residents of a rehabilitative institution following adjudication for a variety of offenses. The scale used to measure unconscious femininity was the Gough Femininity Scale. Contrary to other such studies, the relative proportion of Afro-American adolescent males was evenly distributed throughout all sex role categories rather than heavily weighted in the "high unconscious femininity" and "high conscious masculinity" groups. The implications are that the relationships between delinquent acting out and the task of sexual identification may not be as important an ideology of delinquency among Afro-Americans as among whites. There had been some indication from other studies that sex role stereotyping among Afro-American families might be less in degree than that among white families (Maccoby and Jacklin, 1974). Gough and St. Ange (1974) studied 20 first- and third-grade girls, half of whom were white and the

other half Afro-American. Both white and Afro-American children gave equally stereotyped responses to questions about children. However, Afro-American girls gave fewer stereotyped responses than white girls to questions about adults.

The review of sex role acquisition and typing calls into question the prevalent theme of "mal de mère" in the social science studies of the Afro-American family, especially in terms of the emasculation and rejection of the Afro-American boy by his mother. A closer scrutiny of the psychosocial development of Afro-American boys presents some interesting data.

The Psychosocial Development of Afro-American Boys

In his re-examination of psychosocial development among Afro-American children and youth, Taylor (1976) recapitulates what he articulates as the "fundamental assumptions and empirical evidence, upon which are based conventional views of the nature and meaning of Afro-American self-esteem." Most important, however, he suggests alternative interpretations and conclusions regarding the level of Afro-American self-esteem. He takes note of Rainwater's (1966) study of lower-class Afro-American family life and his view (p. 204) that it is within such families that negative self-concepts are most frequently inspired and sustained.

In lower-class culture human nature is conceived of as essentially bad, destructive, and immoral (and consequently) in the identity development of the child he is constantly exposed to identity labeling by parents as a bad person.

Taylor (1976) rightly notes that such repeated conceptualizations of the Afro-American family, combined with the theories about its matriarchal character and the economic marginality of the Afro-American adult male, pose critical problems for the personality development of

Afro-American children, especially the Afro-American male child. Taylor's (1976) review of the psychosocial development of Afro-American children notes studies that indicate that such problems are especially critical in the development of the male child. Pettigrew (1964a, 1964b) has noted "that father-deprived boys are marked by more immature, submissive, dependent, and effeminate behavior than other boys" and "as they grow older, this passive behavior may continue, but more typically, it is vigorously overcompensated for by exaggerated masculinity" (p. 18). The Afro-American male youth then will project an image of "toughness, smartness, excitement, and autonomy" (Miller, 1958, p. 10).

Taylor's (1976) critique of Rainwater's (1966) study notes that the conclusions drawn are that the problem of Afro-American male identity is caused by the kinds of male models and not by a lack of male models. Rainwater (1966) concluded that the typical Afro-American male models do not display or encourage the values, skills, or aspirations which are required for success in school or in society.

In response to these conclusions, Taylor (1976, p. 10) counters with the fact that:

In any case, there are many individuals in the (Afro-American) community who may not fit the ideal model but who perform competently and often supremely within the definitions of their status in both the white and (Afro-American) world. Are they to be rejected as positive sources of self-esteem? . . . (Afro-American) youth are daily exposed to models of competence and pride who cope with severe privation and adversity. Too little attention has been devoted to such models in the literature. The tendency to view as negative these role models that fail to meet middle-class standards of behavior reveals the inherent value judgments that suffice research on (Afro-Americans).

However, the question remains: Does the socialization process within the Afro-American community lead to the disparagement of the Afro-American male and

the relative enhancement of the female? Has the Afro-American matriarchy resulted in the emasculation of the Afro-American male child?

In reviewing the status of Afro-American women in a racist society, Jackson (1973) gives a comprehensive review of "the bad (Afro-American) matriarch" theme in the social science literature beginning with Rohrer and Edmundson (1960, p. 161):

The (Afro-American) matriarchs make no bones about their preference for little girls, and while they often manifest real affection for their boy children, they are clearly convinced that all little boys must inexorably and deplorably become men with all the pathologies of that sex.

Jackson (1973) also notes as have others (Powell, 1979) that "one of the most rewarding of the recent critiques of the Afro-American matriarchy" is that written by Staples (1970, 1971a, 1971b, 1972, 1973). The Jackson and Powell critiques focus on the fact that "Staples demythologizes Afro-American male economic dependence upon the female, maternal lowering of the sons' educational achievements, and the 'inevitable' maternal hatred by the son" (Jackson, 1973, p. 199).

Reviews on Afro-American college students by Gurin (1966) and Gurin and Epps (1966, 1975) conclude that Afro-American parents do not show partiality among the sexes in deciding on higher education for their offspring, which dispels the notion that girls are preferred and given more consideration than boys in the Afro-American family. However, Vontress (1971) explains that the informal socialization of boys that does take place places a great deal of emphasis on "being a man in a society that suppresses (Afro-American) manhood" (p. 15):

A boy who is weak is often reprimanded by all the women in the household as well as his peers on the street. If there is anything the ghetto culture demands it is obvious, clearly visible manhood. The boy must look, talk, and act like a man, even though he may not feel like one—and usually he does not.

Schulz (1977) takes particular note of the Afro-American boy growing up in the ghetto and reinforces Vontress' (1971) observations of the demands of the ghetto on the socialization of the Afro-American boy. Schulz found no differential socialization by sex during infancy or very early childhood. However, at a very early age boys are relieved of household responsibilities and thus learn the masculine role outside of the family and under the tutorship of peers. Schulz also feels that the Afro-American mother's negative exploitative relationships with men influence her feelings toward her sons (p. 11):

Thus a boy must develop his sense of being a person and a man largely outside of the home and under the negative evaluation of his mother.

He goes on to describe the perceived trajectory of Afro-American boyhood, as well as some of the privileges, the gangs, and the close running buddies, the singing groups, the early attempts at earning money legitimately, and the frustrations encountered, "playing it cool" and "playing the dozens."

Schulz feels that "playing the dozens" is the boy's striving for autonomy against feminine domination by his mother. The game is played primarily by males beginning at age 11 and is a highly rhetorical and witty bantering in which the mother is the target of ridicule and satire. Schulz reinforces his interpretation of the significance of playing the dozens by referencing Dollard's (1939) "The Dozens: The Dialect of Insult." There are some who would disagree with this interpretation of the dozens as a means of disparagement of the dominance of the mother (Powell, 1979; Staples, 1970, 1972, 1973; Jackson, 1973; Willie, 1974) for the mother in the Afro-American family is held in high re-

gard. Indeed, according to Vontress (1971), "playing the dozens is seen as part of the interaction idiom among peers" or an initiation process for survival, as it were, as a member of the peer group.

Indeed, where the author grew up in Roxbury, Mass., the surest way of instigating a fight was to insult someone's mother, even by innuendo. The instigator or challenger would look you in the eye with a mean, sassy look and say, "Your mother!", nothing more. Not to fight after such provocation was an indication that you were a coward or worse still that you didn't love and respect your mother. When I would come home sometimes bloodied by such a fight, my mother would be baffled about why I would fight just because someone said, "Your mother!" and would try to find out what specific insult had been directed at her that would cause me or one of my siblings to fight. It was just the implied insult to your mother that was forbidden. Teasing and jiving were cool, but mothers were left out of it unless a deliberate insult was intended.

Playing it cool is also a survival mechanism and is described by Rainwater (1966) as "the expressive life style" which presents the individual to his peers as clever, witty, and conniving and demonstrates his ability to manipulate others' behavior for his own gain. It is also a face-saving device and a way to create a world with the appearance of success and personal competence.

Schulz's conclusions about patterns of ghetto socialization confirm some important observations noted by other social scientists such as Ladner (1971), Stack (1974) and Lawrence (1975)—the striving for respectability and the inner strength and coping strategies that many families utilize to survive with stability and dignity.

However, Wilkinson and Taylor (1977) present some penetrating questions. Does the lack of an Afro-American male model have as pernicious effects as suggested by many social psychologists? Is a father-absent home in fact without male models? Does the Afro-American mother rear her sons with feminine models, thus producing males who are unable to function as husbands and fathers? Do Afro-American boys hate their mothers? It is difficult to answer all of these questions within the context of this chapter, because it involves a more detailed examination of the Afro-American family. However, the issues surrounding the controversy of socialization to the Afro-American male role arises out of the prevailing views that (1) white society has emasculated the Afro-American male, (2) that as a result the Afro-American male is impeded in his emotional development, and (3) that Afro-American boys grow up to become poor husbands and fathers (Wilkinson and Taylor, 1977).

These (three) postulates are grounded in the experience of slavery and its residual effects, in the contemporary situation in which (Afro-American) males are handicapped by macrostructural forces in performing satisfactorily as husbands and fathers, and in certain socialization practices which tend to convey a view of masculinity that is essentially deviant or psychopathological in extreme. (p. 1)

A review of sex role development has been helpful in shedding light into some of these darkened, unexplained corners. Although children are clearly sex typed, their degree of sex typing is unrelated to that of the same sex parent and children choose to model the more nurturant model. This view dovetails with the theories of the socialization network. The presumption that all Afro-American families are homogeneous reinforces stereotype views. Willie (1974) has pointed out the heterogeneity among Afro-American families and their life styles. Thus, to a large extent the socialization of the Afro-American boy will vary according to the social circumstances and interactional patterns within his family and social network. Sex role acquisition will be influenced and de-

termined by many of these processes. The significance of the absent Afro-American father on the socialization of young Afro-American children will be elucidated by a critique of the father-absence literature. However, the psychosocial development of the Afro-American girl cannot be ignored.

The Psychosocial Development of Afro-American Girls

Although Afro-American girls have been said to be preferred by their mothers and to excel academically compared to boys, the development of Afro-American girls is not without its difficulties. The self-concept development of the Afro-American girl is particularly handicapped by "the stereotypes of Afro-American womanhood so pervasive in American folklore" (Powell, 1979, p. 35). The theme of "black is beautiful" notwithstanding, physiognomy, skin color, and hair texture still may play an important role in the personality development of many Afro-American girls. In a dissonant culture which holds up the Farrah Fawcetts as the models of beauty, a dark-skinned girl with "nappy edges" (Shange, 1980) must struggle to maintain an acceptable appearance, especially after she leaves the comfortable acceptance of her home and community. Indeed, Powell (1970, 1973) and Rosenberg and Simmons (1972) found that Afro-American girls in desegregated schools had lower self-esteem than Afro-American girls in segregated schools. The social world of a desegregated school is a hard world in which to gain entry. In one desegregated school where Afro-American girls rarely had parts in the school plays or as cheerleaders, they formed their own drill team modeled after the ones at many Afro-American colleges. They had to make a place for themselves in the social world of the school. The Afro-American boys, however, are more readily accepted because of their athletic ability and so do not feel the social isolation that Afro-American girls often experience.

Ladner's study (1971) of young Afro-American girls growing up in a housing development showed that socialization into the role of womanhood began at 7 or 8 years of age. According to this study, the most important agent of the socialization process for the preadolescent girl in the inner city is the peer group, a process which resulted in the development of emotional precocity which has some survival value in such harsh environments. Usually, the contact with peers is unsupervised but peer relationships among these girls provided the companionship, psychological support, and nurturance that parents usually provide but can't because of their own struggle to survive financially.

Ladner (1971) takes particular note of the high degree of femininity, the attention to personal appearance, and making one's self beautiful with particular attention to clothes and hairstyles. Here again the importance of hair texture becomes important and a great deal of time and attention is devoted to maintaining one's hairstyle. Indeed, one of the largest and most successful Afro-American industries is that which deals with hair products for Afro-American women. Hot combs and hair straighteners of every type abound. Although the introduction of the "Afro hairstyle" was helpful in setting an alternative standard of beauty for the Afro-American girl, it has not eliminated the preoccupation with hair of the Afro-American girl. A vital part of growing up is learning how to deal with one's hair.

The roots of your hair
what turns back when
we sweat, run, make love, dance,
get afraid, get happy: the tell-tale
sign of living.
            (*Nappy Edges* by Ntozake Shange)

Ladner (1971) makes it very clear that the adolescent process for the inner city girl

in her study is very different than that for the white majority group. Although the poor Afro-American female has problems peculiar to her age period, they are different in kind and consequences. Ideas and thoughts about womanhood are handed down from generation to generation. However, the role models are restricted, encompassing those of their mothers and other women in their immediate communities. "Moreover, the responsibilities she has to assume are often those carried out in other social classes, by adult females" (p. 126).

Among all preadult females the strongest conception of womanhood was that of the strong role of the woman in the family, a concept that is conveyed by mothers to their daughters and indeed by all women to girls. Half of the girls came from homes headed by females and many of them were aware of the fact that they too would probably play this role.

The search for models of womanhood is a prominent and difficult process for the Afro-American adolescent. However, it is the model of the educated middle-class woman that most girls aspired to achieve. Achieving this goal meant avoidance of any serious involvement with boys and sexual activity resulting in pregnancy. Attainment of middle-class status meant sacrifices, i.e., after-school job and strict study habits. In describing such families with middle-class aspirations, Ladner (1971) noted the enforcement of certain moral codes and images of respectability, especially as related to boys, the postponement of marriage as an immediate goal, the importance of school, and the stress put on higher education, and inner sources of strong determination and adaptive coping strategies.

For the middle-class Afro-American girl, education, professional attainment, and marriage to an educated man are stressed. However, education and a profession, independence and self-reliance are stressed more strongly just in case the marital options are limited.

The Effects of Father Absence
on the Psychosocial Development
of Afro-American Children

In a recent scholarly overview of the role of the father in child development, Lamb (1976) stresses that the literature indicated the importance of the father in (a) sex role development, (b) moral development, and (c) academic achievement. In the past, most studies on Afro-American families have emphasized the effects of father absence rather than the role of the Afro-American father within the cultural context of the Afro-American family or the role of the Afro-American father in the socialization of children. In terms of sex role identification and father absence, a review of the literature (Herzog and Sudia, 1973; Lamb, 1976) would seem to indicate the following common characteristics: (1) boys raised without fathers are less masculine in their sex role preferences and behaviors; (2) father-absent boys are more likely to exhibit compensatory masculinity; (3) boys raised without fathers have also been reported to have feminine or non-analytical cognitive styles; (4) father absence has its greatest effect on children who are separated from their fathers at a very young age; (5) father absence is less malignant for girls than for boys; (6) the observable effects of father absence on girls is most noticeable in adolescence; (7) among girls father absence is associated with difficulties in interacting with males; (8) alternative masculine models, e.g., an older brother, may inhibit the effects of father absence on boys.

In terms of the effects of father absence on moral development, Lamb (1976) notes, "Evidently, there is far less unanimity among theorists about the father's role in moral development than about his contribution to sex role development" (p. 17). However, the literature review indicates the following characteristics to be most noteworthy: (1) delinquent boys are more likely to come from father-absent homes, and (2) father absence apparently has no discernible effect on the conscious development of girls (Lamb, 1976).

The literature review on the effects of father absence on academic achievement shows: (1) underachieving boys have inadequate relationships with their fathers; (2) the correlation between paternal nurturance and the child's intellectual functioning is higher for boys than for girls; (3) paternal encouragement is correlated with achievement (though this may not be true of all social classes); (4) the effects of father absence are more consistently found among boys, resulting in a deterioration of school performance; (5) such boys demonstrate an absence of the analytic masculine cognitive style, and (6) the findings on girls and academic achievement are much less consistent.

Hartnagel (1970) reports on father absence and self-concept among lower-class white and Afro-American boys. The effects of fatherlessness and race on the self-concept were measured by using the orientation of symbolic interactionism and the semantic differential. Afro-American father-absent boys had smaller differences among the categories examined than white father-absent boys. There were no differences between white and Afro-American father-present boys in any categories. The smaller difference of the Afro-American father-absent boys was felt to be the result of their more potent actual self-concept. However, a review of the protocol and data could lead to several other interpretations of these results.

A rate study of the relationship between Afro-American fathers and their interaction with their preschool children and subsequent self-esteem was done by McAdoo (1976). The study examined the relationship between the observed behaviors and attitudes of Afro-American fathers and the association of their attitudes with the identity of their preschool children. A total of 21 working- and middle-class suburban Afro-American families were studied. Verbal and nonverbal interactions between the fathers and children were recorded. The fathers of boys were more nurturant than the fathers of girls. There were very few restrictive kinds of father-child interaction. Fathers interacted more verbally with their sons and more nonverbally with their daughters. All children in this study had high self-concept scores, and the fathers' attitudes toward childrearing practices were described as being moderately strict. McAdoo asserts that these findings contradict the prevailing stereotype of Afro-American fathers and their relationships with their children.

Previous research has found a strong association between the acting-out behavior of delinquent male adolescents and an association with high levels of unconscious femininity and conscious masculinity. McNabb (1973) tried to replicate such a study with 14-year-old and 16-year-old residents of a rehabilitative institution following adjudication for a variety of offenses. The Gough Femininity Scale was used to measure unconscious femininity. However, unlike previous studies, the relative proportion of Afro-American subjects was evenly distributed throughout all sex role categories, i.e., high unconscious masculinity and high conscious masculinity, high unconscious masculinity and high conscious femininity, high unconscious femininity and high conscious masculinity, high unconscious femininity and high conscious femininity. They were not heavily weighted in the F-M or high unconscious femininity and high conscious masculinity. McNabb suggests that the relationship between delinquent acting-out and the task of sexual identification may not be as important in the etiology of delinquency among Afro-American youth as among white youth.

Biller's (1968) well-known study explored the relationship of father absence and sociocultural background to masculine development among 6-year-old lower-class Afro-American and white boys. Sex role orientation was judged by Brown's IT scale. His findings showed that white father-present boys were the most masculine. There were no significant differences between white father-absent and Afro-American father-present boys. However, the Afro-American father-absent boys were the least masculine. He concluded that the underlying sex role orientation is more influenced by father availability and family background than are more manifest aspects of masculinity. D'Andrade (1973) studied the effects of father absence during early and late childhood among Afro-American children ranging in age from 5 to 15 years. The 58 Afro-American working-class households were divided into categories based on timing and length of paternal absence. The children's patterns of sex identification and sex identity were measured by the Frank test, by verbal self-description, and by a role preference task. Results showed that children who did not have a father present during the first three years of life exhibited a feminine response pattern on the Frank test. The investigator concluded that paternal absence influenced conscious sex role identity through the indirect processes of reciprocal role learning and perception of sex role advantages and disadvantages. Thus, the mother's behavior in the absence of the father can be a crucial variable in terms of outcome for the children. Longabaugh (1973) tested the hypotheses that father-absent boys have a more feminine semantic style than father-present boys, and that father-absent homes have a higher rate of mother-son interaction than father-present homes. The subjects were 51 Afro-American lower-class mother-child dyads. The children ranged in age from 5 to 12 years, and 18 of them were from homes in which the father had been absent for at least 2 years prior to the study. The results showed no significant relationship between father's absence and masculinity and semantic style of either sons or daughters. Father absence was related to alterations of behavior of mothers toward sons, and it was thus concluded that increased mother-son interaction moderated the impact of father absence on the femininity of the son's semantic style.

It has also been noted by Rubin (1974) that the availability of male role models outside the home and the significance of adult males within the home may modify the negative effects of father absence on Afro-American boys. Likewise, Santrock's (1970) study showed that father-absent boys with only older male siblings were significantly more masculine than father-absent boys with only older female siblings. Also, father-absent boys with a father substitute were signifcantly less dependent than father-absent boys with no father substitute. In Santrock's study among preschool Afro-American father-absent boys, children were significantly more feminine, less aggressive, and more dependent than their father-present counterparts. However, these differences were not noted between father-absent and father-present preschool girls.

The effects of father absence on academic achievement of Afro-American children has been studied by Sciara (1975). Three hundred children from father-absent homes and 773 children from father-present homes were studied. The consistency of test scores in reading and arithmetic was established over a two-year period. The findings indicated significant differences between children from father-present homes with higher academic achievement than children from father-absent homes. Father absence had a much greater effect on the achievement of boys and girls whose measured intelligence quotient was above 100. The Sciara and Jantz (1974) study of father absence among Afro-American children found again that both sexes were equally affected. When the children were analyzed by various ranges of IQ scores, father-absent children achieved lower reading scores than those from father-present homes. The investigators feel, however, that the findings are tentative because several important var-

iables—e.g., length of time living in father-absent home and SES level—were not controlled. They nonetheless conclude that father presence fosters a greater cohesiveness of family with more family activity. This in turn encourages greater adult-child verbal interaction and experiential variety than occurs under father-absent conditions. Such characteristics are directly related to school placement, and particularly to reading achievement.

In a discussion of fatherlessness and the Afro-American child, Wilson (1978) notes that there are more important factors than father presence or absence which aggravate or mitigate the effects of fatherlessness. Such factors include: (a) communal acceptance or non-acceptance of such a family structure; (b) presence or absence of stigmatization of such a family structure; (c) the availability or non-availability of kinship or non-kinship father substitutes, and (d) the commonality of such structures within the community.

On the other hand, Bernard (1966) in her study of Afro-American marriages notes, "The adverse effects reported for children socialized in fatherless families presupposes that the father would have been a suitable model. In some cases the departure of the father results in little loss." In this study of low-income families in Philadelphia, fathers took very little responsibility for child-rearing duties and wives and mothers expected little help in the care of the children. Bernard concluded that it is possible that among the Afro-American lower-class the one-parent family may in reality be the most efficient and functional family type because the presence of the husband-father may in the long run have more negative than positive effects on the mother and the children. She feels that the evidence that fatherless families are handicapped in the socialization of children, particularly sons, should not be overemphasized because not all children from such families suffer irreparable damage. Some of the damage associated with fatherlessness undoubtedly comes from deprivation both of money and of maternal care as the mother struggles to perform both parental roles. However, Scanzoni (1971) in his study of fatherlessness or stepfatherlessness in Afro-American working- and middle-class families found that not having the father present was likely to be less deterimental in terms of later development when the home was relatively well-off than when it was not. Among the working class, either the father was not there or, if a father was seen by the child, he participated only minimally in the child's socialization as compared to fathers in intact middle-class families. Thus, it is the child from the less advantaged, broken home who suffers more from father absence than the one-parent child from better circumstances. Fatherlessness and SES are highly correlated in terms of the effect on children. Therefore, it could be that, rather than fatherlessness, the major problem of the single-parent Afro-American family is the economic deprivation and the blocked access to further opportunity. Wilson (1978, p. 170) concludes:

The major result of fatherlessness in (Afro-American) families seems not to be a confusion of sex identity but a critically reduced ability of the children from these families as adults to successfully fulfill their roles as husbands, fathers, wives, and mothers. The lack of good role models which serve to show the children wholesome husband-wife, father-child relationships deprives the children of workable models that can be used to maintain their own family relations as married adults.

COPING AND OVERCOMING

The basic tasks of coping include (1) satisfaction of basic physiological needs and (2) satisfaction of symbolic needs. The second task of coping involves (a) a sense of reality and a coherent world, (b) some belief system, (c) a sense of self-esteem, (d) a sense of personal control, (e) a sense of social affiliatedness. In addition, the capacity to cope depends on the resources of the child and a balance between the child's strength and the child's vulnerability.

Murphy and Moriarty (1978) have formulated two global concepts of coping. The first is "the capacity to cope with opportunities, challenges, frustrations, and threats in the environment," and the second is "the maintenance of internal integration," that is to say, the capacity to manage "one's relation to the environment so as to maintain integrated functioning" (p. 336).

Coles (1967) in his descriptions of southern Afro-American school children experiencing school desegregation described their capacity to cope with the threats in the environment and maintain internal integration. In another way of speaking, there are two methods of coping: direct coping and indirect coping. Direct coping involves (1) seeking information or establishing a cognitive contract, (2) skill acquisition and practice which involves a mental rehearsal, and (3) appreciation of the other two by establishing and securing helping resources. Indirect coping involves (1) defense mechanism, (2) self-control techniques, (3) task irrelevant behavior, and (4) religious and philosophical activity.

Although the literature on Afro-American children is replete with reference to their poverty status and their deprivation so as to imply that the satisfaction of their basic physiological needs are not met, Billingsley (1968) indicates that this may be so for the very poor but not for the majority.

What often goes unnoticed is how Afro-American families go about the task of meeting the symbolic needs of their children. The symbolic meaning of life is often seen in the names Afro-American parents give to their children. My father named me Gloria because he felt that my life was intended to accomplish something special. I named my son, Daniel Befakadu, an Ethiopian name—Daniel meaning "beloved of God" and Befakadu meaning "The

Father's wish" or "God's will"—following in the tradition of my family to give every child a special name with a symbolic meaning. The practice is more widespread now among young Afro-American parents who give their children African names, again in an attempt to begin the child's life with symbolic meaning, hope, purpose, identity, and direction. Often the names of famous Afro-Americans are given or of a relative who was highly esteemed and respected for certain traits.

In a selection of articles entitled *Growing Up Black* about Afro-Americans who attained fame due to their own efforts or circumstances, David (1975) has included such notables as Walter White (1893-1955), Daisey Bates (1919-   ), Will Thomas (1905-   ), Angelo Herndon (1913-   ), Elizabeth Adams (1910-   ), Isaac Jefferson (1775-1850), Frederick Douglass (1817-1895), Booker T. Washington (1858-1915), William H. Holtzclaw (1870-1943), James O. Corrothers (1869-1917), J. Saunders Redding (1906-   ), Richard Wright (1909-1960), and many others. Although each of these persons grew up at different periods of history, David notes that they all knew in growing up that all individuals were not given equal opportunity in the United States and that for each of them the major motivating force was his or her own "negritude." Indeed, each article was selected on the basis of yielding some "idea of how an (Afro-American) child reacts to the moment of truth"—the fact of being a minority group member in a racist society. The authors learned about the reality of race in their own ways and developed their own method of coping with inner feelings and external circumstances in ways that proved triumphant for them. Each of the authors within his/her article illustrates the development, formation, and preservation of ego strength by refusing to accept the limitations imposed by class or caste status. In short, David's (1975) theme which is recapitulated by the essays advances the view that, as chil-

dren, each of these authors overcame the trauma of negritude in America. David points out the particular importance of parents or a parental figure in helping in the coping process: "When a child is hurt either physically or emotionally by someone outside his family, he will, in all likelihood, turn to his parents for aid and comfort. This is true for children of any race, but the problem takes on added significance if the child is black" (p. 50).

The Murphy and Moriarty (1978) study on vulnerability and coping noted that the child's self-feeling and relation to his home helped the child cope with vulnerability. The particularly important factors in this process were (1) an adequate self-image of the child, (2) his sense of security, (3) his positive orientation to life, and especially (4) the mother's enjoyment of the child as well as the support and active help given to the child in coping. All four of these factors were significantly related to coping capacity. "The parents of good copers neither neglected their children nor overprotected them. They respected their children's capacities, encouraged and rewarded their efforts, and offered reassurance in times of frustration and failure" (p. 349.)

No child is invulnerable, but stress serves as a challenge to evoke new energy to learn how to master stress or else desensitize or get used to it. What is extremely helpful in this process is "the ecological tradition as conveyed by the family and as evoked and supported by various ecological aspects of the setting" (Murphy and Moriarty, 1978). Note the setting in the "patterns of black excellence" described by Sowell (1974, 1976) in the Afro-American high schools he studied. The Gurin and Epps (1975) study showed that the Afro-American college students had a sense of reality in a coherent world—the world of their colleges and the communities in which they lived. They also had a sense of self-esteem, a sense of personal control, and a sense of social affiliatedness. Their coping strategy was to develop a sense of achievement and personal identity within the context of a collective identity of being Afro-American. The achievement needs of the group became part of their personal identity as their personal identity was part of the collective identity. They recognized the system of racism and its external control over their lives, but yet developed personal and group processes that were efficacious in changing the system.

Ghetto children have coping strategies and strengths also. Although not describing Afro-American ghetto children, the processes of coping with vulnerability described by Murphy and Moriarty (1978) are similar to the styles of Afro-American ghetto children:

Some children developed self-protective preventive devices or compensatory measures to manage such problems: timing rest; ability to limit or fend off excessive stimulation; ability to control the impact of the environment through strategic withdrawal, delay, and caution; and the ability to select, to restructure the environment. Involved here as prerequisites were realistic appraisal of the environment, acceptance of people, clear differentiation of fantasy from reality, and many cognitive coping capacities. (Even) tolerance of temporary regression protects against stress by reducing tension (p. 338).

However, ofttimes these processes of coping with stress and decreasing the vulnerability adapted by Afro-American children are given psychopathological labels. In such instances the strengths go unnoticed but strengths which are recognized can be further developed and incorporated into the coping process.

Afro-Americans have survived a harsh system of slavery, repression, and racism. Although there have been casualties, there have been many more survivors, achievers, and victors. The cultural heritage of coping with adversity and overcoming has been passed on from generation to generation, laced with stories of those with remarkable courage and fortitude—"lives of great men all remind us, we can make our lives sublime." The chapter on the Afro-American family will focus also on those processes that have fostered survival by coping and adaptation.

REFERENCES

Barnes, E.J. The black community as the science of positive self-concept for black children: A theoretical perspective. In: R. Jones (Ed.), *Black Psychology*. New York: Harper & Row, 1972.

Baughman, E.E. and Dahlstrom, W.G. *Negro and White Children: A Psychological Study in the Rural South*. New York: Academic Press, 1968.

Bem, D.J. Self-perception: An alternative interpretation of cognitive dissonance phenomena. *Psychological Review*, 1967, *74*, 183–200.

Bernard, J. *Marriage and Family Among Negroes*. Englewood Cliffs, N. J.: Prentice-Hall, 1966.

Biller, H.B. A note on father absence and masculine development in lower-class Negro and white boys. *Child Development*, 1968, *39*, 1004–06.

Billingsley, A. *Black Families in White America*. Englewood Cliffs, N.J.: Prentice-Hall, 1968.

Brigham, J.C. Views of black and white children concerning the distribution of personality characteristics. *Journal of Personality*, 1974, *42*, 144–158.

Campbell, D.T. Stereotypes and the perception of group differences. *American Psychologist*, 1976, *22*, 817–829.

Carmichael, S. and Hamilton, C.V. *Black Power: The Politics of Liberation in America*. New York: Vintage, 1967.

Christmas, J. Self-concept and attitudes. In: R.M. Dreger & K.S. Miller (Eds.), *Comparative Studies of Blacks and Whites in the U.S.* New York: Seminar Press, 1973, 249–272.

Clark, K. The effects of prejudice and discrimination on personality development. In: H. Witmer & R. Kotinsky (Eds.), *Personality in the Making*. New York: Harper, 1952.

Clark, K.B. and Clark, M.P. The development of consciousness of self and the emergence of racial identification in Negro pre-school children. *Journal of Social Psychology*, 1939, *10*, 591–599.

Clark, K.B. and Clark, M.P. Racial identification and preference in Negro children. In: T.M. Newcomb & E.L. Hartley (Eds.), *Readings in Social Psychology*. New York: Holt, 1947.

Clausen, J.A. *Socialization and Society*. Boston: Little, Brown, 1968.

Coleman, J.S., Campbell, E.Q., Hobson, C.J., McPartland, J., Mood, A.M., Weinfeld, F.J., and York, R.L. *Equality of Educational Opportunity*. Washington, D.C.: U.S. Office of Education, 1966.

Coles, R. *Children of Crisis*. Boston: Atlantic Little Brown, 1967.

David, J. (Ed.) *Growing Up Black*. New York: Pocket Books, 1975.

D'Andrade, R.B. Father absence, identification, and identity. *Ethos*, 1973, *1(4)*, 440–455.

Deutscher, M. and Chein, I. The psychological effects of enforced segregation: A survey of social science opinion. *Journal of Psychology*, 1948, *26*, 259–287.

Dill, J.R., Bradford, C., and Grossett, M. Comparative indices of school achievement by black children from different preschool programs. *Psychological Reports*, 1975, *37(3)*, 871–877.

Dollard, J.S. *Caste and Class in a Southern Town.* New Haven: Yale University Press, 1937.

Dollard, J.S. The dozens: The dialect of insult (referenced in D. Schulz, *Coming up Black: Patterns of Ghetto Socialization*, 1977. (No publisher given) 1939.

Dreger, R.M. and Miller, K.S. Comparative psychological studies of Negroes and whites in the United States. *Psychological Bulletin*, 1960, *57*, 361–402.

Dreger, R.M. and Miller, K.S. Comparative psychological studies of Negroes and whites in the United States: 1959–1965. *Psychological Bulletin*, Sept. 1968, *70*, (Supplement), 1–58.

Erikson, E.H. *Identity, Youth, and Crisis.* New York: W.W. Norton, 1968.

Goffman, E. *Stigma.* Englewood Cliffs, N.J.: Prentice-Hall, 1963.

Goodall, J.L. Some aspects of mother-infant relationships in a group of wild chimpanzees. In: H.R. Schaffer (Ed.), *The Origins of Human Social Relations.* New York: Academic Press, 1971.

Gough, A.R. and St. Ange, M.C. Development of sex role stereotypes in black and white elementary school girls. *Developmental Psychology*, 1974, *10(3)*, 461.

Gurin, P. Social class constraints on the occupational aspirations of students attending some predominantly Negro colleges. *Journal of Negro Education*, 1966, *35*, 336–350.

Gurin, P. and Epps, E. Some characteristics of students from poverty backgrounds attending predominantly Negro colleges in the deep South. *Social Forces*, 1966, *45*, 27–40.

Gurin, P. and Epps, E. *Black Consciousness, Identity, and Achievement: A Study of Students in Historically Black Colleges.* New York: Wiley, 1975.

Hall, W.S., Cross, W.E., and Friedle, R. Stages in the development of black awareness: An explanatory investigation. In: R. Jones (Ed.), *Black Psychology.* New York: Harper and Row, 1972.

Harlow, H.F. and Harlow, M.K. Effects of various mother-infant relationships on rhesus monkey behaviors. In: B.M. Foss (Ed.), *Determinants of Infants Behavior IV.* London: Methuen, 1969.

Hartnagel, T.F. Father absence and self-conception among lower class white and Negro boys. *Social Problems*, 1970, *18(2)*, 152–163.

Hauser, S.T. *Black and White Identity Formation: Studies in the Psychosocial Development of Lower Socioeconomic Class Adolescent Boys.* New York: Wiley-Interscience, 1971.

Hauser, S.T. Black and white identity development: Aspects and perspectives. *Journal of Youth and Adolescence*, 1972, *1(2)*, 113–130.

Herzog, E. and Sudia, C.E. Children in fatherless families. In: B.M. Caldwell & H.N. Ricciuti (Eds.), *Review of Child Development Research Vol III.* Chicago: University of Chicago Press, 1973.

Hunt, D.E. and Hardt, P.H. The effects of Upward Bound Programs on the attitudes, motivation and academic achievements of Negro students. *Journal of Social Issues,* 1969 *25*, 122-124.

Hunt, L.L. and Hunt, J.B. Race and the father-son connection: The conditional relevance of father absence for the orientations and identities of adolescent boys. *Social Problems,* 1975 *23*(1), 35-50.

Jackson, J. Black women in a racist society. In: C.V. Willie, B. Kramer, and B. Brown (Eds.), *Racism and Mental Health.* Pittsburgh: University of Pittsburgh, 1973.

Joint Commission on Mental Health of Children. *Crisis in Child Mental Health: Challenge for the 1970's.* New York: Harper and Row, 1970.

Kagan, J. Acquisition and significance of sex typing and sex role identity. In: M. Hoffman and L. Hoffman (Eds.), *Review of Child Development Research,* Vol. 1. New York: Russell Sage, 1964, pp. 137–167.

Kaplan, H.B. Social class and self-derogation: A conditional relationship. *Sociometry*, 1971, *34*, 41–65.

Kardiner, A. and Ovesey, L. *The Mark of Oppression: Explorations in the Personality of the American Negro.* Cleveland: Meridian Books (The World Publishing Co.) (1st Edition 1951), 1968.

Kelley, H.H. Attribution theory in social psychology. In: D. Levine (Ed.), *Nebraska Symposium on Motivation.* Lincoln, NB: University of Nebraska Press, 1967, pp. 192–238.

Kohlberg, L.A. A cognitive-developmental analysis of children's sex-role concepts and attitudes. In: E.E. Maccoby (Eds.), *The Development of Sex Differences.* Stanford: Stanford University Press, 1966.

Ladner, J.A. *Tomorrow's Tomorrow: The Black Woman.* Garden City, N.Y.: Doubleday, 1971.

Lamb, M.E. The role of the fathers: An overview. In: M.E. Lamb (Ed.), *The Role of the Father in Child Development.* New York: Wiley-Interscience, 1976.

Lawrence, M.M. *Young Inner City Families: Development of Ego Under Stress.* New York: Behavior, 1975.

Lewis, M. and Weinraub, M. The father's role in the child's social network. In: M.E. Lamb (Ed.), *The Role of the Father in Child Development.* New York: Wiley-Interscience, 1976.

Lewis, M., Young, G., Brooks, J., and Michealson, L. The beginning of friendship. In: M. Lewis and L. Rosenblum (Eds.), *Friendship and Peer Relations: The Origins of Behavior,* Vol IV. New York: Wiley, 1975.

Longabaugh, R. Mother behavior as a variable moderating the effects of father absence. *Ethos*, 1973, *1*(4), 456–465.

Maccoby, E.E. and Jacklin, C.N. *The Psychology of Sex Differences.* Stanford: Stanford University Press, 1974.

McAdoo, J.L. The relationship between observed paternal attitudes, behavior, and self-esteem of black preschool children. Rockville, MD: National Institute of Mental Health (DHEW), 1976.

McNabb, D.R. Delinquent acting-out and the task of sexual identification in black male adolescents: A replication study. *Smith College Studies in Social Work*, 1973, *44(1)*, 23–24.

Mead, G.H. *Mind, Self, and Society.* Chicago: University of Chicago Press, 1934.

Middleton, R. Self-esteem and psychological impairment among American Black, American white, and African men: Preliminary Report (mimeographed), 1972. (Unpublished.)

Miller, W.B. Lower class culture as a generating milieu of gang delinquency. *Journal of Social Issues*, 1958, *14*, 5–19.

Mosby, D. Toward a theory of the unique personality of Blacks—A psychocultural assessment. In: R. Jones (Ed.), *Black Psychology*. New York: Harper and Row, 1972.

Murphy, L.B. and Moriarty, A.E. *Vulnerability, Coping, and Growth: From Infancy to Adolescence*. New Haven: Yale University Press (2nd edition), 1978.

Nobles, W.W. Psychological research and the black self-concept: A critical review. *Journal of Social Issues*, 1973, *29*, 11–31.

Nobles, W.W. Extended self: Rethinking the so-called Negro self-concept. In: R. Jones (Ed.), *Black Psychology*. Second edition. New York: Harper & Row, 1980.

Pettigrew, T.F. *A Profile of the Negro American*. Princeton, N.J.: Van Nostrand., 1964a.

Pettigrew, T.F. Negro American personality: Why isn't more known? *Journal of Social Issues*, 1964b, *2*, 4–23.

Pettigrew, T.A., Social evaluation theory: convergence and applications. In: D. Levine (Ed.), *Nebraska Symposium on Motivation*. Lincoln, NB: University of Nebraska Press, 1967, 241–311.

Powell, G.J. and Fuller, M. Self-concept and school desegregation. *American Journal of Orthopsychiatry*, 1970, *40*, 303.

Powell, G.J. and Fuller, M. The variables for positive self-concept among young Southern black adolescents. *Journal of National Medical Association*, 1972, *64(6)*, 522–526.

Powell, G.J. *Black Monday's Children: The Effects of School Desegregation on Southern School Children*. New York: Appleton-Century-Croft, 1973.

Powell, G.J. Growing up black and female. In: Claire B. Kopp (Ed.), *Becoming Female: Perspectives on Development*. New York: Plenum Press, 1979.

Powell, G.J. A six-city study of school desegregation and self-concept among Afro-American Junior High School students: A preliminary study with implications for mental health. In: B. Bass, G. Wyatt and G.J. Powell (Eds.), *The Afro-American Family: Assessment, Treatment and Research Issues*. New York: Grune & Stratton, 1982.

President's Commission on Mental Health. Mental Health in America: 1978, Vol. I (Vols. II, III, and IV appendices to the Report). Washington, D.C.: Superintendent of Documents, U.S. Government Printing Office, 20402, 1978.

Rainwater, L. Crucible of identity: The Negro lower-class family. *Daedalus*, Winter, 1966, 172–217.

Rheingold, H.L. and Eckerman, C.O. Some proposals for unifying the study of social development. In: M. Lewis and L. Rosenblum (Eds.), *Friendship and Peer Relations: The Origins of Behavior*, Vol. IV. New York: Wiley, 1975, 293–298.

Rohrer, J.H. and Edmundson, M. *The Eighth Generation Grows Up: Cultures and Personalities of New Orleans Negroes*. New York: Harper and Row, 1960.

Rosenberg, M. The dissonant religious context and emotional disturbance. *American Journal of Sociology*, 1962, *68*, 1–10.

Rosenberg, M. and Simmons, R. *Black and White Self-Esteem: The Urban School Child*. Rose monograph Series. Washington, D.C.: American Sociological Association, 1972.

Rosenberg, M. *Conceiving the Self*. New York: Basic Books, 1979.

Rubin, R.H. Adult male absence and the self-attitudes of black children. *Child Study Journal*, 1974, *4(1)*, 33–46.

Santrock, J.W. Paternal absence, sex typing, and identification. *Developmental Psychology* 1970, *2(2)*, 264–272.

Scanzoni, J. *The Black Family in Modern Society*. Boston: Allyn & Bacon, 1971.

Schulz, D. *Coming Up Black: Patterns of Ghetto Socialization*. Englewood Cliffs, N.J.: Prentice Hall, 1977.

Sciara, F.J. Effects of father absence on the educational achievement of urban black children. *Child Study Journal*, 1975, *5(1)*, 45–55.

Sciara, F.J. and Jantz, R.K. Father absence and its apparent effect on the reading achievement of black children from low income families. *Journal of Negro Education*, 1974, *43(2)*, 221–227.

Shange, N. *Nappy Edges*. New York: Bantam Books, 1980.

Simmons, R.G., Blythe, D.A., Brown, L., and Bush, D.E. Role of school environment and puberty on self-image development. Paper presented at the American Sociological Association Meetings, Chicago, September, 1977.

Simmons, R.G., Brown, L., Bush, D., and Blythe, D.A. Self-esteem and achievement of black and white early adolescents. Unpublished paper, 1977.

Simpkins, G., Williams, R.L., and Gunnings, T.S. What a culture a difference makes: A rejoinder to Valentine. In: *Challenging the Myths: The Schools, The Black and the Poor*. Harvard Educational Review. Reprint Series No. 5, 1975.

Sizemore, B.A. Separation: A reality approach to inclusion. In: R.L. Green (Ed.), *Racial Crisis in American Education*. Chicago: Follett Educational Corporation, 1969.

Soares, A.T. and Soares, L.H. Self-perception of culturally disadvantaged children. *American Educational Research Journal*, 1969, *6*, 31–45.

Soares, A.T. and Soares, L.H. The self-concept differential in disadvantaged and advantaged students. Proceedings of the Annual Convention of the American Psychological Assoc., 1972, *7*, 195–196.

Sowell, T. Black excellence: The case of Dunbar High School. *The Public Interest*, Spring 1974, *35*, 3–21.

Sowell, T. Patterns of black excellence. *The Public Interest*, Spring, 1976, *43*, 28–58.

Stack, C. *All Our Kin: Strategies for Survival in a Black Community*. New York: Harper and Row, 1974.

Staples, R. The myth of the black matriarchy. *Black Scholar*, 1970, January-February, 9–16.

Staples, R. Towards sociology of the black family: A

decade of theory and research. *Journal of Marriage and the Family*, February 1971a, *33*, 19–38.

Staples, R. (Ed.) *The Black Family: Essays and Studies*. Belmont, CA: Wadsworth, 1971b.

Staples, R. The matricentric family: A cross-cultural examination. *Journal of Marriage and the Family*, February 1972, *34*, 156–165.

Staples, R. *The Black Woman in America: Sex, Marriage and the Family*. Chicago: Nelson Hall, 1973.

Sullivan, H.S. Conceptions of Modern Psychiatry: The First William Alanson White Memorial Lectures. Washington, D.C.: William Alanson White Psychiatric Foundation, 1947.

Taylor, R.L. Psychosocial development among black children and youth: A reexamination. *American Journal of Orthopsychiatry*, January 1976, *46(1)*.

Thomas, A. and Sillen, S. *Racism and Psychiatry*. New York: Brunner/Mazel, 1972.

Valentine, C.A. Deficit, difference and bicultural models of Afro-American behavior. *Harvard Educational Review*, 1971, *41*, 137–157.

Vontress, C. The black male personality. *Black Scholar*, June 1971, 10–16.

Weinberg, M. *Minority Students: A Research Appraisal*. U.S. DHEW, National Institute of Education. Washington, D.C.: Soc. & Printing Office, 1977.

Wilkinson, D. and Taylor, R.L. Eds. *The Black Male in America: Perspectives on His Status in Contemporary Society*. Chicago: Nelson-Hall, 1977.

Willie, C.V. *A New Look at Black Families*. Englewood Cliffs, N.J.: Prentice-Hall, 1974.

Wilson, A.N. *The Developmental Psychology of the Black Child*. New York: Africana Research Publications, 1978.

Wilson, W.J. *The Declining Significance of Race: Blacks and Changing American Institutions*. Third edition. Chicago: University of Chicago Press, 1980.

Witmer, H.L. and Kotinsky, R. *Personality in the Making: The Report on the Midcentury White House Conf. on Children*. New York: Harper & Row, 1952.

Wylie, R.C. *The Self-concept: Theory and Research on Selected Topics*. Vol. II. Revised Ed. Lincoln, NB: University of Nebraska Press, 1978.

CHAPTER 5

The Development of
Mexican-American Children

Daniel Mejia, Ph.D.

The majority of the studies relied upon in the development of this chapter are comparative and thus reveal differences and similarities among Mexican-American, Anglo-American, and other minority group children and parents. The myriad of differences in perceptions, meanings, philosophies, and strategies in relation to education, childrearing, achievement and success among the majority and minority groups receives the sharpest focus and most abundant identification and description in these and many other studies.

The assumption underlying many such comparative studies is that what is "Anglo" is "normal" or "ideal." This is an orientation which is coming under heavy and increasing criticism. There is also increasing evidence demonstrating that many studies of minority groups are characterized by conceptual and methodological flaws stemming from investigators' unperceived (and some say, deliberate) perpetuation of cultural stereotypes. For example, a review of the computer-derived bibliography of Padilla et al. (1978),

containing approximately 2,000 citations to the research literature on Hispanic mental health, revealed a paucity of findings based on rigorous methodology and confirmed the impression of Padilla and Ruiz (1973) in their earlier bibliography that the Latino mental health literature is characterized by serious deficiencies: stereotypic interpretations, weak methodological and data-analytic techniques, lack of replicability of findings, and the absence of programmatic research.

In its report to the President's Commission on Mental Health (1979) the Special Populations Sub-Task Panel on Mental Health of Hispanic Americans states:

Typically, research with Hispanics has involved a qualitative definition of culture in terms of group membership (Mexican-American, Puerto Rican, Cuban, etc.). Subjects are then asked to complete a task, a questionnaire, or a battery of psychological tests. Sometimes their performance is compared with that of other ethnic groups, especially the majority group. The results are then generalized to the entire ethnic group under consideration. In those rare instances where the research design is explicitly sensitive to intragroup heterogeneity, the variables most often manipulated have been generation of respondent, age, sex, language proficiency and/or preference, and geographic residency. Finally, comparative studies have typically used univariate approaches in which cultural differences are assessed by means of a single variable or, at best, a very limited set of variables. The implications of differences on other variables, which may or may not be interrelated, are not investigated in a systematic fashion. Furthermore, cross-cultural validity of measurement instruments is rarely tested.

These problems raise serious doubts not only as to the scientific value of that knowledge base, but also with respect to the legitimacy of its pragmatic implications for the delivery of mental health services to the Hispanic population.

While reviewing the contents of this chapter, the thoughtful reader, therefore, will note that "different from Anglo" does not mean "worse." The perceptive reader will be alert to the influence and operation of stereotypes in methodologies, findings, and interpretations, which often mean that these studies raise more profound and troubling questions than they originally proposed to explore and then appear to answer.

Finally, the concerned reader will view the growth and development of many Mexican-American children against the backdrop of a literature replete with statistics revealing acute conditions of systematic stress on a daily basis: high morbidity and mortality rates, substandard schools, unequal pay scales, rampant unemployment, dilapidated housing, high dropout rates, poor nutrition, low educational attainment, repetition of grades in school, high incidence of poverty, and a shortage of relevant, accessible health and mental health care services in their communities. These alarming conditions place many Mexican-American children at an enormously high risk for physical and mental problems.

In this chapter, Mexican-American parental attitudes are first discussed, with a special and separate emphasis on mothers and fathers. The critical roles played by teachers of Mexican-American children, as agents of socialization and self-concept development, are described next. Studies on preschool and school-aged Mexican-American children are then presented. Finally, an effort will be made to pull together salient characteristics of the studies discussed into an overarching social systems or network perspective which is felt to influence the behavior and development of Mexican-American children.

MEXICAN-AMERICAN PARENTS

Childrearing Styles and Philosophies

Historically, Mexican-American parent and child relationships have been associated or equated with Mexican family relationships in Mexico. Staton's (1972) analysis is a very good example of this Mexican perspective on Mexican-Americans. From features ascribed to Mexican parents, the following major themes (or perhaps stereotypes) emerge: A male child is desired. If a female child is born, without the first one or two children being male, the father's machismo or virility is threatened. The birth of a daughter creates strain over guarding and protecting her honor and therefore the honor of the family. The family must make financial adjustments to support the daughter should she become a cotorra (spinster). A daughter is desired, however, after one or two males have been born.

Staton notes that unlike Mexican families, Mexican-Americans do not place importance on having male children. Both groups of children learn submission and strong obedience to the authority of the father, with the mother being the affectionate figure. Unlike Mexican fathers, the Mexican-American father is described as very affectionate in the early years, but demanding respect and much like the Mexican father after the child reaches puberty (i.e., not much contact with the children and holds self aloof).

Staton generally describes the following parent-child relationships as existing in both Mexican and Mexican-American families. The closest relationship is said to exist between mother and daughter, while the most distant occurs between father and son. In fact, the father-son relationship is said to become more distant as the father exerts more authority and demands more respect. The mother-son relationship is also close, with the mother acting as a permissive and affectionate figure. Like the mother-son relationship, the father-daughter dyad also has an affectionate bond—but not as intense as the mother-son bond—with the father also taking on the role of protector.

While to a certain extent some features described by Staton can be observed in some Mexican-American families, the questions are: to what extent and how pervasive are these generalities? Unfortunately, much of the Staton information is ethnocentric, broad, and relies on heavily stereotypic material.

However, other investigators have conducted quantitative research with "real" subjects. Wahab (1973), for instance, studied poor (if not impoverished) Mexican-American families in California. Among the prime characteristics identified, which others might call values, are religion, the extended family, *machismo,* honor, self-respect, and self-sufficiency. Family expectations described by the sample included a hierarchy of respect based upon the individual's age and sex, with older males given the most respect. Demands placed on the person by the family were in the areas of economics, contributions, assigned chores, or other family-related physical tasks. Other role expectations were the protection of the family image, honor, and well-being.

Unlike many researchers of the Mexican-American family, Wahab discusses childrearing and, in particular, the type of person parents are expected to develop in their families and communities. Wahab noted data supporting the finding that *both* Mexican-American parents teach children to conduct themselves with dignity and honor in social interactions. Although parenting does seem to be permissive during the early years when the child is considered to be an *angelito/a,* a drastic change does not occur at puberty, as Staton (1972) and other researchers have indicated. On the contrary, Wahab's sample indicates that the Mexican-American pubescent child still loves mother, obeys father, and respects both.

Perhaps the most interesting aspect of Wahab's childrearing discussions concerns the type of person expected to be developed by the Mexican-American families in the sample. These parents did not view or describe a successful or educated person in an academic or economic sense. Rather, they regularly discussed people who possess *educacion* or, as Wahab says, *urbanidad,* as successful—such individuals have training in human understanding and interpersonal relationships.

In a study of intermediate-grade, working-class children in San Jose, Rusmore and Kirmeyer (1976) studied childrearing among Mexican-Americans and Anglos. Two major reasons were given as to why Mexican-Americans were possibly close to, yet different from, Anglos in childrearing. First, acculturation may ease the divergence between the ethnic groups. Second, differences may be due to urbanization and class disparity rather than culture.

Mexican-American parents were observed as family centered and desirous of close, warm relationships in the family. They were also observed to encourage a similar family-centered attitude among their children through childrearing practices. Beliefs of this parent population included the following six characteristics: 1) parents enjoyed talking with their own parents; 2) relatives had warm and friendly feelings toward each other; 3) parents thought that their child's best friend should be a brother or a sister; 4) the family's neighborhood reputation was important; 5) loyalty to the family was important, no matter who was right or wrong; and 6) Mexican-American families visited their relatives more often than Anglos.

With regard to childrearing, the following differences were also noted: Mexican-American parents encouraged more dependence on family and obedience to authority than Anglos did. They did not allow children an opportunity to bring home friends to play as often as Anglos did, worried more when the child was not at home, required that the child play closer to home, and allowed fewer small decisions by the child (e.g., what to wear). Parents also disapproved more than Anglos when the child argued with authority figures (including the teacher) or interrupted conversations.

Parental Attitudes and Influence

Few investigators have sought to study Mexican-American parents as the primary influence on the child other than as school success factors. We thus have a plethora of information concerning observation and training of mothers in a school context, and a dearth of information on parental reports of involvements with their children, particularly regarding their possible influence on their children.

Tuddenham et al. (1974) studied mothers' reports of the behavior of their 9-, 10- and 11-year-old children. A behavior inventory consisting of "true," "not true," and "uncertain" descriptors was used to differentiate responses for Afro-Americans, Mexican-Americans, Asian-Americans, and Anglo-Americans. Reports from Mexican-American mothers showed the following clusters for boys: "too dangerous," "flares up over nothing," "stays away from home without permission," "seems to relax at home."

For Mexican-American girls, the main differentiating descriptor was that they "did not like to dream." Both boys and girls seemed also to be "easily awakened by noise." Unfortunately, in reviewing this study, a *great* deal of caution must be taken. The Mexican-American sample represented only 2% of the entire population surveyed. Fewer than 80 Mexican-American mothers were questioned compared to 2,212 Anglo-Americans, 641 Afro-Americans, and 117 Asian-Americans. A replication of this study is needed with more equal representative samples. Interestingly, but not surprisingly, although the overall population in this study seemed to be middle class, the Afro-American and Mexican-American groups were selected from the lower or poverty level classes.

Mothers' Attitudes and Influence

In each instance where Mexican-American mothers have been observed with their children, the child has been a preschooler. Of the four studies to be discussed, three used preschool mother-son pairs while the fourth used both male and female preschoolers in the sample. No reports of father-child interaction were found and mother-child interactions dealt with teaching situations only.

In the second of three studies by Steward and Steward (1974a), teacher-learner dyads were observed for Anglo-American, Asian-American, and Mexican-American groups. Mothers were videotaped teaching sorting and motor tasks to their own sons and to other 3-year-old boys. Results showed that teaching approaches (strategies), as well as responses by children, were different both by ethnic group and by mother teaching her own or another's child. In their earlier study, Steward and Steward (1973) noted that the best indicator of child response or maternal teaching was ethnicity. Asian-American and Mexican-American children were characterized by their giving "accepting responses" as a function of childrearing cultural expectations of obedience and respect for elders. Anglo children were not explicitly labeled. One infers from the data descriptions that Anglo preschoolers gave varied responses, perhaps nonaccepting.

With specific regard to maternal teaching styles, Asian-American mothers were characterized as making selective use of specific instruction and providing high and enthusiastic positive feedback. Mexican-American mothers were described as providing fewer teaching loops, slower pacing, original adult wording, and more negative feedback.

It is interesting to note that monolingual English- and Spanish-speaking mothers used more nonverbal cues while bilingual mothers did not. Anglo mothers spent time in setting up carefully embroidered instructions and in giving informational feedback. For lower-class Anglo mothers, a confusing subroutine was observed. Finally, attitudinal differences were also noted in that middle-class mothers among all groups, for example, were concerned with concepts of educational enrichment and quality, while lower-class and minority mothers were described as interested in pressure to modify the schools to meet their special needs.

In a third study, Steward and Steward (1974b) also examined social distance between mothers and their preschool sons as it related to social distance between teacher and learner. Like the previous study, Anglo mothers provided more teaching loops with greater speed than Mexican-American mothers. On the other hand, while Anglos used more elaboration, Mexican-Americans used more originality.

When these parents interacted with ethnically different preschool sons, interesting shifts occurred. Middle-class Anglo and Mexican mothers became more specific when instructing children, while lower-class mothers became less specific. Reinforcement patterns also changed, with more positive feedback given by all. Mexican-American mothers gave more negative feedback than Anglos, but only with regard to nonaccepting responses in the Anglo children. However, when Mexican-American mothers taught Mexican-American male preschoolers who were not their sons, they gave the same kind of negative feedback that they gave to their own sons.

In relation to apparent conflicting teaching approaches, Steward and Steward (1974b) relate how Mexican-American children were faced with the quick Anglo mothers' style (meaning a change in the number of instructions and the speed of delivery). In contrast, Anglo children received fewer instructions and at a slower pace when paired with Mexican-American mothers.

When children requested assistance, two different strategies arose once again. Mexican-American mothers did not immediately accede to requests for help but increased instructional specificity on the next teaching loop. The contrast in feedback and, therefore, teaching styles had similar effects between pairs, e.g., Mexican-American mother/Anglo child, as well as Anglo mother/Mexican-American child. That is, requests for help from preschoolers dropped by 50% among Anglo sons and to one request in every 35 loops for lower-class Mexican-American sons, while middle-class Mexican-American sons slightly increased their demand for help from 2% to 5%.

In addition, all mothers were by and large nicer to the other children than to their own. Another analysis revealed that Mexican-American children received less positive reinforcement from Anglo mothers than from their own, while Anglo children received three to five times more positive reinforcement from the Mexican-American mothers. This information might indicate that, although Mexican-American mothers give more negative feedback to their children, they are also able to give more positive feedback. While Anglo mothers give little, if any, negative feedback, they also give less positive feedback than Mexican-American mothers.

If such feedback frequency is not the case, however, the author would then argue that perhaps mothers displayed behavior stereotyped to ethnicity as learned and taught in the schools and society at large. That is, minorities are taught how to treat and react to the Anglo population by the schools, community at large, and through television's exclusion of minority role models in advertising and casting for films as well as programming. Mothers and teachers might be likewise prone to treat ethnically different children according to these stereotypes.

In a fourth study, Strom and Johnson (1974) devised a parent-as-a-teacher (PAAT) instrument as a self-assessment tool for mothers. The instrument was also paired with a questionnaire displaying the child's perception of parental behavior along the dimensions of control, creativity, frustration, play and teaching-learning. The goal of the approach was to enable mothers to identify their child-rearing strengths and weaknesses through both the child's and their own perceptions. By knowing this, the investigators felt that mothers would be more self-confident in teaching while also being more motivated to change. Results for poverty Anglo, Afro-American, and Mexican-American mothers indicated significant changes in self-concept as teachers; gain in knowledge regarding the teaching-learning process; changes in the child's self-concept as a learner; and increased word recognition, understanding, and elaboration.

Fathers' Attitudes and Influence

The vast majority of parent-child information for Mexican-Americans follows a pattern which also exists in the dominant culture. That is, parent-child relationships are synonymous with mother-child relationships. Consequently, few studies exist on Mexican-American father-child relationships. In view of the unguarded manner in which conceptions of machismo are bandied about in the popular and professional literature, this is a highly undesirable lacuna.

Moerk (1973) contrasted profiles of divorced children with those whose fathers were imprisoned. Specifically, he sought to explore the relationship between deviancy and the fathers' imprisonment, for equal low socioeconomic status (SES) Anglo and Mexican-American populations. Findings indicated that the profiles of children whose fathers were imprisoned more closely resemble those of juvenile delinquents than the control group, while the profiles of divorced children more closely resemble those of the control group than those of the delinquent group. Reasons given for these findings were not attributed to the problem of imprisonment, but to poor family relationships and low SES factors prior to imprisonment.

In a more recent investigation, Orive and Gerard (1975) examined the social contacts of Mexican-American and Afro-American parents of elementary school children (first through sixth grades) in Riverside, California. The study focused on sociometric choices made by Anglo peers for Mexican-American or Afro-American children as related to parental contact with own and mixed ethnic groups. In both samples, fathers were the heads of the households and were matched according to upper and lower SES. Results point toward what is described a "weather vane" character of father—but not mother—contacts and their children's acceptance by classmates. In other words, even though minority fathers had less total contact with their children, both boys and girls modeled *paternal* social contacts, regardless of SES status.

Sons' acceptance by classmates was significantly related to fathers' demonstrated involvement in organizations, while less father contact with relatives was related to daughters' acceptance by class-mates. The investigators provided few explanations for these trends, except to say that mothers may adopt a "conveyor" role and mediate fathers' influence. However, the researchers did conclude, based upon their findings for 322 Mexican-American and 227 Afro-American children, that minority fathers can influence classroom integration and must be brought into mixed ethnic groups.

The author completed a pilot study of middle-class Mexican-American and Anglo-American parents' perceptions of the father role (Mejia, 1975). The purpose of the study was to examine the father role using ethnic populations which have been described as quite divergent in the literature. Six aspects of the father role were investigated with fathers, and sometimes with mothers, through extensive interviews, observations, and survey methods: 1) comparisons of fathers with their own fathers; 2) joys and problems of fatherhood; 3) examples of good and bad fathers; 4) self-evaluations regarding childrearing successes; 5) advice to future fathers; 6) conceptions of an "ideal." In addition to these father role perceptions, data collection also emphasized risk-taking, locus of control, permissive-restrictive childrearing, value systems, and socialization practices.

Results from cross-ethnic comparisons indicate that the fathers' self-descriptions were more similar than dissimilar. In addition, results from observations and interviews likewise depicted this middle-class cross-ethnic group as more alike than unlike. Findings from father role perceptions indicated that, in the enactment of the role, a father must spend time with the family; must not let his occupation dominate; must be patient and nurturant; must be aware of the child's individuality; must provide an example; and must take responsibility. Unanticipated and more surprising findings indicated that fathers were more concerned with their own liabilities—and rectifying

them—than with faults in the child.

Mexican-American fathers did not abide by the published conceptions of an authoritarian-traditionalist extended family, nor to the submissive wife concept also popular in the literature. For example, one father was asked:

Q. What is, in your opinion, society's description of the father role?
A. My Mexican-Indian side tells me that the father should play a very dominant role in the family; almost to the point where the wife is subservient; even as a mother, in all aspects. He is the heavy disciplinarian; the *macho* . . .
Q. How do you feel about that?
A. I don't feel too strongly in favor of that. I am aware of it. In a lot of cases, the *machismo* aspect played a part in my rearing; it had to. When you have 14 brothers and sisters, somebody is providing something. I am aware of that social father role.

On the other hand, the existing non-Mexican role here in the U.S. tends to give more of the rearing practices to the mother, in the sense of running the household. More of an Anglo-Saxon type of outlook, the one I am talking about, where the father is the provider. In a sense, if it is an office he is going to, that is what he does, and the wife runs the whole show at home. His part in the family is not as significant as it should be. I don't like that either.
Q. It sounds like you are talking about extremes?
A. Right. I tend to favor the mutual sharing of responsibilities as much as our social life permits.

Intervention and Training with Mexican-American Parents

Much like reports dealing with observations of parent-child behaviors, studies dealing with family intervention (i.e., parent training) are emphasized in the preschool period. Of those works to be reviewed, only two involved children older than 6 years of age.

At the *Centro Educacion de la Communidad* in Redwood City, California, Hahn and Dunstan (1975) reviewed how attempts were made to provide a bilingual education relating to the child's culture and training of parents, involving teachers in the home, interfacing community, and school. Through such an approach, it was hoped that cognitive and psychological development would be enhanced as self-concept and school success were developed in the classroom and home.

At the Santa Barbara Family Center (Sonquist, 1976), low income mothers were helped to expand their knowledge and skill in childrearing and increase their self-confidence and ability to influence their children's development. The mothers' own development was also emphasized by assistance in developing skills dealing with environmental institutions, expansion of preventive mental health practices, human relations skills and reinforcing involvement and responsibility for the Santa Barbara program. Results indicated positive changes in the areas outlined.

Like the Redwood City program, Wagner et al. (1975) described a study developed to assess parental needs in the preparation of home learning environments for preschoolers. Of the 30 one- to three-year-olds involved (equally divided among Anglo, Afro-American and Mexican-American ethnic groups), 50% were described as developmentally delayed/high risk and were matched with nondelayed children of similar ethnicity. Parents of all three groups, as ascertained through videotapes and observations, showed higher scores for knowledge of child development than performance scores in creating learning environments.

At the Houston Parent-Child Development Center (Johnson et al., 1974, 1976),

the goal of a two-year program was to involve the entire family through parent education. For instance, the first year was characterized by in-house training of mothers along with family weekend sessions. The second year initiated mother-child nursery school activities and father involvement through evening sessions. Goals of the Houston Parent-Child Development Center program derived from the belief that optimum development is a product of parents being affectionate, controlling in a nonrestrictive manner, stressing verbal interaction, and valuing the home as a learning environment.

Education of low income Mexican-American mothers was of interest to the Houston group, but not to the exclusion of developing talents already held. In addition to child care and management training, mothers were exposed to sewing, nutrition, and family health while the children were in nursery school. Findings indicated improvement in maternal involvement and home environment areas. However, clear patterns for home scores and cognitive scores did not appear. In addition, the existence of some negative correlations were thought to show possible cultural differences.

As noted earlier, intervention studies dealing with school-aged Mexican-American children are limited. Henderson and Garcia (1973) instituted a training program designed to teach mothers how to increase the question-asking behavior of their first-grade children. Areas of training included: cueing, modeling, and reinforcement. Quesion-asking on behavior was determined according to baseline examiner instruction on question-asking plus generalization. Results showed that question-asking for both experimental and control groups increased significantly when responding to instructions given by an examiner acting as a model. Overall, the experimental subject displayed more question-asking behavior across all measurement situations.

In another study, McKinney (1975)

trained parents how to tutor their elementary school children in math or reading. Fifty parents—Anglo, Afro-American, and Spanish surnamed—were trained two hours per week for 15 weeks. The parents and children in the experimental groups displayed a more positive attitude toward school than did control group parents and children. In addition, children in the experimental group showed a significant increase in achievement.

TEACHERS OF MEXICAN-AMERICAN CHILDREN

Mexican-American parents are not the only adult models who have come under scrutiny and training when in contact with Mexican-American children. The classroom teacher (typically Anglo) and teacher's aide (typically Mexican, Mexican-American, or other Latino) have also been the subjects of interviews, observation, and sources for assessment and training. Topics involving teachers include the following: competence, expectations, influence, language attitudes, perceptions of child's adjustment, and stereotypes. These topics will be included in this section's discussion of three major areas in the literature on teacher-pupil involvement: 1) teacher evaluations of Mexican-American students; 2) teacher behavior and Mexican-American students; and 3) teacher competence and Mexican-American students. Finally, the children's perceptions and beliefs about their teachers will be examined.

Teacher Evaluations of Mexican-American Students

Fifth- and sixth-grade boys were assessed by teachers on a 15 item semantic differential scale of classroom evaluative criteria (Jensen and Rosenfeld, 1974). Teachers were also presented with videotapes of middle- and lower-class Anglo, Afro-American, and Mexican-American students via audio, visual, or combined stimulus tapes. Data trends showed that although Anglo students were most favorably rated, middle-class Anglos and Afro-Americans were ranked higher than lower-class Anglos and Afro-Americans. Social class made no difference in the ratings of Mexican-American children by teachers.

In a similar vein, Williams and Naremore (1974) presented 120 teachers with audio and videotaped samples of Anglo, Afro-American, and Mexican-American children for determination of ethnic background and teacher expectation. Results revealed that 50% of the sample (Type I teachers) rated the Anglo child as confident, eager, and ethnically nonstandard. Examination of the findings reveals that the Type I teachers came from schools where the dominant attending ethnic groups were Anglo and Afro-American children. The remaining 50% of teachers evaluating the children distributed themselves according to four additional teacher-type categories (Types II, III, IV, and V). Interestingly, Type II teachers rated Mexican-American and Afro-American children high on confidence and eagerness. These minority pupils only represented 24% and 3%, respectively, of the student populations at the schools where these Type II teachers taught (Anglo students represented 66% of the schools' populations).

Type III teachers rated Mexican-American children as ethnic and ethnically nonstandard,* with Afro-American children as higher on confidence and eagerness than the other teachers' ratings (Type I, II, IV, and V). The ethnic mix at the Type III teachers' schools was: Afro-American students 15% (lowest); Mexican-American students 50% (highest); Anglos 20%; other groups 15%.

---

*Ethnic means children were typically Mexican-American. Ethnically nonstandard means that the children did follow expected classroom behavior in spite of their cultural differences.

Among Type IV teachers, the best ratings were for middle-class Afro-American children as high on confidence, eagerness, and ethnic nonstandardness. The ethnic distribution in Type IV teachers' schools was 63% Mexican-American, 25% Anglo, 12% other groups, and no Afro-Americans. Finally, Type V teachers rated both Afro- and Mexican-American students as low on confidence, eagerness, and ethnic nonstandardness (with Mexican-Americans rated slightly lower than Afro-Americans). Representation of the three ethnic groups in Type V teachers' schools was 25% for each ethnic group with the mixed population also having a 25% enrollment.

It is evident from the evaluations of 130 teachers in the Williams and Naremore (1974) study that the lower the minority representation, the higher the ratings for confidence, eagerness, and ethnic nonstandardness. For example, Type IV teachers' ratings of Afro-American children were high, although not a single Afro-American child was in attendance! Also, the higher the representation, or, as in the case of Type V teachers, the more equal the ethnic representation, the lower the evaluations of Afro- and Mexican-American children. Two burning questions occur in reaction to these data: What kinds of problems will such teacher evaluations and pursuant academic expectations cause if busing and school desegregation are implemented? Are school desegregation and busing better than what has existed in the past among ethnically segregated schools (as evidenced by the ratings of Type I, III and V teachers who were from schools where Afro- or Mexican-American enrollments were equal to or greater than 25%)?

Unlike the preceding discussion of teacher expectations based on ethnicity, another investigation (Stedman and Adams, 1973) examined bilingual preschoolers and their teachers' perceptions of the children's adjustments. Results point toward high behavioral ratings for children with high English language proficiency.

The corollary was that there were low behavioral ratings for pupils low in English proficiency.

Bikson (1974) studied the speech of Anglo-, Afro-, and Mexican-American students with both objective (linguistic measures) and subjective (teacher evaluation) methods. The focus of the study, for nearly 150 children and 60 Anglo teachers, was whether minority children were perceived as linguistically deficient in contrast to their Anglo peers. According to the objective measures, the minority students equalled or excelled age-mates. However, the teachers rated these same minority children as inferior to their Anglo peers. Bikson stresses the fact that the regular clustering by classroom teachers of minority evaluations, with the objective/subjective reversal, points toward stereotyping influences. In addition, she mentions that the Anglo teachers in this study displayed an inability to differentiate properties of ethnic speech styles and therefore *did not hear speech differences.* The latter explanation does not get the teacher off the proverbial "hook," however. Even if the teachers were not able to discern what the objective measures were able to evaluate, why did they still display negative behavioral tendencies in assessing Mexican-American children? It appears that language style is intimately related to school success. As a consequence, teacher unresponsiveness, as a product of stereotyping or inability to hear the speech performance of a Mexican-American child, is directly related to ability and performance gains between early and later grades.

Another study looked at teacher stereotyping in relation to presenting ethnic and social-class variation (Rosenfeld, 1973). The results show, once again, that stereotyping occurred on the basis of ethnicity and social class. In a further analysis, the study also concluded that cues, such as ethnicity and social class, are transmitted via audio and visual modes with the audio process providng the teacher with more information for evaluation. This conclusion was stressed by Jensen and Rosenfeld (1974) earlier.

As is evident from the preceding research, language and speech patterns are receiving a great deal of scrutiny. Felice and Richardson (1975), however, studied achievement based upon the effect of teacher expectations of achievement performance and self-concept. Their hypothesis associates low achievement performance of Mexican-American pupils with both teacher-held stereotypes of ethnic inequality and culture plus perceived lack of family support for education. Their approach involved an experimental intervention for previously identified low achievement potential pupils which consisted of academic and family partcipation components. Results indicated that the greatest degree of success in achievement was made by the students whose parents, regardless of SES levels, were involved and supportive at school. In addition, year-end teacher interviews revealed a positive evaluation of the experimental subjects. This was shown by teachers describing these children as less disruptive and as displaying greater academic potential.

Teacher Behavior and Mexican-American Students

A major study used 52 rural, suburban, and urban schools scattered throughout California, New Mexico, and Texas in order to examine verbal behaviors of teachers as a factor in equal educational opportunity for Anglo and Mexican-American children (Jackson and Cosca, 1974). Other data analyzed included 22 school, classroom and teacher characteristics (i.e., school ethnic concentration, SES levels, test orientation, test criteria, education, ethnicity of teachers). Findings for dominant teacher behaviors included these elements: First, teachers praised or encouraged Anglo children 35% more than

they did Mexican-American children. Second, Anglo children's ideas were accepted and used 40% more than those of Mexican-American children. Third, teachers directed 21% more questions to Anglo children. This information is particularly significant because, in fact, the observers were from a federal agency. Most teachers being observed knew this in advance, had ample preparation time, and were "on their toes." In addition, districts with records of federal investigation or prosecution were excluded from observation by the agency. Consequently, the researchers concluded that, based upon the preceding results, the actual "disparities" between teacher behaviors and Anglo and Mexican-American children are much worse. In a nice way, the investigators are saying that they studied the "best" schools, excluded the "worst," and here are the results. Those factors thought to produce the inequities include:

1) There are teacher-student differences in language and culture.
2) Differences were not accommodated by programs in the Southwest.
3) Teacher responses are different for "identical" behavior by pupils from varying ethnic backgrounds, SES, or achievement characteristics.
4) Teacher training institutions had failed to provide relevent coursework and supervised experience.

The theme of Wahab's (1974) research concerned the effects of student attitudes toward self, school, and learning and participation, as a result of "transactions" with the teacher consisting of the following:

1) rewards-praise—hugs, approving smile;
2) punishment-sarcasm—deprivation, scolding;
3) control and management—teacher directing to do or not to do, teacher turning child's head;

4) teacher-assigned tasks—academic, prestigious, calling on child;
5) other teacher-assigned nonacademic tasks—such as being monitors or decorating bulletin boards, room; and nonacademic and nonprestigious tasks—such as cleaning the floor, board, or opening window;
6) nontask academic interaction—teacher helps child or group;
7) nontask and nonacademic interaction—teacher-child socializing, small talk.

For this population of 70% Mexican-American and 30% Anglo school children, five findings were enunciated for the four status categories of Anglo boys, Anglo girls, Mexican-American boys and Mexican-American girls: 1) Anglo students were interacted with more frequently than Mexican-American students; 2) Anglo boys were the highest in rank overall on seven interactions; 3) Anglo girls were second on four of the seven categories; 4) Mexican-American girls were last in all categories; and 5) teachers interacted less with girls than with boys.

More specifically, Anglo children were rewarded more often than Mexican-American children. Teachers assigned three times more tasks to Anglo than to Mexican-American children. Teachers also displayed twice as many nonacademic interactions with Anglo than with Mexican-American children, i.e., small talk or socializing.

In another study, Lecompte (1973) approached teacher behavior in New Mexico from the perspective that "norms and behavior" related to work are learned in school and are expressed by behavior in the classroom. As such, measures related to work (i.e., time, responsibility, performance, academic achievement) were identified. Findings indicate that teacher behaviors are displayed in two categories. First, the management core, institutional demands of the school, and the discretionary area, which may or may not cause

problems since it is based upon teacher style and choice. Second, areas of conflict relative to teacher enunciated rules and expectations as exemplified by being quiet and overtly passive, keeping busy, and dividing up available time.

In examining this study, note that the areas of conflict can all be subsumed under the core of teacher management behaviors. The conflict areas can all be associated with the values of time and responsibility which (according to the investigator) are at variance in Mexican-American and Anglo cultures. In fact, sources of conflict between teacher and child are vested in value differences. There is nothing wrong with this—except that the Mexican-American values identified by the investigator emerged as the same labels promulgated in the 1940s and 1950s. For example, some of the above conflicting values include *machismo*. Therefore, teachers expect conflict with the male Mexican-American child because said child values male dominance, activeness, and superiority. Another stereotype which was incorporated into this study was the alleged difference in time orientation: Mexican-Americans believe in the present time as a "gift of life" and Anglos believe in the proper use of time, or in time as money. Subsequent studies have refuted these stereotypes (McClintock, 1974).

At least one cross-cultural researcher has also studied Mexican-American child-teacher behaviors. Edwards (1970) likened teachers of Mexican-American children to teachers of Maori children in New Zealand. In both instances, the conclusion was that emotional and intuitive reactions of the teacher to the student rest on the fact that background characteristics of the groups are in conflict, with conscious or unconscious stereotypes mitigating behavior. This being the case, the investigator recommended that teachers of culturally different, underachieving children would profit from a degree of detachment and self-observation.

The author has observed that ethnically

different teachers, e.g., teachers who are also Mexican-American, may also interact more with Anglo children. Why? First, these teachers were influenced by their teachers, who modeled one type of behavior for interacting with Anglo children, and another type of behavior for interacting with Mexican-American children. Second, as trainees or student teachers, our prospective Mexican-American teacher of Mexican-American children was no doubt supervised by Anglos who, because of their greater numbers and representation on school faculties, boards, administrative offices, as well as in the university professorial ranks, outnumber new teachers and exert much overall power and supervision. Supervisors and instructors of prospective teachers promulgate behavior established in their own classroom experiences as pupils and teachers. The fact that very few tenured Mexican-American university or college faculty educate prospective Mexican-American teachers projects a model of "white professionalism."

Teacher Competence and Mexican-American Students

Castillo and Cruz (1974) cogently summarize the implications of current studies of the Mexican-American child and school environment according to four elements:

1) Learning and teaching are significantly affected by cultural orientation.
2) Values transmitted in the classroom stem from the teacher's own value system, and this in turn is determined by the teacher's social class identification.
3) Different cultural populations have different learning styles and respond differently to various types of motivation.
4) A child's ability to learn or fail depends to a significant extent on the degree to which the instructional program is compatible with his or her cultural characteristics (p. 343).

Major areas of teacher competencies have been outlined by these investigators in addition to but not as replacements for traditional basic competencies. The aim of this approach is to tailor traditional global behavior traits previously held by and directed toward the dominant Anglo majority to fit current multicultural realities.

The following competencies have been stressed by these and other researchers for enhancing the education of Mexican-American children:

1) Language development. It was felt that in order for many Mexican-American children to develop properly, a need exists for enhancing verbal interactional behaviors in the native or parental tongue of Spanish (Castillo and Cruz, 1974; Gonzales, 1974). However, the form of Spanish emphasized is not Castillian Spanish but Mexican Spanish and *Calo* (the barrio colloquialism and vernacular which has developed through the union of English and Spanish). Language competence can represent a mixture of English and Mexican Spanish and/or *Calo*-Spanish bi- or trilingualism.
2) Culture. Currently, the presentation of cultural elements to the child and the mastery of same for the teacher represents a "catchall" for many needs. Among needs subsumed are the development of knowledge about one's past as well as the enhancement and growth of self-concept and self-esteem. Other factors include stress on the child's community, resource persons, and foods, as well as the nature of his or her "cultural identity," which has persisted and has existed in this country for over 200 years (Castillo and Cruz, 1974; Gonzalez, G., 1974, 1975; Gonzalez J.M., 1975; Garcia 1973a and 1973b).
3) Values associated with cultural democracy (Ramirez, 1972; Ramirez et al.; 1974a).

4) Cognitive development from a field-sensitive perspective (Gonzales, 1974).

5) Parental involvement with curriculum and as liaisons and resource persons (Castillo and Cruz, 1974).

Attempts have been made to incorporate these competencies in their entirety or on a partial basis. For example, California State University at Fresno (1973) conducted a "rural teacher intern program" through its mini-corps. The training was designed for teachers who were bilingual in Spanish and English and who possessed special abilities (because of personal background) or higher probabilities of meeting the needs of rural children from economically depressed or impoverished histories and families.

One researcher has gone so far as to create an environment for peer teaching among Mexican-American pupils in order to improve the child's self-concept by letting the child assume the role of teacher, provide more practice, and tailor teaching to individual needs (Dixon, 1976). However, the investigator does stress the need for adopting five concepts as a means of avoiding the cognitive-style rejection of traditional background Mexican-American children: 1) Mexican-American children identify most closely with family and older siblings as surrogate parents. 2) Motivational orientations are more related to achievement for the family or group and not for the individual. 3) Mexican-American children function better than Anglo children in an atmosphere of cooperation. 4) Interpersonal relationships are important, as Mexican-American children relate better to individual teachers and students in a human environment. 5) From a cognitive perspective, Mexican-American children have been found to be more field dependent and, to a large degree, in conflict with teachers who are field independent. Based upon the above, Dixon (1976) recommended reading strategies which do not conflict with cultural values thus far recognized (pre-dominantly by Ramirez et al., 1974a; Ramirez and Price-Williams, 1974, 1976) for Mexican-American "traditional" children. The next step is to identify how we approach the culturally "nontraditional" Mexican-American child.

A strong move in the direction of providing and training indigenous paraprofessionals is underway. However, efforts must also be made to replace (where possible and/or necessary) the Anglo credentialed teacher to whom many of these noncredentialed aides are assigned. The goal must be to break up the school and schoolroom social systems model which impresses upon Mexican-American children that power, authority and responsibility are vested in the Anglo leader. The provision of adult representatives from the children's own background who are predominantly subordinate to Anglo teachers and districts reinforces this model. If the indigenous paraprofessional's role is always subordinate to the Anglo classroom authority, can Mexican-American children view themselves as competent or independent? On the other hand, in reported situations where indigenous paraprofessionsls have been used, positive gains have been made by the children involved (Jelinek, 1976; Veaco, 1973). In general, children involved with these teacher's aides demonstrated gains, regardless of cultural background.

Aside from competencies learned in the university setting, teachers of Mexican-American children must also demonstrate other, more subtle and less easily measurable qualities. These qualities concern the personal characteristics and individual contributions the teacher brings to the child. Subtle, positive behaviors teachers can bring to the classroom situation include personal receptivity to learning from Mexican-American children and counseling skills for confronting and overcoming the decades of travesty inflicted on them by whatever source and from whatever cause.

Baca (1974), for example, worked with

15 educable mentally handicapped (EMH) Mexican-American children in order to help them first become aware of values for language and culture, and second, overcome fears of using the two languages. It was evident that in creating an environment of "relaxed acceptance," Baca in effect employed counseling approaches which transcended the fact that he was a cultural model. In other words, do not expect problems or difficulties to fade or disappear, just because there is a cultural model.

Torrance (1974) studied teachers of gifted children and their receptivity in learning from their culturally different pupils. Seventy-two instructors responded to questionnaires ascertaining their readiness to learn and the types of information they wished to gain from six culturally diverse groups. In terms of personal growth, these teachers were interested in the traditions and folklore of Mexican-Americans, Native Americans and Cuban-Americans; Mexican-American and Cuban-American dialects; Native American crafts; coping techniques of ghetto Afro-Americans; and philosophy of life and goals of rural and ghetto Afro-Americans as well as rural Anglo-Americans.

The findings are interesting. The most significant element was the fact that these teachers expected to learn from their classroom charges. Such an attitude places a value on the child and culture, enough so that the teacher can recognize this and subsequently change. Here is the crux of the problem: If a teacher is not willing to change personally and grow, or considers teaching "just a job," then some serious reevaluations must be undertaken. This not only applies to new or prospective teachers but also to those who are retraining with bilingual specialties, those who wish to meet the changing needs of school districts in the Southwest (30% to 40% "white flight" is expected in Los Angeles as a result of desegregation), or those who wish to avoid being released for lack of Anglo pupils. The Anglo population has been described as growing dramatically less than that of the Latino population, i.e., 7% versus 43%. Where is the surfeit of Anglo teachers to go, if not into bilingual classrooms in areas such as Los Angeles, San Diego, Denver, Dallas, Houston, and Tucson—to name a few cities with very large Mexican-American populations?

Mexican-American Children's Perceptions of Their Teachers

Thus far, this section has dealt with teachers' evaluations of Mexican-American preschool and school-aged children. In a unique approach, Gustafson and Owens (1971) explored children's self-perceptions and beliefs about their teachers' feelings toward them. The teachers' actual perceptions of the child, in relation to school achievement, were also assessed. Third- and sixth-grade San Jose children were selected because of differing cognitive and social developmental levels between these age groups. The findings indicate that for third graders, no significant ethnic differences existed between self-concept ratings or reading achievement, although on the math test, the Mexican-American 8-year-olds scored significantly higher than their Anglo peers. In terms of the teacher checklist, a more positive relationship was shown between the Anglo children's self-esteem inventory and the teacher evaluation. A correlation was also seen for non-Mexican-American third graders relative to the child's evaluation of "How I See Myself" and "How My Teacher Sees Me."

Differences for the sixth-grade groups were distinct. For example, according to Coopersmith's (1967) Self-Esteem Inventory, no differences in scores between Anglo and Mexican-American third graders were recorded. Results for sixth graders displayed higher and more positive scores for the Anglo sample. Significant differences existed for reading, math, and Lorge Thorndike responses. Once again, scores favored the Anglo sixth graders. As with the third grade sample, responses to the questions "How I See Myself" and "How My Teacher Sees Me" and the teacher's checklist also favored the Anglo child.

It is interesting to note that in reviewing the results of their study, the investigators concluded that Mexican-American children were more independent of the teacher than the Anglo child with regard to "his worth." This conclusion seems to quite easily overlook the fact that young children do not have defense mechanisms of adults. Where preferences are modeled, for whatever reason, a group will be alienated. It would have been of further interest to have examined the findings with regard to whether or not the Mexican-American children's *independence* of the teacher had led them to independently drop out of school and work in the agricultural fields of San Jose before completing elementary school. Especially or only in the lower grade levels of school, we might also note that it appears that "black is beautiful and brown is cute." This is evidenced by the similarity between Anglo-American and Mexican-American third graders in the self and teacher evaluations. Are we to assume that the greatest degree of ethnic equality exists at the kindergarten or preschool level and the range of least to greatest alienation occurs most drastically between the third and sixth grades? The preceding study seems to point in that direction.

PRESCHOOL MEXICAN-AMERICAN CHILDREN

Since 1973, reported data (Mejia, 1973) for Mexican-American preschool children have concentrated on four areas. These include the effects upon development of various types of cognitive intervention and physical grouping. Other areas emphasize the child's self-identity, language,

motivation, autonomy, and behavior. A new area of focus is that of "special" Mexican-American children.

Although all Mexican-American children are special by virtue of their ethnic, cultural, or language differences, "special" in this instance refers to that population which is exceptional due to intellectual differences or physical handicaps, as exemplified by intellectual giftedness or hearing impairedness. Mental retardation will not be elaborated on, since the history of education in the United States with respect to Mexican-Americans is replete with instances of presumed intellectual dysfunctions. In addition, other chapters in this text cover the subject of testing and education.

Cognitive Development

In an effort to enhance school success or reduce school anxiety among Mexican-American preschoolers, two studies have taken apparently diverse yet similar approaches. Plant and Southern (1972) provided a "highly cognitively structured" environment for two successive summers prior to kindergarten entry. Results indicate that treatment and comparison groups displayed differences during the kindergarten year. However, such divergence as measured by the Stanford-Binet, Peabody, and group achievement tests, did not appear on first- and second-grade achievement comparisons.

In contrast, Durrett and Pirofski (1971) sought to observe psychological functioning by grouping Mexican-American and Anglo children according to ethnically heterogenous or homogenous units. Like Plant and Southern (1972), Durrett and Pirofski studied changes utilizing cognitive and behavioral instruments. Unlike the former study, however, results indicated that both forms of grouping facilitated cognitive and behavioral growth or modification. These groups acted as their own ethnic reinforcement.

The foregoing studies can be criticized, as many studies using Mexican-Americans as their subjects have been criticized (Padilla and Ruiz, 1973), for reliance on unproven evaluations from standardized (for middle-class subjects) tests and measures (Padilla et al., 1975; Padilla et al., 1978; Padilla and Romero, 1976). In addition, the Durrett and Pirofski study was further weakened by a lack of sample uniformity. The Mexican-American samples were from low income families and background, while the Anglo-American children were from middle income professional families. Such research typifies a dichotomous cross-class or "apples and oranges" type comparison between Mexican-Americans and Anglo-Americans.

Self-identity

Apart from research into the cognitive development of Mexican-American preschoolers, interest also exists around the child's conceptions of self-identity, person, self-perceptions and ethnic or racial preferences. Along this vein, Rice et al. (1974) noted that Mexican-American subjects could identify photographs that resembled them, although there was some difficulty distinguishing between Anglo and Chicano drawings.

Secondly, Cota-Robles de Suarez (1973) noted that preschool children in her sample were aware of their skin color and showed a significant preference for their ethnic group. Historically, quite the contrary has existed for minority children on this task. Cota-Robles de Suarez, in a review of the literature on skin color preferences (1973), mentions that a sizeable number of minority children select a bizarre color as opposed to preferring their own or the Anglo skin color. This sort of behavior has also been extensively documented among Afro-Americans.

In the social system sense, it is evident that preschool children develop race awareness and preferences at an early age. As a consequence, even prior to entering the public school system, Mexican-American, as well as other minority group children, have a concrete conception of what society favors or decrees as appropriate in the way of skin color. This is exemplified by children's ambivalent and tentative approach in making skin color preference choices. Extensions of this argument lead to the conclusion that knowing society's cultural attitudes and accepting such values places the child in a self-identity "conflict" which is demonstrated by bizarre skin color choice or some other form of avoidant, and therefore "self" denial behavior. The research questions are: How long does this continue? How are other behaviors influenced? What are the methods of intervention?

Language

The influence of language on the development of Mexican-American children receives significant attention through middle childhood. However, investigators do not usually choose to observe how language develops in the Mexican-American (an exception is Lar, 1973). Rather, the emphasis is placed upon assessment and amelioration of, and projections from, the language displayed at the time of contact.

Hickey (1973) compared two monolingual and bilingual groups using the Peabody Picture Vocabulary Test (PPVT) and the Goodenough Draw-A-Man Test. In the second group, items ending with "ing" were deleted since item analysis for the first group had shown that "ing" ending nouns were correlated with failing to identify proper pictures. The above being the case, comparisons between the first group of English and Spanish-English children showed very low scores for the Mexican-American group. However, results for the second group (with "ing" ending nouns omitted) showed both groups as the same. The findings reflect the notion that it is possible to minimize below average ability or reticence of preschoolers with instruments like the PPVT and that bilingualism is not classifiable with other handicaps.

A question is whether bilingualism is really a handicap. For instance, in a review of the literature for preschool bilingual/bicultural education, Padilla et al. (1975) concluded that cognitive development may be facilitated in bilingual children. His review of the research literature revealed the following:

1) Bilinguals outperformed monolingual children on tests involving language comprehension and production.
2) French-English bilinguals from Montreal, because of wider cultural experiences, demonstrate diversification of mental abilities, mental flexibility, and superiority in concept formation.
3) Where bilingual status in a monolingual setting is not commensurate with *ethnic marginality*, bilinguals can outperform monolinguals.

Other language investigators seek to use bilingualism as a fulcrum for predicting such factors as intelligence, verbal learning, achievement, behavior adjustment, and other abilities. One investigator (Hickey, 1972) attempted to measure intelligence and verbal learning ability and concluded that basic Spanish and English language differences were the sources of difficulty. From a systems perspective, this is not the only difficulty. That is, each language carries with it the influences of other interactive systems. Therefore, teaching a child the English language affects the ecology of the other systems attached to the Spanish language.

Behavior

A fourth approach to examining the development of the preschool child involves explorations of behavior factors such as autonomy, maturity, and cooperative or trusting patterns. Results from correlations between personality and intellectual performance with Head Start children show that: 1) preschool inventory scores correlate in a positive direction with extroversion, general adjustment, peer adjustment, and task orientation; 2) preschool inventory scores correlate in a negative direction with distractability and introversion ratings; and 3) no correlations were found between hostility and consideration of others on the preschool inventory (Benson and Kuipers, 1974). It was further concluded that the preschool curriculum ought to require activities which stress explorations, initiative, persistence, and independent behavior.

Durrett and Kim (1973) examined the behavioral maturity of Mexican-American and Anglo preschoolers. The results showed that, on the average, the Mexican-American was less mature than the Anglo peer. However, a reading of the study reveals contradictory evidence. For example, in some areas, Mexican-American children were *more* mature than their Anglo peers. The factor structure of behavioral maturity among Anglos was more complex (therefore more difficult to understand? or does more maturity ensue with complexity?). The implication of the researchers' conclusion seems to be that less complexity for Mexican-Americans is indicative of less maturity. Yet one does not necessarily follow from the other.

In an interesting study exploring cooperation, Parrlman and Pierce-Jones (1974) divided 5- and 6-year-old Mexican-, Afro-, and Anglo-American children by ethnicity and sex. They could choose to cooperate or compete with one another in either an immediate or delayed reward group. Findings for females (which are rare) proved to be of most importance in that female ethnic pairs cooperated more significantly (except for Mexican-American and Afro-American pairs, which also cooperated well) than cross-ethnic pairs. Such behavior did not, incidentally, depend upon delayed or immediate reinforcement. From these findings, are we to assume that these minority children were in a less cooperative situation only when paired with Anglo classmates? Such a hypothesis might be explored with other minority group pairings.

The Adkins et al. study (1972) represents another attempt to show motivation to achieve in school by the comparison of ten "ethnic-cultural" groups. Briefly, the study which included ten groups—Mormon, Catholic, Jewish, Puerto Rican, urban Afro-American, rural Caucasian, Hawaiian, West Coast Asian-American, Mexican-American (Texas), and Native American preschoolers—indicates that middle-class samples usually score higher than lower-class samples. In other words, scores for sex and ethnic-cultural differences in motivation to achieve in school indicate that Catholics, Jews, and Mormons (middle-class sample) scored higher than urban Afro-Americans, Anglos, Puerto Ricans, Mexican-Americans, West Coast Asian-Americans, Native Americans, and Hawaiian children (the lower-class sample). Likewise, results of self-evaluations also show the middle-class samples scoring higher than those of the lower-class. The necessity is not to control for socioeconomic status, but to compare middle-class samples with middle-class samples and lower-class samples with lower-class samples. The caveat remains that one cannot change one part of the social system without altering the entire system. Socioeconomic status, whether of upper, middle or lower class, has individual and environmental influences which cannot always be controlled with certainty in cross-class research.

Attention is also being given to the special bilingual Mexican-American child, such as the hearing impaired, blind, and intellectually gifted. In addition, parental and other adult attitudes toward handicapped Mexican-American children are also being explored. Some of the key conclusions in a study of the hearing impaired

(Grant, 1972) indicated that Mexican-American culture must be studied; personnel must be recruited from the Mexican-American community; and that mothers or their surrogates (grandmothers, aunts or cousins) need to function as evaluators, identifiers, interpreters, and coordinators for hearing-impaired Mexican-American children.

Among populations of special children, Askins et al. (1975) identified "high risk" (as a result of handicaps such as low birth weight) 3- to 5-year-old Mexican-American children in New Mexico. The aim was to provide a responsive environment relative to English and Spanish language development, as well as improve affective and cognitive growth. Findings quite interestingly show that children made gains in self-concept and personality growth, discrimination (perceptual and sensory), and school readiness. However, children did not demonstrate any significant gain in learning aptitude. How this occurred remains a question, since an increase in learning would be anticipated if other measures also showed increases.

No studies since 1973 (Mejia, 1973) were identified which compared Mexican-American neonates with other infants as the research focus. Nor were any studies of expectant parents encountered. Where Mexican-American infants or young children are mentioned, the focal point is usually to provide some form of intervention for the mother (i.e., child care, nuturition, mental health, etc.). Thus far, the intent has not been to observe or to record and analyze the interactions or transactions between Mexican-American parents and their infants. Certainly, preschool parent pairs have been studied, but once again, the focus has been on the mother as teacher and not the mother or father as socializer, model, or transmitter of a myriad of cultural, ethnic, economic, and social material.

Lar (1973) conducted a cross-national study of language development among Anglo-American and Mexican populations. The study was an analysis of infant (birth through eight weeks of age) movement behavior and noncrying vocalizations. An original intent of this study was to follow-up and observe Mexican-American infants at a later date.

Lar categorized and defined movement behavior phenomena according to kinesiology, kinesics, and parakinesic levels. For instance, babbling (noncrying vocalizations) was defined as two or more combinations of noncrying, nonreflexive sounds made with the vocal mechanism along with paralinguistic features. Data were compiled by a combination of handwritten field notes of observations and videotape recordings.

Relative to movement behavior, it was noted that burst patterns were more characteristic of Anglo-American infants while sustained rhythms typified Mexican neonates. In addition, the findings also indicate that rhythmic patterns of English and Spanish were present among nonbabblers at four weeks of age. The preceding led to Lar's conclusions that "infants babble the way they move" and that:

Neonates are preconditioned by experiental uterine timing of events and processes. Rhythms of language are probably learned *in utero*. While the infant experiences mother's movement rhythm, heartbeat, and biochemical routine reactions (which are culturally determined), he or she is also forming certain cellular brain structures that perhaps are imprinted with information about cultural perceptions of timing based upon biological processes.

Two distinct and different cultural patterns were evident to Lar on a kinesiological level. Mexican neonates fisted their hands rarely and customarily were seen with their fingers extended or slightly flexed with open palms. Anglo-American infants ordinarily took a fisted hand position during routine periods. Factors mitigating the hands open versus hands fisted positions were likened to the Mexican culture and Spanish language as relaxed and with no stress-timed rhythms

or situations. In contrast, it was observed that the American sample seemed more "regulated or controlled," with caretakers being preoccupied with routines and schedules. Relative to language, English represents a stress-timed idiom.

Parakinesic behavior among the two cultures shows cultural as well as individual rhythmic patterns, with Mexican infants displaying sustained patterns and Anglo-Americans burst rhythms. According to Lar, Spanish and English languages have characteristic patterns, rhythms, and stresses associated with their communication and expression.

In considering the influence of the pregnant mother, Lar noted the following:

If mother is a sustained mover, which is the typical Mexican rhythm, she is transmitting this culturally determined movement behavior and speech. In response to his or her uterine environment, the fetus may code this experimental information at a cellular level.

Expanding further, Lar implies that rhythms may be the linguistic behavior first learned. Whether Mexican-American school children should first be characterized in terms of language rhythms instead of language competence in either Spanish or English is a question which should be raised.

Based on Lar's initial findings and conclusions, it is evident that much information can be developed in areas such as influences on child and personality development, foreign language learning, and communication (especially intercultural barriers). With respect to interethnic problems, different "bialects" or biorhythms within a culture may decrease rapport and increase ethnic communication barriers.

Extending these findings into the classroom, community or the Mexican-American home, we can easily envision Anglo teachers with burst and standard English rhythms being unable to communicate with Mexican-American children with sustained or undulated Mexican-American English rhythms. The two are simply "out of sinc" and meaningful communication is unknowingly distorted through variable concepts and timing. The research question is whether Mexican-American teachers should instruct Mexican-American pupils or whether Anglo teachers can be either trained or retrained to do so. A corollary question concerns the time and expense involved in designing and completing such an enterprise as opposed to credentialing indigenous bilingual Mexican-American teachers.

SCHOOL-AGED MEXICAN-AMERICAN CHILDREN

Cognitive Development

Cognitive research is currently emphasizing field dependence and field independence differences between Anglo and Mexican-American children. Ramirez (1972) has indicated that intelligence discrepancies may be a product of an ethnic-individual difference variable. Originally incorporating the Witkin (1962) rod and frame test, Ramirez et al. (1974a, 1974b) and other investigators (Buriel, 1975; Kagan and Zahn, 1975) have made significant contributions to understanding aspects of the Mexican-American child's independent and dependent cognitive styles.

Results for field dependence and field independence research indicate that Afro- and Mexican-Americans score more field dependent than Anglo peers. Additionally, the females in the three ethnic groups (Anglo-, Afro-, and Mexican-American) are more field dependent than males. Ramirez and Price-Williams (1974) attribute field sensitive behavior to differences in childrearing and socialization practices. For instance, field-sensistive (dependent) Mexican-Americans are typically described by Ramirez as stressing group identity, respect for family, and religious authority, as well as displaying shared-function family and group characteristics. In contrast, field-insensitive (independent) individuals encourage questioning of convention, an individual identity, and are characterized as having formally organized family and friendship groups.

Ramirez and Price-Williams (1974) have extended the foregoing into analysis of Mexican children experiencing various levels of acculturation. Among a sample of nearly 550 grade-school children from atraditional, dualistic, and traditional Mexican-American communities, it was found that degrees of field-sensitive cognitive style corresponded to identification with traditional to atraditional sociocultural system orientation. Children from traditional families were found to be more field dependent than children from atraditional or dualistic backgrounds.

Aside from this sociocultural orientation, Buriel (1975) studied cognitive styles among Mexican-American children for three generations. The hypothesis for the investigation predicted that field independence was a function of residency in the United States, and that third generation Mexican-Americans would be most field independent (insensitive). Results showed that third generation Mexican-American children *were* most field independent for the samples studied. In addition to supporting previous findings of field sensitivity, Sanders et al. (1976) have observed that Anglo children scored higher on achievement and power measures while Mexican-Americans scored higher on affiliation.

Kagan and Zahn (1975) also explored conceptions of field dependence and school achievement among Mexican-Americans. Two significant findings indicated that, first, Mexican-American children who were more field dependent have greater difficulty with reading than math. Second, field independence has been shown to be significantly related to math and reading achievement. Their data also revealed that the culture gap related to math achievment was supported by field independent constructs while the culture gap related to reading was not.

In the Kagan and Zahn (1975) study, the expectation for children of stricter families, who are more field dependent, was a greater difficulty with math than reading. However, findings showed the opposite to be true; gaps were greater in reading than math. Kagan and Zahn (1975) contend that their results support the premise that field independence and school achievement are significantly related but do not wholly support the belief that Mexican-American children's school failure is explained by field dependence. Their data also did not support the contention that field independence is not related to verbal ability or to quantitative and spatial abilities.

Other research into the cognitive domains of Mexican-American children include classification skills (Walden, 1974), reproduction of direction and orientation (Kerschner, 1972), intelligence as related to neo-Piagetian measure (De Avila and Havassy, 1974), and the identification of gifted Mexican-American children (Bernal, 1974; Bernal and Reyna, 1974).

Kershner (1972) matched eight Anglo and bilingual Mexican-American children according to sex, age (8 to 12 years), SES, intelligence, and amount of stimulation provided by the home environment. Results showed that Mexican-American cognitive style could best be categorized as analytic-spatial as a product of their better spatial ability and poor language abilities. Anglo-Americans were depicted as global-verbal due to better language but poorer spatial characteristics.

Unlike the preceding, Walden (1974) investigated the classification skills of low socioeconomic status 5- to 7-year-old bilingual, biliterate, or monolingual children. Results revealed that the control group made gains in categorical-inferential and relational modes. Categorical-inferential thinking considers objects as whole entities while relational approaches show an understanding of relations for objects in a group (e.g., positional and physical relationships). In all, these lower-class children were described as able to learn in varied and superior ways. Although there were no age differences for language ability groups, there were age differences for categorical-inferential and descriptive thinking. Finally, the varied language experiences displayed by the Mexican-American children were not considered a significant factor in their increasing classifying ability.

The study using the largest sample (nearly 1,300 Mexican-American children) was conducted by De Avila and Havassy (1974) to study Piagetian-derived measures. The purpose was five-fold: 1) to explore the relationship and interrelationships of four neo-Piagetian measures with Mexican-American children who differed according to geography and socioeconomic status; 2) to examine the psychometric status of the measures; 3) to compare standardized measures with the neo-Piagetian procedures and the developmental levels assessed by both; 4) to examine field independence using a water level task; and 5) to explore performance differences according to sex.

Results indicated psychometric homogeneity, reliability, and validity for the Cartoon Conversation Scales, Water Level Task, and Figural Intersection Test (three of the four neo-Piagetian measures). De Avila and Havassy found that the performace of the Mexican-American sample was developmentally appropriate and within the normal levels of cognitive development for chronological age with no sex differences. No performance differences between the geographic regions or between children taking the neo-Piagetian tests in English, Spanish, or bilingually was encountered. The investigators question whether bilingualism really is an obstacle to cognitive development.

De Avila and Havassy demonstrated

that, according to Piagetian constructs, Mexican-American and Anglo children, who are cognitive equals, are observed to be *not* equal in school-related achievement. The assumption, therefore, is that an equal capacity for like status and commensurate rate of cognitive development will not help Mexican-American children succeed equally with the Anglo-American middle-class child. The social implications of this failure are attributed to causes apart from normal cognitive growth and development. Causes for the above include use of traditional capacity and achievement measures (e.g., Otis and Basic Skills), as well as student-teacher relations, curriculum, materials, language and situational contexts used as culturally biased in favor of certain children. De Avila and Havassy state:

Where curriculum meets the educational needs of all children and tests are not biased, there would be a congruence between the neo-Piagetian and standardizing measures. Lack of congruence between the two sets of measures, which is generally due to poor performance on standardized measures, only points to problems in environmental circumstances, including the schools and curriculum. Children are not responsible for such circumstances and should not be penalized for them.

Three hundred Mexican-American adults were surveyed for their definitions of giftedness (Bernal, 1974; Bernal and Reyna, 1974). These in turn were distilled into behavior-rating and adjectival scales for parent evaluations of their children. Along this dimension, Mexican-American parents believed that requirements for giftedness include: verve, style, intelligence, free use of imagination, being more active and aware, as well as associating with adults. For those children studied, it was found that significant differentiations existed for gifted and nongifted and that adjectival as well as behavioral ratings distinguished the Mexican-American groups.

Behavior Studies of Competition

Studies of competition, as they relate to Mexican-American children, were first conducted with Mexican and Anglo samples (Kagan and Madsen, 1972). At that time, the focal point was behavior which lowered outcomes of peers. Results showed that Anglo-Americans were significantly more rivalrous than Mexicans, with cultural differences increasing with age. Additionally, older children were more rivalrous than younger children and greater rivalry developed with age for male Anglo-Americans (over females) but not for Mexicans of either sex.

At a later time, Kagan and Carlson (1975) generalized studies of competition and assertiveness to include Mexican-American samples. For example, Kagan and Carlson compared 5-6, 7-9, and 10-12-year-old boys and girls from middle-class Anglo-American and semi-rural poor Anglo-American categories with Mexican-American and rural poor Mexican children on an adaptive-assertiveness pull scale. The middle-class Anglo-American children were more assertive (competitive) than the semi-rural populations who, in turn, were more assertive than the rural poor Mexican children. It was noted that sex differences were not observed while assertiveness increased for all groups but was lowest among the Mexican sample.

In other studies, Anglo-Americans were most competitive at all grade levels; competition increased with additional trials in a maximizing differences game and with grade level (McClintock, 1974). The investigator associated competitiveness with developmental theory of achievement motivation. Stephan and Kennedy (1975) examined interethnic competition within a triethnic school system. In addition to collecting data on strategy games, the researchers also gathered information in areas where data are typically used to characterize ethnic minorities (i.e., locus of control, authoritarianism, and self-esteem responses). Relative to interethnic comparisons, it was shown that Anglo children were more competitive but less trusting than Afro- or Mexican-Americans. Afro-Americans also scored highest on authoritarianism and externality while Mexican-Americans were lowest on self-esteem.

Another study used two-person choice cards to distinguish competitive behavior among Anglo and Mexican-American children in an absolute gains situation (Avellar and Kagan, 1976). Findings indicated that when the possibility of absolute gains did not exist, Anglo as well as older students gave peers fewer rewards than Mexican-American and younger students. The researchers could not attribute the cultural difference to economic level, and unlike previous rivalry findings, the contention was made that competitiveness was a result of concern for relative gains as opposed to rivalry.

Aboud (1976) comments on interethnic social comparisons and self-evaluations of approximately 50 Anglo and Mexican-American first through third graders. In this study, children were given an opportunity to view their own and peer scores after completion of a test. Anglo children in general decided to look at Anglo peer scores while a large percentage of Mexican-American children also looked at Anglo scores and also sought out Mexican-Americans who had scored better than themselves or Anglos who had scored worse than they. In a replication study, the same tendency was observed among Afro-American college students.

Self-concepts

Much of the literature on Mexican-American school-aged children notes low evaluations of school achievement and success, low perceptions of self-esteem, self-evaluation, self-description, and general self-worth, as reported both by teachers and students.

Redfern (1969) examined Afro-, Mexican-American, and Anglo pupils' levels of expectation, performance, and reactions to success and failure in a ring toss game. Reactions to this situation of "self-test" goals provided the following information: 1) Mexican-Americans were perceived as more capable and more realistic in their expectations; 2) Anglo subjects were described as overestimating the most and having the lowest actual scores; 3) Afro-American children were considered to have the highest expectations; 4) Mexican-American children were described as having a more realistic increase in confidence; and 5) Afro-American children experienced a decrease in anxiety.

Fisher (1974) attempted to assess self-concept and self-descriptions by examining the effect of a first-grade bilingual-bicultural program on nearly equal numbers of Mexican-American and Anglo children. Findings on the program showed that sex differences developed as both self-concept and openness to environmental stimuli (stimulus-seeking activity) changed more positively for girls than boys. With regard to self-descriptions, the investigators concluded that Mexican-Americans did not feel "picked on" anymore after participating in the program, and their initial feelings of unhappiness also dissipated.

Muller and Leonetti (1974) compared low-income Mexican-American and Anglo children's self-concepts in kindergarten through fourth grade. Differences between the groups were found in kindergarten, where Anglo students were described as having significantly higher self-concepts. This finding is somewhat incongruent with previous research (e.g., Gustafson and Owens, 1971; Garcia, 1973a, 1973b) which found that Mexican-American children usually experience greater disillusionment, and, as a consequence, a drop in self-evaluation with increasing age. For example, Miller and Gerard (1975) examined the failure of the Riverside, California, school busing program. The subject involved a 10-year investigation of the self-concept effects of busing Afro- and Mexican-American children into mainly Anglo neighborhoods. Both minority and Anglo students identified pictures of Anglo faces as the students most likely to be happy and to receive high grades. In other words, results were contrary to the goals of a program which expected that there would be a positive change in Afro- and Mexican-American children's values impinging upon achievement. Instead, low achievement motivation and weak self-concepts were said to have remained or increased as a result of the busing.

Attitudes and Behavior

In most research concerning attitudes, one is likely to encounter interest centering around children's racial comparisons or preferences. As an example, Miller (1971) studied the premise that minority group children have been generally shown to display a negative reaction to their minority group status and a preference for the dominant race image (see Cota-Robles de Suarez, 1973; Miller and Gerard, 1975). Working-class 5- to 7-year-old Afro- and Mexican-American children in Detroit and Los Angeles were given the Kenneth Clark Doll Test for racial preference. Overall, preferences strongly favored the Anglo doll at all age levels. However, at increasing age levels, preferences seemed to move toward a position of in-group support. Mexican-American girls displayed a stronger preference for their own ethnic group than Afro-American girls. Afro-American boys showed the weakest own-race preferences, with Afro-American girls next in rank. The investigators concluded that their data supported previous racial preference research for Afro-American children but not for hypotheses concerning Mexican-Americans.

Larkin (1972) also studied preadolescent attitudes as related to class, race, and sex. The study involved explanations of failure as a product of social disadvantage and attitudinal deficits. Unlike many studies correlating lack of achievement and poor self-image with low SES, results showed that social disadvantage and attitudinal deficits did not explain school failure. Among 1,750 Afro-American (20%), Mexican-American (17%), Asian-American (2%), and Anglo-American (61%) fourth through sixth graders from lower, middle and upper-classes, no significant differences existed between SES background, self-esteem, school orientation, peer group orientation, and orientation to family authority. In fact, greater sex differences existed as opposed to ethnic, racial, or social class variation. It was also found that if a family supported higher status for a male child, the self-esteem of the female child was negatively affected.

Since children spend a great deal of time in school, it would be well to discuss student aggression and the school setting. Such a discussion might shed light on children's attitudes, self-concepts, and behavior. Johnston and Krocetz (1976) studied the levels of aggression in pluralistic and traditional schools. Aggressive verbalization and behaviors for first to third grade Afro-American, Mexican-American, and Anglo-American children were tabulated by naive undergraduate experimenters. Results show that less physical and verbal aggression occurred on the pluralistic playground than on the traditional playground. The investigators comment that:

It can be concluded, then, that one particular school which attempts to meet the intellectual and psychological needs of its students through its pluralistic approach to learning has less aggression on its playground during recess than another particular school does.

Achievement

Another area receiving a great deal of attention concerns such topics as achivement, achievement-motivation, or aspirations of Mexican-American children. Some of the elements thought to affect this area include: school-related factors (e.g., mainstreaming), geographic migration, psychocultural effects, and family influences.

Anchor and Anchor (1974) examined school failure as related to parent involvement in the junior high school. Distinct relationships were found between high and low success male students and parent participation in general. For Mexican-Americans specifically, the results were more pronounced in relation to parent involvement in conferences with the teacher.

In another study, the influence of complete geographic removal and migration were explored as factors in educational achievement (Brawner, 1973). A longitudinal study conducted in Racine, Wisconsin, revealed that higher expectations of teachers and administrators, as contrasted with lower expectations in Texas (where many of these children had originally migrated from) led to higher achievement. According to the instruments used, the self-descriptive attitudes and perceptions of parents did not show them as raising high achievers.

Evans and Anderson (1973) studied psychocultural origins of achievement as related to the family. Their conclusion was that depressed achievement was associated more often with values and experiences of the culture of poverty than with ethnic values. Regardless of English competence, Mexican-Americans were found to come from homes stressing education and parents who encouraged them to do well in school. Mexican-Americans were also found to come from homes with less democratic independence training, to experience fatalism, to hold a present-time orientation, to personally have a low self-concept regarding ability and hold lower educational aspirations while at the same time having a high-striving orientation.

Ramirez and Price-Williams (1976) also take a family orientation to school

achievement among Mexican-Americans. In a study of achievement motivation, they asked 30 male and female fourth graders from Anglo-, Afro-, and Mexican-American ethnic groups to tell stories about line drawings concerned with education. The minority groups scored higher on family achievement while Anglo subjects scored higher on need achievement (or individual achievement aspirations). The researchers concluded that the context of the expression of achievement motivation is important, and forms of expressed achievement are culturally defined. These contentions are supported by the fact that Mexican-Americans and Afro-Americans scored higher than Anglo-Americans on need achievement where the line drawings depicted parental figures.

Phillips (1972) studied classroom aspiration reactions to academic and social opportunities for fourth-grade middle-class and lower-class Anglo-, Afro-, and Mexican-Americans. Results showed that Anglo children had higher school aspirations and, in turn, both stronger achievement-oriented motives and more achievement-oriented behaviors than the minority children. On the other hand, desires and hopes for school achievement among minority group children are observed to be just as strong. However, since the methods for minority group children becoming successful did not exist, school stress developed. Phillips concluded that the school stress potential is least for middle-class Anglos, and as such, the minority groups experience the most anxiety.

Political Orientation

There is also an interest in minority group children's perceptions of politics, conflict, and power. Loyola (1973) studied third to eighth graders in Newark and El Paso to determine whether differences in ethnicity portend differences in political attitudes. Among the findings were: 1)

Northeast Anglo- and Afro-Americans had a less positive political attitude than Mexican-Americans; 2) Mexican-Americans' affect and national attachment became less positive with age; and 3) Latin-Americans and Mexican-Americans ranked differently on political items.

Garcia (1973a, 1973b) notes that all his findings on political orientation were influenced by social class. Among the results for Mexican-Americans were: 1) symbolization of the political community developed more slowly; 2) positive affect for the country was at first greater than Anglo peer conceptions; 3) distrust increased with age, even though socialization support system norms occurred at an early age; and 4) disillusionment with the country and its political authorities occurs quickly with youth, and more drastically for rural and working-class Spanish-speaking Mexican-Americans.

Other Factors

Material discussed under this heading concerns data which could not be easily classified within those topics previously mentioned. Some of the information relates to intervention approaches, observations of behavior and background, as well as solicitation of children's impressions or perceptions.

For instance, Zimmerman and Pike (1972) attempted to increase and generalize question-asking behavior of 12 disadvantaged second graders. They presented two situations of praise and found that both produced more question-asking behavior. The most change came with an adult model displaying contingent praise. Overall, generalization of question-asking behavior to a new nonmodeling teacher was observed but only those pupils who both observed a model and were praised for questions produced significantly.

Delay of gratification has also been examined among nearly 200 poor fourth graders (Price-Williams and Ramirez,

1974). In this particular study, children had to trust promises of the experimenter to deliver a bigger reward, and therefore wait for this reward, or to distrust the promises and seek immediate gratification. By and large, Afro- and Mexican-American children accepted immediate gratification rather than the later reward.

The families' sociocultural backgrounds and the impact of an older brother on younger brothers and sisters have also been examined. Lei et al. (1973) examined the families' sociocultural backgrounds as they impinge upon behavioral retardation in a random sample of 2,600 children from a suburban population. Their results indicate a relationship between behavioral retardation and sociocultural elements, such as community origin, ethnicity, residential mobility, and social status. Between ethnic groups, more of the variance was explained by sociocultural factors for Mexican-Americans than for Anglos (while mothers' education defined families with and without behavioral retardation in both groups).

Longstreth et al. (1975) examined the effect of older brothers on younger siblings. Fifty percent of the schools surveyed were attended by lower-class SES Mexican-Americans, while 50% were attended by upper-middle-class SES Anglo-Americans. Results transcend race, sex, and SES levels in that physically active children (as opposed to physically passive) were more likely to have older brothers in both school populations. The results also indicate that the maximum influence for an older brother occurs for age spacings of 0-2 and 2-4 years of age, with nearly nonexistent influence beyond a 4-year age difference. Additionally, the authors comment on the fact that girls experienced self-esteem problems (conflict-inducing effect of an older brother) much more than boys (activating-stabilizing effect). Such an observation would be of high value if it is determined that, in fact, Mexican-Americans highly value male children and show preference for the oldest male.

Maurer and Baxter (1972) studied the neighborhood images of urban Anglo-, Afro-, and Mexican-American 7- to 14-year-olds. The goal of the study was to assess imagery of the neighborhood by using maps drawn by the children. Anglo and Mexican-Americans were shown to prefer structure, natural elements, and pathways while Afro-American children displayed environment, structure, and structure-related preferences. Additionally, Afro-American children in this study omitted human elements in their maps, while Mexican-Americans and Anglos did not. Afro-American children's drawings of home dominated 25% of the neighborhood, while Mexican-American children's homes occupied 5% and Anglo homes occupied 2.5%. Afro-American children drew the home first more than 95% of the time, while Mexican-Americans drew it first nearly 30% of the time, and Anglos drew it first 16% of the time. A striking feature of Anglo drawings of the neighborhoods was that over 25% drew a map without a home. On the other hand, no Mexican-American and only one Afro-American child attempted to draw a map of the city (Houston), while 84% of the Anglos did so.

Based upon the preceding examples, it is evident that images and descriptions of home, neighborhood, and city differed by ethnic group. The author agrees with Maurer and Baxter (1972) that map drawings plus interviews are a profitable means in ascertaining children's physical world impressions.

Language Influences

Linguistic comparisons between ethnically different children run the gamut from bilingualism, psycholinguistic abilities, proficiency, syntax, etc. Programs that exist can be further categorized as: bilingual-bicultural (maintenance), bilingual maintenance, bilingual-bicultural (restorationist), culturally pluralistic, and ESL/bilingual.

Investigators have also attempted to differentiate those linguistic features common to Mexican-Americans. Language abilities of Afro-American, Mexican, and Native American children were studied using the Illinois Test of Psycholinguistic Abilities (Kirk, 1972). Among Afro-American children, the conclusion was that short-term auditory sequential memory was better. Short-term visual sequential memory was better for both Native and Mexican-American children. Other investigators have studied problems affecting English learning as a consequence of Spanish language problems, noting that Mexican-American language patterns were different from English and Spanish (Evans, 1974; Golub, 1975; Ramirez, 1974). The conclusion was that loss of signals (i.e., grammatical and lexical) via perceptual underdevelopment of English phonology, greatly decreased learning ability and language use. Furthermore, there are many indicators that assessment of the children possibly would profit from and is still dependent upon real language abilities and indirect elements, such as parental influences and SES level (Evans, 1974; Golub, 1975; Ramirez, 1974).

Laosa (1975) studied language usage by children and adults among the three major Latino groups (Cuban, Mexican, and Puerto Rican) in the United States. Language patterns in varying social contexts were examined among first to third graders in nearly 300 families. It was determined that Mexican-Americans were experiencing the most mother-tongue (Spanish) displacement; significant differences in child-adult language use also existed for Cuban-Americans and Mexican-Americans. The most extensive mother-tongue language maintenance was displayed by the Puerto Rican-American sample.

A body of data is developing in the area of reading ability and performance. Ziros (1976) discussed Chicano Spanish language interference in learning to read. Among her findings related to syntactic style is the supposition that socioeconomics, and not bilingualism, may determine whether or not English is developed. This being the case, she suggests that we explore standardized test bias (cultural and social) as well as teacher-held attitudes toward nonstandard dialects and syntactic style as they relate to reading.

On the other hand, Lucas and Singer (1975) demonstrate that oral reading interference on the syntactical but not the phonological levels occurs with dialects (i.e., Spanish versus English). Their findings point to negative correlations between amount of Spanish heard at home and syntactic ability and oral reading. In conclusion, they further note that as English syntax competence is acquired, the interference process will be transitory.

In another study related to reading, McCracken (1973) explored sex typing among boys in all-male classes. First through third grade middle-class Anglo and Mexican-American children (all taught by female teachers) sorted reading-related items into sex-role groups. For those male children attending all-male classes, reading was more associated with the male role than for boys attending coeducational classrooms.

SUMMARY AND CONCLUSIONS

The Preschool Child

Published conceptions of Mexican-American preschool children provide little information in the way of the child's individual personal style. In viewing this from a social systems perspective, two factors must be kept in mind. First, the family traditionally makes a systems assignment (or ascribes status) prior to the child's entrance into school. Second, with the advent of preschool intervention programs for Mexican-Americans, changes in the assignment are occuring, or at least being influenced by agents who do not customarily intercede. The author will go one

step further in saying that, prior to the external influence mentioned in the literature, the child's system assignment and status are culturally determined.

Although cross-cultural in nature, the most specific description available for neonatal development is Lar's (1973) study of infant subvocalization and movement in Mexican and Anglo infants. We can infer that subvocalization and movement differences might also exist between Mexican-American and Anglo-American infants, based upon the cultural and genetic links between Mexicans and Mexican-Americans. Once again, this assumption must be explored through further research.

If one can generalize from this important study that rhythmic patterns for Mexican-Americans and Anglo-Americans differ, we could anticipate that cultural system assignments can also differ. The author would argue that his position is supported by the data available for preschool Mexican-American samples. For instance, Wahab (1973, 1974) describes lower-class parental expectations for children and, therefore, system assignments or role expectations. Mexican-American parents in the Wahab study expected their preschool children to have *urbanidad* or, as the author interprets the concept, people who possess *educacion*—being well-brought-up, polite, graceful, socially acceptable, courteous, respectful of elders, and deserving of respect, as well as observing the dignity and individuality of others. Many ethnic communities desire these qualities. What are the socialization approaches used to inculcate these constructs within each group? This research question remains largely unanswered.

Rusmore and Kirmeyer (1976) extend the foregoing in their descriptions of lower- and working-class Mexican-American parental behavior and preschoolers in San Jose. These parents and families expected their children to be family centered; for example, in encouraging their children to play closer to home, in worrying over their children, and in stressing dependence on the family. These results stem directly from Mexican-American samples, in contrast to much stereotypic material referenced from one journal or text to another without questioning its reliability and validity.

Social systems definitions by the dominant culture and by Mexican-Americans appear to be at variance. Intervention programs do not stress system maintenance, for example, but amelioration by introducing child care training, nutrition, or mental health programs (Johnson et al., 1974, 1976; Hahn and Dunstan, 1975; Sonquist et al. 1975). While one cannot criticize the positive aspects of such interventions, one must be aware that where intervention exists to improve behavior or achievement, part of the message conveyed to the child is "something is wrong with you." It is hoped that the other half of the message transmitted is "I want to help you." In either case, the child is in a dependent or vulnerable position by having to rely on programs which are usually Anglo dominated and oriented.

Some intervention styles attempt to change the cultural system, while others attempt to learn from it. An example of building upon an existing system is represented by the research of Steward and Steward (1973, 1974a). Here, the effort was to observe the teaching styles of ethnically different mothers and generalize this information to the classroom. What we now need is research which seeks to learn from the socialization practices of Mexican-American mothers and fathers.

What little we do know about these fathers is that they influence the child's acceptance by classmates (Orive and Gerard, 1975). In addition, we also have data about fathers' self-perceptions regarding their roles (Mejia, 1975); Mexican-American middle-class fathers do not fit the stereotypical description of Mexican or Mexican-American male roles. Such knowledge assists in the determination of adult role behavior or expectations of self.

The father role as perceived by the Mexican-American middle-class can come into conflict with societal expectations of *macho* or submissive behavior from Mexican-American boys or girls by Anglo teachers and institutions.

Early nonverbal and verbal sequences, coupled with such factors as biological or linguistic rhythms, set a trend which will be carried into school and adult life. While the rudimentary interpersonal style of the child is set, it is adjusted when wider aspects of the community and society are encountered. We do not know anything about these early contributions to retained strategies displayed and practiced as a school-aged child, adolescent and adult for Mexican-Americans.

The School-aged Child

The Mexican-American child enters school with conceptions of an assigned status from the family (e.g., be respectful of authority, be courteous, do not shame your family, support your siblings, you do not need to be competitive). In entering a new network, additional system assignments are made (some would call these system reassignments). Unfortunately, what is observed between family and school, parent and teacher, and teacher and child interactions are processes which are largely products of conflict. This being the case, the child attempts to make intersystem adjustments in order to survive both in the school and in the home.

The system orientation held by the child's teachers mediates the teachers' evaluation and behavior toward students. This orientation also ascribes status for the Mexican-American based upon historical definitions by the dominant society, institutional definitions derived from "scientific" instruments, and personal definitions derived from any number of sources. Teachers, parents, playground directors, police officers, and garbage collectors teach Mexican-American children other social system orientations based upon conscious and unconscious roles. These other system orientations add to those observed and learned in the home.

How does the child define a personal status assignment in the school? Jackson and Cosca (1974) noted that teachers praised or encouraged Anglo children 35% more than Mexican-Americans; teachers used Anglo children's ideas 40% more than those of Mexican-Americans; teachers directed questions to Anglo children 21% more often than to Mexican-Americans. In addition, teachers' behavioral ratings were higher for English as opposed to Spanish speakers (Stedman and Adams, 1973). Children in highly concentrated minority schools were likely to get lower evaluations on confidence and eagerness as well as ethnic nonstandardness (Williams and Naremore, 1974). The message conveyed to Mexican-American children about their status in the system should be clear.

The classroom teacher is the next most important socializer of the Mexican-American child after his or her parent. The data presented in this chapter for teacher-child relationships cogently indicate that Mexican-American children are aware of their ascribed status and system assignment. This is explicity evident from Gustafson and Owens' (1971) contrasts between teachers' perceptions and children's conceptions of "How I See Myself" and "How Teacher Sees Me" and the Teachers' Checklist for third and sixth graders. Is it possible that their school phobia and dropout rates represent a process of conflict, survival, and intersystem accommodation by Mexican-American school-aged children?

To briefly recapitulate, the Mexican-American child enters school with a particular system assignment and therefore a particular social identity. The teacher, in turn, possesses a conception of a system assignment for the child which incorporates personal, institutional and societal descriptions. Encountering the latter, the Mexican-American child accepts, rejects, or adjusts to the new social identity and moves on to grapple with teacher, institutional, and parental expectations. Reviews of the literature show that the preceding are not in harmony with each other.

What ensues for the Mexican-American child is negotiation, subordination, or modification of one system for another. The product is psychocultural adjustment or change based upon psychosocial influences. The consequences generally conflict with home, school, or both. The degree of negotiation in this process, however, depends upon the individual style of the child. The author, for example, in the process of accommodating or negotiating, completed the Ph.D. degree in psychology. As a consequence, he has the distinction of being one of perhaps three dozen Mexican-Americans with doctorates in psychology—a sad comment on professional opportunities for a Mexican-American population of over 12,000,000 people. In contrast, many of the author's elementary and high school classmates negotiated their status positions, social identities, and system assignments by dropping out of school, going to jail, joining the military, or dying from drug overdoses.

Psychocultural change need not occur as abrasively as it has in the past. The extreme roles adopted by some of the author's elementary school classmates were not expectations of the family or community. But, unfortunately, the process continues. Phillips (1972) compared classroom aspirational reactions of lower-class Afro- and Mexican-Americans with middle-class Anglo-Americans. The findings indicate that non-white children possess desires and hopes as strong as those of Anglo children for achievement but do not possess the methods for making these a reality. Why is this so?

Non-school approaches have been developing sporadically to improve Mexican-American social identities. That is, other social systems cycles have independently developed to augment or mediate (when necessary) good or bad school and community experiences. Holscher (1976), for example, discusses the function of murals in East Los Angeles and Boyle Heights from the perspective of the artists (Mexican-Americans). Three possible functions are summarized: 1) a protest form and method of educating the community about real problems of society and *barrio*; 2) through cultural and historical themes, the expression, formation, and search for identity; and 3) a cathartic outpouring. Murals for many Mexican-Americans have taken on specific symbols which can be categorized, similar to institutional expressions for weddings, births, birthdays, and funerals. Murals in the Mexican-American community have become revelations of open wounds as well as of a sense of pride and protest. They also offer a glimpse of the murals we carry inside us as a people.

Another form of social identity enhancement is illustrated by Casa de la Raza (Southwest Network, 1974). Casa de la Raza is a K-12 grade school based within the Berkeley Unified School District's Experimental Schools Program. Its reason for existence revolves around cultural, educational, and philosophic themes. Its objectives are personal growth and academic success according to home, culture, language, and values of La Raza.

Aside from the above approaches which exist external to the child's home environment, many Mexican-Americans are actively engaged in or developing programs within their families. For instance, in the author's research with Mexican-American middle-class fathers, one Mexican-American father started a family school within his extended family. In addition, his family has also instituted a "family bank." He states:

I had a study group with their kids. I was teaching a class to my younger cousins. The only way I could have done it was with my uncles and aunts. We have a real strong extended family and we do a lot of things.

Q. Where did the idea for a study group come from?

A. From me. I mentioned it to my aunts and my uncles and they said, "Yeah." The kids were open to it, too. So, I had a school going with them. I was using *Broken Spears* and George Orwell's *1984*, about society projection, about how to act. I think what makes me strong is my extended family. We're open. I may have ideas, they may have ideas and we interact with them. Some of my aunts, and in some ways the kids, have been models for how I should be with my little girl. We've had a food co-op going with them, and we have a family bank going right now because of hard times. I think I have a different family; what we've done has made us strong.

Other families are quietly organizing family banks for emergency economic needs or other types of family programs—educational, recreational, social. In many instances, these types of efforts represent more cultural reinforcement than assimilationist or "melting-pot" tendencies. It would be worthwhile to explore the prevalence of these practices.

Growth Through Psychosocial Harmony

For a long time, a maintenance process in the *barrio* and home has been in existence. If we agree with the definition of a closed system as one which does not exchange information, material, or energy with the wider community (Murrell, 1973), then historically the *barrio* has represented a closed system. And the *barrio* child has become a closed system within the wider community and school.

When a Mexican-American child attends school, the system in the home opens somewhat to accommodate the change. However, we have seen that much of the information transmitted by the child to the home only reinforces the concept of remaining and retaining a closed system. Through a growing movement, whether expressed by murals or school programs, indigenous representatives are attempting to infuse maintenance and restorationist perspectives into the community. In this sense, middle-class Mexican-Americans represent a more open system in the larger community than the vast majority of Mexicans and of Mexican-Americans who are lower-class.

Some middle-class Mexican-Americans may be described as acculturated or assimilated while others may be depicted as aware of society's role expectations of them and as desirous of changing that assigned status. The problems encountered in compensation efforts include the following in the educational sphere:

The assumptions underlying the compensatory education model are that there is a norm in values and aspirations in U.S. society which is just and which most people do and should agree upon; that persons failing to meet the norms are deficient; that the range of experiences which the student brings from his own culture is inferior; and that the educational programs in U.S. public schools are useful in helping the Asian, Black, Spanish-speaking and Indian minority students to compete successfully in contemporary society. Their different cultures and needs are not taken into account (Davis, 1972).

The literature indicates that Mexican-Americans are told the dominant group knows how to train parents, children, teachers, and others through the existence of a plethora of intervention programs and a dearth of programs reinforcing or enhancing minority group perspectives. This ameliorative philosophy and process are pervasive, with role expectations and assigned status of children based upon assumptions inherent in the philosophy. Status passage for the child therefore remains in control of the groups described by Tulkin (1972):

A majority culture can . . . promote a narrow definition of success in order to insure that the power of the society remains in the hands of a relatively select group within the society. Thus, maintaining that any deviation from the white middle class norm represents cultural deprivation, the white middle class is guarding its position as the source of culture and power in this nation. Cultural deprivation, then, is not just a psychological or educational issue: it is also very much a political issue (p. 331).

In the same vein, Murrell (1973) describes morphostatic and morphogenetic states. The morphostatic position desires the maintenance of a steady state while the morphogenetic approach strives for growth. A third element, termed the metagovernor construct, often creates a struggle between those taking a morphostatic position and those taking a morphogenetic stance.

According to the metagovernor concept, various factions within a family, community, or society wish to maintain control. In a deviant family, for example, as soon as the deviant individual attempts to gain some control of his or her own, the system tightens. Mexican-Americans may be viewed as members of the greater American family. The more the person (ethnic group) struggles, the more tightening by the family (dominant society) and the stronger the adoption of a morphostatic stance. The aim of the deviant group (deviancy need not exist in fact, but may be a product of labeling, such as by culturally biased I.Q. tests) is, of course, to inculcate a morphogenetic approach. The metagovernor struggle is one of the reasons a *barrio* or culture remains a closed system. The same struggle is also observable in the classroom, where teachers educate Mexican-American students to defer to Anglo students' status as well as to Anglo society at large. In this process, gatekeepers are designated to ensure the position of the dominant group. Represented by key individuals in the culture, these gatekeepers generally maintain the status quo.

Events such as the Bakke decision, the illegal alien struggle, and the University of California's decision to use SAT scores for admission exemplify metagovernor situations. The SAT decision was made in order to raise standards. The repercussions are enormous: Out of a possible score of 800 points on each section of the SAT, it has been shown that students scoring less than 350 come from families with average annual earnings of $14,500. Students scoring 650 points on the average came from families earning $26,400 or more per year. Even more cogent, college-bound students from families earning less than $6,000 per year score more than 90 points below those from families with incomes of $30,000 (Haber and Smith, 1977). The use of SAT scores thus appears to maintain an elitist academic population. Such a phenomenon, however unintentional, serves to reinforce previous remarks by Davis (1972) and Tulkin (1972).

In a study by Ovando (1977), ethnicity negatively influenced Mexican-American students' college aspirations in high schools where there was a high density Anglo population. Shannon and McKim (1974) and Shannon (1975) have illustrated the relative immobility of Afro- and Mexican-American peoples in Racine, Wisconsin. In the later study (Shannon, 1975), it was concluded that race and ethnicity were the greatest definers of position in the community with regard to occupation, income, standard of living, and housing.

Does the dominant society's fear of adopting a morphogenetic position toward minorities stem from a fear that minorities will treat them as they have treated minorities?

For all ethnic groups, the task remains to struggle for growth but to understand the morphostatic reactions of the dominant group to such growth. In this attempt, the goal is psychosocial harmony. We have observed how social systems influence psychocultural change and behavior as products of psychosocial transition. We now join Murrell (1973) in delineating avenues for reorienting previous approaches:

1) Change the person.
2) Relocate the person.
3) Train the person to fit the system.
4) Modify the system to fit the person.
5) Create new systems.

REFERENCES

Aboud, F.E. Self-evaluation: Information seeking strategies for interethnic social comparisons. *Journal of Cross-Cultural Psychology*, 1976, 7, 289–300.

Adkins, D.C., Payne, F.D., and Ballif, B.L. Motivation factor scores and response set scores for ten ethnic-cultural groups of preschool children. *American Educational Research Journal*, 1972, 9, 557–572.

Alvarez, R. (Ed.) *Delivery of Services for Latino Community Mental Health*. Monograph Number Two, Spanish Speaking Mental Health Research and Development Program, University of California, Los Angeles, 1975.

Anchor, K.N. and Anchor, F.N. School failure and parental school involvement in an ethnically mixed school: A survey. *Journal of Community Psychology*, 1974, 2, 265–267.

Askins, B.E., et al. Responsive Environment Program for Spanish American Children (REPSAC): Fourth Year Evaluation Study. Final Evaluation Report, 1974–75. Prepared for the Bureau of Education for the Handicapped (DHEW/OE), Washington, D.C., *ERIC*, 1975, ED111562.

Askins, B.E. et al., Responsive Environment Early Education Program (REEEP): First Year Evaluation Study. Year-End Evaluation Report, 1975–76. Prepared for the Office of Education (DHEW), Washington, D.C., *ERIC*, 1976, ED127058.

Avellar, J. and Kagan, S. Development of competitive behaviors in Anglo-American and Mexican-American children. *Psychological Reports*, 1976, 39, 191–198.

Baca, M.L.M. What's going on in the Bilingual Special Education classroom? *Teaching Exceptional Children*, 1974, 7, 25.

Benson, G.P. and Kuipers, J.L. Personality correlates of intellectual performance among Head Start children. *ERIC*, 1974, ED097121.

Bernal, E.M. Gifted Mexican American children: An ethno-scientific perspective. *California Journal of Educational Research*, 1974, 25, 261–273.

Bernal, H.H. and Bernal, E.M. Teaching religion to minority groups: Content, method and cultural compatibility. *Notre Dame Journal of Education*, 1974, 5, 232–236.

Bernal, E.M. and Reyna, J. Analysis of giftedness in Mexican American children and design of a prototype identification instrument. Southwest Educational Development Laboratory, Austin, Texas, 1974.

Bikson, T.K. Minority speech as objectively measured and subjectively evaluated. *ERIC*, 1974, ED131135.

Brawner, M.R. Migration and educational achievement of Mexican Americans. *Social Science Quarterly*, 1973, *53*, 727–737.

Buriel, R. Cognitive styles among three generations of Mexican American children. *Journal of Cross-Cultural Psychology*, 1975, *6*, 417–429.

California State University Fresno, School of Education. Rural Teacher Intern Program. *ERIC*, 1973, ED085381.

Castillo, M.S. and Cruz, J., Jr. Special competencies for teachers of preschool Chicano children: Rationale, content, and assessment. *Young Children*, 1974, *29*, 341–347.

Coopersmith, S. *The Antecedents of Self-Esteem*. San Francisco: Freeman, 1967.

Cota-Robles de Suarez, C. Sexual stereotypes — Psychological and cultural survival. *Regeneracion*, 1973, *2*, 17–21.

Davis, R.H. The failures of compensatory education. *Education and Urban Society*, 1972, *4*, 234–248.

De Avila, E.A. and Havassy, B. Intelligence of Mexican American children: A field study comparing neo-Piagetian and traditional capacity and achievement measures. Prepared for Dissemination Center for Bilingual Bicultural Education, Austin, Texas, and the Office of Education (DHEW), Washington, D.C., *ERIC*, 1974, ED106042.

Dixon, C.N. Teaching strategies for the Mexican American child. *Reading Teacher*, 1976, *30*, 141–145.

Durrett, M.E. and Kim, C.C. A comparative study of behavioral maturity in Mexican-American and Anglo preschool children. *Journal of Genetic Psychology*, 1973, *123*, 55–62.

Durrett, M.E. and Pirofski, F. A pilot study of the effects of heterogeneous and homogeneous grouping on Mexican-American and Anglo children attending prekindergarten programs. Paper presented at the American Research Association Annual Meeting, New York, *ERIC*, February 1971, ED047862.

Durrett, M.E. and Pirofski, F. Effects of heterogeneous and homogeneous grouping on Mexican-American and Anglo children. *Young Children*, 1976, *31*, 309–314.

Edwards, S.R. Teacher expectation and influence. *Delta*, 1970, 7, 18–22.

Evans, F.B. and Anderson, J.G. The psychocultural origins of achievement and achievement motivation: The Mexican-American family. *Sociology of Education*, 1973, *46*, 396–416.

Evans, J.S. Word-pair discrimination and imitation abilities of preschool Spanish-speaking children. *Journal of Learning Disabilities*, 1974, 7, 573–580.

Felice, C.G. and Richardson, R.L. Mexican-American achievement performance: The effects of school and family expectations on the bilingual child. *Sociological Abstracts*, 1975, *6*, 63–76.

Fisher, R.I. A study of non-intellectual attributes of children in first grade bilingual-bicultural program. *Journal of Educational Research*, 1974, *67*, 232–328.

Garcia, F.C. *Political Socialization of Chicano Children. A Comparative Study with Anglos in California Schools*. New York: Praeger, *ERIC*, 1973a, ED097153.

Garcia, F.C. Orientations of Mexican-American and Anglo children toward the U.S. political community. *Social Science Quarterly*, 1973b, *53*, 914–929.

Golub, L.S. English syntax of Black, White, Indian and Spanish-American children. *Elementary School Journal*, 1975, *75*, 323–334.

Gonzalez, G. The identification of competencies for child development associates working with Chicano children. Final Report. Prepared for the Office of Child Development (DHEW), Washington, D.C., *ERIC*, 1974, ED118231.

Gonzalez, G. The identification of competencies desirable in teachers working with pre-school Chicano children. *Journal of Instructional Psychology*, 1975, *2*, 15–18.

Gonzalez, J.M. Coming of age in bilingual bicultural education: A historical perspective. *Inequality of Education*, 1975, *19*, 5–17.

Grant, J. Proceedings of a workshop on the preparation of personnel in education of bilingual hearing-impaired children ages 0–4. Prepared for the Bureau of Education for the Handicapped (DHEW/OE), Washington, D.C., *ERIC*, 1972, ED113908.

Gustafson, R.A. and Owens, T. Children's perceptions of themselves and their teachers' feelings towards them related to actual teacher perceptions and school achievement. Paper presented to the 51st Annual Meeting of the Western Psychological Association, San Francisco, California, *ERIC*, April 1971, ED053848.

Haber, J. and Smith, P. Grading UC's admission proposals-The student lobby argues for an alternative approach. *Los Angeles Times*, August 14, 1977, XCVI, Part IV, 15.

Hahn, J. and Dunstan, V. The child's whole world: A bilingual preschool that includes parent training in the home. *Young Children*, 1975,*30*, 281–288.

Henderson, R.W. and Garcia, A.B. The effects of parent training program on the question-asking behavior of Mexican-American children. *American Educational Research Journal*, 1973, *10*, 193–201.

Hernandez, N.G. Variables affecting achievement for middle-school Mexican-American students. Prepared for the Office of Education (DHEW), Washington, D.C., *ERIC*. 1971, ED05987.

Hickey, T. Bilingualism and the measurement of intelligence and verbal learning ability. *Exceptional Children*, 1972, *39*, 24–28.

Hickey, T. Problems of measurement with the bilingual preschool child. *School Psychology Digest*, 1973, *2*, 36–40.

Holscher, L.M. Artists and murals in East Los Angeles and Boyle Heights: A sociological observation. *Humbolt Journal of Social Relations*, 1976, *3*, 25–29.

Jackson, G. and Cosca, C. The inequality of educational opportunity in the Southwest: An observational study of ethnically mixed classrooms. *American Educational Research Journal*, 1974, *11*, 219–229.

Jackson, S.R. and Kuvesky, W.P. Families under stress: An interethnic comparison of disability among selected metropolitan and nonmetropolitan families. Prepared for the Cooperative State

Research Service (DOA), Washington, D.C., *ERIC*, 1973, ED086383.

Jelinek, J.A. A pilot program for training and utilization of paraprofessionals in preschools. *Language, Speech, and Hearing Services in Schools*, 1976, 7, 119–123.

Jensen, M. and Rosenfeld, L.B. Influence of node presentation ethnicity and social class on teachers' evaluations of students. *Journal of Educational Psychology*, 1974, *66*, 540–547.

Johnson, D.L., et al. The Houston Parent-Child Development Center: A parent education program for Mexican-American families. *American Journal of Orthopsychiatry*, 1974, *44*, 121–128.

Johnson, D.L., et al. Measuring the learning environment of Mexican-American families in a parent education program. Prepared for the Office of Child Development (DHEW), Washington, D.C., *ERIC*, 1976, ED127355.

Johnston, K.D. and Krocetz, M.L. Levels of aggression in a traditional and a pluralistic school. *Educational Research*, 1976, *18*, 146–151.

Kagan, S. and Carlson, H. Development of adaptive assertiveness in Mexican and United States children. *Developmental Psychology*, 1975, *11*, 71–78.

Kagan, S. and Madsen, M.C. Rivalry in Anglo-American and Mexican children of two ages. *Journal of Personality and Social Psychology*, 1972, *24*, 214–220.

Kagan, S. and Zahn, G.L. Field dependence and the school achievement gap between Anglo-American and Mexican-American children. *Journal of Educational Psychology*, 1975, *67*, 643–650.

Kershner, J.R. Ethnic group differences in children's ability to reproduce direction and orientation. *Journal of Social Psychology*, 1972, *88*, 3–13.

Kirk, S.A. Ethnic differences in psycholinguistic abilities. *Exceptional Children*, 1972, *39*, 112–118.

Kuzma, K.J. and Stern, C. The effects of three preschool intervention programs on the development of autonomy in Mexican-American and Negro children. *Journal of Special Education*, 1972, *6*, 197–205.

Laosa, L.M. Bilingualism in three limited state Hispanic groups: Contextual use of language by children and adults in their families. *Journal of Educational Psychology*, 1975, *67*, 617–627.

Lar, R. A cross-cultural study of infant movement and preverbalization behavior. Unpublished dissertation, University of California at Irvine, 1973.

Larkin, R.W. Class, race, sex, and preadolescent attitudes. *California Journal of Educational Research*, 1972, *23*, 213–223.

Lecompte, M.D. Who fits the procrustean bed? Spanish-American and Anglo children versus the public schools. Paper presented at the Comparative and International Education Society Meetings, San Antonio, Texas, March 1973, 25–27, *ERIC*, ED104596.

Lei, T.J., Buttles, E.W. and Sabagh, G. Family sociocultural background and the behavioral retardation of children. *Journal of Health and Social Behavior*, 1973, *13*, 318–326.

Longstreth, L.E., et al. The ubiquity of Big Brother. *Child Development*, 1975, *46*, 769–772.

Loyola, J.G. Political socialization, a comparative study of different ethnic school children in Newark, New Jersey, and El Paso, Texas. Unpublished Master's Thesis, University of Texas at El Paso, *ERIC*, 1973, ED115419.

Lucas, M.S. and Singer, H. Dialect in relation to oral reading achievement: Recording, encoding, or merely a code. *Journal of Reading Behavior*, 1975, 7, 137–148.

Maurer, R. and Baxter, J.C. Images of the neighborhood and city among Black-, Anglo-, and Mexican-American children. *Environment and Behavior*, 1972, *4*, 351–388.

McClintock, C.G. Mexican-American children. *Journal of Personality and Social Psychology*, 1974, *29*, 248–354.

McCracken, J.H. Sex typing of reading by boys attending all male classes. *Developmental Psychology*, 1973, *8*, 148.

McKinney, J.A. The development and implementation of a tutorial program for parents to improve the reading and mathematics achievement of their children. Unpublished dissertation. Nova University, *ERIC*, 1975, ED113703.

Mejia, D.P. The Spanish speaking child in the United States: Culture, class and ethnic differences. Paper presented to the XIV Interamerican Congress of Psychology, Sao Paulo, Brazil, April 14–19, 1973.

Mejia, D.P. Cross-ethnic father roles: Perceptions of middle class Anglo American and Mexican American parents. Unpublished dissertation, The University of California at Irvine, 1975.

Miller, J., Jr. A comparison of racial preference in young Black and Mexican American children: A preliminary view. *Sociological Symposium*, 1971, 7, 37–48.

Miller, N. and Gerard, H.B. How busing failed in Riverside. *Psychology Today*, 1975, *10*, 66–67; 69–70.

Moerk, E.L. Like father, like son: Imprisonment of fathers and the psychological adjustment of sons. *Journal of Youth and Adolescence*, 1973, *2*, 303–312.

Mosley, W.J. and Spieken, H.H. Mainstreaming for the educationally deprived. *Theory into Practice*, 1975, *14*, 73–81.

Muller, D. and Leonetti, R. Self-concepts of primary level Chicano and Anglo students. *California Journal of Educational Research*, 1974, *25*, 57–60.

Murrell, S.A. *Community Psychology and Social Systems-A Conceptual Framework and Intervention Guide*. New York: Behavioral Publications, 1973.

Orive, R. and Gerard, H.B. Social contact of minority parents and their children's acceptance by classmates. *Sociometry*, 1975, *38*, 518–524.

Ovando, C.J. Factors influencing high school Latino students' aspiration to go to college: The urban Midwest. San Francisco: R and E Research Associates, *ERIC*, 1977, ED131990.

Padilla, A.M., Olmedo, E., Lopez, S. and Perez, R. *Hispanic Mental Health Bibliography II*. Monograph Number Six, University of California, Los Angeles: Spanish Speaking Mental Health Research Center, 1978.

Padilla, A.M. and Romero, A. Verbal facilitation of class-inclusion reasoning: Children tested in their dominant or subordinate language. *Perceptual and Motor Skills*, 1976, *42*, 727–733.

Padilla, A.M. and Ruiz, R.A. *Latino Mental Health: A Review of the Literature*. Dept. of Health, Education and Welfare, Washington, D.C. Publication No. (HSM) 73–9143, 1973.

Padilla, A.M., et al. Preschool bilingual bicultural education for Spanish-speaking/surnamed children: A research review and strategy paper. Prepared for the Office of Child Development (DHEW), Washington, D.C., *ERIC*, 1975, ED122927.

Parrlman, R.L. and Pierce-Jones, J. Cooperative, trusting behavior in a "culturally deprived" mixed ethnic-group population. *Journal of Social Psychology*, 1974, *92*, 133–141.

Patella, V.M. A study of the validity of language use as an indicator of ethnic identification. Unpublished Master's Thesis, Texas A & M University, *ERIC*, 1971, ED051943.

Patella, V.M. How Mexican is a Spanish-speaking Mexican-American? Prepared for the Department of Agriculture, Washington, D.C., *ERIC*, 1971, ED053852.

Phillips, B.N. School-related aspirations of children with different socio-cultural backgrounds. *Journal of Negro Education*, 1972, *41*, 48–52.

Plant, W.T. and Southern M.L. The intellectual and achievement effects of preschool cognitive stimulation of poverty Mexican-American children. *Genetic Psychology Monographs*, 1972, *86*, 141–173.

President's Commission on Mental Health. Vol. III Appendix. Report of the Special Population Subpanel on Mental Health of Hispanic Americans. U.S. Gov. Pntg. Off.: Wash., D.C., 1979, Stock No. 040–000–00392–4.

Price-Williams, D.R. and Ramirez, M. Ethnic differences in delay of gratification. *Journal of Social Psychology*, 1974, 93, 23–30.

Ramirez, A.G. *The Spoken English of Spanish-speaking Pupils in a Bilingual and Monolingual School Setting: An Analysis of Syntactic Development*. Stanford, CA: Stanford Center for Research and Development in Teaching, Stanford University, 1974.

Ramirez, M. Current educational research: The basis for a new philosophy for educating Mexican-Americans. Austin: Teacher Corps Assistance Project, Center for Communication Research, University of Texas, School of Communication, 1972.

Ramirez, M., Castaneda, A. and Herold, P.L. The relationship of acculturation to cognitive style among Mexican-Americans. *Journal of Cross-Cultural Psychology*, 1974a, *5*, 424–433.

Ramirez, M. III, et al. Mexican-American values and culturally democratic educational environments. New approaches to bilingual bicultural educational environments. New approaches to bilingual bicultural education, No. 2. Prepared for the Office of Education (DHEW), Washington, D.C., *ERIC*, 1974b, ED108496.

Ramirez, M. and Price-Williams, D.R. Cognitive styles of children of three ethnic groups in the United States. *Journal of Cross-Cultural Psychology*, 1974, *5*, 212–219.

Ramirez, M. and Price-Williams, D.R. Achievement motivation in children of three ethnic groups in the United States. *Journal of Cross-Cultural Psychology*, 1976, 7, 49–60.

Redfern, D. Level of expectation, actual performance, and reactions to success and failure in three ethnic groups. Prepared for the California State Department of Education, Sacramento, California, *ERIC*, 1969, ED043704.

Rice, A., Ruiz, R.A. and Padilla, A.M. Person perception, self-identity, and ethnic group preference in Anglo, Black, and Chicano preschool and third-grade children. *Journal of Cross-Cultural Psychology*, 1974, *5*, 100–108.

Rosenfeld, L.B. An investigation of teachers' stereotyping behavior: The influence of presentation, ethnicity, and social class on teachers' evaluations of students. Prepared for the National Institute of Education (DHEW), Washington, D.C., *ERIC*, 1973, ED090172.

Rusmore, J.T. and Kirmeyer, S.L. Family attitudes among Mexican-American and Anglo-American children. *Journal of Cross-Cultural Psychology*, 1976, 7, 450–462.

Sanders, M., et al. Three social motives on field independence-dependence in Anglo-American and Mexican-American children. *Journal of Cross-Cultural Psychology*, 1976, 7, 450–462.

Shannon, L.W. False assumptions about the determination of Mexican-American and Negro economic absorption. *Sociological Quarterly*, 1975, *18*, 3–15.

Shannon, L.W. and McKim, J.L. Attitudes toward education and the absorption of immigrant Mexican-American and Negroes in Racine. *Education and Urban Society*, 1974, *6*, 33–35.

Sonquist, H., et al. A model for low-income and Chicano parent education. Final Report. Prepared for The Children's Bureau (DHEW), Washington, D.C., *ERIC*, 1976, ED113063.

Southwest Network. Casa de la Raza: Separatism or segregation—Chicanos in public education. Southwest Network, Hayward, California, *ERIC*, 1974, ED100581.

Speiss, J.M. and Speiss, M.L. Reinforced readiness requisites: A culturally relevant behavior modification program for Mexican-American, Indian, and Black children. *Proceedings of the 81st Annual Convention of the American Psychological Association, Montreal, Canada*, 1973, *8*, 641–642.

Staton, R.D. A comparison of Mexican and Mexican-American Families. *Family Coordinator*, 1972, *21*, 235–330.

Stedman, J.A. and Adams, R.L. Achievement as a function of language competence, behavior adjustment, and sex in young, disadvantaged Mexican-American children. *Journal of Educational Psychology*, 1972, *63*, 411–417.

Stedman, J.A. and Adams, R.L. Teacher perception of behavioral adjustment as a function of linguistic ability in Mexican-American Head-Start children. *Psychology in the Schools*, 1973, *10*, 221–225.

Steiner, V.G. and Zimmerman, I.L. Assessing bilingual language ability in the Mexican-American preschool child. Paper presented at the Annual Convention of the Western Psychological Association, Portland, Oregon, April 26–29, *ERIC*, 1972, ED073831.

Stephan, W.G. and Kennedy, J.C. An experimental study of interethnic competition in segregated schools. *Journal of School Psychology*, 1975, *13*, 234–247.

Steward, D. and Steward, M. Early learning in the family: A report of rsearch in progress. *Character Potential*, 1974a, *6*, 171–176.

Steward, M. and Steward, D. The observation of Anglo-, Mexican-, and Chinese-American mothers teaching their young sons. *Child Development*, 1973, *44*, 239–337.

Steward, M.S. and Steward, D.S. Effect of social distance in teaching strategies of Anglo-American and Mexican-American mothers. *Developmental Psychology*, 1974b, *10*, 797–807.

Stewart, I.S. Cultural differences between Anglos and Chicanos. *Integrated Education*, 1975, *13*, 21–23.

Stewart, I.S. and Stone, N.K. The identification of Texas anglo, Black and Chicano child rearing practices in relation to child care career competencies. *ERIC*, 1976, ED131331.

Strom, R. and Johnson, A. The parent as teacher. *Education*, 1974, *95*, 40–43.

Thornburg, H.D. An investigation of a dropout program among Arizona's minority youth. *Education*, 1974, *94*, 249.

Torrance, E.P. Readiness of teachers of gifted to learn from culturally different gifted children. *Gifted Child Quarterly*, 1974, *18*, 137–142.

Tuddenham, R.D., Brooks, J. and Milkovich, L. Mothers' reports of behavior of ten-year-olds: Relationships with sex, ethnicity, and mothers' education. *Developmental Psychology*, 1974, *10*, 959–995.

Tulkin, S.R. An analysis of the concept of cultural deprivation. *Developmental Psychology*, 1972, *6*, 326–339.

Veaco, L. The effect of paraprofessional assistance on the academic achievement of migrant children. *ERIC*, 1973, ED086380.

Wagner, B., et al. Parent and child—What's the score? Parental preparation of learning environments for delayed and non-delayed infants. *ERIC*, 1975, ED114211.

Wahab, Z. Barrio school: White school in a brown community. Paper presented at the Annual Convention of the American Anthropological Association, New Orleans, Louisiana, November 28–December 2, 1973, *ERIC*, 1975, ED114211.

Wahab, Z. Teacher-pupil transaction in bi-racial classrooms: Implications for instruction. Paper presented at the Annual Convention of the Pacific Sociological Association, San Jose, California, March, 1974 *ERIC*, ED092294.

Walden, T.A. The classification skills of five, six and seven-year-old children who are bilingual, biliterate, or monolingual, *ERIC*, 1974, ED100529.

Wetzel, R.J. Behavior modification techniques and the training of teacher's aides. Prepared for the Office of Education (DHEW), Washington, D.C. Bureau of Research, *ERIC*, 1969, ED040150.

Williams, F. and Naremore, R.C. Language attitudes: An analysis of teachers' differences. *Speech Monographs*, 1974, *41*, 391–396.

Witkin, H.A. A cognitive style approach to cross-cultural research. *International Journal of Psychology*, 1962, *2*, 233–250.

Zimmerman, B.J. and Pike, E.O. Effects of modeling and reinforcement on the acquisition and generalization of question-asking behavior. *Child Development*, 1972, *43*, 892–907.

Ziros, G.I. Language interference and teaching the Chicano to read. *Journal of Reading*, 1976, *19*, 284–288.

CHAPTER 6

The Growth and Development of American Indian and Alaskan Native Children

Evelyn Lance Blanchard, M.S.W.

When the shadows were gone, and the cliff rock began to get warm, the frogs came out from their sleeping places in small cracks and niches in the cliff above the pool. They were the color of the moss near the spring, and their backs were spotted the color of wet sand. They moved slowly into the sun, blinking their big eyes. He watched them dive into the pool, one by one, with a graceful quiet sound. They swam across the pool to the sunny edge and sat there looking at him, snapping at the tiny insects that swarmed in the shade and grass around the pool.

He smiled.

They were the rain's children.

He had seen it happen many times after a rainstorm. In dried up ponds and in the dry arroyo sands, even as the rain was still falling, they came popping up through the ground, with wet sand still on their backs. Josiah said they could stay buried in the dry sand for many years, waiting for the rain to come again (Silko, 1977).

Partly in good faith, the underlying altruistic influence of the helping professions has stereotyped American Indian and Alaskan Native behaviors. At the same time, the influence of the Euro-Western tradition and its impact on the lives of the indigenous people of North America cannot be discounted or overlooked. Nevertheless, it seems important to approach these behaviors with some knowledge and awareness of the cementing agents that bind the expressions of life as they are understood and accepted by American Indians and Alaskan Natives living today.

In the words of D'Arcy McNickle (1973), foremost Indian historian:

> Thus, the generalized picture today is of a people that has survived in numbers, in social organization, in custom and outlook, in retention of physical resources, and in its position before the law. The situation might be described as a survival of fragments, of incomplete entities—but there we would miss the mark. Any people at any time is a survival of fragments out of the past. The function of culture is always to reconstitute the fragments into an operational system. The Indians, for all that has been lost or rendered useless out of their ancient experience, remain a continuing ethnic and cultural enclave with a stake in the future.

DEVELOPMENT OF THE INDIVIDUAL IN A LARGER SOCIETY

Although there is great diversity among tribes, a philosophical thread, expressed through culture, is woven through the fabric of tribal life today.

Indian people have ancient beginnings, which are recorded in origin stories. Most of these have been maintained in the oral tradition, but all tribes have used other means, such as family histories recorded on totems, skins, bark, and stones.

In these stories, usually only a few people, animals, and other living things participate. As these beings move through space and time, they gain an understanding of how their world would be and the character of life they would assume. These travels and experiences provide an unfolding of life, allowing for continued clarification of their status in the inhabited world.

This process might be compared with Western evolutionary theory first conceptualized by Darwin. There is, however, an important difference. In Indian thought, there does not appear to be a hierarchical

order of being. Even insects share life on a par with humans. Each has its place and responsibility in the natural order of life.

When the final beings emerged onto the land that would be their country, specific lessons about how to live there were taught in addition to what had already been learned. The lessons covered all aspects of living and were concerned with the preservation of the community life and the beings who shared that life.

To live in a world that is shared, there must be order. From the beginning, there was a division of labor and social responsibility in these communities. The performance of certain tasks by specific groups was essential to the continuation of life in that community. The interdependence of the people (or beings) was so strongly emphasized that no one outside the particular group could perform functions assigned to that group. The continuation of these life-preserving functions was ensured through the teachings of the younger members of the tribes. Tribal life has been described as experiments in group living which have continued because they were successful (Coe, 1977).

The maintenance of interdependence formed the foundation for the balance of life that characterizes the tradition of Indian peoples. These influential beginnings are very important to their lives, so much so that they have been maintained to the present day. Tradition and culture, in this sense, are not memories of how it was, but, rather, how it should be and, for the most part, how it is yet today.

Out of these lessons developed the accepted behaviors of the specific tribal community. Accepted behaviors for any individual derived from sex and group membership. Each group and its members had responsibility for certain tasks which might be described as secular or religious in nature.

The life of the tribal community completely established the parameters of behavior. The individual's role and responsibility were clear, and every opportunity was given to learn these well. The accomplishment of specific tasks was necessary. Individual expression developed out of a sensitivity to the uniqueness of role and responsibility. One gained an exquisite sense of his part in the order of the world. From this vantage point, the individual experienced his worth.

Few societies allow for as much individual expression of uniqueness as is available to Indian people. The dominant society allows for individual expression of uniqueness through individualism. The Indian tribal community allows expression through individuality. This is a very important difference in the way a people addresses life. In the former sense, uniqueness must be novel or a departure from the norm; in the latter, uniqueness becomes the refinement of life.

One way of looking at this is to observe some of the traditional art forms. In this art, there are definite limitations of space and style; within these limitations each artist must find room for individual expression. The art of the Northwest Coastal Indians is a clear example of this: for example, the outline of a whale and the raven are set; the differing artistic expressions are within the confines of those outlines.

Art, in this sense, becomes a visual expression of the individual's understanding of the social context in which the dictates of the tribal group are accepted. There is a parallel response to the expected behavior, because it (a) has a life-preserving function, and (b) provides an understanding of one's universe. The world is not recreated in the sense that artistic freedom of expression is generally understood today. Indian art of modern times continues to reflect the traditional base, but the execution is personal and evocative (McNickle, 1973). It is important that the social order is maintained.

The social order was believed to be inherently good and right, because it was based on creative guidance expressed in cultural values that were daily enacted.

The societies were so well-ordered that no aberrations existed. It was possible for homosexuals, for instance, to live life in these societies as anyone else would. Their place in the order of things was not questioned, because they existed. It was possible then for societies like these to institutionalize homosexuality.

Tribal groups exerted pressures of conformity and control on their people. These pressures, in one instance, were developed out of the intricate relational network. Interdependent expectations were strongly felt. Additionally, tribes maintained ceremonies that reinforced both individual and group expectation. The nature and character of tribes provided its members with a sense of security and sureness. The ability to experience this comfort and security derived from the lessons that were taught to the people thousands of years ago when they were situated in their homeland.

Individuality then expresses itself as a refinement of the human experience and reflects the necessity for adherence to a philosophical base that provides understanding of the world and man's relationship to it.

These pressures, born out of the lessons taught, stimulated the development of a high level of sensitivity and allowed tribal people to be acutely aware of balance and imbalance in the natural order of things. Mental illness was considered an imbalance. When an individual's imbalance caused hardship for another individual, it was partly the recipient's responsibility to assist in the return to balance. This individual might sponsor a ceremony, such as a giveaway, for the person who was experiencing the imbalance.

Imbalance or disorders might be caused by disruptions in human relationships, natural disorders, or undesirable influences from within or outside the tribe. Experiences with the imbalances of life allowed people to better understand the balance of life. Threat or danger provided an opportunity for the people to understand better the nature of the world and of man's relationship to it. In this sense, imbalance of any sort took on the character of the natural order of things.

To maintain this kind of society, relationships must be extensive and entwined beyond blood. The education and training of the children was in a very real sense the shared responsibility of the total community. Perhaps this is a characteristic essential to a completely interdependent community.

The importance placed on human relationships necessitated a society that was based on interdependence and responsibility. These were among the first experiences of the Indian person, becoming the cornerstone of the philosophical life. These experiences, which form the basis of tribal tradition and culture, were of such importance that they have persevered through time and today remain an important part of the Indian person's view of life.

The historical-traditional education and training of Indian children encouraged them to be in touch with their world. Their relationships with other beings and things permitted mutual learning experiences. Their sense of community was complete. The experience was a very tangible one. It occurred in close contact with many people who praised, advised, guided, urged, warned, and scolded, but, most importantly, respected. The lessons children learned made sense, because they were directly related to the life of the tribal community and their own place in that life.

Children learned through expectations. As members of the community, they had the responsibility to meet their share of the requirements of living. Disregard of these might cause hardship to themselves and/or other members of the community.

As children grew, they saw that those people who were the most responsible were the most highly valued. They learned that these individuals had acquired their status through adherence to a tribal structure that provided the freedom for people to develop as truly individual persons. Their individuality was an expression of those tribal constructs that allowed the individual to reach his fullest sense of being, in concert with the fulfillment of community needs. In this world, the ends for the individual had the same ends as the community. Today, however, other influences are disruptive.

The emphasis of Western educational and social service planning pulls the child away from this community and thus the connections with tribal life. American Indian children have been forced into an environment that is not only foreign but denies the integrity of their community and, therefore, their own integrity. The pervasiveness and intensity of these experiences create a world of confusion whose impact has been and will continue to be felt for many generations to come.

In this new environment, the community is not only compartmentalized but is a major destructive factor to tribal life and to the individual. Life and its activities do not flow and enfold unto themselves. There are stops and starts. At these junctures, children are required to make new definitions of themselves in relation to the world encountered. There is no longer a way of life but ways of life that are not necessarily connected. Children observe that these different ways are not only in themselves, but also in others. It is extremely difficult to understand how man, who goes in so many different directions, can reach the sense of relatedness essential to the life he has known.

Newness and change were encouraged in Indian life, and often enforced. There was disregard of the old or usual as inappropriate or not worthwhile. Indian societies have never been static but rather dynamic and evolving. Tribes share and trade skills, dress, song, and ceremony. Among some tribes even today, new songs are composed each year for certain ceremonies and never sung again.

The early Western educational experience of Indian children was through enforced separation from their family and community. Children of school age were removed from their families and tribes and enrolled in institutions hundreds or thousands of miles from their homes. This practice currently exists for approximately 30,000 Indian children.

Children did not have available a support system of strong, sensitive elders as their models. They were forced to rely for support on other children whose tribal educations had been discontinued in the same manner. Their tribal education was insufficient to allow them to be teachers to each other. Yet, those beginning precepts of tribal life which they had learned earlier remained as much a part of them as did the first suckling taste of life at the mother's breast.

CHILDREN AND THEIR RELATIONSHIP TO INDIAN SOCIETY

Perhaps the most distinctive aspect of tribal life was the central position of the child. Children in a very real sense represented the renewal and preservation of life. Extended relational patterns, including clans and other groupings, aided the biological family in a support system that centered around children.

Thus, the most destructive forces impeding the social and emotional development of Indian and Alaskan Native children is the systematic removal of these children from their homes and placement in an alien culture. These placements include boarding school and other institutional placements, foster care, adoption, and religious placements. These practices sever the links of the support system that is centered around children and thus encourage the destruction of the basic tenets of tribal life.

Many tribes still maintain practices that are believed to help influence the sex of the unborn child. The particular economic and social system dictated the more desired child for the tribal group. In the southwest Pueblos, girls were often preferred over boys, but in other tribes boys were the preferred children. Infant mortality has been a serious problem with all tribes for a very long time. In times past, the mortality rate might have been an effective population control mechanism. The birthrate might have reflected the environmental conditions and other influences that directly impacted on the survival of the tribe. Tribes made use of various natural contraceptives to limit the size of their families. For all tribes, the successful birth of a healthy child was welcomed, because the child would in time assume the role of caretaker and provider.

The infant had many caretakers. Among numerous tribes, there were several mothers and fathers for a child, and in all tribes child care was a group responsibility. The developing infant was nurtured in an atmosphere much different from that of today. There were not only older caretakers but also older children and other infants, some even of the same age. People lived in small dwellings, lacking the compartmentalized arrangement of modern living. There was a great deal of work required to maintain the community. Mothers worked alongside their growing children. Often, the child might be in very close contact with the parent, resting in an enclosure that hung on the mother's back or next to her breast. The cradleboards used by many tribes continued the enclosed security of the womb.

Among the Plains people, infants were taught not to cry when placed in the cradleboard. It was imperative that the cries of children not reveal a location to an enemy. In more recent times, cradleboards were hung from saddlehorns as these people moved their families from place to place (Niethammer, 1977). In more sedentary times, the cradleboards were hung from the ceilings in rooms where much activity was centered. The child communicated with many people and received this stimulation from the beginning of life.

Children were allowed to develop freely (Morey and Gilliam, 1974). There is not even today a great deal of concern with task timing. Children learned many of these activities through observation. When they were old enough to toddle around, they were in the company of many children. Behavior was observed and copied. The smaller children received encouragement from their older siblings to behave appropriately. Often, these older siblings provided the first demonstrations, and it was part of their responsibility to assist in the formation of certain behaviors.

When the child reached the age at which verbal communication could be remembered, the observable instruction began. At some point among tribes, communication between the sexes was discouraged. This varied according to the specific belief systems of the tribe. Sexes often entered a separation at an early age. Boys had to be instructed by males, because that is the role they would assume. It was the same for girls, as they were cared for by women.

The early communication patterns presented an interesting phenomenon in light of the extremely stringent separation patterns among some tribes. Some individuals, depending on their relational patterns, were not allowed to speak with each other in adult life. However, the shared communication in early life perhaps sealed relational bonds that were developed to support the behavioral taboos in later life. Early closeness provided the security required to maintain separation in later life. Separation from one's family, as through marriage, must have been traumatic for some people. However, the intricate relational pattern allowed for continued and new connections with certain relatives, at the same time that other connections might be discontinued or prohibited.

Much attention was paid to the developing sexual identity of the child. This was accomplished through instruction and participation in sex-related activities. The encouragement went beyond stabilizing sexual identity to include a definition of self as a member of a particular group within the tribe. As children grew, they assumed their specific identity in the intricate tribal relational pattern.

Brothers and sisters were very close. The particular supportive patterns between brothers and sisters usually began in adolescence. There were required exchanges of assistance in the material support of the tribe and in the religious activities. The similarity of cousin and brother-sister relationship allowed people to always have the right kind of support.

These relational groups into which the child entered and grew were with purpose delicately and strongly supported. They are the cementing agents of Indian and Alaskan Native existence, reflecting the philosophy of that life.

This relational system makes Indian and Alaskan Native children extremely vulnerable, because they develop in a world where support of these systems is not encouraged. Indian and Alaskan Native lifestyle fosters the development of a high level of sensitivity. The learning patterns of observation and participation do not require that verbal instruction be the major transmitter of knowledge. Important lessons regarding all spheres of life are learned through nonverbal communication. Children are encouraged to be sensitive to what others think. They are vulnerable to criticism and to influences from the outside society. Perhaps these children do not develop the kinds of defense mechanisms and other habitual patterns that are required by other societies (Bentz, 1977, reference note 1).

The confusion that the child experiences entering non-Indian relational systems causes great psychological pain. The child comes from a world where people gain their status according to a particular competence. Competent status is allowed everyone; even the retarded person might be thought to have special powers.

The particular way in which these systems are affected by the larger socioeconomic system prevents healthy development of the Indian and Alaskan

Native child in either direction. Some studies have pointed to the successful acquisition by Indians of skills used by the larger society. This successful acquisition has occurred in situations where the adaptive skills have been grafted onto persons whose security has been well-established within their life support system. To do otherwise requires complete denial of identity or rebirth (Bahr, 1972).

Competition is a behavior that is not clearly translated. The institutional systems entered by the child operate by rules much different from those learned earlier or those strongly emphasized. These new institutional systems which the children enter require accomplishment, when neither the expectation nor the means to achieve it are made clear, and often have little relevance to previous tribal institutions. In this atmosphere, learning the nature of competitiveness of another group becomes an impossibility for many Indian and Alaskan Native children. Children are forced to use the competitive skills of their group, which may have little applicability in the larger society. Unfortunately, many of these children come historically to this condition, their parents and many previous generations having shared this very same experience.

The close living arrangements required behavior that was tension-reducing. The sharing of children aided in this arrangement. The development of skill was important. One became excellent, because the ability and the encouragement existed. It was not the kind of competition that made one person better than another. The worth of man had been established long before this. Individuals who broke these rules of competition were severely scorned. These are not living arrangements of the historic past; they exist presently and can be witnessed in modern day Pueblos of Arizona and New Mexico (Ortiz, 1969).

Indians and Alaskan Natives are great gamblers. In some groups, women exhibit a greater fondness for gambling than do men. The competitiveness required here is in an atmosphere of fun that is tension-reducing for all. Individual competitiveness and aggression are discouraged, because of the potential threat to community survival. In the tribal context, the competition becomes so intense that the feelings make contact with the activity, rather than the specific individuals involved. The people enter a communal process in which all share in the end product. This is the competitive spirit which is encouraged in Indian and Alaskan Native communities.

The ideal of Dakota life in the old days was cooperation, and, although competition was permitted adults in limited fields of activity, it was not taught the young children. Such competition as existed was to maintain position and good performance relative or equal to others in the band. There were no "stars" and no laggards. Severe criticism was exerted on the child who sought to "shine" in unapproved ways or before he was old enough. The great sensitivity to shame built up from his earlier years, also kept down any desire to excel to the disadvantage of others (MacGregor, 1946).

Any discussion of the social and emotional development of Indian children today must take into account the Indian person's Western educational history. Along with warfare and disease, the Western educational system has probably had the greatest impact on the lives of Indian children.

From a 1976 survey conducted by the Association on American Indian Affairs it was learned that, of the approximate population of one million Indians and Alaskan Natives, 49,249 children under the age of 18 were not living with their families. (A.A.I.A., 1976) These children were in boarding schools, foster and adoptive placements, many of them non-Indian; non-Native. This is an incomplete count, because some states did not provide full information. Nor was it possible to get an accurate account of the children who were in religious placements, either in institutions or in private homes.

The laws, treaties, and reports of the early years give no evidence of attempts to provide a scholastic education to Indians. A notable exception occurred in a treaty negotiated in 1803 with the Kaskaskias in which the following provision was made:

... whereas, the greater part of said tribe have been baptised and received into the Catholic Church to which they are much attached, the United States will give annually for seven years one hundred dollars toward the support of a priest of that religion, who will engage to perform for the said tribe the duties of his office and also instruct as many of their children as possible in the rudiments of literature (Meriam et al., 1928).

This combination of activity and absence of distinction of religious, moral teaching, and scholastic education has characterized Indian education to this day.

The next reference to Indian education originated out of the legislative branch of the government in a report of the House Committee on Indian Affairs of January 22, 1818, in which the following position was taken:

Your committee are induced to believe that nothing which it is in the power of the Government to do would have a more direct tendency to produce this desirable object (civilization) than the establishment of schools at convenient and safe places among those tribes friendly to us (Meriam et al., 1928).

Out of this recommendation resulted the first appropriation for Indian education. Congress made a permanent appropriation of $10,000 for both industrial and scholastic education of Indians. Because the Federal government had no administrative machinery to supervise the education of Indians, this appropriation was meted out to various missionary organizations. Later, as treaty funds became available for education, these were also apportioned to the missionary establishments.

In 1887, there were 227 Indian schools. Of these, 163 were operated by the Indian Service, and 64 were private institutions run mainly by missionary establishments supported through contracts. The philosophy of Christianizing and/or civilizing continued into this era of Indian education. Some of the observations of Indian education of that era would be comical if one did not empathize or identify with the tragic experiences of the children involved in that process.

The following comments were made by Professor C. C. Painter on his visit to a school in the Indian territory in 1887:

I was first introduced into the main room of the (Kiowa) school, where an Hon. Judge from Texas, who had deserted bench and bar in behalf of these people, teaches the young Indian ideas. The Judge, I was informed, was the most distinguished lawyer in the county from which he hails. It is well-known that he has attained distinction in some field of labor; he certainly would not achieve it in the field of pedagogy. He is a little mite of a man—sallow, spiritless. He had two boys and a girl droning away at reading. He never rose to his feet without feeling for his knee pants by way of his breeches pockets, using the stove for a spittoon. He looked as if he had gotten out of his grave to find a "chaw of terbacker," and had lost his way and could not find his resting place. I have never seen such a perfect picture of the old field schoolmaster, and I have seen a number (Meriam et al. 1928).

General Henry Heth, an inspector for the Indian Service, made the following statement in 1889:

The Indian Bureau has been made the dumping ground for the sweepings of the political party that is in power. I have found an abandoned woman in charge of an Indian school. I found a discharged lunatic in charge of another, and he was still there a year after I reported that fact. He would lock himself into a room with the children and light his pipe. As soon as a report that is derogatory to these people goes to Washington, their friends rush to the Interior Department and say that these reports are wrong, and that another trial must be given, and they are kept on and on. . . . If you must go to an Indian school or an agency, and stay only a day or two, everything will seem to run smoothly. But if you stay there a month, and get behind the scenes, into the arcanum, you will find two or three who are physically, mentally or morally incapacitated. You find good, earnest people among them, but they are the exception. You find people who are there only to draw their pay. You will find cliques, wrangles, quarrels going on that are a disgrace to any institution (Meriam et al., 1928).

This contemporary observation (1900) of Indian education was made after a tour of reservations:

There is, as yet, no coherent or comprehensive system or plan for the education of the Indians under Government supervision. It does not appear, indeed, that anybody has thought of the necessity of such a system. The existing arrangements, machinery and methods are highly inorganic, incoherent, and inefficient.

. . . A few good teachers have been sent out, but they are always hampered by association with incompetents in the same school (Meriam et al., 1928).

The Kennedy reports on Indian education in 1969 and the later education reports of the American Indian Policy Review Commission (Association on American Indian Affairs, 1976) revealed that the situation remained unchanged.

In the early years of the Western education of Indians, children of very young age were rounded up from their tribes and forced to attend these schools established by the government. They were required to discard their language, dress, and food. The entire encounter in these educational institutions was with foreignness.

When the children were enrolled, they were required to spend eight continuous years away from their families and tribes. By now the socioeconomic systems of Indian people had been permanently dis-

rupted. Survival necessitated the request and acceptance of food rations. These rations were withheld from families and tribes who refused to enroll their children in these institutions. Today, it is believed to be inappropriate to place elementary school children in boarding institutions; however, in earlier years there was no concern with the age of the child. Not only were the parents denied a voice in the educational program of their children, but so was the tribe.

The impact on the family and the tribe was considerable. Generations of Indian children were denied the education required to survive in their world. Most were unable to invest themselves in the new experience, because the world view was antithetical to what they had previously learned. The handicaps developed from this experience are a major cause for the disruptions of Indian family life today. Most Indian children live in economically depressed communities today, where use of intoxicants has gained prominence.

The educational programs have not improved greatly for Indian children and, consequently, many Indian people leave these institutions ill-prepared.

These conditions converge to place the Indian child in a highly vulnerable position. Because so many children are in these situations, this creates a hardship for the entire tribal community.

THE DEVELOPMENT OF LANGUAGE IN INDIAN CHILDREN

The many people into whose care Indian children are entrusted fondle and communicate with them. The different intonations orchestrate a sound in which there are many expressions. The constancy of this stimulation lays important groundwork for language facility.

It is generally accepted that all children begin to speak at about the same age. However, it is known that "baby talk" is not a characteristic of the verbal interchange of the Indian child and his care-takers and is not encouraged.

From the earliest years the Omaha child was trained in the grammatical use of his native tongue. No slip was allowed to pass uncorrected, and as a result there was no child-talk such as obtains among English-speaking children—the only difference between the speech of the old and the young was in the pronunciation of words which the infant often failed to utter correctly, but this difficulty was soon overcome, and a boy of ten or twelve was apt to speak as good Omaha as a man of mature years (Spicer, 1969).

Mature language acquisition among tribes is fostered from the beginning.

The construction of Indian language is quite different from English. Appropriate use of the Indian language requires a knowledge of and sensitivity to the relational patterns of the individual's community. The way in which something is said is directly related to the status of the speaker, the status of the person spoken to, the sexes of the people, and their relationship to each other. Relationships are an important element in the formation of grammatical structure in Indian languages.

It is known that there are not common roots in Indian and English language. The Indian linguistic structures are entirely different from those of English. While there is disagreement as to the extent to which language shapes thought, there is no doubt that cultural assumptions and values are embedded in language, and concepts are differentially elaborated. Some concepts that are important in some of the Native languages have no counterpart in English, and vice versa (Zimiles et al., 1976).

Indian children's facility in the English language is among the poorest of any group in the United States. They consistently score at the bottom of reading measurements. Even those Indian children who grow up in homes where English is spoken as their first or only language fare poorly in these measurements.

Indian children infrequently receive stimulation from books written in English and are, therefore, extremely handicapped. Most Indians' financial status is below the poverty level, and they cannot buy books for their children. Also, it cannot be overlooked that the themes of most of the children's books written in English may not be stimulating to the Indian child or, as importantly, to the parent who would purchase the book. In some instances, the story may not be relevant to Indian life. In addition, the parents' proficiency in English may not be much better than the child's, and, consequently, the parents and children cannot share in the reading experience.

Physical health has implications for language development. Although the health status of American Indian and Alaskan Natives has shown improvement, it still trails the general population of the country by 20 to 25 years. Poor nutrition among Indians places them in serious danger regarding proper cerebral growth, particularly in the perinatal period, when the brain is undergoing critical development (Zimiles et al., 1976).

Again, according to the Bank Street College Report (Zimiles, et al. 1976):

Otitis media, at a rate of incidence approximating 12,000 per 100,000 for 1972 and 1973, poses the greatest threat to Native American children. Early onset of the first attack (before the child's second birthday) is highly correlated with a tendency toward chronic recurrence of this potentially crippling ear disease. In 1972, 25 percent of all cases reported were in children younger than one year of age; 67 percent of new cases occurred in the under-five age group.

In a study of infants in 27 Eskimo villages in the Yukon and Kuskokwim River Delta areas of southwestern Alaska, a cohort of 378 children were followed from birth to four years of age. Sixty-two percent of the children had one or more episodes of infected and draining ears during the study period. Of these, 65 percent had their first episode before their first birthday.

The data indicated that frequent episodes and hearing impairment occur long before the children reach an age for safe removal of tonsils and adenoids, the usual preventive treatment. These removal practices have been called into question by the medical community, because these conditions can be successfully treated by draining the ear. The social implications of these conditions and others have not yet been acknowledged or acted upon. These conditions not only impair the Indian or Alaskan Native child in the learning of English, but also directly impair his ability to learn and understand his own language. The impact of these conditions, should they continue, presents a serious threat to the social and philosophical quality of Indian and Alaskan Native life.

FROM THE INDIAN CHILD'S PERSPECTIVE

One of the clearest statements of the perceptual beginnings of Indian children is that of Andy Joseph, Councilman, Colville Confederated Tribes (reference note 2)

Mr. Joseph relates that the child reared by his grandparents was considered especially fortunate. Because they were elderly, the grandparents had a much longer experience with life and, therefore, the opportunity to learn more from it. And, as a consequence, they had more to teach and share. They could be more patient with the child's training. Although the child's parents may have been educated in the same way, because of their age and the responsibilities they carried, it was not possible for them to spend as much time with the children as the grandparents might. Additionally, parents often lacked the patience that is developed with age.

Mr. Joseph's childhood education was characterized by its completeness. As a child, he was encouraged to become as fully aware as possible of the environment around him and the activities which took place therein. The first part of this education was concentrated on identification of physical characteristics of beings and things in the world around him. For example, lessons in the identification of a rabbit would include not only its furry coat, its changing colors and its other physical characteristics but also the environmental conditions in which the rabbit lived. Attention was called to the reaction of animals when in the wild. From the animals' reaction the child could see whether the encounter was one of surprise or danger, and thus the child was helped to make a decision about what his reaction should be. This early learning concentrated on the development of the child's individual senses.

From infancy, Indian children were deliberately introduced to their environment. Infants were often placed on the ground so they could learn to hear, feel, and recognize the rumblings of the earth. As they grew older, this same method, for example, was used to alert them to the presence of the deer. The vibrations of the earth could be felt from the deer's first jump. In a deer's first jump, the ground is always hit hard as the deer comes down on all four legs. After that, the impact of the deer's gait is light. It became easy for the child to distinguish the presence of a deer from that of the heavy-footed horse. The recognition of these distinctions was made possible through listening to vibrations of the earth.

These practices developed high levels of sensitivity that were integrated. It is in this area that the most pronounced education of the Indian child took place. Essentially, the method used was rigorous training in problem-solving, assessment or diagnosis. It was necessary that the child have a sense of knowing many things distinctly so that the information could be willfully integrated and thus made usable. Children were encouraged to think about everything around them. Their responses provided their teachers with observable measures of their perceptive abilities and gave indication of areas where their education required further support.

As a young boy, Mr. Joseph was led into the woods and, with his eyes closed, was asked to identify the various trees and other vegetation by smell. His face was rubbed with the blood of the freshly killed and gutted deer and he was required to drag the deer out of the woods. From this, he learned the smell of the deer, so that thereafter he could always identify the presence of the deer in a downwind. Mr. Joseph was reared by a paternal aunt and uncle, who at the time of his birth were in their eighties. He maintains this approach to the development of perceptual abilities through instruction to his children and grandchildren.

This thrust in perceptual learning develops a child quite differently from many other children in this country. From his Rorschach protocols, Hallowell (1942) reported that the psychological characteristics of the traditional Ojibwa personality remained in the relatively unacculturated Ojibwa of today:

The most prominent feature in the great majority of records is the emphasis on strong restraint and control. From the Rorschach evidence alone, one would be bound to infer that the Saulteaux were a people whose personal lives were organized within the ambit of formalized habit patterns and that very little of their emotional and imaginative life escapes these bonds—the sort of social roles the individual conceptualizes are on the whole very passive—standing, sitting, looking, sometimes talking.

A leading Indian educator, Patricia Locke, has proposed that the values inherent in Western education are an assault on the Indian child. It is recognized that the Indian child must learn those activities necessary to survive in his world. However, acquisitiveness, mercantilism, and individualism are values that are antithetical to Indian values. Ms. Locke, President of the National Indian Educa-

tion Association, has encouraged that these specific Western values be taught as skills to Indian children. In this way, the Indian child would be able to exercise his own values, learned from the most sensitive area of his education.

Tribal people often teach their children that they must learn two paths of knowledge. One is the path of the tribal-specific culture, including value systems that are diametrically opposed to the value systems of the dominant society. The Indian child will be inclined to accept this tribal-specific path of knowledge as the good and right way of knowledge for him—or her—as a tribal member. The second path to be learned is that of the dominant society where the value systems (intrinsic to contemporary non-Indian America) of individualism, acquisitiveness and mercantilism prevail. These latter values must be learned by Indian children as social and economic skills and not as values to be internalized. The Indian values of concern for the group, and generosity and disdain for material possessions are reinforced constantly in tribal ceremonies. Youngsters are expected to emulate persons who exemplify such values (Locke, 1977, reference note 3).

Children educated in this way are strongly identified with their family, tribe, and homeland. The perspective of life learned by Mr. Joseph is encouraged and expected in the lives of Indian children. Indian people expect that they are to develop a high level of sensitivity. Possession of a high level of sensitivity encourages the development of what is known as knowledge and intelligence.

This perspective, when developed, was what allowed the Indian child to become sensitive to balance and imbalance. Indian people were taught how to deal with imbalance. As a result, they were able to experience a strong sense of autonomy, because they had knowledge that allowed them to have control in their environment. In this view, long-term planning did not have the some character that it does in Western societies today. Neither was postponement of remedy recommended;

however, the remedial action had to take place within specific conditions.

THE DEVELOPMENT OF COGNITIVE LEARNING IN INDIAN CHILDREN

There is an abundance of data that measures the intelligence of American Indian and Alaskan Native children. The difficulties with the measurements used are that they provide misleading and invalid information.

In recent years, more appropriate attempts have been made to gather information about the distinctiveness of Indian and Alaskan Native children's learning patterns.

In contrast with most assessments of intellectual functioning of Native American children which sample specific knowledge and skills by means of standardized tests, some studies have attempted to examine the processes of cognitive functioning which are assumed to underline test performance. Such work, relatively new and seldom conducted with Native American children, has the potential for revealing in detail how Native American children deal with intellectual tasks—how they define problems and how their thinking is organized—and to identify distinctive features of their ways of thinking and problem-solving.

One form of such investigations examines the degree to which the intellectual functioning of children from a particular cultural subgroup corresponds to patterns shown by children of the majority culture. Silk and Voyet studied aspects of cognitive development among the Oglala Sioux at Pine Ridge. They administered a series of Piagetian tasks to a sample of 75 children from four to ten years of age. They found that Piaget's Theoretical Hypothesis that cognitive development proceeds in a fixed sequence of stages was corroborated by the performance of Sioux children. The age of attainment of these stages of development was in some instances directly comparable to those found by Piaget among Swiss children, and in others was slightly behind that of Swiss children.

An early study by Carroll and Casagrande related the way Navajo children sort objects to aspects of Navajo grammar. In the Navajo language certain verbs require different forms depending on the shape of the object being dealt with. Thus the grammar focuses attention on the form and shape of things. Carroll and Casagrande found that among three groups of Navajo children, Navajo-speaking (or Navajo predominant), bilingual, and English predominant, the most pronounced tendency to sort objects in terms of form as opposed to color was found among the Navajo-speaking children. This study suggests that language and certain kinds of experience influence the bases for making that clarification.

Perhaps the most ambitious effort to study the cognitive style of Indian children is that of John-Steiner and Osterreich who observed, measured, and obtained self-descriptions of learning patterns of Pueblo children, and of selected comparison groups as well. Wide-ranging in both method and scope, the focus of their study is the degree to which the representational behavior of Pueblo children is mediated visually rather than linguistically. They cite Velma Garcia's (Mason) speculation that Pueblo children, in listening to legends, learn to represent them visually because they are not allowed to ask questions or reflect verbally on what they hear. In attempting to show that Indian people use visual imagery a great deal, John-Steiner and Osterreich report on the rich visual details and the unusual reliance on graphic metaphors provided by Pueblo adults when asked to tell of their childhood experiences. When children's drawings were analyzed in terms of their artistic merit, John-Steiner and Osterreich found that kindergarten and first grade children who are primarily Keresan-speaking, and who live in a visually rich environment, obtained the highest scores. At the same time, these and other bilingual children were less effective in retelling stories in English. They rely more heavily on graphic skills as a vehicle for communication and representation. Interestingly, when these children who spoke both languages were asked to retell a story in their weaker language, they included more elements which related to what had been illustrated pictorially. They had difficulty remembering content which was not portrayed visually as well as verbally. On the other hand, white children often retold the purely verbal aspects of the story they heard.

In a similar vein, Collier found that Navajos were exceptionally skillful in identifying and interpreting visual detail in photographs of familiar scenes. Havighurst and Neugarten found that the free drawings of 12-year-old children from the Hopi reservation were judged to have a more advanced sense of realism and spatial representation than a comparison group living in a Northern urban center (Zimiles et al., 1976).

These studies represent the initial efforts to search for distinctive, innate learning patterns of Indian and Alaskan Native children. This only begins to provide information than can form the basis for more discreet forms of learning style. Individuals whose early lives are filled with shapes and colors, as involved in ceremonials, would seemingly approach the acquisition of knowledge in a similar manner.

Efforts in early childhood educational programs on numerous reservations, where the native language is the language of instruction, will certainly assist in better understanding of the cognitive development of native children in the future. Instruction in the native language must go beyond the primary years and recur at important developmental junctures. The current efforts in this area are nascent.

It is important to realize that many Indian children are successfully learning both cultures solely in their tribal languages on some remote cultural enclaves. These fortunate children experience the delight of hearing teachers speak to them, for example, in Yupik Eskimo, Navajo and Miccosukee, the language of their parents, grandparents and extended families. Their grade-level achievement surpasses those of less fortunate children who are forced to learn a foreign language (English) in the early grades. In many situations, a bilingual approach is necessary. This need becomes clear when one realizes that 85 percent of Navajo children start school with no knowledge of English. Exercising their rights as educational decision-makers, parents and tribal leaders have chosen this bilingual path as the desired approach for their children (Gold, 1977).

The use of available information regarding the closeness of alternate generations is encouraging. In some tribal languages, grandparents and grandchildren share the same name in kinship terminology. This situation may greatly influence the acquisitional characteristics of the child. Implications of this sharing are not known, but it is possible that some children may be additionally confused and perplexed by this system, because the cultural system may no longer be intact or homogeneous, or so foreign to the majority culture that it may therefore be overlooked in educational thought, examination and planning where Indian children are concerned.

As these ideas and others are explored, more information will become available to better understand the cognitive development of Indian and Alaskan Native children.

CONCLUSION

Indian children living in today's society are indeed in a sensitive balance of existence. When Columbus reached the New World, there were reported to be at least eight million Indians living in America, and other estimates ranged as high as 75 million. At the beginning of the twentieth century, there were approximately 220,000 Indians left in this country. Today, the Indian population is estimated at about one million persons, representing membership in over 300 different tribes. The tribal diversity is great, making it impossible to depict clearly the social and emotional characteristics of children's development from each of these specific cultures.

The most meaningful and productive programs for Indians are those developed by the Indians themselves. These programs allow for the continuation of the philosophy that forms and guides the Indian child's life. Not only is the tribe's sovereignty respected, but the sovereignty of the individual as well.

There are presently pending in Congress ten legislative actions that would severely impair the tribes' ability to continue their philosophy in the lives of their children. The ideas and practices that stimulate the introduction of these kinds of legislation place the Indian child in a yet more vulnerable position. Indian children are very sensitive to the consequences of these actions. The resurgence of tribalism develops mainly out of a sense of resposibility that Indian children are taught to feel for one another.

And World Maker said:

In life as in the dormant earth, there ever dwells both Good and Evil. Always, in this world, these two elements will oppose one another.

Good is the wisdom of life which I have now awakened from the earth. Evil is nothing more than the ignorance of this life, a drowsiness difficult to know or see; a drowsiness that leads to sleep.

World Maker said nothing else until the sun was hot and high on the third day of creation. Then he spoke once more:

If Evil should ever become all-powerful, if Good should fall back into sleep, then soon again there would be nothing. Life would quickly vanish and the earth would stand naked as it was the first few days of its creation.

Then slowly the sleeping earth would wash back into the sea, and Turtle and Peheipe, once more dwelling on the raft, would wait again for me to come this way.

World Maker lapsed into his silent thoughts and said no more until once again the moon was there:

So Good must resist the pull of the invisible Evil. Thus there comes a third element to the world which will rise from this earth in the form called Coyote.

Coyote looks like Evil should, knows what Evil is doing and always does it first; tries to awaken Good to that which Evil is. In no other way will Good, which never sees true Evil, ever know where Evil is or how Evil works.

Coyote likes the game he plays, ever loud and full of humor, ever full of tricks and cunning. And Good, seeing Evil in Coyote's antics, must flee in mortal fear of games.

No matter what Coyote does or says, always do the opposite . . . only then can life continue. Only then will this tree we sit beneath forever stand, giving nourishment to the greatest life yet to come.

So did World Maker speak during the first days of this world's creation (Simpson, 1977).

REFERENCE NOTES

1. Bentz, M. (Gros Ventre) Doctoral Candidate in Anthropology, Seattle, Washington. Conversation, 1977.
2. Joseph, A. (Okanogan) Councilman, Colville Confederated Tribes, Nespelem, Washington. Conversation, 1977.
3. Locke, P. (Sioux-Chippewa) President, National Indian Education Association, Boulder, Colorado. Conversation, 1977.

REFERENCES

Association on American Indian Affairs, *Indian child welfare statistical survey*. Report submitted to American Indian Policy Review Commission, Congress of the United States, July 1976.

Bahr, H. M. *Native Americans Today: Sociological Perspective*. New York: Harper & Row, 1972.

Coe, R. T. *Sacred Circles: Two Thousand Years of North American Indian Art*. London: Lund Humphries, 1977.

Gold, M. J. *In Praise of Diversity: A Resource Book for Multicultural Education*. Washington, D.C.: Teacher Corps—Association of Teacher Education, 1977.

Hallowell, A. J. Acculturation process and personality change as indicated by Rorschach technique. *Rorschach Research Exchange*, 1942, *6*, 42–50.

MacGregor, G., et al. *Warriors Without Weapons*. Chicago: University of Chicago Press, 1946.

McNickle, D. *Native American Tribalism: Indian Survivals and Renewals*. London: Oxford University Press, 1973.

Meriam, L., et al. *The Problem of Indian Administration*. Baltimore: The Johns Hopkins Press, 1928.

Morey, S. and Gilliam, O. (Eds.) *Respect for Life: The Traditional Upbringing of American Indian Children*. Garden City, N.Y.: Waldorf Press, 1974, pp. 23–27.

Niethammer, C. *Daughters of the Earth: The Lives and Legends of American Indian Women*. New York: Macmillan, 1977.

Ortiz, A. *Tewa World: Space, Time, Being, and Becoming in a Pueblo Society.* Chicago: University of Chicago Press, 1969.

Silko, L. M. *Ceremony.* New York: The Viking Press, 1977.

Simpson, R. *Ooti: A Maidu Legacy.* Millbrae, CA: Celestial Arts, 1977.

Spicer, E. H. *A Short History of the Indians of the United States.* New York: Van Nostrand Reinhold, 1969.

Zimiles, H., Cuffaro, H. K., Ginsberg, S., Mack, G., Sample, W., Shapiro, E. and Wallace, D. *Young Native Americans and Their Families: Educational Needs Assessment and Recommendations, Final Report.* New York: Bank Street College of Education, 1976, pp. 147–151.

CHAPTER 7

The Social and Emotional Development of Filipino-American Children

Rolando A. Santos, Ph.D.

Filipino-Americans comprise one of the fastest growing ethnic groups in the United States, as they approach the million mark. Immigration is the chief source of this increase, with more than half of all Americans of Filipino ancestry foreign-born. Most Filipino-Americans settle in the Pacific states of California, Hawaii, Washington, and Oregon.

In order to work effectively with Filipino-Americans, mental health professionals will find helpful an understanding of the psychosocial dynamics of being, and growing up as, a Filipino-American. As this group increases in number, there will be a corresponding increase in their need and demand for economic, social, educational, and health services. Beyond these requirements for help, however, is the very real need for Filipino-Americans to be understood within a multiethnic and multicultural society.

Understanding the psychosocial development of Filipino-American children re-

quires an understanding of the subculture of their families and social groups. Their development is best viewed as a phenomenon forged in the vortex of competing and conflicting sociopolitical and cultural forces acting on Filipino-American families as their children make the transition from the traditional Filipino culture to that which prevails in the United States.

Filipino-Americans are not a monolithic group. Every Filipino-American occupies a different point on the continuum from traditional Filipino to modern American. However, there are general patterns of beliefs and behavior typical of Filipino-Americans as a group which are different from those of other groups.

DEMOGRAPHIC FACTORS AND AMERICANIZATION

A review of the literature on Filipino-Americans shows a complete absence of

131

significant research on any aspect of the psychosocial development of Filipino-American children. Any reference to or discussion of Filipino-American values or childrearing practices, for instance, relies heavily on studies made on Filipinos in the Philippines. This pratice assumes that what is true of Filipinos must be true of Filipino-Americans. This assumption may be valid for first generation immigrants, especially for recent arrivals from the Philippines. For Filipinos, Americanization does not start at the Los Angeles International Airport or in San Pedro Harbor, but begins in the Philippines, which had been a territory of the United States for over half a century. Most are products of a public school system established by Americans and patterned after the American educational system, with English as the language of instruction and, until recently, a curriculum that was heavily American oriented. For years, every Filipino child in the Philippines was raised and educated as a "developing American." For most immigrants, coming to the United States marks the culmination of years of wanting to come to America and be *Kanos* (Americans). Acquisition of English and tastes for "stateside" goods, often accompanied by conscious or unconscious rejection of Filipino traditions, customs, and languages, are part of the psychosocial baggage many immigrants bring with them to the United States.

For long-time residents and for subsequent generations of Filipino-Americans, the Americanization process is likely to be more advanced, and greater deviations from traditional Filipino culture may be expected. The "old-timers," however, are a group which represents exceptions to the rule of length of residence determining the degree of acculturation and assimilation into the mainstream of American life and deviation from traditional Filipino culture. These are Filipinos who came in the 1920s and 1930s, mostly as farmhands, domestics, stewards in the U.S. Navy, and a few as working students.

Their skin color, accent, limited education, ascribed lower-class status, and national origin made them victims of legal and extralegal prohibitions, e.g., ineligibility for American citizenship and ownership of land and antimiscegenation laws. Racial prejudices, social isolation, and persecution minimized the "old timers'" chances for acculturation and assimilation into wider American society, and resulted in their retention of traditional Filipino culture during the last half century. Ironically, many of the "old timers" are more traditional than many recent Filipino immigrants. The former have not become integrated into or assimilated by the wider American society, nor are they in tune with the more modern ways of recent Filipino immigrants.

Other factors have also been important in the differing degrees of Americanization of Filipino-Americans. Socioeconomic status, age, urbanicity, educational attainment, occupation, place of residence, endogamous or exogamous marriage, fluency in English, and skin color are also critical factors in determining the degree of cultural assimilation or isolation of Filipino-Americans.

However, despite the differences between the traditional and the Americanized, most Filipino-Americans share a core of common values, customs, and traditions. If for no other reasons than skin color and physical characteristics, even when Filipino-Americans consider themselves fully assimilated, they are still Filipinos to others. They are, like other minorities, hyphenated Americans. For those whose light complexion and more Caucasoid features enable them to "pass for white," the memory of a not-too-distant past of Filipino immigrant parents or grandparents remains vivid or, if dimmed, still lingers.

COLONIAL MENTALITY

From the turn of the century when the

Philippines became a territory of the United States until today, American political, economic, and cultural dominance has greatly influenced the history of the Philippines and the lives and institutions of Filipinos. Over half a century of American domination and over three-and-a-half centuries of Spanish rule have contributed to the formation of a colonial mentality that persists in many aspects of Filipino and Filipino-American life. This mentality has created cultural norms and institutions which, in broad configurations, parallel those of other colonized peoples and other colored Americans. In specific manifestations, however, these norms and institutions are uniquely Filipino and Filipino-American. These cultural norms and institutions, shaped and reshaped by history and present-day realities confronting Filipinos and Filipino-Americans, influence their behavior and define both content and context of the psychosocial development of their children.

SKIN COLOR

Even the most Americanized Filipino immigrants find themselves strangers in American society when they arrive in the United States. Initially, the most obvious difference is skin color. Even today many Filipinos equate being light complected with being beautiful or handsome and think that to be American is to be white. When the immigrants finally arrive, exhilaration is mixed with the uncomfortable feeling of being different, and is followed by doubts of ever becoming fully American because they are not white. If these feelings exist and persist, they are transmitted in subtle and nonsubtle ways to the children. These feelings of inferiority and second-class status affect the children's self-image and feelings of self-worth. Negative self-concepts based on skin color are further reinforced by a growing realization that other colored ethnics do not enjoy the same social and economic status as their white counterparts. One immigrant Filipino teenager said, "If there is anything I would change about my Filipino background, it is my color." These feelings complicate relationships between Filipino-Americans and other colored ethnics. Feelings vacillate between commiseration with and disassociation from other coloreds in the immigrants' conscious or unconscious hope for greater acceptance by white Americans.

Thus, to many Filipino-Americans, white Americans constitute a very powerful reference group. At Filipino social gatherings in the Philippines and, to a lesser extent, here in the United States, white Americans are accorded preferential treatment usually reserved for movie stars, important government officials, the clergy, and the rich. Equating light complexion with high social status is often unexpressed verbally but is manifested in the social behavior of many Filipino-Americans.

During the four centuries of Spanish and American colonial rule in the Philippines and the half century of experience as second-class residents in the United States, Filipinos and Filipino-Americans saw power, authority, prestige, and wealth as almost exclusive domains of the white and *mestizo* (mixed blood) rulers. While social and economic realities are gradually changing for them, the colonial mentality remains. In the presence of whites, many manifest a style of behavior characterized by conformity, obedience, obsequiousness, humility, and high sensitivity to the white person's needs and approval. An Anglo waitress, for instance, is perplexed by a Filipino-American waitress not wanting her to do anything ("I'll do it for you, Ma'am"). A Filipino-American vice-principal subserviently pours coffee for her Anglo fellow school administrators. Some Filipino-Americans, on the other hand, affect an air of superiority over and disdain for Anglos. These postures often mask feelings of inferiority mixed with envy, jealousy, and resentment of an inferior status, real or imagined. Among themselves, however, Filipino-Americans in positions of authority tend to be aggressive, paternalistic, and often arrogant. They have learned to behave like, and sometimes to outdo, their colonial masters.

ENGLISH AND FILIPINO LANGUAGES

About 87 Filipino languages and dialects are spoken in the Philippines. Spanish and English, however, have long been the principal languages of the arts, commerce, politics, and education. Spanish and English have enjoyed such importance that, for a long time, Filipinos have tended to judge social status by fluency in Spanish and educational attainment by fluency in English. Pilipino, the Philippine national language which is based on Tagalog, with borrowings from other Filipino languages and vernaculars, has had an uphill battle for acceptance in non-Tagalog regions. However, Pilipino is fast becoming the principal medium of instruction in Philippine schools and is attaining equal status with English and Spanish in the communication and psychology of Filipinos and Filipino-Americans. Bilingualism in Pilipino and English is one of the main goals of the Philippine educational system. Many Filipinos and Filipino-Americans are at least trilingual. They are able to communicate in English, Pilipino, and in their own regional vernacular. Many are also fluent in Spanish. Those who are not fluent in Spanish are at least familiar enough with the language to understand basic conversations.

However, despite the fact that the typical Filipino immigrant speaks English, it is invariably some form of Filipino-English. In the Philippines, they have had mostly Filipinos as English language speaking models, and, because English is a second language to them, their first language influences their accent, intonation, vocabulary, syntax, and idiomatic expressions when they speak English. Again, as in the case of skin color, immigrants find themselves different and not quite American. To many, this situation is disconcerting. Having prided themselves on being English speakers and perhaps having made fun of those who speak *carabao* (water buffalo) or "bamboo English," they now find their own version of English often unacceptable and a cause for embarrassment. Often Filipinos and Filipino-Americans are their own harshest critics in judging the acceptability or unacceptability of their spoken English. This may lead them to taking refuge in using their own vernacular. Ironically, this may be the same vernacular they thought so little of or felt embarrassed about before coming to the United States. Immigrants might also affect an exaggerated version of English which they think most closely approximates American English, or defensively claim that they speak the "King's English," or that, "at least, I spell better and speak more correctly than Americans do."

Regardless of the explanations, however, the brand of English spoken is a critical concern among Filipino-Americans and has important consequences in the language climate of their children. The strong desire to help the children become Americanized as quickly as possible often leads parents to speak to their children only in English, even when they may speak to each other and to other Filipino-Americans in their own vernacular. The children, especially the second and subsequent generations, usually are monolingual in English or are transitional bilinguals. In the latter case, the children eventually forget their native language and function mainly in English. This language situation is a critical factor in the widening generation gap between immigrant parents and their offspring. Often, while parents pride themselves on their children's fluency in English, the children are embarrassed by their parents' and other immigrants' "funny-sounding" language or their accent and pronunciation in speaking English.

EMPLOYMENT

One of the main reasons Filipinos come to the United States is to search for better economic opportunities. The rates of unemployment and underemployment in the Philippines are very high. Those who do work receive low wages, put in long hours, have scant fringe benefits, and little job security. Along with better educational opportunities, family ties with those already here, political discontentment, or simply the spirit of adventure, the chief motive for coming to the United States is economic.

Many Filipino immigrants today are professionals, and many find jobs commensurate with their training and education. Most, however, remain unemployed for long periods of time or have to settle for jobs for which they are overqualified — e.g., dentists working as dental assistants, medical doctors as medical technologists, teachers as cashiers and sales clerks, former government officials as insurance salesmen, engineers and architects as cab drivers or bar tenders. Credentialing and licensing laws, language, age, racism in suble and overt forms, and the tight job market in general are some of the factors that contribute to this situation. Often, what seemed like a high income in the United States when viewed from the Philippines, turns out to be a very limited income in the context of U.S. standards, cost of living, and taxes. Whether or not the immigrants get a good job and good economic income, they miss the psychic income they were used to in the Philippines—higher status, more social privileges, and greater understanding of or tolerance for work habits by others who understood them in the context of Filipino culture. More money and mate-

rial wealth in the United States do not translate into greater self-satisfaction and happiness. However, there is no going back for the immigrant. Typical justifications are: "At least my children are happier because their future is here," and "I owe it to my children to stay and bring them up here because their future is here." The psychosocial climate created in the home by this situation may be less than desirable. Job instability and dissatisfaction, mixed with the shame of doing work below one's dignity often lead to little or no commitment to the job and a lack of creative involvement in it. Many believe: "This is just a stepping-stone, and someday I'll find a better job." Usually, that better job does not come and another career is ruined. In this case, children have to search for success models outside the family and outside the ethnic community.

Despite the fact that their jobs may be similar to those of immigrant Filipinos, American-born Filipinos do not have the added burden of a memory of better days, as a former teacher who laments, "I may not have been paid very much, but I was important and respected in the community."

SOCIAL DISLOCATION

Since the end of World War II, most Filipino immigrants to the United States have been middle-class professionals. During the last few years, more and more upper-class Filipinos have come for political reasons. Whether they come from the middle or upper social echelons in Philippine society, most suffer severe social setbacks in the United States. The recognition and privileges of class are markedly disproportionate to those previously enjoyed in the Philippines. The status symbols of middle-class life in the Philippines, like cars, refrigerators, stereos, color television sets, travel, and lavish parties, are within the reach of even families on welfare in the United States. Family names that mean high social status in the Philippines are now common Spanish surnames that often mean second-class citizenship. Often, because of greater educational and economic opportunities in the U.S., those who have been here longer, although from poorer families in the Philippines, enjoy greater financial and social privileges than the newly arrived families who may have had more in the Philippines. This sudden reversal of roles becomes a source of bitter jealousies: "Why, she was only a Congressman's *querida* (other woman) in the Philippines. Her mother was only a maid. Look at her now! She thinks she's really somebody," or "I remember when we had nothing and they had everything. Look at them now, shopping at Goodwill and Salvation Army thrift stores!" These are expressions indicative of the social-reversal phenomenon. Children from privileged families in the Philippines, who had been catered to and pampered by parents, relatives, servants and chauffeurs, suddenly find themselves in a society less prone to conferring privilege on the basis of name alone. Individual achievement becomes more critical, and both immigrant adults and children find themselves having to compete with everybody else for social and economic rewards. Frustration and resentment often accompany this social dislocation and the loss of ascribed social status. To some Filipino immigrants, social dislocation occasions either an inferiority complex and subsequent resignation to second-class citizenship or exaggerated self-importance. The latter is usually manifested by expressions such as, "I am the only Filipino counselor in Glenn Park," and "I am the Songbird of Santa Maria," or "I am the mother of Filipinism in San Francisco."

FOOD AND FOOD HABITS

Native Filipino food seems to be the most persistent element of traditional Filipino culture among Filipino-Americans. It transcends generational, regional, socioeconomic, educational, age, and other intraethnic differences. Traditional Filipino dishes are served with great pride at most social gatherings of Filipino-Americans. Many food items and their ingredients are imported from the Philippines. Filipino markets, bakeries, and restaurants are popular among many Filipino-Americans and their friends. The familiar tastes, textures, and aroma of Filipino ingredients, sauces, and other foods are reminiscent of life "back home." When ingredients, vegetables, and other food items are not available locally and must be imported with great difficulty and at great expense, substitutions are made, but with attention to preserving the basic integrity of traditional recipes. Many Filipino-Americans raise their own vegetables, like *ampalaya* (bitter melon), eggplant, tomatoes, pepper, squash, and *sayote* in their backyards.

With succeeding generations of Filipino-Americans born in the United States, the taste for Filipino food persists, but is often limited to the more classic dishes, like pancit (noodles), adobo (marinated pork and/or chicken), lumpia (egg rolls), lechon (roasted pig), and fried or steamed rice. Usually the taste for the more exotic foods, like *bagoong* (shrimp paste), *patis* (fish sauce), *dinuguan* (pork meat and intestines cooked in pig's blood), *balut* (partially-incubated duck eggs, boiled), *tuyo* (fried dried fish), and *ampalaya* (bitter melon), has not developed. This becomes a vicious circle. The less children like dishes, the less these dishes are prepared at home in order to spare the children the smells and tastes they find unpleasant. The children then cease to have occasion for developing a taste for these foods. It is not unusual to see hamburgers, hot dogs, and French fries served with rice, sinigang (a fish dish), and adobo, with the ketchup and mustard on the table next to the patis and bagoong. This variety ensures the satisfaction of both traditional and McDonaldized tastes.

CELEBRATIONS AND SPECIAL OCCASIONS

Birthdays, anniversaries, baptisms, confirmations, Christmas, New Year, graduation, arrivals and departures of guests and relatives are special occasions that call for special celebrations. These are usually celebrated in the home. Less usual are celebrations of Filipino-American Friendship Day on July 4, Philippine Independence Day on June 12, and Philippine National Heroes' Day on December 30. The latter holidays are usually not household celebrations but public ones. Often, the meanings of these holidays are lost, especially to the later generations of Filipino-Americans who have grown up celebrating Lincoln's and Washington's birthdays, July 4 as American Independence Day, Thanksgiving, Halloween, Memorial Day, and other typically American holidays.

Whatever the occasion, however, if a celebration is deemed appropriate, the celebrants spare no expense in setting a lavish spread of food and drink for their guests and friends. These celebrations provide opportunities to display one's hospitality and showcase one's material success. Meals for company are very seldom sit-down affairs. Tables are loaded with several entrees, desserts, and other delicacies served buffet style. Usually, an extraordinary amount of food is prepared, more than the company can consume. This is not viewed as extravagance, but as a gesture of generosity. Extreme care is taken not to be criticized for being *kuripot* (stingy) in preparing only enough, or worse, insufficient food and drink for guests. Extra food is usually given to guests to take home with them. Care is also taken to avoid being criticized as *mayabang* (show-off). The hosts usually apologize to the guests for not having prepared more. Before a table groaning with food, some hosts apologize to the guests by saying, "*Paciencia lang kayo* (please be patient with us); this is all we can afford."

These celebrations tend to be very adult centered. Even children's birthdays become occasions for parents to invite their adult relatives and friends, with children, to the festivities. The birthday celebrant is not the "star of the show" as is customary at American birthday parties. Traditionally, presents are not opened during the parties. This custom ensures the avoidance of appearing too anxious and greedy on the part of the birthday celebrant and possibly embarrassing some guests who may not have brought gifts or who may think that their gifts are not as good as those of others. Traditionally, there are no special games or activities planned for the children. They eat and play by themselves while the adults eat and visit or help in the kitchen. Many Filipino-American families are now incorporating some of the more child-centered aspects of birthdays and other celebrations. Again, as in other aspects of a people in cultural transition, a compromise is usually reached in combining traditional Filipino and modern American practices.

WESTERN CLOTHES AND NATIVE DRESS

Filipinos, even in the Philippines, wear Western-style clothes. Whatever is in vogue in Paris and Los Angeles determines what is fashionable in Manila and other Philippine cities. Native costumes like the barong Tagalog, and terno are generally worn on special occasions. Some of these native costumes have been modified to suit present day activities, like the polo-barong for men and the abbreviated balintawak and pantsuits made of Philippine hand-embroidered material for women.

Native costumes aside, however, there

seem to be subtle and not-so-subtle differences in the way new immigrant Filipinos and Filipino-Americans dress, whether American-born or long-time residents of the United States. These differences have occasioned mutual teasing and criticism between "FOB" (Fresh-off-the-Boat) Filipinos and "ABCs" (American-Born Citizens). Recent immigrant males, for instance, are sometimes called "Christmas trees" because they tend to wear tight shiny pants and shirts decorated with studs. Locally born Filipino-Americans are criticized by immigrants as sloppy dressers. Indicative of this conflict are the following comments: "It's a Filipino tradition to dress properly when you go out. I found that people here can wear shorts, tennis shoes, or slippers and hair curlers in public." And a long-time resident stated, "Local Filipinos resent the newly arrived Filipinos' way of dressing. They are overdressed, wear silky pants and bright-colored dresses."

This conflict constitutes another factor in the gap between generations of Filipino-Americans. One mother complained, "Whenever I wear Filipino clothes, my son asks me, 'Why not use clothes from here, Mommy?' and 'Don't be too ancient. We are already in the United States, not in the Philippines.'"

STEREOTYPES AND ETHNIC IDENTITY

Filipinos and Filipino-Americans today find themselves inheritors of a mixed bag of both positive and negative stereotypes. On the one hand, they are thought of as hospitable, neat, hardworking, patient, bright, docile, and honest.On the other hand, they are also called sneaky, dishonest, lazy, gamblers, unreliable, and social climbers. *Manongs* (*manong*, in Ilokano, is used in addressing older brothers and other elders as a sign of respect), *bukbok* (termites), Flips, poke knives, TESOL (Teaching of English to Speaker of Other Languages), or EMRs (Educationally Mentally Retarded) are some of the names given to Filipinos and Filipino-Americans indicative of these stereotypes. The last two terms—TESOL and EMRs—reflect some of the difficulties Filipino immigrant children encounter in school. Because of the initial difficulties in English, many are removed from regular classrooms during a certain period of the day for special instruction in English and are often grouped with others who are classified as educationally mentally retarded. These grouping practices have become socially stigmatizing to the many immigrant children who are inappropriately diagnosed and inappropriately grouped.

Whether the stereotypes are positive or negative, however, they place an added burden on children already confused and hampered by many other aspects of acculturation in American society. In order to avoid the negative stereotypes, many Filipino-Americans choose not to be identified as Filipino-Americans and try to "pass" for Mexican-American, Japanese, Chinese-American, or Hawaiian. Others, when asked, "Are you Filipino-American?" respond by saying, "I'm just an American." This reply sounds noble enough, but often embodies a naive hope of fading into the American mainstream. Typical Filipino-Americans, regardless of how much they may try to be "just an American," remain hyphenated Americans to others because of their high visibility.

There is, however, a noticeably growing pride in being American of Filipino ancestry. This phenomenon has been helped in no small way by affirmative action programs in employment practices, ethnic heritage, and bilingual-bicultural education programs in the schools, and, of course, by the strong trend away from the melting pot concept of cultural assimilation of immigrants toward a culturally pluralistic society where the Anglo model is being replaced or supplemented by various types of more attainable ethnic models.

THE EXTENDED FAMILY SYSTEM

The typical Filipino family in the Philippines is an extended family, usually with three generations living in the same household. Besides grandparents, parents, and minor children, unmarried adult daughters and sons often do not set up households of their own, but remain in their parents homes. Other relatives — aunts, uncles, and cousins — may also live in the same house. Usually, house-workers also share the same family living quarters. The extended family situation, in most instances, is as much an economic necessity as it is a cultural tradition. In a society that has been principally rural and agrarian, the family serves the function that other social agencies serve in more highly urbanized and industrialized societies, e.g., social security, unemployment compensation, Medi-Cal, social welfare, aid for the aged, retirement homes, health and life insurance. Most of these benefits are available in the Philippines, but to a very limited extent. To most Filipinos, the family is not just a haven of family entity and cooperation, but also the only refuge in times of illness, old age, unemployment, loneliness, and for other needs. This phenomenon transcends socioeconomic, educational, and regional differences. Both affluence and poverty are shared by members of the extended family.

The concept of the extended family includes not only blood relations, but also others who have become *compadres* by acting as sponsors at marriage, baptismal, and confirmation ceremonies, or those individuals the family has come to consider family nmembers in less formal ways. Traditional Filipinos and Filipino-Americans tend to view other social institutions as family-type institutions. In jobs, for instance, getting hired or promoted, or receiving a salary increase, is viewed as a favor to be thankful for, not as a reward for a job well done. These benefits are indications of the generosity of

the boss—the parent surrogate—who, in turn, expects from employees something similar to filial loyalty.

The individual works and makes sacrifices for the family. The welfare of the family comes before individual success. A daughter or son, for instance, might postpone marriage indefinitely if the welfare of the family is best served by staying single. A young person in business might refuse a promotion that would mean a transfer to another city or region away from the ancestral home and the extended family. On the other hand, this loyalty to the family could also mean that a young mother of several children accepts a scholarship to go to the United States alone in order to pursue advanced degrees and specialized training in her field because it is viewed as good for the family. A young husband might leave his wife and children and the rest of the family to seek better economic opportunities in the United States as the only way out of the cycle of poverty.

Whether Filipinos come to the United States alone or with only their immediate families, their mentality is still oriented to the extended family. Many Filipino-American families, although nuclear in form, remain extended in their psychology. Many bring their parents and other relatives to the United States at great financial sacrifice. To a great extent, these households mirror their original households in the Philippines. Distance and financial and legal restrictions invariably mean that not all members of the extended family can come to the U.S. Distance, however, does not diminish a Filipino's sense of responsibility for the welfare of those left behind in the Philippines. This help often takes the form of money orders, cash inserted in letters, packages of clothes, household goods, grooming aids, and personal visits to the Philippines, loaded with *pasalubong* (gifts one brings from a trip), as often as economic, political, and other considerations allow.

Relatives and friends visiting from the

Philippines also help in the maintenance of close family ties across the seas. These visitors are often housed, fed, and entertained, often for weeks and months, by their Filipino-American hosts. This arrangement is usually mutually expected. Living in hotels in the Philippines when visiting a hometown may be viewed as insulting to the hospitality and accommodations of friends and relatives. These civilities are observed by visitors to the United States, even when they can afford and prefer to stay in hotels and when doing so might actually be more convenient to the hosts. Traditional Filipino-American hosts, however, welcome these opportunities to catch up on the news at home, be close to the visiting friends and relatives, and to entertain them. The latter is important so that when the visitors return to the Philippines, they will take with them the news that the hosts are doing very well in the U.S. and, even more important, that the hosts have not become haughty and ungrateful. They are still Filipinos!

Subsequent generations of Filipino-Americans may not see these ties to the extended family and close friends from the Philippines as socially and psychologically important. They have their own friends here who may not even be of Filipino ancestry. To them, the constant financial and material assistance to relatives here and abroad may be viewed as dissipation of already limited resources. Questions like, "Why can't they work for what they need?" or comments like, "If you don't send them any money, perhaps they'll be more independent and stop being parasites" are indicative of the lack of comprehension of the cultural context of the situation.

The constant stream of visitors, relatives, and friends, announced and unannounced, is viewed by many U.S.-born Filipino-Americans as intrusion into their privacy, both physical and psychological. Having to share rooms with strangers, crowded households, and being asked "too many personal questions" are common complaints. American emphasis on individual achievement, thus, comes into conflict with traditional Filipino stress on the supremacy of family welfare and the importance of emotional and physical closeness in interpersonal relationships.

AUTHORITY SYSTEM

Traditional Filipino families and other social systems are highly authoritarian. Age, power, prestige, and wealth are the chief sources of authority. Receiving the approval and avoiding the displeasure of authority figures are major concerns in the lives of traditional Filipinos and Filipino-Americans. This concern is socialized in the children early in their lives. Good children obey their parents and other elders. They do not talk back nor do they question authority. Authority flows downward. Older siblings can expect the same respect, deference, and obedience from younger ones. Often when younger siblings address older ones, the honorific word *ale* is used for an older sister and *ate* for an older brother as signs of respect. Thus, Maria is "*aleng* Maria" and Bert is "*ate* Bert" to their younger siblings. Traditional Filipinos kiss the hands of their parents, grandparents, uncles, aunts, *ninongs* and *ninangs* (godparents) when greeting them or in bidding them goodbye. This hierarchical view of authority is best carried out within the extended family. Outside of the family, however, although respect for older persons is traditionally expected of younger ones, other factors supersede age as determining factors in the locus of authority. Social class, and high government and ecclesiastical positions are some of these factors. Young children order maids, chauffeurs, and other servants around. Older employees obey younger but wealthier and more powerful bosses. A young priest is treated with great deference and respect by much older parishioners.

In a society where economic survival and social mobility are strong concerns, power and wealth often transcend age as determinants of the locus of authority. Authority figures enjoy many privileges. Obedience, respect, adulation, gifts in the form of money, material items, and personal service are some of the prerogatives of authority. These gifts are given to seek or return favors or to acknowledge a person's position of authority. The latter ensures favorable attention should the need for attention arise.

Titles are very important to many Filipinos and Filipino-Americans: "I am Captain Gonzales." "Meet Attorney Buendia." "I'd like you to meet my daughter, Dr. Cruz." These titled references are preferred to "Call me Jerry," or "Don't call me Dr. Cuevas. I would much rather be called June."

Respect for authority figures requires the use of much tact in social interactions with them. Use of euphemisms, third parties, and saying "yes" when the opposite is meant, come in handy in avoiding the displeasure or outright wrath and vengeance of the important person. This does not mean, however, that there is no limit to the patience and endurance of traditional Filipinos and Filipino-Americans.

Respect for authority, especially in its traditional manifestations, runs into problems once a Filipino family comes to the U.S. Social, cultural, and occupational dislocations make parents in the new society unsure of themselves, and they are seen by their children as less credible guides in functioning in the new social situations. Cultural discontinuities result. Parents advocate one set of behaviors, while peer groups and the wider society advocate another. A common complaint from children is that their parents do not consider them mature enough to meet with friends outside the home for entertainment and even believe that one must not go on a "date" unchaperoned.

Parents complain that there is less respect among Filipino-Americans. They are dismayed that children have ceased to address their elders as *manong* and *manang*, and that they address older siblings by their first names. Often you hear children bluntly answer "yes" or "no" to their teachers and other elders without saying "ma'am" or "sir." In Philippine classrooms, children stand up when an adult enters the classroom or when called upon to recite. Here, the children remain seated.

Traditional Filipino values come into conflict with the cult of youth and more egalitarian concepts in American society. Immigrant Filipino children, accustomed to highly structured and highly authoritarian classrooms, are usually thought of as shy but good and docile students. Sometimes their shyness is misconstrued as a sign of dullness or mental retardation. These immigrant children find the less restricted atmosphere in American classrooms, especially open classroom situations, unsettling and confusing. Immigrant Filipino teachers find American children "unruly, disobedient, and disrespectful." Thus, the changing context of the nature of authority and privileges is a welcome relief to some and ego shattering to others.

DISCIPLINE AND SANCTIONS

Discipline in traditional Filipino homes depends a great deal on appeals to duties and obligations of family members based on their respective roles as father, mother, oldest son, youngest child, and so on. Traditionally, Filipino children are disciplined by spanking, hitting, scolding, embarrassment through teasing, or reprimanding for being *walang hiya* (shameless), *bastos* (crude), *walang utang na loob* (ungrateful), or for being a source of shame to the family.

Name-calling is another common disciplinary device among adults and children. Derogatory remarks about the person and about other members of the person's family, and calling attention to physical deformities and social deviations are techniques used to punish and to set the offending party straight. Often this disciplinary device takes the form of gossip—a very effective means of social control, especially in closely-knit families and communities.

Indirect methods of discipline which rely more on psychological conditioning and which emphasize positive reinforcement of desired behavior are increasingly being used by parents and are expected by children. Reliance on traditional methods of control through physical coercion and other methods of negative reinforcement, however, constitute another source of conflict between generations of Filipino-Americans.

Traditionally, the mother is the chief dispenser of punishment, especially when the children are young. She spanks, ridicules, and scolds. The mother spends more time with the children, and, therefore, finds more occasions calling for punishment. The father punishes also, but, because he is seldom home, his punishment occurs less frequently. Another reason for the father's less frequent punishment is the children's recognition of his absolute authority. All he usually needs to do is sternly raise his voice or say "Come here!" to keep the children in line. As the children grow older, however, the father takes a more active role, especially in disciplining the sons. Usually, the father does not spank his daughters. His raised voice and stern commands often are still adequate. Besides, for a man to hit a woman or a young girl is viewed as a cultural aberration. In cases where grandparents live in the same household, they are secondary sources of control and often tend to be protective of grandchildren, especially when the punishment meted out by parents becomes harsh and cruel.

In peer group situations, ridicule and physical abuse are not taken lightly. Whether deserved or not, these are embarrassing situations and quite often lead to serious fights. This perhaps partly explains the "poke knife" reputation of Filipinos.

Punishment from teachers is often viewed by parents as deserved, regardless of the children's explanations. Often, the children are punished again when they get home. This attitude has definite limits, however. If the punishment is extreme and parents feel that the family has been shamed by the punishment of the child, parents may confront the teacher and, occasionally, confrontations like this have led to tragedies.

SEXUAL MORES

Most Filipino-American children grow up with minimal direct sex education from parents and other elders. Much of what they know about sex is learned from their peers. Even many of the more Americanized parents avoid any display of affection in the presence of others. This display is considered vulgar and "too American." Ironically, among traditional Filipinos, holding hands, hugging, and touching among those of the same sex and between children and the aged, regardless of sex, are viewed as normal. As the children grow up, the norms of the peer group and those of the wider society are the exact opposites of the norms they have been socialized in. The same behavior with those of the same sex is perverse.

The traditional chaperone of young women when they go out on dates, and the practice of young women entertaining their men friends at home so that parents, especially mothers, can keep track of their activities, come into very serious conflicts with the more permissive expectations of the young male adult and his peers. The double standards are traditionally justified in parents' expectations of their children, especially in matters of sexual behavior: "A girl is like a mirror: Once broken, it cannot be put together again." But, "Boys are boys regardless of what they do."

A basic traditional Filipino assumption is that dating and all activities related to it should have one basic purpose—choosing a marriage partner. The entertainment and socializing aspects of dating are viewed as incidental, frivolous, and may, in the process, render the young people, especially daughters, unfit for marriage. Dating one young man after another, for instance, despite the fact that no sexual relations are engaged in, is viewed as promiscuous and immoral: "No decent man will marry that kind of girl."

A great concern to parents is that the good reputation of daughters be maintained. Daughters should not give any occasion for gossip which casts aspersions on their chastity and, therefore, their fitness for marriage. Concern for the sons is that they do not find themselves in a position where they have to get married and forgo educational and career plans.

Often the parents realize the nature and source of the conflicts. They are not ignorant of the "new morality." They see illustrations on television and in the movies. They observe young men and women in open displays of affection in parks, on the streets, in parked cars, on school campuses, on the beaches, and in other public places. All these observations, however, only tend to reinforce the stereotype many Filipino immigrants have grown up with that Americans are morally decadent.

At one extreme of this conflict, overly strict parents insist on knowing what their children are doing when in the company of the opposite sex, on chaperoning by either parent or by brother or sister, and on strict curfew hours. At the other extreme, many parents helplessly and painfully abandon all traditional restrictions as old-world irrevelancies. This leaves a moral void at home—a void which is immediately filled by the norms of the peer group.

RELIGION

Most Filipinos and Filipino-Americans are Catholics. Some are very devout, practicing Catholics. They attend Mass every Sunday and on other holy days of obligation, receive the sacraments, and govern their lives according to the church's teachings. Many, however, are nominal Catholics with little understanding of Catholic theology, say the prayers in rote recitation, and go through the rituals and ceremonies in church perfunctorily. To many, church occasions have come to mean nothing more than sociocultural events with little religious significance attached to them. Children have to be baptized, one has to attend Mass on Sundays and other holy days of obligation, and one has to marry in the church and die with the church's blessings. More importantly, however, these are occasions for celebrations when Filipino-Americans get together, catch up on the news "back home," eat Filipino food, and just have a good time with other Filipino-Americans. In comparison to the role played by the family and peer group, the church plays a very minor role in children's lives as a source of ideological development or as an agent of social control. This role becomes more and more limited as the children grow older and the peer group influence increases. Generational conflicts result from generational differences in religious beliefs and from parental demands for children to continue the rituals and ceremonies that carry neither the religious nor the sociocultural meaning they have carried for the older generations.

OPTIMISTIC FATALISM

Filipino immigrants to the United States are driven by the search for economic betterment, material well-being, and social mobility. The fact that they left homeland and extended families to come to the United States attests to these overwhelming concerns. Their behavior defies traditional descriptions of Filipinos as fatalists. They work hard on improving their lots. They send their children to school at great personal sacrifice. Often, both parents work and save to buy their own car, house, and household conveniences. They run small family businesses to supplement family income. They buy and lease apartment houses. They shop for bargains and emphasize saving and investing. In these respects, they are thoroughly middle class. On the other hand, their optimism about achieving success through hard work and personal sacrifice is curiously blended with a certain fatalism that class and racial barriers will result in unequal rewards for similar efforts.

Filipinos historically occupied the lower rungs of the socioeconomic ladder during Spanish and American regimes and Japanese occupation and have experienced the rigid social structure of the modern Philippines. They have seen how their hard work and personal sacrifice have often meant more prosperity for their masters and only more work and sacrifice for themselves. These experiences have instilled in Filipinos a philosophical attitude that cushions them from disappointments. They work hard but realize that social recognition and economic reward for their efforts are at the disposition of the socioeconomic elite. Their experiences in the Philippines have been reinforced in the United States where racism, overt or covert, again reminds immigrants of their "proper places."

That which is often viewed as fatalism is really Filipino-Americans' realistic assessments of and coping with limitations imposed by outside realities, much of which they see as beyond their abilities to change. The attitude that one should work as if everything depends on it, while also being resigned to and grateful for any recognition and reward that may come one's way, can best be described as optimistic fatalism. This attitude, however, runs counter to the younger generations' militant demands for equal pay for equal work and other egalitarian concerns.

COMPETITIVE SPIRIT

Filipino and Filipino-Americans are very highly competitive. Often, the object of the competition is not as important as winning, regardless of the prize. Winning and losing are not usually viewed as an individual's victory or defeat, but as a source of pride or disgrace for the whole family.

When a father in the Philippines ran amok because his son had lost an oratorical contest, one Peace Corps volunteer said, "I don't understand how winning an oratorical contest could be that important." What the volunteer did not realize was that it was not the oratorical contest, but winning it, that was important. It could very well have been a fly-swatting contest. This competitive spirit extends to most other aspects of personal, family, and social life. It is important to get good grades and other academic honors, win athletic competitions, beauty contests, and accumulate as many success symbols as possible. This emphasis on winning encourages high aspirations and great personal sacrifices to achieve it. Families, for instance, would sell precious farmland, sell other properties, and get into heavy debt to ensure a daughter's winning a beauty contest. A student with limited financial resources would work all day and study at night and forgo many basic necessities in order to obtain a college degree.

On the other hand, the fear of losing discourages many from taking risks or trying out new ventures. Because so much is invested in winning, avoiding defeat is less risky than trying to win only to end up losing. One competes only when reasonably certain to win. At its worst, this attitude encourages the use of deceit, coercion, and other devious ways to ensure victory and avoid disgrace. This competitive spirit seems to be more prevalent among immigrant Filipinos than among

U.S.-born. It could very well be that the built-in screening devices of the immigration process heavily favor the ambitious, the industrious, and the achievement-oriented. Thus, the locally born often accuse immigrant Filipinos of being "social climbers."

GENERATIONAL PERSPECTIVES ON THE GOOD LIFE

Despite many initial and often persistent racial, social, and cultural adversities, Filipino immigrants tend to see their present lot as economically and materially much better than the one they left behind in the Philippines. Setbacks in the United States, regardless of duration, are seen as temporary. These immigrants optimistically believe that eventually things will be better. Radical discontent with existing socioeconomic and political structures is least manifested in this generation of Filipino-Americans. This optimism is important, if only to validate the great sacrifices immigrants had to make for years in order to come to the United States. Those who would complain about low wages here remember they were paid much less at home. And if there are educational and socioeconomic inequities here, they were certainly worse back home. One should be grateful to Americans for better homes, better schools, more job opportunities and security, higher incomes, more material well-being, greater socioeconomic and geographic mobility, and the ability to help those left behind in the Philippines.

Long-time resident Filipino-Americans in the United States and American-born Filipino-Americans, however, have a different perspective. Much of what they know of the good life is what they have had in the United States, and they cannot compare it with what was, but only with what could and should be. As the younger generation sees the disproportionate number of Filipino-American youth dropping out of school, and many Filipino-Ameri-

cans unemployed, paid low wages, and subtly or overtly discriminated against in housing, interpersonal relations, and other areas of day-to-day life, they cannot make sense of their parents' and other elders' advice to be patient and hope that the next generation will have it better. The young accuse their elders of colonial mentality, and the elders accuse the young of being impatient *walang hiya* (shameless), and *walang utang na loob* (ungrateful).

SOJOURNER'S MENTALITY

Among many immigrant Filipinos in the United States, there is a very marked sojourner's mentality. They are convinced that they are here only temporarily, despite the fact that they may have been here for years. Many become permanent residents out of expediency. Permanent residence eases entry and reentry into the United States, facilitates access to employment, social security, welfare, Medi-Care, aid for the aged, and other social and economic benefits. Many do not become U.S. citizens. This mentality serves the immigrant in several ways. Psychologically, it lessens the feeling of having left forever the home country, relatives, and friends. Citizenship in the new country would make the move seem final and, to many, traumatic. This mentality also provides a psychological cushion for the immigrants in times of failure. They rationalize that disappointment is of little significance because they will be going home someday anyway. This mentality is often reinforced, if not caused, by immigrants' feelings of not fully belonging to the new country and of not really being fully American because of skin color, language difficulties, and other conflicts mentioned earlier. Although America is the place to be for economic and material gain, some immigrants look back to the old country as where they really belong psychologically, socially, and culturally. An oft-repeated dream of the psychological sojourner is to retire in the Philippines. Ironically, the more alienated immigrants feel, the stronger their sojourner's mentality, which in turn leads to greater alienation. This mentality slows down the process of acculturation and assimilation of the immigrant into American society. Most Filipino-Americans refer to themselves and other Filipino-Americans simply as Filipinos.

Despite the fact, however, that many immigrants may have difficulties in considering the United States their home, they realize and accept the fact that their children are Americans who consider the United States as their home. In fact, the parents would not have it any other way. There are no regrets, but only pride in their children being Americans. And yet, unable to forget Filipino customs and traditions and not fully attuned to prevailing American customs, immigrant parents see themselves in many ways raising their own children as strangers.

THE VALUE OF EDUCATION

Filipinos and Filipino-Americans view schooling as of utmost importance for their children. They see education as a passport to good jobs, economic security, social acceptance, and as a way out of a cycle of poverty and lower-class status, not only for their children, but for the whole family. Degrees, diplomas, certificates, good grades, and academic honors are much sought-after symbols. In the Philippines, parents often go into heavy debt and sell property in order to ensure that at least one of their children, usually the eldest, gets a college degree. The rest of the family engage in domestic and farm work and skimp and scrape to enable the chosen daughter or son to go to the city and work for a degree. Education, then, is not an individual but a family concern,

not primarily for culture and enlightenment, but as an economic investment. Once graduated and employed, the graduate has the responsibility of helping the parents and financing the education of the next child. The next child is then responsible for the next, and so on. This practice prevents the dissipation of the limited family financial resources. Dividing these resources equally among the many siblings would mean lower educational attainment for all, which, in turn, would mean no change in the social and economic status of the family. While this practice takes the son or daughter much further educationally and professionally, the debt of gratitude incurred to the whole family is a powerful safeguard in ensuring the graduate's contribution to family welfare. Family welfare then takes precedence over individual economic and social mobility. A violation of this unwritten code of *utang na loob* (debt of gratitude) could make the graduate an outcast from the family as *walang hiya* (shameless) and *walang utang na loob* (ungrateful).

Increased accessibility to free or inexpensive schooling, better economic circumstances, and the availability of more social agencies that provide for the needs of individuals and families in the United States, eliminate much of the need for the traditional system of mutual help. However, the prime importance given to schooling, good grades, and good behavior remains. These emphases result in teachers' and school administrators' evaluations of Filipino-American students as well-behaved, good students who never cause any trouble. These accolades are given especially to recently immigrated children. "The problem is," one school principal complains, "the longer they stay in this country, especially the boys, the more terrible they get. The girls, however, tend to remain good students."

CHAPTER 8

The Growth and Development of Korean-American Children

Keun H. Yu, M.D. and

Luke I.C. Kim, M.D., Ph.D.

Recent studies of Asian Americans have emphasized cultural and historical forces such as acculturation, racism and value transmission as crucially important factors influencing the psychosocial functioning of Asian-Americans (Park, 1976; Man, 1976; Sue and Wagner, 1973; Yoon, 1970). All too often, current research has focused on Asian adults, mostly Chinese and Japanese. A thorough search for literature on Asian children yielded only a few fragmented comments and articles here and there. The paucity of literature on Korean children in the U.S. presents problems in the empirical validation of much of the content of this chapter. Comforted by the "good old" Oriental deductive approach to the search for truth, we have attempted to collect and synthesize the available material with our own, in hopes of exploring the current status of Korean children in America.

We are interested in exploring ways in which the Korean children's adaptation to this alien culture meshes with their Korean cultural heritage; the mastery of their developmental tasks and vulnerability peculiar to Korean children; and some of the hypotheses concerning the psychosocial and personality development of Korean children.

All children of Korean lineage will be collectively referred to as "Korean children," whether they be American-born, Korean-born, or adopted, as long as they have at least one full Korean biological parent. The theoretical framework adopted in this chapter is eclectic, drawing from epigenetic (E. Erikson), psychosexual (A. and S. Freud), sociological, educational, and psychometric approaches.

Korean children are, of course, in different stages of their adjustment and acculturation, but their psychosocial development can best be studied within the framework of normal child growth and development: a group of normal children who happen to be thrust into special sets of circumstances, being displaced into an unfamiliar, strange and new environment as a result of their parents' immigration to the United States. After all, they are children, with an inherent capacity for resiliency and adaptability, as is the case with any other ethnic group of children.

In preparing this chapter, we conducted four surveys in order to compensate for the serious deficits in the existing literature.

Survey I: A survey was conducted by random selection among Korean parents residing in the Washington-Baltimore area during 1976-77, utilizing a questionnaire in which the parents were asked 20 unstructured, essay-type items inquiring into various facets of their children's educational, psychological, and cultural problems and assets. Fifty parents responded and the data will be discussed throughout this chapter.

Survey II: Personal interviews were conducted with school teachers in primary and secondary schools in the Washington-Baltimore area, inquiring into the teachers' experiences, opinions, and subjective appraisals of the Korean children in their classes. Twenty-five teachers were interviewed for this purpose.

Survey III: Personal interviews were conducted with 10 American-born second and third generation Korean young adults in the San Francisco area concerning their subjective experiences of childhood, peer group relationships, family life, school, bicultural and bilingual issues, ethnic identity issues, etc.

Survey IV: Verbal and written inquiries were made of pediatricians in various parts of the United States and Korea with regard to their assessment of physical health and growth of Korean children. Ten pediatricians participated in this survey.

KOREANS IN AMERICA

After the first wave of Korean immigration in 1902–1905 to the end of the Second World War, the Korean population in the U.S. remained static at between 3,000 to 6,000, with a heavy concentration in Hawaii. In the nine years from 1945 to 1956, approximately 4,000 Koreans, mostly students, entered the U.S. Since then, the Korean population has swelled at an accelerated pace, approaching 600,000 by recent estimates. Since the relaxation of immigration laws in 1965, about 15,000 Koreans a year, mostly educated or skilled blue-collar workers, have emigrated to the U.S. (Lee, C.S., 1975). More than 90% of Koreans currently residing in the U.S. are recent immigrants, having arrived here within the past 5–15 years. This figure alone suggests that the largest target population of those Koreans who may need social and mental health services, as well as child guidance, would be among recent immigrants. Of Korean immigrants who arrived since 1970, 24% are nine years or younger. According to a study of Asian-Americans in the Chicago area (Kim and Condon, 1975), almost 70% of Korean families have children under the age of 10 years, with the majority of these being under five years old. This makes all the more compelling the need to study and find ways in which the Korean children can make satisfactory adjustment and adaptation in this country.

The median number of children in the Korean families is 2.5. A higher proportion of Korean adults have completed high school and college than the U.S. population as a whole. In 1970, the average income of the Korean family exceeded the national average. It is noteworthy that Koreans in the U.S. are more widely dispersed in their settlement patterns than other Asian groups (Chan et al., 1975). In 1976, it was found that 44% of Koreans live on the West Coast, 20% in the Northeast, 19% in the Midwest, and 17% in the South.

General understanding of Korean people by the American public has improved over the years, although a perception of Koreans might be still colored at times by the ambivalent or negative feelings once experienced by some Americans about the Korean War. Unfortunately, even today, many Americans believe the myth that Koreans are hybrid or mixed-blooded Chinese and Japanese. The implication that Korean ethnicity occupies an inferior status should not be underestimated. At the same time, the difference of Korean ethnicity from majority Americans must not be overstressed when considering the psychosocial development of Korean children.

Most Koreans are profoundly proud of their natural heritage, rich culture, romantic language and distinctive history of nearly 5,000 years. They love leisure, art and poetry; they love music and love to sing. While they can be temperamental and stubborn at times, earning the expression "Oriental Irishmen," Koreans have an unusually strong will to survive and determination to succeed which have served them well in facing various historical hardships and individual adversities (Chung and Rieckelman, 1974). The struggle of early Korean immigrants in the United States during the first half of the century reveals their immense pride in and dedication to the Korean people, Korean culture, and the Korean Independence Movement (1902–1945).

CHILDREARING PRACTICES IN KOREA

Traditional, native Korean childrearing practices will be described. When a baby is born in Korea, no visitors are allowed to enter the house while the mother is nursing for the first weeks. Even after the first month, the social life of the mother outside of the house is curtailed. The alleged reason for this custom is fear of a contamination of the newborn by germs. This particular custom has a more significant meaning beyond the "germ theory," in that it allows the new mother to pay exclusive attention to the infant's needs through this institutionalized mother-infant togetherness.

Most mothers breast-feed the baby and feed as much and as frequently as the baby demands, without feeding schedules. Weaning is usually quite casual, normally occuring at any time between six and eighteen months. Not uncommonly, breast-feeding continues into three years of age. During this prolonged period of nursing, the mother tends to be overindulgent and pampering of the baby. It seems at times the breasts are used to pacify the infant's rage.

Toilet training is casually introduced to the baby. In the rich and colorful vocabulary of the Korean language, there are no words for toilet training. The Korean parents do attempt to toilet train the child, but no strict demands or harsh measures are practiced. There is no evidence, however, that the toilet training of Korean children is unusually delayed or any more troublesome than for American children.

Another characteristic of the Korean mode of childrearing is the age-old custom in which the baby is wrapped in a shawl or blanket, strapped around the mother's back and carried piggyback. The infant spends a good deal of time on the mother's back while the mother performs domestic or farming duties. The "piggyback" years last variously from one to five years of age. In view of some recent research findings that rocking and kinetic movement of the infant may be essential for facilitating the maturational process of the nervous system, the built-in rocking movement of the piggyback custom seems to indicate intuitive wisdom (Osofsky and Danzger, 1974; Roberts and Thomson, 1976).

As for the sleeping arrangements of Korean babies, most of them sleep in the same room with their parents and other siblings until about five years of age, and some of them until 10 years or older. This practice may sound incredible to Americans in view of possible incestuous connotations in the child's psychosexual development. However, there is no evidence to show that any untoward psychological or psychosexual problems have resulted from this practice (Yu, 1972). Korean mothers are generally reluctant to leave their children with a baby-sitter, unless the baby-sitter is a member of the extended family. They fear that a stranger-baby-sitter may upset the close mother-infant relationship and security of the baby.

When a child reaches six years of age, the parental and social attitude toward the child shifts dramatically from that of indulgence and permissiveness to that of parental prohibition. Strict rules and moral codes are introduced into the life of the child. These rules are practiced repeatedly until it becomes a habit to obey for the child. The child is expected to learn through obedience. The demands are gentle at first when the child is still young, but increasingly firm demands are made as the child matures and advances in school age. However, the overall approach is still one of gentleness.

Confucian philosophy is deeply imbedded in the Korean view of family. Filial respect and ancestor worship are often imposed on the child even before the child can comprehend the reason for them. The child learns that the family is the most important symbol in life and that the preservation of pride and dignity of the family name is regarded as an important duty. The father is the authority figure in the household. A child is not permitted to talk back or disobey. This obedience to the patriarchal family structure is usually ex-

tended to authority figures in school, community, and government. Status, proper protocol and honorific forms of language are stressed in the hierarchical society. The child is publicly shamed and disgraced when he/she violates the code of ethics, resulting in a "loss of face" for his/her family. Due to the patriarchal orientation of the society, the birth of male children and sibling rank become very important. The eldest son customarily inherits the family assets and assumes the major responsibility for supporting his parents and younger siblings. In sum, Confucian ideas and centuries-old cultural conditioning produced a social system with the pattern of submission of individual to the family, of the young to the old, and of woman to man.

Koreans have great respect for learning. Korean school children are under tremendous pressure for high academic achievement in order to be accepted to an "elite" high school or college. Many Korean children study long hours at home after school, with or without a private tutor. The sixth graders and twelfth graders spend most of their time studying in preparation for entrance examinations, with little time left for sports and recreational activities. Trauma and the loss of face ensue when he or she fails in the entrance examination, and this poses a serious social, educational and emotional problem which the Korean child may have to face.

Sex education for pubescent children has been virtually nonexistent. Sexual strivings are generally suppressed and the adolescents are frequently encouraged to sublimate them into school achievement or helping parents with agrarian and domestic chores. Dating is prohibited or under close scrutiny if permitted. Marriage through matchmaking arrangements is still common.

With the introduction of democratic ideals to Korea by the United States after the Second World War, the traditional Korean values have given way gradually to westernization, especially among urban, college-educated Koreans, who have become increasingly individual-oriented. However, traditional value and belief systems still persist and prevail, especially in marriage and family life.

Based on the analysis of traditional Korean childrearing practices, we can draw the following tentative inferences important to the psychosocial development of the Korean child:

1) Basic trust and solid object relationship may be assured by well-nurtured infancy.
2) Prolonged infancy and late resolution of the separation-individuation phase of development is likely to result in psychological dependency and interdependency.
3) Overemphasis on obedience and conformity may hinder developing self-reliance. It may develop a child who functions optimally more in structured settings than in unstructured settings.
4) Shame and disgrace may be the main methods of social and parental control. This is in contrast to the use of guilt in the Judeo-Christian culture. Shame and disgrace may foster the child's need for acceptance and sensitivity to approval and disapproval.
5) Because of constant stress on loyalty to family, partners, and friends, any betrayal of the loyalty may hurt the child severely. This may partially explain why casual dating with different partners is difficult for Korean teenagers.
6) Due to the parents' struggle for survival through the drastic and turbulent periods of social change in Korea, the child may perceive the environment as being hostile, difficult, and unpredictable. A fear of an unpredictable future in Korea as well as a desire for better opportunity for their children has motivated many middle-class, educated Koreans to emigrate to the United States, and this may influence the Korean children's perception and planning of their future.
7) The "surface-passivity" (Yu, 1973) of some Koreans may not be interpreted as weakness or "Oriental inscrutability," but merely a defensive posture toward potential agressors and a "wait and see" attitude toward the new situations or strangers.

DEVELOPMENT OF KOREAN CHILDREN IN THE UNITED STATES

As a culture passes from one generation to the next, so are childrearing practices transmitted, not only between generations but from one locus of settlement to another. We are well aware that many early immigrants to America from diverse ethnic origins maintain their own indigenous cultural life-style for quite some time before attempting to adopt a new way. This is particularly true with Korean immigrants, whose mother culture had provided them with a well-serving cohesive structure for living, including clearcut behavioral norms and guidelines.

For no other reason than their familiarity with the original cultural heritage, and perhaps their desire to have the children maintain the Korean culture, most Korean parents residing now in the United States, especially recent immigrants, raise their children in a manner similar to traditional Korean childrearing.

Our Survey I revealed that most Korean parents had to reexamine their own methods and adopt some of the useful childrearing practices the host culture offers. However, some parents expressed concerns and mixed feelings about the American way of childrearing and wondered what would be the best way to raise a child in this country.

Almost all of our subjects were the biological parents of the children. The Asian-American study in the Chicago area (Kim and Condon, 1975) shows that 88% of adult Koreans are married (with a very low divorce rate), therefore the great majority of Korean children among Korean families in the United States live with both their biological parents. Such stable family life is considered to be a most positive asset for the children in the training of growth-promoting values and emotional stability. Many Korean parents are deliberate in planning children due to their awareness of the high emotional and economic costs of child care in the United States.

From our Survey I, the following picture of Korean childrearing in the United States emerges: Infancy is characterized by tender, loving maternal care, with about 40% of Korean mothers breast-feeding. Although one half of the mothers have out-of-home jobs, most show reluctance in leaving their infants in the care of baby-sitters or infant care centers. A most common solution is for the mother to bring her own mother or mother-in-law from Korea to stay with the family as a built-in baby caretaker. While this kind of arrangement causes considerable inconvenience and difficulty in terms of in-law conflicts and lack of privacy, many Koreans still prefer it to having the baby taken care of by an "outside" baby-sitter or in a day care center.

Toilet training is somewhat less casual than in Korea. This is probably due to the American housing structure which has less constraint and more ready access to the use of the toilet and therefore makes it easier for the parents to formalize demands on toilet training. About 20% of mothers reported some difficulty in toilet training the toddlers.

Sleeping arrangements appear to create some tension for both parents and babies, owing to the separate bedroom arrangement of American housing. No accurate statistics are available at present, but an educated guess would be that 10 to 20% of infants still sleep with parents in the same room. Putting the baby in the crib in another room seems unnatural to some parents and they may feel guilt or anxiety

in doing so. The American custom of separating the infant from the mother during the night beginning at two or three weeks of age may have considerable theoretical as well as clinical implications in terms of psychological and personality development in light of Spitz's (1950, 1965) and Bowlby's (1969) studies on newborn babies and the processes needed for adequate bonding and attachment between the mother and young infant. Further study is needed to throw light on the relationship between sleep arrangements and emotional development of the infant.

The preschool period is characterized by task-oriented mother-child social interplay emphasizing language development. A study done in 1970 reported that about 50% of American-born and 90% foreign-born Koreans listed Korean as their first language (Asian-Americans: Facts and Figures, 1975). Our Survey I data from 50 parents' answers on language development shows that the majority of the children begin to learn Korean as the first language as the mother interacts with the baby. Then two patterns emerge as the child grows into the preschool years. One group continues to use and expand their proficiency in Korean, while acquiring the English language at the same time (the bilingual group); the other group uses less and less Korean in proportion to their acquisition of English, so that, by the time they enter the elementary school, their residual Korean no longer serves a communicative purpose except for understanding some spoken Korean (the monolingual group). The bilingual group seems to develop both languages in verbal and written form without apparent loss of proficiency in either language.

The determining factors between the two groups are not clear. One observation is that the bilingual group is more likely to come from a large extended family including multigenerations or from a family residing in a neighborhood populated by Koreans. Social reenforcement and parental encouragement may be necessary to maintaining the Korean language. Some parents expressed concern and inquired as to whether the bilingual and bicultural orientation is conflictual or complementary to the overall development of the child, including academic achievements requiring English skills (Cummins 1979, 1980). There is no empirical data to answer this simple yet important question (Cummins 1979, 1980). Ultimately, a longitudinal study will be needed to answer this question. Our impression is that bilingual and bicultural children have the advantage of being able to establish a more positive ethnic self-identity and self-acceptance as well as being able to appreciate bicultural enrichment in later years. A problem of the monolingual group that is often presented as a complaint by both the parents and older children is that there is a considerable communication gap between the Korean-speaking parents and English-speaking teens, creating emotional distance between them.

In terms of cognitive development and learning style of Asian-American children, studies have shown that Chinese-American mothers offer significantly less input to their children than Anglo-American mothers in terms of number of teaching loops initiated and completed, but give more enthusiastic positive feedback than the American mothers (Chan et al., 1975). This was further verified by Steward and Steward (1973). It is likely that a similar interactional pattern occurs between Korean mothers and their preschoolers. As far as verbal facility is concerned, many observers commented on a relatively low level of verbal communication and more reliance on nonverbal, implicit modes of communication between the Asian mother and child. This may account for low scores in verbal expression in language development among Asian children, and the tendency for Asian students to go into technical, scientific fields rather than liberal arts. Greater attention needs to be directed toward encouraging and cultivating verbal communication, expressive

language skill and ability to articulate among Korean children so that they may be able to compete and succeed better in the American society which is characterized as a verbal culture.

LeVine (1970) has reviewed a large number of cross-cultural studies of children's cognitive development and concluded that unthinking obedience and passive learning styles often result in the inhibition of cognitive performance. The preliminary report of the UCLA Asian-American Education Project (Chan et al., 1975) has not supported Levine's assertion and has concluded that the cognitive style, conceptual tempo, psychomotor and visual perceptual discrimination of Korean (Asian) children are equal to the American children's norm, except for a possible lower score in certain language functions, i.e., expressive type. Various other intelligence and achievement test scores of Asian children point to insignificant differences between the Asian group and the American group.

Our interview data with 25 school teachers who have had one or more Korean pupils in their classes (Survey II) shows a strong tendency to stereotype Korean students as being "quiet, obedient, respectful, studious and generally very likeable." Some noted that some Korean students are less verbally expressive, less assertive, more sensitive to approval and less self-confident than their Caucasian counterparts. Almost unanimously, teachers commented that Korean children seem emotionally "stable" and thrive on academic work, responding well to concrete and specific instructions. These descriptions are not surprising in view of Korean childrearing practices and the cultural emphases. It is important for teachers to understand that these are culturally determined behaviors, and to get to know the children in the classroom, even if they appear quiet and unresponsive (Kim, 1977).

Peer relationships and social behavior of Korean students appear to go smoothly, once they have overcome initial culture shock and "newness anxiety." Most Korean students, American-born or foreign-born, eventually become conscious of their physical appearance and skin color at some point (Lee, D.C., 1975). Some Korean children view their Asian features negatively and even perceive their physical characteristics as ugly, inferior or shameful. This negative perception may be reenforced by a teasing peer group. Some children overreact to being teased, while others may resent being Asian. A mother reported that her child asked her to dye his hair brunette or blond. By the age of seven, most Korean children seem to come to grips with this problem and arrive at some kind of internal resolution. However, some have not been able to resolve this dilemma, thus affecting their personality function or adjustment (Annual Report of Korean Mental Health, 1975; Annual Service Reports, 1977–1981).

Another interesting area is the Korean father's role in childrearing. Korean fathers traditionally show a great reluctance in participating in child care. Especially in Korea, this is considered an "unmasculine" role. However, all indications are that most Korean fathers in the United States contribute significantly to child care and helping their wives (Survey I). Whether they are willing to do so based on the awareness of a need for more equalitarian roles between husband and wife, or whether they are performing the "womanly" chores out of necessity due to the wives' employment, the fact is that they are doing more chores, i.e., drying the dishes or changing the diapers, than they do in Korea. With Korean wives becoming more liberated and assertive after immigration to the United States, some Korean husbands feel they have to double the effort to "control" the wife; others may become depressed and irritable, or become submissive. The changing sex role in husband-wife relationships, and its influence on childrearing patterns of Korean families living in America will be an interesting phenomenon to study and observe.

Professional help sought from the Korean Mental Health Clinic in Los Angeles was related to marital problems in more than half of all cases, and the new tension created in the marriage with the changing role of the husband and wife was attributed to be the main reason (Annual Report of Korean Mental Health, 1975; Annual Service Reports, 1977–1981).

ADOLESCENT DEVELOPMENT OF KOREAN YOUTH IN THE UNITED STATES

On the surface, most Korean teenagers go through a much less turbulent adolescent period than their American counterparts. While 90% of Korean parents in our Survey I expressed concerns regarding their adolescent children's possible problems with sexual morals, juvenile delinquency, drinking and drug abuse, and disrespect towards parents, only about 5% of them actually reported any major problems with their adolescent children. Korean parents tend to worry about their adolescent children, especially girls, with the fear that sexual morality is too "loose" and their teenagers are trying to assert independence too soon in America. Dating is a frequently recurring topic causing conflict between the Korean parents and their adolescent daughters. Conflict becomes intense when the adolescent wants to be independent and rapidly aspires to adopt American norms of dating while the parents insist on the strict traditional Korean values, each without any effort to accommodate to the other. Korean youth may or may not want to talk about their ethnic roots, but Korean parents tend to dwell on them, while American parents usually do not. The Korean parents usually maintain lofty, idealistic views of their cultural values and heritage and want to impose these on their youth.

It would be fair to say that Korean adolescents do experience a considerable amount of internal tension and turmoil beneath their quiet facade, partly arising from the pressure of their rather rigid and demanding parents and partly from self-doubt and insecurity related to peer group acceptance. This is true for any adolescent to some degree; however, it is intensified for Korean adolescents having immigrant parents.

In this connection, Korean youth are faced with a double dilemma: the absence of a sense of belonging to a vital and nourishing emotional milieu of contemporary American society, and a sense of disconnectedness with their own original ethnic heritage. It is not that Korean youth are unaffected by the original cultural and historical elements which formerly served them well within the group life of the family. Indeed, such elements may be too often present in their mental life. But now they are felt to be irrelevant or inadequate to the perceived demands of complex American society. At the same time they have to deal with the parents as confused mediators of old and new cultures. Parents may seem useless to them in their attempt to assimilate into the new culture, since many Korean parents do not and cannot represent the contemporary American value system. After all, some of the "Oriental culture things" they have tried, at times led to embarrassment or even debilitation. This may be the final blow leading them to disown their parents' culture.

Based on the parents questionnaire in Survey I, three patterns of identity formation can be described. The patterns tend to be correlated with a number of variables, such as with the length of residence in the United States and age at the time of immigration:

1) Full Korean Identity: Those who identified themselves as "full" Korean, but who happen to live in a new country because of parents' immigration.

2) Korean-American Identity: Those who consider themselves as assimilated, acculturated. They wish to retain positive values from both cultures while they strive to participate as fully as possible in the American mainstream. While there is a pitfall of falling into a "marginal" position, this group seems to be the most energetic and ambitious.

3) Full American Identity: Though few in number, they identify themselves as sufficiently Americanized and generally resent Asian physical characteristics. They tend to dissociate themselves from fellow Koreans socially and wish to bury or deny Korean cultural values.

While the second category, the Korean-American Identity, seemingly offers a better adaptive posture than the other two, further research in this crucial area is needed for guiding both Korean parents and their children. It is noteworthy that many Korean parents in our survey were interested in aiding the youth in the struggle for identity formation. Most parents are doing this by encouraging more family input and interaction, giving the youth a renewed sense of love and caring, and promoting close family relationships. This intrafamily approach seems to us unique and promising, in contrast to the social approach adopted by Black and other minority groups in the search for positive ethnic identification (i.e., "Black is beautiful").

So far our discussion has focused on immigrant parents and their foreign-born children. When we direct our attention to American-born, second and third generation adolescents or adults of Korean descent, we discover even more painful growing processes in terms of having been subjected to various forms of institutionalized discrimination, especially during the first quarter of the century. They not only had to contend with constant "Chink Chong Chinaman" since the earliest time they could remember, but also had to explain their ancestral origin and the geographical location of Korea whenever they encountered the question "Are you Japanese or Chinese?" Nobody seemed to have heard of Korea prior to the Korean War. Our interview subjects in California (Survey III) also recounted childhood experiences in which they were discriminated against by other Asians as well as by whites. They were a minority among minorities. Believing that this is the land of "melting pot" and citizenry based on birthright, they believed they were full-fledged Americans, having lived in this country for three generations. A third generation Korean interviewee described how emotionally humiliated and disillusioned he was when someone remarked to him, "You speak English well; how long have you been in this country?"

It is interesting and heartening that, following the ethnic awareness movement, many American-born second and third generation Koreans began searching for their "roots," rediscovering their cultural heritage, and learning the Korean language. Some Korean-American college students even went to Korea to study at a Korean university in an attempt to get acquainted with their own native culture and resolve their identity conflicts. It is heartening to see that the second and third generation Korean-Americans in San Francisco, for example, are dedicated and enthusiastic about working within Korean communities and helping to resolve the unemployment, bilingual education, and mental health problems of recent Korean immigrants, in spite of some language barrier between them.

KOREAN CHILDREN ADOPTED BY AMERICAN FAMILIES

More than 32,000 Korean children were adopted by American families from 1953 to 1974, and many more are being adopted each year (Annual Reports of Holt Adoption Program, 1974). This unparalleled massive number of foreign children being raised by adoptive American parents is a fascinating subject that will provide opportunities to study interracial and cross-cultural childrearing and the psychosocial development of these children.

The first nationwide research on long-term outcome of these adopted Korean children was recently conducted by Dong Soo Kim (1976). These children were typically placed with middle-class, white, Protestant families residing in rural areas or small cities. The families were generally not without children and, in fact, had an average of two children of their own. The family characteristics of the adoptive parents appear to be solid and stable in marriage, somewhat conservative and very religiously oriented.

In reporting on self-concept formation, Kim stated, "In general, the Korean adopted children had a relatively little Korean identity." Even when they were placed in American homes at school age, they tended to lose their Korean cultural patterns rapidly and to identify themselves as "American" or more frequently, as "Korean-American," with little reference to their racial background. As a whole, their self-concepts were remarkably similar to those of other American youth. In short, the racial background and cultural identification of the adopted Korean children had no impact on self-concept formation, although the children older at the time of placement tended to retain Korean cultural factors slightly more than the children adopted before one year of age. Based on their own responses, they seem to be generally quite happy with their new life situations and do very well academically.

According to this study, the Korean adopted children, as a whole, have achieved fairly normal growth and functioning levels, comparable with those of other adolescents in American society.

PHYSICAL GROWTH AND DEVELOPMENT OF KOREAN CHILDREN

Korean children grow and develop physically in as predictable a pattern as any other group of children. Native Korean children tend to be short and small like other Asian children. Second and third generation Korean children, however, demonstrate a significant upward trend in growth pattern, sometimes becoming nearly as big and tall as their American counterparts.

The individual growth of the Korean children is determined by an interplay of hereditary and environmental factors, such as physical and emotional surroundings, quality of nurturing, nutritional, and socioeconomic factors.

Most pregnant Korean mothers appear to have satisfactory prenatal care and follow the obstetrician's instructions, either on a private basis or through public health facilities.

Average birth weight and height of newborn Korean-American infants are approximately 7 pounds and 19½ inches respectively, as compared with 7½ pounds and 20 inches for the American neonate.

According to reports from well-baby clinics and pediatricians (Survey IV), the first year growth curves of Korean babies in terms of all measurements of physical growth show a progressive straight line, nearly identical to that of American babies. Slight slugging of the growth curve begins to appear after two years of age. From five years of age, the Korean growth curve shows a further noticeable drop, compared with the growth curve of American children. This trend continues until the end of puberty.

The "spurt" type of curve, a markedly accelerated rate during a certain time of adolescence, appears among some Korean teenagers and not others. Most American adolescents show the spurt at some point.

The menarch of Korean pubescent girls occurs between the ages of 10 and 13. Boys reach sexual maturity approximately one year later. This onset of Korean adolescence is considered to be about a year later than that of American children.

REFERENCES

Annua l Report of Korean Mental Health Clinic, Los Angeles, CA, 1975.

Annual Reports of Holt International Children's Fund Inc. and Adoption Program. Eugene, OR, 1974.

Annual Service Reports of Korean Social Service Center of Baltimore, MD, 1977–1981.

Asian-Americans: Facts and Figures, UCLA Asian American Studies Center, Los Angeles, CA, 1975.

Bowlby, J. *Attachment,* Volume I. New York: Basic Books, 1969.

Chan, K., Takanishi, R., and Kitano, R. *Asian American Education Project Preliminary Report.* UCLA, CA: Asian American Center, 1975.

Chung, S.H. and Rieckelman, A. The Koreans of Hawaii. In: W.S. Tseng, J.F. McDermott, J.R. and T.W. Maretzki (Eds.), *People and Cultures in Hawaii.* Honolulu: University of Hawaii, 1974.

Cummins, J. Linguistics inter-dependence and educational development of bilingual children. *Review of Educational Research,* 1979, *49,* 222–225.

Cummins, J. Cross-lingual dimension of language proficiency, *TESOL Quarterly,* 1980.

Kim, B.L. An Appraisal of Korean Immigrant Service Needs. *Social Casework,* 1976, *57,* 139–149.

Kim, B.L., *Cultural Conflicts and Behavioral Expectations Among Korean Ancestry Children in American Classrooms.* Paper presented at Forum on Transcultural Adaptations: Asian Children in American Classrooms, Chicago, 1977.

Kim, B.L. and Condon, M. *A Study of Asian Americans in Chicago: Their Socioeconomic Characteristics, Problems and Service Needs.* NIMH, HEW, 1975.

Kim, D.S. Intercountry adoption: A study of self-concept of adolescent Korean children who were adopted by American families. A doctoral dissertation, University of Chicago, 1976

Lee, C.S. The United States immigration policy and settlement of Koreans in America. *Korean Observer,* 1975, *VI,* 4.

Lee , D.C. *Acculturation of Korean Residents in Georgia.* San Francisco: R and E Research Associates, 1975.

LeVine, R.A. Cross-cultural study in child psychology. In: P.H. Mussen (Ed.), *Carmichael's Annual of Child Psychology,* Vol. 2. Third edition. Chicago: Aldine, 1970.

Man, K.H. Social work with Asian Americans. *Social Casework,* 1976, *57,* 195–201.

Osofsky, J.D. and Danzger, B. Relationships between

neonatal characteristics and mother-infant. *Developmental Psychology,* 1974, *10,* 124.

Park, J.S. A three generation study: Traditional Korean value system and psychosocial adjustment of Korean immigrants in Los Angeles. A doctoral dissertation, Univ. of Southern Calif., 1976.

Roberts, D.F. and Thomson, A.M. *The Biology of Human Fetal Growth.* New York: Halsted, 1976

Spitz, R.A. Anxiety in infancy: A study of its manifestation in the first year of life. *International Journal of Psycho-Analysis,* 1950, *31,* 138–143.

Spitz, R.A. *The First Year of Life.* New York: International Universities Press, 1965.

Steward, M. and Steward, D. The observation of Anglo-Mexican and Chinese-American mothers teaching their young sons. *Child Development,* 1973, *44,* 329–337.

Sue, S. and Wagner, N. *Asian American: Psychological Perspectives.* Ben Lomond, CA: Science and Behavior Books, 1973.

Yoon, T.L., *A Study of Koreans from Psychosocial Pesrspectives* (in Korean). Seoul, Korea: Hyunam-sa, 1970.

Yu, K.H. Korean child-rearing practices. A paper read at Department of Psychiatry, University of Michigan, 1972.

Yu, K.H. A cross-cultural study of the genesis of "surface-passivity" among Far Eastern Asiatic peoples. A paper presented at the Korean Psychiatric Association, 1973.

Yun, Hum. The Korean personality and treatment considerations. *Social Casework,* 1976, *57,* 173–178.

CHAPTER 9

Psychological Development of Chinese-American Children

David Sue, Ph.D., Derald W. Sue, Ph.D.

and Diane M. Sue, Ed.S.

A review of the literature reveals a scarcity of sound research or empirical studies on Chinese-American children. This lack is disheartening, since an understanding of minority children is necessary for the development of programs to deal with their needs. Instead, much of the information available is based on impressionistic observations, personal experiences, or college populations. Research on Chinese-American children is scarce for several reasons. There is a general lack of interest in Asian-Americans as compared to other ethnic groups. Also, there is difficulty in obtaining both adequate sample sizes and culturally fair instruments (Kitano and Sue, 1973). Additionally, ethnic groups distrust research, since many of the problems of minorities are discussed in terms of personal maladjustment rather than failure of society (Sue and Sue, 1977). Researchers have also been characterized as more interested in

personal gains than in the needs of the third world community (Lee et al., 1974). These short-comings and problems must be resolved before accurate information on Asian-Americans can be obtained.

Since few studies on Chinese-American children are available, this portion of the chapter will extrapolate from material dealing with Chinese family rearing patterns with an emphasis on the influence of traditional norms and values on the development of the children. The influence of these variables on achievement needs, aggressive behavior, self-esteem, and independence will be discussed, together with the problems of belonging to a minority group.

CHINESE VALUES

In traditional Chinese-American families, the ancestors and elders are viewed with great reverence and respect. Members of the older generations are regarded as occupying a higher status than individuals in the younger generation. The line of authority is clear, and the primary family unit exerts great control over its members. Parent-child relationships are characterized as formal (Hsu, 1955; Sung, 1971). Behaviors which bring honor to the family involve achievement, obedience, and obligation to the parents. It is very important for the child to engage in activities which give the family a good name. Problem behaviors are clearly spelled out; aggression, antisocial behavior, and disobedience bring shame to the entire family and are strictly discouraged. The importance of these values was discussed in a study by DeVos and Abbott (1966) which revealed that, among Chinese living in San Francisco, educational achievement is highly valued, a strong sense of responsibility exists towards relatives, failure to live up to the elders' expectations results in self-blame, and respect for elders is equated with respect for authority. These values influence the types of behaviors that are reinforced by Chinese-American parents in childrearing.

Possibly the strongest value in Chinese families is filial piety. This refers to the obligation and respect that children are expected to display to their parents. Unquestioning obedience to the parents is encouraged at an early age and is maintained throughout life, even after the individual has begun a family of his or her own (Whiting and Child, 1953).

Although American culture also stresses the importance of respect to the parents ("Honor thy mother and thy father"), this injunction is diluted by other values such as independence, self-reliance, and mastery of one's own fate (Kalish and Moriwaki, 1973; Kriger and Kroes, 1972). Chinese families place little value on these behaviors. As Hsu (1953) observed, "The most important thing to Americans is what parents should do for their children; to Chinese, what children should do

for their parents" (p. 75).

In a fascinating study, Tseng and Hsu (1972) examined the content and themes of Chinese children's stories as compared to Northern European stories. The majority of Chinese tales dealt with personal sacrifices performed for the principle of filial piety. In one story, a young couple living with the man's parents was unable to provide food for the entire family. So that the grandparents would have enough to eat, the young couple decided to bury their youngest child. In the process of digging a grave, gold was discovered and filial piety was rewarded. In contrast, Northern European stories, such as Cinderella, Hansel and Gretel, and Sleeping Beauty, tell of the defeat of adults by children. In Chinese stories, the child who defies authority would be admonished, punished, or even killed.

The influence of Chinese values on specific behaviors will now be presented.

AGGRESSIVENESS

Chinese-American children are rarely described as aggressive. Sollenberger (1968) reported that the interactions he observed of Chinese children and adolescents were peaceful and harmonious, and that quarreling or bickering was rare. Similarly, they are characterized as well-behaved, obedient, and responsible by school teachers (Liu, 1950). Rates of juvenile delinquency are low (Abbott and Abbott, 1973; Sollenberger, 1968), even among the Chinese living under ghetto conditions. Chinese mothers are most strict and displeased with disobedience and aggressive behavior (Sollenberger, 1968; Young, 1972). Cultural values of gentleness, obedience, manners, and acquiescence decrease the probability of aggressive behavior and account for elevated scores on the femininity scale of the California Psychological Inventory by Chinese males and females (Fong and Peskin, 1969).

In a study involving 69 Chinese-American families with children under seven years of age, the parents expressed little permissiveness for aggression (Sollenberger, 1968). As compared to a white sample, 44% of the Chinese mothers were "not at all permissive" regarding aggression among siblings; only 6% of the white mothers endorsed this statement. Even when their children faced a provocative situation, the Chinese parents did not feel that their children should defend themselves. Only 4% of the white parents endorsed this response; most of them felt that their children should fight back if bullied. The extent to which white and Chinese parents pressured their children to fight back is presented in Table 1. It is clear that aggression is discouraged by Chinese parents regardless of the situation.

Although the cultural restraints against aggression have resulted in a remarkably low incidence of juvenile delinquency among Chinese youth, the rate has been increasing in recent years, especially in the commission of the more aggressive offenses such as assault and robbery (Abbott and Abott, 1973). Because Chinese youths have traditionally been described as nonviolent and well behaved, many people were shocked to read of gang-related violence in San Francisco's Chinatown. The increase in crime among the youth seems to be related to several factors. First, as the Chinese-American youth establishes more contact with the dominant culture, parental authority may begin to erode. Fong (1965) found that assimilation is occurring among Chinese students, and it is possible that this will lead to increases in aggression. Second, the environmental conditions for children and youths living in Chinatowns are not good. Chinatowns can be described as ghettos. They are densely populated, with the unemployment rate among youths in San Francisco approaching 13% (Asians in Alameda County, 1974). This problem is compounded by the large influx of immigrants from Hong Kong. Forty percent of the Chinese population in Oakland is foreign-born, and the median income for adult males in this area is $6,000 (Asians in Alameda County, 1974). Third, the arrival of immigrant youths who have no knowledge of English compounds the problems. In fact, 40% of the immigrants are between 16 and 19 years, often described as the "problem years" (Lyman, 1973). The youths must learn to adapt to a totally new environment, while limited

TABLE 1

Extent to Which Parents Have
Pressured Child to Fight Back (Percentages)

Pressure exerted by parents	Cambridge (white) (n = 370)	Chinese (n = 66)
Never under any circumstances	18	74*
Occasional slight encouragement	17	18*
Moderate encouragement	38	8*
Urged strongly to defend self	12	0*
Punished child for running home for help	15	0*

*p<.01
Data from Sollenberger, 1968, p. 18.

in the ability to interact, at the same time as they are going through the problems of identity, sexual conflict, and independence from parents. Under these conditions, the immigrants often drop out of classes, hang around pool halls and bars, communicate with other "street kids," and join a gang (Leong, 1972). With the existence of so many problems, it is surprising that the juvenile delinquency rate is not higher.

ACHIEVEMENT

Traditionally, achievement within the family context has been emphasized in Chinese families (Abbott, 1970; DeVos and Abbott, 1966; Sollenberger, 1968). In the face of problems caused by minority group status, the solution has been to excel (Lee, 1966). It is important to note that competition in and of itself is not valued. Hsu (1971) observed that the Chinese oppose "cutthroat competition for individual ends." Instead, the purpose of work and achievement is to enhance the status of the family. Outstanding achievement, especially in educational and occupational endeavors, is a source of pride for the whole family. Chinese families with school-aged children highly value good grades, studying, and the completion of homework (Young, 1972). As compared with Mexican-American and Anglo-American mothers, Chinese-American mothers are more likely to consider teaching to be an important aspect of their maternal role (Steward and Steward, 1973).

This cultural emphasis on achievement is reflected in the data from the H.E.W. Office of Special Concerns (1974). The report revealed that over 24% of the Chinese children who were three or four years of age at the time of the census were in some type of preschool program. This compares to the United States average of 14% for all groups. In addition, the Chinese showed an increased utilization of higher education programs. Over 25% of Chinese males

16 and older had obtained their college degree; this is nearly double the U.S. average of 13%. This stress on education is striking, particularly since most of the older Chinese-American males have received less than eight years of schooling. In San Francisco and New York, half of the Chinese adult population has not gone beyond elementary school. The educational picture for the Chinese population in the United States will remain disparate because of the influx of young and under-educated immigrants.

Chinese children spend more time in formal education than members of other groups. Many of them who are six years or older attend Chinese school after regular school hours (Sollenberger, 1968). In the study by Sollenberger, 41% of Chinese mothers felt that school achievement was "very important" when asked to rate how well they wanted their children to do in school; only 11% of the white mothers felt it was very important. This was especially surprising since, in the Chinese sample, 47% of the mothers and 52% of the fathers had received no more than an elementary school education, and two-thirds of them were in the lower socioeconomic class. The traditional emphasis on education remains strong for both immigrant and American-born Chinese (Young, 1972).

INDEPENDENCE

Although Chinese parents display a very permissive attitude toward their children early in life, a much more restrictive rearing process begins when the children are old enough to understand the difference between right and wrong (Tseng and Hsu, 1972). As compared with Jewish and Protestant mothers, second generation Chinese mothers scored much higher on "control" or strictness. Protestant and Jewish mothers scored higher on the dimension of permissiveness, which is related to the development of independence. Chinese parents are not restrictive for all behaviors, however. They encourage the development of early independence in academic achievement and task-oriented behaviors such as eating alone, dressing, and going to bed by themselves (Sollenberger, 1968). In a study on independence by Young (1972), a group of 20 immigrant Chinese and 32 local Chinese families was compared with a control group of Caucasians. In comparison with the control group, Chinese parents expected their children to interact with peers at a later age, but had similar expectations for academic achievement and self-care tasks. Table 2 presents a comparison of the different group responses regarding their

TABLE 2

Medians of Age Estimates Given to Items of the
Independence Training Questionnaire

Item	Group*	Median Age Estimate
To stand up for his own rights with other children	Cauc	3
	LC	5
	IC	9.5
To know his way around his part of the community so he can play where he wants without getting lost	Cauc	5
	LC	8
	IC	8
To go outside to play when he wants to be noisy or boisterous	Cauc	3
	LC	5
	IC	6.5
To be able to lead other children and to be able to assert himself in children's groups	Cauc	5
	LC	7
	IC	6.5
To do well in competition with other children; to try hard to come out on top in games	Cauc	6
	LC	8
	IC	9.5
To be satisfied to stay with someone he knows well when parents must be away for a few days	Cauc	3
	LC	5
	IC	11
To visit and stay overnight with a playmate	Cauc	7
	LC	8.5
	IC	10
To straighten out most of his difficulties with other children without adult intervention	Cauc	6
	LC	8
	IC	11.5
To take part in group activities, such as clubs, scouts, etc.	Cauc	8
	LC	8
	IC	10

* Cauc = Caucasian
  LC = Local Chinese
  IC = Immigrant Chinese

From Young (1972)

childrens' social interaction with peers. School-aged Chinese children are closely supervised and not allowed to roam about freely; immigrant Chinese parents tend to be even more strict in this area than local Chinese.

SELF-ESTEEM

Self-esteem is associated with an individual's view of self in relationship to the environment and others. If a person has low self-esteem, it indicates that he or she does not feel very sure of him/herself or his/her ability to succeed. In a study by Coleman and his colleagues (Coleman et al., 1972), Chinese school children and youths displayed less sense of control over their environment than whites. About twice as many Chinese endorsed the statement on a questionnaire that "good luck is more important for success than hard work." This is a remarkable finding, especially since these Chinese students spent more time studying than did the white students. Sue and Frank (1973) and Chiu (1971) felt that Chinese-American students suffer from more stress than white students. These studies revealed that the former group was characterized by feelings of isolation, loneliness, rejection, and anxiety.

Problems in self-esteem and self-concept may be brought about by a society which only gives lip service to equality. Chinese-Americans are constantly bombarded by the mass media which uphold Western values as superior. Yee (1973) examined the content of 300 social studies textbooks for elementary and secondary schools and found that 75% of them made no mention of Chinese at all. The others contained brief descriptions of Chinatown in San Francisco, Chinese railroad workers, laundry workers, and the culinary skills of the Chinese. Such an incomplete picture of a people may lead to a lowered sense of self-esteem and little pride in cultural identity. A series of poems written

by Asian students in the fifth and sixth grades demonstrated their understanding of cultural pride, discrimination, and the problems of being a minority group member (Asians are . . . ., 1973). One poem indicates the uselessness of attempting to succeed in a white society (p. 398)

> Asians are silent people
> Never speaking of distress
> Bearing much in their heart
> The burden of the silent one.
> Standing up to their rights
> Trying to prove loyal by working hard.
> America, a place of hopes
> For white people only!

EMOTIONAL RESTRAINT

Fenz and Arkoff (1962) reported that Chinese children learn self-control and detachment by modeling their parents' behavior. They learn to inhibit a show of spontaneity and self-expression; strong control over affective impulses is learned at an early age. Emotional displays are discouraged in the home because of the formal relationship that exists between parents and children (Sung, 1971). Asian mothers are more likely than Black or Caucasian mothers to describe their children as shy, self-effacing, and overcontrolled (Tuddenham et al., 1974). A psychological assessment study involving 104 Chinese males revealed that many of them could be characterized as restrained and controlled (Sue and Frank, 1973).

CULTURE CONFLICTS

A bicultural background can be a positive or negative attribute depending upon the reaction of the dominant culture. Minority group status has proven to be a disadvantage for Chinese in the United States. Chinese children have a special problem involving the use of a different language. According to the H.E.W. Office of Special Concerns (1974), between 61% and 70%

of Chinese children under the age of 14 years still speak Chinese in their homes. The report concludes that the English language will continue to be a major problem in Asian communities. Difficulty with English extends to the college level. Watanabe (1973) reported that of Asians entering the University of California at Berkeley over 50% failed a "bonehead English" exam, twice as many as their Caucasian counterparts. Those who failed were required to make up language deficits in remedial noncredit courses.

Until Chinese students enter school, they are closely supervised by parents, and their interactions are restricted. Most of their behaviors have been shaped by the cultural values transmitted by parents. A San Francisco Chinese Community Citizen's Survey (1969) found that Chinese children were placed in school according to age grade level and were required to compete with English-speaking peers. The Chinese students in these classes experienced frustration and a sense of futility.

Under these conditions, a sense of inferiority can develop causing children to reject their cultural heritage and adopt Western values (Sue and Sue, 1971). Weiss (1970) found that many Chinese-American girls expected the Asian boys they dated to behave assertively and confidently in the traditional Western manner. Chinese-American boys who were unable to fit this image were denounced vehemently by the girls. Under these conditions a youth may feel that he is heir to two different cultures and may find it difficult to decide which one he belongs to, which may result in feelings of alienation from both cultures.

FUTURE DIRECTIONS

Assimilation and acculturation will continue to occur among Chinese-Americans (Abbott, 1970; Fong, 1965; Fong and Peskin, 1969), especially among those liv-

ing apart from Chinatown. "As the American society becomes a positive reference group, its norms and values begin to guide, as well as modify, the perspectives and behavior of the Chinese" (Fong, 1973). However, assimilation will occur much more slowly among individuals living in Chinatown because of the continual influx of immigrants and their greater isolation from the rest of society. Although values such as unquestioning obedience and deference are becoming less acceptable to Chinese youth, not all cultural ties are being rejected. Many Chinese youths are interested in the problems of the Chinese ghettos and communities and are seeking new ethnic consciousness (Fong, 1973; Sue and Sue, 1971). Traditional values will continue to change, but it seems that a large part of the Chinese cultural identity will remain.

REFERENCES

Abbott, K.A. Cultural change, psychosocial functioning, and the family: A case study in the Chinese-American community of San Francisco. Unpublished doctoral dissertation, University of California, Berkeley, 1970.

Abbott, K.A. and Abbott, E.L. Juvenile delinquency in San Francisco's Chinese-American community: 1961–1966. In: S. Sue & N. Wagner (Eds.), Asian-American: Psychological Perspectives. Ben Lomond, CA: Science and Behavior Books, 1973.

Asians are . . . . Personnel and Guidance Journal, 1973, 51, 397–399.

Asians in Alameda County. Mental Health Need Assessment Report, Alameda County, 1974.

Chiu, L.H. Manifested anxiety in Chinese and American children. Journal of Psychology, 1971, 79, 273–284.

Coleman, J.S., Campbell, E.Q., Hobson, C.J., McPartland, J., Mood, A.M., Weinfeld, F.D. and York, R.L. The locus control and academic performance among racial groups. In: S.S. Gutterman (Ed.), Black Psyche. Berkeley: The Glendessary Press, 1972.

DeVos, G. and Abbott, K. The Chinese family in San Francisco. Masters Dissertation, University of California, Berkeley, 1966.

Fenz, W. and Arkoff, A. Comparative need patterns of five ancestry groups in Hawaii. Journal of Social Psychology, 1962, 58, 82.

Fong, S.L.M. Assimilation of Chinese in America: Changes in orientation and social perception. American Journal of Sociology, 1965, 71, 265–273.

Fong, S.L.M. Assimilation and changing social roles of Chinese-Americans. *Journal of Social Issues*, 1973, *29*, 115–127.

Fong, S.L.M. and Peskin, H. Sex-role strain and personality adjustment of China-born students in America: A pilot study. *Journal of Abnormal Psychology*, 1969, *74*, 563–567.

H.E.W. Office of Special Concerns. A study of selected socio-economic characteristics of ethnic minorities based on the 1970 census. Volume II: Asian Americans. Department of Health, Education, and Welfare, 1974.

Hsu, F.L.K. *Americans and Chinese: Two Ways of Life*. New York: Abelard-Schuman, 1953.

Hsu, F.L.K. *Americans and Chinese*. London: Cresset, 1955.

Hsu, F.L.K. *The Challenge of the American Dream: The Chinese in the United States*. Belmont, CA: Wadsworth, 1971.

Kalish, R.A. and Moriwaki, S. The world of the elderly Asian-American. *Journal of Social Issues*, 1973, *29*, 187–210.

Kitano, H.H.L. and Sue, S. The model minorities. *Journal of Social Issues*, 1973, 29, 1–10.

Kriger, S.F. and Kroes, W.H. Childrearing attitudes of Chinese, Jewish and Protestant mothers. *Journal of Social Psychology*, 1972, *86*, 205–210.

Lee, B.H.L. A historical study of discriminatory practices and their effects on the education of American-Chinese in California. Unpublished Master's Thesis, Sacramento State College, 1966.

Lee, D., Hsi, V., Campana, E. and Gonzales, A. Research in third world communities. *Newsletter of the Association of Asian-American Psychologists*, 1974, *1*, 11–24.

Leong, J. Hong Kong immigrants and the public schools. In: A. Chan and J. Surh (Eds.), *Asian American Review*. Berkeley, CA: University of California Press, 1972.

Liu, C.H. The influence of cultural background on the moral judgment of children. Unpublished doctoral dissertation, Columbia University, 1950.

Lyman, S. Red guard on Grant avenue: The rise of youthful rebellion in Chinatown. In: S. Sue and N. Wagner (Eds.), *Asian-Americans: Psychological Perspectives*. Ben Lomond, CA: Science and Behavior Books, 1973.

San Francisco Chinese Community Citizen's Survey and Fact-Finding Committee Report. San Francisco: H.J. Carle and Sons, 1969.

Sollenberger, R.T. Chinese-American child-rearing practices and juvenile delinquency. *Journal of Social Psychology*, 1968, *74*, 13–23.

Steward, M. and Steward, D. The observation of Anglo-, Mexican-, and Chinese-American mothers teaching their young sons. *Child Development*, 1973, *44*, 329–337.

Sue, D.W. and Frank, A.C. A typological approach to the psychological study of Chinese and Japanese American college males. *Journal of Social Issues*, 1973, *29*, 129–148.

Sue, D.W. and Sue D. Ethnic minorities: Failure and responsibilities of the social sciences. *Journal of Non-White Concerns*, 1977, *5*, 99–106.

Sue, S. and Sue, D.W. Chinese-American personality and mental health. In: A. Tachiki, E. Wong, F. Odo and B. Wong (Eds.), *Roots: An Asian-American Reader*. Los Angeles: Continental Graphics, 1971.

Sung, B.L. *The Story of Chinese in America*. New York: Collier, 1971.

Tseng, W. and Hsu, J. The Chinese attitude toward parental authority as expressed in Chinese childrens stories. *Archives of General Psychiatry*, 1972, *26*, 28-34.

Tuddenham, R.D., Brooks, J. and Milkovich, L. Mothers' reports of behavior on ten-year-olds: Relationship with sex, ethnicity, and mothers' education. *Developmental Psychology*, 1974, *10*, 459–495.

Watanabe, C. Self-expression and the Asian-American experience. *Personnel and Guidance Journal*, 1973, *51*, 390–396.

Weiss, M.S. Selective acculturation and the dating process: The patterning of Chinese-Caucasian interracial dating. *Journal of Marriage and the Family*, 1970, *32*, 273–278.

Whiting, J.W. and Child, I.L. *Child Training and Personality: A Cross-cultural Study*. New Haven: Yale University Press, 1953.

Yee, A.H. Myopic perceptions and textbooks: Chinese-Americans' search for identity. *Journal of Social Issues*, 1973, *29*, 99–113.

Young, N.F. Independence training from a cross-cultural perspective. *American Anthropologist*, 1972, *74*, 629–638.

CHAPTER 10

Emotional Growth of Japanese-American Children

Joe Yamamoto, M.D. and

Mamoru Iga, Ph.D.

Except for the first Americans, the American Indians, all the people of the United States are immigrants. Each wave of immigrants has had similar experiences. For example, the Irish, the Italians, the Poles, and others have suffered the similar fate of newcomers and been subject to prejudice and discrimination. Although they were the objects of negative stereotyping, because of their European backgrounds and Caucasian features, these immigrants were able ultimately to become a part of the "American mainstream." For several generations, visible minorities in America—such as Asian, African, or other ethnic groups who do not look like European-Americans—suffered from the misbelief that the United States is truly a "melting pot." The relatively small proportion of immigrants from Asia was ignored in the conceptualization of the "all-American dream."

A pattern of anti-Asian prejudice and

discrimination became especially prevalent on the West coast of the United States prior to World War II. The long history of anti-Asian prejudice and discriminatory acts included denial of citizenship, discriminatory practices in the ownership of land, segregated housing, schools, and work—leading to the relocation of 117,000 Japanese-Americans in the spring of 1942. This infamy was promulgated by President Franklin D. Roosevelt, was encouraged by the military in California and other West coast states, and was concurred in by the Supreme Court (Weglyn, 1976). The ostensible reason for the relocation of the Japanese, who were mainly American citizens of Japanese parentage, was the fear of sabotage, espionage, and disloyal acts against the United States. In truth, during the war and subsequently, there were no known or proven acts of sabotage or espionage (Conrat and Conrat, 1972). Fortunately, the Civil Rights Act of the 1960s and concern about equal opportunity have improved the situation for many Asian-Americans, including the Japanese.

Although we would not want to contribute to another stereotype, whether positive or negative, preferring recognition of each person, the generalizations that we offer are an effort to use stereotyping in a more positive sense in order to understand some of the cultural background and beliefs which may influence the behavior of Japanese-Americans.

When one contrasts first-generation Japanese-Americans, who migrated from Japan to the United States from the turn of the century until 1924 when the Oriental Exclusion Act was passed, with recent immigrants from Japan, one finds educational, social class, and other differences. The Japanese who came prior to 1924 came with very conservative Meiji Era values. They emphasized respect towards one's parents, cohesiveness of the family and the nation, and the work ethic, including frugality and attainment of long-range objectives (Yamamoto and Iga, 1974).

The recent Japanese immigrants are modernized in many ways. First of all, they have been influenced by technological advances. The second important variable has been the influence of the Japanese constitution. The rights of women have been somewhat enhanced, and the influences of the mass media have had a considerable impact on changing the values and customs in Japan. The immigrants who came from Japan prior to the passage of the Oriental Exclusion Act of 1924 came from the working class and generally had the limited education then prevalent among this group; however, they did bring the Meiji Era emphasis on education as a valued objective for their children as a means toward occupational advancement.

For a better understanding of the behavior of Japanese and Japanese-Americans, we will review the contributions of Japanese and American behavioral scientists, focusing on the contributions of Takie Sugiyama Lebra (1976), followed by a discussion of some of the Western views of Japanese patterns of behavior and a discussion of the changing patterns of Japanese-American behavior.

That the Japanese are concerned about human relationships is quite apparent in their group interactions. Many years ago, Ruth Benedict (1946) commented on the many apparent contradictions in Japanese behavior. Takie Sugiyama Lebra (1976) attempted to answer some of these seeming contradictions in behavior. Her position was that Japanese people place great importance on social interactions and relationships and less on individuality. Thus, she contrasts Japanese and Western cultures:

1) In Europe and America, the emphasis is on change and is based upon individuality, equality, rationality, and self-assertion.
2) In Japan, the emphasis is on tradition and groupism, interdependence, vertical relationships, empathy, sentimentality, introspection, and self-denial.

Lebra believes that these differences explain the seeming contradictions in Japanese behavior. For example, in visiting Japan, one is impressed with the politeness and formality of Japanese behavior. In department stores, young ladies attired in uniforms, including white gloves, formally greet you with a bow and smile as you approach the escalator. Quite in contrast, in the subway during the rush hours masses of people push, shove, and rush to get aboard the trains. These seemingly contradictory behaviors must be viewed in the social contexts in which they occur. In a department store, one expects polite and formal greetings, whereas during the rush hour in the subway, one expects that there will be a horde of people crushing towards the trains: Everyone is doing it, and only by joining them can you get aboard the trains.

LEBRA'S CONCEPT OF SOCIAL RELATIVISM

Lebra has taken a different approach from that of other anthropologists. She has managed to describe and explain Japanese patterns of behavior without the pejorative aspects of labeling from an Eastern or European viewpoint. Some studies have taken an exclusively psychoanalytic viewpoint; in her study she has observed the Japanese culture with her own distinctively refreshing views, based on her knowledge of the extensive literature available on the Japanese, her ability as an insider to conceptualize aspects of Japanese behavior, her many years of experience as a Japanese living in Japan, and her experience as a professional observer during her recurrent visits to Japan.

The result of her creative work is a description of the social preoccupation of the Japanese people. Lebra has observed that the Japanese are not only sensitive and concerned about social interactions and relationships, but that this seems to be their major preoccupation. In quoting from a Japanese sociologist, Ikutaro Shimizu (1968), she pointed out that the Japanese tend to communicate through nonverbal means. The Japanese communicate with one another in the process of eating and drinking together. This process does not necessarily include a great deal of verbalizing about important issues, but is more an experience of togetherness. Japanese concern with social interactions and relationships deals with Japanese not as individuals but as a nation. They seem motivated to compare themselves with significant other individuals or nations. Lebra concluded that the Japanese are often motivated by the fear

of being left out, or the need to be a little ahead of others. In the Japanese society, then, it is important that one creates, maintains, or manipulates one's relationship with significant others in order to be able to achieve the sought-for objective. An example is very elegant and elaborate wining and dining on an expense account, an almost invariable part of business transactions in Japan.

In discussing how even symbolic meanings may be relative and dependent upon social relationships, Lebra gave the example of the Japanese underworld (the *Yakuza*, or the Japanese equivalent of the Mafia). In the Japanese underworld, the importance of the social bond of loyalty determines the credibility of the boss. In other words, to his subordinates the boss is never wrong. Among Japanese professors, there is a similar lack of challenge by subordinates. In almost all instances, decisions, whether big or small, are discussed in large groups ad infinitum towards an apparent consensus. It is true that the subordinates do not openly disagree with the professor, but the assumption is that often they have had a chance to express their views prior to the public statement by the "boss."

In focusing on the importance of social relationships to the Japanese, Lebra quoted from Isaiah Ben Dasan (1970): "The Japanese differ from the Jews in a very significant manner: the Japanese consider people to be the most important, whereas the Jews take the law, the words and reasons to be fully as important." An illustration of this concept recently occurred with the hijacking of an airliner. The hijackers demanded the release of revolutionaries imprisoned in Japan. Although Japanese laws prohibited such a release of prisoners, the Japanese government decided that in the interest of humanity the prisoners must be released to save the hijacked passengers aboard the airplane. The Japanese learn to be sensitive about the needs of others, to be compulsive and circumspect, and in these ways to work towards pure, smooth and pleasant social relationships.

Thus, Lebra combines the concepts of social preoccupation and interactional relativism in her concept of social relativism. By interactional relativism,Lebra means the tendency to make less distinct ideological differentiations or separations. That is to say, with interactional relativism, the distinctions are suppressed; the tendency is to blend shades of grey rather than using a distinct white/black dichotomy.

In reference to the internalization of feelings of guilt and of conscience, De Vos (1960) pointed out that the Japanese have a strong sense of guilt. While Westerners have feelings of guilt in reference to possible transgressions related to sexuality or aggression, Japanese feel guilty because of the mother's self-sacrifice which obligates the child to make recompense for her years of effort and endurance. In a similar interpersonal vein, Doi (1971), the foremost Japanese psychoanalytic theorist, described Japanese behavior as being group and socially oriented. Doi said that the Japanese feel guilty about the possible betrayal of one's social group. Lebra concluded that Japanese guilt, like Japanese behavior, is inseparable from social relationships.

Since Japanese ethics tend to be dependent upon the specific situation, the behavior of Japanese people may appear changeable. This may lead Westerners to say that the Japanese are unreliable. Thus, the same Japanese soldiers captured during World War II who asked to be killed, when spared, became model prisoners—because the situation had changed. Lest we believe that Japanese behavior is exceedingly flexible and changeable, Lebra pointed out that once social relationships and bonds have been established, behavior patterns tend to become fixed and persistent. The role of authority figures in Japanese culture has often confused Westerners. Lebra suggested that because of social relativism,

the person in authority is usually as dependent as the subordinates. The price of authority is high in terms of lack of freedom and autonomy. Side by side with increasing authority are increasing social obligations.

Belonging

In Japan, belonging is conceived as being tied to groups. These group ties may be related to blood, geographic, or operational ties such as school or company. Chie Nakane (1970) stressed that a person identifies himself or herself within a social group rather than as an individual. At times this custom makes it delicate to identify a person's social and occupational position. For example, everyone who works for a large Japanese corporation may describe himself or herself as a company member. Thus, it may be difficult to identify a middle-level executive from a production line employee. Indeed, all the men are dressed similarly in conservative dark suits, so it is difficult to differentiate a clerk from a middle-level executive. Another aspect of identity and belonging which should be understood is the emphasis upon belonging as a qualification for employment in government and industry. A concrete example is an applicant who is an orphan, who would not be considered a desirable employee because he or she does not belong to a family group.

In Japan, the emphasis is on collectivism. Group cooperation and participation are taken for granted in everyday activities. Emphasis on the group fosters a tendency towards togetherness and long-lasting relationships. Lebra pointed out that the concern about not being left out of any group situation results in congregation of great masses of people. Certainly, the Japanese are famous for traveling abroad in large groups. An important aspect of this is that even the dead should not be left out; they are included by the daily offerings at the family *butsudan* or *kami-dana* (altar) (Yamamoto et al., 1969). The emphasis on group activities is contrasted to the feeling of loneliness that occurs when an individual is not engaged in social interactions. In Japan, the emphasis on groups promotes physical togetherness, thus eliminating the need for verbal communication. Indeed, among the Japanese there is a distrust of verbal skills as connoting glibness, possible dishonesty, or lack of trustworthiness. This results in a need for conformity requiring that not only subordinates, but also authority figures, conform to group objectives. Lebra concluded that dissension cannot be conspicuous and people in authority cannot be dictatorially suppressive because of socially relativistic group interactions.

Belonging is a part of the social matrix which requires total commitment of the corporation to the employee and the employee to the corporation. This mutual interdependence is hard to explain and even harder to understand for Westerners who have grown up in individualistically oriented societies.

Empathy

Empathy is a highly valued virtue among the Japanese. It is considered a crucial attribute of a human being. This emphasis on empathy is understandable as part of Japanese social relativism. Lebra described the importance of empathy (omoiyari) in the Japanese culture. By empathy, Lebra means the ability to feel what the other person is feeling, and thus to experience the pleasure and pain, and to be motivated to help the other achieve his or her wishes and goals. Ideally, one should be able to enter the other's part and thus to act in a way that would be meaningful and helpful to the other. A part of the emphasis in the empathic interactions is on trying to maintain a consensus or positive feeling of agreement between oneself and the other person. One should be concerned with the other's com-

fort. Thus, hospitality would mean that everything should be planned ahead, including lodging, food, transportation, and so forth, rather than having the guest verbalize preferences. The emphasis in Japan is on anticipating the other's wants and on specifically taking care of them. Part of the mutual interactions crucial in Japanese society, in addition to empathy, is self-restraint (enryo). Self-restraint is exercised to avoid causing problems for others, as well as to avoid obligations which may be difficult to repay.

Dependence

In the American society, independence is a virtue in itself. In Japan, there is a pervasive awareness of mutual interdependence. The common forms of communication include those which reveal the awareness of the dependence of Japanese people upon one another. In discussing the patterns of mutual interdependence in Japan, Lebra showed that the mother is a life-long object of attachment. Long-term breast-feeding and play begin the relationship. Thus, an objective for the Japanese boy is not to grow beyond the oedipal situation, but to learn to develop a masculine identity while still attached to the mother. Close family relationships are followed by close relationships within school groups, and then, in occupational or company groups. Through life, the sense of identity, belonging, and mutual interdependence are related to groups. Of course, the initial group is the family in which the mother functions as the authority figure at home, since the father is absent much of the time. Indeed, the roles of the father and mother are reminiscent of traditional roles of physician and nurse on hospital wards a few decades ago. On the wards, it is the nurse (mother) who is in continuous contact with the patients (children). The titular authority figure is the physician (father). As such, the physician (father) is expected to issue the orders, but these are always subject to improvement and diplomatic correction by the nurse (mother).

THE WESTERN VIEW OF JAPANESE NATIONAL CHARACTER

Previous Western views of Japanese national character suggest that there are three Japanese personality traits: passivity-dependence, nonrationality-intuitiveness, and insecurity-compulsiveness.

1) Passivity-dependence: Dependence need in the sense of *amae*, or the wish to depend on the passive love of a paternal figure, has been emphasized by Doi (1962) as the primary motivating force among Japanese. Caudill (1962) regarded dependence as the root of the two characteristic patterns of Japanese emotions: "emphasis on sexual satisfaction and conscious denial of pleasure and emotion" because "the emphasis on sexual gratification, pleasure and emotion tends to make individuals more competitive, to disrupt the group life and consequently, hamper the satisfaction of the basic wish to *amae*."

2) Japanese nonrationality-intuitiveness: Japanese nonrationality has been discussed by Nakamura (1964), who compared the interpretations of Buddhism by Hindus, Chinese, and Japanese. Through comparison, he showed Japanese "indifference to logical rules," "tendency to avoid complex ideas," "lack of interest in formal consistency," and "intuitive and emotional tendencies." Japanese emphasis on aesthetic experience, neglecting logical rules, is pointed out by Lifton (1965). Because of nonrationality, even when the ideal norm (*tatemai*) and actual wish (*honne*) were contradictory, they were kept harmoniously in the typical Japanese personality. For example, apparent politeness to the ex-

tent of obsequiousness was harmoniously coexistent with a hostile wish and even hatred.

3) Insecurity-compulsiveness: Insecurity was expressed in the diffuse fear which Fischer (1964) observed among Japanese intellectuals (who were expected to be relatively more secure because of their greater capability of self-expression and problem-solving) in spite of the generally high correlation between education and occupational security in Japan. According to Spitzer (1947), "the whole Japanese civilization presents a pattern of a compulsion-neurosis." Erwin Mahler's study (1976), using the Tennessee Self-Concept Scale, appears to confirm this emphasis on the Japanese insecurity.

The Japanese subjects showed significantly lower scores on identity ("Who am I?"), self-satisfaction ("How do I feel about myself?"), and behavior ("What do I do?"). The low scores for Japanese subjects on the physical self, moral self, personal self, family self, and social self are interpreted by Mahler as indicating their poor self-esteem and defensiveness, and wish not to reveal themselves. Results of such verbal tests, we believe, must be evaluated and correlated with observed behavior. The interpretation of Mahler's data would depend on a Western concept of self.

American behavioral scientists have tried to explain Japanese personality using Western concepts of psychosexual development and childrearing. In our opinion, not a great deal has been done to correlate those with adult personality and behavior. The most notable exception has been the contribution of Caudill and Weinstein (1969). In their study comparing middle-class Japanese and middle-class American families, they noted that American infants were left alone more, and American mothers talked and tried to stimulate their babies. The Japanese mothers were almost always with their babies, and rocked and lulled them more, trying to keep them quiet and contented. The result was that the American infants were more active, played more with objects, and gave more happy vocalizations. The Japanese babies were carried and lulled whenever they cried.

Weaning has not been a problem among the Japanese because of their characteristically prolonged nursing period. This has been noted by Lanham (1956). These data support Benedict's (1946) comments that Japanese infants are usually weaned long after they can understand what is said to them. Lebra (1976) commented on the aspects of breast play which are prevalent among some mother and infant pairs.

In Japan, toilet training is not severe. Depending on the family toilet circumstances, usually the training is completed by age two. Infantile sexuality and masturbatory behavior are not condemned (Benedict, 1946; Smith and Beardsley, 1962).

In contrast to the bathing of middle-class American children, where the mother stands outside of the bathtub and bathes her baby, the Japanese mother takes her baby into the bathtub with her. First she bathes the baby and herself, then holding the baby, she sits and soaks herself in hot water in a wooden bathtub. In the first year or two of life, the baby is carried on the mother's back with a strap (ombo). In the wintertime, when she goes out, the mother wears a coat which covers both herself and the child. A child can expect to sleep with parents until about age ten. By the time the child is 16, he/she will sleep with siblings or others (Caudill and Plath, 1966).

Physical punishment does occur. Outside the home, disciplinary measures are usually a discreet pinch or comments that will make other children laugh at the misbehaving child. In contrast to American children, Japanese children react with anxiety when threatened with separation from the family. Thus, when being seriously disciplined, the Japanese child will be locked outside of the home, whereas the American child will be punished by being locked inside the home. Japanese children are also disciplined with threats of harm by strangers, devils, ghosts, policemen, doctors, and other threatening strangers. Lanham (1956) found that a small cone of mogusa powder is burned on the child's skin, causing a third-degree burn which leaves a scar. This procedure was used both for native healing purposes and also for discipline when there were serious problems. Mild disciplinary measures were taken for minor transgressions, and children were often rewarded with sweets for good behavior.

Traditional Japanese Society

Japanese society is a vertical system, as Nakane (1970) represents by Figure 1.

a

b c

d e f g

Figure 1

Each symbol signifies several persons, and lower levels symbolize a much larger number of subordinates than at the higher level. The system has several attributes. First, it is integrated by a sense of collectivism, with an emphasis on mutual obligation and loyalty. Second, the system is rigidly status-stratified, making for keen status consciousness. Third, the relationship between classes is the "serve the powerful" principle (jidai shugi).

Caudill (1962) observed great similarities between nisei (second generation Japanese-Americans) and middle-class Americans; for example, lack of spontaneous interpersonal relationships; difficulty adjusting to strange situations; compulsive emphasis on propriety and respectability; strong concern with money and prestige; not to mention more observable traits such as diligence, industry, stress on education, or postponement of immediate gratification for future happiness. He also noted important differences between the two groups: Japanese-Americans are more sensitive and vulnerable to reactions from others. They show a stronger sense of obligation and duty, and deference to their parents. Although they are similar to the American middle-class in their concern with money and prestige, nisei are more concerned with others' approval of the way they get money and prestige. The sense of being constantly watched by others is traditionally Japanese.

Thus, the nisei show the characteristics of collectivism with emphasis on obligation, interdependence and social concern. Supplemental data were given in Abe's comparison (1958) of Japanese-American norms with American norms in Salt Lake City using the Edwards Personal Preference Schedule. Both nisei men and women are significantly higher on deference, order, abasement, nurturance, and endurance. Nisei men are significantly lower than normative Americans on achievement, exhibition, intraception, and dominance. These data show that nisei generally have strong self-restraint, the essential element of the traditional Japanese personality.

While the second generation had direct contact with Japanese culture through their parents, the third generation (sansei) has lost this contact, with the exception of those living in places where many Japanese live, e.g., Little Tokyo in Los Angeles, Honolulu, Gardena, etc. The fact that most sansei have little knowledge of the Japanese language suggests their almost complete Americanization. Caudill and Frost (1973) studied sansei mothers and found them more like the American mother than the Japanese mother. The sansei mother chats often with her baby. There is a greater and more discriminating use of her voice as a means of communicating with her baby. These babies behave more like American babies than

Japanese babies, with their greater amount of happy vocalization and physical activity, and less unhappy vocalization. The infant's happy vocalization and the caretaker's chatting to him/her are significantly correlated in American, but are not so in Japanese data.

Sansei, however, retain Japanese traits to a notable extent. Caudill and Frost (1973) found the sansei mother closer to her Japanese counterpart in the amount of time she spends in playing with her baby and in carrying and lulling him. A yonsei (fourth generation) baby is more like the Japanese baby in that he plays alone less and sucks on fingers or pacifier less.

The similarity of sansei to Japanese people is also shown in psychological tests. Fenz and Arkoff (1962) found that sansei males in Hawaii expressed greater need (than the American norm) for deference, abasement, nurturance, affiliation, order, and exuberance, with a correspondingly reduced need for dominance, aggression, autonomy, exhibition, and heterosexuality. Meredith (1965) described the sansei as "more reserved, more humble, more conscientious, and more regulated by external realities" than Caucasian American males, and sansei females as "more affected by feeling, more obedient, more suspicious, and more apprehensive than Caucasian American females." He further observed that sansei males exhibited an introverted style of adjustment, and sansei females a heightened, although non-pathological, anxiety pattern.

Japanese-Americans are between the Japanese and the American poles in personality traits; those in the third and fourth generations lean increasingly toward the American side. They appear to have assimilated the dominant culture rather smoothly, but there are also some problems, such as identity conflicts, or over learning the stereotypical attitudes of the majority, or both. With the loss of the old Japanese spirit, it seems more difficult in some ways for young Japanese-

Americans to feel proud of themselves as being responsible, contributing, and important members of a family and a society.

Reischauer (1977) mentioned a Japanese sense of being a separate, unique people. He attributed this to a strong group solidarity which he believes is related to a correspondingly strong sense of difference from others. This group identity, the Japanese spirit (*yamato damashi*), contributed to the determination of the Japanese gymnast to continue in the 1976 Montreal Olympics despite a broken leg. With acculturation, Japanese-Americans can no longer call upon the Japanese spirit. What is to replace this? They may have lost their American identity, as they are often asked, "What are you really?" (the implication being you are not American).

Other than racism, there seems to be very little which prevents the assimilation of Japanese-Americans. Although assimilation varies with social class, generation, geographic locale, and chronology, Japanese-Americans as a whole are willing and eager to be assimilated. The traditional Japanese values of education, hard work, respect for superiors, etc., are shared by the American middle-class and facilitate assimilation (Yamamoto and Iga, 1974). The high level of occupational success which some Japanese-Americans have attained should also be a positive factor (although racism prevents occupational success equivalent to educational success). Their desire to be assimilated is demonstrated by the fact that more than 66% of Japanese-Americans in the San Francisco and Fresno areas intermarried (mostly with Caucasians) in 1975. Kitano (1977) predicted that Japanese Americans will lose their racial identity by the year 2,000.

The Mainlanders

In 1942, 117,000 Japanese-Americans were incarcerated in relocation centers. In various ways this experience had a severe effect on the Japanese-American's personality. First, some elders were imprisoned separately from their families because of membership in groups with ties to Japan. Premature demands of family leadership were placed on sons and daughters; parents lost their authority and status. Second, properties and businesses had to be abandoned. Third, in the confines of the "relocation centers," surrounded by barbed wire fences and guarded by fully armed soldiers, the only jobs available were with the War Relocation Authority, an agency of the United States government. Here the premium was on speaking English and having skills and professions needed in the camp (e.g., cooks, teachers, nurses, librarians, dentists and physicians). All employees were paid $12 to $19 a month. Fourth, in the process of incarceration, a loyalty questionnaire was required of all. This also polarized the group, and a minority who expressed grave dissatisfaction with the imprisonment were segregated for deportation to Japan. Fifth, the military recruitment of Japanese-Americans also strained the camp community because those relatives who remained were still detained. Sixth, the result of the camp experience was to increase Japanese-American identity conflicts, for the popular equation in wartime United States was "Japanese = bad, enemy; American = good, hero." This made more acute the problem of Japanese-Americans who, as a visible minority group living in segregated Little Tokyos, had experienced discrimination in housing, education, and job opportunities, but had the advantage of the Japanese spirit with the positive feelings about Japanese people. Seventh, the wartime dissolution of Little Tokyos hastened the acculturation process, but at the cost of loss of cultural heritage. The only language accepted was English; the only appearance accepted was American.

The Hawaiian-Japanese

The experience of the Hawaiian-Japanese was quite different in several ways. A most important difference was that they were not incarcerated in relocation centers. Thus, even though Pearl Harbor had been bombed, when the United States government decided that the Japanese could be trusted and asked for combat team volunteers, a much higher percentage of the Hawaiian-Japanese volunteered. In contrast, a much lower percentage of Japanese-Americans volunteered from the camps, where feelings of fear and resentment were strong. The 442nd Regimental Combat Team is famous among all Americans as the most wounded, most heavily decorated combat team in the military history of the United States.

Although the Japanese and other Asians have suffered from prejudice and discrimination in Hawaii, being in the majority (among non-Caucasians) until recent years, they have had the advantage of being a visible majority. Gradually increasing numbers of people, especially in education and government, are Asian. The identity conflicts prevalent among Mainland Japanese are often avoided. In Hawaii, the *haoles* (Anglo-Americans) feel that they are the ones discriminated against. Perhaps they are. Certainly, the Samoans and other tiny minority groups are disadvantaged. This shows that no matter where we are in the world, all of us need to be aware that the dominant majority tends to suppress and discriminate against the minority.

SUMMARY

There are so many individual differences among Japanese-American children that it is impossible to generalize about them. They vary in their appearance and in their adherence to the traditional Japanese ways. These include the Confucian values of filial piety, emphasis on the family as the primary social unit and on future achievement in order to contribute towards the well-being of the family. At the other extreme is the typical American child who is raised to be an individual, concerned about his/her achievements, with the objective of a separate nuclear family, not closely connected with the parental home. Indeed, the old Japanese values may have been entirely forgotten and American behavior substituted in every instance.

Statistically, the average child is probably somewhere in between the Japanese and American norms. Third and fourth generation Japanese-Americans lean much more towards the American norms. Even these individuals will vary depending on the geographical locus of their socialization. For example, those who grew up in Gardena in typical middle-class Japanese-American families are likely to maintain more of the traditional values of Japan, although these will be very much overshadowed by the American values. There will be an admixture varying from mild to moderate Japanese influences to practically none at all in the case of Japanese-Americans who have been educated and socialized in parts of the United States where exposure to the Japanese traditions is not possible. Partly due to the efforts of their parents, Japanese-American children will achieve educationally, and to a somewhat lesser extent, occupationally. The recent trend towards outmarriages, especially on the Mainland, will of course decrease even more the number of traditional Japanese families.

Though many Japanese-Americans have achieved a considerable measure of success in education and occupation, the Japanese child in the United States must still face many problems in socialization. A primary problem is the presence of racism, which is hard for the young child to accept, much less to understand. The subtlety of stereotypes and prejudices makes the situation more difficult emotionally, though less difficult educationally and occupationally, in that there are increasing opportunities available, although these do not equal those available to the majority.

With the loss of the old Japanese values, it may be more difficult for young Japanese-Americans to feel proud of themselves as responsible, contributing, important members of family and society. The old Japanese spirit (*yamato damashi*) was a continuation of the use of the amuletic phrase (Ben Dasan, 1970). In the pre-World War II days when anti-Asian prejudices were high, maintenance of the Japanese spirit helped one to counter the negative experiences of racism in educational and job opportunities. One could live with pride and dignity (even lacking equality).

Today, with increasing understanding of cultural pluralism in the United States, paradoxically it may be more difficult for young Japanese-Americans to feel pride in themselves as Americans. It is our prediction that eventually Japanese Americans, too, will combine the traditions and culture of Japan with the technology, culture and values of the United States. Recent successes by Senators Inouye, Matsunaga, and Hayakawa, and Congressmen Mineta, Matsui, and many others have made it possible for Japanese-Americans to feel proud of their identities. It is American to be proud of and aware of one's cultural background and to be able to combine these with American ways (Haley, 1976).

The consequences of this for the health and welfare of Japanese-Americans are problematical. Study of the incidence of heart disease among Japanese-Americans showed that those most acculturated tended to be at most risk (Marmot and Syme, 1976). We hope that, regardless of the problems, we Japanese-Americans will be able to use our achievements and opportunities for the benefit of a future pluralistic society with greater opportunities and benefit for all.

REFERENCES

Abe, S. Nisei personality characteristics as measured by the Edwards Personal Preference Schedule and Mutliphasic Personality Inventory. Ph.D. dissertation, University of Utah, 1958.

Ben Dasan, I. *Nihonjin to Uydayajin* (Japanese and Jews). Tokyo: Yamamoto Shoten, 1970.

Benedict, R. *The Chrysanthemum and the Sword.* Cambridge, MA.: The Riverside Press, 1946.

Caudill, W. Japanese American Personality and Acculturation. Genetic Psychological Monograph, 1952.

Caudill, W. Patterns of emotion in modern Japan. In: R.J. Smith & R.K. Beardsley (Eds.), *Japanese Culture: Its Development and Character.* Chicago: Aldine, 1962.

Caudill, W. and Frost, L. A comparison of maternal care of infant behavior in Japanese-American, American, and Japanese families. In: W.P. Lebra (Ed.), *Youth, Socialization, and Mental Health Research in Asia and the Pacific.* Honolulu: University Press of Hawaii, 1973.

Caudill, W. and Plath, D. Who sleeps by whom? Parent-child involvement in urban Japanese families. *Psychiatry,* 1966, *29*(4), 344–366.

Caudill, W. and Weinstein, H. Maternal care and infant behavior in Japan and America. *Psychiatry,* 1969, *32*, 12–43.

Conrat, R. and Conrat, M. *Executive Order 9066: The Internment of 110,000 Japanese Americans.* Los Angeles: Anderson, Ritchie & Simon, 1972.

De Vos, G. The relation of guilt toward parents to achievement and arranged marriage among the Japanese. *Psychiatry,* 1960, *23*, 287–301.

De Vos, G. *Socialization for Achievement.* Berkeley, CA: University of California Press, 1973.

Doi, L.T. Amae: A key concept for understanding Japanese personality structure. In: R.J. Smith and R.K. Beardsley (Eds.), *Japanese Culture: Its Development and Characteristics.* Chicago: Aldine, 1962.

Doi, L.T. *Amae No Kozo* (The Structure of Amae). Tokyo: Kobundo, 1971.

Fenz, E.D. and Arkoff, A. Comparative need patterns of five ancestry groups in Hawaii. *Journal of Social Psychology,* 1962, *58*, 67–89.

Fischer, J. The Japanese intellectuals: Cliques, soft edges, and dread of power. *Harpers,* September 1964.

Gordon, J.M. *Assimilation in American Life.* New York: Oxford University Press, 1964.

Haley, A. *Roots.* Garden City, N.Y.: Doubleday, 1976.

Ishikawa, T. Personal communication, 1977.

Kitano, H.H.L. *Japanese Americans: The Evolution of a Subculture.* Englewood Cliffs, N.J.: Prentice Hall, 1969.

Kitano, H.H.L. Article in *Pacific Citizen,* Los Angeles, February 25, 1977.

Lanham, B.B. Aspects of child care in Japan: Preliminary report. In: R.G. Haring (Ed.), *Personal Character and Cultural Milieu.* Syracuse, N.Y.: Syracuse University Press, 1956.

Lebra, T.S. *Japanese Patterns of Behavior.* Honolulu, Hawaii: University Press of Hawaii, 1976.

Lifton, R.T. Youth and history: Individual change in postwar Japan. In: E.H. Erikson (Ed.), *The Challenge of Youth*. New York: Doubleday Anchor, 1965.

Mahler, E. What is the self-concept in Japan? *Psychologia: An International Journal of Psychology in the Orient*, Sept. 1976, *19(3)*, 127–133.

Marmot, M.G. and Syme, S. Acculturation and coronary heart disease in Japanese Americans. *Am. Journal of Epidemiology*, September 1976, *104(3)*, 225–247.

Meredith, G.M. Observations on the acculturation of Sansei Japanese Americans in Hawaii. *Psychologia*, June 1965, *1 & 2*.

Nakamura, H. *Ways of Thinking of Eastern Peoples: India, China, Tibet, Japan*. P.P. Wiener (Ed.). Honolulu: East West Center Press, 1964.

Nakane, C. *Japanese Society*. Berkeley & Los Angeles: University of California Press, 1970.

Reischauer, E.D. *The Japanese*. Cambridge, MA: Harvard University Press, 1977.

Shimizu, I. *Nihon-teki Naru Mono* (Things Japanese). Tokyo: Ushio Shuppansha, 1968.

Smith, R.J. and Beardsley, R.K. (Eds.) *Japanese Culture: Its Development and Characteristics*. Chicago: Aldine, 1962.

Spitzer, H.M. Psychoanalytic approaches to the Japanese character. In: G. Roheim (Ed.), *Psychoanalysis and the Social Sciences*. Volume I. New York: International Universities Press, 1947.

Weglyn, M. *Years of Infamy: The Untold Story of America's Concentration Camps*. New York: William and Morrow, 1976.

Yamamoto, J. and Iga M. Japanese enterprise and American middle-class values. *American Journal of Psychiatry*, May 1974, *131(5)*, 577–579.

Yamamoto, J., Okonogi, K., Iwasaki, T. and Yoshimura S. Mourning in Japan. *American Journal of Psychiatry*, June 1969, *125(12)*, 74–79.

PART III

Family Life

Patterns

CHAPTER 11

Black Family Life Patterns, the Development of Self and Cognitive Development of Black Children

Dolores G. Norton, Ph.D.

The term "self" refers to that conglomerate of consciousness, consistent personality traits, attitudes, emotions, and perceptions that make up the individual's identity and influences his behavior. (Erikson, 1968). It is the sense of being that makes the individual an entity to himself, and to others. Most studies in personality relate a positive sense of self to closer development toward individual potential, and conclude that a positive sense of self is important in moving toward a satisfying and fulfilling life for the individual.

Most scholars of human development agree that all individual development occurs as a result of the interaction between basic genetic characteristics and the social and physical environment of the individual. The individual's genetic potential is fostered or constrained by his or her life experiences. The family tends to structure the individual's early social and physical environment, and primarily determines early life experiences. The family's place in the structure of society highly influences the type of physical and social environment available to the child. In the United States, the family's place in the social structure is largely determined by its race and socioeconomic status. Thus, race and socioeconomic status heavily influence the types of life experiences a family can offer a child, and these experiences have a major effect on his development of self.

By approximately age seven, black children in the United States are aware of the social devaluation placed upon their racial group by the larger society regardless of the region in which they live or the socioeconomic status of their families (Baumrind, 1972; Porter, 1971; Williams and Morland, 1976). How, then, do black families provide life experiences that help their children develop positive identities and a good self-image? To answer that question, this chapter focuses on those patterns of black family life that are related to two major aspects of human development: 1) the development of identity and self-image of the black child, and 2) the cognitive development of the black child. These two areas of development are selected because together they explain a major portion of human development and behavior. A strong self-concept is associated with effective social functioning and has been shown to be highly related to cognitive development (Perkins, 1958; Rosenberg and Simmons, 1972). Cognitive development as used in this chapter is far more than questionable I.Q. scores or demonstrated academic ability. It is the mode of operations developed out of human experience that forms our capacity to perceive, evaluate and execute in a manner that makes for successful coping with one's environment. The chapter describes: 1) the black family in the United States today; 2) sets a perspective for viewing the black family as a social system embedded in the larger society, and 3) examines those patterns of interaction within the family itself and in interrelationship with the larger society that influence development on two important dimensions for human functioning: the self-concept and cognitive development.

THE BLACK FAMILY IN
THE UNITED STATES

Of a total of over 200 million people in the United States, approximately 22.5 million, or 11 percent, are identified as black. Despite the increasing absolute numbers over the past years, blacks have remained about 11 percent of the American population since 1900 (U.S. Depart-

ment of Labor, 1971). This seems like a small percentage of the population compared to the enormous judicial, economic and social problems involving blacks in the United States. The time, energy, finances and conflict around desegregation issues, affirmative action cases, and housing problems seem disproportionate when one considers that they are sparked by the existence of only 11 percent of our population. Not only is the population comparatively small, but it is also separate from whites geographically. Most of the black population (over 86%) live in 47 large cities, and in census tracts that are 50% or more black (Cottingham, 1975). This means that despite the diversity of American society, a majority of black children grow up separated from this diversity, among people most like themselves.

Most black children probably live in homes where the median income is lower than that in the homes of most white children. In 1975 the white family median income was $14,268.00 while the black family median income was $8,779.00. By 1980 the poverty threshold for a non-farm family of four was $7,402. The median family income level was $12,674. For Afro-Americans and $21,904 for white families (U.S. Bureau of Census 1979, 1980). There are equally as many poor black families currently as there were a decade ago, but the number of poor white families has decreased (U.S. Bureau of the Census, 1976, 1979).

There is another phenomenon taking place regarding black family income that might mean further division of black children in the future by socioeconomic status among their own racial group. During the 1966–1976 decade, the number of black middle class families has increased. In 1966, 17 percent of black families earned between $15,000.00 and $24,999.00, but by 1976 that percentage had increased to 21 percent (Anderson and Dumpson, 1978). The contrast between the growth of the black middle class due to increased college education among blacks and affirmative action programs and the increasingly jobless lower socioeconomic black underclass is a phenomenon that is beginning to cause concern. The Urban League points to the growing "economic duality" of the black population (Anderson and Dumpson, 1978). Wilson's book employs an economic analysis to discuss what he calls "The Declining Significance of Race" in regard to the growing middle class, as compared to the saliency of race with the black underclass (1978). He has recently suggested that priority be given to those economic issues related to the black underclass. If Kantrowitz's thesis, based on extensive urban population analysis, that "Rich blacks are as segregated from poor blacks as rich whites are from poor whites" is correct, this may mean further division between the worlds of black children themselves on the basis of socioeconomic status (Cafferty and Chestang, 1976). If such a trend is true, and if it continues, we cannot know as yet the implications of such divisions among black families in the future.

Approximately one-half of all black children live in two-parent families. In 1970, 58 percent of all black children lived with both parents. This is compared with a drop from 89 percent to 85 percent for white children during the same period (National Urban League, 1975). It is obvious that increasing divorce and separation, as well as decisions to have children and not marry, have increased the number of female-headed families among both black and white families. Between 1974 and 1977 the number of female-headed black families increased 16 percent (from 1.8 million to 2.1 million) while the number of female-headed white families rose by 13 percent (from 4.9 to 5.5 million). Thus, the proportion of black families headed by women increased from 34 percent to 37 percent between 1974 and 1977, while the proportion of such white families went from 10 to 11 percent.

The importance of the extended family to the well-being of the black family, so often discussed in the literature, is well supported by Census statistics. Many of the black children living in families headed by women are living in family structures composed of some variation of the extended family. Between 1969 and 1975 the proportion of black children living in households composed of their mothers and other relatives increased from 22 percent to 39 percent (U.S. Bureau of the Census, 1976). Another statistic coupled with this one supports the importance of the extended family. It is interesting to note that during the recession years of 1974–1975 the proportion of female-headed black families receiving public assistance declined from 55 percent to 47 percent, and the proportion of male-headed black families on welfare fell from 12 to seven percent (National Urban League, 1975). These figures would be expected to rise during a recession. The fact that more single-parent families were moving in with relatives at this time indicates that during adversity many black families return to extended families to share reduced economic means. Combining households makes it more difficult to qualify for public aid, and the number of black families on public assistance decreased instead of increasing, despite the recession.

Another statistical pattern also supports the importance of the extended family among blacks. One-half (52 percent) of all black children between the ages of three and 13 whose mothers are in the labor force are cared for by relatives. Sixteen percent are cared for by non-relatives, and only three percent are cared for in a formal day-care center (National Urban League Research Department, 1973). It is obvious that black families of all income levels rely on relatives to care for their children while they work. Many middle-class families pay an aunt or cousin or mother to come into their homes and baby-sit, with formal salary arrangements. Having reached financial stability themselves, they not only share that stability by providing economic opportunity for other family members, but also assure that their children will receive responsible, loving and interested family-oriented child-care. Other, less well off families drop their children at the home of relatives, making financial arrangements that are probably lower in cost. For others, there are no financial arrangements, but reciprocity is given in returned child-care, sharing of food, clothing or shelter.

To summarize the current picture of black families:

1) The majority of black children are raised in families living in urban areas in predominantly black communities.
2) Although approximately one-quarter of all black families could be considered in the middle-income range, there is an increasing number of black families who are jobless and whose children will lack certain needs to develop to their maximum potential. The children in these jobless families are growing up not only separate from the larger society but, we suspect, also separate from the privileged black children.
3) About one-half of all black children live in two-parent families.
4) The extended family serves many support functions for black families of all levels of socioeconomic status.

THE DUAL PERSPECTIVE: A SYSTEMS FRAMEWORK FOR VIEWING THE BLACK FAMILY

Billingsley, one of the first social scientists to use Parsons' concept of a social system to analyze black family life, stressed the functions for which all families are responsible and examined the processes through which black families carried out these functions (1968). Parsons defined a social system as an aggregation of persons or social roles bound together in a pattern of mutual interaction and interdependence (1951). The family can be viewed as

such a system with its own aggregate of family members bound together in structural relationships carrying out certain functions towards the goals of family maintenance and development. The family system is embedded in the immediate community system or neighborhood system which in turn is embedded in the wider societal system. All systems interact with each other and affect one another as they carry out various social functions.

Thus, every individual is embedded simultaneously in at least two systems: that of his immediate social and physical environment, and that of the larger major society. The larger system is that of the major society. Chestang calls this system, "the sustaining system" (Cafferty and Chestang, 1976). It houses the instrumental needs of man, the goods, services, political power, economic resources, and large societal institutions. Embedded in the larger system is the individual's more immediate system, the physical and social environment of family and close community. Chestang refers to this environment as the "nurturing environment." The "nurturing environment" can be compared to Erikson's "significant others," those closest and most important in the determination of an individual's sense of identity (Erikson, 1968).

For many groups there is not much difference between the behavior and values of the individual and immediate environmental system and those of the major societal system. For racial minority people, the degree of difference between the systems may be very wide, resulting in value and behavioral conflict between the systems.

This dual perspective of the child's environment is a concept that can be defined as a conscious and systematic process of perceiving, understanding and comparing simultaneously the values, attitudes and behavior of the larger societal system with those of the child's immediate family and community system (Norton, 1978). Such a framework forces one to look at the complexities from different perspectives within the variety of subsystems of each of the two major systems involved. The framework is not a concept to be applied solely to minority people and groups. It can enhance understanding of all people, but is particularly vital to understanding those whose immediate nurturing system might differ or be in conflict with the sustaining system.

The remainder of this chapter will use this framework to examine the relationship between black family life patterns and the development of a self-concept in black children, as well as the relationship between black family life patterns and certain areas of cognitive development in black children. The dual perspective gives us a framework for exploring interaction within the black family as well as between the black family and the larger society.

PARENT-CHILD INTERACTION AND THE DEVELOPMENT OF SELF

The concept of the dual perspective focuses attention on both the immediate social and physical environment of the child and the larger environment. It prevents drawing conclusions based on only one system of the individual's environment. The complexities of the parent-child interaction leading to a positive sense of self cannot be sorted out and evaluated accurately by mental health professionals and educators if viewed only by the norms of the larger society. Use of the dual perspective is imperative in understanding how the behavioral norms set and defined in the larger sustaining society can be experienced in a very different framework in the immediate nurturing society.

Theorists, researchers, practitioners and educators suggest that a positive self-concept is associated with effective social functioning and is highly related to higher levels of cognitive development. Although the concept of self is referred to by various terms such as self-concept, self-image,

self-esteem, and identity, often interchangeably, they all refer to an amorphous concept that implies a person's feelings and beliefs about himself. In a recent study, Rosenberg defined the self-concept as "the totality of the individual's thoughts and feelings having reference to himself as an object" (1979, p. 7). It is the individual's concept of himself that largely determines his behavior. Our self-esteem consists of the positive or negative feelings we have toward ourselves. No matter how the concept is defined, most mental health professionals agree that one of the individual's most basic and continuing needs is for a self-image that is essentially positive. Many studies illustrate that a positive self-image seems pivotal to achievement in school and in social interaction with others (Bayley and Schaefer, 1964: Moss and Kagan, 1958). Maintaining or attempting to maintain a continuity of one's self-concept is a major motivating force of all behavior.

The tremendous importance of the parent-child or primary caretaker-child relationship in the development of a self-concept in the early years has been reaffirmed and substantiated in most mental health research. In a relatively early study, Wylie stated that all personality theorists who were concerned with development of a self-concept gave great importance to parent-child interaction in the development of self (1961). Early consistent, loving, nurturing interaction is the ideal process of interaction leading to a good sense of self. The child who is loved, accepted and supported in appropriate reality-oriented functioning in relationship to others comes to love himself and to respect himself as someone worthy of love.

Self-esteem and self-image are interwoven with group identity and group esteem. What happens to members of a minority group such as blacks whose group has been historically devalued by the wider society? The heavy psychological costs of being black in America have been well documented over the past 20 years (Kardiner and Ovesey, 1951). More recent studies have also documented that regardless of the region where a black child lives or of his socioeconomic group, the child is aware at about age seven of the social devaluation placed on his racial group by the larger society (Baumrind, 1972; Porter, 1971; Williams and Morland, 1976). This information could lead to the conclusion that all black children internalize the poor esteem of the major society that is directed toward their group membership and develop self-hatred or a negative self-image. This is too simplistic an analysis. Since black children do develop a good sense of self, the dynamics are much more complex.

Two basic processes are involved in the development of racial identity by the black child (Proshansky and Newton, 1968). The first is racial conception or identification, and the second is racial evaluation. Racial conception and identification involve when and how the child learns to make a racial distinction at a conceptual level. It is when the child becomes aware that black is a color, that black is his color, and that he is visibly different. According to the early Clark and Clark (1947) and Goodman (1952) studies, children are aware of these racial differences by age three or four. This occurs through observation and comparison of his parents and the incorporation of subtle nuances received in interaction with parents or primary caretakers.

The second process involved in the development of racial identity is racial evaluation. This process involves when and how the black child learns about the evaluation of his own racial group. We have just stated that the child becomes aware of the devaluation placed on his group by age seven. However, the awareness of this devaluation of his racial group does not necessarily extend to the child's evaluation of himself as an individual. The black child, as do all children, forms his evaluation of himself as an individual as a re-

sult of the interaction within his own immediate physical and social environmental system and not from the society at large. Self-image rests highly on the reflected interaction and appraisal of the "significant others" around the child. "Significant others" are those with whom the child is involved emotionally, psychologically and physically, and are to be found in the family and the immediate community.

The idea that positive self-esteem often can be developed quite independently from the child's knowledge and perception of society's view of his racial group is highly supported by much recent research (Rosenberg, 1979; Rosenberg and Simmons, 1971; Taylor, 1976). The family provides the first environment for the child to develop a sense of self. Taylor argues that the Kardiner and Ovesey thesis stating that black self-esteem suffers and can turn into "self-hatred" because blacks must constantly face devaluation of themselves is false. He states that self-esteem is developed through interaction with "significant others" early in life. Taylor further argues that one's identity and self-image depend upon how one is treated relative to others in one's family and the community, how one measures up to one's peers, and the relative position of one's family as compared to others in the community, rather than upon the potentially devaluating larger society (Taylor, 1976, p. 9). Taylor implicitly used the dual perspective when he questioned the findings that the people in the larger society are "significant others" and present the major frames of reference for young black children. By focusing on the interaction in the child's immediate environment of peers and family and comparing this process with that in the larger society, he was able to explain why racism and bigotry in the larger society may not be the major influence on the very early development of self-worth. The sense of self developed in the immediate environment acts as a buffer against the potential devaluation by the larger society.

Taylor's argument is supported by Rosenberg's findings that young children tend to make comparisons only in their immediate environment (Rosenberg, 1979) Therefore, the black child may have a very positive individual self-image and simultaneously be very much aware of how his racial group is viewed by the larger society. If the immediate environment is stable and positive in its nurturing, the child learns from the "significant others" that the devaluation placed on the group is due to hatred, bigotry, or racism on the part of the whites who are external to his immediate subsystem and world, and not caused by his own lack of worth. Black children receiving this kind of nurturing care are ready to evaluate the reflections of devaluation of the larger society in more realistic terms. They possibly understand racism and bigotry quite accurately as reflecting racial devaluation of their collective group. Although they may not understand the reasons or causes, they do not have to relate this to their own sense of self-worth. Except as a member of the "collective group," the child's own self-worth depends on how he experiences interaction within his own family, how he measures up to peers, and his family's position in his own community (Kaply, 1978). The thought is *not* "They hate us because we are so inferior," but "*Why* do they hate us so? What is wrong with *them?*"

Earlier studies of young black children such as the "Doll Studies" presented findings that reflected less positive feelings about self on the part of the black child (Clark and Clark, 1947; Goodman, 1952; Kardiner and Ovesey, 1951). However, as social research methodology improved, reasons for the limitation of these studies became apparent. These include:

1) poor definitions of self-image that could not be quantitatively measured validly;
2) small samples of data drawn from sources that have already come to the attention of society, such as social service agencies and juvenile court records, and should not be generalized from as the norm for black families;
3) the lack of control for variables of education and socioeconomic status.

The result of these flaws flowing into the social science and practice literature created a one-dimensional standard to evaluate black human functioning.

The more positive self-image of black children is supported in more recent research of self-esteem among black children (Powell, 1973; Rosenberg, 1979; Rosenberg and Simmons, 1972). These studies found that the level of self-esteem of black school children does not differ a great deal from that of white school children. Black children in racially homogeneous school situations who do not experience conflicting attitudes of the larger society had even higher images of self-worth than white school children (Powell, 1973; Rosenberg, 1979). Somewhat lowered self-esteem did occur when the larger society moved onto the "significant others" systems level. Black children who were not only in contact with white children but interacted with them on enough levels to experience them as peers and who experienced conflicting racial reactions did reflect lowered self-esteem. However, even in this situation Rosenberg found that most black children did not reject their racial group. They did not automatically translate group rejection into self-hatred. Rosenberg's findings support Proshansky and Newton's thesis mentioned earlier that racial identity is composed of the two processes of racial identification and racial evaluation (Proshansky and Newton, 1968). Knowledge of low evaluation does not necessarily compromise a positive self-identification if early nurturing has been positive.

This chapter is not denying the pervasive destructive impact of racism on the opportunities for the development of positive self-esteem for black children. That is well understood and much has been written about it. Racism in the economic, political and social structure exists but, in spite of it, black families not only have survived but have interacted with their children in ways that foster the development of a positive sense of self. It is easier for those blacks without overwhelming economic and social pressures to aid their children in accomplishing this; however, positive self-esteem is found in black children at all socioeconomic levels.

What happens in the interaction between black parents and their children in those stable nurturing families from any educational or socioeconomoc level who manage to rear children with a strong sense of self? How and with what patterns do these families defy the "mark of oppression"? How can we determine the strengths and healthy coping mechanisms in the interaction between black parents and their children? If these patterns of interaction could be isolated and studied, what social programs and policies could be instituted to aid other families to accomplish this level of functioning?

A fascinating example of the need for a dual perspective in understanding the black family is Baumrind's study on patterns of parental authority and their relationship to the behavior of preschool children (1972). Baumrind studied a sample of preschool black children and white children of middle socioeconomic status with both father and mother present. She hypothesized that authoritarian, rejecting parents would have preschool children who were less confident, less independent, and less competent than the children of parents who were authoritarian but not rejecting. This was a very reasonable hypothesis, given our present state of knowledge that authoritarian rejecting behavior is associated with lower levels of self-worth.

Quite correctly assuming that the effect of the given parental variables might be affected by the racial and cultural context in which black families operate, Baum-rind analyzed black children and their families separately. The major conclusions from this analysis was, "if the black families were viewed by white norms, they appeared authoritarian and rejecting, but that unlike their counterparts, the most authoritarian of these families produced the most self assertive and independent girls" (p. 261). The behavior of those parents assessed by standard research instruments was classified authoritarian and rejecting. Thus, the patterns of interaction that were assumed negative by the larger societal norms and probably should be designated for change paradoxically appeared to produce unusually independent, at ease preschool girls with a good sense of self.

In searching out the reason for this discrepancy, Baumrind moved to examination of the immediate environment of the black girls involved, and compared her findings to those supporting the larger societal norms. She discovered that the authoritarian patterns which best described the little girls' upbringing differed in quality from those which described the authoritarian childrearing practices accompanied by the rejecting authoritarian personality syndrome. The black families were characterized by the practices, but not by the syndrome of repressed hostility, dogmatism, and rejection associated with the authoritarian personality. The families, though authoritarian in their expectations of behavior, were spontaneous and warm with the little girls.

After observation and family interviews with these black families, Baumrind came to a preliminary conclusion that it was of primary importance to the families that a *girl* be self-sufficient and independent, given the one-down position of black women in white American society. Their authoritarian childrearing practices may have the explicit objective of developing toughness and self-sufficiency in the black girls. Their behavior is possibly perceived by the children not as rejection but as nurturing and caretaking (Baumrind, p. 266).

Although much more study is necessary, this preliminary understanding of the different quality and meaning of certain behavioral variables could not have been extricated without careful analysis of the family systems from several perspectives and realization that one must look within the context of the black family to determine the nuances of parent-child interaction that make for the difference in developing a positive self-image. Use of this framework is important in understanding individuals of any group, but it is crucial to understanding behavior and values of a racially or culturally diverse group whose immediate environment may not be congruent in certain aspects with the larger society.

THE BLACK CHILD AND COGNITIVE DEVELOPMENT

One of the major problems involving race in the United States today is that of education. As cited earlier, the majority of blacks live in urban areas, and urban public school systems tend to have larger percentages of black children. These large urban school systems are failing to graduate students with effective cognitive skills, and the majority of these unskilled students are black. Most urban areas must also face the question of de facto school segregation and how to comply with school desegregation rulings. It is not within the goals of this chapter to chronicle the problems of urban education. However, this chapter is interested in those patterns of black family interaction that are related to higher levels of cognitive development. Better understanding of how all children, and especially black children, are prepared to learn is important. If these education problems are ever to be resolved sensibly, schools need to be aware of the cognitive structures and processes young black children bring to the schools and to plan their curriculum building on these processes. There is need for knowledge of the effect of different environments on the early cognitive development of children.

Cognitive development was defined earlier as the mode of operations developed out of human experience that forms the individual's capacity to take in information, evaluate it, hypothesize various solutions and select a solution as being the most effective, and execute some action that makes for successful interaction with one's environment. The key word is "hypothesize." It means that the person is going beyond the concrete reality of the here-and-now and can deal hypothetically with many possible alternative solutions to a problem. This cognitive capacity to organize and hypothesize alternative solutions makes for effective judgment and reasoning. The person can examine his own life situation, taking into consideration many relationships, possibilities and implications, before a decision is made. Although the capacity to make effective decisions will not solve the twin problems of racism and poverty for a black child, if he can be more effective in his decision-making, he can maximize his own efforts to attempt to change the larger system, and he will have more options and alternatives in the given society.

One must look closely at the immediate environment and interaction of the black child in order to determine how this daily interaction differs from that in the overall society. The educational system often misses these differences and therefore may not able to communicate effectively with the child. To further develop the need for the use of a dual perspective, this chapter will briefly discuss the findings from a study on family interaction and cognitive development in which black children and white children and their families were studied and compared (Norton, 1969). The study sample consisted of 109 eight-year-olds who were the firstborn children of mothers between 18 and 40, in good health, with a normal range of intelligence and no birth defects, and who fit into a four-part sample based on race and socioeconomic status. The children were tested and interviewed in their homes ranging through four Pennsylvania counties, from dilapidated urban ghettos, to very upper-middle-class surburbia. Parents were interviewed, the children were tested, and interaction between parents and children was observed in the home. Several findings particularly revealed the need to evaluate the families on their own cultural terms.

One of the most important overall findings on all the children was the strong association between "good" language models in the child's home and the disappearance of what Piaget calls "static and irreversible thought" (Piaget, 1955). Static and irreversible thought is the inability to see the continuous dynamic flow of events leading from one situation or state to another. Thus, one is unable to pursue a series of reasoning and then reverse direction in thought, go back to an original premise, establish new conditions and pursue those hypothetically, and then return to the original premise. The opposite of static and irreversible thought is reversible and mobile thought. Reversible and mobile thought can postulate any number of solutions to a problem by traveling to a conclusion, evaluating it, going back, and traveling to another conclusion. This process is continued until the most effective solution is found. One can begin to see that this is a very important component if one is to learn to think effectively. According to this study, a major environmental condition necessary for development of the capacity for reversible and mobile thought is "good language in the environment. The reason for this is that effective use of language permits manipulation of ideas on an abstract rather than concrete level. "Good" language is not used in any absolute sense here; it means a language with rules which permit the ability to develop concepts which can be used in reverse thought.

In this study there was a strong asso-ciation between "good" language models in the child's home and the disappearance of static and irreversible thought. Mothers who spoke in sentences, used proper names for objects, and had hobbies which reflected reading and good language tended to have children who ranked high on reversible thought. There was little or no variation on the findings among all of the children studied except for the black children from lower socioeconomic families. Among this group of children, "good" language models seemed totally unrelated to high levels of reversible and mobile thought and "defective" language was not particularly related to lower levels of reversible thought. Language models seemed totally unrelated to reversible thought in the case of these children. This was a very different result compared with all white children and with black children whose families were of middle income. For these the correlation was high.

More careful analysis of this phenomenon revealed that the black children from lower socioeconomic families did have effective language models. However, the tests and evaluative methodology used did not tap the dimensions of their language as it was used in the home. This finding was supported by several other linguistic studies. These studies contended that black children from "ghetto" families have a language which has its own internal consistency even though it differs from Standard English (Baratz and Baratz, 1970; Bruck, 1974). The child does communicate with his parents and peers and has learned the rules of his linguistic environment. However, it is not recognized that the child's language is different from Standard English. Thus he is penalized in evaluative tests and the results are taken as manifestations of underlying differences in ability rather than a confusion of language differences.

The implications of this idea for education are far-reaching. If some black children are coming to school with a different language system, the school should be aware of what that system is. How can children learn to read if reading for them is in actuality "translation"? Before they can read Standard English, they must translate it into their spoken or public language. Teachers in the early grades must gear their language teaching and methodology to "begin" where the child is. We know from cognitive development studies that there can be no sudden jumps in learning, but a gradual building upon what is already known.

This finding *again* underlines the need for a dual perspective in looking at the early development and interaction of the black child. When the child is observed or studied from only one system, the child can be penalized and his own learning process ignored in helping him to develop. If this analysis is valid, education that builds upon and is aware of the child's present knowledge and the child's present style of learning may very well be successful in helping the child to reach high levels of cognitive development. To accomplish this, however, the educational system must know the needs and the modes of interaction we have talked about, and it must know the community and the parents or develop methods for obtaining this knowledge.

A complete description of this cognitive study is not within the scope of this chapter. The finding on language was used to point out to mental health professionals, researchers and educators the importance of carefully examining the meaning of the interaction within the child's immediate environment as it related to the "norms" of the larger society. Analysis of the relationship of various aspects of parent-child interaction and specific modes of cognitive development must occur within a framework which permits understanding of the meaning of the interaction within the family, not by external norms.

Yet external norms cannot be ignored entirely. The child's immediate nurturing environment is embedded within the larger sustaining society and very often the

modes of coping which are effective in the immediate environmental system do not serve the child well in the larger environment. All children have to be prepared to operate in the larger environment if they are to have options and alternatives. This is especially crucial with language. If the findings of the studies cited here are valid, we do not accurately evaluate the language development of many black children and they are penalized by our assessment-oriented culture as "inferior." Understanding that the children have a different language which must be taken into consideration and built upon should determine a new direction for early urban education. Piaget saw cognitive development as sequential, with each stage building on the prior stage. If these children have developed a mode of communication different from what is expected of them in the schools, attempts to teach them to read become immensely difficult. The child's existing system of organization in terms of previous experience has no way to assimilate the new language and he or she is often designated as "retarded" or "retarded educable." The cost of such a label is dear to the child, and to society in general.

Mental health professionals must play an active role in bridging the gap between the home environment and the school environment of minority children. They need to be aware of the difference through knowledge of current research, as well as home visiting, in order to interpret to school personnel the more subtle meanings of the child's production in school. There must be active interaction between the home and the school.

As previously stated, a basic assumption of this chapter is that one must learn to operate in the dominant culture of his society in order to have options and alternatives and exercise some control over one's destiny. The goal of the educational system, especially in the unique and diverse culture of the United States, is to respect the differences brought from the diverse environmental systems and build upon them toward aiding the child to operate in the larger sustaining society. This means that what the child brings to school is accepted as good, thus reinforcing the continuity of his self-esteem. However, the child also learns new skills to prepare him for the larger system.

SUMMARY AND CONCLUSION

This chapter has described the black family in the United States as a predominantly urban group dependent on the extended family for many support functions at all levels of socioeconomic status. Although approximately one-quarter of all black families could be considered in the middle income range, there is an increasing number of black families who are still very poor. The children of these families are growing up in a world that is increasingly separate from most whites, and even from more privileged black children.

The chapter presents the framework of the dual perspective for understanding all families, but this is especially crucial for understanding more accurately the development of children from families which are racially, culturally or socioeconomically at variance with the "norms" of the larger society. Without the use of such a perspective, children are at risk of being labeled as "defective" in some areas of development.

Two important areas of development in the black child are discussed: the development of identity or self-image, and cognitive development. These two areas are selected because they explain a major portion of all human behavior. They are also selected because a valid and accurate evaluation of them in the black child can be negated if those doing the assessment use only the "norms" of the larger society and do not carefully examine the child's immediate nurturing environment and the meaning of parent-child interaction within that system. Mental health profes-

sionals, researchers, and educators making these assessments need to be specifically aware of the meaning of racially and culturally determined behavioral patterns.

Providers of service to black children and their families must have knowledge about their unique sociocultural history and the types of interaction that lead to their psychosocial development in order to serve them adequately. They cannot assess a situation correctly without specific knowledge of the immediate nurturing environment and of how it compares with the major society. Searching out such valid knowledge of the nurturing system is a difficult task, but one that those engaged in work with minorities must accomplish. Placing this knowledge in perspective in regard to the wider society completes a process that all social welfare professionals must pursue for effective and appropriate understanding and intervention with black families.

REFERENCES

Anderson, B.E. and Dumpson, J.R. (Eds.) *The State of Black America.* New York: National Urban League, 1978.

Baratz, S. and Baratz, J. Early childhood intervention: The social science base of institutional racism. *Harvard Educational Review,* February 1970.

Baumrind, D. An exploratory study of socialization effects on black children: Some black-white comparisons. *Child Development,* 1972, *43,* 261–267.

Bayley, N. and Schaefer, E.S. Correlations of maternal and child behaviors with the development of mental abilities: Data from Berkeley growth study. *Monographs of the Society for Research in Child Development* 1964, 29, (6 Serial No. 97).

Billingsley, A. *Black Families in White America.* New Jersey: Prentice Hall, 1968.

Bruck, M. Social class differences in acquisition of school language. *Merrill Palmer Quarterly,* 1974, *20,* 205–220.

Cafferty, P. and Chestang, L. (Eds.) *The Diverse Society: Implications for Social Policy.* New York: National Association of Social Workers, 1976.

Clark, K. and Clark, N. Racial identification and preference in negro children. In: T.H. Newcomb and E.L. Hartley (Eds.), *Readings in Social Psychology.* New York: Henry Holt, 1947.

Cottingham, P. Black income and metropolitan residential dispersion. *Urban Affairs Quarterly,* March 1975, *10,* 273–296.

Erikson, E. *Identity, Youth and Crisis.* New York: W. W. Norton, 1968.

Goodman, M.E. *Race Awareness in Young Children.* London: Collier Books, 1952.

Kaply, S.M. Self-esteem and early development: A critical review of the literature. Unpublished paper, University of Chicago, School of Social Service Administration, 1978.

Kardiner, A. and Ovesey, L. *The Mark of Oppression.* Cleveland: World Press, 1951.

Laosa, L.M. Nonbiased assessment of children's abilities: Historical antecedents and current issues. In: T. Oakland (Ed.), *Psychological and Educational Assessment of Minority Children.* New York: Brunner/Mazel, 1977.

Morland, J. Kenneth. A comparison of race awareness in Northern and Southern Children. *American Journal of Orthopsychiatry,* January 1966, *36,* 23–31.

Moss, H. A. and Kagan, J. Maternal influences and early IQ scores. *Psychological Reports,* 1958, *4,* 655–661.

National Urban League Research Department. *1972 Income Tax Deduction on Child Care. Who Benefits?* Washington, D.C.: National Urban League, 1973.

National Urban League Research Department. *Black Families in the 1974–75 Depression.* Washington, D.C.: National Urban League, 1975.

Norton, D.G. *Environment and Cognitive Development: A Comparative Study of Socioeconomic Status and Race.* Bryn Mawr: Doctoral Dissertation, Graduate School of Social Work and Social Research, Bryn Mawr College, 1969. (also on microfilm, University of Michigan).

Norton, D.G. *The Dual Perspective: Inclusion of Ethnic Minority Content in the Social Work Curriculum.* New York: Council on Social Work Education, 1978.

Oakland, T. Using test in non-discriminatory assessment. In: T. Oakland (Ed.), *Psychological and Educational Assessment of Minority Children.* New York: Brunner/Mazel, 1977.

Parsons, T. *The Social System.* New York: Free Press, 1951.

Parsons, T. and Bales, R.F. *Family, Socialization and Interaction Process.* New York: Free Press, 1955.

Perkins, H. V. Teachers' and peers' perceptions of children's self-concepts. *Child Development,* 1958, *29*(2), 221–230.

Piaget, J. *The Language and Thought of the Child.* New York: A. Meridian Book, 1955.

Piaget, J. *Origins of Intelligence in Children.* New York: W. W. Norton, 1963.

Porter, J. *Black Child, White Child.* Cambridge, MA: Harvard University Press, 1971.

Powell, G.J. Self-concept in white and black children. In: C. B. Willie, B. M. Kramer and B. S. Brown (Eds.), *Racism and Mental Health.* Pittsburgh: University of Pittsburgh Press, 1973.

Proshansky, H. and Newton, P. The meaning and nature of negro self-identity. In: M. Deutsch, I. Katz and A. Jensen (Eds.), *Social Class, Race, and Psychological Development.* New York: Holt, Rinehart, 1968.

Rosenberg, M. *Conceiving the Self.* New York: Basic Books, 1979.

Rosenberg, M. and Simmons, R. Black and white self-esteem: The urban school child. Washington, D.C.: The American Sociological Association, 1972.

Taylor, R.L. Psychosocial development among black children and youth: A reexamination. *American Journal of Orthopsychiatry,* January 1976, *46*(1), 4–19.

U.S. Bureau of Census. *Current Population Reports.* Household and family characteristics, March 1976. Series P-20, No. 311. Washington, D.C.: U.S. Goverment Printing Office, 1976.

U.S. Bureau of Census. *Current Population Reports.* Consumer income. Series P-60 and Special Studies Series P-23. Washington, D.C.: U.S. Government Printing Office, 1977a.

U.S. Bureau of Census. *Current Population Reports.* Marital status and living arrangements, March 1976. Series P-20, No. 306. Washington, D.C.: U.S. Government Printing Office, 1977b.

U.S. Bureau of the Census. *Current Population Reports.* School enrollment: Social and economic characteristics of students, October 1976, Series P-20, No. 309. Washington, D.C.: U.S. Government Printing Office, July 1977c.

U.S. Bureau of Census. *Current Population Reports.* Characteristics of population below poverty line. Series p-60, No. 130. Washington, D.C.: U.S. Government Printing Office, 1979.

U.S. Bureau of Census. *Current Population Reports.* Money, income and poverty status of families and persons in U.S. Series p-60, No. 127. Washington, D.C.: U.S. Government Printing Office, 1980.

U.S. Department of Health, Education, and Welfare. *Monthly Vital Statistics Report.* Provisional statistics, annual summary for the U.S., 1976 births, deaths, marriages and divorces. PHS 78–112, *25,* No. 13, December 12, 1977.

U.S. Department of Labor. *Black Americans: A Chartbook.* Bulletin 1699—Bureau of Labor Statistics. Washington, D.C.: U.S. Government Printing Office, 1971.

Wachs, T. Utilization of a Piagetian approach in the investigation of early experience effects. *Merrill Palmer Quarterly,* 1976, *22*(1), 11–30.

Ward, S. G. and Braun, J. Self-esteem and racial preference in black children. In: S. Chess and A. Thomas (Eds.), *Annual Progress in Child Psychiatry and Child Development.* Also in *American Journal of Orthopsychiatry,* July 1972, *42*(4), 644–647.

Wells, E.L. and Marwell, G. *Self-Esteem: Its Conceptualization and Measurement.* Beverly Hills: Sage Publications, 1976.

Williams, J.E. and Morland, J.K. *Race, Color and the Young Child.* Chapel Hill: The University of North Carolina Press, 1976.

Wilson, W.J. *The Declining Significance of Race.* Chicago: The University of Chicago Press, 1978.

Wylie, R.C. *The Self-Concept.* Nebraska: University of Nebraska Press, 1961.

CHAPTER 12

Family Life Patterns of Mexican-Americans

William A. Vega, Ph.D.,

Richard L. Hough, Ph.D.

and Annelisa Romero

There exists today very little consensus regarding the "normative" or "ideal" family system, despite numerous research efforts which have addressed the issue of familial patterning within various historical and cultural contexts. It is certainly possible to speculate with census statistics, as well as with other hard data, about modal family patterns for various subpopulations. However, essentially such analyses only serve to contrast differences in demographic characteristics. The qualitative dynamics of family life and linkage configurations to other consanguineous households are not so easily ascertained by such methods. The issue is further confounded by a host of cultural considerations producing wide variability in family patterns and by the transitional nature of family life cycles. As Moroney (1980) concludes in summarizing the literature of family systems, "there is no one dominant family type." Prototypes abound, including nuclear isolated families (Parsons, 1968), extended families (Van den Ban, 1967), and modified extended families (Litwak, 1960; Sussman, 1959), employing a multiplicity of arrangements, including families with and without children. Parenting is equally complex. High divorce rates in the United States produce diverse patterns of parenting (or surrogate parenting), as well as parents and children who may live in more than one household.

Though the literature on the family has emerged from studies by various disciplines, too often the notion of "normalcy" in family structure is discussed as if incontrovertible scientific evidence exists that such a model institution is a reality. In the absence of plausible evidence, pathology is often linked to family structure and socialization patterns. This dichotomization of "normal" and "pathological" confounds the dialogue concerning a proper conceptualization of this social phenomenon, introducing a large measure of value bias.

It is within this context that we introduce the contemplation of a particular subset of family life patterns—the Mexican-American family. Cultural, historical and linguistic differences necessarily receive special emphasis in this assessment. However, considering these factors in isolation would only serve to oversimplify very complex social processes. The United States is a multiclass, multicultural society even in the absence of its Mexican-American population. Cultural differences can be distinguished by variations in social distance, group interpenetration, and internal differentiation. This cultural panorama has continued to puzzle scholars wishing to describe American culture or any significant part of it. Obviously, in the face of so many cultural groupings in dynamic interaction, social analyses intending to capture so much rich detail are fated to be simplistic. Perhaps the failure of attempts to accurately describe complex cultural systems results from the use of limited and constrictive conceptualizations and terminologies. Certainly, in defining family life patterns among Mexican-Americans, it would seem advantageous to broaden the parameters to allow for temporal, economic, coincidental, historical, and cultural factors as proximate indicators both within and outside the cultural group. Multidimensional development models with elastic attributes are more likely to produce an accurate portrait than broad statistical brush strokes. This chapter will organize its review of Mexican-American family life following this more expansive line of reasoning, buttressed by a critical summary of the existing literature on the Mexican-American family.

DEFINING MEXICAN-AMERICAN FAMILY LIFE

Stereotypes: Strength or Weakness?

The Mexican-American family has been described by various social scientists as basically traditional, patriarchal, rooted in rural extended family values, and exhibiting traits which exemplify the "culture of poverty" Clark, 1959; Heller, 1966; Lewis, 1966; Madsen, 1964). Such traits have been identified as "fatalism," "machismo," "superstitiousness," "religiosity," "female submissiveness," "present-time orientation," etc. A contrast has often been drawn with Anglo-American cultural traits, as if the two cultures had discrete characteristics. Several Mexican-American scholars have adamantly reacted to these stereotypes with a variety of criticisms concerning the scientific rigor of the studies from which these observations were derived. The critique usually encompasses sampling design, conceptualization, data-gathering techniques, instrument validation, and other methodological and theoretical deficiencies which compromise the parsimony of the findings (Monteil, 1975; Padilla and Ruiz, 1973; Romano, 1968; Vaca, 1970; Vega, 1980a). In all fairness to these early anthropological observations receiving such criticism, and their flaws notwithstanding, their findings probably represent the observations of well trained scholars using the appropriate tools of their disciplines within that historical epoch. Unfortunately, an overly literal interpretation of this work can easily lead to distortions that are unacceptable at either the descriptive or conceptual level. Undoubtedly, it is possible to argue that the traits identified by anthropological observation actually exist within some elements of

Mexican-American culture, but it would be just as easy to demonstrate that such qualities exist in some sectors of the Anglo-American culture as well, which does little to explain either cultural group.

Perhaps one of the most interesting factors of this controversy is the fact that the same cultural traits that are often argued to provoke dysfunctional adaptation and socialization, cultural conflict, and limited social mobility in Mexican-American family life (Grebler, Moore, and Guzman, 1970) are also held responsible for a number of positive outcomes. For example, it has been argued that Mexican-Americans are less prone to mental illness because of family solidarity and that their family life absorbs, supports, and protects individual members from stressors (Jaco, 1959, 1960). Similarly, the case has been made that the Mexican-American family, in the absence of other support systems, is the primary source of financial resource concentration and redistribution (Grebler, Moore, and Guzman, 1970), as well as for problem resolution (Keefe, Padilla, and Carlos, 1978). At the risk of pointing out the obvious, the lack of rigorous and comprehensive conceptual models and reliable data bases makes the identification of isolated cultural traits a specious exercise. It should be readily evident that deleterious cultural practices can and do exist in Mexican-American family life (Boulette, 1980). However, what remain to be defined and identified are the conditions under which such practices can be damaging and are likely to be manifested, and Mexican-American subpopulations within which such cultural practices would not be found at all. Such a focus would recognize the inherent complexity of Mexican-American culture resulting from regional diversity, bi-national origins and stratification processes. This approach would also provide a much needed balance to family literature. As Miranda (1980) points out, "attempts to think in terms of strength as opposed to weakness have received limited attention."

The processes of Mexican-American family socialization and internal dynamics also have never been adequately presented in the social science literature (Levine and Padilla, 1980; Monteil, 1975). The stereotypic patriarchal family derived from anthropological observation had quite well defined characteristics, including clear sex-role differentiation, male supremacy, and the unquestioned authority of the eldest male. This view of the Mexican-American family contrasted a fundamentally submissive, devoted and chaste female with an aggressive, arbitrary, and somewhat irresponsible male (Padilla and Ruiz, 1973; Peñalosa, 1968). Childrearing was exclusively the domain of female family members. Children loved their mothers and feared their fathers, with boys generally experiencing much greater freedom and mobility than girls (Staples, 1971). Older males, including fathers, were free to come and go without question or hindrance. Affective support was the responsibility of women. Protection and financial support were masculine role qualities.

Two modifications have been suggested concerning the traditional model. The first basically defends traditional extended/modified or extended family systems as inherently stable and possessing very positive characteristics that can and should be strengthened (Dominguez-Ybarra and Garrison, 1977; Hoppe and Heller, 1975). The second school of thought asserts that the normative Mexican-American family is in transition or has not yet been identified by empirical research (Levine and Padilla, 1980; Miranda, 1980; Monteil, 1975; Vega, 1980a). This assertion would certainly be consistent with general trends in the literature concerning family structures, as noted earlier.

Structure: Nuclear or Extended?

The literature on Mexican-American

culture also includes an extensive review of socialization processes and social networks. The network and social supports literature suggests that a well articulated system of linked households exists through which Mexican-American families meet their various life needs. As Caplan (1976) and Cobb (1976) have noted, support systems exist to transmit information needed for survival, to promote affective sustenance, and to provide access to resources and knowledge. Valle and Mendoza (1978) describe networks operating in Mexican-American social spheres which are both dense and functional. In their research, Mexican-Americans overwhelmingly indicated that family networks are available and useful for solving problems, and that such netowrks are extended by both fictive kin systems (*compadrazgo*) and neighborhood helpers (*servidores*). The extended networks operate as channels or links to resources, as well as providing various forms of direct support (Nall and Speilberg, 1967). The lack of specification of network availability and utilization by differing Mexican-American subpopulations in differing ecological domains is a continuing deficiency within existing data bases. Many observers have commented on the viability of these "umbrella networks" for information dissemination to households in Mexican-American neighborhoods (Cuellar, 1974; Sotomayor, 1973).

An interesting observation provided by Valle and Mendoza (1978) about network utilization is the expression by elderly respondents that self-reliance was important for maintaining self-pride (*orgullo*), and that it was important to avoid becoming a problem to family and friends. These observations indicate an attitudinal ambivalence about using support systems (Steglich, Cartwright, and Crouch, 1968). This tendency should be more fully explored in order to determine the types of problems and the threshold of severity that stimulate the use of helping networks.

The limited research on family structure seems to indicate that Mexican-American families are neither nuclear nor extended in the pure sense. Sena-Rivera (1980) has described the Mexican-American family as historically embodying the elements of the modified extended family (Litwak, 1960; Sussman, 1959), stating: "Typically, the modified extended family centers around a bilateral clustering of essentially independent nuclear family households integrated through an ongoing normative reinforcement process, continuing demographic similarities, services and material interdependence, ongoing affective support and, in a number of instances, a status hierarchy based on mitigated eldest male authority, with the authority manifested differently in the more independent nuclear units" (p. 75). This model of Mexican-American family arrangements would include geographic residence in close proximity and frequent contact. A central household, presumably housing the elders of the family, serves as the focal point for family interaction.

In addition to the sanguinary structure, the family is intersected by the *compadrazgo* system (ritual co-parenthood) which extends responsibility for the well-being of children to a greater number of adults, thus assuring the child's security. However, the relationship is also very functional in providing reciprocal support between the godparent and the child's natural parents (Berruecos, 1972; Mintz and Wolf, 1950). This enlarged protective network is also an important resource for the potential social mobility of the child, as well as of other family members. The extent to which these functions of the *compadrazgo* system continue to be viable has been debated and its presence is no doubt mitigated by numerous cultural and economic factors (Padilla and Ruiz, 1973).

The presence of natural healers in the network system has been reported consistently as a major resource used by Mexican-American families seeking relief from various health, mental health, and life crisis problems (Clark, 1959; Kiev, 1968;

Rubel, 1960; Saunders, 1954; Torrey, 1969, 1972). Though some investigators have negated the importance of healers as an actively utilized support system adjunct (Edgerton, Karno, and Fernandez, 1970; Padilla, Carlos, and Keefe, 1976), some recent research has indicated that, at least in some geographic areas, natural healers continue to be a neighborhood resource (Vega, 1980b). The range of natural healers encompasses a variety of healing modalities and practitioners, including massage (*sobadoras*), herbs (*hierberas*), and spiritual (*espiritualistas*) treatments. Various religious counselors also play a role in Mexican-American family life. Though predominantly Catholic, a high rate of conversions to various evangelical (*evangelistas*) sects is apparent in urban Mexican-American communities. Recent research clearly indicates that religious counselors are a continuing and utilized source of social support in the family life of Mexican-Americans (Vega, Warheit, and Meinhardt, 1982). Again, it is important to interpret these trends cautiously, since wide variations in religious practices are to be expected in such a diverse ethnic population.

Whatever the relative degree of their utilization, community and neighborhood helpers are often considered virtual family members in view of their consistent role as supportive and nurturing allies. Geographic proximity is the key to their social integration within a primary family network. Because they may be present more than some family members, they are capable of offering numerous practical services.

At least in theory, the support system of the Mexican-American family is composed of integrated components, as illustrated in Figure 1. The inner core is the nuclear group. The complementary units are composed of other family households and *compadres*; then we have neighbors, neighborhood helpers, natural healers, and religious counselors. The role certain community agencies play as support sys-

tem adjuncts for the very young and elderly must not be overlooked, since their presence may be well integrated into family life and functioning (Valle and Mendoza, 1978). The literature is inconsistent regarding the actual presence and reliability of these various support system elements. Most likely the "ideal" support system would be found in a relatively stable, homogenous, low-income Spanish-speaking neighborhood, since the research describing its persistence is predominantly from that type of milieu.

CULTURAL TRAITS IN FAMILY LIFE

Despite the absence of consensus in the social science literature concerning the normative and structural configurations of the Mexican-American family, several cultural traits have been identified by field observation which deserve recognition. These traits do not, in themselves,

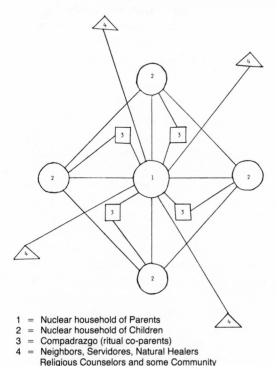

1 = Nuclear household of Parents
2 = Nuclear household of Children
3 = Compadrazgo (ritual co-parents)
4 = Neighbors, Servidores, Natural Healers
    Religious Counselors and some Community
    Agency Personnel

Figure 1. Family Support System Model

constitute modal family patterns. They are orienting values which typify the macro culture of low-income Mexican-American populations. Actual adherence to these values in the family life of Mexican-Americans varies. Nevertheless, these values are pervasive. An appreciation of their existence and potential impact on family life provides an invaluable perspective for understanding cultural behaviors and expectations. The authors present these normative characteristics of Mexican-American families with trepidation, fearing that they will be perceived as "stereotypes" in the classic mold. However, it is important to acknowledge that cultures do "hang together" on the basis of commonly shared value clusters. How these values are actually operationalized in the daily family life of Mexican-Americans remains an outstanding research issue; however, we have no doubt of their importance in the family experience of Mexican-Americans in the United States today.

Mutual obligations and reciprocity are the motivating forces in the support system dynamic. These are mediated by certain values which have received broad attention in the literature: *orgullo* (pride and self-reliance), *dignidad* (dignity), *confianza* (trust and intimacy), and *respeto* (respect). These values must be mutually acknowledged in order for a relationship of reciprocity to be established, and are taught and sternly reinforced in the home. The home is a special environment, with specific status roles for the elderly as well as for parents. Some families will address a highly respected elder using terms that connote deference. Proper greeting, politeness, and maintaining the family's reputation are all indispensable facets of being *bien educado* (well brought up). Within this type of social organization, the roles and expectations of the various family members are not equivalent. Important family decisions are rarely shared with children or adolescents. Parents teach their children that parents are superior in authority and power and that parents have a responsibility to love and care for their children. Children have a responsibility to be obedient and to live by the values respected in the household. Respect for these important values is of critical importance for the child's ability to develop a good relationship with his or her parents.

Physical modesty is an important norm implicit in *dignidad* and *respeto*. Except for the very young, nudity is discouraged and great value is attached to physical integrity (Lawrence and Lurie, 1972). This is interesting, considering the cramped living conditions that are often encountered in Mexican-American families. Sexual topics and reproduction are rarely discussed between parents and children and a veil of secrecy shrouds the subject (Boulette, 1980). Overt evidence of sexual behavior among adolescent females is a form of disrespect for the household.

In general, household responsibilities are assigned early in life. In rural areas, the children work along with their parents. Children who are able to earn money have a responsibility to contribute to the maintenance of the household. Parents reciprocate by providing for the financial needs of their children, which may extend to young adulthood and even during marriage. Reciprocity is lifelong, and when needs (not desires) and emergencies arise, there is an expectation that, to the greatest extent possible, support will be forthcoming. This network reciprocity applies to all family members, whether in the nuclear household or living a great distance away. It also applies to fictive kin (*compadrazgo*), who share the same favored status. Reciprocity is not limited to financial aid. The support system cuts across social class lines and geographic areas. It is considered an insult not to visit relatives with regularity or when in the immediate area. It is normal to ask favors of relatives. The network can be used for solving personal problems, for seeking employment, for information, for child-care, etc.

Because of marginal economic conditions, many Mexican-American families do not have a clearly designated division of labor as wage earners or household members. Generally, in low-income households, any able-bodied adult capable of earning money has a responsibility to do so—there is no gender inhibition. At various points in time, especially in seasonal work, either the adult males or females in the household may be unemployed. There is no stigma attached to being unemployed as long as honest efforts are being made to locate work. Under these circumstances, household tasks are shared and the children have assigned responsibilities to participate in household functioning. Working parents with children place them with relatives or neighbors. In rural areas, the children who are too young to work simply accompany the parents and play within their sight.

Marriage and parenthood are often entered into at an early age. Marriage is perceived as a stabilizing influence on the young and offspring are welcome. Children are loved and revered as a source of happiness and pride. It is considered abnormal for couples not to bear and rear children or to make a voluntary decision to remain childless. Though they are the norm, youthful marriages have a vulnerability to dissolution, and often end in the early years of the union. Under these circumstances, the parents of the couple encourage them to resolve their differences. However, parents of the female are usually supportive of their daughter's decision to terminate the union and return home or form an independent household. The parents consider it their responsibility to give the problems of their married children the same attention as those of their unmarried children. Similarly, children, even after leaving the nuclear household, have a responsibility to stay in frequent contact and be prepared to provide support when it is required, especially when the parents are elderly.

Though relatively recent, some research has emerged which seems to indicate that Mexican-Americans are more likely to have dense and broader social networks in the second generation (Vega, Warheit, and Meinhardt, 1982). While immigrants appear to be limited regarding the extent to which they can "rebuild" the network lost in the migration process, the second generation has a multigenerational family system it can turn to. This research suggests that immigrants also have fewer friends available, but do receive significant support from them. Members of the second generation report having more friends they feel they could ask for help and, in actuality, they ask for such help. This body of research suggests that immigrants are also much more likely to consult natural healers and religious counselors than second generation Mexican-Americans. It remains a research question whether such utilization constitutes the preferred method of problem resolution and care provision or is reflective of limited family resources and lack of access to formal medical providers.

THE ACCULTURATION ENIGMA

One of the most complex issues impeding a thorough understanding of Mexican-American individual and family functioning and adaptation in American society is the confounding impact of acculturation. Many conceptualizations of acculturation in the social science literature inherently imply a unidimensional linear-temporal sequence. The longer an individual or family is exposed to a dominant culture, the more we can expect adoption of the host culture as well as the degeneration and mutation of previously intact cultural systems and personality structures (Kluckhohn and Leighton, 1946). This is essentially parallel to the melting pot formulation (Glazer and Moynihan,

1975) and has its antecedents in both anthropology and sociology. This model assumes that time and economic interdependence dictate intermixture, value diffusion and social integration, though acculturation may be mediated by a number of cultural properties, including boundary-maintaining mechanisms, the degree of flexibility in the social structure of the host society, and the cultural resistance exhibited by the host society (Social Science Research Council, 1954). Though such a formulation has heuristic value, it fails to identify the facets of ethnicity and culture which persist over time or the demographic and social-psychological factors which are more likely to promote, retard, or suppress the acculturation process (Gordon, 1964).

Olmedo and Padilla (1978), in interpreting the results of an acculturation index, found that Mexican-Americans are a heterogenous cultural group distinguished primarily by nationality and language factors. Important intergenerational differences exist which appear attributable to both differential experience and attitudinal predispositions. As these investigators state, "they [Mexican-Americans] exhibit a wide range of individual differences in the extent to which they have assimilated the sociocultural and psychological characteristics of the Anglo society." There appears to be a broad range of "sociocultural profiles" identified by this study that find fundamental concurrence with the literature on acculturation typologies. Mercer (1976) presents evidence that less acculturated Mexican-Americans usually exhibit lower education and occupational status. Ramirez and Castañeda (1974) indicate that the least acculturated Mexican-Americans manifest high family solidarity, ethnic identification, and Mexican Catholicism. Conversely, highly acculturated Mexican-Americans have low identification on these three variables.

Some attention was given by Park (1928)

to the concept of the "marginal man" as an individual who has no singular culture, but exhibits diverse cultural traits, intensified self-consciousness, and actively penetrates two or more cultural domains despite apparent conflicts. This is really a composite or synthetic identity produced by social and historical processes, which may have far-reaching psychological implications. Stonequist (1964) further defined the characteristics of marginal peoples by identifying three possible accommodations: assimilation into the dominant group, assimilation into the subordinate group, or some form of accommodation between the groups. This concept of cultural marginality, derived from early social science literature (Simmel, 1950), is a logical precursor to the emerging paradigm of multidimensional typologies that identify factors associated with various acculturation modalities. Though this research is still in its infancy, Clark, Kaufman, and Pierce (1976) have identified six variations in acculturation that are distinguished primarily by age and generation. Padilla (1980) differentiated his respondent population using an index of cultural awareness and ethnic loyalty which clustered the population into five types, with generation, education, income, ethnic neighborhood density, and language preference being important predictor variables.

It has been demonstrated that ethnicity is a durable social aggregation which persists over time (Glazer and Moynihan, 1975). Exactly how Mexican immigrants are affected by continuing immigration, residential homogeneity and constant exposure to Latin cultural mediums (television, radio, movies, etc.), in the face of stratification processes which tend to standardize culture, has received scant attention in the scientific literature. Perhaps the most cogent statement has been presented by Fabrega (1969) in his stipulation of factors that affect adjustment to migration. Table 1 presents these fac-

TABLE 1

Features That May Affect Behavioral
Responses to Migration and
Acculturation

Migration
1. Sociodemographic features of individuals undertaking the change.
2. Reasons for the migration (voluntary or imposed and in what manner).
3. Extent of preparation and anticipation preceding change.
4. Occupational and/or economic opportunities in recipient nation.
5. Cultural characteristics of both nations or units involved in the migrations and compatibility between these characteristics.
6. Does the individual have relatives or friends in the new environment?
7. Is there a motivation to achieve assimilation?
8. Geographic distance between the two centers involved in the migration.
9. Number and type of relatives left behind and nature of the relationship that the individual has to these relatives.

Acculturation
1. Mechanisms that serve to promote or diminish the sharpness of the boundary between the cultural systems.
2. Degree of rigidity of each cultural system and the extent to which each system promotes flexibility.
3. Degree of compatibility between the two cultural systems.
4. Cultural mechanisms that allow correction of disturbance or inconsistencies resulting from the contact.
5. Ecological, demographic and political characteristics of the contact situation.
6. Nature of the conjunctive relations established between the two cultures.

tors in detail. Fabrega, Swartz, and Wallace (1968) have suggested that links exist among the degree of assimilation, the nature of the acculturation process, and psychological distress. Pathological outcomes are more likely to occur when acculturation processes lead to disruption in customary life patterns and can result in undermining family stability by provoking interpersonal conflicts and altering socialization patterns (Favazza, 1980).

THE IMMIGRANT EXPERIENCE

The American Southwest was relatively unpopulated until after the Mexican-American War of 1848, and no controlled access existed along most of the border until well into the 20th century. It was the upheaval of the Mexican Revolution of 1910 that encouraged the Mexican government (those fragments of it that were still functioning) to urge its citizens to go north to the fields, mines, factories and railroads of the United States to seek relief from hunger. Free rail transportation was provided, enabling large numbers to flee to the border, where desperate Mexicans were sorted out by labor contractors for shipment to work sites throughout the Southwest and Midwest (McWilliams, 1953). It has been estimated that one person in five of the entire Mexican population left Mexico during this period to find refuge in the United States, if only temporarily. This push-pull effect has continued, with periodic abatement, until the present. Though the original motive for immigration (the Mexican Revolution) has passed into history, high birth rates and underemployment continue to inspire millions to seek a better life on "the other side."

The people who arrived in the aftermath of the Mexican Revolution came from middle-sized towns and rural areas. Most went to work in rural areas but later resettled in urban centers. This was the result of a migratory phenomenon that took hold during the Second World War and continues until the present time. The early migratory population had very little, if any, formal education or experience with modern equipment. This pattern has changed significantly. The culture and technology of Mexico have altered to the point where modern Mexico is virtually a different country, with a rapidly expanding technological infrastructure and mechanized, large-scale farming. Modern immigrants are in better health, have more education, and may already be acquainted with post World War II production processes. Similarly, cultural and material standards in Mexico have changed due to a combination of technological innovation, the growth of the middle class, and social engineering. Family size is declining marginally, urbanization is progressing steadily, and sex-role equality is slowly emerging, at least in the major urban centers. Today, many immigrants come from mid-size cities in Mexico, and we would not expect modern immigrants to arrive with the same cultural imprinting as their predecessors. However, according to expert judgments (DeForest, 1981), the actual volume of immigration has not diminished and fluctuates seasonally, totaling approximately one million people per year including undocumented aliens, many of whom either return voluntarily or are involuntarily repatriated.

Common Patterns and Problems

While there were and continue to be many different immigrant experiences, immigrants also share many common patterns and problems. First is the uprooting from friends, family and culture, emotional sacrifices needed to establish a new life, and the hardship on family members left behind. In general, men travel north alone to find work, seeking out friends and family for shelter and employment. This creates a situation of extended father absence. The second phase is the transition process of the family from one country to the other, which may last for months or years, and usually begins with exploratory trips to assess the new situation. Quite rare is the *barrio* family that has not been visited by relatives from south of the border. The attitude of the host family is usually sympathetic, since they were once in a similar predicament. After the male is established in his employment, which may take an extended period, the family is gradually brought over. It is not always possible to bring in all family

members with legal documentation, especially on a timely basis. It usually takes many months to complete legal immigration proceedings and the financial burden may prohibit the process from reaching a successful termination, so that some family members may not be documented.

There are, of course, many variations to this pattern. For example, young adults may be unmarried when they immigrate and then marry in the United States. Some come from backgrounds where substantial resources are available, so everything can be done in a legal and cautious manner. However, as a rule, immigration is a high stress process, and Mexican and Mexican-American folk culture is replete with lore regarding the many facets of this experience, such as the danger, the romance, and the loneliness.

The final phase, which is quite lengthy, is the adaptation process. The most salient quality of the immigrant experience is that it is an endemic cultural process, which produces a profound impact on the family and the entire community. As new immigrants begin to make selective probes of their new environment, they frequently encounter a family network of support which understands and is geared to the needs of their situation. Many immigrants find themselves socially isolated, and the radical change in their life-style, especially the total absence of the street life that typifies Latin countries, is a very depressing part of accepting life in the United States. At the center of this adaptation process are family members who may provide emotional support, resources and access networks for the new immigrants, as well as basic socialization for the entire family. A nearly universal *barrio* experience is having an entire migrating family stay in the household. If a sudden employment loss occurs, this "doubling up" may recur. This requires the Mexican-American host family to be very flexible regarding the value of their intimacy and elastic about their space requirements. While immigrant children rarely seem truly distressed by the physical hardships, this is, to a great extent, a function of age. The least likely to easily accommodate themselves are immigrant adolescents, whose lives are more dependent on contact outside the home. They are poorly equipped for the cultural transition and language requirements demanded by the new environment.

The ethnic identity of immigrants proceeds through a transformative process which creates a psychological dualism. Though most immigrants will always identify themselves as Mexicans, the gradual accommodation to new habits and values undermines the solidity of this self-perception. Furthermore, after years in the United States, many immigrants are quite surprised to realize how both they and the Mexico they remember have changed, and how Mexicans may no longer regard them as their own. Some immigrants resolve this tension by actually returning to Mexico to live for periods of time or even permanently. However, few families have the financial resources to allow such choices and so gradually accept the permanency of their situation.

The immigrant is usually a victim of economic and cultural marginality. Poverty, which continues to be a precursor of the immigrant experience, results in numerous psychosocial stressors. Periodic father absence, primarily in Mexico, but also in the United States, typifies life for immigrant families. This has serious implications for the household and its total ability to survive. In many cases, such absence can be equated to the psychological impact of a disrupted marital status, since it frequently results in the deterioration of any meaningful affective bonding. Recent data also indicate that Mexican-Americans have higher rates of separation and divorce than Ango-Americans (Boulette, 1980), and that Mexican-American mothers have the lowest educational attainment of any Hispanic ethnic group, with only one-third having completed high school (Ventura and Heuser, 1981).

These are demographic indicators linked to health pathology and substance abuse, and the collective impact of these stressors would vary according to the availability and utilization of coping resources in the milieu.

Little research has been done on typologies of adjustment to the immigrant experience. Romano (1968) developed four prospective typologies of cultural adaptation: 1) Anglo-Saxon conformity, for those who have totally eschewed their Mexican roots; 2) stabilized differences, for those who maintain their "Mexicanness", 3) realigned pluralism, for those who have developed alternate cultural institutions paralleling Anglo-American society, and; 4) biculturalism, for those who are fully conversant with both cultures. Most immigrants fall into the second category since they exist in a homogeneous Spanish-speaking world. The remainder, possibly the better educated and more aggressive, would be bicultural. The other categories would be more likely to typify the second generation and beyond. It is difficult to speculate on the representativeness of these typologies, since little research has ever attempted to confirm or modify them. It is doubtful that so few categories are sufficiently comprehensive to capture the dominant variations that would be expected among Mexican immigrants. The process of social differentiation among immigrants is related to multiple demographic factors and psychological attitudes. Therefore, the specification of adjustment processes and typologies would appear to be a multifacted phenomenon. Accurate understanding of these processes is important for understanding the predisposing and nurturing environment of the second generation, which will be discussed in the next section.

THE SECOND GENERATION

Mexican-Americans have the highest

fertility rate of any Hispanic ethnic group in the United States. As Ventura and Heuser (1981) state, "the fertility rate of 114.1 births per 100 women, 15-44 years of age, for Mexican women was 40 percent greater than the rate for Peurto Rican women (81.3) and more than twice the rate for Cuban women (53.9)." Of Mexican-American babies born in 1978, 87.6 percent had both parents of that ethnic background, more than any other Hispanic ethnic group. The 1980 census is providing evidence that, at least in some major metropolitan areas such as Los Angeles, the degree of residential segregation is actually increasing. A clear demographic pattern is emerging: high birth rates, and a low median age population concentrated in urban clusters of high ethnic homogeneity and density. These urban clusters are not limited to the Southwestern states. Several Midwestern cities, including Chicago and Detroit, are experiencing this rapid population aggregation. These population centers are highly varied in their cultural and ethnic composition. This pattern of population and cultural mixture will have an important impact on the second and succeeding generations.

Linguistic and Cultural Marginality

The second generation is usually bilingual, but only functional in English. This is much less likely to be true in rural areas, where social isolation and low population density operate to insulate even the second generation from English language sources. Quite often, the second generation is taught Spanish as a first language in the home, with the school emphasizing English. This process of Spanish language dislocation results in a second generation which understands Spanish, but has quite limited linguistic versatility. Generally, there appears to be an inverse relationship between educational attainment and English language fluency.

Obviously, these are trends with significant exceptions. Yet, the processes seem clearly marked. Immigrant parents converse in monolingual Spanish, and their children respond to them in a combination of English and Spanish. Elderly monolingual family members and visiting relatives from Mexico are addressed in fractured Spanish, which conveys the essential information but is grammatically and idiomatically deficient. This linguistic differential is indicative of socialization attributable to social agencies, educational institutions, and media of the dominant culture, as well as local subcultural influences.

The impact of this socialization quite often provokes conflicts between children and parents. Many observers have often mistaken these differences as a conflict between Latin and Anglo values, or even traditional as contrasted with modern and rational values. Other salient considerations should be noted. Generally, low-income areas possess a cultural style that blends the social and historical forces which typify the area, and may be quite eclectic and discontinuous. The *barrio* has an independent culture and tradition that are neither Mexican alone nor middle-class Anglo-American. This is hardly a new discovery, since an impressive sociological literature attests to the viability of lower-class culture in diverse ethnic settings (Cohen, 1955; Cressey, 1964; Miller, 1958). This local "style" can assume many forms and expressions, including dress, musical taste, speech, mannerisms, dating etiquette, etc. Often, immigrant parents perceive these manifestations as harmless idiosyncracies. However, they may also represent a fundamental affront to values, customs, and decency. It is not that immigrants are static or inflexible. If they have been in the United States for ten years or more, they have usually accommodated themselves to the major cultural differences and can accept some life-style variations. However, most immigrant parents are not prepared to accept behavior which is perceived as degrading or lacking in respect for oneself or others.

It is difficult to equate this parental resistance to "traditional" or conservative values, because the social environment in which it is occurring is not "middle America," where the youth are predominantly conforming and college bound. It may be occurring in depressed areas where delinquent behavior, substance abuse, and school failure are occurring at alarming rates. Under these circumstances, the actions of parents may seem erratic or harshly reactive to children, especially adolescents, who are part of a youth subculture where this behavior is considered normal. Most potential conflicts are usually avoided by discretion and selective "blindness" of parents and children. However, if problems do surface, the resulting conflicts can constitute very severe family stressors.

The second generation is frequently marginal to Mexican culture, especially working-class Mexican culture, and yet not socially integrated into other major cultural domains. They exist in independent subcultures which are, as a whole, negated by the society which produced them. Though the Pachuco is an atypical subcultural variant, the psychological dynamics of marginalization are accurately portrayed by the Mexican philosopher Octavio Paz, in *The Labyrinth of Solitude* (1961). Paz describes the condition of second generation marginality he observed among "Pachucos" in Los Angeles as follows: "They are instinctive rebels, and North American racism has vented its wrath on them more than once. But the Pachucos do not attempt to vindicate their race or nationality of their forebearers. Their attitude reveals an obstinate, almost fanatical will-to-be, but this will affirms nothing specific except their determination—it is an ambiguous one, as we shall see—not to be like those around him. The Pachuco does not want to become a Mexican again; at the same time he does not want to blend into the life of North America." (p. 14).

Cultural Transmutation

Few social scientists have ever recognized the importance of diverse cultural influences on the second generation. As mentioned earlier, the urban barrio is not a traditional Mexican setting for the second generation nor even for many of the first generation. For example, in many cities, black culture, especially idiomatic expressions, musical tastes, and dance styles, have a strong influence on Mexican-Americans, especially the second generation. In other cities, the influence of differing Latin cultural groups is very strong, so that another type of cultural diffusion takes place. Thus, there are multiple cultural influences penetrating the life space of Mexican-Americans, which vary according to the characteristics of specific locations. Youthful urban Mexican-Americans are socialized in a superdynamic cultural intersection, a process which occurs in stark contrast to the continuity and slower rate of adaptation by their immigrant fathers and mothers. For the second generation, synthetic cultural styles will emerge which are uniquely American, a product of multicultural fusion from disparate sources. As Favazza (1980) has written, "In the diffusion process, a receiving culture's patterns and values serve as selective screens which reject some elements and accept others. Cultural objects, traits, or ideas which are transmitted undergo transformation in the receiving cultural systems. Acculturation, particularly when not forced, also may be a creative process leading to reorganizations, reinterpretations, and syncretisms which may enrich old patterns or develop new ones." (p. 104). Some elements may be maintained from each of these sources, some may be transformed, and others discarded altogether. Understanding this process is the key to understanding the identity crisis of young Mexican-Americans, and the complexity that their dilemma poses for the family.

UNDERSTANDING FAMILY PATTERNS IN THE CONTEXT OF SOCIAL STRATIFICATION

It should be restated in relationship to the preceding discussion that any analysis attempting to describe heterogeneous cultural groups is immediately vulnerable to simplistic reduction. It should be clear that there is no single Mexican-American family type in either structure or cultural practice. One essential denominator is social class, for even in Mexico social class is an overwhelming influence producing social differentiation. In the sense the term is used here, social class is not defined exclusively by economic parameters. Social classes represent levels in a prestige hierarchy stratified by culturally defined standards. In American society, most social classes are permeable, diffuse, yet internally cohesive. Johnson (1960) has defined social classes this way: "a social class, then, is a more or less endogamous stratum consisting of families of about equal prestige who are or would be acceptable to one another for 'social interaction' that is culturally regarded as more or less symbolic of equality; as the term stratum suggests, a social class is one of two or more such groupings, all of which can be ranked relative to one another in a more or less integrated system of prestige stratification" (p. 469). Gordon (1964) notes that social class is a preeminent definer of culture and life style, superseding subcultural definers but not totally supplanting them. Social mobility requires rapid adoption of valued cultural patterns. This is true in Mexico and it is true in the United States.

Mexican and Mexican-American middle-class families are concerned with family planning, achieving educational goals,

and creating successful businesses. This is not to imply that members of the poor immigrant generation are not concerned with these objectives as well. However, the historical evidence is quite clear. The immigrant generation starts out too late and has little personal power, limiting their life chances. There are certainly exceptions, and these are usually found among owners of small businesses serving the Spanish-speaking community. In the main, however, it is the highly acculturated, English-speaking and educationally prepared segment of the second generation that benefits from social mobility. These high achievers came from families characterized by constant affective support where hard work and mobility are strongly encouraged.

Social stratification within Mexican-American society does not follow the classic five to six class typologies identified by Warner and Lunt (1941) or Hollingshead (1949). Instead, it is more restricted, reflecting limited social mobility. Table 2 describes a stratification pattern for Mexican-American families that typifies an urban *barrio* and its immediate surroundings. The underclass is composed of new immigrants who are still in the transition process. Their profile is that of poor, uneducated transients who migrate in search of reliable employment and a support system to nurture them until they can cope using their own resources. If the family persists in this situation for several years, the impact on them may be very serious and will be evidenced in the social, physical and mental health of the nuclear unit. These families are typically large, Spanish-speaking households, living in chronically overcrowded conditions; in emergencies, several households may merge.

The low-income family differs from the underclass primarily because of its employment and residential stability. It may also include elderly Mexican-Americans on fixed incomes. This type of family is also large and often unacculturated. The

TABLE 2

Family Life Typologies Derived From Demographic/Cultural Variables

Variables	Under Class	Low Income	Working Class	Middle Class
Nativity and Acculturation	Parents and possibly some children born in Mexico. Some members of household are undocumented; very unacculturated.	Parents and possibly some children born in Mexico, documented, marginally acculturated.	Parents can be immigrants or U.S. born. Most of family are U.S. citizens and children U.S. natives, bilingual; moderate acculturation.	All family members are usually U.S. born with some exceptions. Most are fully acculturated with some biculturalism and bilinguality.
Regional Origins	Predominantly from middle sized cities and small towns in rural areas of Mexico.	Predominantly from middle sized cities and small towns in rural areas of Mexico.	Some rural but mostly urban areas of Mexico and U.S. children born in metropolitan clusters of U.S.	Urban U.S.
Residential Characteristics	Rural or urban, but characterized by transience.	Rural and urban, but are relatively stable.	Mostly urban, with some rural	Urban
Educational Attainment	Very limited, usually 6 years or less for parents, and children will not complete high school.	Very limited, usually 6 years or less for parents, and children will not complete high school.	Immigrants will have 6 to 8 years of school, native born typically have some high school, and some high achievers.	Usually high school and some college. A few with advanced degrees, or technical school.
Language Preference of Household	Monolingual Spanish	Monolingual Spanish	Immigrants will speak Spanish in the home, but have optional English capability; children and U.S. native parents will speak English in the home.	Monolingual English
Household Characteristics	Large family (5-8) with periodic father absence and frequent visitors from Mexico.	Large family (5-8), frequent visitors from Mexico.	Middle sized family (4-6) with periodic visitors from Mexico.	Small to medium (3-5)
Occupational Characteristics	Agricultural labor and unskilled manual labor in service areas.	Stable semi-skilled labor and service work.	Stable skilled and some semi-skilled labor.	Professionals, business and some highly skilled blue collar.

children are unlikely to be high achievers because of deficits in acquired skills, acculturation, and requisite education. The poor working conditions and lifelong manual labor experienced by this group usually result in the early onset of chronic physical health problems and disabilities (Vega, 1980). Both the underclass and the low-income groups may exhibit some of the stereotypic "traditional" traits ascribed to all Mexican-Americans by many social scientists.

The immigrant working-class family has usually passed through both the underclass and low-income status. They would tend to be better educated, with some high school attainment. If the parents are immigrants, they have achieved stable employment in skilled or semi-skilled occupations. This working class does not suffer from the economic marginality of the two types mentioned previously. Their homes are ample, though still overcrowded by the standards of the larger American society. This type of family has the resources to plan, take occasional vacations, and save small amounts of money. The children are more likely to be aggressive, mobile, articulate, and independent. Consisting of middle-size families in bilingual households, this is the most dynamic social class in Mexican-American society.

Some second generation family members may eventually acquire a good deal of wealth from astute business transactions or through career attainment. A substantial proportion of the working-class family type is composed of second generation Mexican-Americans whose parents were underclass, low-income, or working class. They will probably own their own homes and will encourage their children to educate themselves.

The middle class is similar to the Anglo-American middle class, in that it is a nuclear unit in a predominantly monolingual English-speaking household. Education will be highly stressed in the home. Rarely are the parents in such a

household immigrants, unless they were also from the middle class in Mexico. Some will have achieved social status and economic viability through higher education, but a significant proportion has attained economic security through skilled trades and business. They may have family members who remain working class. Their children will probably remain middle class.

These social class typologies, despite some overlap, do represent distinctive lifestyles and life chances for their members. It warrants repetition that individuals and families may move through several of these groupings in the process of establishing their lives and life-styles in this country. However, many families do not change their social status even in the second generation. Given existing patterns of social mobility, education, and demographic trends, the stability of this unique social class structure can be expected to persist.

FAMILY PATTERNS IN VALUE CONFLICT AND SOCIAL CONTROL

Some investigators have speculated that Mexican-Americans have distinct standards for defining deviant behavior when contrasted with middle-class Anglo-American culture (Ramirez and Castañeda, 1974; Sanchez, 1971; Seward and Marmor, 1956). Behavior that would be considered inappropriate and provoke a serious reaction in Anglo culture, it is claimed, would not lead to the same result in Mexican-American culture. This argument seems plausible only within certain domains.

Expectations and sanctions for nonconformity to social roles within the family and support system are probably more rigidly defined and controlled among Mexican-Americans than among their Anglo counterparts. Behavior outside the home may be subject to a different code. The parents may perceive limitations on their ability to control the external environment and feel reluctant to impose severe psychological pressure on children who fail to live up to their expectations. This is not an issue of differences in standards regarding appropriateness of behavior, but a difference in the degree of sanction that Mexican-American parents will impose on their children to demonstrate disapproval in attempting to achieve behavioral conformity. This distinction in behavioral tolerance levels represents a locus of control difference between Mexican-American and Anglo-American parents and may be indicative of a confounding of ethnicity with social class. There is no evidence whatsoever to indicate that the conforming values related to interpersonal behavior and expectations about social mobility are different between Mexican-Americans and Anglo-Americans if social class is controlled. The differences may be primarily situational. Mexican-Americans accept the free will of their children. They may reproach, castigate, and even reject a family member who violates primary group norms. They will impose expectations on their children regarding their social role performance outside the home as well. However, when their expectations are not fulfilled within the external domain, the degree of sanctioning is less severe. Scolding and reproach are appropriate responses for such behavior, but rarely do these conflicts provoke rejection or withdrawal of love.

Behavior which is perceived as supportive of family expectations and reputation is highly rewarded, especially achievements outside the home. The emphasis on rewards can have the effect of differentiating siblings by stigmatizing the nonconformers. While this is similar to a labeling phenomenon, it differs in that it is less an assignment of deviance than a declaration of "no expectations" about the role performance capabilities of the affected family member. While this "limbo" perception of the family member does not imply rejection, it can follow the dynamics of self-fulfilling prophecy by lowering collective expectations about this individual and ultimately affect the person's own self-perception.

Differences in socialization and social control methods are notable among Mexican-Americans of diverse social classes. Parental expectations regarding their children do not vary greatly, but there are vast differences in the personal power of the families to realize these expectations. Stated somewhat differently, the abstract desires of parents of different social classes for the well-being of their children differ little, i.e., education, health, family, financial stability. The ability to recognize, understand, and support the specific activities that result in the fulfillment of their expectations is the poignant difference between the social classes. Underclass and low-income families are mired in the struggle for survival, and their visibility regarding problems external to the household is low. They are socially isolated and minimally acculturated.

Working-class families exhibit broader social perception and community involvement and are more likely to be somewhat bilingual, if not functionally bicultural. This facilitates the social mobility of the second generation. The middle-class families are often physically removed from Spanish-speaking neighborhoods and are likely to be completely fluent in English. This removes many situational factors that could act as barriers to community participation and puts the entire family in a milieu where the dissonance between family expectations and the social environment is minimized. This is especially important with respect to adolescent subcultures, since middle-class neighborhoods are more culturally homogeneous. This residential segregation can and does quite often provoke an identity crisis among middle-class Mexican-American youth, since they are in a distinct minority in such residential areas. Romano's (1968) typologies of Anglo-American conformity and realigned pluralism are examples of possible accommodations to this situation. Middle-class Mexican-Americans can negate their cultural origins, which may or may not cause psychological problems, or they can readjust by joining organizations and participating in networks which provide ethnic support and project a positive image of being Mexican-American.

A MULTIVARIATE MODEL FOR UNDERSTANDING MEXICAN-AMERICAN FAMILY LIFE PATTERNS

A promising framework for contemplating the Mexican-American family is within evolutionary sequences (life stages) and life events. While it is known that families go through several redefinitions of structure and role content in their lifetimes (Havighurst, 1952; Neugarten, 1979), the literature regarding Mexican-American life is practically devoid of such considerations. Existing speculations based on anthropological observation and cross-sectional survey data portray a "static" non-adaptive family. The dynamics of the life cycle (Kellam and Ensminger, 1980) should be discretely disentangled within a culturally specific matrix of present and past experience. Highly relevant to this discussion is the role of traumatic life events as they impact on the life cycle, given the high degree of vulnerability of Mexican-Americans to such events and the known relationship between life events, locus of control, and pathology (Pearlin and Schooler, 1978). There is every reason to hypothesize that the immigration experience and poverty are stressors which increase family instability and are closely related to a number of major stressful life events (disability, divorce, accidents, arrests, death, life-threatening illness, etc.) which have a disintegrating and disruptive effect on family functioning and cohesiveness.

A recent epidemiological investigation concerned with the effects of life events on Mexicans in Ciudad Juarez and Mexican-Americans and Anglos in El Paso, Texas, revealed the tendency of Mexican respondents to have both physical and mental health more adversely impacted by life changes affecting friends and significant others (Hough, 1981; Hough, McGarvey, and Fairbank, 1981; Zippin and Hough, 1981). In addition, Mexican respondents were found to rate events concerning social and geographic mobility as more stressful than Anglos because of the perceived link to family disintegration and support system displacement (Hough, 1981a).

Figure 2 illustrates how the identification of the generic term, "past experiences," intersects with a variety of demographic factors and coping behaviors with resultant implications for general functioning and pathology. Such a model may be usefully applied to the study of Mexican family life patterns. The immigrant experience described in this chapter, for example, subsumes many, if not all, of the stressors identified in this model, and it would be logical to hypothesize that immigrants constitute a very high risk group. There is confirmatory evidence of this high risk status from epidemiologic field studies (Vega, Warheit, and Meinhardt, 1982). As Hough (1981a) has noted regarding the importance of elaborating on past experiences with specificity in order to identify pathogenic factors, "virtually all of the elements under the rubrics of socioeconomic characteristics, stressors, and mediators [in Hough's model] are subsumed under the single general designation of 'past experiences' in the old Rahe-Arthur model. By specifically elaborating on particular elements as factors, it is clear that a more complicated model develops quickly from a relatively simplistic one." (p. 208)

When family life is viewed as a developmental phenomenon with a unique historical content, it becomes possible to perceive the interplay of time, life events and family adaptation. As indicated ear-

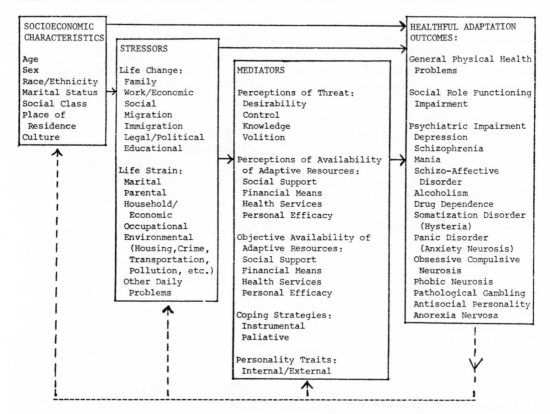

Figure 2. Model of expanded past experiences, major sociocultural variables and impairment outcome linkages: An adaptation of the Hough Model (Hough, 1981a, p. 209)

lier, there is evidence that life events are an important predictor of pathology among Mexican-Americans (Hough, 1981a; Fernandez, Garcia, and Tello, 1981). Stressful life events constitute contingency points in the career of the family which test its resilience and viability at different points in time.

SUMMARY AND CONCLUSIONS

Though the social science literature is somewhat lacking in refinement, methodological rigor, and consensus, there is reason to believe that the Mexican-American family is a flexible institution which adapts to changing environmental conditions. The social phenomena of acculturation and the immigrant experience are poorly understood, especially where a

common border exists between sending and receiving nations and the totality of relevant variables has never been accounted for. The impact of multiple cultural influences and social class stratification has received sparse attention and must also be taken into account, especially when urban Mexican-Americans are involved. Demographic trends underscore the importance of ecological and situational factors transforming family life practices as a function of adaptation.

Attention was given to the social class structure and role content of Mexican-American families and the values that reinforce the system of mutual support. Support system components were described as multidimensional, multipurpose, and buttressed by an explicit set of culturally derived expectations which are mediated by various demographic factors, especially acculturation and social class. Though cultural behaviors which typify the interactional patterns within many Mexican-American households were reviewed, it must be acknowledged that the variations to be found in familial adaptation preclude any closure on this topic. The chapter concluded with the presentation of a comprehensive research model for understanding the Mexican-American family. This model details the factors normally considered in the literature as stressors but relates them within a temporal framework that specifically recognizes the importance of life changes and life events as integral etiologic factors and processes in family life with correspondent outcomes. Only through the use of such a research model can refined conceptualization and parsimony of findings be achieved.

REFERENCES

Berruecos, L. Comparative analysis of Latin-American *compadrazgo*. Unpublished Master's thesis, Michigan State University, 1972.

Boulette, T.R. Priority issues for mental health promotion among low income Chicanos/*Mexicanos*. In: R. Valle and W. Vega (Eds.), *Hispanic National Support Systems*. State of California Department of Mental Health, N80-620047, 1980, pp. 15–24.

Caplan, G. The family as support system. In: G. Caplan and V. Killilea (Eds.), *Support Systems and Mutual Help: Multidisciplinary Exploration*. New York: Grune and Stratton, 1976, pp. 19–36.

Clark, M. *Health in the Mexican-American Culture*. Berkeley: University of California Press, 1959.

Clark, M., Kaufman, S. and Pierce, R.C. Exploration of acculturation: Toward a model of ethnic identity. *Human Organization*, 1976, *35*, 231–238.

Cobb, S. Social support as a moderator of life stress. *Psychomatic Medicine*, 1976, 300–314.

Cohen. A. *Delinquent Boys: The Culture of the Gang*. Glencoe, Il: Free Press, 1955.

Cressey, D. *Delinquency, Crime and Differential Association*. The Hague: Martinier Nijhoff, 1964.

Cuellar, J. On the relevance of ethnographic methods: Studying aging in an urban Mexican-American community. In: V. Benston (Ed.) *Gerontological Research and Community Concern: A Core Study of a Multi-Disciplinary Project*. Los Angeles: Andrus Gerontology Center, University of California at Los Angeles, 1974.

DeForest, M.E. Mexican workers north of the border. *Harvard Business Review*, May-June 1981, *59* (3), 150–157.

Dominguez-Ybarra, A. and Garrison, J. Towards adequate classification and treatment of Mexican-American patients. *Psychiatric Annals,* 1977, 7 (12), 80-96.

Edgerton, R., Karno, M. and Fernandez, I. *Curanderismo* in the metropolis. *American Journal of Psychotherapy*, January 1970, *24* (1), 124–234.

Fabrega, H. Social psychiatric aspects of acculturation and migration. *Comprehensive Psychiatry*, 1969, *10*, 314–329.

Fabrega, H., Swartz, J. and Wallace, C. Ethnic differences in psychopathology, Vol. VII. Specific differences with emphasis on the Mexican-American group. *Psychiatric Research*, 1968, *6* (3), 221–235.

Favazza, A.R. Culture change and mental health. *Journal of Operational Psychiatry*, 1980, *11* (2), 101–119.

Fernanez, L., Garcia, P. and Tello, S. Assessment of the outpatient population in the community mental health center of San Ysidro: An assessment of mental health needs of Mexican-Americans in the community of San Ysidro, California. Unpublished Master's Thesis, San Diego State University, 1981.

Glazer, N. and Moynihan, D. *Ethnicity: Theory and Experience*. Cambridge, MA.: Harvard University Press, 1975.

Gordon, M.M. *Assimilation in American Life*. New York: Oxford Press, 1964.

Grebler, L., Moore, J.W. and Guzman, R.C. *The Mexican American People*. New York: The Free Press, 1970.

Havighurst, R.J. *Developmental Tasks and Education*. New York: Longmans Green, 1952.

Heller, C. *Mexican American Youth: Forgotten Youth at the Cross Roads*. New York: Random House, 1966.

Hollingshead, A.B. *Elintown's Youth: The Impact of Social Classes on Adolescents*. New York: Wiley, 1949.

Hoppe, S.K. and Heller, P.L. Alienation, familism; and the utilization of health services by Mexican-Americans. *Journal of Health and Social Behavior*, 1975, *16* (3), 304–314.

Hough, R.L. Life events and stress in Hispanic culture. In: W. Vega, and M. Miranda (Eds.), *Hispanic Services Delivery: Mental Health Issues*. California State Department of Mental Health, 1981.

Hough, R.L. Socio-cultural issues in research and clinical practice: Closing the gap. In: E.A. Serafetinides (Ed.), *Psychiatric Research in Practice: Biobehavioral Themes*, 1981a, 203–225.

Hough, R.L., McGarvey, J.G. and Fairbank, D.T. *Modeling of Life Change Impacts Across Cultures*. In press, 1981.

Jaco, E. Mental health of the Spanish-American in Texas. In: M. Opler (Ed.), *Culture and Mental Health, Cross Cultural Studies*. New York: Macmillan, 1959.

Jaco, E. *The Social Epidemiology of Mental Disorders: A Psychiatric Survey of Texas*. New York: Russel Sage Foundation, 1960.

Johnson, H.M. *Sociology: A Systematic Introduction*. New York: Harcourt, Brace & World, 1960, p. 469.

Keefe, S., Padilla, A. and Carlos, M. Emotional Support Systems in Two Cultures: A Comparison of Mexican-Americans and Anglo-Americans. Los Angeles: Spanish Speaking Mental Health Research Center, UCLA, 1978, Occasional Paper #7.

Kellam, S. and Ensminger, M.E. Theory and method in child psychiatric epidemiology. In: F. Eares (Ed.), *Studies of Children*. New York: Prodist 1980, pp. 145–180.

Kiev, A. *Curanderismo: Mexican-American Folk Psychiatry*. New York: Free Press, 1968.

Kluckhohn, C. and Leighton, D. *The Naucho*. Cambridge, MA: Harvard University Press, 1946.

Lawrence, G. and Lurie, J. Communication problems between rural Mexican-American patients and their physicians. *American Journal of Orthopsychiatry*, October 1972, *42* (5), 777–783.

Levine, E.F. and Padilla A.M. *Crossing Cultures in Therapy: Pluralistic Counseling for the Hispanic*. Monterey, CA: Brooks-Cole, 1980.

Lewis, O. The culture of poverty. *Scientific American*, October 1966, *215*, 19–25.

Litwak, E. Occupational mobility and extended family cohesion. *American Sociological Review*, 1960, *25*, 9–21.

Madsen, W. *The Mexican American of South Texas*. New York: Holt, Reinhart & Winston, 1964.

McWilliams. C. *North From Mexico. Spanish-speaking People of the United States*. New York: Greenwood Press, 1953.

Mercer, J.R. Pluralistic diagnosis in the evaluation of black and Chicano children: A procedure for taking sociocultural variables into account. In: C.A. Hernandez, M.J. Hough, and N.N. Wagner (Eds.), *Chicanos: Social and Psychological Perspectives*. Saint Louis: Mosby, 1976.

Miller, W.B. Lower class culture as a generating milieu of gang delinquency. *Journal of Social Issues*, 1958, *14*, 5–19.

Mintz, S. and Wolf, E. An analysis of ritual coparenthood *(Compadrazgo)*. *Southwestern Journal of Anthropology*, 1950, *6*, 341–368.

Miranda, M. The family natural support system in Hispanic communities: Preliminary research notes and recommendations. In: R. Valle and W. Vega (Eds.), *Hispanic Natural Support Systems*, State of California Department of Mental Health, N80-620047, 77–78, 1980.

Monteil, M. The Chicano family: A review of research. *Social Work*, 1975, *18* (2), 22–31.

Moroney, M.M. Families, Social Services and Social Policy. *DHHS* Pub No. (ADM) 80-846. U.S. Government Printing Office, Washington, D.C., 1980, p. 49.

Nall, F.C. and Speilberg, J. Social and cultural factors in the responses of Mexican-Americans to medical treatment. *Journal of Health and Human Behavior*, 1967, *8* (4), 249–308.

Neugarten, B.L. Time, age, and the life cycle. *American Journal of Psychiatry*, 1979, *136*, 887–894.

Olmedo, E.L. and Padilla, A.M. Empirical and construct validation of a measure of acculturation for Mexican-Americans. *The Journal of Social Psychology*, 1978, *105*, 179–187.

Padilla, A., Carlos, M. and Keefe, S. Mental health service utilization by Mexican-Americans. In: M.

Miranda (Ed.), *Psychotherapy with the Spanish-Speaking: Issues in Research and Service Delivery*. Los Angeles: Spanish-Speaking Mental Health Resource Center, University of California, 1976, pp. 9–20.

Padilla, A. and Ruiz, R. Latino mental health: A review of the literature. *DHEW* Publication No. (HSM) 78–9143. U.S. Government Printing Office, Washington, D.C., 1973.

Padilla, A.M. The role of cultural awareness and ethnic loyalty in acculturation. In: A.M. Padilla (Ed.), *Acculturation: Theory, Models and Some New Findings*. Boulder, CO: Westview Press, 1980, 47–83.

Park, R.E. Human migration and the marginal man. *American Journal of Sociology*, May 1928, *33*, 881–893.

Parsons, T. The normal American family. In: M. Sussman (Ed.) *Sourcebook in Marriage and the Family*. New York: Houghton Mifflin, 1968, pp. 36–46.

Paz O. *The Labyrinth of Solitude*. New York: Grove Press, 1961, 9–28.

Pearlin, L.I. and Schooler, C. The structure of coping. *Journal of Health and Social Behavior*, 1978, *19* 2–21.

Peñalosa, F. Mexican family roles. *Journal of Marriage and the Family*, 1968, *30* (4), 680–689.

Ramirez, M. and Castañeda, A. *Cultural Democracy, Bicognitive Development, and Education*. New York: Academic Press, 1974.

Romano, O. The anthropology and sociology of the Mexican-American: The distortion of Mexican-American history. *El Grito: A Journal of Contempoary Mexican-American Thought*, Fall 1968, *2*, 13–26.

Romano, O. Historical-intellectual presence of Mexican-Americans. *El Grito: A Journal of Contemporary Mexican-American Thought*. Winter 1969, *2*, (2), 32.

Rubel, A. Concepts of divorce in Mexican-American culture. *American Anthropologist*, 1960, *62*, 795–814.

Sanchez, A. The defined and the definer: A mental health issue. *El Grito: A Journal of Contemporary Mexican American Thought*, Summer 1971, *5*, 4–11.

Saunders, L. *Cultural Difference and Medical Care*. New York: Russell Sage Foundation, 1954.

Sena-Rivera, J. *La familia Hispana* as a natural support system: Strategies for prevention in mental health. In: R. Valle and W. Vega (Eds.), *Hispanic Natural Support Systems*, California State Department of Mental Health, N80-620047, 1980.

Seward, G. and Marmor, J. *Psychotherapy and Culture Conflict*. New York: Random House, 1956.

Simmel, G. *The Sociology of George Simmel* (Kurt, H. Wolff, translation). New York: The Free Press, 1950.

Social Science Research Council Summer Seminar on Acculturation. Acculturation: An exploratory formulation. *American Anthropologist*, 1954, *56*, 973–1002.

Sotomayor, M. A study of Chicano grandparents in an urban barrio. Unpublished doctoral dissertation, University of Denver, 1973.

Sotomayor, M. Mexican-American interaction with

social systems. *Social Casework,* 1971, *52* (5), 316–324.

Staples, R. The Mexican-American family: Its modification over time and space. *Phylon,* 1971, *32* (2), 179–192.

Steglich, W.L., Cartwright, W. and Crouch, B. *Study of Needs and Resources Among Aged Mexican Americans.* Lubbock: Texas Technological College, 1968.

Stonequist, E.V. The marginal man: A study in personality and culture conflict. In: E. Burgess and D. Bogue (Eds.), *Contribution to Urban Sociology.* Chicago: University of Chicago Press, 1964, pp. 337–345.

Sussman, M. The isolated nuclear family: Fact or fiction? *Social Problems,* 1959, 6, 333–340.

Torrey, E.F. The case for the indigenous therapist. *Archives of General Psychiatry,* 1969, *20* (3), 365–373.

Torrey, E.F. The irrelevancy of traditional mental health services for urban Mexican-Americans. In: M. Levitt and B. Rubenstein, (Eds.), *On the Urban Scene.* Detroit: Wayne State University Press, 1972.

Vaca, N. The Mexican-American in the social sciences, 1912–1970. *El Grito: A Journal of Contemporary Mexican American Thought,* 1979, *III* (3) Part I, 3–24,; 1970, Part II, *4* (2), 17–51.

Valle, R. and Mendoza, L. *The Elder Latino.* San Diego: Campovile Press, 1978 51–55.

Van den Ban, A. Family structure and modernization. *Journal of Marriage and the Family,* 1967, *29,* 771–773.

Vega, W. Defining Hispanic high risk groups: Targeting populations for health promotion. In: R. Valle and W. Vega (Eds.), *Hispanic Natural Support Systems.* State of California Department of Mental Health, N8-620047, 123–131, 1980.

Vega, W. Mental health research and North American Hispanic population: A review and critique of the literature and a proposed research strategy. In: R. Valle and W. Vega (Eds.), *Hispanic Natural Support Systems.* State of California Department of Mental Health, N8-620047, 3–14, 1980a.

Vega, W. The Hispanic natural healer, a case study: Implications for prevention. In: R. Valle and W. Vega (Eds.), *Hispanic Natural Support Systems.* State of California Department of Mental Health, N80-620047, 66, 1980b.

Vega, W. Warheit, G. and Meinhardt, K. Mental health and disorders in the Hispanic community. In: W. Vega and M. Miranda (Eds.), *Hispanic Mental Health: Relating Research to Services Delivery.* San Diego: San Diego State University Press, 1982.

Ventura, S.J. and Heuser, R. Births of Hispanic parentage. *Monthly Vital Statistics Report, 29,* 12, Supplement, National Center for Health Statistics, DHHS, March 1981.

Warner, W.L. and Lunt, P.S. *The Social Life of a Modern Community.* New Haven, CT: Yale University Press, 1941.

Zippin, D. and Hough, R.L. *Perceived Self-Other Differences in Life Events and Mental Health: A Multi-Cultural Analysis.* In press, 1981.

CHAPTER 13

The Impact of Macro Systems on Puerto Rican Families

Emelicia Mizio, M.S.W.

Healthy families are the *sine qua non* of a healthy society. Well integrated families are critical to the preservation of our societal structure and its effective functioning. Families cannot exist in isolation and cannot maintain their health without societal supports. There is a reciprocity which must be recognized between society and its members (Zimmerman, 1976).

To understand a family and its operations, one must study its transactions with its environments. The family is an extremely vulnerable institution impacted by and responsive to societal conditions. The degree of a family's vulnerability relates closely to its socioeconomic status. The effects of poverty have been well documented in terms of physical and mental malaise and the overwhelming sense of helplessness, hopelessness and alienation. The generally poor, low-status Puerto Rican family is consequently in exteme jeopardy because its extended family system and differences in its values place it in conflict with a sociolegal system in this country which addresses itself basically

to the nuclear family. Our society, in turn, jeopardizes itself when it does not meet the needs of its citizenry or provide necessary supports; hence, the problems of our inner cities. Major cities such as New York, Chicago, Philadelphia, Cleveland, Newark, and Boston have large Puerto Rican (and other minority) populations. The quality of life for Puerto Ricans (and other minorities) in key urban centers must be viewed as inextricably linked to the general quality of life in those cities (U.S. Commission on Civil Rights, 1976).

A coherent and just national family social policy must evolve and address itself to ethnic differences. Social policy deals with the kinds of benefits that are to be distributed, with the people to whom they are to be distributed, with the amount to be distributed, with the way in which they are to be financed, and with the cost of providing the specific benefit (Zimmerman 1976). Ethnicity is defined as conscious and unconscious processes fulfilling a deep psychological need for security, identity, and sense of historical continuity. Within the family, it is transmitted in an emotional language, and it is reinforced by similar units in the community (Giordano, 1974). Ethnicity refers to a common culture. It operates on both conscious and unconscious levels and shapes basic values, norms, attitudes, and life styles of the group's members even as it is modified by such factors as class, race, religion, sex, region and generation (Giordano, 1976a) Social policy experts and planners and service-delivering professionals must make certain that they take these ethnic differences into account. Considerable research is now being conducted in this area (Giordano, 1976b)

THE EXTENDED FAMILY IN A NUCLEAR FAMILY SOCIETY

The family has been viewed as a goal-oriented, task-performing system. It has the following functions: (1) physical care and maintenance of its members; (2) addition of new members through reproduction and their relinquishment when they mature; (3) socialization of children for various roles as spouses, parents, workers, citizens, and members of social groups; (4) maintenance of order within the family and between the family and outside groups; (5) maintenance of family motivation and morale to facilitate performance of tasks in the family and other social groups; (6) production as well as distribution of services and goods necessary for maintaining the family (Zimmerman, 1976)

There are also different family types characterized by common residence. The one with which we are most familiar in the United States is the "model American family," a nuclear family where special emphasis is placed on the conjugal bond. Typically, a nuclear family consists of wife and husband, and their offspring; kin are generally excluded (Murdock, 1968). In a nuclear family, the family's decision making, and reciprocal controls are weak since few mandatory exchanges are required

(Goode, 1964). In the search for upward mobility, the nuclear family structure has freed its members to seek their fortunes without consideration of in-laws or other kin. It is often said that economic factors have shaped the "ideal" American family pattern.

A specific type of American humor centers around interfering in-laws who attempt to violate the sanctity of the nuclear family. Many mental health practitioners have not placed a high value on extended family ties. They have often correlated a successful analysis or course of treatment with the independence of individuals and their own procreated families from their families of origin. A study by the Jewish Family Service in New York showed that social workers often attempt to help the family change its kin relationships — usually in the direction of less involvement. Social workers were also found to be less kin-oriented than their clients. This fact leads to issues about the significance of value differences in therapeutic practice as well as, of course, in society (Leichter and Mitchell, 1967).

Policy makers, as well as mental health practitioners working with Puerto Rican families, must realize that the Puerto Rican family, in contrast to the American family, is an extended one, with strong ties that are in no way considered or experienced as pathological.

An extended family is a composite form of the nuclear family (Leichter and Mitchell, 1967). It is characterized by intense and frequent relationships. The Puerto Rican family is patriarchal, and roles are clearly defined and strictly monitored. There are important reciprocal obligations and strict fulfillment of each person's role responsibilities. Scheele (1969), for example, writes that a person in Puerto Rico, whether bootblack or bank president, by successfully fulfilling the expectancies of his or her various statuses, maintains *Dignidad*—one of the most important Puerto Rican values. The elderly are respected and have a place in this society. Children are deeply loved; they are not held accountable for their parents' "sins."

To visualize the Puerto Rican family, it is important to understand the interrelated Puerto Rican cultural values of *Dignidad, Respeto* and *Personalismo.* For a fuller discussion of important Puerto Rican values, see Mintz (1973), Wagenheim (1970), Fitzpatrick (1971). A person automatically possesses *Dignidad* (dignity in a broadened sense). This is a belief in the innate worth and inner importance of each individual. The spirit and soul are more important than the body. The focus is on the person's qualities, uniqueness, goodness and integrity.

Persons are born into their socioeconomic roles and, therefore, cannot be held accountable for their status. There is often a *fatalismo* (fatalism) about their position in life. Fatalism and Puerto Rican values should be examined in the context of Catholicism and colonialism. The notion of a "colonialized personality" is found throughout a good part of the literature. Some acquaintance with the history would be essential to an understanding of the Puerto Rican situation. (The beginning reader is referred to Wagenheim, 1970. For an interpretation from an independent point of view, see Maldonado-Denis, 1972. For an understanding of how fatalism comes into play in the helper/client relationship, see Vasquez de Rodriquez, 1973.) They may see life's events as inevitable, (*"Lo que Dios manda"*—What God wills). They feel themselves at the mercy of supernatural forces and are resigned to their fate. This life view is illustrated by a conversation between Piri Thomas, a Puerto Rican raised in the U.S., and his mother, who had spent her formative years in Puerto Rico. "Our parents were resigned to their life. But we, the youngsters, would say, 'Has this life gotta be for us forever?' I remember my own mother's answer one day when I asked her, 'Why can't we have a nice house like this?', showing her a picture in a maga-

zine . . . 'Of course, we can have it in heaven someday' " (Thomas, 1974).

It does not matter, therefore, what people have in this life or what their stations in life are. They possess status simply by existing. Rewards will come in heaven. A person is, however, entitled to be treated in this life with *respeto* ("respect" in a broadened sense) as long as they fulfill their role requirements and adhere to Puerto Rican values and norms. *Respeto* is the acknowledgement of an individual's personal attributes, uninfluenced by wealth or social position (Abad, Ramos and Boyce, 1974). *Respeto* also connotes hierarchal relationships. Elders and superiors of one form or another, are to be accorded respect. The superior, in turn, must always be cordial. There are prescribed cultural rituals to show respect. Puerto Ricans are very sensitive to affronts which would violate their *dignidad.* People who have been insulted must always handle themselves in an honest, dignified, and upright manner. An attempt is made to settle the situation *a la buena* (in a nice way). Generally, an attempt is made to avoid direct confrontation, with *"pelea monga"* ("passive resistance") often employed. Aggression is permitted when a man's machismo is challenged.

As previously stated, tied in with *dignidad* and *respeto* is the concept of *personalismo,* a strong preference for face-to-face contact and primary relationships. As an illustration of the importance and extent of this preference, while the supermarket may be a much cheaper place to shop, the *bodega* (neighborhood grocery store) is much more popular in many communities in the states, taking on the characteristics of a primary social institution (Vasquez, 1974). It is the individual in the organization or institution one trusts and deals with. The concept of a collective welfare generally has little meaning. One thinks instead of adverse or favorable effects on Pablo, José and Juan. Even in terms of their ties to the church, Puerto Ricans experience special and individualistic relationships with the saints. Puerto Ricans do not want their unique personalities absorbed into committees and bureaucracies, Their participation in groups will depend on strong ties to individual group members rather than on ties to a cause per se (Roger, 1971). Puerto Ricans seem to seek charismatic leadership. A recent study comments on the high rate of participation in elections together with the tendency to idolize their leaders and to leave too much policy making and implementation to those they have elected. This relates as well to other leaders, labor and religious (Brameld, 1976). *Personalismo* requires that all social, economic, political relationships proceed on the basis of known face-to-face contact (Mintz, 1973).

Puert Ricans feel most comfortable with a family style in their relationships. It is not surprising that the Puerto Rican extended family encompasses not only those related by blood and marriage, but also those tied to it by custom in reciprocal bonds of obligation and feeling. Important parts of the Puerto Rican family system are the *Compradazgo* and *hijos de crianza*.

The *Compradazgo* is the institution of *compadres* ("companion parents"), a network of ritual kinship whose members have a deep sense of obligation to each other. These responsibilities are taken quite seriously and include economic assistance, emotional support, and even personal correction. Sponsors of a child at baptism and confirmation take on the role of *Padrinos* ("godparents") to the child and *compadres* to the parents. Also assuming this role are witnesses at a marriage or close friends (Fitzpatrick, 1971). The relationship develops a significant religious and even mystical quality.

Hijos de crianza ("children of the upbringing") is the cultural practice of accepting responsibility for another's child, without the necessity of blood or even friendship ties. This child is raised as if it were one's own. Neither the natural parent nor the child is stigmatized for the relinquishment. There is also no stigma attached to an illegitimate child. Following the Roman legal tradition, there is no concept of illegitimacy; the child is viewed as a natural child (Fitzpatrick, 1971). This institutional practice serves as an economic and emotional safety valve for the family and often makes it possible for the child to enjoy a better life. The family, in all likelihood, will not be able to produce documents for the child. As Hidalgo (1972) points out, the helping professional must be prepared, if necessary, to battle the legal system. Previously stated and important to reiterate is that the Puerto Rican family is placed in immediate jeopardy as a result of described differences in family structure and values, bringing it into conflict with the socio-legal system of the U.S., which addresses itself basically to the nuclear family. Consider social security and income tax provisions as illustrations. Income tax regulations do not allow tax deductions for *Compadres* or consensual unions. In many parts of Puerto Rican society, consensual unions are a common and acceptable practice. Consensual unions must, however, be examined in the context of the economic situation. When one owns no property, there is little need for legal entanglements. It is interesting to note that with the rise of the middle class in Puerto Rico the percentage of consensual marriages has dropped and it is basically a phenomenon of the poor (Fitzpatrick, 1971).

Support of an *hijo de crianza* is credited by the Internal Revenue Service if the contribution has been more than half of the year's total support. Social Security benefits are not paid to any of these groups. For those few fortunate Puerto Ricans who hold health insurance policies, coverage is defined without reference to the Puerto Rican concept of family.

There is a gross inequity in the amount of societal benefits and residual services provided to the Puerto Rican population. Young and old receive little from society. One need only look at the conditions in ghetto schools, hospitals, outpatient clinics and housing, at the lack of recreational facilities and activities, at the limited amount of police protection, at the types of jobs available and their salary range, along with the unemployment figures, to be struck by the harsh reality of the Puerto Rican condition. A society which provides so little to the Puerto Rican community also serves in may ways to render the minority impotent in its self-help efforts. Under existing societal conditions, mutual assistance, both financial and emotional, is essential. Puerto Ricans in the United States have been described as having lost their social assets; they are removed from the customary support of tradition, kin, and esteem of hometown neighbors. Housing patterns in New York show that Puerto Ricans scattered throughout the city at a faster rate than was true of other ethnic groups upon their arrival. Housing is not as easy to find as it was in the past. Puerto Ricans are thus exposed to the host culture more intensively and sooner. Isolation from their ethnic groups has been associated with increased rates of mental illness in minorities (Rabkin and Struening, 1976). It is imperative, therefore, that any remaining semblance of the extended family be preserved. Public policy and programs must lend support to the extended family. The extended family system should be viewed as important not only to the Puerto Rican, but to other ethnic groups as well. Moreover, the value placed on the extended family should not be assumed to be solely related to a poverty status. An examination of Anglo-American alternative life styles will frequently reveal attempts to create such an extended family group (Beck, 1976).

Society's restrictions on self help affect the nearly two million Puerto Ricans and their descendants on the Mainland, most of whom live in New York City (New York Times, 1977). New York City Housing Authority regulations prohibit the public housing dweller from extending the tra-

ditional hospitality of an open door to their "kin" in need of a start in the new land; neither can they share the rent when it would be mutually beneficial in financial and child-caring terms. Among Puerto Rican families living in poverty, nearly 60 percent are headed by a woman (U. S. Commission on Civil Rights, 1976). The need for mutual aid arrangements within such families is especially critical. Lack of child care facilities for their children inhibits the participation of Puerto Rican women in the labor force. (U. S. Commission on Civil Rights, 1976). Restrictions on apartment sharing occur at a time when it is virtually impossible to obtain an apartment in a project or to rent a decent apartment elsewhere. In attempting to qualify as foster parents, Puerto Rican families find that they face a serious problem in lack of housing space. Institutional care, rather than foster home care, is stressed by child welfare agencies (Valle Consultants Ltd., 1973). Can institutional care be considered better than the loving concern of a *Madrina* (Godmother) for an *hijo de crianza,* even if in substandard housing? To solve both the housing and child care problems, abandoned buildings in local neighborhoods might be refurnished and made available on a non-profit basis to families who qualify as foster parents (Valle Consultants Ltd., 1973)

On the other hand, the author does not believe self help efforts alone can suffice, nor is sharing a cramped apartment in New York. The Puerto Rican Family Institute in New York has found that migrants may overstay their welcomes when they are unable to find a job or secure housing. Reliance for too long on a *Compadre* may lead to tension between the host and the newly arrived family (Gorbea, 1975). Certainly, day care or institutional programs are needed; however, their use should be dictated by need and cultural preference. Most importantly, the author should not be interpreted as denying society's responsibility to provide a humane standard of living for its poor. But if the poor are not to be helped, let them not be hindered in their communal efforts to solve the problems of their poverty.

SOCIETAL STRAINS ON THE PUERTO RICAN FAMILY

Points of tension in the Puerto Rican family have been classified as:

1) A traditional system of relationships based on social class and family background versus an industrial system based on competition, initiative, and conspicuous consumption as a basis for status.
2) High aspirations and low achievement.
3) The value of dignity, pride, and honor contrasted with the increasing emphasis on material wealth and consumption.
4) A value system that reveres the *jibaro,* (an idolized folk hero of the Puerto Rican) (Wagenheim, 1970) as opposed to one that reveres the successful entrepreneur.
5) The present commitment to democracy compared to the traditional methods of power that prevailed in the colonial system (Vasquez de Rodriquez, 1971).

One cannot truthfully write about the Puerto Rican family living in the United States or in Puerto Rico as if a universal model existed. Families are affected by and deal with potential strains in different ways. The Puerto Rican family system must be viewed along a continuum from the extended family system to the American nuclear family system. There are many possible variations in between. It may be helpful to understand differences in Puerto Rican family structure and values as influenced by industrialization on one hand and by the penetration of the Anglo-American culture on the other (Mintz, 1973). Strains may be caused by either stream of influence. Traditional patterns are also often augmented by

other friendships, such as work relationships (Wagenheim, 1970). Business firms may be quite paternalistic and highly centralized in authority, following a pre-industrial form (Scheele, 1969). A study dealing with acculturation among Puerto Rican women on the Mainland showed that even among those who score high on acculturation there is still respect for and adherence to traditional family-related values (Torres-Matrullo, 1976).

These points of tension exist in Puerto Rico as well as in the United States. Under the impact of American colonialization, industrialization, and urbanization, the family in Puerto Rico has undergone considerable shock. Before emigrating, the poor family has often moved from a rural community to an urban area, where traditional values may have encountered Americanization and the effects of a clash of values may have already begun. The life style in a prosperous urban area in Puerto Rico is different from anything in their past experience. Families often find themselves living in urban shanties, sometimes in the shadow of sleek new office buildings. They exist by doing odd jobs and collecting meager welfare payments (Wagenheim, 1970).

The urban area stateside, especially in New York, is considerably more complex than in Puerto Rico. Lack of proficiency in English, limited education and occupational skills, and possible dark skin add to the problems of Puerto Ricans. Because they are automatically United States citizens, there is little preparation required for emigration to the States. They find themselves suddenly transplanted to an unfamiliar environment, and are expected to know how to negotiate business immediately in an American urban setting and to resolve the complexities of such a life style. The Puerto Rican Family Institute in New York has found that the newly arrived migrant needs assistance in dealing with the vital areas of housing, health, education, employment, and home management (Canabal and Goldstein,

1975). It is to be expected that many migrants would not know how to maneuver in this complicated environment that is so different in culture and institutional arrangements.

Families must be able to deal with an urban environment as well as to cope with major changes in values. These changes usually mean an increase in role failures. Family members will differ in their interpretations of role obligations, and strained relations may well ensue. Family members have not been prepared to fulfil the new expectations. Previously, roles in the Puerto Rican family had been clearly defined. In rural settings there was a sharp division of labor, with wage earning activities generally relegated to men. Women's freedom was severely limited and their relationships with men were limited to kin. The cults of virginity and machismo were combined, with men as innately superior to women, a view reinforced through the societal structure. Boys and girls in Puerto Rico had been basically segregated from each other and this pattern continued in adulthood. Parents had viewed their children as completely dependent, demanding obedience from them. Children should be quiet, submissive, and respectful; achivement is less important than conformity. These concepts were especially applicable to girls. In the middle and upper classes there is less emphasis on these subordination patterns, but they are still interwoven into the overall fabric of Puerto Rican society (Bucchioni, 1965; Stycos, 1952; Wagenheim, 1970) Wagenheim (1970) points to a phenomenon that was once taboo, that of a suburban wife in Puerto Rico driving and shopping alone; while she now shops alone, the same woman today will not venture out alone at night without her husband. While the double standard continues its hold among all classes in Puerto Rico, it is decreasing most rapidly in the urban class. The virginity cult, however, remains largely unmodified, even by the impact of more flexible continental standards (Brameld, 1976).

The traditional family structure and value system come into immediate conflict with the demands of the stateside environment. Women must act independently, work, and carry the same types of burdens as men. They are forced to deal with external systems such as school, police, hospitals, etc., and to be involved with non-kin men in lively interactions. Men cannot protect their women from external pressure. Children must also become assertive in order to survive and often continue this pattern by challenging parental views. While these exchanges and others like them need not become crises, they become critical when compounded by a society that denies access to resources which an individual needs to adequately play the newly defined role. American society denies such access to Puerto Ricans and then judges them by what they have been denied. This is indeed a crucial dilemma for Puerto Ricans. Rabkin and Struening's (1976) review of research on mental illness among New York City residents revealed that epidemiological studies consistently show higher rates of mental illness for Puerto Ricans than for other ethnic groups or for the total population.

It is important to note that the available statistics might not reflect accurately the degree of the problem. Puerto Ricans have great tolerance for the "peculiarities" of others and will lend support to keeping the person at home and in the community. Also, many Puerto Ricans have a belief system which differs from that of Anglos. Spiritualism flourishes hand in hand with Catholicism, the predominant religion of Puerto Ricans. Spirits are believed to be the cause of illness, and a person feeling his or her defenses tumbling may see a spiritualist and attend a seance. Such persons may find community support in dealing with their psychic problems, the origins of which are considered spiritual. However, for some, not seeking psychiatric help may quickly precipitate a more severe breakdown. It is crucial for health practitioners working with the Puerto Rican population to have an understanding of this belief system, as well as of the way in which professionals can cooperate with spiritualism (Lubchansky, Egri and Stokes, 1970; Ruiz and Langrod, 1976).

Rabkin and Struening (1976) write that the development of mental illness in migrant populations relates to the amount of social change experienced in the transition from one setting to another. They view alterations in life style, family organization and role assessment, membership in social networks, and extent of community supports as each contributing to the individual's vulnerability to the experience of stress and illness. We have already noted the great number of social changes experienced by the Puerto Rican migrant. In general, all families handle stress differently. The fact that the great majority of families cannot be classified as mentally ill is a testimony to human resiliency. There are great differences in family structure and value systems. In the case of Puerto Ricans, differences relate in part to whether formative years were spent in the United States or in Puerto Rico, as well as to the level of education. When viewing Puerto Rican families along the continuum described earlier, one should not expect to find too many families at either the traditional or nuclear end. It is important to note, however, that certain Puerto Rican families in the United States may remain in a more traditional form than families in Puerto Rico because of their isolation from the wider society. This tendency may reflect needs to cling to the security of the familiar and to reject what appears to be so unaccepting of them.

To understand variations between families and family members, it is imperative that in our assessments we go beyond ego strength and pathology. It is critical to take into consideration the external systems with which the family and its members have been in transaction. How much stress can any family be expected to tolerate and still maintain a viable homeostatic balance? Families are open social systems and as "living systems are acutely dependent upon their external environment" (Katz and Kahn, 1966)

Sociologists have classified the family as having the following functions fundamental to social life: sexual, economic, reproductive, and educational (Murdock, 1968). The family, along with meeting instrumental needs, must be able to meet the expressive and affective needs of its members. One cannot evaluate the Puerto Rican family's ability to perform its functions or the way in which Puerto Rican culture structures these tasks without examining the environment of the Puerto Rican family in the United States. Goode (1964) pointed out that a family can continue to exist only as it is supported by the larger society. The society, as a larger social system, furnishes the family, as a smaller social system, with the conditions necessary for its survival.

THE PUERTO RICAN AS A MINORITY MEMBER

We have seen that the Puerto Rican family finds itself in a hostile environment which makes life a struggle for existence. Racist practices, along with a highly technological, stratified, closed society, inhibit the upward mobility of Puerto Ricans and relegate them and their family to the lower caste. The Puerto Rican family finds itself defined as a minority group, whereas in Puerto Rico it was part of a majority. Minority is synonymous with an out-group whose worth, culture, values, and life styles are deprecated and stereotyped. Minority is synonymous with blocked access to the fraternity of the in-group and the full benefits of the American way of life. Erikson (1959) notes that the shock of American adolescence is the standardization of individuals and the intolerance of difference. This destructive parochialism permeates the whole American scene. Society even attempts to force Puerto Ricans into defining themselves as white or black, the standardized categories for color in the United States, with no allowances for the Puerto Rican's mixed Indian, Spanish and African heritage.

In fact, the Puerto Ricans' chances for success seem related to their ability, as individuals and families, to obscure their differences from the majority group. Puerto Ricans who, by placing themselves into the proverbial "melting pot," are able to metamorphose as white with an Anglicized name and lifestyle can provide their families with an American standard of living. The price they must pay is denial of self and heritage, and sacrifice of personal integrity. Whether or not society permits them self-definitions, as white or black they are faced with an identity problem. There is no intention here to stigmatize or blame the victims, a procedure Ryan (1969) defines as an "intellectual process whereby a social problem is analyzed in such a way that the causation is found to be in the characteristics of the victim rather than in any deficiencies or structural defects in his environment."

As Longres (1974) points out, the racial experience in the United States goes beyond the individual and family and must be viewed as a collective one where all are forced to confront and question their racial identity. The color question persists as a psychological dilemma even among the seemingly assimiated. It is as if each day the Puerto Rican issue and color question come up even for those who can pass as Anglo. Again and again, one needs to decide whether to confront or let a remark about Puerto Ricans go by. Always at issue is how much racism one can accept in one's "friends." Also ubiquitous is the need to reassess the "fit" of the Puerto Rican stereotype and to place oneself and others in perspective.

This racism and its internalization also threaten Puerto Rican unity and can serve to divide Puerto Ricans along racial lines. For some, a negative internalization of self may work against the interests of their own group in an attempt to deny their own heritage and to secure their new "chosen" identity.

The havoc society wreaks and the problems it creates for the individual and for the family by its measurement of worth in terms of color are vividly protrayed in *Down These Mean Streets*. Thomas's (1967) autobiography describes how his painful identity problem and destructive relationships with his siblings and father were related to the differences in color between him and his siblings and to feelings about self and others tied to these color differences:

It wasn't right to be ashamed of what one was. It was like hating Momma for the color she was and Poppa for the color he wasn't . . . Man do you know what it is to sit across a dinner table looking at your brothers that look exactly like paddy people? True, I ain't never been down South, but the same crap's happening here. So they don't hang you by your neck. But they slip an invisible rope around your balls and hang you with nice smiles, and "If we need you, we'll call you." I wanna feel like a "Mr." I can't feel like that just yet and there ain't no amount of cold wine and pot can make my mind accept me being a "Mr." part time . . . You and James (his brothers) are like houses painted white outside and blacker'n mother inside. And I'm close to being like Poppa—trying to be white on both sides. (p. 8)

Thomas's identity crisis is unfortunately not atypical. How intense this crisis can be is indicated by the fact that admission rates to mental hospitals for non-white Puerto Ricans are the highest among the Puerto Rican group. Second generation Puerto Ricans have a higher total admission rate than their parents. This finding is surprising in its contrast to the usual pattern among immigrant groups (Rabkin and Struening, 1976). It may well be, however, that not being subject to minority status throughout one's formative years provides better insulation than growing up as a minority "non-person." First generation parents can probably maintain their *dignidad* and find comfort in their recollections of their past.

Identifying oneself as Anglo-white, black, or Puerto Rican serves as a locus of orientation to concepts of self and others, to values and to life styles. The kinds of identifications, confusions, and ambivalences experienced by Thomas unfortunately reflect malignancies in our society because individuals and their families comprise vulnerable and open social systems.

It is futile to enter into a debate about whether Puerto Ricans uncontaminated by American society are themselves racist. It is also futile to attempt to determine whether the prejudice observed in Puerto Rico relates to class, as is claimed, rather than to color. What is certain is that Puerto Ricans are totally unprepared to deal with the discrimination to which they are subjected upon arrival in the United States. Both in statistics and in literature, the devastating effects of color discrimination and ghetto existence on the Puerto Rican family in this country are clear. Thomas's excruciatingly painful identity struggle over what and who he was and his pathological relationships with his family over color differences would not have happened in Puerto Rico.

THE SEARCH FOR THE POT OF GOLD

The United States has traditionally attracted immigrants seeking their fortunes. Though the Puerto Rican has not found a fortune in America, Anglo-Americans have found a fortune in Puerto Rico. Puerto Ricans have filled labor shortages in many important stateside industries: in Illinois' electronic industries; in Wisconsin foundries; in the steel mills of Ohio, Indiana and Pennsylvania; in East and Midwest farms; and in the textile and gar-

ment industries of New York (Migration Division, 1975). Puerto Ricans initially were recruited to serve as a source of cheap labor. Some employers now consider minorities an "excess population" because machines are increasingly being substituted for low-level positions. Current migration therefore differs from previous immigration in that the opportunities for work are no longer available.

White immigrants did not have to deal with the degree of racism that permeates our society with respect to "rainbow" people. There are other important differences which should be noted. For example, the Puerto Rican migration is an airborne one. It has a back and forth flow, significant in that the feeling of need to adjust to the stateside environment tends to be less than if travel were more difficult. In fact, it is difficult to find a Puerto Rican adult who has not spent some time in the United States (U. S. Commission on Civil Rights, 1976).

Though Puerto Ricans come to the States for many reasons, migration has been seen to have an economic regulator (Migration Division, 1975) that serves as the primary motivation for migration. Puerto Rico's economic situation at present is devastating. It should be noted that the means of production, resources, and capital in Puerto Rico are mainly in the hands of North Americans. The dollar value of United States business holdings in Puerto Rico is exceeded only by its holdings in Britain, Germany, and Canada. Strategic considerations are also critical in Puerto Rico's proximity to Cuba and the Panama Canal. Also, Puerto Rico may prove in the future to be an oil resource, as preliminary seismic studies show potential deposits off the northwestern coast (New York Times, 1977).

In Puerto Rico, present conditions are deplorable. The myriad of economic problems necessitate a continuation of patterns that are cruel and divisive to the family. It is not uncommon to find wives separated from husbands and children, or vice versa, with children cared for an ocean away from their parents. With part of the family in Puerto Rico and part in the United States enough is earned to keep the family from starving. Yet, stateside the Puerto Rican is by no means doing well. Puerto Ricans have had the dubious distinction of being poorer, having less education, and being more dependent upon welfare than the national average (U.S. Commission on Civil Rights, 1976). In the general population, about 64 percent of all persons 25 years old and over were high school graduates compared to 30 percent in the Puerto Rican population. By 1976, in the overall population, about 3.8 percent of all persons had completed less than 5 years of school; the figure was 18.7 percent for the Puerto Rican population (U.S. Bureau of Census, 1976).

We should, however, take note that official census figures often belie existing conditions. As an illustration, a 1966 report by the U.S. Department of Labor stated that the unemployment rate for Puerto Ricans in slum areas in New York was 33.1 percent, which contrasted with the 10 percent official unemployment rate (U.S. Commission on Civil Rights, 1976).

With reference to education, the dropout problem becomes acute in the 18-24 age group. In Chicago, a study showed that the dropout rate for Puerto Ricans in grammar and high school was 71.2 percent; 12.5 percent dropped out of grammar school while 58.7 percent dropped out of high school. It is important to understand that reasons for dropping out are not purely academic. Of the 30 percent of the Puerto Rican U.S. high school students who drop out each year, one-third have already completed most of their required courses and are in their senior year. Most dropouts are bored, feel the need to find a job, or find the school unresponsive to their cultural background.

Studies of schools in Chicago and New York revealed that schools with heavy Puerto Rican enrollments had students with reading averages lower than pre-

dominantly black or Anglo Schools. Lags increased with each succeeding grade. Birthplace, language, and dropout rate were interwoven. Young Puerto Ricans born on the Island are more likely to be doomed to a life of poverty (U.S. Commission on Civil Rights, 1976). The Chicago report discussed its interviews of 140 dropouts (better termed "pushouts"). The pushout's personal reason for leaving school was a major crisis in self-identity that made staying in school more and more difficult. The pushout had learned that his or her position in society was clearly lower than that of an Anglo. This newly acquired consciousness of societal rejection was in violent opposition to the internalized sense of *respeto* and *dignidad*. "Social schizophrenia," a conflict of great intensity, resulted. The easiest way out was to dissociate oneself from school, a major establishment symbol. Aspirations for the future decreased and a sense of defiance developed. Some students joined gangs, which provided an environment where they could find recognition, new respect, and leadership roles. Such students concluded that academic achievement often does not bring the expected reward (Lucas, 1974).

While census figures and findings paint a grim picture of the Puerto Rican condition, what is perhaps of even greater concern is the fact that the situation has worsened greatly.

The . . . stresses and strains burdening the Puerto Rican family have resulted in an escalating increase in children without homes, delinquent children, addicted youth, and youth poorly prepared to compete for higher education or employment. It remains rather amazing that, despite these burdens, the majority of Puerto Rican families have been able to make an adjustment to their new environment, recreate some of their cultural ambience (for example, food, religion, and recreation), and create communal institutions and organizations that contribute to the community's wellbeing and progress. It is a strong, vibrant community, often resisting forces that attempt to assimilate it or eradicate it, linguistically or culturally. One commentator has suggested that the tenacity to exist as a distinctive group has been stubbornly embedded in Puerto Ricans as a result of 450 years of colonialism (Miranda, 1973).

To round out the picture, we should note that the situation is not uniformly bleak. One hundred and four thousand Puerto Ricans earned $10,000 or more in 1974. About 25,000 earned in excess of $15,000 and around 5,000 had earnings in excess of $25,000. Thousands of mainland Puerto Ricans are high school and university graduates. The figures for 1975 show 198,000 high school graduates, 12,000 college graduates, and more than 17,000 enrolled college students. Forty-two thousand Puerto Ricans held professional, technical, or managerial jobs in 1975. Three-fourths of the Puerto Rican families on the mainland are entirely self-sufficient and do not receive any government aid (U.S. Commission on Civil Rights, 1976).

Nevertheless, the overall statistical picture is a dismal one. The figures in human terms mean that it is often difficult for a Puerto Rican man or woman to find employment. When secured, jobs are frequently seasonal or temporary, and the norm is dead-end employment. Doors are often closed for reasons having nothing to do with willingness to work. Qualifications are unrelated to the task at hand. As an illustration, written examinations for some sanitation workers require a college education; high school diplomas are required of airplane maintenance personnel; there is a height requirement for police personnel; Puerto Ricans in union construction jobs are token workers (U.S. Commission on Civil Rights, 1976); fluency in English is required for dishwasher jobs, etc. For a Puerto Rican seeking employment, discrimination exists at all levels, not only in the private sector but in public service as well as in employment and training programs. Discriminatory practices in government are well documented

by the United States Commission on Civil Rights (1976). This is a matter of gravest concern, for how can Puerto Ricans expect to make gains in the private sector if they cannot rely on the governmental sector to set an example and enforce its own regulations.

A minority group woman can at times secure employment more easily than a man, perhaps as a sewing-machine operator or as a domestic, because our society still needs to have these functions performed. In those instances where a husband must stay at home to care for young children, family roles are reversed. Recall that in the Puerto Rican family system the male is expected to be the breadwinner and a dominant figure. Hence, role reversal is of tremendous importance in a family system where *machismo* is valued; the extent of valuation, of course, varies with the family. American psychiatrists have ethnocentrically defined *machismo* as "belligerent masculinity" and "sexual dominance" that such men are expected to display under any possible challenge or situation. They have viewed *machismo* in terms of sexual overcompensation, and as related to generic problems in masculine identification (Group for the Advancement of Psychiatry, 1970). *Machismo*, however, in its ramifications does not appear to be too different from the combination of male chauvinism, with its implicaions for female-male roles and rewards, and the double standard of sexuality (Sirjamaki, 1969).

The difference seems to be that Latin American *machismo* is not disguised or subtle so that its impact is more readily discernible. *Machismo* in its individualized expression can be viewed in the context of a society denying a male his manhood by societal castration. This situation has been found by social workers to create panic, confusion, marital discord, and the breakdown of family ties (Giordano, 1976a, 1976b).

A man needs to work. The significance of work to a man's self-concept is well understood. Peter Drucker states:

Social effectiveness, citizenship, indeed even self-respect depend on access to a job. Without a job, a man in industrial society cannot possibly be socially effective. He is deprived of his citizenship, social standing, and of the respect of his fellow man, if not his family, and finally of self-respect. (Mayfield, 1972, p. 108).

A man needs avenues for achievement. Being a *macho completo* (complete man) provides an avenue of gratification when there are few other opportunities for status or reward. This sense of being a *macho* must go hand in hand, however, with being able to provide for and protect one's family. It is not necessary that these functions be a man's exclusive domain. It is recognized that government has taken over more and more family functions. Consequently, the family's authority in relation to such concerns as parental discipline and legal systems has lessened. A Puerto Rican man with no employment, power, or status can be expected to be impotent in protecting his family in relation to these external systems. A principal strain on Puerto Rican family life is the disparity between the presumed dominance of the male and the actual facts of the situation (Group for the Advancement of Psychiatry, 1970).

Some women may experience contempt for their husbands because they can no longer view them as *machos*. A husband can be expected to strive to reassert his dominance, but due to all the external pressures, he will often in the end experience defeat and lose his sense of *dignidad*. Many women feel torn apart at seeing the men they love destroyed by forces over which they have no control. Children, experiencing the friction in the home, seeing the family structure undermined, and probably having had no contact with successful Puerto Rican families, internalize contempt of parents, Puerto Ricans, and themselves. Funnye and Shiffman (1967) note that the ghetto im-

poses a pervasive sense of worthlessness on its children, with implications of undesirability and inferiority. There are situations in which the impact of these feelings is such that even after the parents' struggle to provide the child with a college education, the child is fearful of leaving the ghetto to achieve in the larger community.

In working with a group of Puerto Rican adolescents at Aspira, the author learned that for many youths the image of what a family should be was related to models derived from television. Media influences often mean that Puerto Rican parents and children, literally and figuratively, do not speak the same language in speech or in values. In the adolescent's eyes the Puerto Rican family can never be expected to compete with families in programs such as Life with Father. Studies conducted by Hickel among Afro-Americans revealed that young black television viewers regard whites as more competent than blacks, and model their conduct accordingly (Newsweek, 1977). Models on TV have been changing, with minorities, particularly Afro-Americans, being depicted in a more positive light. Yet the harsh realities of ghetto existence seem in many ways to be romanticized in the TV programming. Even with the limited changes, however, neither Afro- nor Anglo-American models are Puerto Rican models.

There are few Puerto Rican professionals in any area with whom the adolescents have contact and can identify. It is hoped that the further development of bilingual, bicultural school programs will help these adolescents establish goals for themselves and to recognize the worth of their family and their group. This author will never forget her first day on a job in a settlement as a Field Instructor of a student unit and as an Assistant Professor from a University. A youngster came running after her an said in disbelief, "Are you really Puerto Rican?"

Puerto Rican adolescents in contact with external systems in the larger society have been stripped of their cultural heritage.

When Juan Ortiz began bringing his homework back from the second grade in Brooklyn, his mother noticed he had changed the spelling of his first name. "Well," the nine-year-old explained, 'My teacher tells me my name isn't Juan, it's John.' " (New York Times, 1972)

The stripping process continues today. Many professionals are inadvertently guilty of taking part in this without any awareness of the racism involved. On one occasion the author served as speaker and discussion leader at a program designed to help social workers deliver relevant services to the Puerto Rican community. Under discussion were the difficulies students encountered in school in terms of both cultural and language issues. One day-care worker pointed out proudly how the children who were in her program would never face these difficulties, since from early infancy only English was spoken and Anglo values were stressed. The other professionals seemed convinced that the solution to Puerto Rican problems was socialization in the Anglo culture during infancy or at least in early childhood. They appeared taken aback when the author pointed out the racism in such an approach.

Our definition of cultural pluralism must include the concept that our language and our culture will be given equal status to that of the majority population. It is not enough simply to say that we should be given the opportunity to share in the positive benefits of modern American life. Instead, we must insist that this sharing will not be accomplished at the sacrifice of all those traits which make us what we are as Puerto Ricans (U.S. Commission on Civil Rights, 1976).

In the futile search for the "pot of gold," children may often experience their parents' pain and feel tremendously responsible for the family's burdens and "failures." They often have had to learn to negotiate

various systems for the family and may be crushed in the process. Some children exhibit acting-out behavior which may have primarily sociological determinants and great sociological and psychological ramifications (Cressey and Ward, 1969). Whatever the antecedents of Puerto Rican delinquency, for example, the authority of the parents, especially of the father, is destroyed. Clearly, not all families disintegrate. Great credit must be given to those families that maintain their strength and balance in a society where the "pot" discovered is not filled with gold but is a melting pot filled with sterotypes of the middle class Anglo-American family unit.

CASE ILLUSTRATIONS OF FAMILIES IN TRANSACTION WITH THEIR ENVIRONMENT

Several case vignettes from the files of family agencies demonstrate some of the transactions of the Puerto Rican family with the stateside environment.* No claim is made that these cases are a statistically representative sample of the Puerto Rican population stateside, but the situations are not atypical. Nor should these family agency clients be viewed as more or less pathological because of their relationship with the agency. Identifying data have been disguised so as to protect the client's right to confidentiality.

Case #1 (Gonzales)

Mr. and Mrs. Gonzales both came from Puerto Rico as adults. Both have some college education. Their financial situation is adequate in that their combined income makes it possible for them to live comfortably with their two children. They had just come back from a Florida vacation

*The agencies are not being identified in the interest of protecting further the identity of the client. The author, however, would like to thank these agencies for their cooperation.

when they made contact with the family agency social worker. Mrs. Gonzales was working in a semi-professional position in a day-care center, in an Eastern city, where a family agency worker served as a consultant. When her 16-year-old daughter was arrested for shoplifting, she immediately turned for help to the family agency worker. An unsuccessful attempt was made to involve the father in the family sessions. Coming for help, especially to a female worker, seemed to be too great an affront to his machismo. His wife was quite accepting of the male-female role dichotomy in the home. Nevertheless, from the content of the sessions it was clear that Mr. Gonzales was very much involved in the counseling process and with his family. His affection and concern were very evident to the worker despite his difficulty in expressing his feelings directly.

The need for that clear communication by this family of feelings, ideas, and needs was also apparent to the worker. The daughter Dolores was feeling extremely lonely and misunderstood, and the parents in turn were feeling quite hurt. Dolores experienced herself as different from all her friends. She had stolen some clothing in order to dress like all the other teenagers and so that she could go to a school dance. The parents were very strict in keeping with the tradition of protecting the female. They did not approve of the typical teenage attire and the freedoms allowed to Anglos.

The parents came to see that they had to accept the reality of the stateside culture and that they would cripple their daughter were they to continue to deny her the right to participate in teenage activities. They gave up setting limits in an automatic way and tried to balance the traditional value system with the needs of their teenage daughter in an Eastern city environment. The 16-year-old daughter had internalized the traditional Puerto Rican value system with some modifications. Her rebellion against her heritage did not mean she was truly desirous of throwing it all off. She needed to feel she had options. She assessed her group of friends and recognized certain behaviors of which she did not approve. Nor did she herself truly wish to dress in any extreme fashion. The daughter was able to modify her dress in the way that was satisfactory to all. She pleased her parents and willingly went to family affairs. (All age groups socialize together in the Puerto Rican culture.) The parents recognized she needed to be allowed her own separate life.

Basically, what happened in this situation was a cultural clash that went beyond a clash of generations typical in families with teenagers. The family was able to handle a crisis by opening up channels of communication and build upon their foundation of love and caring. Fortunately, this was not a situation where poverty compounded the difficulties.

Case #2 (Garcia)

The Department of Public Assistance of an Eastern city referred Mr. Garcia to the family agency for a number of problems. The client was drinking heavily and showed no interest in the W.I.N. program to which he had been referred for employment. He needed assistance with his medicaid eligibility and had great difficulty taking care of his 9-year-old daughter who was acting out. Also, they were living in a deplorable housing situation. Mr. Garcia, a man in his early fifties, had come to the States eight years ago, leaving a decent civil service job as a foreman in construction. His wife had moved herself and five children to the States against her husband's wishes.

Mrs. Garcia had insisted that in the States the family would have better economic and educational opportunities. Hoping to get his family to return to Puerto Rico, he took out a loan from a credit union and bought a home in Puerto

Rico. Not succeeding in getting his wife to relent, he came to the States. His wife died from alcoholism shortly after his arrival. While in Puerto Rico he had had no idea of his wife's condition. The money that was left after selling the home in Puerto Rico and repaying the loan was used for her funeral expenses. The family had been receiving supplemental assistance while he was in Puerto Rico, as what he had been able to send was insufficient for their basic needs. He decided after his wife's death against returning to Puerto Rico and was able to secure a construction job to which he had to commute daily. Though his income was still inadequate, he withdrew the family from welfare on the basis that ". . . if I can work to take care of my family, I don't want them acting like beggars." He had a series of lay-offs and when he was no longer eligible for unemployment benefits he had to go on assistance.He tried hard looking for work. He picketed with the Puerto Rican construction workers for more jobs, having met up with job discrimination. When some jobs did finally open up, he was not able to obtain one because of his age. He was so defeated and depressed that he increasingly took to drink.

Mr. Garcia feels that basically he has been a happy man. He equates happiness with being in Puerto Rico where he feels he can function at his best. Puerto Rico is a memory which triggers a smile on his face. He does not speak, however, of returning to Puerto Rico. His children are very important to him and they intend to remain. His depression is clearly a reactive one.

It is not unusual for part of a family to come to the States and the other member(s) to feel forced to follow. A woman may very well take the lead in such a situation. Mrs. Garcia wanted what she thought would be the best for her family. She was especially concerned about educational opportunities. Puerto Ricans value education. Mr. Garcia valued his family and, despite the upheaval he knew it

would cost him, came to reunite himself with his family. Little by little the force of circumstances and the environment tore this proud man down. All he had was in his past and like many Puerto Ricans he turned to his past for solace. He had not come to the States looking for handouts. He responded well to the combination of counseling, advocacy efforts and the concrete interventions of the family service worker. Importantly, through the worker's efforts he was again able to resume construction work, which gives him a sense of well being. His daughter is doing well. It is a sad commentary on this society that a man should have to depend on a social worker to obtain employment.

Case #3 (Santos)

The Santos family was referred to the family service agency by the school their 11-year-old daughter attends. The mother was acting in a bizarre fashion and was interfering with the teacher's functioning and her daughter's schooling. The father is a factory worker. The mother was a former practical nurse in Puerto Rico and because of her inability initially to speak English worked on an assembly line for a while. Mrs. Santos has had a mastectomy, is terminally ill and undergoing chemotherapy. Due to her irrational behavior, there is fear that she may hurt herself as she wanders about or that she may hurt others as she is easily upset. When she takes her medication, she is under better control.

Mrs. Santos has always been a devoted mother and has become obsessed with her daughter. Until her illness the mother functioned well. She now no longer allows her daughter to visit girlfriends and limits all her activities.

The Santos are members of a Pentecostal congregation. The mother carries a Bible in her pocketbook and says, "God will help me," but will not discuss her condition. The minister and his congregation have been extremely supportive of the family. All the Santos find comfort and draw strength in the church experience. The minister takes the daughter to school and in an effort to contain and watch over Mrs. Santos the minister's wife has tried to stay with her during the day. Mr. Santos cannot continue to miss days from work without jeopardizing his job. If money is secured from Cancer Care, a member of the congregation will stay with Mrs. Santos. Plans are for the daughter to go and live with an aunt in Puerto Rico upon the death of her mother.

Mr. Santos is deeply concened about his wife. He is at a loss about how to handle her. Under no circumstance, however, does he wish her institutionalized.

This family has ties to the Puerto Rican community in its affiliation with the Pentecostal Church, which is serving as a sustaining force in a difficult situation. The Pentecostal Church, a storefront variety, is a native organization and an important social institution both as a religious force and a community resource. This family, as many other Puerto Ricans have done, is able to draw emotional support from the religious experience. Mrs. Santos' belief that God will help her reflects the resignation to their fate that is not uncommon to many members of the Puerto Rican community.

Puerto Ricans, in general, have a wide tolerance for idiosyncratic behavior, which explains the acceptance of Mrs. Santos' irrationality. Families are willing to put up with a great deal and are not quick to institutionalize their own even when this seems absolutely necessary. A Puerto Rican social worker in New York recently reported to me how difficult it is to get families to accept placing the elderly in nursing homes when they, under their living conditions, cannot possibly care for them. There is tremendous guilt to work through. Nevertheless, it is my understanding from her that there is a long waiting list in Puerto Rico for nursing homes. Changes are clearly taking place.

The hope is that the changes will reflect need and not the Anglo rejection of the elderly.

As to be expected, their daughter upon her mother's death will be cared for by family. Puerto Ricans are very protective of their female children. Mrs. Santos has become irrationally protective of her daughter. It is understandable that her anxiety over her impending death would manifest itself in this way.

Case #4 (Castro)

The family was referred to the family agency by the Visiting Nurse Association. The family is known to just about every social agency in the community, including protective services. Mrs. Castro's husband had deserted the family about a year ago, just prior to the birth of the youngest child. The oldest child is five years old. All children and Mrs. Castro appear retarded. The children have totally lacked stimulation. Mrs. Castro refuses to allow the children out of her sight. She is quite paranoid and has had a number of psychiatric hospitalizations. This is not to deny that some paranoia in a minority person is necessary for survival. Mrs. Castro carries a knife constantly in her skirt pocket and people are frightened of her. She has tremendous difficulty managing the care of her home which is in chaos. A student social worker had finally managed to gain Mrs. Castro's trust and, hopefully, there will be some changes in the home.

The family agency has tried to no avail to involve Mrs. Castro's blood kin and in-laws in an attempt to provide her with the emotional support of family, to avoid the possibility of placement, and in the hope of providing the children with the warmth of family contact and interaction. They say she is too crazy and refuse to involve themselves with her or to assume any responsibility at any level for the children. The relatives feel greatly burdened by their own difficult circumstances. They clearly state they do not want to take on anyone else's troubles or to involve themselves at all with this nuclear family. In fact, it is felt that Mrs. Castro's sister has actually stolen food stamps from her in the past. The extended family system has clearly broken down in this situation and traditional values seem to have no place. Neither is there stateside a community that can serve as a mechanism of social control which demands the meeting of one's obligation to one's family if one is to remain in good standing and in turn obtain community support. Environmental pressures can exert such force that the culture of poverty seems to have greater impact than ethnic roots and may destroy the humanity of people. This must not be allowed to continue to happen.

Many social agencies are now involved with this family and it is costing society huge sums of money for these residual type services. Society will pay thousands to keep an individual in jail but not one cent for a guaranteed income. We can only speculate at this point about the kind of environmental and psychological stress that made Mr. Castro a runaway husband. One also needs to ask how much of the retardation of Mrs. Castro and the children relates to nutritional factors and how much to lack of intellectual development because of inadequate early stimuli. Projects such as the highly successful and replicated one originated by the Family Service Association of Hempstead, New York, need expansion. Trained personnel go into homes of two- and three-year-old children and attempt to foster verbal interaction by teaching mothers to play with their children. They demonstrate the use of toys and books. They work toward the development of a closer mother-child involvement and improvement of mother's self image. The children's I.Q. scores have been shown to rise through such efforts. Preventive societal supports at all levels can enable families to make their proper contribution to society.

SUMMARY AND CONCLUSIONS

In attempting to understand the Puerto Rican family, it is important to gain knowledge of its cultural heritage and the degree of each family's identification with the Puerto Rican or Anglo cultures. A unique blending is found in each individual and family. Class factors enter into this blending. Gordon (1964) has formulated the term, "ethclass," a subsociety created when ethnicity and social class intersect. He speaks of two types of ethnic identification: historical, which primarily focuses on the ethnic group, and participational, which focuses on the ethclass. He points out that members of similar ethnic groups from different social classes share peoplehood (historical identification) but do not necessarily have similar behavioral styles (participational identification).

All classes in Puerto Rican society seem to maintain both the historical and participational identifications. The degree of the identifications varies with the individual and family. On the mainland, it is, of course, difficult to identify the numbers of those who have completely assimilated into an Anglo life style. No culture will remain static, expecially if it is to remain viable. In addition, all cultures have functional and dysfunctional aspects. As in all societies, subordination patterns in male-female roles must continue to undergo changes without females developing into superwomen. Extended families remain critical to individual members in an alienated world. This should not, however, negate a person's individuality. The humanitarian value system of the Puerto Rican needs to influence Anglo culture. Nevertheless, Puerto Ricans should not accept that the fruits of their efforts will be rewarded only in heaven. A humane standard of living must be available to all.

Caution must be taken not to stereotype any individual, class or group. The author affirms Cafferty's and Chestang's (1976) view that it is as dangerous to ignore an individual's ethnic identity as it is to assume certain behavioral characteristics based on that identity.

Therefore, the characteristics of the Puerto Rican culture that have been discussed in this chapter should be utilized as guidelines for comparisons and applied with a respect for the differences and similarities among Puerto Ricans and Anglo-Americans.

Most of what is written in the literature and experienced by the Anglo in relation to the Puerto Rican relates to the lower-class Puerto Rican. Because this is the case, it is critical to recognize that our knowledge of Puerto Rican culture, even with attention to ethclass, is insufficient without reference to the Puerto Rican's transaction with the environment. We know that external macro systems furnish the conditions for a family's existence. As members of a minority group, Puerto Ricans have suffered greatly from institutionalized racist practices.

Mayfield's (1972) definition of powerlessness distinguishes the type of powerlessness imposed from without. The ecological conception and redefinition of pathology are also relevant to the Puerto Rican family situation. Behavior is not seen as sick or well, but as transactional, the outcome of reciprocal interactions between specific situations and the individual (Kelly, 1969).

Admittedly, the helping professions by themselves cannot restructure society and achieve a more equitable distribution of opportunities and rewards. The helping professions can, however, help the Puerto Rican family deal with suffocating external systems and, through joint advocacy efforts, work toward systems change. Helping professionals are certainly in a position to examine with honesty their own delivery system to the Puerto Rican consumer, noting the ways in which their services are functional, dysfunctional, or nonexistent. Services must be culturally

syntonic and not geared to an Anglo value system.

To avoid continued polarization between groups in our society (McGready (1976), the helping professions must work toward an acceptance of the concept of social utilities as developed by Kahn (1969) building on the Wilensky and Lebeaux (1958) concept of institutional and residual services in social welfare. We need to accept that by the very nature and complexity of modern society, services and supports will be necessary. A social utility, then, is a social invention, a resource or facility designed to meet a generally experienced need in living. These services must be accessible and be non-stigmatized, in the manner of public utilities.

Social utilities must be delivered in culturally relevant ways. Flexibility must be allowed for in their neighborhood design and implementation. Minimally, the helping professions must advocate a public social policy and a delivery system which takes ethnic factors into account. This includes working toward helping the Puerto Rican community have a part in its definition of its problem. Solutions must not be superimposed.

The Puerto Rican family must be permitted and assisted to utilize its own strength, draw upon its humanitarian values, and support its kin and the Puerto Rican community at large. The helping professions must work as agents of change if they are to be instrumental in the Puerto Rican family's efforts to manage its tasks effectively, in harmony with its values and life style, as well as with the realities of the mainland environment and urban existence.

REFERENCES

Abad, V., Ramos, J., and Boyce, E. A model for delivery of mental health services to Spanish-speaking minorities. *American Journal of Orthopsychiatry,* 1974, *44,* 584–595.

Beck, D. *Marriage and the Family Under Challenge. An Outline of Issues, Trends and Alternatives.*

Second Edition. New York: FSAA, 1976.

Betances, S. Race and the mainland Puerto Rican. In: A. P. Campos, (Ed.), *Puerto Rican Curriculum Development Workshop: A Report.* New York: CSWE, 1974, 55–66.

Brameld, T. Explicit and implicit culture in Puerto Rico: A case study in educational anthropology. In: J.I. Roberts and Akinsanya (Eds.), *Sociology in the Cutural Context.* New York: David McKay, 1976, pp. 44–57.

Bucchioni, E. Home atmosphere and success in school. A sociological analysis of the functioning of elementary education for Puerto Rican children. Unpublished Doctoral Dissertation, New School for Social Research, 1965, pp. 55–66.

Cafferty, P.S.J. and Chestang, L. (Eds.). *The Diverse Society: Implications for Social Policy.* Washington, D.C.: NASW, 1976.

Canabal, J. and Goldstein, D. The Puerto Rican family institute: A laboratory for therapeutic techniques to aid Spanish-Speaking families. In: D. J. Curren (Ed.), *Proceedings of Puerto Rican Conferences on Human Services.* Washington, D.C.: The National Coalition of Spanish Speaking Mental Health Organizations, 1975, pp. 61–85.

Cressey, D. R. and Ward, D. A. *Delinquency, Crime and Social Process.* New York: Harper & Row, 1969, especially pp. 244–253.

Erikson, E. *Identity and the Life Cycle.* New York: International Universities Press, 1959.

Fitzpatrick, J. J. *Puerto Rican Americans: The Meaning of Migration to the Mainland.* Englewood Cliffs, N.J.: Prentice Hall, 1971.

Funnye, C. and Shiffman, R. The imperatives of deghettoization: An answer to Piven and Cloward. *Social Work,* 1967, *12,* 5–11.

Giordano, J. Ethnics and minorities: A review of the literature. *Clinical Social Work Journal,* 1974, *2,* 207–220.

Giordano, J. Introduction. Group identity and mental health. *International Journal of Mental Health,* 1976(a), *5,* 3–4.

Giordano, J. Ethnicity and community mental health. *Community Mental Health Review,* 1976(b), *1,* 4–14.

Goode, W. J. *The Family.* Englewood Cliffs, N.J.: Prentice Hall, 1964.

Gorbea, C. The institute's program for new arrivals. In: D. J. Curren, (Ed.), *Proceedings of Puerto Rican Conferences on Human Services.* Washington, D.C.: The National Coalition of Spanish Speaking Mental Health Organizations, 1975, pp. 73–79.

Gordon, M. *Assimilation in American Life.* New York: Oxford University Press, 1964.

Group for the Advancement of Psychiatry. *The Case History Method in the Study of Family Process.* New York: Group for the Advancement of Psychiatry, 1970.

Hidalgo, H. *Ethnic Difference, Series #4.* Washington, D.C.: National Rehabilitation Association, 1972.

Kahn, A. Theory and Practice of Social Planning. New York: Russell Sage Foundation, 1969.

Katz, D. and Kahn, R. *The Social Psychology of Organizations.* New York: John Wiley and Sons, 1966.

Kelly, J. Ecological constraints on mental health services. In: A. Bindman and A. Spiegel (Eds.), Chicago: Aldine, 1969, pp. 93–100.

Leichter, H. J. and Mitchell, W. E. *Kinship and Casework.* New York: Russell Sage Foundation, 1967.

Longres, J. F. Jr. Racism and its effects on Puerto Rican continentals. *Social Problems,* 1974, *55,* 67–75.

Lubchansky, I., Egri, G. and Stokes, J. Puerto Rican spiritualists view mental health: The faith healer as a paraprofessional. *American Journal of Psychiatry,* 1970, *127,* 88–97.

Lucas, I. A profile of the Puerto Rican dropout in Chicago. In: A. P. Campos (Ed.), *Puerto Rican Curriculum Development Workshop: A Report.* New York: CSWE, 1974, pp. 20–30.

Maldonado-Denis, M. *Puerto Rican: A Socio-Historic Interpretation.* New York: Vintage Books, 1972 (Translation).

Mayfield, W. Mental Health in the Black Community. *Social Work,* 1972, *17,* 106–110.

McGready, W. Social utilities in a pluralistic society. In: P.S.J. Cafferty and L. Chestang (Eds.), *The Diverse Society: Implications for Social Policy.* Washington, D.C.: NASW, 1976, pp. 13–25.

Migration Division, Department of Labor, Commonwealth of Puerto Rico. *Puerto Ricans in the United States,* 1975 (Xerox).

Mintz, S. W. Puerto Rico: An essay in the definition of national culture. In: F. Cordasco and E. Bucchioni. (Eds.), *The Puerto Rican Experience: A Sociological Sourcebook.* Totowa, New Jersey: Littlefield, Adams, 1973, pp. 26–90.

Miranda, M. (Ed.) *Puerto Rican Task Force Report.* New York: CSWE, 1973.

Murdock, G. P. The Universality of the Nuclear Family. In: N. Bell and E. Vogel (Eds.), *A Modern Introduction to the Family.* New York: The Free Press, 1968, pp. 37–44.

Newsweek, February 21, 1977.

New York Times, Jan. 9, 1977.

New York Times, July 30, 1972.

Rabkin, J. G. and Struening, E. L. *Ethnicity, Social Class and Mental Illness, Working Paper Series No. 17.* New York: Institute on Pluralism and Group Identity, 1976.

Roger, L. *Migrant In the City: The Life of a Puerto Rican Action Group.* New York: Basic Books, 1972.

Ruiz, P. and Langrod. The role of folk healers in community mental health services. *Community Mental Health Journal,* 1976, *12,* 392–398.

Ryan, W. Fretting About the Poor. In: W. Ryan (Ed.), *Distress in the City.* Cleveland: The Press of Western Reserve University, 1969, pp. 262–267.

Scheele, R. The prominent families of Puerto Rico. In: J. Steward (Ed.), *People of Puerto Rico.* Urbana: University of Illinois Press, 1969, pp. 418–462.

Sirjamaki, J. Cultural configurations in the American family. In: R. J. R. King (Ed.) *Family Relations: Concepts and Theories.* Berkeley, CA: The Glendessary Press, 1969, 42–54.

Stycos, J.M. Family and fertility in Puerto Rico. *American Sociological Review,* 1952, *17,* 572–580. National Council on Family Relations, Reprint.

Thomas, P. Puerto Ricans in the promised land. *Civil Rights Digest,* January 1974. *6.*

Thomas, P. *Down These Mean Streets.* New York: New American Library, 1967.

Torres-Matrullo, C. Acculturation and psychopathology among Puerto Rican women in mainland United States. *American Journal of Orthopsychiatry* 1976, *46,* 710–719.

U. S. Bureau of the Census. *Current Population Reports.* Persons of Spanish origin in the United States, March 1975. Series P-20, No. 290. Washington, D.C.: U.S. Government Printing Office, 1976.

U. S. Bureau of the Census. *Current Population Reports.* Persons of Spanish origin in the United States, March 1976. Series P-20, No. 302. Washington, D.C.: Printing Office, 1976.

U. S. Commission on Civil Rights. *Puerto Ricans In The Continental United States: An Uncertain Future.* Oct. 1976.

Valle Consultants Ltd. *What Holds Sami Back: A Study of Service Delivery in a Puerto Rican Community.* New York: Valle Consultants Ltd., 1973.

Vasquez de Rodriquez, L. *Needs & Aspirations of the Puerto Rican People, Social Welfare Forum, 1971.* New York: Columbia University Press, for the National Conference on Social Welfare, 1971, 15–22.

Vasquez de Rodriquez, L. Social work practice in Puerto Rico. *Social Work,* 1973, *18,* 32–40.

Vasquez, J.D. La Bodega - A social institution. In: A. P. Campos (Ed.), *Puerto Rican Curriculum Workshop: A Report.* New York: CSWE, 1974, pp. 31–36.

Wagenheim, K. *Puerto Rico: A Profile.* New York: Praeger, 1970.

Wilensky, H. L. and Lebeaux. *Industrial Society and Social Welfare.* New York: Russell Sage Foundation, 1958.

Zimmerman, S. The family and its relevance for social policy. *Social Casework,* 1976, *57,* 547–554.

CHAPTER 14

The Japanese-American Family

Joe Yamamoto, M.D.

and Mitsuru Kubota, Ph.D.

The situation of the Japanese-American family today can best be understood by first studying the family in Japan, by analyzing the characteristics and cultural values of Japanese society, then by looking at the effects of migration to the United States, and finally by evaluating the present status of the Japanese-American family in the United States. That we chose this historical view is no accident. The people of Japan have long valued their history and culture and have held tightly to their ancestral past (Yamamoto et al., 1969).

The folktales and myths of Japan abound in gods and goddesses. In the beginning, it is written, out of the primeval sea a reed-like substance emerged which became a deity (Piggott, 1969). From this deity evolved numbers of gods and goddesses among whom is the important Amaterasu, the sun goddess.

One of the many myths connected with Amaterasu is of her withdrawal into a cave, which caused the world to become dark. She had become angry with her

brother Susano, a troublesome character who had destroyed her rice fields. Because the world was dark without her, all the other gods and goddesses came to the cave to plead with her to come out and restore the light. But she remained in seclusion until a dance was performed by a goddess outside the cave. This dance, described by some as merry and by others as obscene, aroused Amaterasu's curiosity, and she peeked out and saw her reflection in a mirror which had been hung on a tree outside the cave by the gods and goddesses. This was the first mirror. Intrigued by her reflection, Amaterasu decided to come out, thus restoring sunlight to the world and creating the normal periods of day and night.

This explains the important symbolism of the mirror in the history of Japan. It is both a sacred object of the Shinto religion and a symbol of the sun. More important, it is believed that the emperor of Japan is a direct descendant of the sun goddess. Thus, the emperor of Japan, Emperor Hirohito, is a direct descendant of Amater-

237

asu, the sun goddess. This belief in the creation myth of the Japanese empire persists despite the fact that the emperors of Japan have not always been descendants of previous emperors; members of the extended family have been substituted when there was no direct descendant. These facts have not dissuaded the Japanese from believing in the direct lineage from the sun goddess to the present emperor.

Primogeniture and lineage are an integral part of Japanese culture. Before the loss of World War II and the subsequent initiation of democratic and equalitarian values, centuries of Japanese history had been founded on primogeniture and lineage. The elder son became the head of the household and was responsible not only for his parents in their old age but also for his brothers and sisters. Consequently, sexual preference for the male predominated, specifically for the firstborn male.

Japan continues to be a vertical society (Nakane, 1970). From the time a Japanese infant awakens until the time he or she goes to sleep, education focuses on the importance of behavior towards elders and awareness of position in the vertical hierarchy. In the family, the rankings are related to seniority and sex. The father has the most authority, followed by the mother in an unofficial capacity, then the eldest son, then the next eldest brother, etc. In the Japanese language there are no words denoting brother or sister, only words which describe the family position of the brother or sister. For example, older brother (*niisan*) or younger brother (*ototo*), older sister (*nehsan*) or younger sister (*imoto*). And, there are special words to describe the firstborn son (*chonan*) and firstborn daughter (*chojo*).

Vertical relationships are generalized to the larger society where rank is important and superior and inferior relationships are clearly prescribed. The language used by an individual varies according to whether the other person is higher or lower in rank. For example, a person of higher rank does not bow as deeply as a person of lower rank, while a person of lower rank makes certain that his or her bow is deeper than that of the superior. To Americans, such concern about details may seem trivial, but these rituals have played a vital role in Japanese social relationships.

The importance of intrafamily relationships is paramount in Japan—past, present, and future. In contrast to the emphasis on individuality in the United States, Japanese society is oriented toward the total family. This difference is significant and must be considered no matter which aspect of Japanese family behavior is evaluated. American behavioral scientists must keep in mind that the value of independence as the goal of maturational and emotional development is a typically American value. In Japan the socialization processes aim not towards the individual but towards the interdependent member of the family team.

A lifetime reciprocal obligation operates between the parents and the children. The Japanese person's scan of time includes the past, present, and future. Ancestors are worshipped, and one is accountable to them (Yamamoto et al., 1969). To honor them and the family name, good behavior and high performance are demanded. In the *present* there are the relationships between the parents and the children. Parents, taking a long-range view into the *future*, are frugal so that their offspring will have the best possible educational advantages. With reciprocal obligations, the children are expected always to show filial piety and to take care of their parents in old age. This is difficult to picture in the United States, where Social Security is designed for financial security for the aged. In the Japanese society there is no need for "social security"; the children are expected to provide for comfort and care of their parents in old age.

This family team must be understood. From morning to night the Japanese family does everything together—eating, relaxing, sleeping, bathing, etc. This is done with due respect for the hierarchical status of each family member. Thus, a prediction can be made as to who will be served first, who will bathe first, etc. In the typical Japanese family the children sleep with the parents in one common sleeping room. Here the status hierarchy is reversed with the youngest sleeping closest to the mother.

The attachment of the Japanese child to the parents, especially to the mother, is very strong. This strong attachment may be related to the mother's indulgence and focusing of her attention on the child. The child is looked upon as the center of the universe, and indeed, never again will a Japanese experience this sort of lavish affection and attention. A Japanese child-rearing has been indulgent, with prolonged nursing, weaning at a much later age, and a view of the child as an integral part of the mother's destiny. Ishikawa (1977) describes breast and bottle feeding and weaning in Japan as similar to the United States. In Japan, the mother is valued in her role as a mother. The expectation is that the mother will take care of the children and focus her attention upon making sure that the children are well prepared for educational achievement.

The father is respected as the head of the household, but it is the mother who spends most of her time with the children. The exception is on Sundays which is the usual day off for the Japanese man. He will spend the day with his wife and children, and they will enjoy themselves as a family unit. The Japanese father's home is very important to him. It is his private area where he can relax in grace and comfort. It is a tradition in Japan that, when one enters the home, shoes or slippers are removed before one steps up onto the tatami floor. This stepping up to the tatami floor represents the feeling that the home symbolizes all that is clean and acceptable. When one leaves the home and puts on shoes or slippers, one must be prepared

for the dirt of the outside world.

Tatsuzo Suzuki et al. (1972) have published a study of Japanese-Americans in Honolulu. In this cross-cultural study, they have compared the responses of a scientifically selected sample of Japanese-Americans in Hawaii with data from past surveys in Japan. There are some interesting differences between the approaches of Japanese-American parents in Hawaii and Japanese parents in Japan. For example, if asked about their child coming home with a rumor that the teacher had done something to get into trouble, and the parents knew it to be true, in Hawaii only 8% of the parents would deny the rumor and 76% would tell the truth; whereas in Japan 29% of the parents would deny it and 52% would tell the truth. Attitudes about the importance of money also differ. In Hawaii only 9% agreed that money is all important, while 88% disagreed; but in Japan 57% said that money was the most important thing and only 28% disagreed. On the question of discipline the responses were nearly equivalent: In Hawaii 14% valued freedom and 70% discipline; in Japan 20% valued freedom and 68% discipline. Parents were asked if they would adopt a child in order to continue the family line, even if there was no blood relationship: In Hawaii 52% said they would adopt, whereas 27% said they would not; in Japan 43% would and 41% would not adopt.

The Japanese in Hawaii and in Japan were asked, "Would you rather be a man or a woman?" In Hawaii only 15% of the women said they would prefer to be a man and 73% said they preferred to be a woman; in Japan 43% of the women said they would prefer to be men, while only 48% preferred being women. Similarly, when asked about which sex had the more difficult life, in Hawaii 25% of the women said that the men had the more difficult life and 48% said women; in Japan 47% of the women said the men have more difficult lives, and only 33% said women. When asked who gets more pleasure out of life, Japanese in Hawaii and Japan concurred: 52% of the Hawaiian women said men and 14% said women; 60% of the women in Japan said men and 15% women.

When asked about Japanese character, the respondents in Japan said the Japanese tended 1) to be diligent, 2) persevering, 3) proper and formal, and finally 4) kind. Fewer of the respondents described the Japanese as being 5) idealistic, 6) cheerful, 7) open, resilient, matter-of-fact, 8) free, 9) rational, or 10) original. These responses could be interpreted as representing the sort of behaviors felt to be the most important among Japanese. In contrast, the Hawaiian-Japanese consider themselves to be 1) free, 2) cheerful, 3) kind, and 4) diligent. Also, they more often described themselves as being 5) open, resilient, and matter-of-fact, 6) idealistic, 7) persevering, 8) rational, 9) original, and finally, less often 10) proper and formal. From this review of character in Japan and Hawaii, it can be seen that the values have changed somewhat. While it is important in both groups to be diligent, the rank has changed. Perseverance is more highly valued in Japan than in Hawaii; while the Hawaiian-Japanese consider it most important to be free and cheerful, followed by kind and diligent. The difference in ideal characteristics shows the gradual Americanization of the Hawaiian-Japanese population.

Let us now consider the Japanese-Americans on the mainland United States. The vast majority of the Japanese migrated prior to the passage of the Oriental Exclusion Act in 1924. The first generation, or issei, are quite elderly now. The second generation, the nisei, are middle-aged or older. The third and fourth generations, the sansei and yonsei, are respectively young adults, or children and teenagers. These generations of Japanese-Americans show varying degrees of acculturation to the American way, yet all have suffered discrimination and prejudice. During their lifetimes in the United States, the majority have been incarcer-

ated in the relocation centers of World War II, suffering poverty and deprivation. Yet, many have seen their sons and daughters achieve educational and vocational success. Compared to all other ethnic groups, it has been repeatedly pointed out that the Japanese have the highest level of educational achievement (Breslow and Klein, 1971; De Vos, 1973; Nishi, 1982). The subsequent vocational achievement of the group has been commensurate.

Along the way there have been many cultural conflicts which, of course, are often also generational conflicts. Two major dramatic conflicts between traditional Japanese values and American values are the focus on the family unit as more important than the individual and the general respect for authority figures and the elderly. Other areas of difference include the vertical structure of the traditional Japanese society, the formality of relationships, the importance of filial piety and respect for elders, and the emphasis on long-range planning and future goals which encompass being frugal and saving. In contrast is the emphasis on youth in the American culture today.

In the traditional culture, as Ruth Benedict (1966) pointed out, Japanese society places great emphasis on the relationships between superiors and inferiors. The emphasis is not only on deference to and respect for the superior by the inferior, but there is a reciprocal and mutual respect by the superior person who acknowledges responsibilities and obligations to the inferior person. Thus, it is not a picture of the authoritarian individual functioning willy-nilly, but quite in contrast, a picture of vertical relationships with due respect to the individual's station in life.

Immediately after World War II there was a significant series of studies done by Caudill and associates (1952, 1969, 1973) and De Vos (1954, 1955). Caudill (1952) proposed that Japanese values and personality structure importantly contributed to the achievements of Japanese in the United States. He was aware of the extended family relationships in Japanese society and the emphasis on the family rather than the individual. The Japanese child is valued in terms of not only the potential of helping the parents in the future, but in the case of the male child, of the importance of carrying the family line. The child is socialized with concern about what others will say and how others will respond. The child learns to adapt to society.

De Vos (1954) describes the differences in the childrearing practices of second generation mothers in comparison to first generation mothers. The younger mothers modified the traditional Japanese practices. These modifications were towards the practices found among American middle-class mothers: a tendency away from breast feeding, an emphasis on bottle feeding, and relatively more abrupt weaning. These younger mothers also tended to emphasize early bowel and bladder training. However, the second generation Japanese mother was different from the American middle-class mother because she tended to feed the child whenever he or she was hungry and to bottle feed the child for a longer period of time. This latter practice is consonant with the practice of mothers in Japan who usually breast feed for several years.

Childrearing patterns in which the Japanese and the middle-class American culture seem to resemble one another are: the insistence on polite manner and social grace, encouragement of competition between siblings, the emphasis on the longer preparation necessary for the goals of a professional education and a "good" marriage, the attendant expectation that gratification of immediate economic and sexual desires will be postponed, and the suppression of aggression, or the necessity of masking aggression as competition or as ambition.

De Vos (1955) studied two generations of Japanese-Americans in the United States with the Rorschach Projective Test.

He described the issei and the nisei and noted the differences from the kibei, the second generation Japanese-Americans who had been sent back to Japan to stay with grandparents or aunts or uncles to receive the traditional Japanese education. The kibei had especially traumatic experiences being uprooted from their homes and placed in unfamiliar homes in Japan, albeit homes of close relatives. These children must have suffered at being left abruptly to be raised by relatives they did not know in a "strange" culture where the emphasis was on strict conformity to the customs. Then they returned to the culture shock of reentry into American society and its different emphasis on individualism and freedom. De Vos found that the nisei tended to be more like middle-class Americans than either the issei or kibei. De Vos commented that the ease of the acculturation of the nisei was due in part to a number of consonant behavior patterns: the formation of the superego in the Japanese culture, and certain compatibilities between the value systems of traditional Japan and those prevalent in American middle-class society. De Vos felt that the Japanese children learned to conform to community standards rather than internalizing parental authority. Thus, De Vos assumed that the nisei conform to the dominant social values communicated to them through the mass media and contacts with the majority culture. He observed personality traits such as tact, compliance, cleanliness, ability to delay gratification for long-term achievements and a strong achievement drive, all of which he felt helped the nisei adapt to situations in school and on the job to win acceptance from the majority culture.

Kitano (1961) compared the different attitudes between first and second generation Japanese using the Parental Attitudes Research Inventory. He concluded that the similarity in behavior of the nisei and the middle-class American was the product of education and acculturation.

Kitano (1962) pointed out that there

was a changing pattern of achievement among the Japanese. The third generation college students were now acculturating, and they were behaving much more like the American middle-class. In contrast to the great emphasis on academic achievement of the nisei, the sansei were more often interested in participation in extracurricular activities as well as in academic achievement.

Arkoff et al. (1963) compared the attitudes of Japanese-Americans and Caucasian-Americans towards marital roles. The Japanese-American men were more male dominant, while the Japanese-American women were more American in their family attitudes. Although Arkoff did not so conclude, this may well be due to the conflict between the traditional roles of Japanese women and the equalitarian roles of American women. The authors concluded that they thought the evidence showed that Japanese-American women were acculturating in a superior manner compared to the men. This, of course, is a value judgment which reflects the emphasis on conformity to American values.

McMichael and Grinder (1964) compared Japanese-American and Caucasian-American children. They speculated that the Japanese children would show weaker internal control of their behavior than the American children. Their results showed there were no significant differences between the two groups in resistance to temptation. The majority of the subjects yielded to temptation in terms of guilt after transgression. The results also indicated no significant differences in the degree of guilt. However, the findings did suggest that the Japanese group tended to confess and make amends more often. This fits the Japanese emphasis on obligation, responsibility and repayment of debts. They concluded that the resemblance in the development of conscience between the Japanese and Caucasian children appeared to be due to the effect of the American culture. However, it could just

as easily have been concluded that in both cultures there is a similar degree of emphasis on responsibility and the development of appropriate behavior.

In 1969, Caudill and Weinstein published the results of observations of middle-class Japanese mothers and their infants compared with middle-class American mothers and their infants. They time-sampled behavior of the respective pairs and found that the Japanese mother had greater physical contact with the infant but demonstrated less verbal behavior. Also, she stayed within eyesight of her child. The objective of the Japanese mother seemed to be a contented and quiet child. In contrast, the American mothers tended to be more vocal in their interactions with their babies, and to encourage physical activities and the exploration of the environment. The American infants, therefore, were more outwardly active, vocal and curious in terms of exploring their bodies as well as their physical surroundings.

Caudill and Frost (1973) studied the behavior of third generation Japanese mothers and their infants in the Unted States and compared it to the Caudill and Weinstein (1969) data. The authors concluded that the behavior of the sansei mothers and infants is closer to that of Americans than to Japanese. The sansei mother spends a greater amount of time in lively chatting with her baby, who in turn learns to respond with increased happy vocalization and physical activity. The sansei mother is like the traditional Japanese mother in more often carrying the baby, although not as often lulling the baby. This may be a sort of compromise adaptation to the American way. To illustrate, one Japanese mother carried her baby and danced around the room, clearly a substitute for carrying, rocking and lulling the child as the traditional Japanese mother would.

In talking about communication methods, Barnlund (1975) presented interesting hypotheses contrasting the Japanese and Americans. His speculations concerned the inclination of Japanese to be less revealing, less open, and less communicative than the Americans. He felt the Americans were more open, communicative and, when under stress, would tend to defend themselves actively, in contrast to the passive defense of the Japanese. The Japanese are socialized to be contented and quiet, while the socialization of Americans is towards activity, communication, and exploration.

Yamamoto and Iga (1974) described how the Japanese in America have been able to progress. Their ability to get on was attributed to several factors including: 1) Japanese tradition of enterprise; 2) positive group identity; 3) cohesive group response despite adverse conditions due to racism; 4) Japanese values which were consonant with American middle-class values; 5) financial responses in the community; and 6) emphasis on education for advancement. Many Japanese-Americans have been better educated, often thanks to parents who saved and encouraged achievement.

Kitano (1974) notes that in Honolulu, Fresno, San Francisco and Los Angeles recent studies have shown that intermarriage rates of the Japanese with other ethnic groups have increased 50%. Eventually this will result in the diminution of the visibility of Japanese-Americans. Many will no longer belong to visible minority groups. Only time will indicate the extent of maintaining of some of the important traditional values.

Considering the past history of discrimination, prejudice, and victimization of Asians in the United States, the situation has improved significantly. The fact that an American of Japanese ancestry has been elected Senator recently from the State of California is an incredible change.

This then is a part of the American dream, that America is comprised of people from many different ethnic groups. This recognition of the cultural plurality of America is important for the benefit of visible minority groups.

Table 1 illustrates the differences between the Japanese and American family. In order to be sufficiently flexible and inclusive in discussing the Japanese-American family, the various combinations of the traits attributed to the Japanese are considered as combined with, augmented by, or altered by American values. The key note here is heterogeneity. This heterogeneity of Japanese-American families is in a constantly changing and interacting relationship, not only with the Japanese values in Japan (which also are changing and interacting with those throughout the world), but also with the American values and culture (which are changing due to both technology and urban growth and also the realization that the world's resources and access to them are limited).

Many of the differences in ideals in Japan and the United States (see Table 1) have been absolute in the past, but because of the changing nature of the society and culture in Japan, they have become relative. With the democratization of Japan in the post World War II Era, the roles of men and women have been more equalized.

From generation to generation there has been an increasing trend towards the adoption of American values. However, despite the successful incorporation of many American values, it is the authors' opinion that most Japanese-Americans retain some of their cultural heritage. There are many reasons for this, including the racism prevalent in the United States. When a Japanese-American is asked repeatedly, "Where were you born?" he or she realizes that to be an Asian in America means having to be aware of one's cultural heritage. The alternative would be to be considered an un-American American and thus a second-class citizen.

It is important to emphasize the overriding importance of the group in Japan in contrast to the emphasis on the individual in the United States. In Japan, one

TABLE 1

JAPANESE	AMERICAN
1. Familism	1. Individualism
A. Common Activities 1) eating, sleeping, recreation	A. Individual Activities

B. Interdependency
    1) dependence
    2) restrained
    3) other-directed or externally
    4) group achievement
	B. Independence
	    1) self-responsible
	    2) spontaneous
	    3) inner directed or internally controlled
	    4) individual achievement

C. Arranged Marriages	C. Individually Arranged Marriages
D. Intact Family Background Crucial	D. Family Background Not Crucial
2. Vertical Relationship	2. Equalitarian

A. Patrilineal
    1) male dominant attitude toward marriage role
	A. Nonpatrilineal
	    1) equalitarian attitude toward marriage role

B. Eldest son favored	B. Equal favoritism
C. Emphasis on child	C. Emphasis on each other or adults
D. Significant other in socialization of child is the mother	D. Significant other in socialization of child is more equal between mother and father
3. Socialization	3. Socialization

A. Goal is to conform to society
    1) good behavior is based upon conformity, duty, responsibility
	A. Goal is to adjust society to one's aim
	    1) good behavior is based upon independence

4. Social Control	4. Social Control
A. Based upon shame, guilt, comparison, appeal to duty and responsibility, ridicule, teasing	A. Based on love and punishment

belongs to the college family, the factory family, the store family, or the bank family. One's identity is a group identity. In the United States the focus is on the individual like the cowboy who rides off on horseback alone to explore not only unknown country but himself, with little or no group support.

Environmental destruction by this em-

phasis on individuation and consumer satisfaction has reached its peak during the last decade. Now society is in a phase of limited expectations and floundering as to directions which will make the most of our scarce natural resources and yet maintain those values and behaviors that this society has learned to believe are important. It is difficult to say, at this point, with increasingly limited expectations, whether group or individual identities will be superior in the future. With both types of identities, it is apparent that there will have to be a sharing and a mutual respect for the rights, privileges, and need gratifications of all others.

To return once again to the comparison of the Japanese and Americans, social control in Japan is different from social control in the United States. There is evidence of extreme indulgence in infancy and early childhood. The child is the center of the universe. Then, increasingly control is based upon shame, guilt, and appeal to concern about the criticism and rejection by others. The young child is ridiculed and teased towards better behavior. In the United States on the other hand, the child is less indulged in infancy, and is socialized to be much more active and verbal. This is based upon not only verbal interactions with the infant or child, but expressions of love for appropriate behaviors and punishment which is much more frequently physical and at times even harsh.

An analogy with the roles of an attending physician and a hospital ward nurse clarifies the traditional relationship between the husband and wife in Japan. Although she is respectful and defers to the doctor's opinions, nonetheless the responsibility for care is directly the nurse's. She expresses opinions, preferences, and points out needed improvement in treatment regimens. Similarly, the Japanese mother is deferential to and dominated by the father; nevertheless she serves as the most important socializer for the children. Paradoxically when the husband returns home with his paycheck he hands it over to his wife. She then deposits the money and gives the husband an allowance which will take care of his bus fare and incidental expenses. So despite the apparent and open male dominance in the Japanese family, in terms of practical day-to-day operations, the influence of the Japanese woman is very strong. Indeed, the empha-

sis on the role of the woman as a very special self-sacrificing, patient, enduring mother who lives for the betterment of her children is the foundation of Japanese families. In contrast, American families have become increasingly individually oriented, so that everyone has to have things his or her way. This stress on individualism has fostered a lack of concerned involvement with other members of the family.

The much more frequent incidence of divorce and ruptured family relationships leads to more difficult lives for many Americans. It is well-known that individuals who have no spouses or families are much more vulnerable to diseases of stress and adaptation. In Japan divorces would have been unheard of; people married to have families and to continue the lineage of the family. Thus, on a continuum of socialization for Japanese-Americans, the issei tended not to divorce at all, the nisei infrequently and the sansei more frequently. This is also connected with the increasing rate of marriage outside the Japanese group; 50% or more of recent marriages are with non-Japanese spouses. Intermarriage will lead to the development of different relationships and a dilution of the old Japanese values.

Most likely the Japanese male in the United States will want to have a male dominant marriage and the Japanese female will prefer the American equalitarian family roles. Doi (1973) discusses the loss of traditional values, including the *enryo* syndrome. *Enryo* means to be reserved, inhibited and not to express one's wishes or preferences directly. Doi gives a beautiful example of *enryo* in his description of a visit to an American friend's home in Topeka, Kansas. The friend asked, "Would you like some ice cream?" Doi, a recent visitor from Japan, could not answer such a question "yes" even though he was hungry and would have liked some ice cream. In the Japanese way, he said, "No, thank you." What the host did not realize was that if he had said that he really wanted Dr. Doi to have some ice cream if he were hungry, then Dr. Doi would have said, "Yes, of course, thank you." This reluctance, this inhibition to express direct wishes, preferences, needs, is referred to as the *enryo* syndrome.

Also, there is *amae* which Doi describes as passive love. In childhood, this is related to the tendency of the very young infant and child to depend entirely on the mother. As the child gets older, there are times when he or she wants to return to this state of passive love. Doi believes that this is the central conflict for the Japanese in Japan. Certainly, with the American emphasis on independence, even the normal interdependency of Japanese kinship relations must be dampened in the United States. This may not be necessarily tragic, if satisfactory mutual relationships can be established. *Amae* is in the context of the vertical society with the inferior person passively depending on the superior person. Perhaps, the loss of opportunities for *amae* by both men and women adds to the increasing tendency to divorce?

SUMMARY

Heterogeneity is the keyword in evaluating the Americanization of the Japanese. The range of behavior is from the relatively pure Japanse patterns of the first generation (issei) to the almost all-American behavior of the fourth generation (yonsei). In between are variations determined by social class, generation, recency of immigration, and geography. Experiences in the United States also vary. However, the experience of preventive detention for the mainland Japanese has left an indelible consciousness of racism.

In addition to racism, a continuing problem for Japanese-Americans will be in gaining a sense of positive identity. The emphasis is often on being one-half Japanese or one-quarter or less. Less often is there a positive emphasis on being an American of Asian heritage.

Thus Japanese-Americans, both of mixed and unmixed heritage, will continue to need to be aware of their cultural heritage and to draw strength from it. Gone is the time when the Japanese in America could call on the "Japanese Spirit" (Ben-Dasan, 1972) and weather the hardships of discrimination and prejudice with a countering positive prejudice about the Japanese. Now we Japanese-Americans need to remember that we have roots we can be proud of and to aim towards lives participating in a new American dream—an America peopled by men and women and children from many different backgrounds. Our strength derives from heterogeneity, tolerance, knowledge of differences, and mutual respect.

REFERENCES

Arkoff, A., Meredith, G., and Dong, J. Attitudes of Japanese and Caucasian-American students toward marriage roles. *The Journal of Social Psychology*, 1963, *59*, 11–15.

Barnlund, D.C. *Public and Private Self in Japan and The United States*. Tokyo, Japan: Simul Press, 1975.

Ben-Dasan, I. *The Japanese and the Jews*. Translated from the Japanese by Richard L. Gage. New York: John Weatherhill, 1972, p. 193.

Benedict, R. *The Chrysanthemum and the Sword*. Boston: Houghton Mifflin, 1966.

Breslow, L., & Klein B. Health and race in California. *American Journal of Public Health*, 1971, *61*, 763–775.

Caudill, W. Japanese-American personality and acculturation. *Genetic Psychology Monographs*, 1952, *45*, 3–102.

Caudill, W.and Frost, L. A comparison of maternal care and infant behavior in Japanese-American, American, and Japanese families. In: W. Lebra, (Ed.), *Mental Health Research in Asia and the Pacific, Volume III*. Honolulu: East West Center Press, 1973.

Caudill, W. and Weinstein, H. Maternal care and infant behavior in Japan and America. *Psychiatry*, 1969, *32*, 12–43.

De Vos G. *Socialization for Achievement*. Berkeley: University of California Press, 1973.

De Vos, G. A comparison of the personality differences in two generations of Japanese-Americans by means of the Rorschach Test. *Nagoya Journal of Medical Science*, 1954, *17*, 153–265.

De Vos, G. A quantitative Rorschach assessment of maladjustment and rigidity in acculturating Japanese-Americans. *Genetic Psychology Mono-*

graphs, 1955, 52, 51–87.

Doi, T. The Anatomy of Dependence. Tokyo; Kodansha International, 1973.

Ishikawa, T. Personal Communication, 1977.

Kitano, H.L. Differential child-rearing attitudes between first and second generation Japanese in the United States. The Journal of Social Psychology, 1961, 53, 13–19.

Kitano, H.L. Changing achievement patterns of the Japanese in the United States. The Journal of Social Psychology, 1962, 58, 257–264.

Kitano, H.L. Japanese Americans: The development of a middleman minority. Pacific Historical Review, 1974, 43, 500–519.

McMichael, R.E., and Grinder, R.E. Guilt and resistance to temptation in Japanese- and White Americans. The Journal of Social Psychology, 1964, 64, 217–223.

Nakane, C. Japanese Society. Berkeley and Los Angeles: U. of California Press, 1970.

Nishi S.M.: The educational disadvantage of Asian and Pacific Americans. P/AAMHRC Research Review, January 1982, 1, (1).

Piggott, J. Japanese Mythology. New York: Paul Hamlyn, 1969, pp. 13, 15, 31, 32, 46.

Suzuki, T., Hayashi, C., Nisihira, S., Aoyama, H., Nomoto, K., Kuroda, Y., and Kuroda, A. A study of Japanese-Americans in Honolulu, Hawaii. Annals of the Institute of Statistical Mathematics, Supplement 7, 1972.

Yamamoto, J. and Iga, M. Japanese enterprise and American middle-class values. The American Journal of Psychiatry, May 1974, 131 (5), 577–579.

Yamamoto, J., Okonogi, K., Iwasaki, T., and Yoshimura, S. Mourning in Japan. The American Journal of Psychiatry, June 1969, 125(12), 74–79.

CHAPTER 15

Family Life Patterns of Pacific Islanders: The Insidious Displacement of Culture

Faye Untalan Muñoz, M.P.H., D.S.W.

Anthropology has been the basic source of general knowledge of the peoples of the South Sea Islands of Melanesia, Micronesia, and Polynesia. Theories as to the origin of these peoples are inconclusive. However, much is known and written about the friendly, hospitable, and noncompetitive nature of the Island people. These qualities, in addition to their strong family ties, support a tight social-psychological-economic bond among family members which extends to distant relatives and other social relationships.

Over the past 300 years, the Islands have been inundated with the explorations, colonizations, and Christianization of different European countries. The impact and consequences of these cultural intrusions and exploitations are not only immeasurable, but also, in most cases, irreversible. The beneficial or concurrently destructive effects on native cultures and lives of these often sudden and unpre- dicted cultural changes can only be estimated. A wise Samoan chief was once heard to liken Western civilization to the parasite which kills Island coconut trees. Once on the tree, the parasite remains until eventually the tree dies. As Western civilization comes to the Island people, their traditional ways are irrevocably changed.

In recent years, growing numbers of people from the South Pacific Islands have been arriving in the U.S. Many are brought by tourism and the entertainment industry, as is the case with Polynesians. Natives of American Samoa, Guam, and Hawaii have also migrated to the mainland for similar reasons. Military draft and induction have played an important role in effecting migration, with the quest for better educational and economic opportunities running a close second. It is estimated that a substantial portion of the native populations of American Samoa and Guam now live on the U.S. Mainland. The primary place of entry is the West Coast, with concentrations of Island populations found from Seattle to San Diego. American Samoans, Guamanians, and Hawaiians all share something in common. Their islands are part of U.S. territory, making these Islanders U.S. subjects or citizens, unlike some of their other island neighbors. Hawaii has the added status of statehood; American Samoa and Guam are still territories. As U.S.territorial citizens, Samoans and Guamanians do not have full voting rights and representation in the U.S. government. However, like other U.S. citizens, they are subject to federal legislation, including the draft laws. American Samoans, because of their status as nationals rather than citizens, were not subect to the draft. Their enlistment and involvement in the Vietnam conflict were, however, higher per capita than any other group in the U.S. (*Pacific Daily News*, 1977).

Apart from exotic and romantic stereotypical descriptions of the Islanders, little information has been published concerning them. Especially lacking are data which provide comparable analysis of the different island groups on political, social, economic, and religious experiences that have affected their lifestyles and living conditions. Each island has had its own unique culture and language, even if under a general rubric. Each island has been subjected to different European countries: France, Germany, and Spain, for example, with distinctive political and religious ideologies. In addition, each island has had a different history with differing impact on the lives of the Islanders, as exemplified by World Wars I and II.

Friendliness, hospitality, and generosity are common characteristics of many Pacific Island peoples. Such qualities are essential in a small area where survival depends upon people's relations to each other and to nature. The social patterns of the Islanders and the relationships between families and within families serve economic, social, and psychological functions. Further, food is naturally abundant. There are breadfruit, taro, coconuts, and bananas; yams either grow wild or require little care. Thus, there is no need to struggle, to compete; no reason not to share and exchange. In fact, some Islanders believe that to exploit natural resources is to grieve the gods. They believe one should take only what one needs from nature and leave the rest for others.

On a recent trip to Guam, the author was with a Chinese visitor who made a comment that Chamorros are lazy because they do not market mangoes, papayas, and breadfruit, but allow much of this fruit to go to waste. An astute Chamorro responded, "Well, we give them (referring to the mangoes, etc.) to friends and relatives who need them; what is left goes back to nurture the soil and the plant so it will yield again next harvest. Besides, God did not intend for us to take advantage of the harvest; such abuse will lead to smaller harvests." In this person's mind, there is a taboo against exploiting nature. The "wasted" produce does in fact nurture the soil, and in return, the soil will yield a greater harvest. In any event, there is a high value placed upon generosity, while greediness is valued negatively.

Extended intergenerational families and child adoption among relatives are characteristics more common and typical among Island peoples than among other minority groups. The extended intergenerational family differs from the extended family where relatives maintain a social network of close communicaton. Under the roof of the intergenerational family, any combination of grandparents, parents, and children, plus single aunts, uncles, or cousins, may live in one household.

Among Pacific Islanders, it is not uncommon for relatives to adopt at infancy the child of another relative and raise this child as their own. The "adopted" child is not necessarily unwanted or a burden. In some cultures, older unmarried aunts and grandparents look forward to the birth of a new family member ("their" potential child). Although complex and confusing to welfare agencies who must deal with this type of family situation in the context of contemporary American family life, this cultural practice is very useful to the Islanders. Sharing or exchange between families corresponds to what one economist, Polanyi (1953), called "reciprocal" economy, or what others have called "redistributive" economy. Child adoption as a form of sharing provides social, economic, and psychological security to the adopter, who can in turn anticipate care in later life. It provides additional sustenance for the child, since parents by themselves do not always have adequate means to support their offspring. The child is also provided with other persons with whom to relate. As well as learning about different personalities, the child benefits from other skills, opportunities, goods, and psychological comforts, and is thus further enriched in life. Intergenerational and child-adopting practices maintain closeness among families beyond mere physiological connections, assuring control and continuity of family traditions and social practices. In most of the South Sea Islands, children are highly cherished. In their traditional language, Islanders lack pejorative and negative concepts regarding children. For example, no word for "illegitimate" exists in their vocabulary. When such a term is heard, it can usually be traced back to a European word or concept.

Though some basic commonalities may be expected, it is beyond the skill and competence of the author to illustrate and describe family patterns of all Pacific Islanders. Therefore, the people of Guam, the Chamorros, will be used to describe some of the Islanders' cultural patterns that have been changed as a result of historical, social, or other events. Chamorros are the indigenous inhabitants of Guam and the other Mariana Islands in the Mi-

cronesia group. The term describes the people, the culture, and the language. This chapter will attempt to illustrate cultural alterations and transformations as Islanders try to adapt to colonization, Christianization, and Western civilization, and to survive as a unique civilization. Further, this chapter will illustrate how the traditional culture is being changed and family roles and relationships are being altered and sometimes undermined as a result of the influx of Western culture and economy, especially the introduction of the money exchange system. Observations in this chapter correlated highly with a description of the changing status of elders in Polynesia by Watson and Maxwell (1977).

For a long time in Chamorro culture, the family has been the primary social group on the Island. It has functioned not only as the means for bringing members into society, but also as the main nurturing and socializing force. In this role, the family has maintained order and enforced social mores, values, and beliefs. Traditions have been maintained and transferred from one generation to the next. In a society which relies primarily on oral history, family cohesion and strong cultural ties are essential factors in the continuity of cultural heritage. Chamorro cultural continuity and survival can be attributed to these factors, despite a history of colonization and indoctrination to new cultures, ideas, and social systems.

The family is the center of a Chamorro's personal life, from birth to death. Personal identity, social status, and responsibility are tied to the family, as indeed is one's total being. The Chamorro family is a whole network of relationships among kin; belonging to a family is comparable to belonging to a clan or to a tribe in other cultures.

The family is traditionally sustained economically and psychologically from within as a result of a strong, cohesive relationship among its members. Proximity of living has enabled family members to share in the care and rearing of children. Grandmothers and aunts have also commonly cared for children.

In close-knit Chamorro families, one may often find parents living near married children or married children living with parents and unmarried brothers, sisters, aunts, and uncles in the same household. Such a system enables close cooperation with and sharing of family responsibilities. In many instances, the mother is the manager of the household. She delegates responsibilities and manages income. She is also the primary decision maker on practically every aspect of family life—from what to do with a sick child to what the family should eat. The father might share some of these roles; however, they are usually the mother's responsibility. A mother's responsibility with regard to her children often extends to overseeing her married children's lives and providing support and control in various aspects of their marriages. The wife's mother of a Chamorro couple, married for 28 years, lives with the couple in their home in California. If the couple desires to go out for an evening, they will ask the mother's permission. If she says no, they don't go out. This is a traditional relationship. Working unmarried mothers living at home normally contribute their salaries to the mother.

Prior to World War II, Chamorros had an economic lifestyle based on a subsistence level. People raised their foods or used local food sources. Family members clustered around common family land and shared available food, such as breadfruit, yams, taro, coconuts, fish, and wildlife, such as the coconut crab.

The traditional life patterns of the Chamorros were changed drastically during World War II. The war separated people from their relatives and from family owned land. The need for manpower in military activities caused people to work as part of the labor force. Wartime survival needs superseded the usual family concern over land and farm. People saw the war as a crisis which would eventually be overcome. They believed that things would normalize after the war, and that they would then be able to return to their former lifestyles. This was not the case. Instead, conditions forced greater separation and breakdown of the family social structure. The use of private land by the federal government to build military facilities for defense purposes, along with wartime destruction, contributed to family disorganization. Military induction caused a number of young men to leave the Island, many never to return.

Wages became the primary source of family income. Business brought a monetary economy to the Island. Families purchased cars, television sets, and other modern appliances. Electricity and running water, in fact most modern conveniences, were costly. Families went into debt to keep up with payments. Women, including wives, took jobs to help meet their families' financial needs. As wives and other women went to work, the care of children could no longer be confined to family members. Paid babysitters and child care services became popular. Responsibility for the care of children was transferred to nonfamily settings. At the same time, certain attitudes persisted concerning child care. Some believed that leaving a child in the hands of others indicated a lack of concern for the child. A mother who left her children in the care of others was often seen as a poor mother or a noncaring one. Although this may have been untrue, envy or jealousy of the mother, or the belief she was noncaring, affected the care provided by others. In other cases, the children of working parents were inadequately cared for because of a lack of supervision. Such new child care arrangements caused a rapid change in child-rearing practices and other integral Chamorro family relationships. There was an evolution of relationships, not only of parents to younger children, but also of parents to older parents, brothers, sisters, and aunts.

The family's economic resources, along with other family resources, and the parents' beliefs as to what constitutes good child care, determine the quality of a care a child receives. Where it is still possible for families to live together or close to each other, grandparents and nonemployed aunts take care of their grandchildren, nieces, and nephews. When relatives are able to care for the young, the children obtain not only the social-psychological sustenance which the nuclear family provides, but also the cultural, emotional, and economic nurturance provided within the traditional context of Chamorro family life.

If one examines exposure of Guamanians to nonfamily child care practices in an historical context, one realizes the limited nature of their experience in light of the rapidly changing social and economic structures of their lives. Thoughtful analysis and planning are not yet employed in meeting the many changes that have drastically affected the circumstances of people's daily lives.

Since World War II, and especially in the past 10 years, the island of Guam has continued to undergo rapid economic and political changes, with the opening of the Island to tourism, the political change toward greater local government control, and the effects of military activities during the Korean and Vietnam conflicts. Two severe natural catastrophes, Typhoon Karen in 1962 and Typhoon Pamela in 1976, which made Guam a disaster area, caused severe and extensive damage to property and natural food resources on the Island. These conditions helped change the social, economic, and political lives of Chamorros, as did the increasing flow of immigration from Korea, Taiwan, the Philippines, Hong Kong, and Japan.

The size of Guam has been important in the degree of change in the Chamorro family structure. Because the Island is a small contained area of land, social control within the family is much more effective. There is less deviation from social mores and tighter adherence to cultural values and behavior. Individual family members still rely to a great extent on their immediate families.

Family structure functions dynamically to adapt, adjust, and cope with societal and environmental conditions. It has evolved historically, modifying and gradually altering its cultural/anthropological configurations. This approach toward understanding family patterns is particularly useful in looking at Chamorro families.

Chamorros, though U.S. citizens, are the most isolated citizens of this country, not only because of the distance between the Island and the U.S., but also because of the manner in which the U.S. deals with its territorial possessions and citizens. Despite this isolation, Guamanians are still highly committed and loyal to the U.S. government. This attitude can be attributed to the "Americanization" process of education and to the Islanders' experience in World War II. In addition to this loyalty, however, Guamanians have a stronger loyalty to their cultural values and heritage. This has been clearly demonstrated by the Chamorros' ability to maintain their culture and language while surviving 300 years of Spanish rule, American rule since 1900, the Japanese occupation of World War II, and subsequent changes affecting the Island and its people. One can see countless examples of the remarkable resiliency of the Chamorro family in its accommodation and adaptation to change. The traditional family structure has needed enormous strength in order to maintain its cultural values against outside pressures. This adaptive, accommodating cultural characteristic cannot be overemphasized. It is inherent in the Chamorro family's ability to survive and is essential to the survival of values, beliefs, and language, and in passing them on to the next generation.

On the U.S. mainland, however, geographic distance between extended family members and subsequent lack of contact have caused many individuals to be rather independent and unrestrained by Chamorro social/cultural mores. With the disintegration of the extended family as a support system, contemporary Chamorros needed to develop a new family system. Thus, Guamanian families have adopted new social relations on the mainland. One example is a pseudofamily structure, in which relationships with neighbors are developed and they are treated as relatives, helping out with child care, and sharing food and other resources. Lacking family support and social control, individuals in need are sometimes forced to alter their lifestyles drastically. Young, divorced women, coming to the U.S. after their divorce, and living in apartments away from families and relatives, may resort to the welfare system. Though Guamanians are predominantly Catholic, divorces are becoming quite common both on Guam and on the mainland. When apart from the family structure, Guamanians are likely to follow the lifestyles of their new neighbors and associations.

Wives in families that have broken away from other Guamanians, particularly those married to nonGuamanians, often express severe "loneliness" and "emptiness." Their lives lack the traditional responsibilities of the Chamorro mother as head of household. Without useful meaningful activities related to family coherence, the wife makes housework a compelling task. As one housewife told the author, "I clean house every day. I have to pick up the dog hairs with scotch tape." Though neatness and cleanliness are highly valued by Guamanians, this form of compulsiveness is uncommon. Further, this condition is not found among wives living in communities with other Guamanians or maintaining frequent communications with relatives (Munoz, 1977a).

Crises require adaptation of existing behavior patterns to meet the demands of new situations. The stresses of cultural change and the continuing impact of Western culture have not only altered traditional values and attitudes, but also have produced such social problems as increased divorce, broken marriage, drug abuse, juvenile delinquency, and crime. The new economic pattern of living, money exchange, and so-called free enterprise have increased hypertension and mental illness. Changes in economic patterns have caused changes in eating habits; refined and canned products have replaced naturally grown food products. These changes in eating, along with a more sedentary lifestyle, further the propensity toward obesity among the Islanders and greatly increase health problems.

In a society with rapid social change, problems outnumber solutions. The resulting uncertainties are absorbed by society, which is made up for the most part by members of families. The family is the bottleneck through which all troubles pass; no other group so reflects the strains and stresses of life. The family's sympathy, understanding, and support rehabilitate personalities bruised in the course of competitive daily living.

Family adaptability and integration, affectional relations among family members, good marital adjustment of husband and wife, companionable parent/child relationships, family council control in decision making, and social participation of the wife are all important factors in enabling families to adjust to crisis (Hill, 1958). These attributes of Chamorro families enabled them to survive a multitude of changes and crises. Rapid changes now occurring are, however, producing stresses and strains beyong their usual resiliency and tenacity. Thus, overwhelming problems of loneliness and depression exist among wives and older people, and violence and aggressive behavior among the young. An increasing incidence of drug use and criminal behavior is plaguing the Island.

Inadequate educational programs on Guam and insensitive educational systems on the U.S. mainland have failed to provide the educational and technical competence necessary for Guamanians in the job market and salary competition in the U.S. Many Guamanians are found working as construction workers and guards, and loaders and ramp workers for the airline industries. Retired Navy men are working as janitors, cooks, and service station attendants (Munoz, 1977b). Chamorro families have had to adapt their traditional customs in order to survive in a competitive and money-oriented society. These adaptations sometimes restrict their capacity for upward mobility.

To illustrate this phenomenon on the mainland, we will look at the migration patterns of three Guamanian families in the U.S. We will note the year in which the first family member migrated to the U.S., and in particular, the locations where the family members subsequently settled. We will also mark the proportion of traditional Guamanian marriages in relation to intermarriages. We will then determine the extent to which members of nuclear families have stayed in close proximity to one another on the mainland as well as the number of migrating family members who have returned to Guam.

Family A lives in Long Beach, California. In 1940, Mr. A's mother's brother joined the Navy and left Guam. Since his retirement, Mr. A's mother's brother and his wife, an Anglo woman, have been living in Pleasonton, California. Mr. A's brother left Guam in 1941 after enlisting in the Navy. He, too, married an Anglo woman and has resided in Hayward, California, since retirement. Mr. A's mother, then a widow, came to the U.S. in 1967 and settled with her widowed daughter and grandson's family in Fairfield, California. Mr. A and his wife and six unmarried children settled in Long Beach in 1965. This followed a short stay in Fairfield after having been attracted to Southern California by job opportunities provided by a distant uncle. Mr. A's sister, her husband and their 13 children also came to the U.S. in 1968. They settled in Castro Valley, not far from Hayward, California,

where Mr. A's brother lives. All of Mr. A's siblings have since moved to California and have remained in the U.S., with the exception of his widowed sister, who remarried and returned to Guam in 1973. Of the A's married children, all have married Guamanians and remain in residence near their parents. One married daughter who remained on the Island after her parents' departure recently moved to California with her family. Mr. and Mrs. A have returned to Guam several times to visit their other married daughter and other relatives. Three of Mr. A's nieces and nephews married Anglos or Mexican-Americans. The rest of this third generation married Guamanians in the United States.

The B Family also lives in Long Beach. Mr. and Mrs. B, now in their 70's, came to the U.S. in 1964. All but one of their 13 grown and married children live in Long Beach. Two of Mr. B's sisters and their families have also moved to California. Mrs. B's sister and her husband moved to California with their nine unmarried children after his retirement from the government of Guam in 1974. They settled in Carson, a city near Long Beach. Another sister of Mrs. B married a Mexican-American serviceman on Guam; they moved to California in 1964 with their six unmarried children. Their married children remained behind with their own families. Married sons and daughters bringing their families and following their parents are not unusual among Guamanian migrants to the U.S. The B family illustrates the transfer of a clan from Guam to California. This particular family maintains close ties and frequent contacts; an almost daily visit is made to Mr. and Mrs. B by their children and grandchildren. Cousins visit and play with each other as in the traditional lifestyle on Guam. Here again, older children, siblings, and cousins take care of younger children.

The C family lives in Gardena, California. Mrs. C was married on Guam to Mr. C, a Filipino immigrant. They came to the

U.S. with their nine children in 1969. They were initially helped by Mrs. C's aunt, who was married to a retired Guamanian serviceman. Mrs. C's aunt and family had been living in Carson for some years. Mrs. C comes from a large family on Guam; three of her sisters married non-Guamanians (Anglo, Japanese, and Mexican). However, only two of her siblings reside in the U.S., in California. Two of Mrs. C's chidren have married since their arrival in the U.S., one to a person of Guamanian ancestry, and one to a person of Puerto Rican ancestry. The older daughter, after finishing college, returned to Guam and is now working for the Island government. She also wanted to be close to her aunts and other relatives on Guam. The other married children remained near their parents' residence.

These three families illustrate the patterns of migrating Guamanian families: The first person who comes to the United States is usually a member of the military. The earlier family members come to the U.S., the greater are the chances that they will have left a majority of their siblings on Guam. The more recently settled Guamanians have a higher percentage of siblings already in the United States. Brothers and sisters who stay in the U.S. tend to live in close proximity to one another. Older Guamanians usually marry other Guamanians. In the second and third generations of Guamanian immigrants, however, there is an increasing proportion of intermarriage. There is some flow between Guam and the mainland in each family. However, by the third generation the nuclear family is usually living on the mainland in close proximity to one another.

Guamanian as well as other Pacific Islanders away from home often develop a common social unit with fellow transplanted Islanders. Whether consisting of a few families or a highly structured organization containing many friends and family members, this primary social group remains the basic social unit of many overseas island communities. This participation in the social group reaffirms the Islander's sense of cultural identity and heritage. The social unit also provides roots in the new environment. For the basically gregarious Islanders, group activities and relationships have a continuing importance. On the mainland, relationships are formed with persons from home with whom they might never have had the opportunity of socializing had they remained on the Island. The need for hospitality and friendship creates a desire to help fellow Islanders cope with the problems of social survival in an alien environment. The social group not only provides roots and reaffirms a sense of identity, but also functions as a means, in itself, to sustain group life. Often, social obligations are important enough to an Islander to supersede school or job obligations (Munoz, 1977b).

Islanders are often mistaken in the United States for members of other minority groups. They are often discriminated against and made to feel insignificant. Because Islanders are often initially inarticulate in English, they are unable to express complaints adequately if exploited in any way. Their self-image is immediately influenced by Anglo-Americans' attitudes and responses to them. Their values, beliefs, and customs are condemned for being different. They are made to feel that their ways must be changed if they are to become "civilized." They feel they must change to accommodate American values. And when they do change, they are still not Americans, because, with their "funny" or "terrible" English accents, they are told, "You don't sound like a . . ." Islanders then begin to deny their own values and accept the premise that Western quality is better than Island quality.

Thus denied integration into the main social structures in the United States, Islanders seek association with fellow Islanders by forming social groups. The social groups link the Islanders, not only with immediate friends and family, but also with a "nation" of "people" in terms of identity as well as roots. Mainland family and friends are the chief support for new arrivals, but their own progress may be delayed by the drain upon their limited resources demanded by these social groups.

Islanders know that they are Americans, yet they also know that Americans understand little and care less about their welfare. They receive no recognition as part of this country. They feel little empathy from Americans for the social conditions and problems of the Pacific peoples in America.

Islanders, beset by many problems on the mainland, worry about the future for their children and their people as a distinct ethnic group. They would like to eliminate the racism and oppression that they have suffered. At the same time, they want to preserve their language and culture for their children. The experience of the Hawaiians indicates to the Guamanians the possibility that not only may their language and culture become extinct, but they might lose their home island to other groups (Munoz, 1977b).

Children and other family members may be required to postpone or sacrifice education or personal development (including marriage) in order to help the family. Although such sacrifice is beneficial to the economic survival of the family, it deprives individuals of the education and individual development required to support themselves and their own families in later life or to attain full development of their potential. As new families develop Western values, they also break away from the traditional Chamorro family ways of unity and support. The traditional family-centered values of Chamorro culture are tested continuously against the individualism of American society. The cultural values of family unity and responsibility will continue to have tremendous problems surviving in a capitalistic society and will eventually disappear.

As a group, Pacific Islanders have yet to achieve full development in the fields of higher education and the professions. Both American Samoa and Guam suffer from inadequate health services. They have not been able to use federal resources effectively to develop and to maintain mental health and other social programs on the Islands because of the serious lack of trained indigenous personnel. Cultural and linguistic differences are extremely important considerations in the development and delivery of human services to these Islanders. Their lack of participation in the U.S. in determining policies for dealing with human needs further exacerbates their problems. Political participation and opportunities are limited by the Islands' territorial status and their remoteness from Washington, D.C. The size of the islands and their lack of natural resources limit any full-scale economic development which would sustain the economic survival of each island as an entity.

The problems facing the Islanders are complex and very difficult. This brief discussion is an attempt to describe the problems and dilemmas many Islanders face today and, it is hoped, to spur thoughtful investigation for future solutions. American Samoans, Guamanians/Chamorros, Hawaiians, and other Pacific Islanders will continue to face these dilemmas until a more sensitive response can be found. One hopes that these Islanders, as unique people with a rich humanitarian culture, will survive.

In summary, some of the problems experienced by Pacific Islanders on the U.S. mainland begin with economic alienation. Low-paying jobs which result from inadequate education and lack of skills cannot support the large families and extended family obligations of many Islanders.

Political alienation is a second gripping problem for transplanted Islanders. Sensitivity on the part of the receiving community to assist Islanders as well as other minority groups to organize and relate to the political system is extremely important.

Service alienation is a third outstanding problem. Social service agencies and public service programs, most notably in the field of education, have thus far been extremely insensitive and unresponsive to the Islanders' problems and needs. This is especially noticeable in areas like Los Angeles County which have highly concentrated populations of Islanders.

Public attention and concern for the problems plaguing the Islanders are long overdue. A comprehensive examination of their health and welfare is essential in order to map out both meaningful and realistic programs which take into account their genuine interests. The Island governments are young and far removed from the center of the nation where major political decisions are made. Worst of all, the Islanders have no voice in the politics of this country. Unless the welfare and interests of the Islanders become a genuine concern of political leaders in the U.S., Guamanians and American Samoans are likely to disappear as a people, just as the Hawaiians have disappeared as a people. As matters stand, Guamanians have no choice but to succumb to a political and economic structure with which they are ill equipped to cope.

REFERENCES

Hill, R. Social stress on the family. *Social Casework*, 1958, *39*, 139–150.

Munoz, F. U. Unpublished dissertation manuscript, 1977(a).

Munoz, F. U. Pacific Islanders—A perplexed, neglected minoity. *Social Casework*, 1977, *57*, 179–184(b).

Pacific Daily News, April 14, 1977.

Polanyi, K. *Semantics of General Economic History*, revised edition. New York: Columbia University Research, Project on Origins of Economic Institutions, 1953.

Watson, W. H. and Maxwell, R. J. *Human Aging and Dying: A Sociocultural Gerontology*. New York: St. Martin's Press, 1977.

CHAPTER 16

Indian Family Values and Experiences

John Red Horse, Ph.D.

INTRODUCTION

The objective of this chapter is to explore the dynamics and consequences of American Indian cultural behavior. The reader will be introduced to cultural patterns which demonstrate that American Indians tenaciously cling to a separate reality. The selected unit of analysis is family values and experience.

Critical in this analysis are the interactive patterns between American Indian families and a field of professionals commonly identified with mental health; i.e., psychiatrists, psychologists, pediatricians, social workers, teachers, and lawyers. As such, the work does not represent a definitive piece of American Indian family theory; rather, it focuses upon significant areas of conflict between culture and practice.

The theoretical orientation guiding this writer follows a social conservation model in which mental health is tied to a sense of selfhood that is accomplished through an adherence to a historic culture and transmitted principally through family interaction. Value systems, expressive behavior, and child rearing patterns are crucial factors in a developing sene of selfhood. Moreover, the family is the basic unit of group identity (Levine, 1976). Thus, a constellation of variables emanating from and attributed to the family and group are crucial to understanding human behavior.

CONTINUITY OF VALUES

American Indians continue to prefer a separate value system from mainstream society. This preference often escapes professionals who are inclined to confuse cultural values with technological adaptations. Thus, an Indian who possesses a new car, a modern equipped home, or other technical accoutrements has assimilated. Such a perception allows for sim-

258

plistic theory building in mental health. One major family service organization, for example, continues to distribute a 1968 fourth printing of a literature review which states that culture is not important to American social casework practice (Frankiel, 1968). Bell (1973), however, significantly clarifies social structure by defining differences between technical and cultural realms. Technical realms are concerned with instrumental, economizing modes. Cultural realms are concerned with expressive, self-fulfillment modes.

Adding to the confusion of social realms is the obstinacy of Indian resistance. Deloria (1969) identified the historical character of American policy which has long attempted to move Indians into the social mainstream. Violence and bad feelings have resulted. Few Indians appreciate the price of admission: a loss of land, a distortion of cultural history, a plastic identity, and a destruction of religion.

Religion and land serve for issue analysis. Contrary to popular notions, the last religious battle between the American government and Indians did not take place at Wounded Knee in 1890. A telling photograph was taken in the 1930s during Franklin Delano Roosevelt's official signing ceremonies converting Indian land for dam construction. Rather than smiling, a Mandan observer was crying because religious land had been lost. The Taos Pueblo more recently struggled against government insensitivity toward spiritual land. Tribal leaders fought valiantly and retained Blue Lake as a religious sanctuary. One Congressman, however, irately suggested that Indians could very well build a church like every other American (Cahn and Hearne, 1972).

The Congressman's attitude does not represent minority opinion. Mental health practitioners are generally aware of a relationship between land and emotional well-being. Urgency for living and recreational space is universally advertised. Indian land represents a major resource to meet national needs irrespective of spir-itual values. Obviously such prevailing attitudes contribute to an Indian sense of separate realities.

Americans, moreover, have developed elaborate defense mechanisms to combat Indian rejection. Indian existence is simply denied Wahrhaftig and Thomas (1972) point to the folly of white denial in Eastern Oklahoma. A current vogue among many professionals is to romanticize reservations. Consequently, whites who have never before met Indians become instant authorities on Indian culture. They employ a simple rule of thumb: An Indian on the reservation has retained his culture; an Indian off the reservation has assimilated.

Many non-Indian professionals fail to realize that cultural retention is not necessarily affected by geographic movement. Cultural values are retained and transmitted through family and ethnic networks (Giordano, 1974; Papajohn and Spiegel, 1975). Moreover, values tend to persist even under adverse conditions. Hallowell (1967) points to this in an investigation of Ojibway personality. He controlled for four levels of acculturation. Levels were governed according to measurable indicators; e.g., language, religion, housing, location, schooling, employment, and marriage patterns. It was assumed, for example, that Indians who had married white, converted to Christianity, and spoke only English would be quite acculturated and would not possess Ojibway personality patterns. Obversely, Indians who married Indian, practiced Midewiwin, and spoke only Ojibway would not be acculturated. Hallowell's findings, however, indicated that core personality patterns remained constant across all levels of acculturation.

A more recent investigation tested an hypothesis on child rearing patterns in urban Indian families. Families were discretely classified according to whether they were urban or traditional oriented. An assumption was that urban-oriented families would be inclined to rely upon mainstream, non-Indian standards of child rearing. According to the study, "the majority of Indian families, irrespective of their traditional identity status, failed to use high degrees of white child rearing techniques" (Miller et al., 1975). Another investigation explored the impact of familial imprints and injunctions upon attitudes of Indian adolescents regarding expectations surrounding early childhood development. Findings indicated that Indian adolescents had expectations that varied considerably from mainstream, non-Indian expectations (Red Horse, 1976). At issue are family injunctions during early socialization periods. Red Horse's investigation supported Miller's findings that Indian families are inclined to raise children according to an independence orientation.

Obviously some gradual change occurs in adherence to values. Cross-cultural and cross-tribal variables have become critical since numerous Indians have intermarried along racial and tribal lines. Caution, though, must be exercised in identifying Indian personality change associated with social class movement. Such movement does not necessarily assure that one will adopt adult middle-class values as a standard for living.

The complexity of value assessment is introduced in Table 1 which illustrates Kluckhohn's value orientation and preference model (Kluckhohn and Strodtbeck, 1961). Three discrete value orientation preferences are possible for each of five

value modalities. Statistically, this provides for 243 (3^5) variable combinations. Each must be addressed in cultural assessment.

A study at Flandreau Indian school (Krush et al., 1969) administered a Kluckhohn test to measure value orientation of 503 Indian students. Several tribes were represented. This investigation employed four value modalities: relational, man-to-nature, time, and activity.* Acculturation represented the theoretical focus. The scale allowed comparison of adult middle-class orientation with contrary orientations. Indian girls differed significantly from adult middle-class in man-to-nature and time dimensions. Indian boys also differed significantly in these two dimensions, but appeared more middle-class than girls. Both sexes differed significantly from middle-class on the relational dimension. No significant difference appeared between students and middle-class on the activity dimension.

Briefly, the aforementioned data suggest that American Indians are far from assimilated. Their present beliefs and life styles depart from adult middle-class norms. Moreover, their choice to remain different confronts mental health profes-

---

*Each modality is concerned with a common human problem: relational—man's relationship to other man; man-to-nature—man's relationship to nature; time—man's temporal focus; activity—man's mode of human activity. A more thorough discussion of value orientation within a family context can be found in Papajohn and Spiegel, 1975.

TABLE 1

Value Orientation: Modalities and Preferences

Modalities		Preferences	
Activity	Doing	Being	Being-in-becoming
Relational	Individualism	Collaterality	Lineality
Time	Future	Present	Past
Man-nature	Master-over-nature	Subjugation-to-nature	Harmony-with nature
Human-nature	Evil	Mixed	Good

Source: Papajohn and Spiegel, 1975.

sionals with compelling ethical issues concerning the rights of individuals, families, and groups to behave in culturally appropriate ways. The following case illustrations demonstrate important aspects surrounding culture conflict and family process. They obviously do not exhaust the issues.

SUPERVISION OF CHILDREN

William and Mary lived in a three-room house. They had six children: five girls aged 18, 16, 14, 12, and 10; and a boy aged 15. The girls shared a small bedroom with two double beds. The boy slept in the living room on a couch. He had a large closet-type room for his clothes and other personal belongings. The living room had no divider; thus, on one side was the kitchen and dining area. The house had no plumbing. It was heated by an oil stove.

William and Mary were Midewiwin and spoke mostly Chippewa in the home. Neither had graduated from high school, but they knew enough English to communicate with non-Chippewas. They were cooperative with the schools and placed a high value on education. The children were bilingual; however, they were beginning to have difficulty speaking Chippewa well. Their understanding of the language, however, was fluent. This concerned the parents because all Midewiwin ceremonies are conducted in Chippewa. The concern was communicated to the children through nonverbal behavior. Double messages regarding the importance of school led to reduced attendance by the children. While this is a traditional family, school withdrawal appears as a common characteristic among a large number of American Indian children, especially at the middle-school age. Bryde defines this as a crossover phenomenon*

(Fuchs and Havighurst, 1973).

School authorities reported the family to court services. A caseworker was assigned to assist William and Mary in supervising the children. The couple's previous experiences with the "welfare" had concerned financial assistance. No difficulties arose on these occasions because welfare officials recognized the lack of employment opportunities in the area. William and Mary had come to take for granted a low-key relationship with welfare personnel. The new worker, however, was not representing an income maintenance section; she was a representative of child protective services acting "in the best interests of the children." The family was not prepared for this type of intervention.

The family did not change its behavior. This concerned the new worker. She valued explicit discipline and wanted William and Mary to direct family activities with authority. In her opinion, all the parents ever did was watch television. One visit appeared especially galling. The worker arrived for a home visit at the same time the children were returning from school. The worker failed to note that all the children had gone to school which, of course, was the presenting problem. She was more concerned that apparent chaos reigned as the children negotiated for household chores.

The boy spilled the garbage. He was gone for a long time since some trash had to be burned. When he returned, it was for only a short time. He had to go to a cousin's for water. He did both these routines daily because they were too hard for the girls. The girls did not have a specific task. They had to negotiate among several: dinner had to be prepared, the table had to be set, dishes had to be washed and dried. Lively argumentation erupted as the girls parried for a task. Obviously, the

---

*The term crossover is descriptive of an overt change in school behavior by Indian children. Its characteristics are that children who were cooperative in

class behavior and attendance in elementary school years will begin to tune-out and/or drop-out during middle-school years.

one who had washed dishes at breakfast did not want that chore again at dinner. All wanted to set the table. Moreover, all were required to explain their reasons for deserving an easy chore and usually did so with shouts and giggles.

The caseworker became furious. She scolded the parents regarding their lack of concern for the children's behavior and suggested more active methods of meting out discipline. She was convinced that both parents were too lazy to set good examples for their children.

The worker obviously lacked a basic understanding of Indian family process. She contaminated product with process. A common characteristic among Indian families is freedom of interaction among children. This process may certainly be chaotic, but chaos need not necessarily undermine parental authority. The caseworker completely overlooked that the children never once disputed the tasks. The work was done. That is product and is governed by parents.

The caseworker developed a good-bad behavior continuum and demanded that the parents adopt her child-rearing philosophy. Good parents supervise their children closely. Good parents demonstrate authority. Good parents tell and direct children in all activities. The caseworker confused process conflict with family values. Actually, the parents had a high regard for authority. They simply had a different way of transmitting this value to children. While it appeared that no communication existed, the parents were keenly aware of the children's interchanges. Significant nonverbal communication had been employed to assure that no child was bullied or treated unfairly by another.

Indian families place a high regard on interpersonal process in child rearing. Appropriate relationship behavior represents a key value injunction. Children are taught to respect the presence of others. Parents, other adults, and older children set relationship examples for young chil-

dren to follow (Morey and Gilliam, 1974).

Interpretations of family behavior often cloud issues of discipline. Investigators have identified permissiveness as a characteristic in Indian child rearing (Morey and Gilliam, 1974). This is presumed because physical punishment is generally devalued by parents in their relationship to children (Lewis, 1970; Morey and Gilliam, 1974). Such assertions may mislead one to assume that children have undisciplined freedom. Such is not the case. Sanctions and discipline are characteristically administered through relationship behavior which may at times be extremely stern and demanding.

William and Mary were obviously proud of their traditional home. While some differences appear, their home correlates closely to what child specialists refer to as a democratic authority structure. Data indicate that such a structure is a viable, salubrious, and legitimate setting for child rearing (Frankiel, 1968). In such settings, parental injunctions may be rigorous. Children, however are given a great deal of freedom to act out their feelings, since this is a necessary process in sharpening interpersonal skills. Placing a value on this process involves parental commitment which is at times questioned even by parents. This writer has found that in such instances, the pattern is generally reinforced by other family members or by grandparents. In my own family, I have found that children play an active role in maintaining this standard: they have a way of informing grandparents or namesakes when harsh treatment has occurred. The family network in turn responds to maintain the integrity of child-centeredness.

CHILD ABANDONMENT

Indian families have a long standing tradition of organizing supportive networks around children. A common method is the naming ceremony (Densmore, 1970).

This ceremony develops a natural network consisting principally of family members; i.e., aunts, uncles, cousin.* This allows the extended family to serve as a protective social fabric to provide for the health and welfare of children.

Namesakes assume major social responsibilities. A normal expectation is that personal contact between namesakes and children will be frequent. They are able, therefore, to act as role models. Moreover, if hard times were to befall parents, namesakes would care for any children. They would do so with unconditional, nonjudgmental behavior and without undermining the sanctity of parent-child relationships.

Outside observers may contend that naming ceremonies have diminished in importance with a general demise of Indian religion. This writer's experience, however, is that religious injunctions remain significant in Indian behavior. In situations where the natural child welfare network is absent in family social organization, behavior often remains as if the network still existed. Behaviors that have become expected through time remain constant. Obvious family dysfunctions result during periods of stress (Boggs, 1956, 1958). Demands of urban adjustment, for example, have introduced stresses detrimental to Indian family organization. On occasion, some parents have developed alternative, pseudo family networks following expected ways of behavior. These attempts to introduce an understandable coping mechanism into the social fabric of a family in crisis have been misinterpreted by many non-Indian professionals. A single case cannot explore all cultural and circumstancial variables present in these situations; however, Margaret's case

*A name also serves two other important functions. First, one's name sets a path from which life shall proceed (Momaday, 1976). Second, and often less recognized, one's name sets a path from which a spiritual afterlife shall proceed. Without a name, one is not really Indian; hence, one's spirit will never come to rest in the afterworld (Bearheart, 1976).

regarding child abandonment is illustrative of a few puzzling pieces.

Margaret was 36 years old. She had two children: a daughter aged 11, a boy aged 3. The daughter had lived continuously with her mother. She was well-adjusted and bore considerable responsibility in the home. Social caseworkers believed that the daughter's role in the home was inappropriate and that the young girl was a victim of her mother's poor health. The mother suffered from a heart condition. Regardless, few family support services were offered by caseworkers. Rather, several attempts were made to remove the daughter for foster placement. All failed because the daughter was able to complete home chores without disrupting other important, measurable obligations of her life; e.g., school attendance.

The younger child was born with a heart defect. This required specialized and expensive medical care immediately upon birth. Moreover, considerable parent involvement would be necessary for transportation, supervision of medication, and other predictable health related emergencies following the child's hospital release. This unnerved the mother. While she would receive medical assistance and would be able to meet other financial obligations to raise her baby, Margaret was necessarily concerned about her own health. She had suffered two recent heart attacks prior to childbirth. Margaret realized supervision assistance was necessary. No in-home support services were offered. Margaret was persuaded to place her boy into a foster home that would be more prepared to give special attention.

The baby required round-the-clock care for several months. Margaret was pleased that the foster mother was emotionally involved and gave such great care of the baby. The welfare department provided considerable and unquestioned social and financial support services for the foster home. The foster mother became a prominent figure in the family's life. She and Margaret became very close friends. Her mothering role with the boy over a three-year period gave her an obvious psychological and emotional tie to the baby. Margaret recognized and accepted this development and asked the foster mother to be a godparent to the boy. This formal role was accepted and religiously enacted.

During the first two years of placement no apparent difficulties emerged among the caseworker, foster mother, and Margaret. A crisis developed, however, in the third year. Margaret suffered several medical relapses. During each medical crisis, Margaret was confined to bed. The daughter became a homemaker because no public in-home services were offered. Margaret was unable to visit her boy during this period. Margaret had visited three months prior to a severe attack. Her physical deterioration started shortly after that visit. Hence, approximately one year passed without contact among the boy, foster mother, and Margaret. Interestingly, the foster mother made no attempt to bring the baby to Margaret's home for a visit.

Casework visits were infrequent. Visits to both the foster mother and Margaret were conducted on the average of once every six months. During the year of Margaret's severe illness, she was never visited. Margaret, however, did not feel ignored or mistreated. She did not issue a complaint. She knew her boy was being well cared for, and her daughter was home to respond to any emergencies. Therefore, Margaret did not call the foster parent or caseworker.

Margaret's nondemanding behavior was misinterpreted by the caseworker who charged that Margaret appeared not to care for the boy. When casework contact was reinitiated, the content of discussions was unclear. Two contrary accounts developed. Margaret had always been assured that voluntary placement under the circumstances would protect her from neglect charges. The caseworker now insisted, however, that Margaret had been negligent through a demonstrated lack of interest and visits. She advised Margaret of pending court action to terminate parental rights. Margaret, however, understood that the caseworker had simply conducted a health inquiry and decided that Margaret was too sickly to care for the boy.

Following a few casework sessions, Margaret visited the foster home. The reception was abrasive. The foster mother was hostile. She thought that Margaret had no right to interfere with the child care routine. This behavior by the foster mother was different and unexpected. Margaret was surprised. She had expected a warm visit, as always, between friends. The foster mother subsequently complained about Margaret's interference and received support from the caseworker. A charge of abandonment was filed against Margaret.

The charge appeared bizarre. Margaret's physical condition was not considered mitigating, but causative. The caseworker indicated that Margaret did not have an emotional attachment to the child. Nor could one be developed, since the baby was three years old. Margaret was so unprepared for this behavior that she could not muster answers to charges. Indeed, she completely withdrew. She did not visit her boy again until court procedures started, at which time an Indian family advocate became active in the case.

A complex and contrary set of expectations governing interpersonal behavior emerged. Margaret's behavior followed culturally defined expectations which she took for granted, but could not isolate, define, or articulate. Consequently, she appeared incompetent and indefensible. The ability to articulate behaviors normally taken for granted, however, does not appear uncommon. Hall (1969), for example, indicates that cultural rules are divided into three modes: technical, formal, and informal. Technical rules are set in writing and provide obvious guidelines for behavior. Formal rules are taught through an active process, e.g., verbal admonition. Thus behavioral alternatives are clearly understood. Informal rules are transmitted through role models. They are learned without an actor knowing they are being learned. Thus, definitions of incorporated behavior surrounding informal rules are often unknown to an actor. Margaret's behavior appears both circumstantially and culturally appropriate. Public officials, however, did not want culture introduced as a behavioral variable. Margaret was not entitled to treatment different from any other person. She lived in an urban environment. She was Catholic. Consequently, she was not eligible for special treatment. Her withdrawal from the casework process simply indicated a lack of interest in the child and constituted grounds for termination of parental rights.

Several interviews were necessary to confirm that Margaret's behavior followed rules based on early childhood injunctions. Margaret was a late convert both to an urban world and to Catholicism. She was raised on the reservation within an extended family, and her parents were Midewiwin. She had been an urban Catholic for less than 10 years. Early behavior patterns remained a strong influence in her life. Margaret began to articulate her behavior quite by accident when talking about religion. She was struggling to explain astonishment over the foster mother's behavior. She was really unhappy with herself because a malicious and possessive person had been selected as a namesake. However, she was reluctant to enter openly into conflict with a namesake. She chose to withdraw rather than to destroy a spiritual bond.

EXTENDED FAMILY

Nancy was 18 years old. She was seven months pregnant when making application for welfare services. During the application process, welfare workers developed a petition for Nancy to sign. The petition diagnosed Nancy as mentally retarded and subject to epileptic seizures. It proposed that Nancy receive mothering-skills training under the supervision of a caseworker. Nancy refused to sign.

Nancy's family contacted an Indian family advocate unit. Meetings were initiated with welfare officials who proved unresponsive. Advocates, for example, could not trace the source which labeled Nancy retarded. No tests had been administered by the welfare department. Advocates concluded that this opinion may have been based upon interpretation of tests taken by Nancy in public school. If so, the tests were inappropriate. Advocates, however, did not question the diagnosis of epilepsy. This, though, did not seem sufficient grounds to withhold a child from its mother. Regardless, the welfare department ordered the hospital not to release the child. The hospital complied.

A court hearing was scheduled. Nancy's parents were outraged and insisted that the family network was available for assistance, if necessary. The caseworker considered this offer untenable. According to her, the grandparents were too old and senile to care for the infant. They were in their early fifties and had just finished caring for three other grandchildren. These children appeared well-adjusted. No social or medical visits had occurred during the intervening time since these children's departure. Nevertheless, the caseworker did not accept that the grandparents were competent to assume child-caring roles and responsibilities.

The court followed welfare department recommendations. Grandparents do not legally possess family rights and, as such, had no claim before the court. Emergency foster placement was ordered. Issues of cultural appropriateness were introduced by the grandparents' attorney. The court responded by setting two placement guidelines. First, any foster home selected should be within reasonable distance of the child's family. This would facilitate daily visits which were court mandated and were to include four hours daily training in mothering skills for Nancy. Second, a foster home with at least one Indian foster parent should be secured. The legality of placing the child directly from the hospital without prior observation of Nancy's parenting skills was ignored.

Indian advocates responded with three activities. First, they tracked the social planning activities of the welfare department. Second, they implemented a parallel Native American social planning apparatus. Third, they secured the services of a different attorney.

Available plans offered by the welfare department and the Indian advocates differed significantly. The welfare department "miraculously" secured an Indian foster home. The department accentuated its hard work because available Indian foster homes were in short supply. The home, however, did not comply with the first court directive: it was located two counties away, 45 miles from Nancy's residence. Moreover, the main parent substitute was a white woman who had married an Indian. This hardly appeared culturally appropriate, since parent training was involved. In their parallel work, the Indian family advocates had secured an appropriate all-Indian foster home seven miles from Nancy's home.

The tribal Council which was the governmental body of the tribe in which Nancy was enrolled became active in the case. The Council took issue with the welfare department's interference in Indian family affairs and seriously explored kidnapping charges. A new attorney prepared a series of arguments around issues of due process. Furthermore, a contempt motion was filed because the welfare department had not complied with original court orders. The court ruled the welfare department's plan improper. Temporary placement in the grandparent's home was ordered. A condition to this placement was that the Indian family advocate should continue to provide support services. Nancy

was scheduled for a series of psychological evaluations. Three days after this hearing, the welfare department withdrew the petition against Nancy. Seventeen days intervened between the original placement order and return of the child.

Aside from obvious legal issues, several questions regarding casework ethics may be drawn from this case. Chief, of course, is the sanctity of family vis-à-vis welfare services, including recognition of the extended family. Another compelling issue concerns provision of culturally relevant services, especially in regard to foster home placements and diagnostic procedures. Nancy, for example, was eventually "diagnosed" as average intelligence with special learning disabilities, not retarded. Moreover, Nancy's experience is not considered unusual. A recent publication by the Association on American Indian Affairs (Unger, 1977) points to an undermining of Indian families through social service delivery systems. The volume includes articles by Indian and non-Indian professionals who condemn a universal trend in welfare services to arbitrarily and capriciously undermine Indian families.

Few social caseworkers understand Indian extended family units. Most rely upon a nuclear family conceptual framework in organizing service dlivery. Consequently, family becomes a unit of analysis with specific household parameters. One observer, for example, points to a decline of vertical generations in single households as an indicator of Indian extended family deterioration (Miller et al., 1977). Reductionism occurs, of course, when household is translated as family. Wahrhaftig (1969) describes a Cherokee village in Northeastern Oklahoma in which families consist of several households. This understanding of family has remained unchanged for most Indians regardless of location; i.e., reservation, rural, or urban.

Following this conceptual framework, Indians develop an extremely strong sense of family along both vertical and horizontal extensions. Grandparents and older namesakes become active superegos in families: They provide child rearing guidelines. In most families, children become participants in setting discipline standards. If harsh discipline has been received, for example, children may talk with grandparents who in turn approve or disapprove of parental behavior. Curiously, the role of Indian grandparents is too often ignored by child development investigators. This obviously represents a primary resource for collation of child-rearing standards.

Vertical family structure is reinforced with horizontal organization. Thomas (1969) describes the important role of uncles in Cherokee families. This, of course, contributes an important standard for discipline. It provides for development of a positive relationship between fathers and children. Moreover, it introduces moderation in adult-child relations: Children are seldom punished in heat of anger. Indeed, Indian parents are noted for seldom meting out extreme physical punishment in discipline relationships with children (Lewis, 1970).

Indians often practice open family behavior extending through second cousins. This relationship degree is equivalent to brother or sister in nuclear families. Tragic diagnostic errors may result when this horizontal structure is misunderstood. On one occasion, this writer attended a chemical dependency program's staffing session which discussed the sexually loose behavior of an Indian adolescent. Description of the boy's behavior provided the counselors with some levity. The issue, however, was serious because the boy was on parole. His behavior warranted a revocation order. A counselor indicated that the boy had lived with several girls during a three-week period. Moreover, to his amazement, the girls knew about it and were even observed in groups with the boy. Simply by chance, the counselor presented the girls' names to the staffing committee. I was stunned. I knew the family well. The children were all first cousins. The boy had not been involved in sex behavior; he had simply been visiting different members of his family.

The above case confirms the opinion of many Indian professionals who believe that the structure and process of extended family networks escape the grasp of non-Indian caseworkers. A common result is iatrogenic casework intervention which undermines the family. Data from the Association on American Indian Affairs study (Unger, 1977) would lead one to presume that the Indian family is rapidly becoming qualified for endangered species status. The Association documents the capricious removal of Indian children from families followed by subsequent placement into non-Indian homes. Moreover, this appears as a characteristic welfare plan in every state having a large Indian population.

The Association's data are under attack from several State Departments of Public Welfare. Other sources, however, corroborate the Association's. Tables 2 and 3 illustrate two perspectives on casework intervention derived from alternate sources. Table 2 presents comparative data on race of child in placement and race of foster family. According to the data, an overwhelming number of Indian children are placed in homes in which neither parent is of Indian descent. Table 3 presents comparative data on interventive techniques used by a county social service department. According to the data, an overwhelming interventive technique used with Indian families is removal of children. Hence, substitute care prevails as a principal interventive plan with Indian families. Data in Table 3 do not allude to frequency or types of intervention offered prior to removal of children. Westermeyer (1977a, 1977b), however, tracked welfare interventions and found that Indian children are removed from their homes disproportionately more often than children of other races. Moreover, he indicates that the removal of children appears as an in-

TABLE 2

Characteristics of Child Placement Settings: Race of Children Compared with Race of Foster Parents

Child	Total in Foster Care	Number of Children Placed with Foster Parents Neither of Which are Same Race	Percent
Caucasian	730	5	1
Black	136	41	30
Spanish	17	11	65
Oriental	4	3	75
Native American	77	59	77

Source: Ramsey County Welfare Department, 1976. Percentages are rounded off to nearest whole number.

TABLE 3

Comparative Interventive Techniques Used by a Selected Welfare Department Serving Native American Families

Type of Intervention	Number of Indian Children	Percent of Children
Foster Placement	29	49
Emergency Foster Homes	9	15
Termination of Parental Rights - Awaiting Adoption	12	20
In-Home - Court Supervised Placement	9	15
Total Interventions	59	99

Source: Urban Indian Child Resource Center, Oakland, California. Percentages are rounded off to nearest whole number (unpublished data).

itial welfare plan; supplemental in-home support services were not offered to Indian families.

CLOSED COMMUNITY NETWORKS

Speck and Attneave (1974) conceptualize a family network counseling technique which purports to have a retribalization effect. I personally have difficulty working with such a large unit of analysis. Within an Indian casework context, network couseling is simply a means to re-

confirm the structural and cultural integrity of the extended family.

Contrary to numerous professional opinions, primary Indian family units remain very stable. In fact, at this level of analysis, Indian families are more cohesive than other minorities in America (Levitan and Johnson, 1975). Family deterioration is often the result of stress through adverse situations; e.g., relocation programs which disrupt family structure without providing culturally relevant social support services. The principal objective of relocation programs is employment, not family unity. Family members, however, do not immediately change behaviors simply because an employment program has disrupted the network.

Moreover, Indian family networks follow what has been identified as an open family-closed community pattern (Mousseau, 1975). Outsiders do not gain entrance easily. The family network represents a relational field characterized by intense personal exchanges which have lasting effect upon one's life and behavior (Speck and Attneave, 1974). Understanding this family relational field is a necessary prerequisite for analyzing conceptual terms, such as noncompetitive, nonjudgmental, or noninterfering behavior. Many caseworkers, for example, have experienced and observed interference among Indians. Moreover, intratribal conflict is well documented between "fullbloods" and "breeds" (Wax, 1969). Such radical departures from thoroughly documented concepts become empirically manageable to observers who comprehend the family relational field. The concepts simply deteriorate with social distance.

Moreover, formal competition among Indians is not necessarily a means of increasing personal power. Tracking the behavior of a champion dancer and his family serves to illustrate. Dancing competition is keen among Indians. Major social dances are held throughout the country each year. It is not unusual for 500 dancers to compete for honors at each event. A champion dancer is a source of pride and status for a family. Strict rules of behavior, however, govern dance contests. Few judges can observe all rule violations. Consequently, young men must disqualify themselves. This self-enacted behavior is a norm. Occasionally, a feather will be seen on the dance floor. Losing part of the costume is reason for disqualification. Many times nothing will be said even by judges who may have seen the feather fall. A dancer must check his costume and leave if he discovers a feather missing. A family's honor is more important than victory.

The family of a champion also assumes an obligation to share. This often takes the form of giveaways at selected dances. An old Mandan indicates that this represents the difficulty of being Indian: one must not only learn to win with honor, but also learn to share the winnings (Little Owl, 1972). Learning to share, of course, results from long-term imprinting through a family relational field. Family is a safe environment. Sharing is an expected behavior pattern which is taken for granted. Nothing is really ever lost; everything is retrievable.

The value of sharing has obvious impact upon behavior outside the closed community network; i.e., in mainstream society. The impact is not always visible. I isolated myself from extended family a few years ago to resume academic work. I took residence in a large apartment, and my son soon had several friends. He began sharing toys with other children. This developed a spiral effect. First, only he would share. Then, a few others reciprocated. Shortly, a majority of children started sharing toys. A parent committee soon organized and objected to my son's behavior. An insistent committee directive ordered him to quit giving toys away. Parents would troop their children to my apartment ordering them to "give those expensive toys back; they belong to Giese." My son had difficulty understanding their complaints about monetary value and private property. He still does. What had never occurred to us was that this was his first experience playing with non-Indians. His previous transactions had taken place within the safe confines of family. Rather than attempt to explain this issue, I withdrew. We moved back to our family.

Many Indians withdraw. Consequently, many urban Indian communities become noticeably closed to outside influence. Factions, of course, develop. These may follow family, reservation, tribal, or other political lines. They truly form a network of networks (Speck and Attneave, 1974). This generalized, closed community network is a critical factor in health and welfare service utilization patterns. Ninety percent of Indians in Minneapolis responding to Indian health behavior questions indicated a preference to receive services from Indian workers (DeGeyndt, 1973). This preference is clearly demonstrated by Indian clients in the Twin Cities Metropolitan Area of Minnesota who rely solely upon Indian service agencies. This contrasts with non-Indian health and hospital programs located in the same community which are continuously involved in strategies to recruit Indian clients and are unable to serve a representative number (Red Horse and Feit, 1976).

Non-Indian professionals have developed a host of explanations to distort the behavior of a closed community network. A common one is that Indians do not value preventive health care measures. Indians, however, have a historical tradition of sophisticated health and welfare practices. Moreover, most contemporary Indian-controlled health programs follow the Twin Cities experience: They are understaffed, underfinanced, and overutilized.

The closed community network points to a need for mental health professionals to develop a social conservation model for service delivery (Levine, 1976). This model would recognize and respect three basic principles. First, individuals are strengthened through group identity; therefore, Indian family history, customs, and traditions all contribute to a sense of selfhood. Second, natural networks within neighborhoods represent foundations for human services; therefore, Indian extended family units represent natural helping systems. Third, mental health programs should offer preferred forms of help based on ethnicity and differential environment; therefore, Indian extended family units should become cornerstones

in planning for health and welfare services.

SUMMARY AND DISCUSSION

The objective of this chapter was to explore American Indian family values and experiences. A critical factor in the analysis was the interactive process between professionals identified with the field of mental health and Indian families. The theoretical orientation followed a social conservation field. Thus, an underlying assumption was that cultural patterns remain an influence upon Indian behavior and must be considered a critical desideratum to any mental health service plan.

Data overwhelmingly suggest that services offered by mental health professionals may be culturally detrimental for Indian families. A reader may misinterpret the material and point to social caseworkers. They often become convenient scapegoats. No profession identified with the field of mental health, however, can escape responsibility. An Augsburg University investigation of judicial sentencing patterns, for example, confirms that Indians receive disproportionately harsh sentences in comparison with other races (Grams and Rohde, 1976). Hence, incarceration represents a principle rehabilitative service offered to Indians. An investigation of diagnostic procedures in an adolescent psychiatric unit (Robbins, Red Horse, and Iungerman, 1976) disclosed that Indian youth received detrimental labels disproportionately to youth of other races. Hence, Indian adolescents were more prone to be professionally labeled as "sneaky" or "shifty." Finally, the Government Accounting Office investigated the medically dominated Indian Health Service and revealed an alarming rate of sterilization among Indian women between ages fifteen and forty-four. The investigation also questioned a misuse of consent forms by Indian Health Board

Service (Dillingham, 1977). Results of this study generate Indian fears of government-sponsored genocide.

Indians have obvious and compelling reasons for being suspicious and for maintaining a closed community network. Responding to a national Indian study on child welfare, one wag identified this behavior as "Indian Paranoia" (Denver Research Institute, 1976). Following the data, this is not a disease; it is dis-ease. Hopefully, recent trends in Indian self-determination will prevail in law, health, education, and welfare programs. Self-management of culturally relevant mental health models may provide for accumulation of data focusing on normal growth and development in Indian families. Tracking of such data is a necessary prelude to the development of responsible and effective professional services.

REFERENCES

Bearheart, E., Jr. Religion as a variable in family practice. Paper presented at the Minneapolis Indian Alcoholic Counselor Workshop, 1976.

Bell, D. *The Coming of Post-Industrial Society.* New York: Basic Books, 1973.

Boggs, S.T. An interactional study of Ojibwa socialization. *American Sociological review,* 1956, *21,* 191–198.

Boggs, S.T. Cultural change and the personality of Ojibwa children. *American Anthropologist,* 1958, *60,* 47–58.

Cahn,E., Jr. and Hearne, D.W. (Eds.) *Our Brother's Keeper: The Indian in White America.* New York: New Community Press, 1972.

De Geyndt, W. Health behavior and health needs of urban Indians in Minneapolis. *Health Service Reports,* 1973, *88,* (4), 360–366.

Deloria, V., Jr. *Custer Died for Your Sins.* NewYork: Macmillan, 1969.

Densmore, F. *Chippewa Customs.* Minneapolis, MN: Ross and Haines, 1970.

Denver Research Institute. *Indian Child Welfare: A State-of-the-Field Study.* Washington, D.C.: U.S. Department of Health, Education, and Welfare, 1976.

Dillingham, B. Indian women and IHS sterilization practices. *American Indian Journal of the Institute for the Development of Indian Law,* January 1977, *3,* (1), 27–28.

Frankiel, R.V. *A Review of Research on Parent Influences on Child Personality.* New York: Family

Service Association of America, 1959. Fourth Printing, 1968.

Fuchs, E. and Havighurst, R.T. *To Live on this Earth: American Indian Education.* Garden City, N.Y.: Anchor Books, 1973.

Giordano, J. Ethnics and minorities: A review of the literature. *Clinical Social Work Journal,* Fall 1974, *2* (3), 207–219.

Grams, R.W. and Rohde, R. Race and the sentencing of felons in Hennepin county. Unpublished research, Department of Sociology, Augsburg College, Minneapolis, Minnesota, 1976.

Hall, E.T. *The Silent Language.* New York: Fawcett World Library, 1969.

Hallowell, A.I. Ojibwa personality and acculturation. In: P. Bohannan and F. Plog (Eds.), *Beyond the Frontier.* New York: The Natural History Press, 1967.

Kluckhohn, F.R. and Strodtbeck, F. *Variations in Value Orientations.* Evanston, IL: Row and Peterson Company, 1961.

Krush, T.P., Bjork, J.W., Sindell, P.S. and Nelle, J. Some thoughts on the formation of personality disorder: study of an Indian boarding school population. In: *Hearings Before the Special Subcommitte on Indian Education of the Committee on Labor and Public Welfare United States Senate, Part 5.* Washington, D. C.: U.S. Government Printing Office, 1969.

Levine, I.M. Ethnicity and mental health—a social conservation approach. Paper presented at the White House Conference on Ethnicity and Mental Health, June 1976.

Levitan, S.A. and Johnston, W.B. *Indian Giving.* Baltimore: The Johns Hopkins University Press, 1975.

Lewis, C. *Indian Families of the Northwest Coast: The Impact of Change.* Chicago: University of Chicago Press, 1970.

Little Owl, R. Material received through field interview at the Sisseton, South Dakota, July Fourth Pow Wow, 1972.

Miller, D., et al. *Native American Families in the City.* San Francisco: Institute for Scientific Analysis, 1975.

Miller, P.J., et al. *Annual Report: Formative Evaluation of the Innovative Demonstration Projects in Child Abuse and Neglect.* Washington, D.C.: CPI Associates, 1977.

Momaday, N.S. *The Names.* New York: Harper & Row, 1976.

Morey, S.M. and Gilliam O.L. (Eds.) *Respect for Life.* Garden City, N.Y.: Waldorf Press, 1974.

Mousseau, J. The family, prison of love. *Psychology Today,* August 1975, *9,* 3, 53–58.

Papajohn, J. and Spiegel, J. *Transactions in Families.* San Francisco: Jossey-Bass, 1975.

Ramsey County Welfare Department. *Ramsey County Foster Care Placement Report* (mimeographed) St. Paul, Minnesota, 1976.

Red Horse, J.G. Pre-parent testing: An analysis of early childhood development expectations among Indian adolescents. Unpublished research. Minneapolis: School of Social Work, Universty of Minnesota, 1976.

Red Horse, J.G. and Feit, M. Urban native American preventive health care. Paper presented at the American Public Health Association meeting, October 1976.

Robbins, S., Red Horse, J.G. and Iungerman, K. Differential diagnosis and stereotyping in native American mental health treatment. Unpublished research. Minneapolis: School of Social Work, University of Minnesota, 1976.

Speck, R.V. and Attneave, C.L. *Family Networks*. New York: Vintage Books, 1974.

Thomas, R.K. Lecture on nationalism. In: G. Wilkerson (Ed.), *The American Indian Reader*. Prepublication draft designed for use in Clyde Warrior Institutes in American Indian Studies. Albuquerque, New Mexico: National Indian Youth Council, 1969.

Unger, S. (Ed.) *The Destruction of American Indian Families*. New York: Association on American Indian Affairs, 1977.

Wahrhaftig, A. The folk society on type. In: G. Wilkerson (Ed.), *The American Indian Reader*. Prepublication draft designed to use in Clyde Warrior Institutes in American Indian Studies. Albuquerque, New Mexico National Indian Youth Council, 1969.

Wahrhaftig, A.L. and Thomas, R.K. Renaissance and repression: the Oklahoma Cherokee. In: H.M. Bahr, B.A.Chadwick and R.C. Day (Eds.), *Native Americans Today: Sociological Perspectives*. New York: Harper and Row, 1972.

Wax, M.L., et al. Formal education in an Indian community. In: *Hearings Before the Special Subcommittee on Indian Education of the Committee on Labor and Public Welfare, United States Senate, Part 4*. Washinton, D.C.: U.S. Government Printing Office, 1969.

Westermeyer, J. The drunken Indian: Myths and realities. In: S. Unger (Ed.), *The Destruction of American Indian Families*. New York: Association on American Indian Affairs, 1977(a).

Westermeyer, J. The ravage of Indian families in crisis. In: S. Unger (Ed.), *The Destruction of American Indian Families*. New York: Association on American Indian Affairs, 1977(b).

PART IV

Mental Health Issues for

Minority Group Children

CHAPTER 17

Mental Health Issues in the Development of the Black American Child

Hector F. Myers, Ph.D.

and Lewis M. King, Ph.D.

A (country) that proves incapable of solving the problems it creates is a decadent (country). A (country) that chooses to close its eyes to its most crucial problems is a stricken (country). A (country) that uses its principles for trickery and deceit is a dying (country).

Aimé Césaire (1972)

INTRODUCTION

The paraphrase of the words of the great Martinican poet Aimé Césaire reflects the catalyzing principles that motivate the nature of the critical examination of the mental health condition of the black American child. The central theme of this chapter will be the relationship between the social order and the social problem, i.e., the relationship between the social structure (in our case, the theory of our mental health guardians) and the social

process (in our case, the quality of life of our children).

Dr. Irving Zola (1970) tells the story of a physician trying to explain the frustrations of the modern health practitioner:

You know, sometimes it feels like this ... I am standing by the shore of a swiftly flowing river and I hear the cry of a drowning man. So I jump into the river..., pull him to shore and apply artificial respiration. Just when he begins to breathe, there is another cry for help. So I jump into the river, reach him, pull him to shore, apply artificial respiration, and then-just as he begins to breathe, another cry for help. So back in the river again, reaching, pulling, applying, breathing and then another yell. Again and again, without end goes the sequence. You know, I am so busy jumping in, pulling them to shore, applying artificial respiration, that I have no time to see who the hell is upstream pushing them all in.

We would, indeed, be quite fortunate if we were able to rescue our children at the same rate at which they were being pushed in upstream. Not only is our rescue operation woefully inadequate, we are yet to attack the problem "upstream," i.e., the social order. Clearly we have thousands of black children increasingly less capable of negotiating the rough waters of modern American society. It is equally clear that this "underpreparedness" is a product of the social order. Our examination of the process of the victimization of the child must be accompanied by the examination of the structure of victimization.

In this chapter, we outline two major objectives which we address in separate sections. In Section I, we examine the objective situation of the mental health of black children, paying particular attention to the role of the established mental health system in addressing the objective situation. Central to this analysis and critique will be the issues of incidence and prevalence of mental health disorders, diagnosis or attribution of cause, and the social response (i.e. treatment, etc.) to the diagnosed problems. In Section II, we propose a reanalysis of the data based on an understanding of history and the objective social structures. Historically, blacks have occupied in American society a particular class position that is clearly and excessively stressful. Our reanalysis will lay emphasis on this socioecological stress as a pathogenic by-product of the dynamic, historical transaction between black individuals, families and communities and the established structures, institutions and practices in society. It is the essentially oppressive nature of these transactions which accounts for the mental health

status of the black child. The mental health of the Afro-American child, and of Afro-Americans generally, can be accurately described as the product of efforts to adapt to insidious social processes that manufacture illness and social incompetence.

A note of caution: The very attempt at a scientific exploration of the problems of the mental health structure that result in the conditions of underdevelopment of black children is itself fraught with difficulty. There is always the fear of writing too much or too little on the limitations of the social structure and the failure of social institutions. It is no accident that the United States, the third richest nation in the world (after Kuwait and Switzerland), is ranked 15th in infant mortality; if we exclude white children from the statistic, the ranking drops to 27th. It is no accident that the figures are almost identical if one does the analysis looking at class distribution. We will try to at least highlight the major critique of the social structure. A second problem grows out of the fear that in the honest exploration of issues data will be pulled out of context and used unfairly to continue to perpetuate social myths. We have numerous examples of this in our recent history (Moynihan, 1965). Nevertheless, we will try, as black scholars, to take up the challenge to face up honestly to the reality of our black children. Finally, we acknowledge that fundamental social change often emerges out of the clear articulation and sharpening of the social contradictions and the struggle to collectively forge new syntheses.

SECTION I—THE OBJECTIVE SITUATION

In this section we report and analyze the data as the scientific community reports it on the mental health probems of black children. We are concerned here with the range and extent of mental health problems among black children. A recent publication of the National Academy of Sciences (1976) states:

There are no government survey programs attempting to assess the social development or psychological well-being of American children. Well-validated instruments to measure their characteristics do not even exist. Hence discussions of changes over time in the psychological health and social behavior of children must rely not on careful analysis of scientific data but on institutional records, such as juvenile arrest rates or the number of admissions to psychiatric facilities. Administrative statistics such as these have serious limitations as indicators of change: they are subject to distortion by changes in administrative definitions and practices; they provide little background information on the children who are counted as "cases" and they reveal nothing about children who do not come into contact with particular agencies or services. (p. 107)

This problem becomes even more severe when one considers a segment of the children's population, namely, the black child. We know, for example, that there has been an increase in recent years in psychiatric services for persons under 18 years (see Tables 1 and 2), but we fail to comprehend the reason. Is this because of earlier detection? Or is this because of greater awareness, availability and acceptance of psychiatric care? We cannot answer these questions without adequate survey data on the psychological well-being of the black child.

While we focus first on the statistics on juvenile arrest rates, we do not want to lose the opportunity to examine a whole range of children's psychiatric problems, including schizophrenia, various brain syndromes, depression and suicide, neuroses, hyperactivity, and behavior and learning disorders. We shall examine these in turn, but first we explore the general trends in available statistics on children's psychological well-being, using juvenile arrest rates and psychiatric hospitalization.

A study by Condry and Siman (1974) found that at every age and grade level children show a greater dependency on their peers than a decade before. This trend is even greater among black youth. Myers (1976) reports one out of five black junior high school students and three out of five black high school students as gang members. The susceptibility to group influence is higher among children in homes where there is less parental supervision, either due to limited interaction (Bronfenbrenner, 1958), parental absence (Condry and Siman, 1976) or the destruction of the family (King, 1978).

The implications of this increased attachment to age-mates are reflected in diminished psychological and emotional development which could lead to mental illness. Peer-oriented children have a more negative view of themselves and friends, are pessimistic about the future, show lower responsibility, and are more likely to engage in antisocial behavior (Siman, 1973). A more serious manifestation of this psychological impairment is reflected in the precipitous climb in the rates of juvenile delinquency. The estimated trend for black youth ages 10-17 is reflected in Figure 1.

Paralleling the reported increases in juvenile delinquency rates is the rate of admissions to psychiatric facilities. One report on the rate of admission to psychiatric hospitals in units per 100,000 population for youth under the age of 15 years shows that in New York, non-whites are hospitalized at almost three times the rate for whites; the rates for non-white males in this age group was almost five times the rate for white males and females (Shiloh and Selavan, 1974). A later report, on a similar population between the ages of 11-24 who were hospitalized with a diagnosis of schizophrenia in 1969, showed that almost twice as many non-white males and females were hospitalized with this diagnosis as were whites (DHEW, 1977). From these statistics we note the significant difference both in the rate of institutionalization and the severity of the

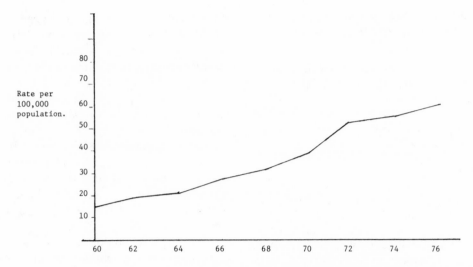

Figure 1. Rate of Delinquency Cases Disposed of by Juvenile Courts Involving Black Youth Ages 10-17.
Source: (Prorated from Juvenile Court Statistics, 1977, DHEW No. OHD-OYD 78-2604)

diagnosis given to children and youth under 18 years of age as a function of race (Table 1).

This racial trend in mental health becomes even more striking when we review the statistics on the pattern of institutionalization of young children as a function of race and social class. Comparing the rates of institutionalization of black children and youth under the age of 18 from 1966 to 1971 as reported in a DHEW publication (1977), we find that the rate of institutionalization in 1966 was 696 per 100,000 population. By 1971, this rate had almost doubled to 1,091. Furthermore, if we look at the types of institutions to

which these youngsters have increasingly been referred, we find that between 1966 and 1971 a significant decrease of 47 percent in the rate of institutionalization in psychiatric hospitals was paralleled by a 38 percent increase in the rate of institutionalization of black youth in juvenile institutions and an 11 percent increase of blacks in the populations of homes and schools for the mentally retarded. The positive nature of the first statistical item should not be overestimated, because this significant decrease in the psychiatric hospitalization of blacks may not be primarily the result of the national trend away from psychiatric hospitalization

TABLE 1

Admissions to Psychiatric Hospitals by Race & Sex & Diagnosis: 1962, 1969

	Whites			Non-Whites		
	Total	Male	Female	Total	Male	Female
Admissions to Psychiatric Units Per 1,000 population, N.Y., 1962 (Age 15 Years)	0.2	0.2	0.3	0.7	1.2	0.2
Admissions/100,000 population, ages 11-24, diagnosed as schizophrenics, 1969	-	120.3	84.4	-	285.8	142.0

From *Psychiatric Services and Changing Institutional Scene,* 1950–1975. DHEW Publication, 1977.

generally and the increased use of community mental health centers for the care of the psychiatrically impaired—but may only reflect expanded methods of black incarceration (Table 2).

This note of concern is futher justified if we look at the overall race x sex institutionalization rates for youth under 20.

TABLE 2

Psychiatric Services and the Changing Institutional Scene, 1950–1975

NIMH SERIES B, NO. 12

Rates	1966	1971
	2.8 Million	4.0 Million
	1,433/100,000	1,968/100,000
Ages 25-44	2,096/100,000	
Child under		
18	696/100,000	1,091/100,000

Distribution X Psych. Diagnosis (All Facilities)

	Males	Females
Schizophrenia 23%	22%	23%
Depressive Disorder 15%	10%	21%
Alcohol 9%	14%	4%
Organic Brain Syndromes 5%		
MR 3%		
Drug Disorders 3%		

Changes in Population by Institution

Mental Institutions	− 47%
TB Hospitals	− 84%
Correctional Institutions	− 8%
Juvenile Deliquency Schools	+ 38%
Homes and Schools for MR	+ 11%
Homes for Aged	+ 133%

1970 compared to 1950
Race X Institution X Sex (Under age 20)

1. All Institutions
    - White Males   − 21%
    - White Females   − 39%
    - Non-White Males   + 56%
    - Non-White Females   + 14%

   Comparable Rates: Non-White Male 2.3 X White male
                       Non-White female 1.4 x White female

2. Correctional Institutions
    Non-white male 5 X White Male

3. Juvenile Training Schools
    Non-white male 4 X white male

From *Psychiatric Services and Changing Institutional Scene,* 1950–1975, DHEW Publication, 1977

While white male and female institution-alization rates show decreases of 21 percent and 39 percent respectively, the rates for black males and females show increases of 56 percent and 14 percent respectively.

These general social indicators, examined thus far, appear to point to a rapid increase in the number of black children and youth having problems keeping afloat in the rough waters of society. A more detailed examination of the available statistics on the specific "problems in living" may afford some scientific insights into the nature of "the drowning."

Psychosis

The psychiatric nomenclature in the field of children's mental health is still very confusing. There are several terms utilized to describe psychiatric disorders in children. These include autism, infantile psychosis, symbiotic psychosis, and atypical child. Autism differs from other child psychotic syndromes in age of onset (Makita, 1966). It almost always starts in the first years of life. Other psychoses almost never occur before ten years. Its defining symptoms are lack of social interest or responsiveness, delayed or deviant development of language, and resistance to change. The reported prevalence in the general population of autism is 2.0 to 4.5 per 10,000 children under the age of ten years. The ratio of boys to girls was found to be roughly three to one (Lotter, 1966). A search of the literature found no study which indicated autism as a problem among black children. One can find little solace in the evidence, however, since this finding is also true among poorer classes. Since the syndrome is so closely associated with lower intelligence and speech difficulty, one must ask questions pertinent to the diagnosis. There may be a tendency to overrepresent black children in cate-gories other than autism. On the other hand, this may also reflect black parents as "unrefrigerated" (i.e., open, warm and accepting). The research on these questions is yet to be done.

In the other psychotic syndromes, and primarily childhood schizophrenia, the key symptoms are avoidance of people, delusions, hallucinations, thought block-ing.Although there are no national surveys on the prevalence of these schizophrenic syndromes; there is some evidence from what is reported that black children are overdiagnosed as psychotic. The same is true for all children of low socioeconomic status. This finding for children is identical to the reported inverse relationship between the frequency of psychotic disorders and social class (King, 1978). Although we understand a little of the clinical picture of schizophrenia in children and young adolescents, we have not yet developed ways of adequately assessing this picture, especially in differing social and cultural groupings. We, for instance, quite recently, had to "rescue" an eight-year-old troubled girl from the diagnostic category of "psychosis" by pointing out to the clinician how her responses on a Wechsler test were quite in keeping with the culture and indeed very perceptive. On one question, as an example, "What would you do if you were lost in the forest?" her response was, "Take off my clothes and put it on backwards." This was clearly a culture specific response indicating an attempt to reverse the process of being lost. It was not autistic thinking but symbolic action to begin to correct a series of events. A further probe by the clinician would have revealed clear steps to the resolution of the problem. The resolution in this culture may appear to begin with superstition or magical thinking. Yet, the psychology of the culture is more sophisticated than the deodorant commercials which have us believing that one product gives more sex appeal than the other.

Brain Syndromes

We are dealing here with acute brain syndromes and their associated neurologic dysfunctions which tend to be reversible, and chronic brain syndromes which are often irreversible (Wilson, 1972). Acute brain syndrome is primarily due to disordered physiology. Its defining characteristics are clouding of consciousness and disorientation. The disorientation is usually of recent and rapid onset. On the other hand, chronic brain syndrome is primarily due to lesions in the brain which may affect activity level, ability to concentrate, emotional reactivity, and general ability to control or organize behavior. The hallmark of chronic brain syndrome is progressive dementia (i.e., reversal in changes in cognitive functions and social development).

Many kinds of conditions and injuries of childhood can lead to brain syndrome. These include prenatal stress, obstetrical complications, maternal starvation, prematurity, low birth weight, respiratory distress, neonatal hypoglycemia, neonatal jaundice, infant malnutrition, lead poisoning, head injury, and frequent infant diseases.

Researchers have shown that brain damage or dysfunction is associated with a higher prevalence of mental illness. Graham and Rutter (1968) found six times as much psychiatric disorder among children 5-14 with a brain disorder than in the general population. Again, there is little or no work on this subject or on the general black youth population. There is, however, clear evidence for more severe conditions, including greater stress, malnutrition and diseases, in black children during both prenatal and neonatal phases. The extent of damage to black children is not really known, but on all indices of stress, at least twice as many black children suffer as white children (National Academy of Sciences, 1976). While there is certainly an overrepresentation of black children on the rolls of those labeled minimally brain damaged, this should not cloud the issue of the relationships between stress and brain syndromes established by adequate research.

Depression and Suicide

There is still a question as to whether affective disorders as known in adults exist in childhood (Graham, 1974). Increasingly, however, there is a tendency to accept their existence.

Descriptions of childhood depressive disorders represent two general viewpoints: (1) that childhood depressive disorders are similar to adult syndromes with a few additional unique overt features (Ling, Oftedal and Weinberg, 1970); (2) that childhood depressive disorders are different from adult syndromes and are not manifested in overt depressive syndromes (Gross, 1977). Despite this apparent disagreement on syndromes, there are some remarkable similarities. These include self-dislike, a sense of failure, difficulty sleeping, indecisiveness, dissatisfaction, poor school performance. The two approaches differ in how they view significant mood changes, social withdrawal, temper tantrums, hyperactivity.

There is still some question as to the relationship between these symptoms of depression and different disorder syndromes, including behavior and learning problems, chronic illness and physical handicaps. The implications for black children, however, seem quite clear. These are the children most vulnerable because of the attack on their self-concept in school, the threat or actuality of abandonment due to the destruction of family, and the insurmountable obstacles of society. As Anthony and Gilten (1976) state, "Depression may be natural, developmental and existential, but for the most part, it is brought into being by bad conditions — rejecting parents, systematic cruelties, deprivations, losses, failure and the general inhumanity of man to man." Black children, especially, become victims of the human condition. There is evidence to suggest that a very large percentage (10-25 percent) of black children are at high risk for clinical depression during childhood and adolescence.

Suicide and other self-destructive behavior which are closely associated with depression are extremely rare in young children although it has been argued that "accident proneness" has some connection with suicidal or self-injurious behaviors. Burton (1968) found that accident-prone children have a high incidence of families with severe problems.

The incidence of adolescent suicide has been well recorded. Schaffer (1974) quotes a figure of 0.6 percent as the proportion of suicides in all deaths in the 10-14 age group. No such estimates are available for black children of a similar age range. According to Seiden (1972), blacks between the ages of 15-24 commit suicide at a rate higher than that of the total black population of all ages. This is especially true for young black females. Marvis (1969) notes that the suicide rate among U.S. black women is the14th highest in the world and has risen 80% in the two decades prior to this report. Allen (1973) reports that in California the rate of black female suicide during 1970 was 30.2 per 100,000 population as compared to 13.6 per 100,000 for white females ages 20-24. Kiev and Anumonye (1976) state that suicide is the most common cause of death among young black women. Black females report the highest suicide rates for ages 15-19, while black males report the highest rates for ages 20-24. There is a problem with these figures, however, because we are still not sure of what constitutes suicide among black adolescents. Our traditional concepts of self-poisoning, hanging,

jumping out windows and cutting wrists, which are the most common methods, will have to be modified to include drug overdose, victim precipitated homicide, and some deaths by accident due to driving while drunk. When all these facts are considered, suicide is indeed on the very rapid increase in our black youth.

The authors of this chapter, in their own clinical work with black children and youth, find precipitating events to be very substantial. More frequently, the youth had struggled for a long time and had attempted varying solutions, none of which apparently worked. What often works against the youth is the mistaken assumptions by their families about childhood problems and the false belief that black youths will not kill themselves. There is even a more callous attitude by the larger society which in many instances fosters self-destructive behaviors.

Behavior and Conduct Disorders

Grouped under this heading are acting-out behavior in the home and classroom, and physical aggression and antisocial behavior on the streets. Children in this range are in frequent fights, do not follow directions, damage others' property and are often revengeful or cruel. There are two parallel syndromes—the unsocialized aggressive disorder and the socialized conduct disorder.

Children who qualify as "unsocialized aggressives" fit into a truer psychiatric syndrome which probably begins in early childhood. There is a pattern of behavior which parents are able to recall and a pattern of relationships with the social world, including other children, parents and adults. It is difficult to differentiate between this clinical syndrome and hyperactivity; and particularly in the black child they are often confused. The disorder is most common among foster and adopted children (Bohman, 1971), twice as high among boys, and higher in the urban areas of large cities (Rutter, 1973).

It is reported that as many as 3 percent of black 10- and 11-year-old children may have this problem. There is no definitive national survey to validate this finding, but general clinical evidence from the Los Angeles area seems to support this finding. There is clear evidence for an association between this antisocial conduct and reading disability. At least one-third have much difficulty. There is *no* evidence for genetic determination, and brain injury accounts for only a minor proportion of cases (Rutter, 1973). A good deal of the evidence seems to indicate social influence in the home as the major cause of the problem. Children are in some way prevented from mastering the developmental tasks and developing the intellectual and emotional tools for making normal age-related transitions.

The second group of conduct disorders, socialized conduct disorder, seems to have a different pattern and source of origin. The behaviors can be better characterized as "negative street behavior" resulting in crime and delinquency. There is no history of behavior problems. The onset is in middle childhood or earlier. Its major source of origin is peer group pressure or influence. This type of conduct disorder is growing at a most rapid rate in the inner cities of our nation among all youth, but particularly affects the black youth. It results in the third largest killer of black youth in the U.S., and includes massive drug and alcohol abuse, as well as crime and vandalism.

At the height of juvenile gang activities in 1972, the State of California's report on juvenile crime noted an increase of 35.7 percent in homicides, a 20.6 percent increase in robberies, 20.0 percent increase in assaults, a 26.7 percent increase in forcible rape, and a 33.2 percent increase in the use of heroin and other narcotics. The national rate of institutionalization of children and youth under 20 reflects the major societal means of coping with this wave of youth violence. In 1970, the rate

of institutionalization was 12 percent lower for white males than in 1959. For non-white males, however, the rate in 1970 was 8 percent higher than in 1959. As of 1970, the rate of institutionalization of non-white males in correctional institutions was six times that of white males; for non-white females about seven times the rate for white females. A substantial number of youth are now included among the heavy and habitual abusers of marijuana, PCP (Angel Dust), and even heavier drugs like cocaine and heroin. A pilot epidemiological study (Fairchild, 1978) reported estimates among users of PCP in the Southeast Los Angeles Health Region to range from 15.6 percent of youth ages 12-15 to 69.4 percent of youth 16-21. In a 1975 planning report from the same county area in Los Angeles, 34 percent of the drug abuse clients served were 21 years or younger.

Some Further Trends

The above brief exploration of the problems in living faced by black children does not exhaust the picture. The latest statistics reported by the Office of Education and the National Institute of Mental Health show that despite a significant increase in the fiscal allocations for urban education and mental health resources, a greater percentage of urban children are performing poorly in school and are being diagnosed (and perhaps misdiagnosed) as emotionally disturbed and mentally retarded; a significantly wider range of academic problems are being attributed to emotional disorders and, consequently, more of these children are being referred for psychiatric evaluation and treatment (Shiloh and Selavan, 1974). There is a similar trend in the statistics for children with problems of hyperactivity, physical handicaps, disorders of speech, language, vision and hearing. The net result of all of this is that in a hypothetical community of 100 children, close to 45 would be carrying the baggage of a psychiatric label, while 30 would be at high-risk for being thus labeled.

While we have thus far focused on the "hard" signs of mental health and illness, what is even more alarming to the authors are the statistics on the "soft" signs for potential mental health problems. We refer to the statistics on child abuse, pregnancy rates in teenagers which are now gaining recognition as a national problem, and infant mortality rates. Let us for a moment focus on the implications for birth and fertility rates in teenagers 14-19.

Briefly, to set a context, age-wise patterns of fertility and birth rate across races further demonstrate that whites generally have their children at an older age, 25-29 years for mother and father, while blacks generally have their children when mother and father are both 20-24 years of age. Whites seem to wait to have their children after the college years and after several years of employment. Blacks, on the other hand, seem to have their children soon after high school or during the college years, and prior to the establishment of an employment pattern. Of course, it is important to note that a larger percentage of blacks than whites go directly into the job market from high school rather than going to college. As such, therefore, the probability of starting a family at an earlier age is greater. Nevertheless, this race differential suggests that a substantial number of black children are born to parents who are younger, less well-trained and educated, and less secure economically.

In recent years there has been growing concern nationally about teenage pregnancy. In the black communities across the country, we are beginning to see the development of a new black family structure (i.e., the teen family within the original adult unit).

During the 60s and 70s, the overall U.S. birth rate decreased, but the births to teenagers increased overall, as well as in

proportion to all births. In 1973, 20 percent of all births were to teenagers, as compared to 17 percent in 1968 (Menchen, 1975). The majority of teen births are to non-white women, many of whom are black. In a comparative study of the percentage of change in the birth rate as a function of age and race from 1961-1973, Menchen (1975) reported that between 1961 and 1968 the birth rate to white mothers under 20 dropped by 9.4 percent, but only dropped by 0.2 percent from 1968-1973. Black teenagers, on the other hand, reported birth rate increases of 27.2 percent from 1961-1968 and 9.4 percent from 1968-1973. Thus, blacks are disproportionately producing children during their teen years when they are least equipped physically, emotionally, socially, and economically to raise children.

The incidence of pregnancy and birth among the youth of a group is a good index of the state of mental health of a group because it provides, at the very least, a rough estimate of the number of children from that group whose parenting will be provided by a parent who is going through major developmental crises. In addition to the social and economic handicaps faced by the adolescent parent and offspring, the child of the adolescent is at serious risk for prematurity, both in terms of gestational age and birth weight, for birth complications or defects, for malnutrition and ultimately infant mortality.

In terms of prematurity, it was estimated that in 1967, 12.5 percent of white mothers under 15 and 8.5 percent of white mothers 16-19 delivered premature infants. For non-white mothers during the same year, 19.5 percent of those under 15 and 15.7 percent of those 16-19 delivered premature infants. Even when we control for age, non-white adolescents are almost twice as likely to deliver a premature infant as whites (Menchen, 1975).

The infant mortality rates by race and age of mothers are equally enlightening. Overall and regardless of age, infant mortality is highest among non-whites, with rates almost double. Both groups, however, report the characteristic U-shaped function between rate of mortality (1000 live births) and age of mother. The highest rates are for girls under 15 and for women 45 and over. The lowest rate is for women 25-29 years of age. These statistics once more show that the greatest risk for prematurity and infant mortality is run by the offspring of girls under 15, especially of non-white girls.

These health statistics paint a rather bleak picture of the developmental process of the black child. If that child is from a low income urban background, he or she begins life exposed to great health and environmental risks. This pattern of risks is compounded by economic, social and political vicissitudes that later on produce the mental health problems described earlier.

Social Response to the Problems

If we accept the research findings, the projections about black children and youth, and the generalized intrapsychic explanations of cause, then one logically should find an effort on the part of society to develop individual, group and family psychotherapy and/or assistance. This pattern, however, does not prevail among black children and youth. Institutionalization and incarceration are the interventions of choice. A few statistical examples should underscore this point. Reports of the rate of admissions to psychiatric units per 100,000 population for youth under 15 years of age show that non-whites in New York are hospitalized at almost three times the rate for whites. The rates for non-white males in this age group was almost five times the rate for white males and females (Shiloh and Selavan, 1974). The social responses to the mental health problems and needs expressed by black children are increasingly becoming drug treatment (e.g., the excessive misuse of Ritalin to control school children), incar-

ceration and psychiatric hospitalization.

A later report on a similar population between the ages of 11 and 24 who were hospitalized with a diagnosis of schizophrenia in 1969 showed that almost twice as many non-white males and females were hospitalized with this diagnosis as were whites. From these statistics we note the significant difference in both the rate of institutionalization and the severity of the diagnosis given to children and youth under 18 years of age as a function of race.

Reasons for the Present Social Response

There is a principle that one's theories or assumptions, implicit or explicit, guide one's methods or actions. If we are able to examine the theoretical perspectives, we may find reasons for society's perceptions of mental health among black children and youth and, indeed, an explanation of the social response. The intent of this section is to briefly examine the theoretical perspectives. We find that an earlier exposition by Rainwater (1970) is closely aligned with our analysis.

In this very provocative article, Rainwater identified five conceptions of the poor or the "disinherited". The conceptions were: (1) the Moralizing, (2) the Medicalizing, (3) the Apotheosizing, (4) the Normalizing, and (5) the Naturalizing. The first four represent combinations of two basic dimensions: potency (i.e., the poor are either weak or they are potent) and virtuosity (i.e., the poor are either basically virtuous or they are basically evil). The fifth perspective combines the essential elements of the other four and extends them to their logical conclusion.

According to the Rainwater analysis, the most basic perspective on poverty is the *Moralizing* which characterizes the disinherited urban black as evil and potent. The urban black poor are basically evil and sinful and drawn to a "less civilized" way of being in the world. As such, therefore, they tend to gravitate to environments where debauchery, sin and immorality are the rule (i.e., drug addiction, broken families, school failure, and the other negative features of these environments are legitimate by-products of this state).

By "social standards," the victims are sinful and need to be "born again"; if this fails, then why not try some "benign neglect." We see this very pervasive influence in our social policies and programs in "this nation under God."

The second perspective, the *Medicalizing* or Medical Model, characterizes the urban black poor as essentially evil and weak (i.e., sick, helpless products of their unhealthy selves and unhealthy environments). The central theme in this perspective is that the lives of the poor and black reflect the pathologizing of normal personal and social processes. Both the individual (i.e., the black child) and the social institutions (i.e., the black family, the black community) are sick.

Elements of this perspective may be described as "psychopathological persons," wherein the attribution of cause is centered on the deficits in the personality and cognitive and emotional structures of the individual black child. The "pathological environment" is another related subelement in which the primary causal agent is the inadequate black family and community; the root cause is not individual pathology, but social disorganization and social pathology (i.e., the pathological cycle of poverty in the ghetto culture).

Much of social science and mental health evolves from this perspective. We can characterize most mental health theory, research, and practice as psychopathologizing insofar as the primary basis for the analyses of the causes of emotional and behavioral disorders rests on the psychodynamics of the individual. The environment is generally considered as a pathological context that contributes to the development of a distorted, inadequate ego in the individual. Thus, black child abuse, black youth violence, black youth suicide are all explained as the products of fundamental deficits in the character structure of the individual child or parent. These deficits result from the deleterious influences of a pathologizing environment.

The social responses (i.e., treatment) that evolve out of this pathologizing perspective emphasize the diagnosis of "disease" in the child and family and prescribe clinical interventions to achieve symptomatic relief. The pathology assumed to be endemic to the environment remains essentially untreated because "it is too political, too difficult, and falls outside of the expertise of the social scientist and mental health practitioner." Thus, from this perspective, the emphasis is on the diagnosis and treatment of symptoms in the person. The pathogenic social structure processes that lead to the disordered behavior are essentially ignored.

The third and fourth perspectives, the *Apotheosizing* and the *Normalizing,* characterize the urban black poor as essentially virtuous. The negative experiences of poverty and oppression in the first case serve to create a striving individual and culture engaged in a perpetual struggle for survival against insurmountable odds. From this struggle emerge special skills, life styles, philosophies and a special quality of existential humanity that are adaptive to the stark reality of their existence. From the *Apotheosizing* perspective, therefore, black language, cognitive styles, behavior patterns, and native preferences represent healthy, adaptive attributes forged within the context of a vibrant and creative black culture.

The *Normalizing* perspective, on the other hand, denies the concrete reality of being black and poor as having any meaning and significance in accounting for black behavior and mental health. This perspective starts from the basic premise of the "equality of all people." The assumptions then are that although blacks may have been discriminated against, the effects of these experiences over several generations are essentially minor. What characterological, cognitive, emotional and behavioral differences may exist between blacks and whites are basically superficial and minor variations in form and expression and not in substance. The material and social restrictions black children have been forced to live under are not assumed to be severe enough to have had any lasting effects on the internal dynamics of black individuals and families, or on the transactions between blacks and the larger society.

The basic model of intervention suggested by these two perspectives can be parsimoniously described as "non-treatment," or ignoring the existing social conditions and simply letting "the natural creative and generative energies of blacks take their course."

Both of these positions, and especially the *Apotheosizing*, can be found in the writings of liberal white and black social analysts. While they do not attribute the current mental health status of blacks to either moral decadence or illness, they nevertheless confuse important issues and make erroneous assumptions. First, they make the assumption that "we are all basically the same (i.e. equal), and if given the right opportunity we would all rise to our natural level in society." In reality, we must distinguish between "existential equality" and "functional equality." Existential equality is an ideological principle that affirms the essential humanity of people and the rights of each to be granted the same respect, valuing and opportunity to be. Functional equality, on the other hand, is based on performance—i.e., the demonstrated product of ability, effort and opportunity to function within our social structure. This is a political dialectic or interaction between natural, personal attributes and the political structuring of options, opportunities, barriers, and constraints to the development of these personal attributes. Failure to acknowledge this critical inter-

action reduces the ideas articulated by these two perspectives to nonsubstantial, platitudinous statements.

Second, these positions confuse adaptation with health. While the moralizing and medicalizing perspectives characterize black behavior as essentially negative and pathological, the apotheosizing and normalizing views commit the error of reacting to the deficit model by postulating its opposite—strengths and assets. This approach, while more palatable, still fails to portray reality accurately and honestly. While black children are not essentially deficit ridden, by the same token neither are they heroic, striving creatures. Their efforts to adapt and cope in the face of great odds are admittedly heroic. However, adaptation to oppression comes at a price. That price often entails the development of necessary strategies to ward off extinction, but these strategies do not allow for mastery and truly creative development and growth. Thus, it is not sufficient in the fostering of the mental health of oppressed people to simply reaffirm culture and advocate for greater opportunities. It is necessary to radically remove the internalized "mentality of the oppressed" and to radically restructure the social order to allow for the free development and growth of all people (Fanon, 1967a, 1967b).

The fifth and final perspective as identified by Rainwater, is labeled the *Naturalizing*. This viewpoint is advocated by those who attempted to assess the cause of the behavior of blacks and the poor from a presumably value-free position. The assumption made is that science with its "value-free," objective methods can ascertain the "truth" about black behavior by comparing objectively the behavior of black children against the "universal standards for all human behavior." Two major value perspectives or themes coexist under this naturalizing heading: *Biological* or *Genetic Determinism* and *"Cultural Relativism."*

According to the genetic determinist, there is "scientific evidence" to support the contention that the poor and blacks are biologically different from—i.e., inferior to—the more affluent and the whites. This genetic difference is used to explain why many urban black children fail at many socially defined developmental tasks, and why they are disproportionately represented among "the mental health" casualties. This assumed biological deficit is seen as an immutable barrier to the successful participation of black children in society. Therefore, expectations and aspirations should be realistically adjusted downward and the inferior status of black children should be accepted as fact.

This perspective is particularly evident in the work on the intelligence and cognitive capabilities of the black child. All deficits identified in the black child, whether behavioral, emotional, cognitive or physical, are attributed directly to natural biological weaknesses that impede his/her effective functioning and healthy social adjustment. No amount of manipulation of social and environmental conditions can overcome the immutable effects of this biological barrier. Therefore, black children are doing as well as can be expected, given what they have to work with. This view elaborates on the basic premise of the moralizing and medicalizing perspectives, but locates the "essential weakness" of blacks in their genetic structure rather than in their bodies or in their spirits.

The *Cultural-Relativism* perspective is related to the genetic determinist view although opposite in its locus of attribution. This perspective views the behavior and social system of the black poor as perfectly valid entities in their own right. Black children are neither inferior nor superior to whites; they are simply different. Black language, cognitive styles, behavior patterns, and value preferences are socialized by-products adaptive to the black world. As such, therefore, black behavior should be evaluated within the context of the black culture and not against standards developed to assess the behavior of whites. Those who assume universal norms of behavior and use assessment tools normed according to these criteria are viewed as committing a transubstantive error—i.e., assuming that the substance and meaning of concepts, images and behavior are "essentially the same" across cultures because they are "similar" in form (King, 1978).

Like the apotheosizing perspective, the cultural-relativist position affirms the essential difference of blacks. It is similarly limited in its analytic position by its failure to locate the present status of the black child organically within a concrete historical reality. The black child *is* different from the white child; black culture *is* different from white culture. These differences result, in part, from the different cultural roots from which they emerge (i.e., African vs. European). The differences also result from the fundamentally different existential positions of the black child and white child in this society. White children develop within a concrete social reality defined as white. The obstacles that they may face can be attributed to their social class, sex, or religion, and ultimately to their individual abilities. Race, for the white child, is not an existentially meaningful entity. It is a fact, a minimum common denominator taken for granted.

The black child, on the other hand, begins with a dual existential reality: to be black and to be American. Race is an existential factor that is primary. Being black sets the tone of one's existence throughout the entire lifespan. As our data bases clearly show, the cards are often stacked against the child primarily on the fact of being black. Additionally, the factor of social class for blacks appears to interact in a multiplicative relationship with race (i.e., race x sex). As we noted earlier, to be black in America is difficult; to be black and poor is disastrous. Add to this reality sex, religious ideology, and individual capacity and we get a more accurate picture of the true basis for the differences between black and white children.

Therefore, the cultural-relativist perspective is humanistic but limited as a perspective for analysis. It is significant to also note that although they make different attributions of the causes of black behavior, the cultural relativist (difference) and the genetic determinist (deficit) prescribe similar solutions—leave the black child and the black family alone. The perspectives differ, of course, in the motivation for the "hands off" policy (cultural difference vs. limited ability) and lead to different social policy (cultural pluralism vs. cultural normative élitism). Nevertheless, according to these viewpoints, the mental health of the black child should ultimately reach an acceptable level if we assume a noninterventionist position.

From all of these five perspectives we see the black child as both hero and villain, as both superior and inferior, as both the normal product of an organized social response to oppression and a pathological deviation from the normal social order. Black society is simultaneously evil and decadent and vibrant and heroic. It simultaneously provides a healthy context in which necessary survival skills are socialized and a context that inflicts handicaps and encourages incompetence. The fact that these unexamined contradictions have coexisted without resolution for several decades is in part responsibile for our failure to devise a means of grasping the reality of the black child and devising an effective social response to that reality. We shift between positions without a heightened consciousness informed by an understanding of history, devoid of a method for the analysis and understanding of the historical reality and therefore without a vehicle for the transformation of our children and youth. What remains unexamined are the deep structures of the traditional mental health and social science epistemology, with sin, sickness, and genetic determination as root issues.

The task of the next section is to initiate this exploration by heightening the contradictions endemic to this social structure, exploring a method for the understanding of the condition of black children and youth, and suggesting a vehicle for the transformation of their condition.

SECTION II—MENTAL HEALTH AND THE URBAN BLACK CHILD: A REFORMULATION

The responsibility for the failure of our social change programs must rest at least in part with the scientific community and the failure to examine the deep structures of our assumptions, concepts and methods used in the analysis of social phenomena. Although social science is not the only force influencing social policy, it does play a critical role in defining the nature of social problems and directing the formulation of social response. An illustrative case in point is the infamous Moynihan report on the black family (Moynihan, 1965) and the subsequent Nixonian policy of "benign neglect." In a recent review of 50 years of social science research on the black child (Myers, Harris and Rana, 1979) the authors documented evidence of the rigid and narrow definition of black child development and mental health as essentially negative products of deficits in the child and in the black family. What was clearly absent in the literature was the conceptual and empirical specification of the fundamental problems and the role of social scientists in helping set policies and practices that establish the conditions that can lead to different outcomes.

An analysis of the mental health condition of the black child/youth must look at the interactions between the child and the social context. Human development is dependent upon this interaction which is reciprocal. The black child is born into a social context (familial as well as economic) which must be understood and revealed. It is the basis for a truly scientific exploration of the psychology of the black child. Understanding the conditions of the community now implicitly raises the questions of history as to why these conditions prevail, persist or remain largely unchanged. The black child is not a "thing" apart from his/her condition. The psychology of the black child is a product of the dialectical interactions between the child and his/her social space.

Let us examine the social context of the black American child, paying particular attention to those indices that appear to most directly interact with his/her mental health condition. To do this we have abstracted the data relative to the 20 major urban centers and created an illustrative, theoretical city of 1,000 people (King and Myers, 1978). The comparative quality of life and mental health for the black and white residents of this city would look like this:

Housing: In this city there would be 200 whites with about 800 blacks. About 400 would be above the poverty line, 600 below the poverty line, in this case the line being $5,000 per year. Of the 800 blacks, fully 620 would be living in substandard housing as opposed to 15 whites; most of the blacks (i.e. 500), would be below the poverty line. There would be 28 percent overcrowding (i.e., more than one person per room) among the blacks as opposed to 5 percent for whites; 86 percent of the blacks would be renting as opposed to 43 percent whites. When new homes or apartments are built, blacks would occupy only 4 percent of them due to rapid urban renewal.

The relatively few blacks who were working class or middle class and were able to move to the outskirts of the city would spend 60 percent of their income for housing, while their white neighbors spent 30 percent of theirs for housing.

Health: Only 38 percent of the black population and 40 percent of the poor would report excellent health, as opposed to 60 percent of the white population and 64 percent of those above poverty. The 200 whites would have an average life expectancy of 76 years, the 800 blacks less than 64 years on average. The above-poverty-to-below-poverty difference

would be 70 to 58. Blacks would die almost twice as often from hypertension, cirrhosis of the liver, influenza and pneumonia. The poor would also most likely die from these conditions at the same rates. The source of care for blacks and for the poor would mainly be public sources while that of whites and those above poverty would be mainly private. Blacks and the poor would be less likely to visit the physician and even less likely to visit the dentist or eye doctor. As to hospital insurance coverage, only 50 percent of blacks under 65 would have health insurance in contrast to 80 percent whites; 43 percent poor as opposed to 87 percent non-poor would be covered. The picture and direction are similar when one examines nutrition by caloric, iron, protein and calcium intake.

Perhaps the most devastating data bases would be in the area of the care and protection of children. Pregnancy complications occur in 25 percent of blacks vs. 15 percent whites, and 22 percent of poor vs. 16 percent above poverty; maternal mortality per 100,000 live births, for blacks is 60, for whites 14; for poverty 58, for above poverty 17. Note the fact that race appears to be the more significant variable in this instance. The birth weight statistic continues the trend. Birth weight is significant because it is a good predictor of moderate to severe handicaps—mental retardation, mental illness, etc. The lower the birth weight, the higher the incidence of handicaps. On an average, the birth weight for black babies would be 250 grams less than for whites, and for poor babies 150 grams less than those above the poverty level. In the area of prenatal care, the negative trend continues. In infant mortality rates (fetal deaths per 100 live births), the United States ranks 15th at 17.7 percent when the so-called 48 advanced nations are considered; roughly twice as many black babies would die at birth as white babies. This statistic drops by almost 20 percent for below poverty when compared to above poverty.

For the health status of this child who is able to survive the first major trauma, the pattern is repeated with regard to nutrition, immunization against common disease, dental and eye doctor visits, physician visits. The net result is that black children under 17 would report only 40 percent of the time to be in excellent health vs. 65 percent of whites; 43 percent of those under the poverty line and 72 percent of those above.

A cursory glance at three other data bases would complete the picture and help to further establish the nature of the problem. These data sources are in education, income, and family composition (King and Myers, 1978).

Education: The Bakke decision confronted blacks halfway up the stairs and much of the gains of the 1960's may be lost summarily; the trend in desegregation does not help the picture. The gap between racial groups by income continues at a minimum of 13 percentage points at all levels of education. In 1978, whites are still three times more likely than blacks to be college graduates.

Income: If Karl Marx lived in America in this last decade, he might have been willing to consider the new black urban underclass as real products of the class formation under the ideology of capitalism and not as lumpen proletariat. Blacks are severely limited in their participation in the labor force, and the ratio of black to white unemployment has remained virtually constant for the past 20 years. In 1978, there was a 40 percent unemployment among black youth which is over twice that of white youth; the annual average unemployment for the total population was twice as high for blacks (13.3 to 6.0). There is nothing "lumpen" about groups who face persistent racism, who are the last hired and the first fired, who face real institutionalized barriers to progress at every turn, from education to the building trades.

Family Composition: This final index is important because the family has indeed been the bedrock of support and protection for the black individual in the face of the most overwhelming forces against the individual. The statistics do not, in this case, reflect an accurate picture because of the "nuclear family" proliferation. In 1975, 61 percent of the 5.5 million black families had husband and wife both present, a decline from 73 percent in 1965. In 1973, the proportion of black families with female heads and no spouse counted was 35 percent. The most recent statistic of 1978 quotes a new figure of 51 percent. In 1974, there were 3.2 million black children in families headed by women or 40 percent of all black children; the

increase was almost entirely for families with incomes under $8,000.

This is the social condition, this is the quality of life and health context faced by the majority of our black children and youth.

There is no question in our minds that black children are being devastated. We remain amazed at the creativity and ingenuity of all the children who survive these conditions. One of our major premises is that there is a deep structure, coterminous with the capitalistic social order, that maintains these social conditions. This is a history of economic and social exploitation, designed to benefit the few, that has resulted in the data revealed. The reference to a deep structure in society emphasizes the notion that social deprivation and discrimination are factors that are rooted in the social structure of society and not in the individual. That is, individual ability, coping strategies, and experiences influence the relative impact that poverty will have on their lives. The established social priorities and practices determine the existence of poverty, as well as those groups most likely to be dispossessed.

A second major premise is that the child who is part of this condition *interacts* with, changes and is changed by this condition. The changes brought about by the child however (necessarily only at the survival level) are insufficient to balance the changes imposed on him/her by the society. For example society has built new prisons to deal with the revolt of youth.

A third major premise is that the influence on the child by the society, generally labeled stress conditions, is mediated internally by the child in an interaction that results in coping strategies which we dimensionalize into mental health states of well being.

The basic debate among scientists faced with accounting for the mental health condition of black children lies in the specification of the critical causal factors (i.e., genetic vs. environment), and the elaboration of predictive models that specify the nature of the relationship between these factors and the mental health outcomes. The model for the analysis of the mental health of black children which we now propose draws upon two distinct theoretical sources: (1) the theory and research on urban stress and its effects, and (2) the theory of social dialectics of oppressed and colonial people as articulated by Frantz Fanon. These two perspectives share in common an emphasis on the critical dialectic between the appraisal and adaptive processes within the person, and the transactional processes between the person and the sociopolitical context to predict mental health outcome.

The Urban Stress Model of Mental Health

In a series of very provocative articles, Dohrenwend (1961, 1967), Dohrenwend and Dohrenwend (1969, 1970) and Myers (1976, 1977a,b) review the available theoretical literature on psychosocial stress as a heuristic model for the analysis of the epidemiological findings on the physical and mental health of the poor and ethnic minorities. The basic paradigm consists of an elaboration of the Selye (1950, 1974) and Lazarus (1966, 1974, 1977) models of the stress-adaptation process as precursors to disease and system malfunctions. The paradigm contains five basic elements: (1) *the antecedent stress state,* defined as the basal level of stress usual for the individual or group; (2) *the eliciting stressor,* the objective stressful social stimulus that requires adaptation or change in the usual level of functioning; (3) *the mediating factors,* which are the internal and external factors that increase or decrease the relative impact of the stressor; (4) *the adaptation process,* the complex physiological, cognitive-affective and behavioral response process of coping with the stressor, and (5) the *health outcome* resultant from the coping effort. This paradigm is diagrammed in Figure 2.

Several assumptions are made in this paradigm. First, that the greater the amount, intensity and duration of the stress experienced, the greater the likelihood of illness and the greater the severity of the disorder (Holmes and Rahe, 1967). Second, that the amount of stress experienced and the severity of the impact of stress are related to factors of social

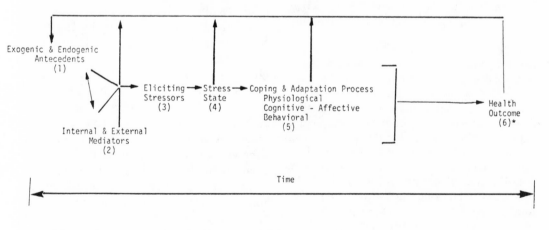

*(6) Represents both the point along the Health (+) -- Illness (-) continuum as well as the specific disorder(s) that may result

Figure 2. Simplified conceptual and research paradigm depicting the role of stress in health and illness

class and race (Dohrenwend and Dohren-wend, 1970; Myers, 1976). Third, that the impact and meaning of any stressor or class of stressors is influenced by internal and external mediating factors related to the person's social class and ethnic background. Fourth, that the person's or group's state of relative health can be meaningfully predicted from his race x social class stress dynamics (Myers, 1976, 1977a).

Following an extensive and critical review of the theoretical and epidemiological literature on black mental health, the urban stress model suggests that individuals who are both black and poor are exposed to a greater amount of stress, and are often forced to cope with stress over an extended period of time; consequently, the severity of the impact of that stress on their lives is substantially greater.

1. Antecedent stress state

Myers (1976) contends that the negative interaction of the two factors of race and social class serves to create a cross-generational pattern of stress induction and stress accumulation in the urban black poor. This pattern is created by the greater exigencies of daily living and the greater risk of facing troubles that place even greater demands on already over-taxed resources (Koos, 1946; Dohrenwend and Dohrenwend, 1970; Brenner, 1973). Thus, the black urban poor can be reasonably characterized as likely to be functioning at a higher basal stress level than the norm. This means that they are physiologically and psychologically primed to perceive a wider range of stimuli as stressful and to react to them accordingly (i.e., stress primed). If this hypothesis is in fact true, then black children from poverty backgrounds begin to develop, even in utero, in chronically stressed environments. The previously reported race x SES trends in prematurity, infant mortality and birth defects may be the outcome of this state of greater vulnerability to stress and greater stress reactivity in black par-

ents. Similarly, the recently reported higher mean heart rates in low-income black neonates as compared to their white peers also supports this hypothesis (Schachter et al., 1974).

Thus, a critical antecedent in the stress dynamics of black low-income children is the higher basal stress level at which they function even before birth.

2.Mediating factors

In addition to being exposed to insidiously stressful environments, there are important internal and external factors that influence the degree to which specific stressors will impact on each black child. These factors mediate the effects of the stressors and help to account for individual differences in vulnerability to stress and risk for disease, disability and dysfunction.

External mediating factors would include the host of experiences and exigencies associated with a low-income ethnic status. Included among them are poor sanitation, crowding, inadequate nutrition and health care, unemployment, poor education, marital instability, and the general oppression of parents and of the communities. Myers (1976, 1977) also postulates the critical role that racism plays via the inconsistent and discriminatory manipulation of response options and rewards that are institutionalized in the larger social order. Behaviors that are rewarded and held in high esteem for some (e.g., assertiveness in white males), are severely punished in others (e.g., assertiveness in black males); assumptions and expectations that are made about some (e.g., basic competence for white children) are denied in others (e.g., basic incompetence for black children); behaviors that are socially devalued (i.e., passive acceptance and compliance) are the expected norm for blacks. In fact, much of the frustration, resentment and feelings of impotence and worthlessness often attributed to these children can be said to emerge from the basic conflict between the black child's natural urge and strivings for competence and mastery and the external barriers that impede and stifle these strivings. Therefore, blacks and the poor can be said to be sociopolitically trapped in a pressure cooker. The objective sources of stress are many, yet the coping options are controlled restrictively by societal forces outside of the self.

People as acting and transacting beings are continuously assessing themselves and the social context and elaborating transactional strategies to maximize personal gains. Urban black children, on the other hand, must confront and operate in a social order in which the rules appear to be stacked against them. The degree to which they perceive the odds against them as manageable or overwhelming will depend to a significant degree on the transactional competency and success of their parents, the competence of the models in their primary community of identification, their ability to overcome odds and to develop their own level of competency, and, finally, on the availability and accessibility of resources and supports to help them in their coping efforts.

A host of internal mediating factors can also be identified that contribute to the relative success or failure of black children's coping efforts. Central among these are their individual temperaments (i.e., tendency to overreact or to underreact under stress), their native abilities and developed competencies and skills (Dreger and Miller, 1968; Pettigrew, 1964; Watts, 1974; Sewell and Severson, 1975), their past experiences with successful coping efforts, whether personal or vicarious, (Lazarus, 1966, 1967, 1974, 1977), the accuracy and sophistication of their analytical skills (i.e., the ability to read situations and to determine the best course of action), and, finally, their relative perception of themselves as capable of manipulating and controlling their environments and themselves (Dohrenwend and Dohrenwend, 1970; Baron et al., 1974; Epstein and Komorita, 1970; Gurin et al., 1969; Guttentag and Klein, 1976; McAdoo, 1973, 1976).

This last factor, personal effectiveness, is perhaps the most critical of all the internal mediators. This factor subsumes jointly the variables of self-esteem and locus of control. The scientific literature has consistently reported that low-income black children are characterized by low levels of self-esteem and by external attributions of control over their successes or failures (Pettigrew, 1964; Lefcourt, 1966; McDonald and Gunther, 1965). While the validity of the interpretations of these empirical findings is still being debated, it would be naive of us to deny that low-income black children are more likely to have doubts about their ability to manipulate and control events in their lives. The fact is unarguable that there are insidious social processes that consistently remind blacks of the need to prove themselves. This is especially evident when blacks interact with and compete against whites. The mistake that many social scientists make is to evaluate this sensitivity and doubt as a personal deficiency rather than to appraise it as a by-product of accurate reality testing.

Unfortunately, despite their reality base and adaptational utility, doubts about one's power or ability reduce the effectiveness of stress coping efforts. Thus, urban black children are highly vulnerable to stress not only because of the antecedent stress conditions and the presence of mediating external stress-inducing factors, but also because of the existence of internal factors that reduce their stress-coping effectiveness. The latter are part of the legacy of oppression and racism and are still being reinforced by the social processes that continue to manufacture black incompetence (e.g., class oppression, the remediation mentality in education, the graduation of functional illiterates, etc.).

3. Social stressors

Much of the research on psychosocial stress effects on health emphasizes the importance of episodic, major social stress events that have a disruptive effect on daily functioning (Holmes and Rahe, 1967; Dohrenwend and Dohrenwend, 1970, 1974; Dohrenwend, 1973).

This literature consistently reports that individuals from low-income backgrounds experience more major stresses in their lives and these events are more disruptive for them than for their more affluent counterparts (Srole et al, 1962; Myers et al, 1974; Dohrenwend and Dohrenwend, 1970; Brown et al., 1975).

This emphasis on major stressful experiences is, however, only one small part of the stress picture. For the poor, and particularly poor black children, the fact of greatest significance should be the insidiousness and pervasiveness of stress in their everyday lives (Dohrenwend & Dohrenwend, 1970; Ilfeld, 1977). Not only are they more likely to experience many more major life-disrupting events than the white child, but these demands are added onto an already taxed system. It is this insidious pattern of accumulated stress that seems to offer a better explanation for the high incidence of health and mental health casualties that we reported earlier in this chapter.

4. Coping and adaptation process

Selye (1950, 1974) and Lazarus (1966, 1967, 1976, 1977) have consistently affirmed the fact that health outcomes are more the products of efforts to cope with stress than the direct results of the stressors themselves. This suggests, therefore, that a useful approach to the analysis of the mental health needs and problems of the black child should include an analysis of their stress-coping processes. Unfortunately, very little work has been done in this area. We do not know, for example, what coping strategies are used by urban

black children to adapt to the myriad of stresses they must face daily. Consequently, we can only speculate about the nature of these coping efforts from the casualties and from what we know about the life styles of the urban black poor.

It is apparent from what we have been discussing thus far that the coping strategies that are used by black youngsters are inadequate to meet the demands faced. It is important, however, that we not fall prey to the traditional practice of blaming the victim, but go beyond that and assess the constraints imposed on those coping efforts. We know that how one copes with stress is influenced by the nature of the stresses faced, by one's experience with similar stresses in the past (i.e., learning) and by the availability of adequate coping resources, both personal and external. If we analyze the concrete reality of urban black children we would have to recognize the seriousness of their plight. First, they are born into a reality that is itself stress-inducing (stress-primed). Second, they must develop effective coping strategies for a myriad of stressors in a context of severely restricted parental and communal resources and must face institutionalized barriers to access to societal resources (i.e., racism, discrimination, etc.). Third, there are few models of competent coping available that define appropriate standards, methods and processes of functioning that have been tested in their reality. Finally, and most importantly, the basic thrust of coping efforts is to reduce the impact of stress on the individual. In the reality context of the urban black child, that is akin to trying to hold back the oceantides. What is fundamentally absent is a personal and collective black theory and method of functioning dedicated to the transformation of the basic social processes that creates the reality of poverty and oppression in which black children must live. Illness, dysfunction and incompetence are the natural and legitimate by-products of the concrete reality of the urban black child. Adapting to it and learning to cope with its pressures can result only in survival, not mastery. The evidence suggests that black children are surviving despite great odds. However, they are not thriving. It is our assertion that thriving is neither a reasonable nor realistic outcome of the concrete reality of poverty and oppression. Oppression and poverty allow adaptation, while thriving and mastery require a more supportive and enhancing environment.

The Social Dialectic Model of Mental Health

The urban stress model accounts for differential incidence of mental illness as a function of social class and race-related differential exposure to stress and stress-coping efforts. Primary emphasis in the analysis is placed on the degree to which the individual is affected by the stress endemic to the environment as mediated by his or her personal assets and coping styles. External sociopolitical factors are important, mediating factors that influence both the amount of stress exposure as well as the relative impact of that stress on the individual. However, the stress model stops short of articulating precisely how the external context of reality predetermines the degree of susceptibility to mental disorder. Similarly, with its emphasis on coping and adaptation, the stress model does not articulate a social change strategy. Thus, as a model of mental health for the urban black child it is still not complete enough for our purposes.

Therefore, in elaborating our alternative model of mental health for the urban black child, we looked to the dialectical analyses of the mental health of colonial societies in the Caribbean and Africa as articulated by Frantz Fanon, the Martinican psychiatrist. Fanon elaborated a color x class analysis of the colonial society as the critical dynamic that defined the state of mental health of the society (Fanon,

1965a,b; 1967a,b). The mental health of colonial societies was broadly defined as the product of the dynamic between the institutionalized interests of the ruling classes and the identity defense and ego elaboration of the oppressed masses. Central to this dynamic was the systematic negative definition of the values, life styles and culture of the oppressed masses by the ruling classes and the imposition of the colonial culture, values and standards.

King (1978, 1979) applied this analysis to the mental health of urban black communities and affirmed that "the present mental health dilemma (of the urban black child) is not (simply) one of personal maladjustment, but rather of class conflict and of crisis in the historicity of society". It is indeed incomplete and misleading to account for the mental health statistics on the black child as reported earlier simply on the basis of their presumed greater inherent maladjustment (Rainwater's Medicalizing and Moralizing approaches), or greater psychological vulnerability (Rainwater's Psychopathologizing approach). Both of these explanations, which are central to the present thinking in mental health, continue to ignore the critical conflicts and contradictions in the sociopolitical situations in society that operate oppressively on the excluded members of society to create the state of vulnerability and high casualty rates which we see.

King notes further that if we accept the personal maladjustment concept as central to our analysis of the mental health of the black child, then we also implicitly assume that we live in a positive, growth-enhancing social structure to which all members of society should ideally adapt in order to function optimally. However, even a cursory analysis of the peculiar history of black Americans would suffice to belie that assumption. The historicity of the transactions of blacks and the larger American society is one characterized by exclusion from full participation, oppression, and alienation. To this blacks have developed response systems characterized by mistrust, fear, hostility and reactive rejection. This peculiar transactional process between oppressed and oppressors results, as suggested by Fanon, in the creation of a social majority of disinherited people condemned to a marginal social and psychological status. They are trapped ambivalently between self-affirmation and self-denial, between self-recrimination and self-idealization, between the idealization of the oppressing other and the vituperative condemnation of all associated with that idealized other.

On the other hand, this transaction also creates a social minority of the inherited (ruling class) deluded by their false sense of superiority, blind to the ethnocentric, self-serving value basis of their evaluations of the oppressed, and trapped in an oppressive self-perpetuating social structure.

The analysis of mental health in a class-caste society such as ours cannot, therefore, be made simply on the basis of the presence or absence of illness symptoms. Rather, it must necessarily include the analysis of the transactional processes between individuals and social classes, on the one hand, and the social structures, on the other, that create the conditions of differential mental health vulnerability as a function of social class and race. Similarly, mental health cannot simply be defined on the basis of adaptive capacity, because in societies with oppressive institutional practices, adapting to the reality of these unhealthy conditions is itself an unnatural state—a state of illness. Therefore, the concept of mental health in an oppressive reality must also include the active commitment to personal and social transformation.

Consistent with these premises, the social dialectic model of mental health defines a two-factor matrix that structurally represents the dialectic between the psychological state of the person as impacted by the external social structure, and the nature of the transaction between the person and the social structure. This dialectic evolves developmentally in the individual and historically in the society.

The first factor in the dialectic defines the internal state of harmony or disharmony in the individual as influenced by the external social structures. The person can be said to be in a state of high or low crisis to the extent that there is an internalization of external oppression. Thus, the individual who, by virtue of his or her social class or color, is in a state of struggle and disharmony and engages in self-destructive or otherwise damaging behavior can be said to be in a state of high crisis. If, on the other hand, social class and color oppression is acknowledged but successfully circumscribed such that a significant state of internal struggle does not develop and behavior is not destructive, then the person is said to be in a state of low crisis.

Similarly, the second factor in the dialectic, the nature of the transaction between the person and society, can be dichotomized consistently with the degree of developed conflict that is central to this transaction. If the individual has a heightened awareness of the fundamental structural contradictions in society and is actively engaged in a struggle to articulate and remedy these contradictions, then he or she is said to be in a state of developed conflict. If, on the other hand, there is little awareness of these structural contradictions, and little or no concern for understanding and correcting them, then he or she is said to be in a state of undeveloped conflict.

In this two-dimensional matrix, a state of mental health exists only when there is both low personal crisis (i.e. low stress) and a developed consciousness of and conflict with the contradictions in the social structure. The other three conditions resulting from the combination of these two factors represent states of mental illness: (1) low crisis and undeveloped conflict = psychosis; (2) high crisis and undeveloped conflict = anxiety, suicide, depression, substance abuse, etc; and (3) high crisis and developed conflict = violent outburst, acting-out behavior, mass revolts, etc.

We can now apply this reformulated model of mental health (stress-dialectic) to the analysis of the mental health and needs of the black child.

As depicted in Figure 3, we are conceptualizing the black child as both influenced by and influencing self and the social context of his/her reality. In turn, the social context serves as a powerful shaping force continuously acting on the black child and reacting in turn to the child. The relative weight (strength) that can be assigned to child (personal) and to context (person-society transaction) in predicting behavioral outcomes should vary considerably. However, we can make some general observations based on the stress and dialectical models of mental

health. As the thinking of the Dohrenwends, Myers, and King suggests, the factors of race and social class are critical determiners of where the primary power and strength of influence rests. For the black child, especially the urban, low-income black child, extrapersonal factors seem to have inordinate significance as mental health predictors. In fact, it can be said that a major developmental task for the black child is to develop the self-transformative and social transformative competencies necessary to alter this balance of power and influence. He/she must ultimately wrestle this power away from the primary control of those outside of the self, and to seize and control it for self. A functional definition of racism, class oppression and discrimination may be said to be that process wherein the ability to achieve

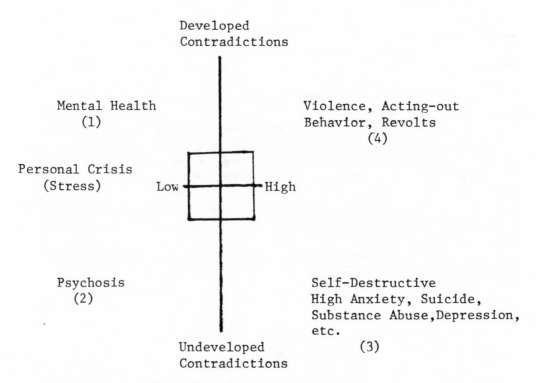

Figure 3. Dialectic matrix of mental health

this affirmation of personal power is restricted on the basis of color and social class.

Many of the "illnesses" and behavior disorders that are often reported in urban black children may be viewed as products of the intersect between the amount of stress generated by external social processes (person-context conflict) and the level of internal crisis resulting from the struggle to capture personal power and influence over self and the world. Acts of youthful acting-out (perhaps better described as ineffective and inappropriate assertiveness) and violence illustrate this line of reasoning. The young black child who "acts-out" in the classroom, home or community is in a state of high crisis within himself and conflict with his social context of reality. One of the messages that seems to be transmitted by this behavior is the child's failure to develop the behavioral attitude and repertoire necessary to influence the social order to obtain that which is needed to achieve a state of harmony. The child, therefore, vents anger and frustrations at those targets and in those situations in which this crisis state is frequently triggered.

It is not unusual for mental health professionals to receive a referral of a child who has violent outbursts in school, yet receive no such reports from his/her family, or vice versa. In many cases, of course, the dysfunctional pattern of behavior is reported across both contexts. This represents a more severe form of the crisis described. What we now have is a black child whose pattern of interaction with most of the major social demand and support systems has been such that he or she feels powerless and incompetent in all. Thus, he or she is in a perpetual state of crisis and is developing a response repertoire characterized primarily by frustrated outbursts. Radical changes in the child, in the context, and in the transactions between the two will have to occur if this pattern of destructive relating is to be resolved.

The example above is not suggesting, with naive and irresponsible simplicity, that the solution to this crisis-conflict rests simply in the context of "giving in" to the child. Rather, we are underscoring a process of transaction between that black child and the world in which the child is not allowed to gain the control over himself or to develop the skills and confidence necessary to act effectively on the world. Instead, he/she is perpetually in a state of being acted upon. As suggested by Myers (1977a), this state of manufactured social incompetence is due in part to inconsistent and discriminatory manipulation of behavioral contingencies and response options which is structurally integral to our existing social order. These discriminatory practices have become institutionalized in our major social institutions, and in the black communities and families as extensions and reactions to the larger social ideology and praxis.

We can extend our analysis of black child mental health using the dialectical crisis-conflict model by looking at the issues of black youth drug and alcohol abuse. Current literature on these issues tends to emphasize personality characteristics of the users, family structure and relationships, and life styles as primary etiological factors in these disorders. These findings are meaningful but limited because they address only the issue of crisis within the individual and family and essentially ignore the role that social structural dynamics play in the development of these disorders. We can illustrate the importance of the latter by (1) exploring and contrasting the drug preference of lower-class black youth and their middle-class white peers, and (2) discussing the social and economic factors that determine the differential availability and accessibility of drugs and alcohol in urban ghettoes.

First, the issue of pattern of drug usage. Recent evidence suggests a difference in the pattern of drug usage as a function of race and social class (Newman et al., 1974;

Single et al., 1974; Kleinman & Lukoff, 1978). By and large, low-income black youth seem to prefer downers and drugs like PCP, while their middle-income white peers seem to prefer uppers and mind expanding drugs. Why does one group seek perceptual screens while the other chooses perceptual expansion? One wants to shut out the world, while the other seeks thrills and the expansion of his/her range of experiences.

The dialectical, crisis-conflict model would suggest that the central dynamic in substance abuse is the state of high personal crisis and an undeveloped consciousness and conflict with social realities. Similarly, the black-white differences in drug usage may be due to race and class difference in the nature of the personal crisis and in the nature of conflicts between self and context. Both youngsters engage in the same generic behavior (substance abuse). However, the agent of choice is symbolically different. Both abusers seem to share the same crisis over feelings of personal competency, problems of restricted options, and limited meaningful contacts with significant adults and institutions. However, for black children and youth, the struggle seems to be related to feelings of being overwhelmed by the demands of a basic struggle for survival. Their wish seems to be to say to the world, "Get off my back and leave me be. I am tired of always being conscious and fighting everything and everybody. I just want some peace and quiet, to live pleasantly and not have a care in the world". This retreat from consciousness of the perpetual state of crisis serves as the major reinforcer of the behavior. In addition, there are the secondary gains of being "hip" and of emulating adult models who are themselves seeking escape from pressures, from oppression, from failure.

Unlike his black peer, the young middle-class white addict's choice of drugs appears to be a response to a crisis of experience. The struggle for propriety, competition and achievement striving as primary orientations makes life orchestrated, not lived. Consequently, although these youth possess many of the physical "possessions" associated with comfort and success, they nevertheless are in a crisis of personal responsibility, a struggle to achieve personal meaningfulness and growth through risks and experiences. Thus, they gravitate to the use of agents that temporarily provide those experiences. They also derive secondary gains from the opportunity to negate the validity of a sociocultural milieu which they perceive as stifling and constricting.

In summary, the essential core of the struggle for autonomy, power and responsibility for self underlies the substance abuse behavior of both black and white youth. However, the manifestation and experience of this struggle appear to be different for each. For the black substance abuser, the desire to escape demands and to avoid the conscious experience of failure poses the greatest problem for treatment. What can the therapist, drug counselor, or parent provide the youngster that can match the pleasures of escape? Teaching competent behavior as a more lasting problem-solving strategy takes time, especially when the child's history is one of frustrated problem-solving efforts. Furthermore, growth is a process of struggle in itself and struggle is exactly what is being avoided. Finally, even if the counselor can convince the youngster that drugs are dangerous weapons, and that there are better ways of coping with his/her problems, how does the counselor address the fundamental nature of the context with which the youngster has been struggling? Unfortunately, the model of mental health that underlies the current treatment of substance abuse is essentially incapable of addressing these issues. With it we can only perceive and respond to the personal and familial crisis. As such, therefore, we hold the victim as the primary culprit in his/her own victimization (Ryan, 1971). The context, although recognized as an important co-

conspirator, is functionally absolved as "untreatable" by our present methods.

The dialectic crisis-conflict model, on the other hand, demands attention to the context as a coequal partner in the social dialectic that produces mental health casualties. There is a saying that in urban ghettoes there are three things that are rarely in short supply—religion, alcohol and dope. Observational evidence validates this folk wisdom. At almost every street corner in every major urban ghetto there is a storefront church, a liquor store and the opportunity to make a score (a dope connection). This fact cannot be ignored. While alcohol and drugs are not generally manufactured in ghettoes, their supply is usually plentiful. We submit that the social structures and processes that create the feelings of despair and hopelessness in urban ghettoes (e.g., racism, discrimination and class oppression) serve to manufacture the demand for these goods and are therefore critical factors in the etiology of substance abuse. Equally important is the mercantilist social ideology of money and profits above all else which also underlies and feeds the growing problem of black youth addiction.

The question of black youth suicide is even more complex. As initially articulated by Durkheim (1951), central to suicide are the feelings of anomie, hopelessness, personal alienation and marginality. These feelings can often be traced to early problems in relationships with parents and other relatives, with the resulting feelings of being alone, of being different, and of being excluded from significant familial connections. Many suicide victims also grow up in multiproblem families (Hendin, 1971), and have few personal friends, close relatives or other resources (Allen, 1973; Marvis 1969). They often have difficulties in their adult lives in developing close interpersonal contacts and tend to experience many disappointments in their romantic relationships, and in life generally (Allen, 1973; Marvis, 1969; Hendin, 1969).

Young black women attempt suicide with greater frequency and at an earlier age than young black men. Men, however, tend to be more lethal. The pattern of life described above is one of considerable stress, instability and confusion where there are few resources and supports. The black child or youth at risk for suicide develops a pattern of isolation and has difficulty establishing intimate and meaningful connections with significant others. This pattern of limited options and resources in the face of great stress and demands creates a state of existential crisis. Questions about the meaninglessness of life and the value of continuing to exist in the face of few pleasures are often reported by these youth. Young blacks frequently use drugs in their suicide attempts, seemingly as a perceptual screen against both the concrete reality of their world and the suicidal act itself. Marvis (1969) and Breed (1970) note than many young black suicide victims often get high and then go to secluded places far away from the possibility of rescue. Perhaps this is a symbolic description of their feelings of aloneness in life and now, also, in death. The wish to reduce the possibility of rescue reflects the seriousness of the intent and of the crisis motivating it.

Both the traditional mental health formulations and the dialectical crisis-conflict models recognize the significance and depth of the personal crisis which leads to suicide among black children and youth. However, the dialectical model also emphasizes the etiological significance of the undeveloped consciousness in the victim of the fundamental social contradictions that he/she faces. The frequently reported multiproblem family origins, difficulties in communicating with parents, and absence of significant adult others among black suicide victims underscore the true seriousness of the impact of social oppression on black families and communities. These destructive processes are so pervasive as to virtually strangle these social systems to the point where they are unable to provide significant and meaningful support and buffering for their children and youth. These children, in fact, are very aware of the families' problems and their inability to successfully cope with the needs and problems of their members. In other words, the children are conscious of the inadequacies of their families and communities as well as of their own inadequacies. However, they remain unaware of the oppressive social system as the real source of their failures, frustrations, and pain. Consequently, they perceive themselves as hopeless and inadequate in the face of the demands placed on them. Neither they nor their significant others possess the necessary resources to meet these demands. Therefore, in hopeless despair, they opt to end their lives and the struggle. Black youth suicide is an indictment against chronic familial, community and societal failures to recognize and meet the basic human needs for dignity and a sense of personal competence so dramatically displayed by these children and youth. To simply respond to their individual cries (i.e., suicide gestures and attempts) without addressing the structural sources of their despair and that of their families is to treat the symptom but ignore the basic causes of the disease.

Implications and Recommendations

We have briefly reviewed the statistics which provide us with a gross index of the state of mental health of the current generation of black children and youth. We have also provided a brief critique of the current explanations that are offered in the social science and mental health literature. Finally, we have offered a reconceptualization of the mental health needs and casualties of the urban black child, placing particular attention on the critical dialectic between internal, personal processes and extrapersonal, societal processes which interact to create conditions of stress (conflict) and crisis. The intersect of conflicts between the black child and the social context of reality, on the one hand, and the internal crises that result from his/her struggle to achieve control and competency, on the other, is suggested as an etiological factor predictive of black mental health outcomes.

There are several specific recommendations that can be made from the framework of this dialectical crisis-conflict model that are pertinent to research, service, training and public policy needs.

This conceptual model argues for a dramatic shift in the thrust of mental health research on the urban black child. The questions asked, the assumptions made, the conceptualization of the hypothesized relationship between variables, and the research methodology need serious reconsideration. New research efforts need to be mounted that are founded on the assumption that the black child is an entity independent of the white child, and not an entity to be known mainly by comparison. Questions about the basic nature of the black child—his/her coping styles, pressures and demands actually faced, pattern of life span development and the crises and conflicts therein, factors that interact to predict successful mastery over the vicissitudes of life—should be central to this research effort.

Similarly, research is needed that concretely specifies the critical variables that define social class for blacks. These variables should be identified not as generalized criteria for all groups, but as specifically significant and meaningful to blacks. The extent to which these variables are, in fact, useful in defining social class for other groups should be secondary to the major research objective.

Additionally, specific studies are needed that address the issue of mental health outcomes by attempting to specify the developmental process of transaction between the urban black child and the significant context, taking into account the history of that context. An example of an effort to approach such a task is the

research by Brenner (1973) that looked at the relationship between economic downturn, social class and ethnicity in psychiatric hospitalizations. This study defined the context of economic reality and traced its historical effect on mental health. The study stopped short, however, of assessing the true incidence of emotional disorder in the population and did not address the process of demands and coping efforts that is central to the etiology of disease.

Finally, research is needed that is multidisciplinary and multifactorial. Such studies would address specific issues from several disciplinary perspectives simultaneously, each discipline specifying a variety of variables that are presumed to contribute to our understanding of the issue studied. Thus, questions about the etiology of black youth violence would be addressed by looking simultaneously at economic factors in the society, community and families, the demands and pressures faced by family members and the youngsters themselves, the availability and usefulness of resources, changes in the juvenile justice procedures and policies, changes in the attitudes and practices of police departments, merchants, school personnel and city officials, changes in the availability and quality of mental health resources in the community, changes in patterns of migration, and mobility in the community, among others. The major goal would be to determine the nature of the relationship between these factors in accounting for the mental health outcome studied.

Similarly, mental health training and services need to be reconceptualized and targeted consistently with this model. The training of mental health caregivers needs to reflect perspectives and competencies that go beyond the assessment and treatment of disorders in individuals to include the assessment and treatment of social systems and environments. This includes the revision of our current diagnostic practices and nomenclature to reflect the basic premise that individual disorders result from disordered transactions between persons and environments (Barker, 1964, 1973; Rappaport, 1977). Therefore, the diagnostic nomenclature and the treatment approaches must reflect the coequal treatment of both factors—person and environment.

Mental health services concurrently need to be reconceptualized away from the individual disease (medical) model to a social action, preventive model. The primary thrust would be to alleviate and prevent individual pain and disorder by assessing and removing the social realities that engender that pain and suffering. This proposition is not new. In fact, it forms one of the bases of the public health model—identify the significant pathogens and the environmental conditions that breed them and proceed to control and eradicate both.

Finally, the dialectical crisis-conflict model has several major implications for public policy. Foremost is the assertion that the mental health needs of urban black children are intimately tied to the basic societal structures and practices. Thus, efforts to address and correct the former require direct confrontation with the policies and practices in society that create and maintain our existing social order. Treating the individual casualty is folly if we ignore the policy and priority decisions which create the high unemployment, inadequate health care, inadequate education, poor nutrition and quality of life that have become synonymous with urban ghetto living. A radical change in the current mental health status of the urban black child will require radical changes in our economic policies, our social policies, our policies on health, education and welfare.

In this chapter, we have struggled to articulate a mental health reality of the urban black child. From our analysis of that reality, it appears that the task and challenge facing the black parent, the mental health provider, the scientist-scholar, the black child himself, and society in general are to act aggressively to transform the fundamental nature of our social structure, and to redefine the nature of the relationship between the black child and society. This massive task may appear idealistic and unachievable. However, the alternative of manipulating surface structures (e.g., headstarts, early screening, diagnosis and treatment programs, integrated schools, etc.) is a superficial, time-limited palliative that is likely to produce modest results at best. The mental health problems of the black child and of the entire black society are firmly connected to the fundamental structures and processes of a society that endorses the manufacture of black incompetence rather than fostering the creative growth and full and equal participation of all.

REFERENCES

Advance Report, Final Natality Statistics, WCHS Report (HRA) 76-1120, *24*, 11, Suppl 2, February 13, 1976, 6, 1974.

Allen, N.H. *Suicide in California 1960–1970.* Monograph, State of California, Dept. of Public Health, 1973.

Anthony, S. and Gilten, P. *The Discovery of Death in Childhood and After.* Baltimore: Penguin, 1976.

Askenasy, A. Dohrenwend, B.P., and Dohrenwend, B.S. Some effects of social class and ethnic group membership on judgements of the magnitude of stressful life events: A research note. *Journal of Health and Social Behavior,* 1977 *18,* 432–441.

Barker, R.G. *Ecological Psychology: Concepts and Methods for Studying the Environment of Human Behavior.* Stanford, CA: Stanford University Press, 1964.

Barker, R.G. and Schoggen, P. *Qualities of Community Life.* San Francisco: Jossey-Bass, 1973.

Baron, R.M. Cowan, G., Ganz, R.L., and McDonald M. Interaction of focus of control and type of performance feedback: Considerations of external validity. *Journal of Personality and Social Psychology,* 1974, *30* (2), 285–292.

Bohman, M. A comparative study of adopted children, foster children and children in their biological environment born after undesired pregnancies. *Acta. Paediat.* (Suppl.), *221,* 1, 1971.

Breed, W. The Negro and fatalistic suicide. *Pacific Sociological Review,* 1970, *13,* (3), 152–162.

Brenner, H. *Mental Illness and the Economy,* Cambridge, MA: Harvard University Press, 1973.

Bronfenbrenner, U. Socialization and social class through time and space. In: E.E. Maccoby (Ed.),

Readings in Social Psychology, 3. New York: Holt, Rinehart & Winston, 1958.

Brown, G.W., Bhrolchain, M., and Harris T. Social class and psychiatric disturbance among women in an urban population. *Sociology,* 1975, *9,* 225–254.

Bureau of the Census. *Current Population Surveys: 1974–1975.* Washington, D.C.: U.S. Dept. of Labor.

Burton, L. *Vulnerable Children.* London: Routledge & Kegan, 1968.

Cesaire, A. *Discourse on Colonialism.* New York: Monthly Review Press, 1972.

Condry, J.C. and Siman, M.A. Characteristics of peer and adult-oriented children. *Journal of Marriage and the Family.* 1974, *36,* 543–554.

Condry, J.C. and Siman, M.A., An experimental study of adult versus peer orientation. Unpublished manuscript. Ithaca, N.Y.: Cornell University, 1976.

DHEW Publication No. (ADM) 717–433, NIMH Series B, No. 12. Psychiatric Services and the Changing Institutional scene, 1950–1975. 1977. 27.

Dohrenwend, B.P. The social psychological nature of stress: A case for causal inquiry. *Journal of Abnormal and Social Psychology,* 1961.

Dohrenwend, B.P. Social status, stress, and psychological symptoms, *American Journal of Public Health,* 1967, *57,* 625–632.

Dohrenwend, B.P. and Dohrenwend, B.S. *Social Status and Psychological Disorders: A Causal Inquiry.* New York: John Wiley and Sons, 1969.

Dohrenwend, B.P. and Dohrenwend, B.S. (Eds.) *Stressful Life Events: Their Nature And Effects.* New York: J. Wiley and Sons, 1974.

Dohrenwend, B.S. Life events and stresses: A methodological inquiry. *Journal of Health and Social Behavior,* 1973, *14,* 167–175.

Dohrenwend, B.S. and Dohrenwend, B.P. Class and race as status-related sources of stress. In: S. Levine and N.A. Scotch (Eds.), *Social Stress.* Chicago: Aldine, 1970, pp. 11–140.

Dreger, R. and Miller, S. Comparative psychological studies of Negroes and Whites in the United States: 1958–1965. *Psychological Bulletin Monograph,* Supplement, 1968, *70,* (3), Part 2.

Durkheim, E. *Suicide.* New York: The Free Press, 1951.

Espstein, R. and Komorita, S.S. Self-esteem, success, failure, and locus of control in Negro children. *Developmental Psychology,* 1970, *4,* (1, part 1), 2–8.

Fairchild, H. *The Epidemiology, Treatment and Prevention of Phenocyclidine (PEP) Abuse: A Pilot Investigation.* Research Report, Central City Community Mental Health Center, 1978.

Fanon, F. *Black Skin White Masks.* New York: Grove Press, 1965a.

Fanon, F. *The Wretched of the Earth.* Preface by Jean-Paul Sartre. Translation by Constance Farrington. New York: Penguin Books, 1965b.

Fanon, F. *A Dying Colonialism.* Translation by Haakon Chevalier. New York: Grove Press, 1967a.

Fanon, F. *Towards the African Revolution.* New York: Monthly Review Press, 1967b.

Gelles, R. Preliminary results from a DHEW grant. *Child Protection Report*, Feb. 21, 1977.

Glaser, K. Masked depression in children and adolescents. *American Journal of Psychotherapy*, July 1967, *21*, (3), 565–574.

Graham, P. and Rutter M. Organic brain dysfunction and child psychiatric disorder. *Boston Medical Journal*, 1968, *3*, 695.

Graham, P. Depression in pre-pubertal children. *Develop. Med. Child Neurol.*, *16*, 340–347, 1974.

Gross, B. Parent-child development centers: Creating models for parent education. *Children Today*, 1977, *6*, 18–22.

Gurin, P., Gurin, G., Lao, R.C., and Beattie, M. Internal-external control in the motivational dynamics of Negro youth. *Journal of Social Issues*, 1969, *25* (3), 29–53.

Guttentag, M. and Klein, I. The relationships between inner vs. outer locus of control and achievement in black middle school children. *Educational and Psychological Measurement*, 1976, *36* (4), 1101–1109.

Hendin, H. Black suicide. *Archives of General Psychiatry*, 1969, *21*, (4), 407–422.

Hendin, H. *Black Suicide*. New York: Harper & Row, 1971.

Hollingshead, A.B. and Redlich, F.C. *Social Class and Mental Illness*. New York: John Wiley and Sons, 1965.

Holmes, T.H. and Rahe, R.H. The social readjustment rating scale. *Journal of Psychosomatic Research*, 1967, *11(2)*, 213–218.

Ilfeld, F. Current social stressors and symptoms of depression. *American Journal of Psychiatry*, 1977, *134* (2), 161–166.

Jensen, A.R. How much can we boost I.Q. and scholastic achievement? *Harvard Educational Review*, 1969, *39*, 1–123.

Kiev, A. and Anumonye, A. Suicidal behavior in a black ghetto, a comparative study. *International Journal of Mental Health*, 1976, *5* (2), 50–59.

King, L.M. Social and cultural influences on psychopathology. *Annual Review of Psychology*, 1978, *29*, 405–433.

King, L.M. The future of mental health research on the black population: Outline of an alternative deep structure. *Fanon Research Bulletin*, 1979.

King, L.M. and Myers, H.F. *Mental Health Research in a Black Community*. Unpublished paper, Fanon Center, 1978.

Kleinman, P.H. and Lukoff, I.F. Ethnic differences in factors related to drug use. *Journal of Health and Social Behavior*, 1978, *19*, 190–299.

Koos, E.L. *Families in Trouble*. New York: Kings Crown, 1946.

Lazarus, R.S. *Psychological Stress and the Coping Process*. New York: McGraw-Hill, 1966.

Lazarus, R.S. Cognitive and personality factors underlying threat and coping. In: M.H. Appley & R. Trumbull (Eds.), *Psychological Stress: Issues and Research*. New York: Appleton-Century-Crofts, 1967, pp. 95–117.

Lazarus, R.S. Psychological stress and coping in adaptation and illness. *International Journal of Psychiatry in Medicine*. 1974, *5* (4), 321–333.

Lazarus, R.S. Psychological stress and coping in adaptation and illness. In: Z.J. Lipowski, D.R. Lipsitt, and P.C. Whybrow (Eds.), *Psychosomatic Medicine: Current Trends and Clinical Applications*. New York: Oxford University Press, 1977, pp. 14–26.

Lefcourt, H.M. Internal vs. external control of reinforcement: A review. *Psychological Bulletin*, 1966, *65*, 205–220.

Ling, W., Oftedal, G., and Weinberg, W. Depressive illness in childhood presenting as severe headache. *Am. J. Dis. Child*, 1970, *120*, 122–124.

Lotter, V. Epidemiology of autistic conditions in young children. *Social Psychiatry*, 1966, *1*, 124.

Makita, K. The age of onset of childhood schizophrenia. *Folia Psychiat. Neurol. Japonica*, 1966, *20*, 111.

Marvis, R.W. *Social Forces in Urban Suicide*. Homewood, IL: The Dorsey Press, 1969.

McAdoo, H.P. An assessment of racial attitudes and self-concepts in urban black children. Final Report. Washington, D.C.: Children's Bureau (DHEW) 1973.

McAdoo, H.P. A re-examination of the relationship between self-concept and race attitudes of young black children. Paper presented at the Demythologizing the Inner City Black Child conference, Atlanta, Georgia, March 25, 1976.

McDonald, R.L. and Gunther, M.D. Relationship of self and ideal self-description with sex, race and class in southern adolescents. *Journal of Personality and Social Psychology*, 1965, *1* (1), 85–88.

McKinlay, J.B. A case for refocusing upstream—The political economy of illness. In: A.T. Enslow and J.B. Henderson (Eds.), *Applying Behavioral Science to Cardiovascular Risk: Proceedings of a Conference*. Seattle, Washington June 17–19, 1974. American Heart Assn., 1975.

Menchen, J. Recent trends in teenage births, birth rates and abortions. The published report of data abstracted from *Vital Statistics in U.S.*, 1961, 1968, 1969, 1970: Monthly Vital Statistics Reports, 1971, 1972, 1973; *Advance Report*, 1974. Paper presented at the NICHD Conference on Teenage Pregnancy, 1975.

Moynihan, D.P. The Negro family: The case for national action. U.S. Dept. of Labor, Office of Policy Planning and Research. Washington, D.C.: U.S. Government Printing Office, 1965.

Myers, H.F. Holistic definition and measurement of states of non-health. In: L.M. King, V. Dixon and W. Nobles (Eds.), *African Philosphy: Assumptions and Paradigms of Research on Black Persons*. Los Angeles: Fanon Center, 1976, 139–153.

Myers, H.F. Cognitive appraisal, stress coping and black health: The politics of options and contingencies. Paper presented at the Tenth Annual Convention of the Association of Black Psychologists, Los Angeles, August 1977a.

Myers, H.F. Stress and health in the black child: A conceptual and action research paradigm, Paper presented at the National Medical Association Convention, Los Angeles, August 1977b.

Myers, H.F., Harris, M., and Rana, P.E. *The Black Child in America 1927–1977: An Annotated Bibliography*. Westport, CT: Greenwood Press, 1979.

Myers, J.D., Lindenthal, J.J., and Pepper, M.P. Social class, life events and psychiatric symptoms: A longitudinal study. In: B.S. Dohrenwend and B.P. Dohrenwend (Eds.), *Stressful Life Events: Their Nature and Effects.* New York: John Wiley and Sons, 1974, pp. 191–206.

Myers, J.K., Lindenthal, J.J., and Pepper, M.P. Life events, social integration and psychiatric symptomatology. *Journal of Health and Social Behavior,* 1975, *16,* 421–429.

National Academy of Sciences. *Toward a National Policy for Children and Families.* Washington, D.C.: Author, 1976.

Newman, R.G., Cates, M., Tytun, A., and Werbell, B. Narcotic addiction in New York City: Trends from 1968 to mid-1973. *American Journal of Drug and Alcohol Abuse* 1974, *1,* 53–66.

Pettigrew, T.F. *A Profile of the Negro American.* Princeton, NJ: Von Nostrand, 1964.

Powell, G.J. *Black Monday's Children: A Study of the Effects of School Desegreation on Self-Concepts of Southern Children.* New York: Appleton-Century-Crofts, 1973.

Rainwater, L. Neutralizing the disinherited. Some Psychological Aspects of Understanding the Poor. In: V.L. Allen (Ed.), *Psychological Factors in Poverty.* Chicago: Institute for Research on Poverty Monograph Series, Markham Publishing, 1970, pp. 9–28.

Rappaport, J. *Community Psychology: Values, Research and Action.* New York: Holt, Rinehart and Winston, 1977.

Rutter, M. Why are London children so disturbed? *Proc. Roc. Soc. Med.,* 1973, *66,* 1221.

Ryan, W. *Blaming The Victim.* New York: Pantheon, 1971.

Schachter, J., Ken, J.L. Winberly, F.C., and Lachin, J.M. Heart rate levels of black and white newborns. *Psychosomatic Medicine,* 1974, *36* (6), 513–524.

Schaffer, D. Suicide in childhood and early adolescence. *Journal Psychology and Psychiatry,* 1974, *15* 275.

Seiden, R.H. We're driving young blacks to suicide. *Psychology Today,* August 1970, 24–28.

Seiden, R.H. Why are suicides of young blacks increasing? *HSMHA, Health Reports* 1972 *87* (1), 3–8.

Selye, H. *The Psychology and Pathology of Exposure to Stress.* Montreal: Acta, 1950.

Seyle, H. *Stress Without Distress.* New York: J.B. Lippincott, 1974.

Sewell, T.E. and Severson, R.A. Intelligence and achievement in first grade black children. *Journal of Consulting and Clinical Psychology,* 1975, *43* (1), 112.

Shiloh, A. and Selavan, I.C. (Eds.), *Ethnic Groups in America: Their Morbidity, Mortality and Behavior Disorders, Vol. II: The Blacks,* Springfield, IL: Charles C. Thomas, 1974, p. 233.

Siman, M.A. Peer group influence during adolescence: A study of naturally existing friendship groups. Doctoral dissertation. Ithaca, N.Y.: Cornell University, 1973.

Single, E., Kandel, D.E., and Fauat, R. Patterns of multiple drug use in high school. *Journal of Health and Social Behavior,* 1974, *15,* 344–357.

Srole, L., Langer, T., Michael, S.T., Oplu, M.K., and Rennie, T.A.C. *Mental Health in the Metropolis.* New York: McGraw-Hill, 1962.

Thomas, A. and Sillen, S. *Racism and Psychiatry,* New York: Brunner/Mazel, 1972.

Warfield, J.L. Black people and suicide: A review from a black perspective. *Journal of Black Health Perspectives,* August-September 1974, 11–28.

Watts, G. New Evidence in the argument about race and intelligence: How about it, Jensen? *World Medicine,* 1974, *9* (13), 77.

Wilson, J. Investigation of degenerative disease of the Central Nervous System. *Arch. Dis. Childhood,* 1972, *47,* 163.

Zola, I.K. Helping does it matter: The problems and prospects of mutual aid groups. Paper presented at the United Ostomy Assn. Conference, 1970.

CHAPTER 18

Clinical Issues and Techniques in Working with Hispanic Children and Their Families

Frank J. Trankina, Ph.D.

The need to understand the mental health issues of the Hispanic* child and those of his or her family continues to take on increasing importance and even urgency. This is true from a humanistic and psychiatric, as well as a social and economic point of view. The matter also comes to reflect standings on issues central to the cultural, social, and political bases of the country. The Hispanic people, particularly the Mexican people, have been part of the history of the United States since its beginning. Consequently, the concern of the present day reflects not so only an awareness of the number of

persons of Hispanic descent living in the country, but also on emergent awareness of the cultural bases of our history and the human rights and conditions of minority groups, considerably fostered by the Civil Rights movement of 1964.

The population of Hispanics in this country numbers more than nine million. The concentration of Hispanic families occurs particularly in the five southwestern states of California, Arizona, New Mexico, Texas and Colorado. Pupils of Spanish-speaking families comprise 35% of the school population in Hartford, Connecticut, 52% of the school population in San Antonio, and 45% of the school population in Los Angeles (Ylvisaker, 1980). Almost 75% of the children in Headstart Centers in Los Angeles are Hispanic, many being only Spanish-speaking. The majority of the children entering kindergarten in the public schools of Los Angeles

---

*This chapter is written primarily from the point of view of the Mexican-American child and family; however, the same issues would apply to various other Hispanic and Latino groups in varying degrees. Therefore, the terms are used interchangeably throughout.

will be of Hispanic descent in the coming years.

If we combine the above information with other data, such as the findings from the Joint Commission on the Mental Health of Children, which was submitted to Congress in 1969 and is still relevant to the present, the significance of mental health issues for Hispanic children becomes even more urgent. Some of the major findings (Joint Commission, 1973a, 1973b), accumulated from masses of data were:

1) that the prenatal period and the first three years of life are the most critical to a child's development;
2) in terms of service, these years are the most neglected;
3) poverty is the single most important cause of physical and mental illness;
4) a developmental preventive approach is the most effective in the long run; and
5) racism is a major mental health problem (Berlin, 1975; Lourie, 1975).

To this data we can include the fact that the American Orthopsychiatric Association recently concluded in a special report that 25%-30% of all children entering first grade are identified as having behavioral and emotional problems (Bower, 1978). Further, the preponderance of this group comes from the poor and minority groups (American Orthopsychiatric Association, 1978). In a seven-volume comprehensive, nationwide study and assessment of child mental health needs and programs, prepared for the United States Department of Health, Education and Welfare, Sowder (1975) concluded that:

1) in urban and city areas 3.5% of children are severely disturbed and 22% are less-severely disturbed;
2) in rural areas 2.3% of children are severely disturbed and 12.2% are less-severely disturbed; and
3) in suburban/mixed areas 2.7% children

are severely disturbed and 16.8% are less-severely disturbed.

CHILDREN AT RISK

Factors placing children at risk for the development of mental health problems can generally be grouped into three clusters. These would be health variables, family-social variables, and educational variables. Latino children are at risk in all three of these areas. Health data suggests that the majority of the poor are from ethnic minorities, and poverty is concomitant with poor nutrition and lack of prenatal and pediatric care. Family disruption is suggested by a high incidence of unemployment, substandard housing, alcoholism and drug abuse, overrepresentation in juvenile and adult court statistics (Morales, 1967, 1976). With regards to school, Mexican-American children have the highest dropout rate of all groups in the southwestern United States after the sixth grade; 60% of Mexican-American children entering the first grade will graduate, as compared with 90% of their Anglo counterparts (Carter, 1974).

All of the factors placing the Hispanic child at risk may produce the devastating effects of dehumanization and alienation. Alienation can be viewed as a concept for integrating social and psychological processes in understanding the development of mental health problems, particularly for minority groups. Srole (1956) operationalized five elements characteristic of alienation, which seem particularly useful for understanding the development of alienation so often characteristic of the minority child. These include:

1) the individual's sense that community leaders are indifferent and detached from his or her needs and concerns;
2) a perception of the social order as unpredictable and without order, creating an impossibility for achieving one's

goals and desires;

3) the view that one's role and position in life are actually deteriorating rather than improving;

4) a sense of meaninglessness with loss and confusion about one's internal values and norms; and

5) a feeling of not knowing whom one can trust, with a concomitant loss of predictable and supportive immediate personal relationships.

Seeman (1959), in his classic paper, similarly characterized alienation by the five elements of powerlessness, meaninglessness, normlessness, isolatedness, and self-estrangement.

HISPANIC CHILD AND THE SCHOOL

The Hispanic child's experience with alienation often begins quite early within the educational setting. The school is probably the second most significant agent, after the family, in the formation of a child's personality (Sullivan, 1953). There is a close connection between a child's mental health and his or her experiences in the school. Moreover, the school is in the powerful position of being able to provide corrective emotional formative experiences (Sullivan, 1953).

When Hispanic children enter school, they may be faced from the start with many of the factors that breed apathy. This is fostered by the children not finding reward within the school, which often becomes a negative, punishing experience. The children may be treated less favorably than their Anglo counterparts, experience isolation, and cultural and language exclusion. Schools in minority areas usually have inadequately financed programs. All of this results in a 40% dropout rate for Hispanic children before graduation (Nava, 1970; Ramirez et al., 1971).

Further, Hispanic children are often faced at school with an Anglo middle-class value structure which may be different from what has been taught and fostered at home. In a sense, the children may be forced to reject their own heritage in order to succeed. While all children usually have some difficulty in the adaptation process of beginning school, Mexican-American children have many more problems. Some of these include the following (Carter, 1974):

1) *Underachievement*—Mexican-American children can expect to achieve significantly below national norms in reading, probably the most crucial learning skill; further, while Mexican-American children start school close to Anglos in measured achievement in all areas, they will fall behind Anglo children at each grade level (Coleman, 1966);

2) *Cultural Exclusion*—schools may rely upon a cultural deprivation theory to explain the low social status of minority groups; the children may be seen as a product of a rural folk culture, and failure is assumed to be with the socialization provided by the home and culture; the children may be seen as "dirty" and "passive"; bilingualism may be viewed as a detriment, though research is showing the opposite (Padilla and Liebman, 1975); the children may be viewed stereotypically as "lazy" and satisfied with a subordinate role.

3) *Cultural Marginality*—faced with a social system that is often unaware of the strengths and beauties of the cultural differences, and not being able to articulate or understand what is happening, the children will experience rejection and confusion and begin to not know to which culture they belong or want to belong (Fabrega, 1968); it is not uncommon to observe a classroom in the Los Angeles area, for example, as early as at the preschool level consisting almost entirely of a Spanish-speaking child population and yet be staffed with teachers who speak only English; the older Hispanic child may turn to and use the peer group to help buffer this type of conflict; these groups serve an important psychological func-

tion, but may be viewed as a threat to the stability and safety of the school by school personnel and administrators.

4) *Discrimination*—this may take the form of grade retention, ability grouping, placement in educable mentally retarded classes, and use of culturally biased psychological and educational tests; further, teachers might typically praise and encourage Anglo children considerably more frequently than Mexican-American children in the classroom.

5) *Impersonality and Rigidity for the Minority Child*—impersonality has been found to increase as the child progresses through the school system; moreover, it has been found that the most rigidly run schools occur in the *barrios* and have the most inadequately equipped facilities (Carter, 1974); this is probably the opposite from what should be the case if the system were culturally sensitive; for example, Mexican-American children may be operating from the premise that they should not speak out in class unless called upon, resulting in the pattern of consistently being excluded from the give and take of the classroom environment unless a sensitive teacher invites the children's contribution.

UTILIZATION OF MENTAL HEALTH SERVICES

If we can make a case for the fact that the Hispanic child is at risk for the development of mental health and social problems, we are faced with somewhat of a paradox. This is the dilemma that the Hispanic family underutilizes mental health services. Moreover, it has been estimated, based on careful analysis (Sowder, 1975), that mental health centers are seeing only one out of 14 disturbed children. This would mean that the school systems are dealing with all of these children, usually without the help and backup of mental health professionals. And, if we can make a case for the fact that many

institutions of the society, including the schools, are not sensitive and aware of cultural differences, the utilization issues become further complicated and confusing. In a sense, the mental health institutions are shaped by the same forces as any other institution. Writers and commentators have addressed the underutilization issue fairly extensively in the past decade (Karno, 1966; Philippus, 1971; Padilla et al. 1975). Essentially, concern is with the fact that Latinos, including children, are significantly underrepresented in mental health facilities in proportion to the percentage of the population they represent. This was particularly apparent in utilization studies of the 1950s (Jaco, 1959) and the 1960s (Karno and Edgerton, 1969). However, an interesting development occurred in the 1970s. During this decade, there was an overall increase in the number of utilization studies for ethnic groups; in addition, a number of studies indicated that Mexican-Americans were utilizing mental health services in numbers that were proportionate to their population in their respective communities (Lopez, 1979). While this matter lends itself to various tenable interpretations, it may be due to the fact the many centers have successfully embarked upon an approach of cultural sensitivity.

Explanations for the underutilization of mental health services by Hispanic families have taken various lines of thought. Some have argued that Hispanic families have less need for services because they, in fact, experience fewer emotional problems. Epidemiological and "at risk" issues do not lend support to this contention (Hollingshead and Redlich, 1958; Bloom, 1975). Some have maintained that Latinos have less emotional disorder and this is due to certain cultural patterns. This includes the view that the family and extended family network offer sufficient support and assistance when a member is experiencing difficulty. Thus, in the long run, the family members protect one another from the development of serious emotional disorder (Jaco, 1960).

Still other views include the findings that the Hispanic family will turn to outside sources for help, but these sources may not typically include mental health facilities. Rather, the Mexican-American might typically turn to the family doctor or priest/minister, if not a relative (Padilla, Carlos and Keefe, 1976). Some explanations have proposed a high reliance upon folk medicine and faith healings (Creson, McKinley and Evans, 1969; Kiev, 1968; Torrey, 1972). This approach is usually collectively referred to as *curanderismo* and a *curandero* is a type of "faith healer" or "witch doctor" who often uses various combinations of herbs and prayers to evoke a "cure." Many case studies have been published illustrating this approach; however, it appears to be the case that *curanderos* are consulted primarily among persons in the lower socioeconomic groups and among first generation immigrants (Keefe, 1979).

A further line of thinking regarding the utilization issue and the one primarily accepted among minority mental health practitioners and those working with minority groups is that the Hispanic family chooses not to use or is simply not able to use the available mental health services as they presently exist. This view would maintain that there is no viable reason for mental health problems to occur less frequently among Latinos than for the population as a whole. It would further state that Hispanic families have at least as much need for mental health services as persons of any other group. Moreover, it could be maintained that Hispanic children and their families are really at risk for the development of mental health problems and that these children and families may well have need for services in a proportion that is greater than that of the population as a whole (Green, Trankina and Chavez, 1976). Van Oss Marin et al. (1980) have presented strong evidence that lack of utilization of medical services by Mexican-Americans is significantly due to lack of money to pay for services, and the same may be the case for the use of mental health services.

An additional issue to consider is that even when Mexican-Americans are referred for mental health care, the services received may be inferior to those received by the Anglo population. For example, surveys have shown that Mexican-American patients were less likely to be referred for psychotherapy and, when referred, received services for a shorter period of time (Karno, 1966; Lorion, 1973; Yamamoto, James and Palley, 1968).

CULTURAL PLURALISM

There are two general and dominant views or models operating today regarding cultural diversity in the United States. One model is the *melting pot*. This view assumes that various immigrant groups coming together in the United States should shed their distinctive identities and become merged into a great American amalgamation. This model is widely accepted consciously or unconsciously by many major institutions of the society. This view rests on anglicization for its ideology and assumes the superiority of the English language and culture and its perpetuation through an anglocentric public education, producing a monocultural, English-speaking child (Mercer, 1977).

An alternative model is pluralistic or diverse. This model assumes that each of the various ethnic groups in the United States should maintain its own cultural autonomy. The supporting ideology is that of cultural democracy and assumes that all languages and cultures have equal value, that both English and other languages should be taught, with the goal of a multicultural, multilingual child (Mercer, 1977).

A crucial element, however, that might be added to the pluralistic model, or even result in a third model, is that of optional membership such that an individual can choose to move about and identify with either group, and, consequently, no one from inside or outside either group should have the right to force either identity upon any individual.

An additional consideration here is that behavior patterns and world views are transmitted from generation to generation. This may occur through imitation of parents, passing on of cultural or subcultural norms and values, or through the functioning of the family structure, and the reward patterns within its structure. This all occurs whether or not one bothers to think self-consciously about one's own ethnicity.

WORLD VIEW DIFFERENCES

What then are the cultural differences between the Hispanic and Anglo worlds? This question is approached from the point of view of understanding the differences for their implications for clinical practice, while excluding negative stereotypes.

The Mexican-American child is indeed a product of two cultures. Awareness of the differences and similarities will help the therapist or practitioner function effectively. A consideration of historical world view differences can serve as a useful introduction. The cultural and historical heritage of Hispanic-Americans is rich and strong; they are descendents of an advanced Indian culture, as well as of a historically powerful and strong Spanish culture. In a sense, the Mexican-American may be thought of as tricultural. Beginning with the Indian roots, Castaneda (1977) views the average Mexican-American in the United States as caught in the middle of a perennial struggle between values of traditionalism and values of modernism. As used, neither of the terms is thought of as more positive than the other, but simply as different. The

most important characteristics of traditionalism include:

1) a sacred sense of life;
2) a sense of community where the benefit of others is of utmost importance and identity is linked with the group; and
3) a sense of hierarchy, based on age, sex roles, and status.

The most salient characteristics of modernism, critical to democratic philosophy and brought to high levels of formulation in the United States Constitution, include:

1) rational science;
2) individualism; and
3) egalitarianism.

The traditional world view, further, may include emphasis on harmony, communality, interdependence, cooperation, and obedience; humanity is in a sacred relation to nature. On the other hand, the modernist view may emphasize stimulation, individuality, independence, competition, and power; humanity is seen in a conquering relation to nature. It is these two world views that the Mexican-American child may have to reconcile; acculturation difficulties and identity problems for him or her occur above and beyond the stresses that everyone must deal with in day-to-day living. Moreover, psychology, psychiatry, and mental health workers in general have evolved in a modernistic fashion; while a typical therapist might respond to a severe marital problem by helping the couple to get divorced, the priest may well help the couple to remain married (Castaneda, 1977).

HISTORICAL PERSPECTIVES AND
SELF-IDENTITY

World view differences have a long history. For example, the culture and society of the early Indians were based on nature religions. While the Indians felt themselves a part of nature, the conquering Spaniards viewed nature as an obstacle and barrier getting in the way of the conquest. This was most difficult for the Indians to understand. The Indian view was rather powerfully expressed in the following anonymous writing:

They [the Spaniards] taught us fear and withered the flowers. In order that their flower might live, they hurt and consumed the flower of others. There was no Higher Knowledge, no Sacred Language, no Divine Teaching in the substitutes for Gods which came here. Castrate the Sun! That is what the foreigners came to do here (Bolio, 1941).

The great structure, control, and power of the Spanish empire lasted from the time of the conquest in the fifteenth and sixteenth centuries to the eighteenth century when the New World empire began to fall. The economy was changing from mining to agriculture, wealth increased, and a "New World" self-identity was emerging. Uprisings and rebellions occurred throughout South America and Mexico. At the same time the Catholic religion of the missionaries was merging continuously with Indian beliefs. Though the revolutions were beginning, the Spanish stamp was to be left on the language, literature, family, and society.

The wars, struggles and movements for independence lasted from 1810 to 1825, beginning in Mexico, Venezuela, and Argentina (Franco, 1969). This occurred at a time when Napoleon was invading Spain. Independence for many countries did not occur until the mid 1820s. Fifteen years of bloodshed left its impact on the people. Yet, many of the new governments were authoritarian and oppressive. In addition, Mexico was conquered by the French. Later, Mexico was on a collision course also with the United States and its conquest of Mexico's northern territories (Wolf, 1959).

Some writers have maintained that the many drastic upheavals that have been the plight of Middle America have left their effects on the national and social identity and personality development (McWilliams, 1968). Some have spoken of the extreme difficulty of establishing a historic sense of self, resulting in a spiritual sense of defeatism (Paz, 1961). The Hispanic child is a product of a long history of oppression, complicating his or her identity within Anglo society.

ACCULTURATION

In describing and talking about the Hispanic-American person, child or family living in the United States, one must realize that cultural differences cover a wide range (Miranda and Castro, 1977). One individual may differ considerably from another within the same subculture as well as differ from members of the dominant culture. Latinos in the United States also comprise many different generations; a second, third, or fourth generation Latino may function quite similarly to his or her Anglo counterpart generally, yet function differently when visiting his or her parents and grandparents.

A number of writers and researchers have attempted to tap the acculturation variable. Miranda and Castro (1977) found that Mexican-American women remaining in therapy for at least five sessions demonstrated higher levels of psychological and behavioral acculturation, as compared with women who dropped out of treatment. Some researchers have focused on sociocultural variables, such as occupation of head of household, being raised in urban or rural environment, and number of family members, to determine the degree of similarity to the dominant culture (Mercer, 1976). Other investigators have focused on semantic variables and studied the affective meanings attached to certain key words and concepts such as "mother," "father," "male," and "female"

(Olmedo et al., 1978). In general, these studies have demonstrated that Hispanics vary considerably among themselves in cultural characteristics and differences.

The clinical implication of these studies is that acculturation levels and differences must be taken into consideration in working with a particular family or child. Castro and Gonzalez (in press), for example, have proposed that a therapist might rate himself or herself on key variables, such as English or Spanish language dominance, education, and occupation. Other factors that might be considered are nationality, traditional versus modernistic family orientation, Catholic versus Protestant religion, and degree of urbanization. The therapist might then rate the Hispanic family with whom he or she is working on the same dimensions. The greater the differences between the two ratings, the more the therapist would need to think in terms of disparity between himself or herself and the client.

The acculturation issue takes on an added dimension in work with children. The child is, of course, first socialized within the family. However, the school plays a significant role in this process also. Consequently, the child and the parents may be at different degrees of acculturation. A bright teenager or college student may be counseled similarly as would an Anglo in regards to a peer relationship problem. However, the approach taken to a family problem may be considerably different than what would occur with an Anglo teenager and his or her parents. The therapeutic intervention with the Latino children and families must assess the level of acculturation of all members of the system, and how any changes in one part of the system could affect other parts of the system.

The developing child may, as a result, experience considerable difficulty in developing a positive self-identity. Spanish-speaking preschool children in a classroom with only English-speaking children have been observed by the author to go off by themselves, often in small groups, and interact only among themselves, with little or no interaction, verbal or nonverbal, between themselves and the teachers. This conflict may become particularly painful in adolescent years. The teenager may become rebellious or may develop exaggerated "in group" behavior and attitudes. Recently, a teenage client needed to choose between a new outpatient bilingual therapist or continue with his Anglo therapist whom he'd known for six months in an inpatient unit. In a rather interesting manner, the adolescent said he would prefer the new therapist; his stated reason was "he speaks English, I speak English; he speaks Spanish, I speak Spanish." This person may have been in the process of developing a nonconflictual, flexible, bicultural identity, hopefully incorporating the best of two worlds.

Mercer (1976) has attempted to take the acculturation issue into account in the area of intelligence testing, resulting in the development of the SOMPA—System of Multicultural Pluralistic Assessment. This is a system of testing which attempts to take into account the linguistic and sociocultural functioning of the child. The approach also attempts to be socially and culturally nondiscriminating. In addition to use of formal IQ tests, this system assesses the child's social role functioning and adaptive behavior in general and outside the school setting. Measures of psychomotor functioning and medical history are included, as well as an assessment of the family's socioeconomic status on several variables.

Consideration of all the factors results in an adjusted IQ score, usually raising the score for Hispanic and Black children. This adjusted score is used to estimate actual learning potential. The estimated learning potential is the most controversial aspect of the SOMPA in that it assumes that the tests are ethnically and culturally biased in favor of a white, Anglo, English-speaking, middle-class child. The adjusted IQ, then, attempts to take biasing variables into consideration, thereby raising the score and hopefully resulting in a true measure of actual learning potential. This amounts to having separate norms for different ethnic groups. SOMPA is becoming increasingly used as it is in accord with the spirit of the recent legal and legislative history in the area of psychological testing. Study and development of SOMPA II is currently underway and will attempt to determine if the separate norms for the different ethnic groups are, in fact, predictive of level of functioning (Figueroa et al., 1980).

THERAPEUTIC EXPECTATIONS

Psychotherapy research has generally shown that there is a greater likelihood of success and greater probability of preventing premature termination of treatment when there is a mutuality of expectations between client and therapist. Before a Latino family seeks mental health services, the family is likely to go through several phases. The most important of these, suggested by Burruel (1975), is that the family members might first attempt to handle the matter themselves. The various phases of recognizing an emotional problem might include:

1) noticing unusual behavior;
2) attempting to understand the problem;
3) handling the problem within the family; and
4) taking some direct or indirect action—taking action might include anything from seeking mental health services, to consulting a priest, to searching out a *curandero*.

The Mexican-American family may then come for mental health services with some clearly defined expectations. Chavez (1975) found that families may often have, by this time, three primary types of expectations. These include:

1) receiving *consejos* (counsel) in which mutual sharing and discussion occur between client and therapist, leading to problem definition and eventual resolution;
2) receiving *dirreción* (advice, direction) in which the client expects to receive some direct advice and suggestions for the problem; and,
3) relief from *los nervios* (nerves) in which help is expected for relieving anxiety and depressive symptoms or psychophysiological symptoms.

Clients expecting *consejos* or relief from *los nervios* were found to be most likely to remain in treatment; those expecting *dirección* were least likely to continue.

Chavez (1975) also found that those Mexican-American clients who perceived themselves as active were most likely to continue treatment, in contrast to those who were reluctant to reveal themselves. Moreover, those clients who perceived the therapist as a person to help them "sort things out" and understand their feelings in a personal and warm manner were also most likely to continue treatment, in contrast to those who expected a "faith" or "omnipotent parent" role in their therapist.

Various views have been expressed regarding the Mexican-American's willingness to talk about personal matters once in treatment. Some have felt that open discussion of feelings outside the family is discouraged (Heiman, Burruel, and Chavez, 1975). Others have maintained the opposite, viewing the Hispanic person as turning to the outside for help with problems (Grebler et al., 1970). In one of very few empirical studies of the matter, it was found that both Mexican-Americans and Anglo-Americans were considerably willing to disclose to therapists. This pattern held across occupational levels and for males and females. The Mexican-American group though, was lower than the Anglo-American group in overall self-disclosure tendency (Acosta & Sheehan, 1976). The matter becomes confounded when acculturation is taken into consideration as a moderating variable. For example, Edgerton & Karno (1976) reported that many Mexican-Americans perceive mental illness similarly to Anglo-Americans; however, the more likely an individual is to speak primarily Spanish (is therefore less acculturated), the more likely he or she is to maintain a traditional viewpoint.

CULTURAL SENSITIVITY AND THERAPEUTIC IMPLICATIONS— PROGRAM VARIABLES

If a clinical service is to be viable and relevant to a particular ethnic group, the service must examine itself as to whether it is meeting the needs of the group to be served. In the past several decades, a number of variables have been identified and discussed as particularly relevant to providing services to Hispanics. After the initial identification of these variables, the decade of the 70's saw a number of mental health centers giving particular emphasis to them in setting up services. Some of these centers were successfully used by Latino families, suggesting that the overall effect of attending to these variables was beneficial and resulted in higher utilization rates.

These variables can be grouped into two general clusters—program variables and cultural variables. Program variables refer to the general structure, form, and visibility of services. Cultural variables refer to interpersonal awareness of potential differences in behavior, attitudes, and values between different groups. The program variables are summarized in Table 1.

Center Characteristics

The program variables can themselves be grouped into several categories, including center characteristics, staff characteristics, and client knowledges. Center characteristics of importance are physical location, degree of formality, and amount of "red tape." Mental health facilities are often located in the "better" parts of town and in middle-class neighborhoods of larger cities. The services can therefore appear foreign, unfriendly, and "really not for us." Centers that have been located within the *barrio* have been having greater success in reaching the people. Padilla (1975), in describing different types of service delivery modes, reviewed characteristics of a *barrio service center model*. These particularly include location in the area to be served and deliberate active efforts to attract clients from the catchment area.

TABLE 1

Program Variables of Importance for Hispanic Mental Health Services

Center Characteristics	Staff Characteristics	Client Knowledge
Location	Bilingualism	Knowledge of services
Degree of formality	Biculturalism	Overcoming *verguenza*
Amount of "red tape"	Training and development	Language preference
Translation of forms	*Personalismo*	Freedom from fear of legal
Waiting Periods		threat
Baby-sitting facilities		Community involvement
Hours of service		
Continuity of services		
Appropriate publicity		

Some centers have utilized "satellite" clinics to serve these areas, as well as the media, such as radio.

The degree of formality may be another variable influencing service delivery. Many Latino families will feel considerably more comfortable in an atmosphere (*ambiente*) of personalism. This might be fostered by warmly decorated waiting areas. Some therapists have made coffee available. The amount of "red tape" and paperwork is often another barrier. Poor people, in general, are often not acculturated to the massive amount of paperwork characteristic of middle-class Anglo society. This matter is further complicated for Hispanic families because there may be a family member, relative, or friend who is an illegal alien. The more forms and the more often a name appears on an official form, the greater the concern of possibility of detection. In many centers and institutions, forms have not been translated; this is particularly problematic with medical information forms which are often required for services to children. It is also helpful to have all directional and information signs in the center, hospital, or institution in both English and Spanish.

An additional barrier to services are waiting periods. A Hispanic family may think of seeking mental health care as somewhat similar to medical care. The family may then expect a relatively expedient appointment, as well as recommendation for some prescriptive course of action. This need could be met by utilizing some type of specialized intake department that could screen all cases, determine priorities, provide crisis intervention services, and be available to the family during an interim period if there is to be a wait.

Other center characteristics that could facilitate use of services include provision of baby-sitting facilities, perhaps through volunteers, since many families cannot afford a baby-sitter. Also, flexible hours of service, including evenings, are particularly important if the father is to be involved and if he were to lose money if taking off time from work. Continuity of services might help maintain the therapeutic relationship as there occurs greater risk of losing a family with each transfer or additional agent involved; lack of continuity disrupts the development of the personal relationship and increases formality.

In general, in considering center characteristics, the Latino family may not be familiar with nor feel comfortable with a bureaucratic type of agency. Moreover, the family may already be beginning the process with a considerable amount of fear and mistrust. A great deal of initial personal questioning may further reduce self-esteem and arouse feelings of vulnerability. It probably would have taken a great deal of effort and difficulty for the family to make the first contact; consequently, the first contact may determine whether the family will continue and set the whole stage for what is to follow.

Staff Characteristics

Staff variables, also summarized in Table 1, which lend themselves to utilization of services include bilingualism, biculturalism and appropriate and relevant training and development for all staff. The language barrier can, in fact, be critical. Marcos et al., (1973a), for example, found that Spanish-speaking schizophrenic patients interviewed in English were judged by experienced raters as significantly more pathological than when interviewed in Spanish. In a further development and refinement of this same issue, an attempt was made to study specific behaviors in the two types of interview situations. It was found that, when interviewed in English, the primarily Spanish-speaking patients presented more content indicative of pathology, more frequent misunderstandings of the interviewer occurred, as well as briefer responses, and higher frequency of speech disturbances characteristic of anxiety (Marcos et al., 1973b). All of these factors may lend themselves to a greater likelihood of being interpreted as reflecting increased pathology. In addition to language, similarity of cultural background may facilitate the relationship (Bloombaum et al., 1968). Further, it would seem critical to provide inservice training and development for all staff working with ethnic minorities. For example, a primarily English-speaking therapist may be able to provide culturally sensitive treatment in working with a bilingual Latino if the therapist is sufficiently familiar with the cultural factors and differences.

Personalismo (personalism) is a particularly important therapist variable for working with Latino families. This variable is similar to the concept of empathy, but it implies something more. It includes an attitude of warmth and equality between therapist and client. The therapist might, for example, be willing to talk about his or her own place of birth and background as part of the therapeutic inquiry into the client's background. It further includes a willingness to be outgoing and friendly at times. It implies an attitude of respect and an underlying awareness of the strengths and beauties of the Hispanic history and culture. Also, it is considerably important to act politely and tactfully at all times, no matter what the content or purpose of a particular communication. Therapeutic topics may often need to be approached slowly and cautiously. Confrontations should be avoided. Interpretations should be discussed carefully and clearly. Even if a therapist were to make a therapeutic or cultural blunder, an overriding attitude of *personalismo* would probably consolidate a strong, positive relationship and keep the relationship from deteriorating. Chavez (1975) has also maintained that a constructive attitude of *personalismo* on the part of the therapist may prevent a premature dropout rate for the Mexican-American.

More frequent use of touching than what usually occurs in Anglo society is characteristic for many Latinos. Handshakes are used more frequently; it may be advantageous for the child therapist to put his or her arm on the child's shoulder after or before a session; and it is considerably more acceptable for males to use such gestures with other males as signals of acceptance or gratitude. A final aspect of *personalismo* is the communication of a sense of caring, an attitude that the therapist sincerely cares for the welfare of the family, whether it be a matter of an emotional-social problem or concern about housing or an unemployment problem.

Client Knowledge

A third group of program-related variables include characteristics that reside more in the knowledge and behavioral repertoires of the clients. Because many Latino families have limited knowledge about mental health services, it would seem that the providers should assume some responsibility for adequately informing clients of the existence and type of services that are available. Such attempts can be linked to already existing agencies, and information can be provided through the schools, medical facilities, and churches.

Adequate and correct information is crucial for the Hispanic family, which may experience considerable *verguenza* (shame, embarrassment) when faced with a mental health problem. The first reaction of family members and parents may be to blame themselves for causing or not having done everything possible to have prevented the problem. This could even occur in situations of developmental delay with the mother searching for the things she could have done wrong during pregnancy. Besides helping the parents with this unrealistic sense of guilt, it is incumbent upon the therapist to help the family to do everything within their capability in the present to provide the best for the child. Some authors have maintained that *verguenza* stems from a sense of pride. While this may partly be the case, it could also stem from a lack of appropriate information, leading family members to blame themselves, since family members are supposed to care for each other.

If services are to be provided in Spanish, families should have this knowledge and all brochures and service descriptions should be in the two languages. Even if a particular family speaks English well, members should know of the availability of bilingual staff and be able to make a choice, since the bilingual individual may be able to express some difficult emotional issues better in Spanish, or feel more comfortable in doing so. This choice should be available to children and teenagers, as well as adults. The family should further feel comfortable in knowing that it is not the business of the mental health agency to search for unnaturalized immigrants.

And, finally, it would seem that the ideal state of affairs would be a service that has direct input from the consumer and receiver of services about the relevancy and adequacy of services. When community members feel that they are part of the service, they will achieve some sense of power and control in shaping its destiny. Community members then become part of the problem-solving process.

COMMUNITY AND SOCIAL SERVICES

In reviewing the culturally sensitive program variables of importance for Hispanic mental health services, it becomes apparent that the use of innovative approaches is indicated. These would include particularly approaches involving community and social services. Ruiz (1977) has proposed a particularly useful and viable conceptualization, which presents a continuum termed "the intrapsychic-extrapsychic dimension." It would assume that Latinos and Anglos alike are subject to similar intrapsychic stresses. If, for ex-

ample, a Latino woman or man and an Anglo woman or man were both going through a divorce, they would both be subject to possible stress, anxiety, and depression, and might both be in a crisis state. However, it may be the case that, while the Anglo woman might receive help and support from her family, the Latino woman's family might view the matter as a failure for the woman and might even expect her to remain married no matter what. Thus, the "extrapsychic" dimension includes additional social stresses. A family with a child having serious school problems, whether Anglo or Hispanic, will be in a state of disequilibrium and stress; however, the Hispanic family may be in a considerably added state of stress if, in addition to the child's school problem, the family does not have sufficient space in the house or if the father has recently been laid off from work.

If it is determined that a particular presenting problem is intrapsychic, then the usual forms of psychotherapy may be indicated. It frequently occurs, though, that a presenting family or child problem is assumed too quickly to be "intrapsychic" when, in fact, the problem is "extrapsychic" and requires other than traditional methods (Ruiz, 1977). A comprehensive approach may need to take into consideration all of the following types of services:

1) medical
2) optometric
3) dental
4) food
5) clothing
6) housing
7) employment
8) financial
9) vocational
10) educational
11) school placement
12) legal.

These services may be needed for the whole family or for various family members, even though the presenting problem may be a child behavior problem. Many services might be obtained with the help of a community worker with expertise in guiding a client family through the bureaucratic systems.

Advocacy is also a significant community and social service. This was somewhat vividly illustrated when a family was referred to the author for "child abuse" because the child was reported to have been playing unattended. An investigation was made by Protective Services, who determined that the family lived in "substantial housing." Also, interviewing had not been done in Spanish. It was determined that the parents were, in reality, very loving and caring parents. They were from Mexico relatively recently and were living in an apartment which was the most they could afford. However, the children had been placed out of the home indefinitely. When all of this was explained to the couple by the therapist, they both broke down in tears at the prospect of not having their children back. The therapeutic role in this case involved considerable advocacy and helping the social agency deal with their negative feelings toward the family and serving as an intermediary.

CULTURAL SENSITIVITY AND THERAPEUTIC IMPLICATIONS— CULTURAL AND FAMILY VARIABLES

Each Hispanic family and each individual is different from one another. Each is at a different point on a hypothetical continuum of acculturation, varying in the degree of emphasis on traditional values. Some writers have proposed that focusing on the traditional value structure of the Mexican-American can do more harm than good, because of the danger of perpetuating stereotypes (Romano, 1968). However, this would be true only if it were first assumed that modern values or American values are more desirable, im-

plying that the values of traditional Hispanic families were not in themselves sources of strength and beauty. Moreover, an argument could be made for the fact that there are many aspects of a traditional Hispanic value structure that are considerably more beneficial than modernistic values. Lopez (1977) did, in fact, find that therapists and clinicians rated the average healthy Mexican-American as closer to their concept of a person functioning at an ideal state of mental health, as compared with the healthy Anglo-American. These positive ratings were primarily in the areas of emotional expression, assertiveness, and family orientation. Kagan (1977) has also discussed many adaptive aspects of the Mexican family's socialization process and social motivation.

Table 2 summarizes the key aspects of the value structures of Hispanic Americans which may differ from Anglo views. This table groups the concepts in two general categories, one emphasizing family aspects, and the other aspects referring more specifically to children.

Primacy of the Family

In Hispanic culture, the family is generally viewed as primary to the individual (Diaz-Guerrero, 1975). Family values are established very early in the lives of the children. The family is expected to be a source of support and ego strength throughout life. Consequently, outside help for a mental health problem may be sought only as the last resort. Therapists would generally need to be aware that a child or any family member would consider the possible implications for the whole family of any sort of change.

The parents, family members, and the children, particularly when young, are encouraged to spend time together. It might, thus, be perfectly acceptable for the mother to accompany her children to and from school even if not particularly

TABLE 2

Different Cultural and Family Value Emphases for Traditional
Hispanic Families and Children

Family Values	Corresponding Child Values
Primacy of family (*la familia*)	Respect toward elders and authority (*respeto*)
	Different emphases in child-rearing
	Cooperation
Male roles and *machismo*	Male and the *palomillo* or *chollo* group
Female roles	Home emphasis
	Female "honor"
Role of extended family and *compadrazgo*	
Influence of folk beliefs	

necessary. It would be incorrect to assume that the mother was fostering dependence or was overprotective. Because of the primacy of the group welfare of the family, it could be necessary for an older child to remain home from school if the mother has a doctor appointment for a new baby and the older child is needed to help translate. If the child is then expected to attend school or is criticized for missing school, a difficult conflict is set up.

Also, because of the primacy of family ties, it may be difficult for the older adolescent in a traditional family to leave home for college or for work or to establish a separate identity if he or she chooses to do so. Many women are seen who are experiencing considerable conflict because of wanting to meet their own needs outside of the family and establish independent lives; yet they cannot leave home because of the guilt they would feel for the apparent rejection of the family.

Of particular relevance here is the concept of *respeto* (respect). Children are expected to be polite, respectful, and dignified with their parents and other adults. It frequently happens that a young adolescent is brought to the clinic and is viewed diagnostically as withdrawn or mildly depressed. Clinic personnel may be struck with the fact that the young teenager is not going through a normal stage of rebellion, particularly toward parents, which is generally viewed as normal by Anglo therapists and as a prelude to establishing increased self-identity. It would be a considerable mistake to encourage the teenager to become more assertive or rebellious as, again, a conflict would be fostered. If it is carefully determined that the child is feeling rebellious toward the parents, much caution is needed in handling its expression and the process may need to take longer than usual. Similarly, a school counselor may see a child individually in his or her office and be struck with the child's politeness (*respeto*); it could be a mistake to assume automatically that the child is incapable of aggression which may have been the original reason for the referral to the counselor's office.

Generally, adolescent rebelliousness will be expressed in avenues outside the home, or in an indirect manner. A young, very depressed female child was seen who was internalizing very considerable hostility toward a parent, and the anger seemed realistic and justified in view of how she was being treated. It would have been a disservice to encourage the child to express the anger and further exacerbate the guilt. If, in fact, a Hispanic child readily expresses anger toward a parent, which occasionally occurs, one can usually hypothesize that an extremely distructive relationship exists between the parent and the child.

In some situations, a very traditional family value structure can impose considerable hardships for a child. A teenage pregnancy could result in the teenager being "disowned" and perhaps having to live with relatives or friends. A homosexual orientation of a child may be virtually impossible for parents to accept no matter how much of an effort is made to educate the parents.

Cases of physical and sexual abuse of children may present some special difficulties. While it is frequently difficult for any child to report or talk about these situations, it may be even more difficult for the Latino child, who, consciously or unconsciously, may feel a need to protect the honor of the family. A number of adult women from Mexico have been treated by the author for ostensibly child-related problems. After some time of treatment with good rapport established, and when the women had the chance to talk alone, they broke down in tears and spoke of having been sexually molested by relatives; they each went on to say that they were frightened to tell their mothers because they were afraid that their mothers would scold them, become angry with them and, in various ways, put blame on them. Within a traditional family, a sexual abuse incident may result in the girls becoming viewed as "violated." It is crucial in these situations to assess the whole family, and, particularly the family members' perceptions of the events. Unfortunately, little work has been done and few, if any, case studies have been reported in the literature in these areas of physical and sexual abuse. However, Mitchell (1980) recently found that the Mexican-American mothers of child-abused children experienced themselves a very significant number of interpersonal losses and separations as compared with a matched control group of Mexican-American mothers in which no child abuse had been reported.

Childrearing Differences

Childrearing practices have been found to differ in some respects among Hispanic families. Cooperation is very strongly stressed. Kagan (1977) has presented a very considerable amount of evidence leading to the conclusion that Mexican-American children are more concerned than other children with cooperative behavior. They are particularly concerned about group enhancement, welfare of the whole group, and altruism. These differences were found across different situations, suggesting that the behavior is not determined by the nature of the situation, but is a more enduring trait. Of further interest is the fact that the results were found across different types of populations—subjects from different states, from middle and lower-classes, from urban and semirural settings, and from several different generations. Moreover, cooperativeness increased as the children grew older, particularly from ages 5 to 9.

Because of the emphasis on cooperation, less sibling rivalry may occur. An older child may be expected to take over some parental functions in relation to the younger children, and sibling status may be more clearly defined by age. An elder brother may need to contribute to the support of the family and an older sister may need to care for the younger children. A possible result is that the adolescent child may assume more responsibility and become more socially mature than his or her Anglo counterpart. If the adolescent has, in fact, assumed much responsibility and views himself or herself as a young adult, it would be a therapeutic error to treat the person with expectations that one would normally have for adolescents.

Male Roles

The more traditional a particular family, the greater the likelihood of differences from an average Anglo family regarding socialization processes and sex role development. For example, sex roles may be more clearly differentiated. Though there is considerable danger in stereotyping, it could be said that any therapist working within the Latino community will eventually have to work with a male who has many characteristics embodied in the concept of *machismo*. The usual view of *machismo* is that men are expected to be forceful and strong and not show tender or affectionate emotions. A male operating primarily from such a concept of himself frequently must deal with considerable dissatisfaction from his wife, particularly if she views herself in a more equal fashion. However, if the wife is herself functioning in the counterpart traditional role—nurturant and self-sacrificing—less conflict would be expected.

It is unfortunate, however, that the word *machismo* usually has negative connotations. The Latino male receives self-esteem primarily from raising a successful family, and, secondly, from his standing in the community and with nonfamily members. Thus, the male is expected to be responsible, hard working and to place his family quite high in priority. He would almost always be expected to do what is best for the children and his wife. This point was quite beautifully stated by Ruiz (1977):

When I think of the *machismo* of my father and uncles, the emotional responses elicited are in terms of a strong sense of personal honor, family, loyalty, love for children, and respect for the aged (p. 243).

Machismo can have a negative side and can cause difficulties for families when extreme. The male child may identify strongly with his father and the therapist has a responsibility of not interfering with this process if it would create additional problems. The therapist should also iden-tify the family system effects of any behavioral changes for the child. The author was referred a child of four who was acting very aggressively in the preschool classroom. In talking with the child it was determined that he had been spending much time with his dad and his dad's buddies who told him it was OK to fight with kids bigger than him. The young male may also join social groups called *palomillos*; prestige and status may result if the male is able to effectively demonstrate masculine traits with his friends (Murillo, 1978). A male may also obtain social reward by demonstrating perseverance through drinking with friends and being able to hold the alcohol well. It may thus be acceptable for the Latino male to spend a lot of time drinking with friends; however, such gatherings may serve considerable social support functions. If, for example, a husband were having marital, family, or work problems, he could meet with friends who would be expected to offer help and support. Fabrega et al. (1967) has observed that Hispanic males in treatment sometimes present emotional problems as physical symptoms to avoid the inference of subjective vulnerability which might be interpreted as weakness by friends.

A very common complaint presented by a Latina mother is that her husband is not sufficiently involved with the children. She may, in reality, be trying to communicate that she perceives her husband as not emotionally involved nor supportive of her as well. Such situations might be a prelude to the need for crisis therapy in preparation for divorce. The wife may, however, be fearing that her husband will retaliate with violence and fear for her safety. Divorce is generally much less acceptable than in Anglo society, and considerable guilt may be engendered. Further, it might be more beneficial to help find ways that the family members could remain together, particularly if this would be more acceptable for the wife.

Ramirez (1979), in examining the therapeutic implications of *machismo*, has suggested capitalizing on the positive qualities in the following manner:

1) the therapist actively invite the participation of the male;
2) the therapist respond to the male's role by explaining that his involvement is needed in making important family decisions; and
3) the therapist adopt an attitude of service (*servirle*), including flexible appointments and meeting at the home "on his grounds."

Female Roles

The Hispanic female child may be socialized primarily in the direction of taking care of children and the home; she may be allowed less freedom that is allowed for the male child and be allowed to spend less time away from home. This situation is probably undergoing rapid change both in this country and in Mexico at the present (Senour, 1977). Consequently, it is not uncommon for a woman to want to work or to seek professional training in areas other than those dominated by women; this may create conflict and be opposed by the husband, or any of the grandparents. In some sense, it may even be necessary for the Hispanic woman to overcompensate in order to succeed. For example, Hernandez (1976) found that, contrary to the impressionistic literature, Mexican-American college student females had more competitive attitudes than the Mexican-American males. The females were also found to have significantly higher levels of state-transitory anxiety and lower self-esteem than Anglo-American women. The interpretation offered was that the Mexican-American women are undergoing extremely rapid change, producing conflict and high anxiety. Latina women in these states of conflict frequently benefit most from a group therapy experience, which offers peer support and helps in assuaging guilt for wanting to be more independent.

Extended Family

An additional cultural variable to be considered is that of the extended family. The extended family includes the generations living and the relatives. Extended family members are expected to aid and support one another. The grandparents have a particularly important role. The extended family may also include the *compadrazgo*, which is an extension of the family through godparents who are usually selected from close friends or relatives. It is probably through such an extended system of support that many Hispanic persons are, in fact, able to acculturate and deal with the impersonality, complexity, and bureaucracy of so many aspects of life in United States society.

Awareness of the role of the extended family is critical for a therapist to function effectively. For example, a young Mexican-American couple sought help for marital difficulties. It was determined that much of the difficulty was caused by interference from the wife's mother, particularly in the handling of various matters with the children. This is a frequent complaint among families seeking help, though the parents may have considerable difficulty in stating the matter directly and comfortably because of the operation of *respeto* in relation to the elders. The therapist first took an approach of encouraging the grandparents to stay out of the picture, which resulted in a broken next appointment, perhaps due to the couple's feeling that the therapist was not sensitive to their dilemma. The couple did return and a more successful approach involved fostering the couple's strength more gradually, including the grandparents' involvement, but at a level determined by the couple themselves mutually. It might also be necessary to exercise special care that therapeutic interventions are not undermined by grandparents or other closely involved extended family members.

Folk Beliefs

Some mention should be made of folk beliefs and illnesses. Folk beliefs usually occur in older and very traditional Hispanic persons. A therapist should expect to be faced with such a presenting problem, though the frequency is generally decreasing. In these beliefs, a spiritual or supernatural factor is assumed to cause some problems which may be physical or psychological. The author has been referred cases in which older persons suffering from endogenous depression, which may have had a physical basis, used a "hex" as a last-resort explanation.

A few of the more common types of folk illnesses which may involve children include the following (Farm Workers Health Service, 1970; Gonzalez, 1976):

1) *Mal ojo* (evil eye)—believed to be produced by "strong sight" in which the child is coveted, leading to diarrhea, sleepiness, and crying;
2) *Caida de la mollera* (fallen fontanel) — believed caused by jolts or a fall of a baby or by a blow to the head; resulting in fever and diarrhea;
3) *Susto* (fright)—believed to result from an emotionally traumatic experience resulting in restlessness during sleep, loss of energy and depression; and
4) *Empacho*—resulting from food clinging in the stomach and interfering with digestion and believed caused by quality of food consumed.

The folk belief system also encompasses various religious practices, propitiatory rituals, and some magical elements. Noll

& Speilberg (1978) have grouped these practices into the following summary categories:

1) making promises and sacrifices (*manda*);
2) visiting religious shrines;
3) offering medals and candles; and
4) offering prayers.

Curanderos (healers) may be consulted and some "healers" may achieve very considerable fame. *Curanderos* may give specific advice, use various types of herbs and teas, and offer prayers. A priest might also be sought out. The author, for example, knows a case in which a psychotic woman was able to refrain from swallowing pins after a priest was brought by the mental health center to bless the house with holy water. Similar to what mental health staff working with American Indians have suggested in regards to Indian "medicine men" (Kahn et al., 1975), it could be beneficial to form some type of liason with a *curandero* whose services might be used as needed. After a careful analysis, Holland (1978) has, in fact, concluded that many Mexican-Americans in the Tucson area adhere to both traditional and modern medical concepts simultaneously and the former older medical system is slowly being assimilated into the more modern.

Explanations of the continuation of folk beliefs include the study of the historical roots and their function within the culture (Gonzales, 1976; Kiev, 1968). Some have focused on the stress-reducing aspects and functions of the illnesses (Klein, 1978). Other authors have given particular focus to the acculturation process that the families are experiencing and how acculturation problems are expressed through the folk illness and "cure" process (Kiev, 1968; Klein, 1978).

SOCIAL SYSTEMS INTERVENTION

Beyond the realm of mental health program issues, social services, and cultural issues lies the vast area of social systems intervention. The idea of social systems intervention is itself relatively new within the mental health professions. It has received considerable impetus from the community mental health movements. Several issues and examples of social system intervention in work with Hispanic children will be discussed here, though it should be realized that the field is ripe for considerable originality.

Two principles which integrate issues of community mental health and Latino minority needs are:

1) prevention of mental health problems may be the most beneficial approach in the long run; and
2) progress can be made more rapidly if the mental health worker can align himself or herself with forces already accepted and respected by families within the ethnic group.

Such an approach, for example, might have as its target agent, well-baby clinics. The public health nurse is often already a source of support for many Hispanic mothers, and the mothers might actually seek advice at the well-baby clinic. A mental health staff person could be available to the nurse for consultation, could join the medical staff during phases of the examination, or be available to talk to all families during screening and while the family is waiting for the physician. Immediate discussion of difficulties could occur, as well as referral; hopefully, the referral process would have been made considerably more comfortable because the family would have already experienced some nonthreatening, caring assistance. One such approach resulted in approximately 100 referrals to a mental health clinic from 800 parents seen; 53 of the families referred became clinic clients (Trankina et al., 1975). Very similar issues and techniques could be utilized with

children and families at the preschool level such as at Headstart Centers.

For the older child a similar approach might be taken by the mental health professional working in close collaboration with the school. Teams could be formed consisting of school personnel and mental health practitioners knowledgeable about the cultural and social issues of relevance for Hispanics. Such an approach could result in increasing reinforcement of the student within the school setting, sharing of information and recommendations, coordination of services, assuming mutual advocacy functions for the children, and making for ease of referral for mental health services when indicated. An approach such as this, for example, found that school personnel were more willing than usual to try alternatives to a special class placement for emotionally disturbed children and were quite willing to allow classroom observations and have clinic personnel join the school's staffing meeting for the child (Trankina et al., 1975). In addition, the schools eventually requested help in establishing child groups, parent groups, teacher inservice training, and intervening in a housing crisis in which the manager of a low-income housing project was planning on raising rent to unrealistically high amounts.

SUMMARY

The mental health care of children, in general, is critical, and the need is even greater among minority children. Hispanic children may be at risk when one considers health, family-social, and educational variables. Social and cultural factors have resulted in alienation, beginning early in the life of the minority child. Hispanic families may have a need for mental health and social services that is greater than their Anglo counterparts. Yet, services are underutilized by Hispanic families. This situation has improved in the decade of the 70's. Various explanations have been offered to account for the underutilization of services. However, it is probably the case that the Hispanic family chooses not to use or is not able to utilize services as they frequently exist.

An understanding of cultural differences is critical in promoting effective clinical intervention. An acceptance of cultural pluralism in the United States allows this approach. An understanding of cultural differences encompasses world view differences, historical perspectives and the influences of these on self-identity. Each Hispanic person and family is different in the degree of acculturation to the dominant Anglo society. Therapeutic sensitivity might well begin with awareness of the level of acculturation of the client. Possible differences in therapeutic expectations must also be considered.

A number of variables on a program level can be identified as relevant to providing culturally sensitive services. These variables refer to the general structure, form and visibility of services. They include characteristics of the mental health facility, staff characteristics and client awareness and knowledge. Community and social services may be needed as well.

A second major group of variables include potential family, social, and cultural variables which may be characteristic, to varying degrees, of the Hispanic population. Awareness of the following family values is needed by the mental health practitioner: primacy of the family, male roles, female roles, role of extended family, and influence of folk beliefs. Corresponding child-related values include: importance of respect toward authority, different emphases in child-rearing, importance of cooperation, and the learning of male and female roles.

Various approaches to social system intervention can be utilized to foster prevention, as well as provide innovative, culturally relevant services.

REFERENCES

Acosta, F. X., and Sheehan, J. G. Psychotherapist ethnicity and expertise as determinants of self-disclosure. In: M. R. Miranda (Ed.), *Psychotherapy with the Spanish-Speaking: Issues in Research and Service Delivery* (Monograph #3). Los Angeles: Spanish Speaking Mental Health Research Center, UCLA, 1976.

American Orthopsychiatric Association. Developmental assessment in EPSDT. *American Journal of Orthopsychiatry*, 1978, *48*, 7-21.

Berlin, I. N. The impact of the Joint Commission findings on community programs. *Psychiatric Annals*, 1975, *5*, 51-68.

Bloom, B. L. *Changing patterns of psychiatric care.* New York: Human Sciences Press, 1975.

Bloombaum, M., Yamamoto, J., and James, Q. Cultural stereotyping among psychotherapists. *Journal of Counseling and Clinical Psychology*, 1968, *32*, 99.

Bolio, A. M. (Ed.), *Libro de Chilam Bolam de Chumayel.* Mexico: Ediciones de la Universidad Nacional Autonoma, 1941.

Bower, E. M. Early and periodic screening, diagnosis, and treatment: Realities, risks and possibilities. *American Journal of Orthopsychiatry*, 1978, *48*, 4-6.

Burruel, G. The definitional process among Mexican-Americans and its effects on the utilization of mental health services. Unpublished doctoral dissertation. University of Denver, 1975.

Carter, T. P. *Mexican-Americans in School: A History of Educational Neglect.* New York: College Entrance Examination Board, 1974.

Castaneda, A. Traditionalism, modernism, and ethnicity. In: J. L. Martinez, Jr. (Ed.), *Chicano Psychology.* New York: Academic Press, 1977, 355-360.

Castro, F. G. and Gonzalez, H. I. A conceptual approach for culture sensitive therapy with Hispanic clients. In: C. Hernandez, M. Haug, and F. Castro (Eds.), *Chicanos: Social and Psychological Perspectives.* Third edition. St. Louis: C. V. Mosby, in press.

Chavez, N. Mexican-Americans' expectations of treatment, role of self and of therapist: Effects on utilization of mental health services. Unpublished doctoral dissertation. University of Denver, 1975.

Coleman, J. *Equality of educational opportunity.* Washington, D.C.: U.S. Department of Health, Education, and Welfare, Office of Education, 1966.

Creson, D. L., McKinley, C. and Evans, R. Folk medicine in Mexican-American sub-culture. *Diseases of the Nervous System*, 1969, *30*, 264-266.

Diaz-Guerrero, R. *Psychology of the Mexican: Culture and Personality.* Austin: University of Texas Press, 1975.

Edgerton, R. B. and Karno, M. Mexican-American bilingualism and the perception of mental illness. In: C. A. Hernandez, M. J. Haug, and N. N. Wagner (Eds.), *Chicanos: Social and Psychological*

Perspectives. St. Louis: C. V. Mosby, 1976, 230-236.

Fabrega, H. Value identification and psychiatric disability: An analysis involving Americans of Mexican descent. *Archives of General Psychiatry*, 1968, *19*, 45-49.

Fabrega, H., Jr., Rubel, A. J., and Wallace, C. A. Working-class Mexican psychiatric outpatients: Some social and cultural features. *Archives of General Psychiatry*, 1967, *16*, 704-712.

Farm Workers Health Service. *English-Spanish glossary for health aides*. Sacramento: Health and Welfare Agency, State Department of Health, 1970.

Figueroa, R. A., Vickovich, D. H., and Sandoval, J. Validation of the system of multicultural pluralistic assessment. Symposium presented at The American Psychological Association annual meetings, Montreal, 1980.

Franco, J. *An Introduction to Spanish-American Literature*. New York: Cambridge University Press, 1969.

Gonzalez, C. The role of Chicano folk beliefs and practices in mental health. In: C. A. Hernandez, M. J. Haug, and N. N. Wagner (Eds.), *Chicanos: Social and Psychological Perspectives*. St. Louis: C. V. Mosby, 1976, 263-281.

Grebler, L., Moore, J. W., and Guzman, R. C. *The Mexican-American People*. New York: The Free Press, 1970.

Green, J. M., Trankina, F. J., and Chavez, N. Therapeutic intervention with Mexican-American children. *Psychiatric Annals*, 1976, *6*, 60-75.

Heiman, E. M., Burruel, G., and Chavez, N. Factors determining effective psychiatric outpatient treatment for Mexican-Americans. *Hospital and Community Psychiatry*, 1975, *26*, 515-517.

Hernandez, A. R. A comparative study of fear of success in Mexican-American and Anglo-American College Women. Unpublished doctoral dissertation. Los Angeles: California School of Professional Psychology, 1976.

Holland, W. R. Mexican-American medical beliefs: Science or magic? In: R. A. Martinez (Ed.), *Hispanic Culture and Health Care: Fact, Fiction, Folklore*. St. Louis: C. V. Mosby, 1978, pp. 99-119.

Hollingshead, A. B. and Redlich, F. C. *Social Class and Mental Illness: A Community Study*. New York: John Wiley & Sons, 1958.

Jaco, E. G. Mental health of the Spanish-American in Texas. In: M. R. Opler (Ed.), *Culture and Mental Health: Cross-Cultural Studies*. New York: Macmillan, 1959.

Jaco, E. G. *The Social Epidemiology of Mental Disorders: A Psychiatric Survey of Texas*. New York: Russell Sage Foundation, 1960.

Joint Commission on Mental Health of Children. *Crisis in Child Mental Health: Challenge for the 1970's*. New York: Harper & Row, 1973(a).

Joint Commission on Mental Health of Children. *The Mental Health of Children: Services, Research, and Manpower*. New York: Harper & Row, 1973(b).

Kagan, S. Social motives and behaviors of Mexican-American and Anglo-American children. In: J. L. Martinez, Jr. (Ed.), *Chicano Psychology*. New York: Academic Press, 1977, pp. 45-86.

Kahn, M. W., Williams, C., Galvez, E., Lejero, L., Conrad, R., and Goldstein, G. The Papago psychology service: A community mental health program on an American Indian reservation. *American Journal of Community Psychology*, 1975, *3*, 81-97.

Karno, M. The enigma of ethnicity in a psychiatric clinic. *Archives of General Psychiatry*, 1966, *14*, 516-520.

Karno, M. and Edgerton, R. B. Perception of mental illness in a Mexican-American community. *Archives of General Psychiatry*, 1969, *20*, 233-238.

Keefe, S. E. Mexican-Americans' underutilization of mental health clinics: An evaluation of suggested explanations. *Hispanic Journal of Behavioral Sciences*, 1979, *1*, 93-115.

Kiev, A. *Curanderismo: Mexican-American Folk Psychiatry*. New York: Free Press, 1968.

Klein, J. Susto: The anthropological study of diseases of adaptation. *Social Science and Medicine*, 1978, *12*, 23-28.

Lopez, S. Clinical stereotypes of the Mexican-American. In: J. L. Martinez, Jr. (Ed.), *Chicano Psychology*. New York: Academic Press, 1977, pp. 263-275.

Lopez, S. Mexican-American usage of mental health facilities: A re-examination of more than two decades of research. Paper presented at the Western Psychological Association annual meeting, San Diego, 1979.

Lorion, R. R. Patient and therapist variables in the treatment of low-income patients. *Psychological Bulletin*, 1973, *79*, 263-270.

Lourie, R. S. Introduction to the Joint Commission on Mental Health of Children's progress report. *Psychiatric Annals*, 1975, *5*, 6-11.

Marcos, L. R., Alpert, M., Urcuyo, L., and Kesselman, M. The effect of interview language on the evaluation of psychopathology in Spanish-American schizophrenic patients. *American Journal of Psychiatry*, 1973, *130*, 549-553 (a).

Marcos, L. R., Urcuyo, L., Kesselman, M., and Alpert, M. The language barrier in evaluating Spanish-American patients. *Archives of General Psychiatry*, 1973, *29*, 655-659 (b).

McWilliams, C. *North from Mexico*. New York: Greenwood Press, 1968.

Mercer, J. Pluralistic diagnosis in the evaluation of Black and Chicano children: A procedure for taking sociocultural variables into account in clinical assessment. In: C. A. Hernandez, M. J. Haug, and N. N. Wagner (Eds.), *Chicanos: Social and Psychological Perspectives*. St. Louis: C. V. Mosby, 1976, 183-195.

Mercer, J. Identifying the gifted Chicano child. In: J. L. Martinez, Jr. (Ed.), *Chicano psychology*. New York: Academic Press, 1977, pp. 155-173.

Miranda, M. R. and Castro, F. Culture distance and success in psychotherapy with Spanish-speaking clients. In: J. L. Martinez, Jr. (Ed.), *Chicano Psychology*. New York: Academic Press, 1977, pp. 249-262.

Mitchell, M. C. Physical child abuse in a Mexican-American community. Unpublished doctoral dissertation. Los Angeles: California School of Professional Psychology, 1980.

Morales, A. Historical and attitudinal factors related to current Mexican-American law enforcement concerns in Los Angeles. Paper presented at Council of Mexican-American Affairs, Police-Community Relations Committee, Los Angeles, 1967.

Morales, A. The impact of class discrimination and white racism on the mental health of Mexican-Americans. In: C. A. Hernandez, M. J. Haug, and N. N. Wagner. *Chicanos: Social and Psychological Perspectives*. St. Louis: C. V. Mosby, 1976, pp. 211-216.

Murillo, N. The Mexican-American family. In: Martinez, R. A. (Ed.), *Hispanic Culture and Health Care: Fact, Fiction, Folklore*. St. Louis: C. V. Mosby, 1978, pp. 3-18.

Nava, J. Cultural backgrounds and barriers that affect learning by Spanish-speaking children. In: J. H. Burma (Ed.), *Mexican-Americans in the United States*. Boston: Schenkman, 1970.

Noll, F. C., II and Spielberg, J. Social and cultural factors in the responses of Mexican-Americans to medical treatment. In: R. A. Martinez (Ed.), *Hispanic Culture and Health Care: Fact, Fiction, Folklore*. St. Louis: C. V. Mosby, 1978, pp. 51-64.

Olmedo, E. L., Martinez, J. L., Jr., and Martinez, S. R. Measure of acculturation for Chicano adolescents. *Psychological Reports*, 1978, *42*, 159-170.

Padilla, A. M., Carlos, M. L., and Keefe, S. E. Mental health utilization by Mexican-Americans. Paper presented at the annual meeting of the Western Psychological Association, Los Angeles, 1976.

Padilla, A. M. and Liebman, E. Language acquisition in the bilingual child. *The Bilingual Review/La Revista Bilingue*, 1975, *2*, 34-55.

Padilla, A. M., Ruiz, R. A., and Alvarez, R. Community mental health services for the Spanish-speaking/surnamed population. *American Psychologist*, 1975, *30*, 892-905.

Paz, O. *The Labyrinth of Solitude: Life and Thought in Mexico*. New York: Grove Press, 1961.

Philippus, M. J. Successful and unsuccessful approaches to mental health services for urban Hispanic-American population. *American Journal of Public Health*, 1971, *61*, 820-830.

Ramirez, M., Taylor, C., and Petersen, B. Mexican-American cultural membership and adjustment to school. In: N. N. Wagner and M. J. Haug (Eds.), *Chicanos: Social and Psychological Perspectives*. St. Louis: C. V. Mosby, 1971.

Ramirez, M., III. Recognizing and understanding diversity: Multiculturalism and the Chicano movement in psychology. In: J. L. Martinez, Jr. (Ed.), *Chicano Psychology*. New York: Academic Press, 1977, pp. 343-353.

Ramirez, R. Machismo: A bridge rather than a barrier to family and marital counseling. In: Martin, P. P., *La Frontera Perspective: Providing Mental Health Services to Mexican-Americans* (Monograph #1). Tucson: La Frontera Center, 1979, pp. 61-62.

Romano, O. I. The anthropology and sociology of the Mexican-Americans: The distortion of Mexican-American history. *El Grito: A Journal of Contemporary Mexican American Thought*, 1968, *2*.

Ruiz, R. A. The delivery of mental health and social change services for Chicanos: Analysis and recommendations. In: J. L. Martinez, Jr. (Ed.), *Chicano Psychology*. New York: Academic Press, 1977, 233-248.

Seeman, M. On the meaning of alienation. *American Sociological Review*, 1959, *24*, 849-852.

Senour, M. N. *Psychology of the Chicana*. In: J. L. Martinez, Jr. (Ed.), *Chicano Psychology*. New York: Academic Press, 1977, pp. 329-342.

Sowder, B. J. *Assessment of Child Mental Health Needs and Programs. Volume IV—The Impact of Part F: An Analysis of 76 Child Mental Health Programs*. McLean, VA: General Research Corporation, 1975.

Srole, L. Social integration and certain corollaries: An exploratory study. *American Sociological Review*, 1956, *21*, 709-716.

Sullivan, H. S. *The Interpersonal Theory of Psychiatry*. New York: Norton, 1953.

Torrey, E. F. *The Mind Game: Witch Doctors and Psychiatrists*. New York: Emerson Hall, 1972.

Trankina, F. J., Hinds, P., Guerrero, P., and Green, J. Intervention programs implemented in serving ethnic minority children in a community mental health center. Paper presented at the National Council of Community Mental Health Centers annual meeting, Denver, 1975.

Van Oss Marin, B., Marin, G., and Padilla, A. Utilization of traditional and nontraditional sources of care among Hispanics. Paper presented at the American Psychological Association annual meetings, Montreal, 1980.

Wolf, E. *Sons of the Shaking Earth: The People of Mexico and Guatemala—Their Land, History, and Culture*. Chicago: University of Chicago Press, 1959.

Yamamoto, J., James, Q. C., and Palley, N. Cultural problems in psychiatric therapy. *Archives of General Psychiatry*, 1968, *19*, 45-49.

Ylvisaker, P. N. Bilingualism sounds hard only to adults. *Los Angeles Times*, August 17, 1980.

CHAPTER 19

Mental Health Needs
and Puerto Rican Children

Enrique Rivera Romero, M.D.

and Victor Bernal y del Rio, M.D.

"Crisis in Child Mental Health: Challenge for the 1970s." This was the title of a report on American children by the Joint Commission on Mental Health. When reflecting on the mental health of our children in Puerto Rico, the authors could not help but think about a frequently used saying: *The virus that gives you a cold on the mainland gives us pneumonia in Puerto Rico.* When we think about a crisis in child mental health on the mainland, the authors frankly and boldly state that what we have today in Puerto Rico is chaos in mental health. And when we make a closer inspection of the mental health needs of children in general and Puerto Rican children in particular, the authors cannot help but call it what it is: a disaster. The title of a report today on this topic would substitute only one number: "Crisis in Child Mental Health: Challenge for the 1980s."

SOCIAL AND POLITICAL BACKGROUND

The Secretary of Health has repeatedly stated that mental health is the number one health problem. This statement has been supported by the findings of the Commission on Mental Health (Woodbury, 1976b).

How did Puerto Rico arrive at this state of affairs? Puerto Rico was to have been the "window of the world;" the pathfinder for underdeveloped countries. It is relevant, at this point, to digress from the specific concern of mental health and briefly highlight Puerto Rican history. An understanding of the past is necessary for an understanding of the dynamics of Puerto Rican mental health problems today.

Population

Puerto Rico's population has reached 3.2 million people. The ratio is 1,000 + per acre (Demographic Report, 1976). Seventy percent (2.24 million people) are medically indigent. Puerto Rico's Mental Health Commission reported that 60,000 people earned $1,000 or less a year and that 40,000 make less than $100 per year in Puerto Rico (Woodbury, 1976). At present, the official unemployment figure is 21 percent and it is calculated that about 400,000 families, or 50 percent of the population, are on food stamps (Woodbury, 1976). Forty-nine percent of the population are 25 years of age or younger (1.5 million). Thirty-five percent are 19 years or younger (1.1 million children). While Puerto Rico is recognized as an industrial commonwealth, it is heavily burdened with a poverty-stricken population.

Socio-Political Changes During and After World War II

When World War II began, Puerto Rico was headed by Luis Muñoz Marin, a new leader, a man who peacefully transformed Puerto Rico from an agricultural country into an industrial one. Marin replaced the semi-feudal life style of the Puerto Rican with national pride and dignity. His administration brought about many social changes and eliminated many social inequities. Marin initiated "Operation Bootstrap." Factories were established throughout the island and new and better school programs were developed. Illiteracy was almost eliminated. Special scholarship programs for postgraduate study on the mainland were instituted. Puerto Rico's first school of medicine was established in 1951 and became a significant training and research health center. In 30 years, Puerto Rico had made more progress than many countries in the world had been able to accomplish in centuries.

At that time, Luis Muñoz Marin emphasized strong economic development to raise the economic standards and living conditions of the Puerto Rican. He overlooked two basic areas of transition: the social implications and complications of a sudden shift from an agricultural society to an industrial one, and the resolution of the island's political status with respect to the United States.

Concurrent with the improvement in living standards, a new social phenomenon arose: Many Puerto Ricans who had been in the U.S. Armed Forces during the war found it difficult to readapt to Puerto Rican life. They had heard about the "American dream;" consequently a second wave of Puerto Ricans emigrated to the United States (the first was during the 1920s). Among the emigrants were farmers with "dreams of glory." Marina (1962) called them "Quixotes that went to conquer the mainland with the ox and the pick." These emigrants embraced a common hope to return to Puerto Rico as successful people and to retire in the mountains with *dignity* and *respect*—something they did not have when they left Puerto Rico.

In 1952, after heavy pressure from the United Nations, Muñoz Marin revived the old concept of the commonwealth (previously defeated by Congress in 1922). Since 1952, the island has been the "Commonwealth of Puerto Rico." Its status is not that of a federal state, nor is it a colony or incorporated territory. While Puerto Rico is autonomous in many ways, it is restricted in many important areas by Federal control. Because of this, it is difficult for Puerto Rico to cope with its internal sociopolitical problems.

The Latin-American Invasion of Puerto Rico and the "Neo-Ricans"

Within the last 17 years, Puerto Rico has experienced a "Latin-American invasion" as many Cubans, Dominicans, Chileans, Argentinians and others left their countries for political reasons. Entering the mainland as refugees, they proceeded to Puerto Rico and helped compound the island's unemployment problem (especially since 1969). The Federal Government has thus become the Gate of Puerto Rico for the Spanish-speaking refugee. At present, there are some 80,000 Cubans and 60,000 Dominicans in Puerto Rico.

As the problems of recession in the United States have deepened, Puerto Ricans who found themselves without jobs and on food stamps began to return to Puerto Rico. They arrived not as realizers of the "American dream," but as defeated, angry Americans bringing with them children known on the mainland as "second generation Puerto Rican" and identified in Puerto Rico as "Neo-Ricans."

FACILITIES FOR THE CARE OF EMOTIONALLY DISTURBED CHILDREN

There are 10 *Community Mental Health Centers* strategically distributed around the island. These began operations in 1969. Only two of the Centers employ a Child Psychiatrist as a consultant (Auxiliary Secretary of Mental Health, 1976).

According to the Auxiliary Secretary of Mental Health Statistics for the year 1975-1976, 19.8 percent of the patients served by the Community Mental Health Centers were 19 years old and younger. During this same year, 35.5 percent of the new cases handled by the Auxiliary Secretary of Health in different facilities were younger than 18 years.

None of the Community Mental Health Centers is under the direction of a psychiatrist and two are even directed by non-physicians. No inpatient services for children or adolescents are available. In its last report for the years 1975-76, the Auxiliary Secretary of Mental Health reported that 1.8 percent of those admitted to adult inpatient services were children under 19.

There are no governmental or private day hospitals for the treatment of children and adolescents in Puerto Rico. Adolescents in need of daily care are treated with adult patients, as no programs specifically designed for adolescents exist. Where a "day care" facility ostensibly exists, it constitutes part of one of the poorly staffed Community Mental Health Centers.

There are innumerable nurseries in Puerto Rico, mostly located in San Juan. They are not licensed by the Department of Health or the Department of Education but by the Department of Social Services. Caretakers are usually middle aged or older and are not trained in basic child personality development. The nurseries are generally overcrowded and can precipitate early anxiety in the children, leading to inappropriate and overwhelming psychic stress. In general, Puerto Rican nurseries can be characterized as factories promoting psychopathology in preschool children and producing predisposing factors for later school difficulties.

Problems of Puerto Rican nurseries include government budget limits on the funding of the program. Motherly-looking but untrained women are available on government salaries. Private nurseries reflect two different situations. On the one hand, some nurseries are under the leadership of foreign-born women interested in financially successful ventures. These nurseries merely provide custodial care during a child's most important developmental years. On the other hand, there are nurseries under the leadership of young and talented teachers sincerely interested in the quality care of preschoolers. Financial stability too often becomes the deciding factor in quality care, even in the most ideal settings. Nurseries thus become overcrowded. It is important to note that none of these nurseries are psychiatrically or psychologically oriented.

The Department of Social Work, Department of Education and Department of Health have assumed a passive, observant stance. Children in Puerto Rican nurseries are invisible citizens whose developmental emotional needs are not met appropriately. Consequently, they begin to display emotional problems early in life.

There are no residential, psychiatrically-oriented treatment facilities for the care of emotionally disturbed children or adolescents in Puerto Rico. What exist are various penal institutions established for the care of young offenders, called detention homes. Detention homes are poorly staffed, with no psychiatric orientation at any level. They resemble jails more than residential detention "homes." Homosexual aggression is a first-day ritual known by all, yet no corrective action is undertaken. One of these institutions is reminiscent of the old El Morro Castle's dungeons.

The young offender is irreversibly damaged when placed in one of these supposedly "corrective" environments. One case documented in 1969 describes the fate of a 19-year-old placed in a detention "home." The author, who was then acting as the Psychiatric Consultant for the Juvenile Court *(Tribunal Tutelar de Menores)* held a consultation with the young man because he had "gone crazy" after spending three days at a detention home. This youngster had been submitted for three consecutive days to the homosexual initiation ritual. The "home" authorities brought him to the psychiatrist because they could not understand his assaultive behavior and suicide threats.

The recommendations for placing him in a psychiatric unit could not be implemented because there is no such facility in Puerto Rico. He was sent back to the same detention home under medication and "protective vigilance." Cases like this repeat themselves with unbelievable frequency. Since 1969, conditions do not seem to have improved at all. In fact, they have worsened.

The reason for the lack of inpatient psychiatric services for children or adolescents in Puerto Rico is cultural. Puerto Rican parents can conceive of their children becoming sick or being jailed because of an overt crime or offense, but they cannot understand that children or adolescents can become emotionally disturbed due to a more covert and subtle psychopathological process. They cannot allow their children to be hospitalized because of the social stigma placed upon them as a family and the intolerable guilt that they would have to face. A second consideration in evaluating the reasons for the lack of in-patient service for children is the indifference of the island psychiatrists. Little, if any, efforts are made to influence the decision-makers regarding this need. Community Mental Health Centers ostensibly meeting this need have no such facilities anywhere on the island.

What alternative is employed to meet this need? The chemical jacket is the only alternative when a psychotic patient falls under your responsibility, whether that patient is in a clinic, in a private office, or in one of the residential homes that offer services to children and adolescents in Puerto Rico.

Governmental outpatient services for children and/or adolescents are centered around the nucleus of the Community Mental Health Centers. There are ten such centers distributed throughout the island. Even in San Juan, the services for children in these centers are lacking specialized psychiatric personnel, whether psychiatrists, social workers, psychiatric nurses, or psychologists. Children are usually seen by the so-called "psychosocial specialist." This group of mental health workers is inadequately trained. When a psychiatrist is available, it is very difficult for a child patient to see him or her. The children must first follow the sequence of mental health workers in the clinic. When the children are seen by a psychosocial specialist, they are given appointments for the following month. When the children come in the next time, if they have not improved, they are referred to social workers who will "take a look" at the problem. If these social workers have any questions or are not too sure of what can be done with the children, they then consult their immediate supervisors. These immediate supervisors will decide whether children will be seen or "the problem" reviewed by a psychiatrist. When the social worker takes the consultation case to the psychiatrist, the psychiatrist reviews the case and advises the social worker as to special medications or specific treatment strategies. The case is then referred back to the psychosocial specialist with the psychiatrist's prescribed medication and/or advice. The child leaves the clinic with a routine monthly appointment schedule. Many months have been lost in most cases. Only complicated problems are reviewed by direct personal contact or indirect consultation with the psychiatrist.

The prescription problem is another one of the realities which falls within the mental health disaster area. Innumerable prescriptions have been given to youngsters who have never seen a psychiatrist or a clinic. Prescriptions without an appropriate psychiatrist's signature have been filled and delivered by the mental health pharmacy. This flagrant violation of the law went unchecked until a new Auxiliary Secretary of Mental Health took over in 1977.

Until 1977, the irresponsible prescription of psychotropic drugs was widespread. At present, the new Auxiliary Secretary of Health is doing his best to change this state of affairs, but his hands are tied by the rigidity of a closed budget and the unavailability of child psychiatrists, social workers and other specialized personnel. The situation is such that the structure by which the psychosocial specialist became the substitute for the psy-

chiatrist must be completely dismantled and a new delivery system for mental health established. In sum, outpatient governmental services for both adults and children have been unprofessional, inhuman, immoral and illegal. At present, health officials seem highly aware of the seriousness of the situation and of the need to undertake a total restructuring of the Division of Mental Health and to raise children's services to a first-level priority. Whether they will be able to achieve these goals within the present budgetary contraints remains to be seen.

There are several private institutions that provide services to children and adolescents on an outpatient basis. One of these is the Puerto Rico Institute of Psychiatry, Child Psychiatry Division, the only private, nonprofit institution on the island to offer psychiatric services to children at low cost. Service is given on a one-to-one basis to families, employing the highest standards of psychiatric practice on the island. However, this is a very small clinic and can help only a few of the many thousands of children in need of psychiatric service in Puerto Rico.

According to the 1975-76 statistical report of the Department of Health's Sub-Secretary of Mental Health, 37.4 percent of all new cases admitted for service in that department were 18 years old or younger. Of these, 63.6 percent were males. The same report of the services offered to the entire mental health population states that 2.6 percent were preschool children and 25.9 percent were students. 25.3% of the total population served through the Mental Health Program during 1975-76 were 24 years of age or younger. Despite these figures, service offered to the younger population is almost nonexistent compared to that offered to the rest of the population. It is obvious from this report that although the governmental institutions presided over by psychiatrists have made a great leap forward in service for children and adolescents, in the final evaluation, real service provision for children and adolescents is still in a state of serious travail.

During 1969, the S.S.S. Insurance program in Puerto Rico decided to cover emotional disturbances in their insurance program. It was because of a great effort by the psychiatry, neurology and neurosurgery section of the Puerto Rico Medical Association that this insurance company was able to include emotional disturbances. It must be noted that children were covered, but child psychiatrists were to be paid less than the usual fee paid for adult patients for the same amount of time. The rationale was that "children should pay less because they are physically smaller." Such medieval thinking is still prevalent among Puerto Rican insurance companies, health planning coverage programs, and many of the decision-making professionals in Puerto Rico.

MANPOWER

As of 1980, there are 33 child psychiatrists in Puerto Rico. Thirty-one are located in the metropolitan area of San Juan. One of the two remaining child psychiatrists on the island practices in Ponce and the other practices in Mayaguez.

Of the child psychiatrists practicing in San Juan, 29 work on a full- or part-time basis for the government, rendering services to adults as well as to children. Much of the time and money spent in the training of this specialized group of child psychiatrists is "lost," since they are not practicing full-time in their specialties. It is curious to note that most of these child psychiatrists have been trained in Puerto Rico at the State School of Medicine, Psychiatric Department. Many of them have remained on the periphery of the School of Medicine in an academic setting on a consultation basis. They are not involved in direct patient care. Their consultations are miles away from any direct contact with their patients.

The School of Medicine in Puerto Rico had made a tremendous contribution to the country in terms of physical health. This contribution is of such magnitude that the life span in Puerto Rico at present has advanced to 71.5 years. The same thing cannot be said about the mental health conditions of Puerto Ricans and specifically of Puerto Rican children.

One of the reasons for the Medical School's lack of development in mental health can be traced to the 1950s and 1960s when the Department of Psychiatry acquired the reputation for a philosophy devaluing both inpatient and children's services. In the Department's 1960 "Ten Year Proposal for Mental Health Programs," for example, only two sentences were written to summarize the needs of Puerto Rican children and adolescents. The Department suffered from an ambiance of professional feudalism still influencing the people in charge of mental health services at the School of Medicine today. The presence of such a structure and such a philosophy lasting many years at the highest authority level in the government as well as in the School of Medicine has done irreparable damage to the advancement of mental health for all of Puerto Rico and to the building of quality services for children and adolescents in Puerto Rico.

There are few formally trained psychiatric nurses in Puerto Rico. Psychiatric nurses become so designated through "on the job" experience. There is no special training designed for them. Social workers, too, are very poorly trained in the area of psychiatry, especially child psychiatry. During the years 1969 to 1972, the senior author was in charge of developing a school psychiatry program for the prevention of drug addiction and drug abuse in Puerto Rico. The major problem encountered was trying to recruit a staff of social workers trained in psychiatry. The curriculum for social workers in Puerto Rico is designed to create a good general social worker capable of handling all kinds of cases, including psychiatric ones. Their total exposure to psychiatry is in the form of a short course devised by the School of Medicine and taught by personnel at the University of Puerto Rico. Such social workers are thus inadequately trained in the field of mental health. They have little insight into psychiatric illnesses or how to handle psychiatric patients. It took several years to train these social workers to shift their orientations from general practice to a more specific psychiatric focus—several years and several resignations of social workers.

In very recent years, psychologists have been in great demand in Puerto Rico. With the emergence of the Caribe Psychological Institute (*Centro Caribeno de Estudios en Sicología*), the great need for psychologists in Puerto Rico is slowly being met. This center is graduating Masters in psychology who are working in the mental health centers throughout the island and in different clinics.

As the idea of a psychosocial specialist became increasingly implemented in the United States, the Sub-Secretary of Mental Health began to experiment with the concept in Puerto Rico. The eventual result was the creation of a group of psychosocial specialists with different educational backgrounds. Most Puerto Rican psychosocial specialists are high school graduates and have become substitutes for psychiatrists, child psychiatrists, social workers, and other highly trained personnel. Services for children and adolescents have consequently deteriorated. At present, this type of practice is being evaluated as to its impact and credibility.

SCHOOL PSYCHIATRY

As in other mental health areas, school psychiatry is a virtually abandoned cause

in Puerto Rico. In 1969, when the problem of drug addiction reached almost epidemic proportions, the Department of Education undertook the task of organizing at the school level a prevention program for drug addiction. The senior author was recruited to help set up a preventive drug addiction program as a pilot study in eight different schools in Puerto Rico. The work moved with great enthusiasm. Teachers and school supervisors remarked that, up to that time, all the help that they had received in terms of mental health in schools had been limited to "investigations." They had been left "without any practical feedback." A program in drug education was developed for teachers and all school personnel from kindergarten to ninth grade. Programs were devised to care for those children who were suffering from behavior disorders and learning difficulties in school, both at the elementary and high school level. It was the first time that an active program involving children and teachers had been implemented in Puerto Rico.

Abruptly in 1974, however, the program was discontinued when a new political administration took office. It was absorbed into different preventive programs outside the schools by the new Department of Drug Addiction and Alcoholism. Gains in school mental health were lost, knowledge derived from the pilot study was bypassed, and the schools regressed in terms of mental health prevention programs. At present, mental health clinics as such do not exist in any school in Puerto Rico. There are several psychiatrists assigned to the Department of Education on a part-time basis for consultation purposes, but only to high level personnel. Social workers do not receive necessary feedback from continuous psychiatric consultations to improve basic knowledge in the understanding of children with emotional difficulties. The school systems lack a pedagogic philosophy and orientation to guide the staff towards any direct involvement with children, especially at preventive levels.

In sum, schools in Puerto Rico, whether public or private, are not involved in any organized psychiatric program for their children. Psychiatric education for teachers, social workers, or other school personnel is nonexistent. As long as the Department of Education maintains its archaic belief that schools are simply and only places to learn the basic skills of mathematics, science, history and language, a school program encouraging child personality development and detecting early signs of psychopathology in the child or adolescent remains a dream. It is of crucial importance for personnel involved in the pedagogic program design in Puerto Rico to understand that the affective development of the child is as serious an issue to cover in their curriculum as mathematics and science. The philosophy that schools are only in charge of teaching basic knowledge and that personality and character development are relegated to parents is outmoded.

THE PUERTO RICAN MENTALLY RETARDED

Although services exist in Puerto Rico for children in need of special education and for the mentally retarded, these can be characterized as fragmented, unstructured efforts covering a very limited population.

There have been some attempts by the Department of Education to develop special schools for children with emotional problems. These efforts all have failed because of the basic fact that key personnel are not psychiatrically oriented. They are "specialty oriented," depending upon whether they are specialists in dyslexia, learning disorders, or mental retardation.

There are three different institutions for the mentally retarded in Puerto Rico, theoretically serving an estimated 50,000

such persons. Of the three institutions, two are government controlled—one in Trujillo Alto and the other in Mayaguez. A private nonprofit institution, the Psychopedagogic Institute, is located in the metropolitan area. All three facilities (especially the governmental institutions) are inadequately equipped and staff members require specialized training in order to deal with the mentally retarded (Willer and Intagliata, 1977). In 1976, the Psychopedagogic Institute came under a new administration emphasizing the "psychiatrization of the institution." New training programs for teachers and all personnel in charge of the mentally retarded were established. Innovative and creative ideas are being implemented to mobilize the mentally retarded population. The goal is to prepare them to return home as soon as possible. The Psychopedagogic Institute is one of the most progressive institutions in Puerto Rico in this respect, with inpatient services for severe cases of mental retardation, a school serving both mentally retarded inpatients and outpatients of the community, and a clinic that detects new cases and brings them into early treatment and management. While this institution is very limited in terms of staff, the new psychiatric orientation has changed the ambiance dramatically for the good. At present, this facility delivers one of the best services for children in Puerto Rico. While it is still far from meeting the demand for mental retardation care in Puerto Rico, the Psychopedagogic Institute is successfully working towards a reality of attaining its goal of excellence.

In sum, programs for the mentally retarded are in need of restructuring, beginning with whole treatment philosophy. The archaic concept of institutionalizing patients until old age or death should be replaced with a modern philosophy of training, educating, and preparing the mentally retarded to enter the mainstream of society to the fullest extent possible. The aim is to help these people achieve maximum development in their cognitive and affective growth. To further this aim, decision-makers and politicians, in the exercise of their responsibilities in our society, must understand the meaning of mental retardation—not as a political instrument, but as it affects human beings.

RESEARCH IN CHILD PSYCHIATRY

In Puerto Rico, research on the mental health of children and adolescents is almost nonexistent. Budget limitations are great, academic resources are scarce, and policymakers do not consider research a first priority.

Nonetheless, each year, some isolated piece of research is presented at the yearly convention of the Psychiatry, Neurology and Neuropsychiatric section of the Puerto Rican Medical Association. These represent individual efforts toward research stemming mainly from the Puerto Rico Institute of Psychiatry and from the private sector of psychiatry practice. It is interesting to note that child psychiatrists have been among the most active in these efforts.

In terms of research data and potential, it must be emphasized that while the talent is available to carry out a research program on the mental health of children, there is no budget for this purpose.

MENTAL HEALTH FACTORS IN THE DEVELOPMENT OF PUERTO RICAN CHILDREN AND ADOLESCENTS

The limited facilities available in Puerto Rico for the mental health care of children have been described. There are very few public or private institutions directly and effectively dealing with the mental health problems of the children of Puerto Rico. Mental health centers and school clinics lack staff, equipment and internal cohesion. Where personnel lack training, efficiency is very low. At this point, it

becomes relevant to explain how such a state of affairs evolved.

There are several factors to consider in any attempt to understand what is happening to Puerto Ricans today.

First, consideration must be given to the political and governmental organization making all decisions from 1940 to the present. The attempt to industrialize Puerto Rico, to develop its potential, to bring it up to the "American standard" was an excellent idea. The advances in housing, education and welfare were great. However, new challenges emerged as a result of these gains: the political status issue and the psychosocial development of the Puerto Rican.

Since Americans landed on the shores of Puerto Rico in 1898, concern about the political destiny of this island has been an ubiquitous feature of Puerto Rican life. Once Puerto Rico developed a better economic situation and improved quality of life, political status and restructuring of systems became pressing issues that usurped precious time, talent, and energy from other areas. At present, it appears that the political status of the island does not satisfy anybody in Puerto Rico. Chronic dissension about independence and statehood have created obstacles hindering Puerto Rico from solving problems of population explosion, emigration, and unemployment. Politics drains Puerto Rico's energies away from other issues that should rank high on the national priority list and that can neither be denied nor ignored. They are a part of the country's heritage as much as they are a part of her future.

A second factor influencing mental health in Puerto Rican children and adolescents is the psychosocial development of the Puerto Rican returnee. In the early 1940s, a second wave of emigrants left Puerto Rico for the United States and reached its peak after the war. People began to leave Puerto Rico in great masses. They travelled to the mainland mostly in cargo ships, some in two-motor airplanes, in numbers almost comparable to the European emigration years before. One of the cargo ships was called the "Marine Tiger." Any Puerto Rican new to New York in those days was called a Marine Tiger. When the senior author arrived in New York in 1948 to study medicine, he found himself referred to as a "White Shoe Marine Tiger" each time he visited the barrio to see friends. The beginning of the "dream to return home," discussed below, occurred at this time. Puerto Ricans began to organize themselves according to their towns of origin in Puerto Rico. During the forties and early fifties, entire blocks, streets and buildings served as places for people to meet according to the town of origin in Puerto Rico. The barrio's social clubs emerged from these first geographic arrangements. As old buildings were destroyed and new housing projects were erected, the "Puerto Rican towns arrangement" by streets and buildings disappeared, and were replaced by "social town clubs," such as Club Cabo-Rojeño, Club Comerieño, Club Corozaleño, etc. Town togetherness was a way to preserve a sense of the extended family living arrangements Puerto Ricans had back on the island. In many ways, Puerto Ricans on the mainland have preserved the extended family system not as the defensive survival strategy of a minority group, but as part of a Puerto Rican cultural heritage they need to keep. When many Puerto Ricans returned to the island in 1977, they found that the Puerto Rican extended family system had been "Americanized" into the *nuclear* family system. This was and still is a shock to them.

In certain respects, emigration was healthy for Puerto Rico because those who left became employed. The more successful sent money back to their families in Puerto Rico. This contributed a great deal to the income level of Puerto Ricans for many years. As the society became more industrialized and more powerful financially, many of the island's indigenous cultural values were dropped. The family,

which up to 1954, had been of the extended family type, became *nuclear* almost overnight. The nuclear family slowly began to disintegrate and the divorce rate rose to one for every three new marriages. The prolonged economic recession of 1975 affected Puerto Rico in two ways: The direct impact of the recession on Puerto Ricans themselves resulted in gross unemployment, further compounded by the large number of returnees from the mainland.

It is calculated that from January to June, 1977, about 80,000 Puerto Ricans returned to the island. During the author's years of living in New York, he found a very interesting characteristic of Puerto Ricans and their children on the mainland. They all carried within them a "dream (fantasy) to return to Puerto Rico." Second-generation children were found to "carry the dream" (*llevo el sueño*) consciously or unconsciously. This fantasy served the Puerto Rican on the mainland as a cushion for rebounding from "bad days." In their children, it became an unconscious wedge that made it more difficult for youngsters to identify with the mainstream, whether in New York, Boston or Chicago. Puerto Rican youngsters on the mainland suffered an eternal ambivalence in their identity. This created difficulties for them in making a successful sociocultural adaptation. The task of the mainlander born Puerto Rican was to work through this ambivalence and convert it into an asset.

Many of those who returned with their families to Puerto Rico brought with them children born in the U.S. This created still more difficult problems to deal with. Returnees have frequently become a burden on the unemployment sectors. Their children find themselves lost as they witness the stark reality of the "dream" of returning to Puerto Rico. Many Puerto Ricans returned from the United States as the vanquished, rather than the victors they were in their dreams when they left Puerto Rico. Their children constitute a great psychological problem for Puerto Rico. Neo-Ricans,* as they are called in Puerto Rico, find themselves caught in a tremendous identity crisis.

Paradoxically, while neo-Ricans do not consider themselves Puerto Ricans, they simultaneously experience anger resulting from the rejection and prejudice they were subjected to on the mainland as Puerto Ricans. Although born on the mainland, they were not allowed to be mainlanders, i.e., New Yorkers, Chicagoans. When they moved to Puerto Rico, they realized that they were also not Puerto Ricans since they could not understand Puerto Rican values and customs of the 1970s. The "returnees" are likewise out-of-joint. They are shocked that their expectations of returning to "our Puerto Rico" are not met. The familiar Puerto Rico they left now confronts them with the bitter reality of a different society, unknown to them. Their children find themselves in a land that is foreign to them and, in many cases, hostile. Most cannot even speak Spanish. While these children and adolescents resist the Puerto Rican heritage, they have no roots as mainlanders. These identity crises constitute a basic substratum and a basic vulnerability to delinquency and/or drug-addiction.

Special programs are needed for these children and their families to prepare them for the new life they will experience in the new Puerto Rico—a life completely different from that of the 1940s. These children need more than a history class and a visit to El Morro Castle. They need to be taught the Puerto Rican experience by people who are knowledgeable, loving, and patient, and this preventive education must be psychiatrically oriented.

Another factor affecting the mental health of the Puerto Rican child was "Operation Bootstrap," which brought to Puerto Rico many jobs, urban development, and new economic gains. No one suspected that Puerto Rico would attain so much, so fast and so intensively. The extended family, where godfathers were responsible for the upbringing of the family, was the prevailing family style at that time (Marina, et al., 1969). Negative consequences of Operation Bootstrap included the dislocation and, in many cases, the total fracture of traditional family ties that had served so well in guaranteeing children the satisfaction of their basic emotional needs and the provision of the social restraint needed for growth into a psychologically balanced individual. The "community" disappeared from the Puerto Rican family system. Suddenly, relatives became unimportant and grandparents were just used according to how they met the nuclear family's needs. The outcome today is a fragmented nuclear family at odds with the relics of the extended family. The remnants of what used to be the extended family resent their losses in the family hierarchy. Their roles are secondary and ineffectual in terms of being meaningful authority figures for the growing child.

At present, the Puerto Rican family lives in a time of crisis where children have lost the strength and protection of their extended families. They have also lost the effectiveness of a strong nuclear family, since parents work and when at home, they are tired and emotionally unavailable to the growing child. Quarrels between parents and the rest of the extended family are frequent, creating more

---

*Neo-Rican is a label initially heard for the first time among college-level youngsters who began to organize themselves as a sociocultural group in Puerto Rico. Initially, they called themselves "New York Rican," meaning New York Puerto Rican. This phrase was shortened to "New Yorican," with the same meaning. A newspaper columnist for *El Mundo* (San Juan) called them "neo-Ricans." This label included all Puerto Ricans born on the mainland who had returned to Puerto Rico to live. The columnist considered them a different type of Puerto Rican, describing them as verbally aggressive, unaccepting of Puerto Rican values, and orienting themselves more toward a model of an undifferentiated sociocultural individual somewhere in between the Hispanic and Anglo-Saxon cultures, but unable to stabilize themselves in either.

social disorganization which affects the children.

The nuclear family has failed in Puerto Rico because there are no public or social institutions that can provide child care or assume the roles of the absent working parents. As mentioned above, divorce has risen to alarming levels: one divorce for every three marriages (Woodbury, 1976c).

Against this background of sociocultural family disorganization, Puerto Rican children have to somehow survive their own identity crises and the effects of a fragmented, overcrowded society surrounding them.

SUMMARY AND CONCLUSIONS: SOME SUGGESTIONS AND A PROPOSED PROGRAM FOR THE MENTAL HEALTH CARE OF CHILDREN AND ADOLESCENTS

The authors have attempted to describe the current state of mental health in Puerto Rico and its impact on children. The authors experienced some initial resistance in writing this chapter because it is uncomfortable and difficult to discuss issues which are essentially negative and where there are few positives. They hope that what they have presented here is taken not as an attack on individuals in any past or present administration but as an attempt to be frank and honest in their appraisal of the present mental health status of Puerto Rican children, both in Puerto Rico and in the United States, from a historic, sociological and psychological point of view.

The entire existing program for mental health in Puerto Rico must be reconstructed on the basis of first deciding that the mental health needs of children must be the top priority and that mechanisms should be instituted to deal effectively with the basic and fundamental problems of the island, such as the political status issue and the decision to adopt a policy toward improving the quality of life. The proposed organization sketched below represents an alternative, first attempt, just one of the possible solutions to the problem of structuring such a program.

In the senior's author paper entitled "A Blue Print for Child Psychiatry in Puerto Rico" (Rivera-Romero, 1969),· a two-point program was recommended; despite the passage of a decade, those suggestions still stand as basic. As mainlanders read these suggestions, they may strike them as nothing new and perhaps a bit old-fashioned, but it must be kept in mind that in Puerto Rico, we are perhaps 25 years behind the times in the area of psychiatry.

The first proposition is the creation of both a neuropsychiatric institute for children and adolescents and an independent department of mental health that could initiate programs with an institution of this type. The central concept is that the proposed neuropsychiatric institute would offer basic training for all people who must deal with children or adolescents —teachers, nurses, social workers, psychiatric residents, medical students. The idea is to create an institution in the metropolitan area with satellite clinics of an ambulatory nature that would move periodically from one regional section of the island to another. Important cities such as Ponce, Humacao, Fajardo, Carolina, Bayamon, Arecibo, Aguadilla, Mayaguez, Guayama, Yabucoa and Aibonito would be selected for the training and service clinic stations. This Ambulatory Satellite Unit—consisting of a child psychiatrist, a child social worker, a child psychologist, and a child psychosocial specialist—would move into regional areas where medical centers are located to begin to see patients and to use this experience to teach local personnel how to deal with emotionally disturbed children and adolescents. It would be essential to note the strength and weakness of a particular area and to make the necessary recommendations for that area in terms of service, training and future research.

The Ambulatory Satellite Clinic would

serve as a beginning in that particular area to study its problems and begin to solve them. Once needs are known, the neuropsychiatric institute in the metropolitan area would take care of the training needs in that particular region and provide solutions for particular problems. When regional people have been trained, they would be sent back to their regions of origin. They could also receive on-site training by the ambulatory team. Once this task is accomplished, the Satellite team could move to another region. In this way, the program could cover the entire island in about ten years. There would therefore be two levels of simultaneous training: people in training at the proposed San Juan Neuropsychiatric Institute and the people in the local training programs in the regions and small towns which would work directly with patients in these communities. This type of program would require a special budget. This is why it becomes necessary to establish a new Department of Mental Health beforehand, with its own budget.

As a complementary solution to the problems of mental health in Puerto Rico, governmental programs to help private institutions that are already dealing with the psychiatric care of children and adolescents in Puerto Rico are also recommended. These institutions, such as the Family Living Institute, the Puerto Rico Institute of Psychiatry, the Psychopedagogic Institute, and many others are lacking necessary financial support from the government. It must be noted here that Puerto Rico does not have the philanthropic institutions present on the mainland that provide financial backing to many local programs. We do not possess the financial affluence of a community that can afford to give thousands or millions of dollars for a specific mental health program in a community. As previously explained, 70 percent of our population is medically indigent and incapable of financially supporting a mental health program for children or adolescents at a local

level. The 15 percent of our population who are wealthy do not contribute financially to alleviate the needs of the medically indigent group.

A digression is indicated here in order to point out some differences between the socioeconomic classes on the mainland and in Puerto Rico. In third world countries, socioeconomic status cannot be translated literally, utilizing American measures. What is considered a lower socioeconomic status in the United States is considered, in Puerto Rico, middle and even upper middle class. Members of the high socioeconomic class in Puerto Rico comprise an elite of 15 percent who can meet their particular health care needs by travelling to the best medical or psychiatric centers on the mainland. Any attempts to extrapolate programs for minorities on the mainland as applicable to Puerto Rico thus remain doubtful in view of these socioeconomic differences.

Even if the above recommendations were instituted, it would still be necessary to devise a program to deal with the basic factors that perpetuate the crisis of unemployment and family fragmentation, including the failure of the nuclear family system, the devaluation of the still lingering extended family system, and the return of second generation Puerto Ricans (neo-Ricans). The latter deserve special attention and research in order to create the appropriate social, educational and treatment approaches required.

Finally, although the physical health of our children and adolescents is improving everyday, there are many pockets of extreme poverty in Puerto Rico, especially in rural areas. These constitute a unique in-vivo setting where changes in cognitive and affective patterns evolving from 1940 to 1970 can be studied.

In these rural areas, life has remained at a standstill since the early 1950s. Television has not reached these isolated areas. The communities consist usually of about 600 to 700 people who are proud of their heritage and are still living with the extended family and community system. They are in great need of schools, health programs and social services. Puerto Rico has the responsibility to improve the quality of life of these people without adulterating their growing community process, as it occurred after 1940.

In 1976, the senior author recommended that a conference be held to include the heads of governmental departments, consultants, and members of the private sector who are involved with the mental health of Puerto Rican children and youth (Rivera-Romero, 1976). The objectives of this meeting were to have been discussion, decision, and operationalization of programs to deal comprehensively with the three most important aspects of mental health: prevention at different developmental levels, environmental strategies, and delineation of treatment responsibilities. Issues such as infant hospital psychiatry, nurseries, inpatient services for children from infancy to adulthood, special schools and day care programs were to be dealt with in this conference with special reference to delegation of responsibilities in the delivery system. It was hoped that the Department of Education, the Department of Social Services, and the Department of Health could agree upon a comprehensive policy for the mental health of Puerto Rican children, adolescents, and their families, with private institutions sharing the responsibility.

The authors and their fellow Puerto Ricans are still waiting for such a conference to be convened.

REFERENCES

Auxiliary Secretary of Mental Health, Community Mental Health Center Report, 1975-76. Unpublished government report. San Juan, Puerto Rico.

Auxiliary Secretary of Mental Health, Report of total services offered, 1975-76. Unpublished government report. San Juan, Puerto Rico.

Coelho, G. V. and Stein, J. Coping with stress of an urban planet: Impacts of uprooting and overcrowding habitat. *International Journal of Psychiatry*, 1977, *34*, 379-390.

Demographic Office Report on Estimated Total Population from 1970 to July 1976. Unpublished government report. San Juan, Puerto Rico.

Marina, F. Personal Communications, 1962.

Marina, F., Von Ekhard, L., and Maldonado, M. D. *The Sober Generation.* San Juan, Puerto Rico: University of Puerto Rico Press, 1969, pp. 3-92.

Rivera Romero, E. A blue print for child psychiatry in Puerto Rico. Paper delivered before the Annual Psychiatric Meeting of the Puerto Rico Medical Association, 1969.

Rivera Romero, E. Present state of child and adolescent psychiatry in Puerto Rico. Paper delivered before the Annual Psychiatric Meeting of the Puerto Rico Medical Association, 1974.

Rivera Romero, E. The Puerto Rican perspective: Report of the Commission on Mental Health. Unpublished manuscript. San Juan, Puerto Rico: 1976, pp. 89-101.

Willer, B. and Intagliata, J. Residential services for the mentally retarded in Puerto Rico: Observations and recommendations report. Paper presented at the State University of New York at Buffalo, July 1977.

Woodbury, M. Food stamp program: Report on the life cycle, mental health and the quality of life in Puerto Rico. San Juan, Puerto Rico: The Mental Health Commission of Puerto Rico, 1976a, p. 31.

Woodbury, M. Mental health is the number one public health problem in Puerto Rico. San Juan, Puerto Rico: Mental Health Commission, Monograph Number VII-A, 1976b.

Woodbury, M. Divorces in Puerto Rico: Report on the life cycle, mental health and the quality of life in Puerto Rico. San Juan, Puerto Rico: Mental Health Commission on Puerto Rico Pages 23-29, 1976c.

CHAPTER 20

The Mental Health of the American Indian Child

Fred Wise, Ph.D. and

Nancy Brown Miller, M.S.W., Ph.D.

The mental health of American Indian children is an area of increasing interest and concern in our society. To understand the processes by which mental health or, conversely, mental health problems develop, it is imperative to understand something of the American Indian culture and the unique position of the Indian within our society. This chapter is an attempt to present an overview of the issues in defining mental health problems of Indians by professionals who represent the dominant culture, and the social and legal context within which any understanding of the American Indian must take place. The focus will be on the various forces and conflicts which impact upon the American Indian child throughout his or her development and on various treatment modalities which may increase the effective delivery of services to this complex, heterogeneous group of people in our society.

There are no simple solutions to understanding the unique needs of American Indians today. Some of the views expressed by the authors may be controversial. It is also probable that no Indian individual will "fit" all of the generalizations made. Each person has his or her own personal experiences and perceptions of those experiences and, therefore, must be considered as an individual first. For example, while most Indians in our society share a similar history in relation to their status within the dominant society, their perceptions about that relationship will vary, as will their attitudes and behaviors regarding mental health and the utilization of mental health services. While much of this chapter deals with general issues related to American Indians, these issues are deeply related to the mental health of Indian children growing up today as they attempt to define their identities and their roles both within the Indian culture and the dominant society.

WHO IS AN INDIAN?

In contrast to any other cultural group in our society, a person is not a "real" Indian unless he or she fits into categories defined by the Federal government, including blood degree and tribal status. In order to be eligible for Federal Indian programs, a person must be able to prove he or she is at least one-quarter Indian "blood," and his/her tribe must be one that is officially "recognized" by the Federal government. For many programs and services, he or she must also reside on a Federally-defined reservation.

American Indians are generally perceived as a homogeneous group, a composite of certain physical and personality characteristics which have become stereotypes reinforced by the media. Trimble (1976) notes that the common view of the American Indian is the media portrayal of a person with black hair, brown skin, high cheekbones, and most often dressed in clothing typical of Plains Indian life 100 years ago. Bromberg and Hutchinson (1974) note personality characteristics of stoicism, nature/ecology orientation and noncompetitiveness. History has seen Indians alternately described as savages, nuisances, objects of curiosity, research subjects for social scientists, people to be pitied and helped and, in light of recent land, fishing and water rights claims, people to be feared or despised.

Obviously, the idea that there is an "Indian" stereotype that could fit all or even most Native Americans today is naive and simplistic, no more valid than any similar attempt to describe a "white" person. Vine Deloria, a respected Indian leader and author, sums up the frustration among Indian people of this stereotyping: "People can tell just by looking at us what we want, what should be done to help us, how we feel, and what a 'real'

Indian is like" (1969, p. 9).

There are, however, some important distinctions regarding Native Americans which must be noted. One is the wide disparity among tribes with respect to such variables as size, geographic location, language, traditions and customs, and fiscal and natural resources. There are over 400 tribes recognized by the Federal government, about 280 of which have a land base or reservation. There are also tribes which have never been recognized by the Federal government and tribes which have lost trust status through termination policy.

Just as tribes represent a wide range of characteristics, so do Indian individuals. About half of the more than one million Indians in the United States today live on reservations; the other half live in urban and rural areas. Clearly, the social and cultural influences that come to bear on these populations are very different. For example, while the reservation group may have the benefit of a number of Federally supplied services such as health care, the urban group is often isolated from these services. Indians living on reservations continue to have regular access to traditional customs, while those in urban areas are generally cut off from many Indian cultural influences. Conversely, opportunities for employment and higher education are often greater for Indians living in urban areas.

Another difference among Indians is "quantum blood" or biological "Indianness," referring to the degree of Indian ancestry an individual possesses. Many Indians believe that the arbitrary blood requirement of the government is a dominant culture policy which has resulted in divisiveness and dissension among Indians who have had to fight for limited funds and services. In addition, it has provided an economically advantageous excuse for not recognizing certain individuals for trust-status benefits. Indeed, the idea of legislating who is an "Indian" is very foreign to the Indian belief system; Indians know who is and is not an Indian.

While this is not to say that a universal definition exists among tribes or even among individual Indians within a tribe, it points out that the issue in most cases has not been theirs to decide. Indians also represent a wide range of phenotypic characteristics with respect to body size, skin and hair color, and facial features. The conflict of cultural identity is often increased for those Indians who do not fit the traditional physical stereotype, as they may encounter prejudice and rejection from both Indians and non-Indians alike.

Also to be considered is the degree to which an individual has been assimilated into the dominant society. Many Indian people live in isolated reservation areas with little contact with the dominant society, often in very primitive living conditions, and retain their traditional language and customs. Other Indians have "melted" into the dominant culture and retain few, if any, traditional beliefs. Still others have acculturated to the degree that they exist comfortably within the dominant society, but retain many of their original beliefs and practices. What is emerging, particularly among urban Indians, is an increasing pan-Indian identity, both as a means of establishing ties with those of similar backgrounds and experiences, and as a defensive measure for greater political strength (Ablon, 1972; Price, 1972).

Thus, there are vast differences among Indian people which challenge the stereotypes held by the dominant culture. Yet, there is a pervasive view that Indians are the way they were a century ago, and that Indians are not Indians unless they live on a reservation with a marginal existence and maintain all traditional beliefs and customs. Consistent with this belief is the view that for Indians to possess or desire the artifacts of our modern world seems, in some way, to diminish their "Indianness." In addition, there is still a tendency to view such traits as education or affluence as antithetical to being In-

dian. In fact, other than the romanticism of the "simple" life-styles of Indians, rarely does the dominant culture attribute success or positively valued behavior to Indians. These views have obvious detrimental effects, not only on the perpetuating aspects of stereotypes, but also on the self-concepts of Indian children who often see economic and educational advancement as a threat to losing their identity.

Paradoxically, there is also a belief that all Indians want to be assimilated and supposedly "equal." This view appears to be based on the assumptions that: 1) all Indians are alike; and 2) the dominant culture is better; therefore, Indians should *want* to be part of it. It is as if the prerequisite for change is assimilation.

As Steiner notes in *The New Indians* (1968) there is, however, a great deal of change occurring within Indian cultures. Many Indians are becoming educated and are improving their economic status despite the hindering aspects of negative stereotypes. Concurrently, there is a strong resistance to assimilation, both among Indians on reservations and in urban areas (Ablon, 1972; Bowman et al., 1975; Chadwick and Strauss, 1975). This resistance attests to the strength and belief in the values of Indian culture and traditions. It should not be forgotten that Indian culture has withstood removal from traditional lands, attempts at extermination, boarding schools, attempts at assimilation through "termination" and "relocation" policies, and other direct attacks.

INDIAN VALUES

Although no Indian tribes are identical in their cultural beliefs and practices, there are some unifying concepts which set Indians apart from the dominant society. These concepts derive from their common aboriginal backgrounds, from their common experiences during the past nine or ten generations, and have probably also been influenced by the fact that Federal programs and non-Indian people have a tendency to treat them as if they are alike. Current pan-Indian movements also tend to blur subtle distinctions (understood by Indians) in order to "explain" Indian culture to others and to present a united front for protecting Indian lands and rights. The following list is not meant to be exhaustive, but rather illustrative of some of the ways Indian values differ from the values of the majority culture. Nor is it meant to apply rigidly to all Indians because of the individual differences previously described.

1) Sharing and Generosity

Indians have an extremely strong ethic for sharing, which is tied to the notion that respect is given to those who share what they have. An example is the ritual of gift giving, common among many tribes, in which a family will give to another that which is most prized. It is a way of gaining honor and respect, and it is no honor to give what is not valued. In contrast, the majority culture judges an individual's worth in relationship to what he or she has acquired. This trait of sharing is often difficult for Anglo-American professionals to understand and accept since, for example, they may see overcrowded, impoverished families opening their homes to a host of friends and relatives for extended visits.

2) Cooperation

Indians believe in working together and getting along with each other; the family and the group take precedence over the individual. This stems from an integrated view of the universe where all people, animals, plants, and objects in nature have their place in creating a harmonious whole. This is in sharp contrast to Anglo-American values, which stress individuality and competition. Indian children in school are often mistakenly seen as "unmotivated" because of their reluctance to compete with peers in the classroom or on the playground.

3) Noninterference

Traditionally, Indians are raised not to interfere with others. From childhood, they learn to observe rather than to react impulsively to situations. They learn to respect the rights of others to do as they will and not to meddle in their affairs. Unfortunately, this trait is often viewed by the dominant society as either aloofness or withdrawal; in child rearing, it is mistaken for "permissiveness". (For an excellent review of this personality characteristic, see Wax and Thomas, 1972, and Hallowell, 1955.) This trait is also difficult for Anglos to understand, as members of the dominant society seek and offer advice continually and verbally "move into" situations rather than impassively observing.

One reason for the trait of noninterference may be that, at least until recently, expected norms for behavior were well defined and communicated by example. In child rearing, the use of multiple caretakers with congruent values and expectations has been a standard practice. In contrast, the majority culture reflects a multitude of cultures attempting to define the "right" way to raise children, resulting in a plethora of books, articles, and professionals giving advice, much of which is contradictory.

4) Time Orientation

An Indian is very much grounded in what is happening in his or her life at the moment, rather than making specific plans for future endeavors. Indians are busy living their lives rather than preparing for them. Synonymous with this belief is a time consciousness which emphasizes that things get done or take place within a natural order and not according to deadlines or artifically-imposed time frames. While this time orientation may be partially related to the nature of traditional Indian economies and the need to focus on daily survival, it is also related to the Indian world view of events moving through time in a rhythmic, circular pattern. Artificial impositions of schedules disrupt the natural pattern. The dominant society, in marked contrast, is highly clock-oriented, with punctuality and schedules having high value. Indians are, therefore, often viewed as lazy, inefficient, and unmotivated.

5) Extended Family Orientation

Indians have a strong family orientation that goes far beyond the immediate nuclear family. The extended family may have as many as 200 members, including both blood relatives and clan members. Within this framework, there is a strong respect for elders and their knowledge and wisdom about the world; in traditional family networks, the older people were the primary educators of the youth. In contrast, the primary orientation of the Anglo culture is towards the nuclear family, with little respect for elders, and with much child training and supervision delegated to outside institutions or non-family members. Thus, family involvement in discussion of problems and decision making is much greater in Indian families than in those of the dominant society.

6) Harmony with Nature

Indians hold nature as extremely important, since they realize that they are but one part of a greater whole. There are many rituals and ceremonies that express both their reverence for nature's forces and their observance of the balance that must be maintained between them and all other living and nonliving things. The Indian view of the earth is that it is larger than anyone's right to desecrate it. In contrast, the dominant culture has repeatedly shown a value system that seeks to control and often destroy the balance of nature, with the view that human beings are superior to all other forms of life and have, therefore, the right to manipulate nature for their comfort, convenience, and economic gain.

In summary, Indian people place interpersonal relationships over the individual and have a holistic view of the world. Indians value others by who they are, rather than by what they have acquired. Their holistic view of life is in conflict with the dominant society, which views the world atomistically, separating the whole into parts such as health, religion, family, and occupation. This contrast is particularly evident with respect to the medicine man, who serves as healer, priest, and counselor to an individual and families. Traditional healing serves not to relieve symptoms, as Western medicine so often does, but to restore harmony to the individual within the total universe.

Although we have presented some specific Indian values, it should be noted that there is no way to totally understand the Indian culture by dissecting the surface layer of its many parts. The attempt to isolate and define Native American values is an Anglo-American preoccupation with analyzing and categorizing all aspects of life. Indian belief systems result from an integration of their values; one value cannot be thoroughly understood without exploring them all.

ISSUES IN DEFINING MENTAL HEALTH PROBLEMS

It is deceptively easy to formulate assumptions and generalizations regarding mental health and/or mental health problems. The real issue, however, is that neither mental health nor mental illness lends itself to easy definition. While some conclusions and recommendations will be presented at the end of this chapter, it is not a definitive analysis of all the issues relating to either the mental health of the Indian child or the relationship of culture to personality development.* Rather, it is an attempt at examining some of the underlying assumptions regarding the assessment and treatment of mental health and/or mental illness within the Indian subculture.

We must first look at the question of what is mental health. Is it the absence of mental illness or psychopathology? Is it appropriate adaptation to the social and physical environment? Or is it merely not deviating from the accepted social mores of the dominant culture? It is probably tied to all of these, and more. However, in lieu of any clear cut definitions, a logical place to begin is to address some of the related issues: 1) Who defines mental health and mental illness? 2) What are the situational determinants? 3) How are mental health and mental illness measured? 4) How are they perceived inter- and intraculturally? We propose no new classification schema or operational definitions. There is an abundance of these already, and our position is that there must be a sounder data base before any new generalizations are made.

First, one essential point of contention between the Indian culture and the dominant culture is *who* defines what is appropriate behavior. While there is some validity in the position that mental health should be defined by the majority because it is they who institutionalize the most prevalent standards for everyone, this view denies the right of another culture in our society to be different and to define its own behavior. Essentially, this is the assimilationist perspective; i.e., since you have to live in our society, you will have

to abide by its mores. The underlying requisite in this position is that one must not only abide by those mores, but must also give up one's primary cultural values and become a part of the majority culture. The fact that a great many Indians today remain far from being assimilated and with many of their core values still intact is an indication of their unwillingness to do so.

A second and related issue concerns the situational determinants in which behavior is defined as adaptative or maladaptive. For example, what is appropriate on a reservation may not be appropriate in the city. It is naive to assume that someone who is raised in a certain value system in one place will easily make the transition to another value system just because the place of residence has changed. An excellent example is found in Stewart's (1964) research on relocated Indians in Denver, Colorado. He notes that the orientation of Indians not to do things according to clock-oriented priorities did not fit well with a 9:00-5:00 working day. Many lost their jobs when they could not follow this artificially imposed time schedule. In contrast, Steiner (1968) notes an Indian-run housing program in which they accomplished as much as others would on a rigid time schedule.

Perhaps central to both the aforementioned issues is how mental health or mental illness is measured. Western thought has a firm basis in the scientific method, of drawing cause-and-effect relationships. The heavy reliance on supposedly objective intelligence and personality assessment instruments in defining and diagnosing psychopathology is an example. Few of these tests are culture-free or even culture-fair. As a result, Indian children are often erroneously deemed intellectually inferior, with poor self-concepts, withdrawn and passive, and with a greater susceptibility to psychopathology.

In addition to "objective" instruments, the assessment of mental health on an observational level should also be examined. One of the authors is reminded of an

*For a comprehensive discussion of the latter, the reader is directed to two excellent literature reviews of the social and cultural factors of psychopathology: King, 1978; Dohrenwend and Dohrenwend, 1974.

Ottawa girl in an urban public school who was referred for psychological testing and counseling because her teacher felt that she had a poor self-concept and her school work was suffering because of it. On further inquiry, it was found that the teacher, who had previously had very little contact with Indian children, based her assumptions on the girl's shyness and lack of eye contact when she spoke to the child. Unfortunately, the teacher was unaware that in many Indian subcultures, it is a sign of disrespect to maintain eye contact with an elder. This is only one of many examples that could be mentioned to underline the point that the dominant society is ethnocentric, often quick with its judgments, and that these judgements can have destructive effects.

A final level of analysis is in the interpretation of data that is gathered in naturalistic observation. Again, the problem is not so much in the data, but with the inferences that are made from it. Examples of these types of data include arrest rates, hospital admissions, and other such social statistics which can be used to infer underlying psychopathology. One case of mistaken inferences is noted by Bergman (1977) in a discussion concerning the psychiatrist's role in Indian mental health. He reported that in a mental hospital in the Southwest, the majority of Indian schizophrenics were violent. The conclusions drawn were that Indian schizophrenics were more violent than those of other ethnic groups. Closer analysis, however, revealed that one of the few behaviors that the Indian family system was unprepared to deal with was violence. Hence, violent people were the ones who found their way into hospital statistics because the family could not take care of them.

This last example also underlines another important issue regarding Indians and their perception of mental illness. There is a rather striking difference between Indians and the dominant culture, not only in what is labeled as psychopath-

ology, but in how it is received. The dominant society has traditionally seen the mentally ill as people to be feared and isolated from the rest of the society. In contrast, Indians are very tolerant of deviant behavior. It is not so much that the range of behaviors that is acceptable is greater, but that the range of what is tolerated is greater. As an Ojibway medicine man once told one of the authors, "We place a lot of emphasis on family and community and having people be part of that. We are not like the white man who seems to look for reasons to exclude people." He went on to relate a story of a mentally retarded individual who lived on a reservation in Minnesota. He said that everyone knew how he was different, and how at times he would exhibit strange behaviors like moaning and echolalia. He was, however, very gentle and liked to be around people, especially children. Consequently, many mothers felt no hesitation having him play with and help care for their children. The emphasis was on what he could do, and not on how he was different or inadequate. All efforts were made to incorporate him into the social system, rather than to exclude or isolate him. The lesson for the children was by example: everyone is valuable.

In conclusion, defining what is mental health or mental illness yields cloudy results at best. Psychopathology is not absent among Indians, but as mental health professionals, we must be careful not to draw cause-and-effect relationships without a good understanding of both the values of the culture to be judged and the culture that is doing the judging. Too often, the assumption of pathology is made by professionals as a result of their lack of understanding about cultural diversity. Perhaps a more proper perspective can be gained by noting Deloria's statement, "But the right thing for many people who want to do good is always in terms of their own value system. God help us from those who want to help us" (Steiner, 1968, p. 256).

CONFLICTS IN PSYCHOSOCIAL DEVELOPMENT

Family

Many Indian children today live within and between two highly divergent cultures. Child rearing for Indian families is an exceedingly complex task if they wish to pass down traditions and language, yet assure their children improved chances for education and for employment as adults. Many parents feel caught in the conflict between opposing value systems and may express or model ambivalence to their children.

Families on reservations have traditionally relied on large extended families with multiple caretakers, all of whom shared consistent values. Today, with families broken apart physically for reasons of employment and moves to urban areas and increasingly disjointed because of the change or breakdown of traditional values, many Indian children are exposed to a range of values and behaviors which not only are incompatible, but may be conflict-laden. For example, as children enter school, they often receive divergent messages from their families both to "keep the old ways" and to abandon these traditional ways in order to compete successfully in the economy of the dominant society.

Indian children today must essentially learn to be "white on the outside and Indian on the inside" if they wish to be able to compete successfully in the larger society. They must be able to reconcile the dissonant values of the Indian culture with the daily necessity to compete in school and to become assertive in dealing with Anglo institutions. In order for an Indian child today to learn such skills as competitiveness and assertiveness, he or she must first have pride and belief in the value of being Indian. To balance the two value systems requires a secure psychological base, ego strength, and reinforcement from others in the family and peer group. Indian children must have good models and, often, they are unavailable (Leon, 1968).

Bryde (1971), in citing his own and other research, reported that Indian adolescents show a significantly high incidence of feelings of rejection, depression, anxiety, and alienation from both Indian and the majority societies.

As he looks around him, it dawns upon him that in order to make a decent living for his future family, he must eventually leave his Indian home and go into the non-Indian world to learn the necessary skills. It also dawns upon him for the first time that the norms by which the dominant culture judges a worthy person are those of material achievement . . . He begins to believe that he does not measure up to their norms . . . that they reject him as a person . . . He slowly learns with growing dismay that the outside group expects all Indians, including him, to be no good, undependable, lazy, and to get drunk every chance they get . . . eventually, he begins to view himself in this way. (p. 38).

An example of the negative influences of these role models and stereotypes is the Indian child on a reservation who learns that Indians are of superficial, fleeting interest to the white man, an attitude exemplified by the short-term investment by researchers and by whites who come to live and work there for brief periods. As McNickle (1968) states, "at the level of native crafts or dance costumes or tribal lore . . . 'being ethnic' has a kind of glamor" (p. 119). Thus, these Indian children learn that they are objects of curiosity for the dominant society, but also experience prejudice and discrimination, resulting in exclusion from full participation in the dominant system.

The most obvious consequences for the excluded person are his acquisition of conflicting or fragmented values and goals from the dominant system and his subsequently constricted range of ego defensive and adaptive techniques. These influence his character structure and his vulnerability to illness. His excluded status also influences his relationship with his normative reference group . . . If the major institutions of his society are controlled by members of a dominant system to which he cannot belong, many of the values which they uphold will only symbolize his inferior status and reduce his already low self-esteem. (Brody, 1966, p. 855)

Education

When Indian children begin school, their academic achievement is comparable to the cultural majority for the first several years. By the fourth grade, however, achievement scores begin to drop and continue to decline progressively through high school (Bryde, 1971). There is a 60% drop-out rate among Indian children compares to 23% nationally, with the highest rate in grades 8 and 10 (Pepper, 1976). Particular problems are noted in the acquisition of verbal skills. In terms of higher education, 18% of students in Federal Indian schools go on to college; the national average is 50%. Three percent of Indians who enter college graduate; the national average is 32% (Vogel, 1972).

School thrusts Indian children into the value system of the dominant society. Historically, this was particularly true when boarding schools were the only educational alternative for Indian children on reservations. These schools placed the children in large dormitories and separated them from their families for most of the year. Sadly, the stories of boarding school suppression of language and customs are well known (Beiser, 1974). Over 40,000 Indian children have been educated in boarding schools, and although public schools are increasing rapidly on reservations, they continue to be primarily Anglo schools, encouraging such majority culture values as competition with peers and achievement motivation. Even the textbooks on American history reflect the attitudes of the dominant society toward Indians. A review of more than 300 history texts demonstrated that, "most of the books were, in one way or another, derogatory to the Native Americans. Not one could be approved as a dependable source of knowledge about the history and culture of the Indian people in America" (Costo, 1970, p. 11).

The educational system serves to question the child's sense of trust in his or her earlier experiences. According to Saslow and Harrover (1968), "The identities of the children are weakened and the possibility of diminished initiative is presented, as well as a subsequent breakdown of adequate self-image and competence with which to manifest subsequent achieving behavior . . . the school system contributes toward the feelings of alienation by virtue of the abruptness of change in culture that it presents and by its concentration upon the defense of that culture" (p. 228).

Academic achievement is related to self-concept. Academically successful children must have belief in themselves as a worthy individual and feel a sense of worth from others and a sense of trust with the significant adults in their lives. As the school system continually and subtly discourages "Indianness," Indian children need to integrate dissonant values into their cognitive frameworks. To obtain a higher education in most cases requires leaving the reservation and competing in the dominant society's system and life style. Eventually, the Indian student must decide within a range of choices, which includes assimilation into the dominant society, returning to the reservation, and perhaps even having to choose between the family and the outside world. "Higher education means, of course, that more Indian individuals may choose the path of non-tribal, assimilated life. But it also means that Indian community life will soon be in the hands of a generation of educated Indians" (Lesser, 1961, p. 143).

For most Indians, however, the choice is not clear-cut. Deloria (1979) has eloquently described the dilemma:

No matter how well educated an Indian may become, he or she always suspects that Western culture is not an adequate representation of reality. Life, therefore, becomes a schizophrenic balancing act wherein one holds that the creation, migration, and ceremonial stories of the tribe are true and that the Western European view of the world is also true. Obviously, this situation is impossible although just how it becomes impossible remains a mystery to most Indians. The trick is somehow to relate what one *feels* to what one is taught to *think*. (p. viii)

In summary, depending on their background (traditional or nontraditional), geographic location (urban vs. rural vs. reservation), and socioeconomic status, education can represent a number of dilemmas to Indian children. Some of these include: 1) whether or not education is a betrayal of traditional values, family norms, or parental expectations; 2) conflicts about whether school is to better themselves or to better Indians in general; 3) possible guilt tied to preferential treatment; and 4) conflicting expectations by school officials and others which range from intense pressure to succeed to pressure to fail. There are also other problems revolving around lack of Indian peers and appropriate social contacts.

Media

Television, movies, and popular literature are primarily produced by individuals and groups who both reflect the attitudes of the dominant majority and cater to the pleasures of the mass society. The American Indian man has consistently been stereotyped, with a few exemplary exceptions, as the dominant society has wanted him to be portrayed: a painted, feathered, warring savage with animal-like cunning who is always "defeated" by the superior strength possessed by the white man. His religion and customs are portrayed as exotic, often barbaric and superstitious, and always futile in resisting the encroachment of civilization. The contemporary Indian usually takes the form of a stoic, often mystical, marginal member of society who not infrequently behaves like a fool.

Indian children are aware of the ways their people are represented in the media, and while they may know that the stereotypes are false, they become sensitive to the negative expectations and attitudes that non-Indians exhibit. Even if the message that Indians are second-class citizens is not clearly stated, the subtle influences still come through. In time, they may come to believe in themselves and to treat non-Indians with distrust and hostility. Their self-concept may be negatively affected by the repeated messages they receive from the media about both themselves as individuals and about their people.

Urban Influences

An increasing number of Indians are moving to urban areas, primarily for employment. It is estimated that about one-third of Indians today live permanently on reservations, one-third in urban areas, and one-third move back and forth between urban areas and their reservations. Most families who move to urban areas still consider their reservation "home" and many would return if jobs and housing were available.

The relocation movement beginning in the 1950s has brought thousands of Indians to cities with hopes of training and jobs. With few jobs available on reservations and in rural areas, the program offered promise for improved living and for economic gains to share with families on the reservation. For many Indians, however, training ends with no jobs available (Graves, 1971). Allowances for living are meager for city dwelling, families are often separated, and friendships are difficult to establish. Accustomed to a relatively clear system for obtaining medical and financial help on reservations, many

Indians find services in the urban area to be a maze of complex bureaucracies. Urban Indians are the poorest, least educated and most highly unemployed group of people in our society (Chadwick and Strauss, 1975).

The children of these families, meanwhile, are being raised with fewer contacts with traditional life and little knowledge of the native language. Daily they observe the frustrated hopes of their parents. The choices for these Indian children may be even more limited than their parents'; reservation life is unknown to them, and they may eventually become members of the urban under-class. Their peers are often non-Indian and they increasingly grow up to marry non-Indians, diluting the cultural heritage they will teach their children (Price, 1972).

In an intensive study of 120 Indian families living in the San Francisco Bay area, the Native American Research Group (Bowman et al., 1975) found that the majority of mothers wanted their children to learn their heritage and to retain their cultural identity and practices. Unfortunately, many of the mothers felt unequipped to carry out their child-rearing roles successfully because of several factors: None of the mothers had been raised in cities themselves and had few effective coping skills to teach their children; many had attended boarding schools with subsequent feelings of ambivalence about authority and education; contacts with other Indians did not occur naturally, but had to be actively sought out; and the children were continually exposed to competing value systems.

Summary

The outlook for the mental health of Indian children can appear bleak when considering the complex interactional effects of changing family values, poverty, educational conflicts, and negative stereotypes portrayed in the media. Yet, while the Indian cultures are undergoing enormous changes on some levels, many Indian families continue to provide their children with the values of the traditional Indian culture. There are strengths in Indian families, often unnoticed or misjudged by non-Indian professionals, such as the richness of family life available through multiple caretakers and the cohesiveness of families and clans in providing support and care for each other. While families may often live in small and crowded housing, and children may be deprived of many of the tangible aspects of middle-class life, these factors alone should not be used to judge the adequacy of a family's ability to care for its children. The extended Indian family considers loyalty to the family and tribe as a primary value, and can serve as a valuable resource, even when members reside several states away from each other.

In spite of the many conflicts facing Indian children today, the reality is that increasing numbers of Indian people are becoming educated and working with their own people to preserve their culture. Additionally, the Indian population is steadily increasing and Indians are becoming a potent political force in our society, as well as better realizing their goal of self-determination.

PRESENT SERVICE DELIVERY SYSTEMS

The present mental health delivery system for Indians is alarmingly inadequate. On a Federal level, the delivery of mental health services is the responsibility of the Indian Health Service (IHS). An American Indian Policy Review Commission report on Indian health problems (1976) reviewed the current state of affairs and concluded that the ability of the IHS to deliver mental health services suffered greatly from lack of funds, severe understaffing, an absence of a comprehensive needs assessment, a lack of training programs for professionals and paraprofessionals, and inadequate facilities. In general, these remarks applied only to reservation populations, and when the needs of Indians living off reservations are also considered, it is clear that the problem is immense. Regarding this second group, the report explains, "With few exceptions, no mental health programs (or general health care), even today, are reaching the balance of the Indian population, about 50% which lives off reservations in either urban areas or in tribal settings never federally recognized" (pp. 86-87).

On state and local levels, mental health services to the off-reservation population are available through agencies such as Community Mental Health Centers, family service agencies, and religiously based help groups. These agencies, however, are rarely utilized by Indians (Wise, 1979). This has led to some rather myopic conclusions, the most obvious of which is that, if Indians do not use existing mental health services, they must not need them. This often serves as a convenient way of avoiding the frustration of rendering service to a population that does not readily accept existing methods of delivery.

It is as if the programs are beyond reproach, and their failure is in the recipient's ability or willingness to take advantage of them. Essentially, an elitist attitude has developed that externalizes the responsibility for the failure of existing programs. Unfortunately, the outcome is often either termination of the program or the development of yet another program to help "those poor people" take advantage of the first program. It is amazing how much time and money are spent in programming, and how little is devoted to questioning how those efforts can be made more relevant.

Yet social statistics regarding alcoholism, crime, juvenile delinquency, and school drop-outs among Indians are inescapable and clearly point out the need for development and use of effective mental health interventions. In order to better plan effective programs that will reach more Indian families, it is necessary to understand some of the reasons why underutilization occurs.

At one level, many Indian parents are simply not aware of the services available, or if they are, policies and procedures are often confusing and highly impersonal, require a great deal of motivation in filling out complicated forms, and necessitate having reliable transportation to use the services (Miller, 1978a). The problem of explaining what mental health professionals do or have to offer is difficult in general and can only be compounded for Indians, whose understanding of the dominant culture may itself be lacking. Additionally, the value systems and therapeutic approaches are frequently inappropriate or conflicting with an Indian's view of the world.

For many Indians, however, there is a much deeper reason for nonutilization of services. Through experience, they have arrived at a strong mistrust of the dominant culture and its institutions. They know of the boarding schools that took Indian children from their families, of the uninformed sterilization of many Indian women, and of the many broken treaty-obligations. Prejudice in such areas as employment and housing just serves as a reminder of what the dominant culture has done to them. Many Indians are ambivalent, if not resentful, of the dependent and often powerless position they find themselves in with respect to Federal and state services. To ask them to become dependent once more is often highly threatening, especially when the interaction involves intrusion into their feelings, emotions, and thoughts, many of which they feel will be judged negatively by the dominant society.

There is a psychological distance that many Indians maintain not only out of mistrust, but out of fear. They are afraid that the dominant culture will swallow them up, take away their traditions and culture and, thus, their identity. More than anything else, they fear loss of spiritual identity. They see what the dominant culture has done in respect to what they value, and they do not want to be part of that. It is understandable that they are truly frightened of dominant culture mental health professionals whom they may view as "trying to make them white."

One last reason for nonutilization has a more positive tone. The traditional family system and its tolerance for deviation both serve to develop an excellent support system where many personal problems can be solved (Weibel, 1977). When personal or family problems arise, Indians may tend to exhaust all primary resources (family, friends) before considering taking their problems to a "stranger." Often, the decision to seek professional help is the result of many hours of family discussion and consensus to take that step.

SERVICES TO HANDICAPPED CHILDREN

One area which demonstrates the lack of needed services on reservations and the failure to provide them to Indians in urban areas is services to handicapped children. While the past 15 years have seen a virtual explosion of programs, funds, and legislation from both public and private sources, few of these resources have reached Indian people.

In May, 1976, the First Inter-Tribal Symposium on Mental Retardation was sponsored by Project Impact of the National Association for Retarded Citizens and the Navajo Tribe. This meeting was held in the Navajo Nation. Members of eight tribes and Federal and state officials discussed the status of services to handicapped children on reservations (Miller, 1978b). The enormity of the need for appropriate services was staggering, and until a few years ago, no services were available. Handicapped children were either given no education or services, or were sent off reservations to state institutions, where they usually remained with no attempts to return them home or to involve families in their on-going care.

In the past 10 years, several small schools, both residential and day schools, have been established on the Navajo, Hopi, and Sioux reservations; funding and staffing are major problems. Funding problems arose out of disagreement among Federal and state agencies regarding responsibility, with the Bureau of Indian Affairs, Department of Health, Education and Welfare, and other agencies all considering the responsibility of educating handicapped children on reservations to be under someone else's domain. BIA boarding schools have historically provided no special programs, and the public schools are just beginning to develop special education programs.

Thousands of handicapped Indian children continue to be unserved due to lack of facilities, the isolation of families, and transportation difficulties. The result of the Symposium was to identify and document the need and to begin to develop strategies for developing programs on reservations.

Off-reservation Indians with handicapped children may also be failing to receive services for reasons less clear. In a survey conducted in Los Angeles in 1975 of Regional Centers which serve as a registration point for developmentally disabled individuals, there were no Indians known to be registered. Additionally, according to the Los Angeles City Schools, with 4,500 Indian children registered, only 21 were in any kind of special education program—less than one half of one percent (Kahan and Miller, 1978). Either Indian children with special needs are not being identified, families are not reporting their Indian ethnicity, or they are receiving services somewhere else, which is unlikely.

A one-year, state-funded case-finding project at the Indian Free Clinic in Huntington Park, California (Los Angeles area) resulted in locating 33 Indian children and adults with handicapping conditions who were not receiving services. Most families were either unaware that any services existed, had tried to locate help but were confused about what was available, had been put on interminable waiting lists, or had no money to pay for services. In many situations, institutional systems such as schools, public welfare, and medical facilities knew of the problems, but had not helped the families obtain needed services (Miller, 1978a). Two case examples demonstrate the problem:

Marlene was a 12-year-old severely retarded girl who had been seen regularly by a pediatrician, but never attended school. The doctor had advised the mother to "keep her home and treat her as normally as possible." Both parents had been raised on reservations, thought schools were only for normal children, and had never inquired about special education.

Jim did not begin talking until the age of 4, and was always slow in all areas of development. His parents had not consulted a doctor because he was healthy, and had assumed that he would learn speech when he began school. When he was taken to the school for enrollment at age 5, the school said they had no place for him and that the mother should keep him home until they called. When the family was located by the outreach staff, Jim was 7 years old and still waiting for the school to call. A referral was made to a psychologist in a public agency for evaluation; the psychologist called protective services and filed a complaint of neglect against the mother for keeping the child out of school.

Both of these examples point out the isolation that many Indian families feel in urban areas. Never having expected services to exist, they did not know they could seek them. Jim's family also exemplifies the divergent value system regarding the seeking of help for developmental and learning problems. The majority culture is medically oriented, and the failure to begin talking at an early age is viewed as within the realm of pediatric care; to Jim's mother, doctors are consulted only when you are physically ill. Her belief system is not "wrong," but was viewed as such by a mental health practitioner who filed a complaint of neglect against the mother.

If Indian families, whether on reservations or in urban areas, do not seek services for relatively obvious handicaps, either because they do not exist or because of fear that the child may be taken away from them, how much more difficult it is to expect that they would seek professional help for "emotional" or behavior problems of their children.

FUTURE APPROACHES

The successful delivery of mental health services to Indian children and their families is dependent on a number of factors. Perhaps overriding in importance is the previously mentioned issue of relevance. Many of the reasons for the failures and nonutilization of past mental health programs by Indians relate to the fact that most of these methods of delivering service are simply not appropriate. They fail to recognize not only the differences among tribes and individuals, but more importantly, the differences between Indians and the dominant culture. Often these programs, as well as the professionals who carry them out, reflect the values of the dominant culture. These values may include: work is good; affluence and education make people happier; and individualism and competition are desirable traits. The assumption that these values are universal can have profound effects on service delivery interactions. Because of the basic differences between the two cultures, some Indians feel very strongly that they will be misunderstood or negatively judged if they express their values and attitudes. The greater the perceived distance between the values of the client and the service provider, the more difficult it is to establish contact and develop rapport (Mazur, 1973).

Some of the value differences that can

create problems within the therapeutic relationship include: the efficacy of relying on many of the mainstream, intrapsychic theories, such as the rational/cognitive approaches used by the majority of professionals, which may not be appropriate with some Indian clients who have a more emotional and spiritual view of the world; an atomistic approach that attempts to categorize problems and deal with symptoms, which is often in conflict with an Indian's holistic view of harmony with nature; and an approach which advocates a belief system divergent from that of the client and attempts, either explicitly or implicitly, to assimilate him or her into the dominant culture.

In general, an effective therapeutic relationship will be based on many of the same tenets that characterize effective psychotherapy with any population: sensitivity to the individual client's needs, interests, and background; the development of trust; and the communication of care and sincerity. There are, however, some important therapeutic variables which deserve special attention when serving Indian clients.

One is the speed of therapy. The traditional Indian way of dealing with problems is to sit and talk with friends. In the course of talking, sometimes not even about the specific problem, a solution is found. This is similar to the concept of "working through," and in this context may be viewed as a comparatively slow process that does not fit well with the conventional notions of many mental health professionals who believe that problems should be talked about directly until they are solved. In contrast to the sense of immediacy that characterizes many Western-thought therapies, Native American clients may not respond well to being "pushed." A therapist who expects quick disclosure of sensitive material may be frustrated with an Indian's reluctance to speak about personal matters before a sense of trust has been built. Instead, a Native American may prefer to talk of other things until they understand and trust the situation better. To move too quickly may precipitate withdrawal, if not the termination of their participation altogether.

An approach which stresses confrontation may also meet with considerable resistance, since many Indians do not usually respond favorably to such overt intrusion. The therapist must remember that for many Indians, noninterference is strongly valued. In the same vein, directive interventions that seek to prescribe behavior will probably not be as effective as an approach which relies on more nondirective techniques, such as clarifying and empathizing. As noted before, Indian clients are often extremely wary of dominant culture institutions and their representatives; therefore, it is important for them to get a sense that they have a say in the direction of the therapeutic process.

Mental health professionals must be careful not to be overly active and appear to direct the course of therapy with their interventions. The therapist who tries to impress a client with dynamic interpretations, especially early in the course of therapy, stands the chance of being rejected by an Indian who is less interested in this show of intelligence or knowledge than would be a member of the dominant culture. Quick interpretations also have a greater risk of showing cultural insensitivity. At the same time, the Indian client will not usually be active or overtly display his or her emotions until he or she feels comfortable and trusting of the therapist.

There must also be a great deal of flexibility in the delivery of mental health services. The prevailing notions of the "50 minute hour/once per week/at my office" routine can seem very odd to many Indians. The idea that personal problems could be isolated so as to need attention on a regular time schedule is very foreign. Service workers must be willing to go outside their offices and into the community. Home visits can, in fact, be very useful, since they represent a willingness to adapt to the Indian's social system rather than an attempt to change it. In this way the outreach worker becomes a more accepted part of the community.

A case example illustrates this point best. One of the authors had the opportunity of working with an Indian Center in a large metropolitan area of Michigan. Among the Center's services were health, employment, and educational counseling. It was found that the best identification of problems in all these areas was done by the educational specialists who had close contact with many Indian families through their home and school visits with Indian children. The families learned to accept and trust these outreach workers because the workers had come to them and demonstrated their concern for the children. Eventually the families confided in the workers and reported other problems, at which time appropriate referrals could be made.

This example also points to perhaps the most important issue in developing effective delivery systems: that is, the knowledge and use of existing social support systems. As mentioned before, the importance of the extended family for Indian children is great. Family members are sources of support and understanding and provide a rich resource of personalities and access to traditional customs and beliefs. A survey done of an urban Indian community has shown that the family is an extremely important support system and link-up with service agencies for Indians seeking help for health and mental health problems (Wise, 1979).

It would, therefore, seem only logical to aim interventions at working with and strengthening the family. A fine example of this type of program is seen in the work done at *Ah-be-no-gee*, a family and child services program for Indians living in the Minneapolis area (Red Horse, 1977). This program stresses the importance of utilizing natural family networks and is based on the idea that the family is the foundation for both Indian culture and individual mental health.

Future approaches with Indian children and their families also raise several questions which can only be answered by the individual practitioner. What are the responsibilities and the limitations of a professional working with an Indian family today? Should the professional encourage the parents to provide more opportunities for the child to have more exposure to their Indian people and Indian cultural practices? Should the professional take an active role in helping the children learn social skills that will enable them to be "white on the outside," while choosing whether they want to identify as Indians. Or should the professional maintain the position of nonjudgmental neutrality espoused by the mental health system?

The authors maintain the position that effective work with Native American children and their families must include an assessment of the child's developing cultural identity, and that treatment must include an educational dimension for the parents to assist them in enabling the child to better know his or her cultural heritage.

SUMMARY

The delivery of effective mental health services to Indian children and their families in the future requires heightened sensitivity by professionals to the relativity of culture. The values of the dominant society permeate all of our political, economic, educational, and mental health systems. Mental health professionals are taught to define adjustment and deviance according to those values. While they often possess intellectual understanding and acceptance of divergent cultural values and behaviors, the assessment and treatment of individuals continues to be based on dominant society norms.

Most mental health professionals would

deny feelings of prejudice and judgmental attitudes in their practice, yet the policies of agencies result in the underutilization of services by many ethnic minorities. In working with bicultural children and their families, it is imperative for professionals to understand the dynamics of biculturalism, particularly for the developing child who is exposed to multiple and often dissonant models in the family, school, and peer groups, and inconsistent consequences for behaviors displayed at home and away from home.

The personality and development of the Native American child cannot be understood by simply knowing more about Indian cultures. Mental health professionals must be aware of their own values and expectations, and have an understanding of the complex interaction of Indian and Anglo societies on political, social, and economic levels in order to have an appreciation of the conflicts faced by Native American children in their development.

REFERENCES

Ablon, J. Relocated American Indians in the San Francisco Bay area: Social interaction and Indian identity. In: H. Bahr, B. Chadwick, and R. Day (Eds.), *Native American Today: Sociological Perspectives.* New York: Harper and Row, 1972.

American Indian Policy Review Commission, (Final Report) *Report on Indian Health.* Washington, D.C.: Government Printing Office, 1976.

Beiser, M. A Hazard to mental health: Indian boarding schools. *American Journal of Psychiatry*, March 1974, *131*(7), 305-306.

Bergman, R. Panel Participant, Issues in Contemporary Psychiatry. Audiotape produced by Smith, Kline & French Laboratories, 1977.

Bowman, B., Carlin, W., Garcia, A., Maybee, C., Miller, D., and Sierras, P. *Native American Families in the City: American Indian Socialization to Urban Life.* San Francisco: Institute for Scientific Analysis, 1975.

Brody, E. Cultural exclusion, character and illness. *American Journal of Psychiatry*, January 1966, *122*(7), 852-858.

Bromberg, W. and Hutchinson, S. Self image of the American Indian: A preliminary study. *International Journal of Social Psychiatry*, Spring/Summer 1974, *20*, 39-44.

Bryde, J. *Indian Students and Guidance.* Boston: Houghton Mifflin, 1971.

Chadwick, B. and Strauss, J. The assimilation of

American Indians into urban society. The Seattle case. *Human Organization*, Winter 1975, *34*, (4).

Costo, R. (Ed.) *Textbooks & the American Indian.* American Indian Historical Society, 1970.

Deloria, V. *Custer Died For Your Sins.* New York: Avon, 1969.

Deloria, V. *The Metaphysic of Modern Existence.* New York: Harper & Row, 1979.

Dohrenwend, B. P. and Dohrenwend, B. S. Social and Cultural Influence on Psychopathology. *Annual Review of Psychology*, 1974, *25*, 417, 52.

Graves, T. Drinking and drunkeness among urban Indians. In: J. Waddell and O. Watson (Eds.), *The American Indian in Urban Society.* Boston: Little Brown, 1971.

Hallowell, A. *Culture and Experience*, Philadelphia: University of Pennsylvania Press, 1955.

Kahan, M. & Miller, N. *Developmental Disabilities Project* (Final Report). Huntington Park, California: Indian Free Clinic, 1978.

King, L. Social and Cultural Influences on Psychopathology. *Annual Review of Psychology*, 1978, *29*, 405-33.

Leon, R. Some implications for a preventive program for American Indians. *American Journal of Psychiatry*, August 1968, *125*(2), 128-132.

Lesser, A. Education and the Future of Tribalism in The United States: The Case of The American Indian. *Social Service Review*, 1961, *35*, 135-143.

Mazur, V. Family therapy: an approach to the culturally different. *International Journal of Social Psychiatry.* Spring-Summer 1973, *19½*, 114-120.

McNickle, D. The sociocultural setting of Indian life. *American Journal of Psychiatry*, August 1968, *125*.

Miller, N. Utilization of services for the developmentally disabled by American Indian families in Los Angeles. Ann Arbor, University Microfilms, 1978(a).

Miller, N. (Ed.) Proceedings of the First Annual Inter-Tribal Symposium on Mental Retardation. National Association for Retarded Citizens, Arlington, Texas, 1978(b).

Pepper, F. Teaching the American Indian child in mainstream settings. In: R. Jones (Ed.), *Mainstreaming and The Minority Child.* Reston, VA: Council for Exceptional Children, 1976.

Price, J. The migration and adaptation of American Indians to Los Angeles. In: R. Bahr, B. Chadwick, and R. Day (Eds.), *Native Americans Today: Sociological Perspectives.* New York: Harper & Row, 1972.

Red Horse, J. G. Culture as a variable in human services. *Protective Services Resource Institute*, August-September 1977, *2*(7), 11.

Saslow, H. and Harrover, M. Research on psychosocial adjustment of Indian youth. *American Journal of Psychiatry*, August 1968, *125*(2), 224-231.

Steiner, S. *The New Indians.* New York: Harper & Row, 1968.

Stewart, O. Questions regarding American Indian criminality. *Human Organization*, Spring 1964, *23*(1), 61-66.

Trimble, J. Value differences among American Indians: Concerns for the concerned counselor.

Journal of Counseling Across Cultures. Honolulu: University Press of Hawaii, 1976.

Vogel, V. (Ed.) *This Country Was Ours: A Documentary History of the American Indian.* New York: Harper & Row, 1972.

Wax, R. and Thomas, R. American Indians and White people. In: H. Bahr, B. Chadwick, and R. Day (Eds.), *Native Americans Today: Sociological Perspectives.* New York: Harper & Row, 1972.

Weibel, J. Native Americans in Los Angeles: A cross-cultural comparison of assistance parents in an urban environment. University Microfilms, Ann Arbor, 1977.

Wise, F. Help-seeking behavior and support systems within an urban Indian community. Unpublished manuscript. Michigan State University, 1979.

CHAPTER 21

Mental Health Issues of Japanese-American Children

Lindbergh S. Sata, M.D.

Mental health issues surrounding Japanese-American children in the United States are only understandable to the extent to which the children and their families have acculturated and assimilated into mainstream America. It is with this in mind that an overview of Japanese immigration to the United States and an examination of the intergenerational differences and similarities will be explored in setting the stage for identifying mental health issues facing third and fourth generation Japanese-American children in the United States.

HISTORICAL PERSPECTIVE TO IMMIGRATION

Japanese immigrants and their offspring generations continue to attract the attention of ethnographers and social scientists because of the uniqueness of their patterns of immigration to the United States. The principal wave of immigration was time bound, and the majority of first generation Japanese or Isseis arrived between 1900 and 1920. An anti-oriental sentiment had already been established on the West Coast and within twenty years of the initial arrival of Chinese immigrants in the United States, the pejorative term *coolie labor* had been established by 1869 (Hill, 1973). The Chinese Exclusion Act of 1882 was established in response to the presence of 104,000 Chinese who were part of the labor force in the railroad, mining and timber industries. As is true with most immigrant groups, orientals were first viewed as providing cheap labor in the settlement of the West but subsequently as economically competitive and threatening to White Americans as the Chinese moved into urban areas.

The impact of the Chinese Exclusion Act of 1882 was devastating to the fewer than 150 Japanese immigrants present in the United States. It set the stage for racial discrimination directed towards all orientals and eventually led to the Gentlemen's Agreement between Japan and the

United States in 1909. The influence of labor unions and the effects of restrictive legislation and practices are well documented and provide insights into the understanding of discrimination as a function of numbers and economics, as well as of visibility on the basis of color (Hill, 1973).

Thus, while Western European immigration patterns continued unabated and 17,000,000 individuals arrived beneath the welcoming arms of the Statue of Liberty, the backdoor to the United States was closed and Japanese immigrants were excluded as their numbers approached 70,000. The period between 1906 and 1921 enabled single male immigrants to marry Japanese women by utilizing culturally approved marriage brokers (Kikumura and Kitano, 1973) or to be reunited with their wives in forming the Issei or first generation immigrant population.

THE ISSEI GENERATION

Little was known of Japan until Commodore Matthew Perry's visit in 1853 which opened trade between Japan and the United States. Japan had barely emerged from a primitive feudal system ravaged by one hundred years of civil war and was struggling for existence in a preindustrialized society (Sata, 1973). The immigrant generation of Isseis were a product of the Meiji era, still clinging to the traditions of caste and class. Most were poorly educated, with respect to both the Japan they had left and the land to which they had turned.

The historical accounts of the settlement of Issei are well documented by historians, sociologists and ethnographers. While equally valid, the documentation of the blatant racism thrust upon Isseis has remained buried in newspaper accountings of violence (Kitano, 1969) and racist editorials of West Coast newspapers of the 1900-1920 era, and in restrictive land law legislation and anti-miscegenation statues wherever oriental immigrants settled.

The cultural, religious, philosophical and racial disparity between America and Japan appeared minimized among Issei in a variety of adaptive mechanisms incompletely appreciated or understood by social scientists. Virtually every family album contained photographs taken in Japan in Japanese traditional dress which, conversely, is conspicuous by its absence in photographs taken in the United States. The adoption of Western dress may have reflected identification with the ruling group or with those cultural values supporting inconspicuousness of presentation of self in the presence of others. Outward behavioral manifestations of performance, dedication, allegiance and politeness were congruent with Protestant ethics (Yamamoto, 1974) and facilitated some degree of acceptance by Westerners in an otherwise hostile environment.

The evolution of Japanese ghettos retained self-sustaining sociocultural, educational, economic and religious institutions that permitted social distance and coexistence with the majority community without the problems of "racial contamination" or a threat to the economy of the larger community. Being preoccupied with survival issues, Isseis had little time or opportunity to master English and thus were interdependent on members within the Japanese community for emotional sustenance and economic support.

For Isseis, the family unit was central for the transmission of cultural values and beliefs as well as for the teaching of children to survive in America. The next level of organization included the Ken-ji-kai, which were social membership organizations based upon the prefecture in Japan from which they came. Other community organizations were business-related such as growers' organizations, hotel associations or Japanese community-wide social organizations. In the presence of such community organizations, engagement with representatives of the larger community became formalized and largely restricted to organizational leaders who could communicate in English to represent the Japanese community.

Among Isseis and their families there were clearly established roles and functions which were hierarchically determined with rigid adherence to defined roles. Status was determined on the basis of lineage and geographic origins in Japan. Those whose families were of the Samurai or warrior class received unusual distinction within Japanese communities and were accorded respect and leadership functions. Priests, clergymen, educators and professionals were also respected since many came from the upper social strata of early 20th Century Japan. Businessmen, trades people and farmers represented descending status within the community, as was true in Japan, but this was further influenced by genealogy and geographic origins. Isseis from rural prefectures were accorded low status as contrasted to those from prefectures adjacent to large urban centers.

The majority of Issei immigrants were poorly educated, averaging 4-6 years of formal education in Japan. Isseis tended to be from rural areas, were themselves disadvantaged educationally and culturally, and had been without employment opportunities in their native country. Thus, in settling in their new home, daily discourse centered around the problem of survival, and cultural teachings were minimal or nonexistent. Japanese was the primary language of communication with their second generation offspring, hereafter designated as Nisei.

What is central to the understanding of the Issei is that the teachings transmitted to their children reflected parataxic distortions of impressions of the larger community without their having directly experienced membership in that community. Because of their overriding concern for survival, such teachings reinforced a need for hypervigilance, stoicism, non-offensive conduct vis à vis the larger community, non-disclosure of emotions suggesting weakness of character, etc. Hard work, politeness, diligence, conscientiousness, personal appearance and avoidance of conflict were common topics discussed within the home to prevent drawing negative attention to the family unit.

The combination of ethnocentrism reflecting Japanese cultural values coupled with the loss of dignity in a hostile environment contributed to the phenomena of cultural paranoia. In its adaptive sense, it permitted the survival of the immigrants and their offspring in their ability to withstand psychological insults; the hypervigilance further facilitated early diagnosis of situations leading to possible physical injury. In a maladaptive sense, it constrained Isseis in exploring the potential of their new homeland and contributed to the "ghettoization" of the mind.

The shame and/or guilt culture of the Issei evolved negative views regarding mental illness and tuberculosis, both thought to be inherited diseases and reflecting poorly upon the family unit. Virtually no information is available regarding the incidence of mental disorders, although tuberculosis was known to exist in significant numbers.

While purely speculative, several mechanisms may have been involved in the extremely low numbers of identifiable mentally disordered Isseis. The immigrants themselves were prescreened, and those who came and survived required both physical stamina and adaptive character traits to withstand hardships. Those who were physically weak died early deaths, many from pulmonary disorders aggravated by hard rock mining and working out of doors in the railroad, mining, and timber industries. It is also known that substantial numbers returned to Japan. Among these could have been those Isseis whose psychological makeup was such as to be unable to cope with the rigors of immigrant life. Suicides occurred with rarity or were disguised in their reporting to reflect death by natural causes.

Issei immigrant survivors are rapidly dwindling in numbers and most are over 80 years of age. With few exceptions they communicate in Japanese, continue to maintain cultural and social ties with other Isseis, and pursue culturally relevant activities such as calligraphy, classical Japanese singing, flower arrangement and writing Japanese poetry. In their waning years Isseis are pursuing activities for which neither time nor opportunity was available earlier in their lives. In a poignant manner Isseis appear to have returned to the cultural pursuits of early youth as if to close the circle in a uniquely Japanese style with neither a beginning nor an end. Simultaneously they are seen attending funerals almost weekly, paying final respects to friends who have preceded them in closing the chapter on this generation known simply as Issei.

NISEIS

Niseis are American-born offspring of Issei immigrants and are considered second-generation Japanese-Americans. Niseis vary in age from 35 to 65, with the largest numbers between 45 and 60 years in age. They have been described variously as the model minority (Kitano, 1962), the Quiet American (Hosokawa, 1969), the most educated and successful ethnic group in the United States (Sue and Frank, 1973).

In contrast to their parents, Niseis who were raised in families prior to World War II (1941) were bilingual, with Japanese as their primary language. The extent to which they mastered spoken and written Japanese is directly correlated with the person's age at the outbreak of World War II when Japanese language schools were for all intents and purposes abandoned as a community activity. Furthermore, the

majority of Nisei males who entered the armed services and were not assigned to the European theatre of war were further trained to serve as translators in the South Pacific theatre and have retained their language proficiency.

While physical hardships and marginal standards of living plagued Isseis in their initial 30 years in America, they were relatively free of psychological stress. Their community was self contained with culturally consonant support mechanisms and a communal form of living with interdependency upon one another for cultural and social cohesiveness.

Niseis raised in such an environment developed as do most transitional generations with clearly defined expectations within the family unit as well as within the community. Many of their experiences with family and community were alien to those experiences in school with non-Japanese-American friends. The culturally valued experiences, including martial arts training for males and dancing and playing Japanese instruments for females, as well as Japanese language school, clearly set Niseis apart from their parents' generation on the one hand and from their non-Japanese peer group on the other. Incompletely and superficially immersed in both Western and Eastern cultures, Niseis became a marginal generation without understanding how it was to be American or how it was to be Japanese (Sata, 1973).

The ambivalence characterizing Nisei is best illustrated in the response to discriminatory land laws prohibiting ownership of land by their parents' generation. Niseis represented families as the paper owners of land in which decision making or even opinions were construed as disrespectful and intolerable by their Issei parents. On the other hand, by virtue of their facility in expressing themselves in English, Niseis negotiated and mediated at the direction of their fathers. The prohibition of dating until early adulthood, the insistence on maintaining social distance with non-Japanese, particularly with respect to dating and marriage, coupled with the severely autocratic role of Issei fathers, created ongoing generational conflicts reflected in psychological decompensation of some members of this generation. Again, the numbers of Nisei schizophrenics or the incidence of the seriously psychologically disabled are unknown because of the secrecy and shame surrounding their beliefs regarding mental illness. For those institutionalized prior to 1941, the majority of schizophrenic patients were women who were hospitalized only following many years of manifest psychotic symptoms hidden from public view by family members. Of clinical interest is the finding that some of these chronic patients still make themselves up in bizarre white faces reflecting their earlier developmental conflicts within the family and the psychotic expression for the wish to be someone other than Japanese-American.

With the bombing of Pearl Harbor and the hysteria that followed, West Coast Japanese families were uprooted and placed in concentration camps in the Spring of 1942. The majority of known Japanese community leaders were arrested several months earlier, separated from their families and placed in a segregated facility in Crystal City, Texas, and designated as dangerous aliens. The precipitous nature of arrest and detention without formal hearings or public charges and the subsequent developments leading to mass evacuation of Japanese families destroyed their communities as functional sociocultural entities. Those few Nisei who resisted and questioned the constitutionality of incarceration without due process were labeled traitors and imprisoned. The blatant racism against and economic exploitation of Japanese families is well documented (Weglyn, 1976), as is the response and record of Niseis during and following World War II (Hosokawa, 1969).

The simultaneous loss of leadership among Isseis and the necessity of communicating with federal representatives escalated Niseis into roles of prominence overnight and contributed to the erosion of established roles and functions within the family unit. Sleeping quarters were barely sufficient to contain the necessary number of army cots, while bathroom, laundry and mess facilities were centralized in blocks containing approximately 200 people each. The lack of privacy, the communal facilities and the establishment of English as a primary mode of communication both emancipated and deprived Niseis of the stabilizing influence of family life.

Peer groups by age formed quickly as the primary socialization unit and organized around athletic competition between blocks. Parent surrogates were self selected from older Nisei who acted as coaches, and parental supervision gradually dissipated over time.

The educational experiences for most school-age Nisei during this period were grossly inadequate, lacking textbooks or course options, and staffed with poorly trained teachers. Absenteeism for weeks on end was common and uncontrolled, creating increasing restlessness as well as stimulating the wish to increase self controls over their own destiny.

Since it was possible to leave the camps under special dispensation between the years 1942 and 1946, many Niseis who could qualify left to attend colleges and universities in unprecedented numbers, making Niseis the most educated racial subgroup within the United States. In addition, they successfully demonstrated their loyalty to the nation in the creation of the 442nd Regimental all-Nisei combat unit which became the most decorated battle unit in World War II (U.S. News & World Report, 1966).

Given the aforementioned developments, Niseis began anew, starting new lives in the midwestern and eastern United States. With the end of World War II, many gradually returned to be reunited with families and communities on the West Coast. Unable to return to former neighborhoods now occupied by other minority groups, they resettled wherever housing was available.

The reestablishment of lives of Niseis in the post World War II era contained elements of starting over similar to their parents' generation but with several clear distinctions. They were far better educated, had a realistic view of the world around them, and had demonstrated sufficient flexibility in abandoning ghetto life and its attitude of coexistence in exchange for an assimilated form of living with mainstream America. Their education enhanced employment opportunities previously denied them and facilitated increased acceptance by the majority culture.

SANSEI

The Sansei, or third generation, represents the grandchildren of Issei immigrants and, as a group, resembles middle class white American children in attitudes, beliefs and life style. Most have lost the ability to communicate in Japanese. Friendships among Sansei continue to reflect the strong emotional ties among Nisei, with concentration camp experiences as a primary reference point for friendships continued over a span of 35 years. As contrasted to Isseis whose ties were traced to the prefecture or origin in Japan, Nisei and their Sansei offspring tend to identify themselves with respect to the camp in which their Nisei parents spent four impressionable years between 1942 and 1946. Because of this phenomenon, Sansei children have developed and maintained friendships based upon socialization patterns of their parents' generation as well as those resulting from school and community functions.

Sansei continue to show some characteristics of their parents' generation and, while not as apparent, continue to be less aggressive socially and tend to over-achieve, but continue to enjoy the reputation of being model children in school

(Sata, 1974). The majority do well academically, and the incidence of school maladjustment is small and constant from year to year.

For the behaviorally deviant, social institutions are gradually replacing both the family and the community in their monitoring and treatment functions. Traditional Japanese community gatekeepers such as family physicians and clergy continue to function as first line interveners with families experiencing social and behavioral deviance. Younger Nisei of the age group 35 to 50, together with older Sansei between 20 and 35 years of age, have worked together to create social and health agencies within the community and have become increasingly sophisticated in seeking avenues of funding outside the Japanese community.

Parameters of Mental Health

Examination of higher education career choices for Sansei based on University of Washington graduates during 1975-1976 reflects a climate of optimism in the wide diversity of majors selected as well as a trend away from seeking careers primarily in education, engineering, health and natural sciences, nursing and sociology. Of particular mental health significance are increasing numbers of graduates in psychology (16 percent), architecture and urban planning (11 percent), and the social and humanistic sciences (32 percent).

Indirect inferences drawn from such data include the reflection of increasing career options as well as competence of Sansei in competing in career choices requiring verbal facility (Table 1). There also appears to be heightened social awareness and psychological mindedness less demonstrable among their parents' generation.

The continued reinforcement of education for evolving generations of Japanese Americans is reflected in the following data. Of the 6,330 Japanese males in Se-

TABLE 1

Asian Student Graduates by Major
University of Washington 1975-76

	JPN	CHN	FIL	OTHER
Architecture	5	—	—	—
Business Administration	6	7	1	1
Communications	4	2	1	1
Economics	4	4	3	1
Education	—	—	—	—
Engineering	—	3	1	1
Forestry	1	—	—	—
General Studies	1	—	2	—
Health Sciences	3	2	3	1
Humanities	2	5	3	1
Natural Sciences	4	3	1	—
Nursing	—	1	2	1
Psychology	7	4	4	—
Social Sciences	5	3	1	1
Social Work	2	—	—	—
Total	44	34	22	8

attle in 1970, 20.7 percent of Nisei males were college graduates in the 45-64 age group. Contrasting with the educational achievements of older Nisei, the 25-34 year age group of older Sansei have 49.6 percent who are college graduates (Ong, 1976).

Of the 8,798 Japanese females in Seattle, 6.8 percent of Nisei women were college graduates in 1970 in the 45-64 age group. The 25-34 year age group of older Sansei show impressive gains with 25.3 percent being college graduates (Ong, 1976).

The numbers of successful college graduates of younger Sansei will continue to increase the total pool of college graduates which, for all Japanese Americans, was 22.6 percent for males and 10.2 percent for females in 1970.

Since the early 1970s, Sansei and the still emerging fourth generation, or Yonsei, have increasingly identified with the Chinese, Filipino, Korean and Samoan communities as Asian-Americans in preference to the term Japanese-Americans. In West Coast schools from junior high

onward are social groupings with designations such as the Asian student coalition, Asian study clubs, cultural heritage programs, ethnic minority studies, Asian-American studies, etc.

Sansei appear less preoccupied with miscegenation previously seen as culturally proscribed and pejorative and view interracial marriage as a further option in seeking marital partners. In this regard, Sansei females tend to marry outside their racial grouping more so than do Sansei males, as appears validated in several studies (Tinker, 1973; Kikumura, 1973).

In the process of seeking an Asian identity, young Sansei have provided volunteers in a variety of Asian community-based human service projects in health, mental health and community development. They appear to be seeking an identity which is neither wholly Japanese nor American but an amalgamation of desirable elements of Asiatic and Western cultures. Increasingly, Sansei and other Asian youth are beginning to utilize entitled services such as economic aid to students as well as legal, social and human services previously avoided by the Nisei and Issei generations. The issues of entitlement to services and their increased utilization have not reduced the continued tendency towards reliance upon self initiative and the family as a primary method of solving potential problem areas.

Physical Size and Educational Preparedness

Physical stature continues to be a curious but important determinant underlying occupational choice among Sanseis. For all intents and purposes, those occupations in which physical size is important are closed as viable occupational choices. While Sansei youth are taller than their parents' generation, they continue to have difficulty competing for employment in law enforcement, fire fighting, heavy equipment and the construction trades industries.

As was true with their parents' generation, Sansei continue to gravitate towards professional careers and are utilizing higher education as the competitive arena with relative success. Since college plans are reinforced early in the child's life, some degree of preselection of friends with similar educational goals occurs in junior high and on the high school level. The adaptive nature of such associations of friends drawn from educationally oriented families protects Sansei from excessive and overt racial discrimination as contrasted to the experiences with blue collar classes which tend to discriminate more openly.

The relative freedom from overt racial discrimination that Sansei college-bound youth enjoy is not the reality shared by Sansei whose education stops with high school or earlier. Those youngsters continue to bear the brunt of discrimination on the labor market, increasing the gap between their college-bound peers and themselves. The alienation resulting from the disparity of viable options available to working vs. professional classes places such Sansei at specific risk psychologically and is reflected in drug abuse, narcotic addiction, and conflicts with family, peers and agents of social control.

Drug Abuse

In a survey conducted in Seattle among 1031 Asians composed of Chinese, Filipino and Japanese youth and young adults, 57 percent admitted to the use of marijuana; 30 percent amphetamines; 18 percent barbiturates and tranquilizers; 15 percent cocaine; and 13 percent LSD. The 54 known drug users in the sample tended to be from low-income families with patterns of drug abuse initiated at the junior high and early high school levels. Of the 17 admitted heroin users in the sample, 82 percent had not sought drug counseling, reflecting the view that existing drug treatment programs do not meet the needs of Asian drug users (Masuda, 1973). Distrust of professionals and treatment agencies as well as ignorance of services available accounted for 80-85 percent of the negative responses by known drug users (Okimoto, 1975).

Behavioral Disorders Among Sansei Children

While racially specific mental health data are available in Hawaii, it is not as useful in the understanding of mainland populations since their developmental and acculturative patterns differ markedly for Hawaiian and Western United States Japanese-Americans. For example, while it is recognized that Asian clinicians encounter individual cases of minimum brain damaged and/or hyperkinetic Sansei children as confirmed by studies in Hawaii (Werner, 1968), there are few systematic studies of Sansei children in the United States. Data available through the Seattle

Public Schools document extremely low numbers of Sansei children identified as behavioral or special education problems and suggest several possible explanations. Those who are considered hyperactive in the context of culturally normative values may be misidentified as being within the range of normalcy when compared to majority culture hyperactive children. Nisei parents may tend to minimize or deny hyperactive behaviors, which therefore are not brought to the attention of physicians and school authorities.

Of the 1458 Sansei students in the Seattle School District in K-12 years, there was a total of 2 students suspended annually during 1974 and 1975. Additionally, 1 child per year dropped out for emotional and/or physical reasons, suggesting both inadequacy in the sensitivity to Sansei youngsters and the perpetuation of the stereotype that Sansei children are free of emotional problems.

Delinquency

In a similar manner, delinquency reflected in juvenile arrest rates in the Seattle area is probably underreported as Nisei parents become actively alarmed and involved in correcting delinquent behaviors when called to their attention. Such parental actions frequently determine whether arrests and formal charges are instituted against minor children. Related to such phenomena is the proportionately high incidence of juvenile arrests amongst Sansei children who are products of interracial marriages or from divorced single-parent families. Similar observations have been noted in Japanese delinquency studies elsewhere (Kitano, 1969).

Changing Socialization Patterns

One of the vulnerable periods for Sansei is early adolescence and the establishment of dating patterns. Preadolescent friendships for Sansei are frequently mul-

tiracial until the onset of dating when Sansei are confronted with the realities of ethnicity and color; the level of acceptance by other racial groups and the majority may reflect restrictive convenants regarding marriage. Sansei youngsters with a substantial Sansei peer group are less affected than their suburban counterparts residing in White middle-class communities.

The identification of Japanese families with the mainstream culture is reflected in identical rates among Whites and Japanese in decreasing school enrollment in the Seattle urban schools of 6 percent annually since 1970. While the movement to suburban communities reflects a wish to improve educational experiences and avoid interracial conflicts, new challenges will face Sanseis, placing them under further psychological stress.

Critical to the past survival of Isseis and Niseis in the United States has been the cohesiveness of the nuclear and extended family. Social breakdown syndromes were uncommon as reflected in low indices of divorce rates, juvenile and adult crime, unemployment and illegitimacy. Such attainments were at the expense of isolation from mainstream cultural influences and the retention of ethnocentric views of the world around them.

The clear trend towards acculturation is best illustrated in the increasing incidence of interracial marriages, totalling 50 percent of Sansei marriages. Conversely, the decision to marry outside their racial group makes Sansei vulnerable psychologically to problems previously unencountered amongst most Japanese in the United States.

Since social relationships in marriages tend to mirror in large part work relationships of the husband, adjustment requirements for Sansei women will continue to place emotional demands upon them. As importantly, the selection of non-Japanese spouses generally severs continued social relationships within the Japanese community, forcing the person to rely upon individual resources without assurance of culturally relevant community support. It is reasonable to assume that those who are better educated, stronger psychologically, and marrying within upper-middle socioeconomic classes would have fewer incidents of rejection as contrasted to lower socioeconomic counterparts. Studies of marital adjustment, interracial couples across demographic variables, and child rearing patterns should provide interesting mental health data for Sansei and their offspring who are designated Yonsei or the fourth generation.

CONCLUSION

With each successive generation, the Japanese-Americans have moved increasingly into mainstream America with reasonable success. At the same time, it is clear that there continue to be problems of underutilization of mental health services and arising from the distrust of non-Asian-oriented mental health professionals (Kitano, 1969; Sue, 1975). While major psychiatric problems become inescapable over time, neuroticism appears not to attract the attention of parents in seeking professional assistance. While the issues of bicultural and bilingual approaches to the treatment of Asians have critical significance to the Issei and Nisei generations (Yamamoto, 1968), they have less applicability to the Sansei generation. The need for continued education of Nisei parents appears warranted in order to increase their sensitivity to the psychological needs of Sansei and to provide more appropriate role models for help-seeking behaviors. The more recent developments of community-based mental health services have encouraged utilization and served the transitional function of linking patients with comprehensive mental health services in the larger community. The evolving generation of psychologically oriented mental health professionals of Japanese descent can more effectively offer therapeutic intervention with Sansei who, themselves, are Western in their orientation.

Lastly, as the acculturative process continues and the incidence of interracial marriages increases, the distinctive Asian racial features will gradually give way and within several generations become indistinguishable and lost. In three short generations we have successively moved from Isseis identified as Japanese aliens to their Nisei offspring referred to as Japanese-Americans to Sansei, more appropriately designated American-Japanese.

REFERENCES

Hill, H. Anti-Oriental agitation and the rise of working-class racism. *Society*. January/February 1973, 43-68.

Hosokawa, B. *Nisei: The Quiet Americans.* New York: William Morrow, 1969.

Kikumura, A. and Kitano, H. H. L. Interracial marriage: A picture of the Japanese Americans. *Journal of Social Issues*, 1973, 29(2), 67-82.

Kitano, H. H. L. *Japanese Americans: The Evolution of a Sub-culture.* Englewood Cliffs, N.J.: Prentice-Hall, 1969.

Masuda, M. Drug abuse in Seattle Asians. Task Force Report of Seattle King County Drug Commission, Seattle, Washington, 1973.

Okimoto, D. Asian keyperson: Survey on drug abuse. Task Force Report of Seattle King County Drug Commission, Seattle, Washington, June, 1975.

Ong, P. M., Fujita, J. T., and Chin, S. Asians in Washington: A statistical profile. Commission on Asian American Affairs, Olympia, Washington, September 1976.

Sata, L. S. Musings of a hyphenated American. In: S. Sue and N. Wagner (Eds.), *Asian Americans: Psychological Perspectives*. Ben Lomand: Science & Behavior Books, 1973, pp. 150-156.

Sata, L. S. Asian culture and learning styles. In: L. A. Bransford, L. Baca, and K. Lane (Eds.), *Cultural Diversity and the Exceptional Child*. Reston, VA: Council for Exceptional Children, 1974, pp. 50-56.

Sue, D. and Frank, A. A typological approach to the psychological study of Chinese and Japanese American college males. *Journal of Social Issues*, 1973, 29, 129-148.

Sue, S. and McKinney, H. Asian Americans in the community mental health care system. *American Journal of Orthopsychiatry*, 1975, 45, 111-118.

Tinker, J. N. Intermarriage and ethnic boundaries: The Japanese American case. *Journal of Social Issues*, 1973, 29, 49-67.

U.S. News and World Report. Success story of one minority group in the U.S., December 1966.

Weglyn, M. *Year of Infamy*. New York: William Morrow, 1976.

Werner, F., Bierman, J., French, F., Simonian, K., Conner, A., Smith, R., and Campbell, M. Reproductive and environmental casualties: A report on the ten year follow-up of the children of the Kauai pregnancy study. *Pediatrics*, 1968, *42*, 112-127.

Yamamoto, J., James, Q. C., and Palley, N. Cultural problems in psychiatric therapy. *Archives of General Psychiatry*, 1968, *19*, 45-49.

Yamamoto, J. and Iga, M. Japanese enterprise and American middle class values. *American Journal of Psychiatry*, May 1974, *131*, 577-579.

CHAPTER 22

Mental Health and Vietnamese Children

Daniel D. Le, D.Th., M.S.W.

There are two distinctly separate groups of Vietnamese in America. The first group consists of about 20,000 students, permanent residents, and the war brides who had been living in the U.S. prior to the fall of the Saigon government in April, 1975. The second group comprises over 140,000 adults and children who fled the fighting in their homeland during and after the sudden change of government of Saigon. Their departures took place amidst shooting, mortar shelling, fires, and sirens. Adults and children alike were screaming, running, pushing, and shoving, all trying to get away in order to survive. A number of people died en route, and the 140,000 who survived the escape eventually arrived in the U.S. as refugees. This refugee group represents the majority of Vietnamese now in the U.S. The aftereffects of their tumultuous relocation and the severity of their losses are the themes of this chapter.

The survivors of any disaster are subject to tremendous psychological pressures.

For the refugee, all the forces of disaster—war, death, injury, loss of home, possessions, family memorabilia—are joined with the crushing losses of country, culture, language, tradition, and history, endlessly inflicting painful memories down to the lowest trivia of life.

We know that feelings and behavior are the results of what has been learned in the past. In order for health care professionals to understand the special needs and problems of Vietnamese children and to provide effective service to them, they must grow in knowledge and appreciation of the refugees' cultural heritage, of the changes in their country as a result of the war, and of their postwar experiences and those of their parents and significant others, including evacuation, refugee camp, and resettlement experiences.

VIETNAMESE CULTURE

The Vietnamese have a rich cultural

heritage that goes back several thousand years. Since 600 B.C., they have developed their land for rice farming by the construction of dikes. The Chinese script, technical vocabulary, and Confucian methods of administration have been incorporated into their culture. Unfortunately, the country also has a long history of invasions. The Chinese ruled it for a millenium; the French held it as a protectorate for 80 years; and the Japanese occupied it during World War II. Throughout the thousand-year Chinese rule, there was a continuous evolution of national identity in what subsequently became Vietnam. Nationalism developed particularly during the periods of colonial rule and in the unsettled atmosphere of the 20th century, it found political expression.

The unity which binds the Vietnamese people is not one of political necessity or social contract as in the West. Rather, it is a continuing search for the "harmony" in life and a commitment to the salvation of an identity. A major aspect of Vietnamese personality is a Confucian belief in the value of harmony in social relations. Only by achieving such harmony between father and son, husband and wife, employer and employee, etc., can tranquility of the soul be achieved.

The family is the first loyalty of the Vietnamese, combining their religious, social, economic, and political units. Vietnamese consider themselves primarily members of their families, with well-defined places within them and well-defined rules of behavior depending on their places within the family structure. Vietnamese call their fathers "my father," their mothers "my mother," their uncles "my uncle," and never use first names of family members as do Americans. First names are used only by the elderly when they address children.

Ancestral veneration is evident in their selection of days for celebration within the family. The most meaningful familial events are not birthdays or wedding anniversaries, but annual memorial anniversaries of the deaths of their ancestors. Such days are important events for the family, opportunities for all members to get together to remember their common origin, thus enhancing familial solidarity.

Vietnamese friendships are built upon high expectations and acceptance of responsibility. A friend in need feels free to ask for help and friends expect to be asked. Americans have many acquaintances with whom they have friendly relationships, but a much smaller number of close friends. The Vietnamese refugee may expect an American sponsor to fulfill requests for help and responsibility like a friend. Americans may misinterpret Vietnamese requests for assistance as failures to take the initiative and solve their own problems.

Vietnamese are urged to emphasize self-control or, in other words, to repress feelings which might bring them into conflict with others. The high value they place on harmony in interpersonal relationships is expressed in everyday situations through the use of delicacy, tact, politeness, and gentleness in dealing with others. Therefore, Vietnamese may tell Americans what they think Americans want to hear, rather than giving an objectively truthful answer. Vietnamese do not understand American forthrightness.

"Yes," when spoken in Vietnamese, does not mean the same as "yes" in English. Very often it means, "Yes, I hear you," rather than "Yes, I agree with you." The American asks "Do you understand?" The proper answer for a Vietnamese at work or at home is, of course, "Yes." It would be impolite to say "I do not understand," for it would imply that you could not explain. In a job situation, it would imply the Vietnamese could not perform the task.

Changes Wrought by War

Until the date of evacuation, Vietnamese refugees were living in a country in which war had been fought continuously for 30 years. No one in the country escaped the effects of the war. Fear, anxiety, hatred, distrust, despair, depression, withdrawal, and sadness became a way of life for millions. Preservation of sanity too often meant indifference to or ignoring the violence, the fighting, the bombing, the sirens, and death around them every day. Refugees born and raised in war, that is, under 30 years of age, account for over half of the total refugee population in the U.S. Whether they liked it or not, they had to adapt their behavior and coping mechanisms to this reality. Most Vietnamese found it difficult to expand the horizons of their thinking and feeling beyond the next bowl of rice. There was little confidence in surviving even to the next day.

A team was sent to South Vietnam in 1973 to conduct an in-depth study and evaluate conditions there. On January 27, 1974, their report was presented to the Senate Judiciary Subcommittee investigating problems connected with the refugees. Among the findings which contribute heavily to mental health problems in Vietnamese today were:

1) Over half of South Vietnam's population—some 10 million people—have been forced to move, often many times over, as refugees since 1965.

2) New refugees continue to flee the violence in the countryside, some 6,000 to 8,000 each day during the first months of the ceasefire in 1973, and several hundred each month since. A total of 818,700 new refugees moved during all of 1973.

3) The ceasefire reduced somewhat the level of violence, but the rate of civilian casualties remained tragically high. In 1973, the monthly average of civilian war casualties admitted to hospitals was 3,597—for a total of 43,166. This monthly average was down only 900 compared to 1972.

4) The total number of Saigon govern-

ment and Provisional Revolutionary Government (PRG) civilian and military deaths, during one year of ceasefire, was greater than the total number of American soldiers killed during a decade of war.

5) The dislocations caused by the war have shattered the social fabric of Vietnamese life . . . Once a predominantly rural society, Vietnam now has over 65% of its population in urbanized areas. South Vietnam is now an agricultural deficit area. A massive social welfare problem has emerged in the needed care of 880,000 orphans or half orphans, 650,000 war widows, and some 181,000 disabled amputees, paraplegics, blind and deaf. For the first time in Vietnamese history, there is a need for institutions to help the aged person, normally cared for in the extended family. To many people, the social support systems—especially the extended family—were destroyed.

6) Mines and unexploded ordnance remain among the principal causes of civilian casualties. No U.S. assistance in ordnance removal has been offered.

7) There continues to be a critical shortage of simple rehabilitative and medical devices, such as prosthetic devices and other equipment to help the handicapped . . .

In the desperation of war, many Vietnamese eliminated every value other than survival and did anything to improve their chances of survival. The war thus destroyed not only human lives, but human values as well. It undermined all government structures and systems of society, thus destroying the foundations of freedom. Those Vietnamese born in the last 30 years have sustained deprivation and scars that are with them still.

Evacuation

Early in 1975, when some provinces in

central Vietnam were lost to the communists, the people of South Vietnam felt that there would be an eventual end to the everlasting war. The rich, the intelligentsia, and Northerners who had left North Vietnam in 1954 planned to leave the country, expecting a politically neutral regime, at least during the transitional period, which would allow them time to make a considered decision and to pack. Then, evacuation began, suddenly. Rumors spread and people panicked. Those who had left their homes in the North—Hue, Da Nang, Nha Trang — immediately embarked on any ship bound for safety. Those in Saigon used any means to evacuate. Some planned thoughtfully, but most became caught up in the feverish evacuation movement and could not think of anything except getting out before the communists came in or took over. They wanted to avoid possible horrors during the transitional period, but they thought they would return later when peace had come. Many died during this period of panic, many families were split, others arrived safely in the Philippines and Guam, and a few were scattered on some islands in the Pacific.

Refugee Camps

Conditions in the refugee camps were deplorable. The word "camp," their supervision by military personnel, conformity to military discipline, barbed wires and seclusion, and unfamiliar food all made the refugees feel as though they were prisoners. Some tried to understand and adopted stoicism as a means of coping. Some became exasperated and likened the refugee camps to concentration camps. All wanted to leave the camps as soon as possible but had to undergo bureaucratic sponsorship procedures. In the feverish hunt for sponsors, some signed papers without thinking or understanding. Some managed to leave the camps in a few days,

while others remained for months.

Resettlement

Resettlement has created a new set of problems. Some families have been fortunate and are very happy with their sponsors. Others did not get along with their sponsors and fled. Some misunderstood the meaning of sponsorship, equating it with the concept of Vietnamese friendship; expecting too much, they were disappointed. Still others discovered they had been impulsive in signing documents without first asking for the meaning. Without knowing, many agreed to give up their children or to work under unbearable conditions. Resettlement problems proliferated in their dimensions and numbers. While charitable groups, associations and individuals have volunteered or have been funded to provide help, the need for assistance still exists, especially with psychosocial aspects of resettlement. Disillusionment has culminated in suicide for some refugees and has brought others to the verge of nervous breakdowns.

CURRENT MENTAL HEALTH NEEDS AND PROBLEMS

Cultural Problems

Like other immigrants, Vietnamese refugees are confronted with racial discrimination, an unfamiliar culture and economy, a lack of information on their rights and obligations, and a foreign language and social environment. Special problems of this group include ambivalence about their presence here on the part of many Americans of all races; their coming from a country torn by war for more than a generation, their distorted picture of Americans created by their experiences with U.S. military forces; the fact that many arrived without any kind of preparation or resources after seeing their families divided and their educations and careers interrupted. Furthermore, upon arrival in the U.S., they found no supportive, established ethnic communities of relatives into which they could integrate.

Food, clothing, and even climate are minor difficulties compared to the barrier of language. Differences between American and Indochinese value systems add to these difficulties. Vietnamese refugees are lost in contradictions—sentiment vs. reason, clanism and dependence vs. individualism and independence, spiritualism vs. materialism, covert and indirect attitudes and manners vs. overt and direct attitudes and manners. These cultural clashes generate social, moral, and psychological conflicts which bear very heavily on the refugee's mental health.

Social Problems

Many refugees cannot cope with the moral standards typical of American society. There are clashes between husbands and wives. Children hover between what they learn at school from their classmates or teachers and what their parents teach at home or what they learned while living in Vietnam. Parents are confused about how much freedom their children should be given, and how and what type of restrictions should be instituted. Extremes exist in situations where the parents are traditional and their children are becoming Americanized.

In addition, parents have problems between themselves. Many Vietnamese wives are attracted to the Western women's emancipation movement. The typical problem is what degree of emancipation is tolerable to the husband. Some couples cope with the new situation easily and find satisfaction in it, but others reach the point of divorce. In some families, problems surface and are dealt with. In others, problems are latent and waiting to explode, contributing to the uncertainty of tomorrow.

Economic Impacts

It might be possible for family problems to fade with time and effort if the economic situation of the refugee family were satisfactory. Financial troubles exacerbate psychosocial problems and retard the adjustment process. Most Vietnamese refugees are unemployed, some are underemployed, and only a very limited number find jobs in their fields. Issues contributing to the employment problem are language difficulties, differences in training, and the rate of unemployment in the United States at large. Most refugees require retraining either in their own fields or in other fields.

In March of 1976, on behalf of the Inter-Agency Forum on Resettlement of Southeast Asian Refugees in Los Angeles County and under the sponsorship of the State of California Department of Health, the International Institute of Los Angeles conducted a human services needs survey of approximately 300 Vietnamese families living in the county. Preliminary findings on 893 individuals from 157 families included the following factors as indicative of socioeconomic and personal instability leading to subsequent personal and intrafamily emotional stress:

1) Of the adults, 41% had elementary school educations only, 11 percent had received high school or college level technical/vocational training, 24 percent attended college preparatory high school, and 22 percent completed college/professional training.
2) The typical family had 5.7 people and an earned income of $370 per month, 33 percent of the families were on welfare, 44 percent received food stamps, and 64 percent applied for Medi-Cal.

3) The average monthly rent per family was $183.
4) Uncertainty or dissatisfaction with the adequacy of their sponsoring relationship was reported by 44 percent of the families.
5) Problems reported by refugees related to language difficulties, loneliness, homesickness, isolation, uncertainty about the future, lack of financial stability, need for job training and better jobs, experiences of discrimination, and a lack of acceptance by American society.

Psychological Problems

Cultural, social, and economic pressures have critically affected the psychological stability of the refugees. Nostalgia for their native land and for the "good old days" has become more and more acute. Feelings of shame and guilt have become unbearable.

Unemployment and lack of English proficiency are major sources of stress because they involve losing face—an anathema in Vietnamese society. Many refugees are highly competent with marketable job skills but are not employable because of the language problem. If they obtain work, usually they are underemployed.

In addition to language limitations, many former Vietnamese soldiers who trained for a lifetime of war in their homeland now find they have no vocational skills to compete in limited labor markets. They are frustrated and resentful. They tend to exhibit apathy, passivity, and a lack of motivation in relation to the goals of the larger society. In many cases, hostile feelings are turned inward and joined with feelings of frustration to produce serious waves of depression.

A large number of women and aged cannot communicate in English at all. They feel alienated from U.S. society and they cannot even communicate with their next door neighbors. Such isolation may result in personality disturbances.

Most of the refugees have large families. Because of financial problems, they cannot afford adequate housing and find themselves in congested, limited living space. Many must live in low income, high crime areas, which causes constant stress.

The author has seen many persons with clinical syndromes of depression, interpersonal conflict, somatic distress, and various types of mental illness during the past six years, in working with Vietnamese refugees in the U.S. Many appear to be suffering from guilt and remorse about significant others—especially wives, husbands, or children—left behind in Vietnam. Loss of their former status greatly affects their self-image and self-respect. They are ashamed of not being able to support themselves or their families adequately or of having to be on public assistance. A number of them have no family members or any other social support system. They are desperately lonely and isolated and feel totally out of place in the U.S. While they feel they have no future and don't want to live here, they know they cannot return to their homeland. With no alternative, they live in a perennial paradox. Those who are motivated to adapt to a new life have been hindered by seemingly unsurmountable barriers on the road to acculturation.

MENTAL HEALTH NEEDS AND PROBLEMS OF VIETNAMESE CHILDREN

Among Vietnamese children there are three main groups: babylift orphans, unaccompanied children, and children of refugee families. The exact number of these uprooted refugee children is difficult to estimate. According to U.S. government reports, there were 2,043 young children who came to the United States on the babylift, 440 to 500 unaccompanied minor children between two and sixteen years of age, and 50,000 to 60,000 children of refugee families. All groups of children have been scattered throughout the 50 states. However, the largest concentrations of refugee families and children settled in California, Texas, and Florida.

Refugee children from Vietnam are different from other children who come to the attention of mental health professionals. The differences lie in their cultural background, their language, and their reasons for being refugees. In addition to the specific problems of either being orphaned, unaccompanied minors, or children of refugee families, they all have common problems.

According to Dr. Jean E. Carlin, an American psychiatrist who visited Vietnam, the consideration of age at time of arrival in the U.S. is an important factor in understanding and anticipating the future psychosocial and mental health problems of Vietnamese refugee children.

Those involved in Operation Babylift may have been spared the difficulties of growing up in an economically depressed family, but they must nonetheless face the problems of growing up "different" in an Anglo community. Children between a few months and six months of age at the time of leaving may have the best chance for successful adjustment if their families adjust well. Children between six months and two years of age at the time of leaving Vietnam may have the most serious psychological problems in the future because of preverbal memories of terror. Also, for children between one year and three years of age, the time of rapid speech development, severe problems might be encountered in having partially learned one language and suddenly having an entirely different set of foreign sounds reinforced. For children over two years of age and up to nine years of age, there is the problem of personal memories about the departure and transition. Another critical time that the move might be expected to adversely

affect the child is between 9 and 15 or 18 years of age. The difficulties of being an Asian in America are compounded by the identity crisis that is usually experienced at that age. Continued aid to the refugees in solving their problems is essential if children are to have secure homes in which they can work out their own problems (Carlin, 1979).

ADJUSTMENT PROBLEMS OF VIETNAMESE CHILDREN

Uprooted Vietnamese children, recently transplanted in a totally new situation, are faced with many adjustment problems. They have to learn English to be able to communicate with their teachers and friends. They must learn new ways of behaving, thinking, and learning. They have to sort out and decide what part of their cultural values and heritage to retain, what parts to modify and replace to function effectively in their new country.

Vietnamese children were born in a war-torn country. They witnessed many violent and brutal scenes in their homeland. The fathers of many Vietnamese children spent most of their time in the battlegrounds, army outposts or camps. Many mothers were left alone to take care of the children's emotional and physical needs and problems. Many of them had been refugees in their home country since birth and had moved many times to different places. The effects are often seen in the introverted personality, unstable behavior, and distressful attitudes of these children.

During the evacuation process, especially among the "boat people" who escaped from Vietnam, refugee children were faced with many real dangers of death, family separation, and physical and emotional deprivation. The evacuation experiences were very traumatic for many of them. The depth of their imprint on Vietnamese children is hard to measure. However, it is obvious that there are underlying causes for fears, nightmares, hostility and depression.

In Vietnam, generally speaking the child was quite secure within the family and there were well-defined roles expected of members in the family. Once in the U.S., these roles changed. Many fathers are unemployed or underemployed and the mothers have to work full-time to supplement the income for the family. The father is no longer the sole support for his family. Very often, the father has to depend on his children for English interpretation, shopping, and other information. This changing role of a person whom the child respects is a confusing factor causing emotional conflict and insecurity. Many parents are having emotional problems themselves and therefore are unable to provide effective leadership and emotional support for their children.

Many children are having problems in the area of home-school interaction. At school, the child is encouraged by teachers and peers to be open in expressing feelings, attitudes, and certain behaviors. At home, those feelings, attitudes, and behaviors are discouraged by parents. Many parents are trying to hold on to their traditional values and are concerned that their children are "too Americanized." Because of the fear of rejection by their parents, many Vietnamese children tend to repress their negative feelings toward them. As a result of the inhibition of angry feelings, personality disorders or certain neuroses could emerge in their later adult lives.

These adjustment problems are real; however, they are not completely unsurmountable obstacles. It has been reported that many Vietnamese children are making excellent adjustments and good progress in schools. In fact, a number of them are top students in their classes and exhibit a fairly good self-image.

In a supportive environment, with the help of understanding parents and teachers, there is every reason to believe that these children could develop a strong bicultural orientation. In general, Vietnamese children are bright, adventurous, and hard-working students. They show a real interest in exploring new cultural avenues and are preparing themselves to make contributions to their adopted country in the years to come.

PSYCHOLOGICAL AND INTELLECTUAL ASSESSMENT OF VIETNAMESE CHILDREN

Psychological and intellectual assessment of Vietnamese children is needed for an increasing number of those having unusual emotional problems and poor school performance, as well as for those who are seen as having developmental disabilities by teachers or counselors, or those having problems in class placement. Most of the existing psychological testing instruments are cultural and class bound, applicable mainly to white and middle-class American children. Many Vietnamese children, especially the new arrivals (the boat refugees), do not speak English. This kind of testing is foreign to them and their parents. Many test questions are not applicable or make no sense to them. At the present time, there are no valid and reliable psychological tests standardized on Vietnamese children. Until certain norms are established for this group of children in the U.S., the following issues are to be considered when psychological testing and evaluations are required:

1) The Indochinese cultures can be characterized as highly prescriptive and proscriptive in comparison to American and other Western cultures. For example, the expectation is generally to take care of one's parents and not rely on the nursing home, agree to an arranged marriage,

not to consider divorce, obey one's husband or parents, etc.

2) Under the American Psychiatric Diagnostic System, mental disorders are classified under major categories as enumerated in DSM-III. However, classifying refugee mental health problems according to that nosology may result in a highly misleading picture of the Indochinese client. For instance, most Indochinese problems generally consist of transient or reactive personality disorders, but the uninitiated clinician who does not understand the cultural manifestations of a transient disorder may give the patient a more severe diagnosis.

3) Using American categories can offer a false and misleading sense of resolution to a case and little in the way of useful information.

4) Various system pressures exist to use the American diagnostic system, including issues related to fee collection and accountability. Indochinese mental health projects which rely alternatively on individual case formulations are often made to feel that what they do is either not legitimate or unimportant.

5) Since the mental health problems of Indochinese tend to be reactive personality disorders, environmental stress or cultural precipitants can often be clearly delineated. Interpreters who are not trained in mental health will frequently fail to take account of these variables and may distort or delete important information or give disparaging interpretations to mental health problems ("His people were lazy there and they are lazy here." "What do you expect from a fishing family?").

6) Tests of intellectual ability can sometimes help to identify specific abilities and deficits. IQ subtests in both native and English languages can be administered to answer such questions as the degree to which language acts as a handicap, familiarity with American culture and ways of thinking, and ability to engage in abstract processing. Reports can be prepared to discuss the client's abilities and deficits, but specific scores should never be reported due to their misleading nature. The Bender Gestalt and Development Test of Visual-Motor Integration have both been found to be useful screening devices for Organic Brain Disorders, particularly when they are used in conjunction with a Weschler.

7) Vietnamese and H'Mong generally will give very open, unguarded and undefensive responses to projective tests, and the use of these tests will often prove useful either when corroboration of interview findings is needed or when the client is unresponsive or uncommunicative in an interview.

The mental health problems of Indochinese generally involve situational or reactive personality disorders which frequently appear as psychoses, character disorders, neuroses, medical disorders, or learning disabilities. Since the problems are reactive and situational, Indochinese mental health problems typically respond to culturally appropriate interventions quickly and favorably, but also have a greater potential for becoming chronic if they are given a chronic diagnosis and consequently treated as such.

As Minsky (1980) has concluded, the history of the use of tests in the United States has been promulgated as being beneficial to the minority group members exposed to them without revealing their underlying discriminatory uses. Only SOMPA (System of Multicultural Pluralistic Assessment), developed by Jane Mercer, meets the assumptions of pluralistic assessment in a non-biased manner. SOMPA has not yet been standardized for other than black and Hispanic children in the age range 5-11 years. Psychological tests used for other minority groups are clearly discriminatory and in violation of existing federal regulations. Interim measures for evaluating Indochinese students who are refugees must not be permitted to continue as the technology exists for adapting the SOMPA techniques for these students.

SUGGESTIONS FOR ACTION

At this writing, there are just a few mental health facilities in the country which are adequately prepared to deal with the emotional and mental health problems of Vietnamese refugees and their children. Lacking further training in the cultural and language differences, American mental health practitioners will remain unable to offer effective direct services to emotionally troubled refugees. The problem is made more acute by the fact that Vietnam offered no training in psychiatry or mental health fields, and very few Vietnamese were trained abroad in mental health. In view of the shortage of appropriately trained mental health professionals and given the current critical situation of Vietnamese refugee adults and children, the remainder of this chapter will propose short-term and long-term approaches to the problems.

It is crucial to understand that to most Vietnamese refugees the term "mental health" is frequently used and understood as "mental illness." The degree of stigma attached to mental illness is so great that they are not amenable to seeking help. Therefore, one should not assess the mental health needs and problems of the refugees merely by counting the number of people who enter the offices of mental health professionals or appear on one's case load. Because of their cultural background and environmental conditions, most of the refugees attempt outwardly to suppress their feelings and to conform to those around them. We must note, however, that they and their children are survivors of a 30-year war and are limited in the means with which to express, discharge, or cope with their internal lives. For many of them, the time for an emotional upheaval is approaching.

In the short term, it is recommended that in-service training workshops for social workers, counselors, and mental health personnel be conducted in areas of high refugee concentration. These workshops should initially address differences in cultural patterns, coping mechanisms stressed in Vietnamese culture, situational problems presently being faced by the refugees, and culturally-sound basic intervention strategies that can be utilized to assist emotionally disturbed refugees. The establishment of family counseling programs and crisis intervention programs with "hotlines" manned by trained bilingual Vietnamese staff members should be supported. Social and cultural programs and, in particular, Vietnamese community centers and other mutual associations of Vietnamese need to be encouraged and supported, as they may provide the emotional, social, and cultural support needed to help refugees combat isolation and preserve their identity and cultural heritage.

For the longer term, it is important that intensive training programs in mental health fields be developed for Vietnamese professionals and paraprofessionals. It is recommended that emphasis be given to the training of Vietnamese who already have proficiency and experience in allied fields—for example, medical doctors, social workers, and school counselors—in order to minimize the time required before actual practice. Special incentives and assistance in education could be given to already trained refugees who express an interest in the mental health field.

In addition to the above mentioned efforts, social structures needed to respond optimally to Vietnamese refugees must include:

1) *Economic support systems* until the refugees became self-sufficient, including effective English classes and vocational counseling and training for adults. These systems are necessary to assist refugees in gaining a sense of

family stability so that they can proceed to deal with their own psychosocial adjustments from a secure base.

2) *Community education programs* through mass media on the historical and cultural backgrounds of Vietnamese, their philosophies of life, values, customs, and behavior. This information will help reduce provincialism and discrimination and benefit the refugees by hastening their acceptance and giving them a new sense of pride and belonging in this society.

3) *Utilization of bilingual Vietnamese* personnel and resources. There are a number of Vietnamese professionals in mental health and allied fields who could assist in planning and service delivery to their people. It is strongly recommended that the desires and needs of refugees be ventilated and that the assistance of such professionals be enlisted. In every local community, a list of resources should be established and utilized.

4) *Consultation and education.* Ongoing consultation services should be offered to clergymen and leaders of the Vietnamese community by local community mental health services. Continuing educational programs in the Vietnamese language should be undertaken, utilizing mass media and forums to disseminate information on basic principles of child care and development, sex education, drug abuse, juvenile delinquency, and generational conflict. In regard to children, there is a real need for culturally and linguistically relevant *parenting training* for Vietnamese parents. Also there is a need for cultural awareness training for teachers and counselors who are working with the Vietnamese children in schools.

5) *Community organization.* This involves participation of mental health personnel in projects to facilitate social and institutional changes that are relevant to primary prevention of mental illness and educational programs specifically designed for the Vietnamese community (e.g. more effective English as a second language programs and expansion of pre-school and child care programs) and various self-help programs for the elderly, adults, and adolescents.

Above all, it is important to stress that although Vietnameses refugees have come from a culture which is entirely different from American culture and their thoughts, actions, and physical appearance differ from Americans, they experience the same feelings and emotions as every human being. When dealing with them, therefore, we should treat them with sensitivity and as individuals worthy of the same human dignity we all would expect if the situations were reversed.

CONCLUSION

There appears to be a consensus that Vietnamese refugees are facing many mental health problems arising from the necessity to start a new life almost from scratch in a new land, surrounded by a foreign culture, and handicapped by self-images as victims and survivors of the long war in Vietnam. Opinions differ, however, in their estimates of the prevalence of severity of these problems and about the mode of intervention for prevention and treatment. One line of thought is that there is no real urgency and that everything can be handled with the existing resources in the community. In the author's work with refugees in Vietnam and in the U.S. over the past eight years, it has become evident that the mental health needs of the refugees have specific and unique features. Furthermore, the mental health situation of Vietnamese refugees is critical and may soon become disastrous. Immediate, positive intervention is indicated with the use of more informed and innovative approaches.

It is hoped that the facts presented and actions recommended in this chapter will help mental health professionals view the problems and needs of Vietnamese refugees in a better perspective. Factual knowledge is the foundation of social progress, and it remains incumbent upon concerned professionals to seize opportunities to translate the information presented here into meaningful action. In the final analysis, the Vietnamese community — with all its hopes and manifold problems—is a microcosm of our imperfect society. The betterment of this segment of our interrelated culture can only serve to strengthen the society as a whole.

REFERENCES

Allport, G. W. *The Nature of Prejudice.* Garden City, N.Y.: Doubleday, 1958.

Aylesworth, L. S. Psychological and intellectual assessments with Indochinese: The socio-cultural case formulation. A paper presented at the Southern California Indochinese Mental Health Conference, August 1980.

Call, J. D. Helping infants cope with change. *Early Child Development and Care,* 1974, *3,* 229-47.

Carlin, J. E. The catastrophically uprooted child: Southeast Asian refugee children. In: J. Nosphitz (Ed.) *The Basic Handbook of Child Psychiatry. Volume 1.* New York: Basic Books, 1979.

Coburn, J. The war of the babies. *Village Voice,* April 14, 1975, 15-17.

Emerson, G. Operation babylift. *The New Republic,* April 26, 1975, 8-10.

Flaste, R. U.S. may airlift refugee youngsters. *New York Times,* April 9, 1975, 1, 48A.

For people in need. *New York Times,* April 16, 1975, 36.

Forrest, D. V. Psychiatric casualties in Vietnam. *Roche Medical Image and Commentary,* 1970, *12*(8), 27.

Goldstein, J., Freud, A., and Solnit, A. *Beyond the Best Interests of the Child.* London: Macmillan, 1973.

Grinker, R. R. and Spiegel, J. P. *War Neurosis.* Philadelphia: Blakiston, 1945.

Hafner, H. Psychological Disturbances Following Prolonged Persecution. *Social Psychiatry,* 1968, *3*(3), 80-88.

If America rejects the refugees we all lose. *Los An-* *geles Times,* May 8, 1975.

Indo-Chinese refugee resettlement program. In: *Inter-Agency Task Force Report.* Washington: Department of HEW, July, 1976.

Inter-Agency task force for Indochina refugees. In: *Report to the Congress,* September 15, 1975.

Jacobson, D. S. The influence of cultural identification on family behavior. *Social Service Review,* 1972, *46*(3), 413-26.

Joint Commission on Mental Health of Children. In: *Crisis in Child Mental Health: Challenge for the 1970's.* New York: Harper and Row, 1970.

Klein, D. C. *Community Dynamics and Mental Health.* New York: Doubleday, 1958.

Kushner, F. H. All of us bear the scars. *U.S. News and World Report,* April 16, 1973, 41.

Language chief obstacle for Viet refugees. *Los Angeles Times,* July 3, 1975.

Margolies, M. and Gruber, R. *They Came to Stay.* New York: Coward, McCann, and Geoghegan, 1975.

Minsky, R. Psychological assessment of Indochinese refugees. Paper presented at the Meeting of the American Psychological Association, September 1980.

Polner, M. Vietnam war stories. *Transaction,* 1968, *6*(1), 8-20.

Rathbun, C., DiVirgilio, L., and Waldfogel, S. The restitutive process in children following radical separation from family and culture. *American Journal of Orthopsychiatry,* 1958, 408-415.

Rathbun, C., McLaughlin, H., Bennett, C., and Garland, J. A. Later adjustment of children following radical separation from family and culture. *American Journal of Orthopsychiatry,* 1965, *35,* 604-9.

Refugees feeling depressed. *Los Angeles Herald-Examiner,* May 17, 1976, A3.

Relief and rehabilitation of the war victims in Indochina one year after the ceasefire. In: *Study Mission Report.* U.S. Senate Judiciary Subcommittee on Problems Connected with Refugees, January 7, 1974.

Strange, R. E. and Brown, D. E., Jr. Home from the wars. *American Journal of Psychiatry,* 1970, *127*(4), 488-92.

Varocas, H. Children of purgatory: Reflections on the concentration camp survival syndrome. *Corrective Psychiatry and Journal of Social Therapy,* 1970, *16,* 51-8.

Who will say what is best for the orphans? *New York Times,* April 13, 1975, 4E.

Wright, H. L. A clinical study of children who refuse to talk in school. *Journal of American Academy of Child Psychiatry,* 1968, *7,* 603-17.

Zigler, E., Butterfield, E. C., and Capobianco, F. Institutionalization and the effectiveness of social reinforcement: A 5- and 8-year follow-up study. *Developmental Psychology,* 1970, *3,* 255-63.

CHAPTER 23

The Mental Health of Chinese-
American Children:
Stressors and Resources

Stanley Sue, Ph.D.

and Robert Chin, Ph.D.

In discussing the mental health of Chinese-American children, we feel the necessity to preface our comments. First, Chinese in the United States represent an extremely heterogeneous group. Some are recent immigrants while others are fourth or fifth generation Americans. Differences among Chinese can also be found in terms of area of residence (Chinatowns versus nonChinatown communities), socioeconomic status, ability to speak English or Chinese (including the question of which Chinese dialect), and exposure to and internalization of conflicting cultural values. Such heterogeneity limits the appropriateness of making generalized statements on Chinese-American children. Second, because of the lack of more research investigations, it is virtually impossible to provide much empirical data

on the personality characteristics or the rates and distributions of mental disorders among Chinese-American children. We have no reason to believe that the rates are any higher or lower than those of other Americans. Third, there is a great deal of misunderstanding as well as lack of information on Chinese-Americans. Indeed, the collection of readings in this book is intended to provide a more accurate view of ethnic minorities. Fourth, contemporary research and theory on Chinese-Americans have fostered controversy. Many research studies perpetuate inaccurate stereotypes of Chinese-Americans, and many traditional social science theories may be culturally relative and biased. These problems must be acknowledged and appreciated. Nevertheless, they are not so serious that analysis or speculation on the mental health of Chinese-American children cannot proceed and be instructive.

Our perspective in discussing the mental health of Chinese-American children is that ethnic minority group status and living in the United States create unique experiences. More specifically, *being* Chinese and *living* in this country interact in a complex fashion. This interaction results in (1) unique kinds of stressors and (2) unique kinds of adaptive resources (see Table 1). By using the term "unique," we are not implying that these stressors and resources can be found only among Chinese-Americans or that all Chinese-Americans inevitably encounter these factors. Rather, the interaction seems to apply more clearly to Chinese-Americans. The focus on stressors is due to the fact that they often affect mental health and that majority-minority group relations have been found to be associated with tension, stress, and discrimination. However, stressful situations can bring about increased adaptation and personal well-being as well as decreased mental health. Available resources such as the personal strengths of individuals and the accessi-

TABLE 1
Stressors Relevant to Chinese Americans That Influence Mental Health

1. Cultural Factors
    a. Exposure to different cultures
    b. The cultures conflict in a significant manner
    c. Conformance to each culture is rewarded and encouraged within the culture
2. Race Relations
    a. Racism including prejudice and discrimination
    b. Inability to control outcomes
3. Social Change
    a. Rapid and unexpected
    b. A large number life events requiring major social readjustments
    c. Few techniques or resources

bility of institutionalized support systems also influence well-being.

Another underlying assumption is that the concept of mental health includes both mental disorders (psychiatrically defined) and positive mental health (e.g. environmental mastery, autonomy, and self-esteem). Thus stressors as well as resources affect mental disorders and positive mental health.

A CONCEPTUAL MODEL

An explicit assumption is that mental health can be examined from different time periods or ages in people's lives and that early life experiences, however indirect or non-visible, can interact with later life circumstances (or stressors) to influence mental disorders and positive mental health in the later stages of life. One's theoretical predilections can substitute causative connections or non-determinative relations between childhood patterns and behaviors in later stages. In any event, it is necessary to remind ourselves of the potential consequences of childhood patterns for the identification of interventions and preventive mental health programs. Early intervention and "prevention" may be the wisest allocation of study and of mental health delivery system resources.

The establishment of a heuristic framework for both treatment and prevention necessitates the assessment of (1) the impact of environmental circumstances or stressors (e.g., cultural diversity, racism, and social change), (2) key personality areas (e.g., achievement, power, affiliation, and independence), and (3) age periods (i.e., children, adolescent-young adult, and adult-elderly). This three-dimensional framework is used because it allows us to cover most of the studies of personality development and echoes many of the issues encountered in psychotherapy and treatment as well. The more clinical aspects of psychopathology and the planning of treatment programs are not taken into account within this framework.

The three dimensions are represented by a cube, composed of many smaller cubes. In Figure 1, the upper cube on the left-hand corner represents the intersection of cultural diversity on achievement in children. Lying below it is the cube representing racism and achievement in children, with social change and achievement in children below it. Lying behind these small cubes are those representing the period of adolescence and young adulthood on these issues. There are cross-relationships between factors in a small cube to another small cube, for example, the influences of racism and of cultural diversity, or the influence of the front of the cube (i.e., childhood) on the later stages of Chinese Americans.

These four personality areas have been used in cross-cultural studies and in the study of Chinese social or political behavior (Brislin, Lonner, and Thorndike, 1973).

Achievement issues include motivation, goal attainment, and accomplishments. They encompass school and academic achievement, income and status gains, and the pressures and reactions of children to the achievement demands from the elder generation. *Power* issues become transformed into control over fate, authority relations, and political participation. The formation of political protest movements, civil rights equities, and the competence to change the power structures derive from power issues. *Affiliation* includes the issues of intimacy, affect expression among persons, sexual relations, and group belongingness and support. Finally, *independence* becomes issues of personal autonomy versus the group, individualism, and identity as a person.

In reviewing the studies on the mental health of Chinese-Americans, we can to a large extent place the variables studied into these categories, according to age periods and to the kind of stressors involved.

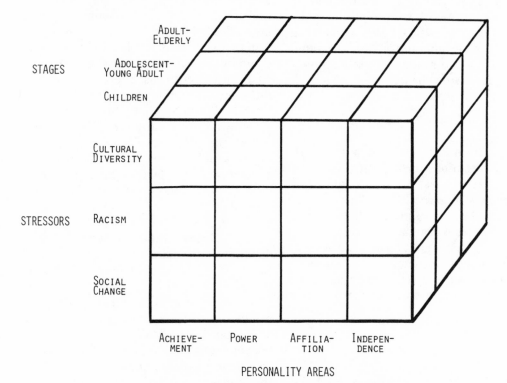

Figure 1: Chinese-American Mental Health

The dynamics leading to disorder and to healthy adjustment-adaptation can be deduced from the levels of reaction to these variables and to the community, family, and personal strengths as support systems. It should be noted that the cube model provides a structure for analysis. Because of the lack of more research studies, few definitive statements can be made for the dynamics of all the smaller cubes or for the interactions between various smaller cubes; moreover, the large cube can be considerably increased in size by the addition of other variables (e.g., another personality area or stressor variable). Most of what we know—indeed, most of the literature on Chinese-Americans—is located in the small cubes involving the effects of cultural diversity on the affiliation and independence of adolescents and young adults.

With this perspective in mind, let us examine the social stressors of cultural diversity, racism, and social change that are likely to influence mental health. Since mental health is also influenced by available resources, Chinese-American families, the community, and personal strengths are discussed. Finally, implications for mental health are drawn.

SOCIAL STRESSORS

All individuals are confronted with stressful situations throughout their lives. Some stressors are brief and unexpected—e.g. the loss of a job or a car accident. Others are more long-term and systematic. It is this latter type of stress that is our primary interest. Chinese in the United States encounter pressures or tensions because of conflicts in cultures, racism, and the rapidity and turbulence of social change.

Cultural Diversity

For a long time, social scientists have emphasized the process of culture conflict in the socialization of ethnic minority children. Culture conflict presumably exists whenever (1) members of one culture come into contact with the norms, values, and behavioral patterns of another culture, (2) the two cultures conflict or significantly differ from each other, and (3) conformance to each culture is rewarded and socialized. All of these conditions appear to be satisfied. Chinese-Americans have been found to be more oriented toward the dominant American culture as a function of the number of generations that one's family has been in the United States, the area of residency (outside versus inside of Chinatown), and the citizenship status (American instead of nonAmerican). These findings by Fong (1965) suggest that Chinese are exposed to American values and that progressive exposure to these values changes the orientation of Chinese-Americans.

There is also evidence that Chinese and American cultures significantly differ in certain values and practices. While we reject the notion of a national character and acknowledge the tremendous variations within what has been traditionally considered "Chinese" and mainstream "American" cultures, there are cultural differences in emphases. For example, A. Chin (1976) notes that Chinese have traditionally been influenced by generational continuity and the solidarity of one's kinship system which includes ancestors and relatives in a particular clan. Other values stem from the Confucian family system where elders were given considerable respect and authority. In the United States, American values deemphasize generational continuity and kinship. The status of elders is undermined by the youth-oriented perspective in the United States. Kinship alliances are more restricted to the nuclear family and, even here, children are encouraged to eventually raise their own families and become independent and autonomous from the family in which they were raised. The American way of life, encouraging rugged individualism, results in what Hsu (1970) calls individual-centeredness. Chinese, on the other hand, are more situation-centered and attached to the kinship system. Abbott (1976) has found that Chinese from Taiwan and Chinese in San Francisco on the California Psychological Inventory showed self-restraint, interpreted by him as an apparent subordination of individual impulse to the will of the group. He feels that Chinese are more likely than Americans to perceive the family and one's group rather than the individual as the primary reference point.

Exposure to different cultural values is a necessary but not a sufficient condition for stress. To a large extent, culture stress occurs when there are dual pressures to conform to both (conflicting) cultures. Many Chinese-American children are socialized by their parents to appreciate the continuity of their family, to respect elders, and to forego individual gratifications that are at the expense of the family or group. Contact with mainstream American society has created a different system in which individualism, adaptation to peer group influences, and the exaltation of youth rather than elders are rewarded. Individual creativity, assertiveness, and initiative are encouraged in American schools, although these characteristics may be frowned upon in Chinese homes (Chun-Hoon, 1971). Furthermore, aspects of Chinese contributions and culture may be ignored or actively discouraged in public schools. For example, Yee (1973) has found that the vast majority of social studies textbooks used in elementary and secondary schools made no reference to the Chinese or to their contributions in American society. What coverage of Chinese there was in the textbooks tended to be stereotypic, superficial, and brief.

Many social scientists feel that exposure to different cultural demands creates problems for Chinese-American children. For example, Sommers (1960) in reviewing a case study of a Chinese-American client noted the difficulty in developing a stable identity because of culture conflict. Similarly, Bourne (1975) found that young Chinese-Americans who were clients at a mental health clinic exhibited anxiety over the inability to reconcile their parental wishes concerning filial piety, achievements in academics, and conformance to the family with the roles and values of youths in the larger society. Males perceived problems centered around social isolation, passivity, and academic achievement, while females experienced guilt feelings in their liaison with Caucasian males. These findings are very similar to those of Weiss (1970) who postulated that the acculturation process for Chinese-Americans can create intense conflicts. He believes that Chinese-American females are more acculturated and have received fewer invidious stereotypes than males. Therefore, they are better able to date Caucasians. Chinese-American males, on the other hand, are under strong pressures to achieve academically and have fewer opportunities to learn adaptive social skills. Fong (1973) also believed that the American public school system teaches children to assert one's independence and autonomy which undermine parental authority. Furthermore, those Chinese living in a Chinatown ghetto face particular problems. Both parents often have to work long hours away from home so that their children are greatly influenced by peers or youth gangs or by the American public school system. In either case, parental values and authority are weakened and parent-child conflicts increase. Discrepancies in acculturation between parents and children appear to have detrimental effects in certain areas. In an interesting study, Kurokawa (1969) examined the relationship between acculturation and medically-attended injuries or accidents for Chinese-American and Japanese-American children, 10-15 years of age, enrolled in the Kaiser Medical plan. Mothers were interviewed in order to determine their child rearing practices and acculturation, while medical records were available for the analysis of injuries. Three acculturation types were developed: Acculturated children of acculturated mothers, acculturated children of nonacculturated parents, and nonacculturated children of nonacculturated parents. Results indicated that acculturated mothers were more likely than nonacculturated mothers to rear the child in a manner that permits exposure to hazards. The acculturated children were more likely than nonacculturated children to be independent and venturesome, which increased the probability of being exposed to hazards. It was also found that acculturated children have more accidents than do nonacculturated children, due to greater exposure to hazards. Furthermore, children who have *acculturation conflicts* at home (i.e., acculturated children of nonacculturated parents) appear to have a higher accident rate. Kurokawa speculates that the tension and conflict at home lead these children to have more accidents because of their inability to cope with hazards they encounter.

In terms of our cube model, the effects of cultural diversity have been demonstrated for children and young adults in the related areas of affiliation and independence. The affiliation issues involve identity and allegiances with the family versus individualism; with the family and the influence of elders versus American schools and the peer group; and with other Chinese-Americans versus Caucasians, particularly in dating patterns. Similarly, conflicts over conformity to self-desires, to parental wishes, to values of other youths, and to the values and patterns fostered in the educational system can be seen as independence issues. Achievement demands on Chinese-American students and their fears of not living up to parental expectations can be seen. For older Chinese-Americans, the necessity to work hard in order to make ends meet or the aspirations to gain status and financial security in this country may also cause family problems.

All of these studies indicate that culture conflict can lead to personality difficulties, tensions between parents and children, and accident "proneness." Are Chinese-American children inevitably caught between opposing cultural forces that are detrimental to mental health? In order to resolve the conflict, will Chinese-Americans have to completely assimilate to American or Western values? We believe that cultural conflict does create stress. However, many Chinese-Americans have developed a healthy *bicultural* orientation. A similar observation was made by R. Chin (1976) who examined the Chinese-Canadian community in Montreal. Being exposed to different cultures does not inevitably lead to a detrimental identity crisis, because identity is a dynamic process in which a stable, healthy, and consistent self-reference as a Chinese-American or Chinese-Canadian can and often does develop. The task is to specify the conditions that foster a healthy bicultural identity, an issue discussed later.

Racism

Chinese-American children have also been raised within the context of American racism. Although most studies of racism have focused on Black Americans, there is growing realization that Chinese-Americans have had a long history of experiences with prejudicial attitudes, stereotypes, discrimination, and institutional racism within American society. These experiences are more than the problems encountered in culture conflict where individuals are exposed to different cultural values. Rather, racism implies an active oppression of a group on the basis of race. For Chinese-Americans, oppression ranges from overt discriminatory laws (such as the Chinese Exclusion Act of 1882) to more subtle, complicated, and insidious processes. For example, Wang (1976) describes the problems that Chinese-Americans have in obtaining equal and quality education in public schools. Chinese-American children who are limited in their English speaking skills have been denied quality education. Simply providing Chinese students with facilities, textbooks, teachers, etc., does not make schools meaningful for many students who are unable to compete with peers in English-speaking classes. This points to very major problems in American society where equal opportunities for education are not provided to minority groups with different language skills and cultures. The United States Supreme Court in 1974 ruled in *Lau vs. Nichols* that the educational needs of Chinese-American students had been denied. The ruling has resulted in the development of bilingual and bicultural education programs.

We do not want to dwell on the documentation of racism in the case of Chinese-Americans. Numerous examples can be given. Rather, we would like to speculate on the effects of racism on mental health. Sue (1977) has argued that racism can be viewed as a situation in which a person's outcome or status is largely determined by race rather than by personal actions or merit. For example, an employer may believe that Chinese-Americans are not sufficiently aggressive to be business executives and consequently will not promote a particular Chinese-American employee. In this case, the employee's individual actions or merit are not considered; the employee's race (or racial stereotype) is the determining factor. Repeated exposure to situations where outcomes are independent of actions can result in what Seligman (1975) calls "learned helplessness," or a feeling that one's fate is influenced by chance factors or external forces (i.e., an external locus of control). Note that helplessness may also occur when a Chinese-American is given a socially desirable stereotype. A teacher may believe that Chinese-Americans are intelligent and hardworking. By inappropriately applying this stereotype to a particular child, and by giving the child good grades, outcomes are again independent of actions.

Seligman believes that learned helplessness has an effect on psychological well-being. If this is the case, then Chinese-American youths who are exposed to conditions involving noncontrol over their fate may be under stress. Hsieh, Shybut, and Lotsof (1969) have found that Chinese-American students are more external in perspective than Caucasian students. An external locus of control refers to the perception that one's fate or life is controlled by luck, chance, or circumstances beyond one's control. Furthermore, those Chinese-Americans who are external rather than internal in locus of control exhibit greater psychological distress (Kuo, Gary, and Lin, 1975). Obviously, some cultures may instill in their members the belief that much of life is beyond control. It seems likely that the learning of such attitudes is relatively "benign" since they are socialized as a normal part of culture. However, when an external locus of control is determined by racism and the resulting feelings of helplessness, the situation is probably quite stressful. Racism may have its greatest impact in reducing the ability of Chinese-Americans to control their fate (i.e., the power issue), whether the age period being considered is childhood, adolescence, or adulthood. In addition, racism reduces one's opportunities to achieve and to gain a measure of personal independence.

Social Change

The United States is a rapidly changing country. Technology, economic and political fluctuations, the energy crisis, and so on have had a profound impact on our lives. Social change can be quite stressful to the extent that it (1) is rapid and unexpected, (2) requires extensive life changes, and (3) occurs faster than the ability to find adjustive techniques and resources. Many Chinese-Americans are especially confronted with social changes. Between 20,000 and 30,000 Chinese immigrate to this country each year. The Chinese population in the United States is becoming more and more an immigrant group. Although there are many reasons for this immigration, one of the primary factors has been economic: Chinese are seeking a better life style for themselves and their families. And yet, aspirations have far exceeded reality. In order to live in more familiar surroundings, many Chinese immigrants locate in Chinatowns where there are housing shortages, unemployment, poor health facilities, etc. Many children are unable to compete in schools because of language difficulties. Both parents must often work long hours, leaving children unsupervised. This is a particular problem since the close family relationship, valued by Chinese, is undermined. Parental control is supplanted by peer group influences. Even if children adapt and become accustomed to the values and expectations of the public school system, there are difficulties. The children may lose their ability to speak Chinese and may be socialized to values that conflict with those of their parents, causing a severe generation problem. The rapidity, turbulence, and unexpected nature of these changes cause stress.

There is growing evidence that major life changes can diminish physical and psychological health. Holmes and Masuda (1974) have found that life events can be reliably measured as to the magnitude of social readjustment required. For instance, death of spouse, marriage, change in residence, a new job, a vacation, etc., can be assigned numerical values that indicate the intensity and length of time necessary to accommodate to these life events. Furthermore, the accumulation of many life changes over a short period of time was related to well-being. That is, the greater the number and magnitude of life events (over a specified time period), the greater the likelihood of physical and psychological ill health (Dohrenwend &

Dohrenwend, 1974). This is particularly true if the life events are undesirable (e.g., being fired at work) rather than desirable (e.g., marriage). Apparently, too many intense life changes over a short period of time create stress and strain the adaptive capacity of individuals. Such findings have been confirmed across different cultures (Holmes and Masuda, 1974).

Immigrants to this country undoubtedly experience severe life changes. Being in a new country, trying to find a job, living in a foreign culture, and encountering prejudice and discrimination are major life events that demand a great deal of social readjustment. Persons who do not have techniques to facilitate transition from one culture to another are likely to be at risk for physical and emotional disturbances. Hinkle (1974) investigated a sample of China-born persons living in the United States. These Chinese had undergone considerable cultural and social changes. Medical histories as well as physical and psychological tests revealed a greater tendency for illnesses than a comparably aged group of Americans. Hinkle concludes that exposure to cultural or social change may lead to poor health if the change occurs in a person who has preexisting susceptibility to illness and who perceives the change as being important and if the change requires significant readjustment in activities, habits, ingestants, and the physical environment.

It is apparent that rapid and unexpected social change can have far-reaching effects on personality issues. The uprooting of familiar social and familial relationships (affiliation), uncertainties in finding employment or in one's status (achievement), inability to control the tempo and direction of life changes (power), and loss of personal mastery over the environment and of autonomy (independence) are all implicated. The impact is probably the most profound on Chinese-American adults and the elderly who, unlike children, have already established life-style patterns.

Nevertheless, children are affected by social change and by its disruptive influence on parents.

MENTAL HEALTH

It is our belief that the three major stressors discussed above reduce mental health. Does this mean that Chinese-American children are at high risk for mental disorders? Do we see large numbers of "psychological causalties?" Again, there have been no studies of the rate of mental disorders among Chinese-American children. Sue and Frank (1973) did find that Chinese-American college students exhibited greater feelings of loneliness, anxiety, and alienation on personality tests than the general student body of students. From our personal experiences, a large number of Chinese-American youths are struggling with the issue of identity as Chinese, as American, as Chinese-American, or as Asian-American. These problems may be a direct reflection of culture conflict, racism, and social change. However, three points must be considered. First, all human beings encounter stress. Although an attempt has been made to delineate conditions that are particularly relevant to Chinese-Americans, stress is a common phenomenon. Second, stressful life events can result in increased adaptive strengths as well as in deterioration. Antonovsky, et al. (1971) speculate that a large number of Jews who had been imprisoned in concentration camps during World War II seemed to have developed tremendous adaptive capabilities as a result of the experience. Some social psychological factors that appeared to be important in resisting stress were (1) homeostatic flexibility, or the ability to accept alternatives and the perception of the availability of such alternatives; (2) relationships and ties to concrete others for personal and mutual support; and (3) community ties, or a sense of belongingness. Third, to the extent that

Chinese-Americans have resources to resist stress, then the impact of culture conflict, racism, and social change may be reduced.

Let us now examine resources such as the family, community, and individual strengths in fostering adaptation and mental health.

RESOURCES

Adaptive skills are often learned in the family and in community settings. These settings also provide resources and supports in times of stress. Thus it is important to understand the family and the community as transmitters of skills to children and as support systems during stress. As mentioned previously, our analysis is necessarily an overgeneralization in which individual differences are submerged.

Chinese American Families

The family (nuclear or extended) is the primary force for socializing Chinese-American children. Most families have maintained some aspects considered under the general rubric of "Chineseness": cultural practices, value patterns, language, food, calendar celebrations and rituals, music, and home decorations. Some of the value patterns noted earlier include respect for elders and male supremacy (A. Chin, 1976). Hsu (1970, 1971) indicates that Chinese families have two value patterns that may act as psychological resources. These value patterns revolve around the meaning of family for Chinese. The first is the transmission of values that encourage a *situation-centeredness* in individuals. Chinese are socialized to appreciate the maintenance of harmonious social relationships rather than to act according to individual needs and desires—i.e., individual-centeredness. The second value is the importance of fulfilling *affective* needs. Hsu believes that human beings have affective needs for human intimacy. For Chinese, these needs are satisfied within the kinship system because children are taught that bonds with family members are continuous with a past, a present, and a future. Thus, even when male Chinese immigrants came to this country in the 1800s separated from their families, there was still a psychological sense of belongingness, identity, and bondage with their families. Affective needs are satisfied through conformity to family and elders. Again, we would like to emphasize that in our discussion of the family, the family *role* is considered. By choice or by reality constraints, many traditional characteristics may not be seen in particular families. Many parents living in Chinatown ghettos must work long hours; hence, the family may lose its influence over children. In other situations, some families may simply socialize children toward Western values, or Western values may be learned from contact with schools.

Translated into resources against stress, the family satisfied affective needs, provided a sense of belongingness and identity, and gave mutual support despite physical isolation and other hardships. It is unclear how Chinese families deal with emotional stress in children and how successful these efforts are. Because of kinship ties and desire to preserve a good family name, disturbances in the family are not likely to come to public attention. Our speculation is that there may be a series of steps taken when a child begins to exhibit emotional disturbance. First, there are direct cognitive appeals (admonitions, advice-giving, appeals to shame and guilt) to the child for proper behaviors. A cognitive approach may be used because many Chinese believe that will power and self-control determine behaviors (Sue, Sue, and Sue, 1975). If these measures fail, respected third parties or intermediaries (discussed in more detail later) are called upon. Finally, the family may turn to Western forms of psychotherapy and treatment as a *last* resort. We

do not know of any studies that examine the efficacy of family or cultural resources. There is evidence, however, that traditional forms of public mental health services in American society are inappropriate for a large number of Chinese Americans (Sue et al., 1975).

Community Resources

In addition to the family, resources against stress can be found in Chinese-American communities. The concept of community encompasses a physical sense (e.g., Chinatowns) and a psychological sense (e.g., ethnic identity) that we would like to address. During times of stress, children often work with teachers, ministers, or physicians. R. Chin (1976) has also indicated that in Chinese communities other third parties or intermediaries (shopkeepers, friends, respected elders, community leaders, etc.) are available. These intermediaries often translate English, write letters, provide information, or otherwise act on behalf of persons in need of help. In view of the importance of respect for elders and for the opinion of others, parents may ask intermediaries to talk with a child who is experiencing problems. For example, if parents are having difficulties communicating with their son who is doing poorly in school, they may ask an uncle (respected by the parents and the son) to intervene. Such informal assistance systems are found in all cultures. For Chinese-Americans, these systems may be quite prominent because formal mental health services are frequently avoided. Homma-True (1976) found that Chinese Americans underutilized mental health services in the Oakland Chinatown area. By surveying a sample of Chinese, she found that many respondents would utilize community mental health facilities if these facilities had bilingual staff. Brown, Stein, Huang, and Harris (1973) also note that the formal mental health services need modification so that treatment approaches form a better match or fit with Chinese-American life styles.

In summary, there are important resources that can be found in Chinese families and in Chinese communities. The presence or absence of stressors is but one determinant of mental health. As indicated by Antonovsky et al. (1971), relationships to concrete others and ties to the community can well influence reactions to stress.

Not all Chinese-Americans live in communities with large numbers of Chinese-Americans. Available evidence seems to indicate that large numbers of Chinese who do not live in Chinatowns nevertheless make frequent visits to local Chinatown areas (R. Chin, 1976). But what about those who reside far away from Chinese communities? What is their sense of identity, belongingness, and community? Despite physical isolation from Chinese communities, many Chinese-Americans have a strong psychological sense of community which is discussed in the final section.

Individual Resources

So far, we have examined stressors and resources that influence the mental health of Chinese-American children. Culture conflict, racism, and social change must be dealt with and the family and the community resources are means by which adaptation to life demands can be achieved. However, the process of mental health is more than the sum of stressors and resources (family and community). Consideration must also be given to individual strengths and weaknesses that act upon stressors and can properly utilize resources. For example, the aversive effects of culture conflict can be minimized. Many children are now growing up with strong *bicultural* identity as Chinese and as Americans. There is an active attempt to integrate bicultural experiences. Sometimes the integration involves *discrimi-*

native control, or acting in accordance with the situation. A Chinese-American student may defer to family elders; yet in the presence of adult Caucasian teachers, the person may be quite assertive. We also see young Chinese adults who marry Caucasians, leave their parents' homes, and presumably lose their Chineseness, nevertheless, return to Chinatowns and volunteer to help other Chinese-Americans. There may also be a *unique blend* of Chinese and American patterns. Some Chinese-American families may eat Chinese food for dinner and have apple pie for dessert. Young married couples may consider their own nuclear family as being the most important relationship, yet the strong affective bonds to their parents are still present. In other words, ethnicity and acculturation are not necessarily mutually exclusive or incompatible. Biculturalism is not merely the selection of behavioral patterns that represent the best of the Eastern and Western cultures. Rather, through bicultural experiences there is an interaction effect that yields a distinct identity.

Children are also growing up with a greater awareness of social contradictions and racism. In recognizing these phenomena, they are better able to build adaptive strategies and to have a greater psychological sense of community with others who share the same experiences. The formation of an Asian-American identity is becoming more of a political force to combat racism, to foster positive self-esteem, and to devise group (community) means of controlling outcomes. Furthermore, biculturalism may result in greater personal flexibility to manage social change. Individuals can learn how to cope with the turbulence of social change.

The main point in our discussion of family, community, and individual resources is that within the conditions that cause stress are also the seeds for tremendous growth and development. This is not a romantic or idealistic view. We can acknowledge both the stressful situation of

Chinese in the United States and the positive strategies that have evolved. Past research has emphasized a "deficit" model where minority groups are perceived as exhibiting deficits because of stress. This view needs to be balanced with an analysis of resources in minority groups.

Examination of stressors and of resources also provides some direction for our preventive efforts, ideally aimed at Chinese-American children. Efforts should be made to reduce the conflicting nature of cultural diversity. Children should be taught to recognize aspects of culture conflict and differential demands. Involvement of parents with the educational system and the responsiveness of schools to the needs of Chinese-Americans must be fostered. Not only schools but also churches, mental health agencies, Chinese associations, and other community organizations should actively deal with the problems of culture conflict. With respect to racism, we have no magical solutions. Efforts must continually be made to bring racism to the attention of others and to combat it. It is clear that community organization and participation in the political arena are benefitting Chinese-Americans in reducing prejudicial and discriminatory actions. Finally, in minimizing the disruptive effects of social change, self-help groups, bilingual-bicultural programs, social service agencies, etc., designed for Chinese-Americans are reducing the impact of rapid and unfamiliar social and environmental change. Thus, by decreasing stressors and by improving family, community, and personal resources, we can move toward the promotion of mental health.

CONCLUDING COMMENTS

In examining mental health studies on Chinese-Americans, we have adopted a cube model involving the dimensions of stressors, personality areas, and age periods. The model is necessarily incomplete, and its use was for heuristic purposes. Our view is that culture conflict, racism, and social change are stressors that affect personality areas such as achievement, power, affiliation, and independence, as well as psychological well-being. Furthermore, the stressors and personality areas may show differential impact depending upon the age of individuals. While stressors may act to lower mental health, our speculation is that family, community, and individual resources can and often do provide means for adaptation and increased functioning.

REFERENCES

Abbot, K. Culture change and persistence of the Chinese personality. In: G. DeVos (Ed.), *Responses to Change: Society, Culture, and Personality.* New York: Van Nostrand, 1976.

Antonovsky, A., Maoz, B., Dowty, N., and Wijsenbeek, H. Twenty-five years later: A limited study of the sequelae of the concentration camp experience. *Social Psychiatry,* 1971, *6,* 186-193.

Bourne, P. The Chinese student—Acculturation and mental illness. *Psychiatry,* 1975, *38,* 269-277.

Brislin, R., Lonner, W., and Thorndike, R. *Cross-cultural Research Methods.* New York: Wiley, 1973.

Brown, T., Stein, K., Huang, K., and Harris, D. Mental illness and the role of mental health facilities in Chinatown. In: S. Sue and N. Wagner (Eds.), *Asian Americans: Psychological Perspectives.* Palo Alto, CA: Science and Behavior Books, 1973.

Chin, A. The Chinese family in Montreal. Unpublished report, 1976.

Chin, R. Montreal Chinese: Studies of personal and cultural identity. Unpublished report, 1976.

Chun-Hoon, L. Jade Snow Wong and the fate of Chinese-American identity. *Amerasia Journal,* 1971, *1,* 52-63.

Dohrenwend, B. S. and Dohrenwend, B. P. (eds.) *Stressful Life Events: Their Nature and Effects.* New York: Wiley, 1974.

Fong, S. Assimilation of Chinese in America: Changes in orientation and social perception. *American Journal of Sociology,* 1965, *71,* 265-273.

Fong, S. Assimilation and changing social roles of Chinese Americans. *Journal of Social Issues,* 1973, *29*(2), 115-128.

Hinkle, L. The effect of exposure to culture change, social change, and changes in interpersonal relationships on health. In: B. S. Dohrenwend and B. P. Dohrenwend (Eds.), *Stressful Life Events: Their Nature and Effects.* New York: Wiley, 1974.

Holmes, T. and Masuda, M. Life change and illness susceptibility. In: B. S. Dohrenwend and B. P. Dohrenwend (Eds.), *Stressful Life Events: Their Nature and Effects.* New York: Wiley, 1974.

Homma-True, R. Characteristics of contrasting Chinatowns: 2) Oakland, California. *Social Casework*, 1976, *57*, 155-519.

Hsieh, T., Shybut, J., and Lotsof, E. Internal vs. external control and ethnic group membership: A cross-cultural comparison. *Journal of Consulting and Clinical Psychology*, 1969, *33*, 122-214.

Hsu, F. *Americans and Chinese*. Garden City, N.Y.: Doubleday, 1970.

Hsu, F. Psychosocial homeostasis and jen: Conceptual tools for advancing psychological anthropology. *American Anthropologist*, 1971, *73*, 23-44.

Kuo, W., Gary, R., and Lin, N. Locus of control and symptoms of psychological distress among Chinese-Americans. Paper presented at the meeting of the Society for the Study of Social Problems, San Francisco, August, 1975.

Kurokawa, M. Acculturation and childhood accidents among Chinese and Japanese Americans. *Genetic Psychology Monograph*, 1969, *79*, 89-159.

Seligman, M. *Helplessness: On Depression, Development, and Death*. San Francisco: Freeman, 1975.

Sommers, V. Identity conflict and acculturation problems in Oriental Americans. *American Journal of Orthopsychiatry*, 1960, *30*, 637-644.

Sue, D. and Frank, A. A topological approach to the psychological study of Chinese and Japanese American college males. *Journal of Social Issues*, 1973, *29*(2), 129-148.

Sue, S. Psychological theory and implications for Asian Americans. *Personnel and Guidance Journal*, 1977, *55*, 381-389.

Sue, S., Sue, D. W., and Sue, D. Asian Americans as a minority group. *American Psychologist*, 1975, *30*, 906-910.

Wang, L. C. Lau vs. Nichols: History of a struggle for equal and quality education. In: E. Gee (Ed.), *Counterpoint: Perspectives on Asian America*. Los Angeles: Asian American Studies Center, 1976.

Weiss, M. Selective acculturation and the dating process: The pattern of Chinese-Caucasian interracial dating. *Journal of Marriage and the Family*, 1970, *32*, 270-273.

Yee, A. Myopic perceptions and textbooks: Chinese Americans' search for identity. *Journal of Social Issues*, 1973, *29*(2), 99-113.

PART V

Educational Issues Regarding

Minority Group Children

CHAPTER 24

Services in National Preschool Programs

Rosslyn Gaines, Ph.D.

This chapter is based on a project report (Gaines, 1979) to the Authority for Child, Youth and Family Bureau (ACYF) of the U.S. P.H.S. Department of Health, Education and Welfare. The main purpose of the project was to evaluate the integration of handicapped children into the Head Start Program. However, after visiting white rural children in Appalachia and Eskimo and Tlingit Indian Children in Alaska, I realized that it was impossible to consider the question of attitudes toward handicap outside of the context of cultural and ethnic traditions and values. Cultural and ethnic values form the roots of belief and action systems. These determine the roles given to the children, dictate child rearing and socialization methods, and influence response styles toward handicapped and non-handicapped children.

Within a few years, I was able to observe, play with, and talk to rural white Appalachian children; native Alaskan children; Southern black rural children;

urban and rural Spanish-American children; Navajo and Pueblo Indian children; migrant children; urban Polynesian children; and urban black and white children. I was impressed and fascinated with the differences between these children. Many studies of Head Start children take the similarities between children as a central focal point. Their message is that a child is first of all a child, regardless of heritage, environment, physical condition, or emotional status. In contrast, I want to emphasize the unique aspects of children's environments, cultural traditions, and lifestyles. The exquisite differences between children enable us to differentiate between them. As we experience their differences, we come to appreciate these children as unique humans. Certainly, all children have the same basic need for nurturance, nutriment, and physical and social development. But the form in which these are given to children in transaction with the characteristics of the receiving children produces extraordinarily diversified human beings. If these differences are not considered in careful detail, there is no way to understand any child fully. Perhaps the single most important thing I have learned is that social, cognitive, and educational preschool experiences must be assessed within the context of the child's community and social heritage. The main focus of this chapter will be on normal children and their families, but the problems of handicapped children and their families within the various cultural contexts will not be ignored.

All of the children observed were enrolled in Authority for Child, Youth and Family Bureau programs (ACYF) such as Head Start, Home Start, and Parent-Child Centers. The age range in Head Start Programs is three to six years although Parent-Child Centers include younger children. With few exceptions, all the children were from families with poverty level incomes and were able to attend the programs without tuition fees.

Head Start programs began in 1965 and by 1976 had served six and one-half million children (Zigler, 1977). All children receive health, vision, hearing and dental screening. Children receive at least one hot meal and a snack while attending the program. The teacher-child ratio is usually ten to one. The main services of the program are physical health, nutrition, education and mental health.

The data show that as early as 1977, 12 percent of the children being served by the Head Start program of ACYF were handicapped. This large percentage of children with handicapping conditions is in response to the 1974 Congressional mandate that the enrollment of Head Start must include ten percent handicapped children. There are ten categories of handicap defined by ACYF. These categories have definite limits and do not, for example, include children with treatable physical impairments, children whose "vision with eyeglasses is normal, or nearly so," or children whose speech development includes transitory articulation problems.

The method selected to observe was a modified case study method. I chose this rather than an interview or experimental intervention procedure. Although I am primarily a research psychologist, it seemed to me that questions concerning the well-being of handicapped and non-handicapped children could not be answered by a controlled experiment using rigorous experimental procedures. Such procedures do not offer adequate information about dynamic, continuing interpersonal interactions in relatively large groups, particularly groups which meet frequently and regularly. So there are no random samples, control groups, counterbalanced designs or parametric statistical analyses. Rather, this chapter presents the opinions of a developmental psychologist who engaged in relatively systematic short-term observations. The observational method has the advantage of making available to the reader a gestalt picture of the process. Doubtless other trained psychologists could visit the same Centers and select different variables to observe or draw different conclusions from the same variables. The veridicality of the informational base and the characteristics of the process of mainstreaming handicapped children would be enhanced if several other professional persons repeated this same type of study. But for now, it is my picture of the Centers which will be presented through my particular filters.

Three topics will be presented: first, parent involvement in child rearing processes and socializations of children; second, social and cognitive training for normal children; last, the integration of handicapped children into Head Start and its effect. These will be followed by a brief section of conclusions.

PARENT INVOLVEMENT

The most characteristic types of parent involvement across different programs are political and administrative activities and classroom experience. Parents are involved in helping to determine the selection and retention of personnel in Head Start Centers by membership in the Parent Activity Council (PAC) or Parent Planning Council (PPC). So, some parents have some power. However, in certain PAC or PPC committees, parents' votes are only straw votes because the director can exercise a veto. In an American Indian Center, parents were angry because the Director did not call parent meetings for several months. It should be noted that although a deliberate effort is made to hire directors and staff of the same ethnic background as the parents, the ultimate success of the parenting program rests on the individual motivations of and resources available to each director and the teachers. Some teachers, particularly in the rural and urban South, were highly motivated, but could not enlist parent interest because resources available to attract parents were too limited to attract parents.

A second major method of involving parents is to have them serve as classroom volunteers and, in some cases, as paid aides in the Center. There is also an intensive child development training course offering a Child Development Degree, which gives Head Start teachers (some of whose children are enrolled) an opportunity for career development and lateral mobility. Some programs are smothered in volunteers, as in Appalachia where there were 12 adults and 20 children in one large room. Other programs in the rural South and in the rural Alaskan Centers had hardly any assistance from parents.

However, the paramount purpose of parent involvement, as I understand it, is to assist parents in rearing children. Throughout all minority and majority groups, it has been found that the degree of parent involvement in rearing their children is the single most effective predictor of children's positive adjustment to and learning in school. For example,

Bronfenbrenner (1974) found that "all of the children whose preschool experience had included a parent intervention component made significantly higher gains than . . . those without." If this statement is true for normal children, then certainly it is reasonable to consider that as least as much gain could accrue to handicapped children if their parents participated in an intervention program. Parents who rear handicapped children often find that the handicapping conditions create severe problems for themselves and the other family members. Such parents are more likely to need special services more often than parents of non-handicapped children, although there is no lack of problems in rearing any child. Most ACYF programs have made serious efforts to obtain services for children whose physical needs are apparent: somehow, a wheelchair is built or found; somehow teeth are fixed; somehow leg braces are obtained. There is often no systematic way of obtaining equipment and the less dramatic the problem, the less likely that extra services are obtained. Children with no spoken language or inarticulate speech sometimes do not get speech training; children with impaired sight may receive special visual aids, but not receive training in using them; children with hearing losses sometimes do not have hearing examinations or hearing aids. Professional services are sometimes difficult to obtain in urban areas because of costs and crowded conditions. Extensive professional services are not readily found in most rural areas (Brewer & Kakalik, 1974).

Helping parents to cope with the psychological distress associated with child rearing seems largely random within the Head Start Programs. If a teacher is willing to listen to the problems of a parent who is willing to talk, some degree of help is given. Occasionally, professional counseling is made available, as in urban Alsaka and the urban Pacific Northwest, but more often counseling is not available even in metropolitan areas. Occasionally, parent programs and workshops are offered on problems of child rearing, but most parent programs described to me were largely suggested by parents and ranged from income tax to cake frosting to furniture building. (In this culture it is often difficult for parents to suggest a program of help or emotional support—it is easier to frost cakes with pink waves and rosebuds.) Again, few of the child-centered programs are focused on the handicapped child. I have seen a few good films on understanding handicapped children but films, as good as they are, cannot wrestle with parental guilt, shame and disappointment. The only systematic attempt to even edge into parents' distress was in the Home Start experimental Eastern and Northwestern programs with supplemental funding.

Most Home Start visitors are not trained to consider psychological problems as their domain. Their purpose in visiting the home, as I understand it, is largely to educate or prepare the child for school, show the mother how to teach the child, and assist in some aspects of family nutrition. However, some naturally sensitive home visitors find themselves listening, advising, and supporting a distraught mother or father. Many Home Start visitors really cannot function adequately in this role, but at least the mother often obtains some sympathetic attention. In the Appalachian program, home visits were made systematically to parents of handicapped children, although not as frequently as Home Start. I have accompanied the special instructors and also Home Start visitors on several home visits in various parts of the country. In general, these visits seem useful to both parents and child, particularly when a consistent program is structured and maintained. Nonetheless, individual attention has only been offered to a small fraction of parents. Some Home Start programs mandate one teacher home visit per month, but when a teacher is responsible for two shifts of classes or more than 30 children, most visits must be brief and superficial.

Overall, it appears that, as yet, helping parents to gain ways of being loving and helpful toward their children is the least frequent form of parent involvement in the Head Start program. The main issue, then, is, how can such services be made available to parents within the Head Start programs? The major kinds of services required are, first, training parents in techniques known to modify handicapping conditions; second, making counseling services available when parents are in crisis or have deeply disturbing personal problems; third, providing parents with assistance in child rearing problems; fourth, forming a social community for parents of children with chronic handicapping conditions; and, last, providing an information base on normal child and abnormal child development.

The format for these five services includes home visits, individual professional or paraprofessional consultations, group meetings, or some combination of these. In general, the first two services, parent training and counseling, are more frequently scheduled individually; the third, assistance in child rearing, is either on a group or individual basis; the last two services, a social community and information base, are primarily offered in groups. Some of these variations in format will be discussed in the following section describing each type of service.

A. Understanding Child Development

An informational base for normal and abnormal child rearing should be made available to all parents of Head Start children, not only to the parents of handicapped children. Over and over, the research literature shows that poverty parents are more likely to have turbulent, chaotic lives and poor nutritional standards, to be single parents, and to have a low level of education and low income (e.g. Birth and Gussow, 1970). It is also clear that poverty parents, given these conditions, are less likely to be informed about child development processes, good nutrition, and good hygiene. To be effective, all of this information must be presented in a way which is consonant with the parents' cultural and ethnic values and mores. Most important, information must be presented in a fashion that keeps the parents wanting to attend sessions.

The conditions both of providing cultural consonance and maintaining engagement of the individuals in a group can be enormously difficult to meet. Although it is not possible to characterize large groups of people with any single statement, nonetheless many people within a given ethnic, cultural, or social group share a few cardinal traits. For example, it is well known that in urban ghetto settings, there are large numbers of depressed and apathetic single parents. Rural settings also can be characterized by difficulties: Among the native Alaskans, economic depression in combination with their sensitivity to intrusiveness has made it difficult to reach parents. Moreover, native Alaskans are not responsive to learning about things which apparently cannot be changed. Thus, even if they learn to observe symptoms showing that their children are sick, direct medical services are not available during most of the winter and all of the spring thaw in much of Northern Alaska. If they teach their children to wash their hands before eating, there is often no clean water supply. In these instances, social action would have to be combined with parent counseling.

Rural Southern black families, who show considerable affection toward their children within the family, generally believe that it is the responsibility of the schools or appropriate institutions to educate and help their children—the families provide shelter, food, authority, and love, but the rest should be provided by the institutions. In these settings, it might be necessary to offer the parents an incentive program which has personal benefits in addition to the increased well-being of their children.

The traditional Navajo not only prefers his own healing methods and medicine, but does not share the value system of white America. The latter is also true for a large segment of the Mexican-American culture who maintain much stronger family bonds than are commonly found among Anglos. The Polynesians make almost no decisions without church approval and also believe that fat is beautiful. Moreover, there are language and strong dialect differences among these groups which limit verbal communication to persons who share the language or understand the dialect. For example, many Mexican-American parents seem to be very open to their feelings and emotions and, despite some initial reserve, could probably readily use the group process. In most of these communities, the chief barrier to parent involvement appears to be the language difference rather than social or psychological difficulties commonly encountered in attempts to form black or Indian groups. So, particularly in rural Mexican-American communities, any group leader needs to be thoroughly conversant in the local Spanish patois.

With all these differences, no single group format could fit. Some groups would need church or government council approval. Others would require many home visits before parents would consider participating. Some groups could meet in the homes of parents so that a more relaxed environment could prevail. In some areas, improved medical conditions would have to be legislated before it would be reasonable to pursue parent education. Many different methods would be required, with no single answer except that parent involvement groups must be geared to the local ethnic and social values and to the specific problems of parents.

The group structure would probably have to be as varied as the methods to start groups. One thing is certain: no one wants lectures. Some group processes which have been successful are role-playing, group discussion, and brainstorming. Another approach is to offer some sustained program desired by the group, such as leather working or home gardening, with an experienced group person as the class teacher. A television program with a format as appealing to parents as Sesame Street is to children could be an approach in areas where television is available in the homes. Short tape-recorded messages on specific child-rearing problems could also be moderately helpful in areas where most homes have telephones. Commercial group process videotapes have proved useful in some communities.

Above all, regardless of the way the information is conveyed, these parents would have to be treated with care and respect by people with the skills to lead parent groups. If the support and loyalty of the parents cannot be enlisted, the group will fail. It takes a good deal of patience, understanding, and flexibility to develop a cohesive group. There are many people who, with some training in group processes, could be excellent leaders—but strong empathy and flexibility are not universal and there is no point in training everyone who would like a job.

In summary, parental involvement in the Centers was primarily administrative and bureaucratic.

B. Counseling for Parents

Counseling services should be made available to parents as required in crises or by emotional problems. A Midwest single parent became depressed after a radical mastectomy and was not able to cope with her normal sons. She sought crisis counseling, but was unable to obtain help. A mother in the rural South was so obsessed with guilt over her child's cerebral palsy that her interference terminated her son's therapy. She was not able to find adequate counseling. A Texas mother also

was not able to find counseling when her daughter's handicapping condition became a problem for her new husband and herself. Such stories are legion. The reality is that a handicapping condition of children or parents often creates additional severe problems and attendant stress in the parents' lives. Many of these parents become psychologically more fragile and less able to cope with marriage, child rearing, community, or economic problems. For all these reasons, counseling must be available for parents as needed.

C. Parent Training for Modifying Handicapping Conditions

Twelve per cent of the children in the Head Start programs are handicapped. These children, across all ethnic groups, require special service. Some require gross motor exercises, others require speech training, language enrichment, concept development, perceptual discrimination training, social competency skills, fine motor coordination training, or more mature self-help skills. Even in the rare situations where teachers or aides have had special training to assist these children and there is adequate classroom time for such training, it would also be desirable to have most parents work with their children. The purpose is to develop a positive relationship between parents and the handicapped child, and to give the child further assistance. Parental assistance could provide the benefits of stable, reliable, and motivated help to the child, as well as economic benefits to society.

The handicapped child's self-image is largely derived from the people he spends most time with—his family. This family is part of our culture and, as such, is likely to be prejudiced against handicap. One need only to read the classic *Stigma* by Goffman (1963), or Gledman and Roth's *The Grand Illusion* (1976), to be aware of the depth of prejudice against people who are physically different. The consistently poor quality of national services to deaf and blind children (Brewer and Kakalik, 1974) reinforces the belief that the basis of neglect is prejudice. This prejudice can be minimized in families who learn to cope with their handicapped child and relate closely to their child: in a word, to value that child as a person.

The development of a positive relationship between a parent and a handicapped child is largely determined by the combination of the parent's attitudes, the type and extent of the handicap, and the child's personality. As each parent learns to be increasingly competent in rearing his handicapped child, positive attitudes and feelings toward the child increase. To experience a sense of competency, one must have a way of knowing that what one is doing has a positive or desired effect. To participate endlessly in giving exercises without being able to discriminate change begins to seem pointless to any trainer. So, the first requisite in any parent training program would be to start with a baseline and show parents how to observe or measure increments of change. With a growing child, the odds are that change will occur. But if you are working with a child on a daily basis, small increments of change are often overlooked or quickly accommodated. The parents cannot recall these changes without some record system. If the changes are not recallable, the experience of feeling competent is often diminished or absent.

It is not easy to ask parents to keep records, but records need not be conventional. Parents could make any kind of mark, be given an abacus, a chart, or even a pile of stones. The problem lies in teaching them to discriminate change. It might be necessary for a trainer to work with parents and show them changes, perhaps even reward them when they begin to observe adequately. For these reasons, I believe that a system of home visits should be developed for parents of handicapped children, particularly the severely handicapped.

All children need a positive relationship with their parents, but severely handicapped children are more dependent than any other group on parents for the opportunities to learn independence (Gaines, 1969). It also should be noted that programs other than home visits could be useful to parents. For example, some children receive one-half to one hour of special individual training sessions one or more times a week. Parents could observe these sessions and learn the techniques modeled. There would have to be some follow-up time with the specialist after each observation in order to discuss the procedures and teach the parents to observe change.

Last, some parents will not be able to train their children because of interference from crises, serious family problems or personal incapacities, such as alcoholism, depression, etc. Other parents will choose not to do so for a variety of cultural and social reasons. When parents are not able to help their children, additional efforts will have to be made to assist the family and give the handicapped child more training during school periods.

In brief, a training program for parents would not only ameliorate the child's condition, but could stimulate feelings of effectiveness and competency in parents which in turn could promote a more positive relationship between child and parent.

D. Childrearing Techniques

Parents rearing handicapped children are often in the position of having to invent methods for socializing children: How do you train a Down's syndrome child to eat solids? How can you establish a relationship of trust with a deaf child? What can be done about the blind child's automatisms? When and how do you toilet train an emotionally disturbed child? All too often I have seen parents stumbling over these basic child-rearing issues because handicapped children often do not fit into the normal patterns of development or cannot be communicated with in a normal fashion. There are hundreds of child-rearing books, but few of them deal with handicapped children and those that do cannot cover all the variables in all handicaps which modify or interfere with normal socialization processes.

But it isn't only the standard socialization problems which bother parents of handicapped children. Many handicapped children are irritable, some are apathetic, others are emotionally labile. Again, parents often do not know what to do. Some parents overindulge or overprotect their handicapped children. Others demand the impossible and then reject their children for not meeting the demand. Certainly, the attitudes of parents with normal children are often like those of parents of handicapped children and vice versa. But developmentally detrimental attitudes are more common among parents of handicapped children because handicapped children often promote these attitudes. Many of these parents find it more difficult to love their child—no one really prefers a handicapped to a non-handicapped child—and many parents are guilt ridden about their role in bringing such a child into the world.

These attitudes and methods of socializing children can be handled on an individual basis and probably should be if the parent has deep emotional difficulties in regard to the child. On the other hand, groups for parents of handicapped children would bring together parents who could share different successful socialization methods and would also provide an emotional support system for parents (Gaines, 1970).

Starting these groups may be very difficult because capable leaders must be found and a format devised which will continue to attract parents. But immediately, the important issue is that help in child rearing ought to be made available to par-

ents of handicapped children—and it is not now available.

E. Creating a Community

A special community should be provided for parents of children with chronic, severe handicapping conditions, although this community could include any parents who wished to participate. It seems to me that some of the problems of parents of handicapped children are also the problems of minority parents with normal children. Severe handicapping conditions are present in a minority of the population (approximately five percent) and while handicapped children number almost eight million (Mondale, 1970), the presence of one or more severely handicapped children in any given community is rare. While the child can often be integrated in the community, the parents' child-rearing problems are usually alien to their normal social community and the parents are isolated from sharing them. The problems of some minority parents and of many parents of children with chronic, severe, handicapping conditions are:

1. Cultural aversiveness to handicap (or to visible differences)

Persons reared in our society often respond to handicap or to visible differences from current standards of beauty with a strong aversive reaction. Goffman (1963) poignantly describes the effects of this aversion on the handicapped individual, but no one writes of the effects on parents. Parents continually experience this aversive attitude toward their child and it is highly unsettling. They see people repelled by their child and can do little about it except perhaps glare. It must also be remembered that severely handicapped children are usually born to parents without handicap. These parents are subject to the same aversive prejudice as the rest of the population, just as minority parents can prefer skin, hair, eye or physical variations other than those common to their group. There is a classic experiment by Wittreich et al. (1961) which demonstrates the emotional shock associated with extreme physical differences. Subjects were viewed in the Ames distorted room. This room was designed to create the compelling illusion that people were giants or midgets. However, physically disabled people were never seen as other than normal size (other strangers were seen as larger or smaller than normal). Gledman and Roth (1976) and Siller et al. (1967) also discuss public prejudice toward handicap. In brief, parents have to cope with their own reactions as well as with the aversive reactions of others toward their handicapped child.

2. Fear of the future

Parents of handicapped children often have a premature concern about their children's future. The reality is that the more severely impaired the child, the more limited will his occupational and educational achievements be. Parents are aware of this and very early begin to worry about what will become of their child. Some of these concerns could be ameliorated by group discussion. The group could also request services of a vocational rehabilitation counselor for one or more meetings. Individual families are unlikely to arrange this for themselves.

3. Difficulty in loving a handicapped child

We live in a largely child-oriented culture and it is expected that parents love their child. No parent prefers a handicapped child, and many of these children create multiple problems for their parents. Some have communication defects, others have needs which consume an inordinate amount of time, and so forth. Parents need to talk about painful feelings. Talking often relieves emotional

pressure and enables parents to find helpful solutions.

4. Personal guilt

Many parents feel personal responsibility for a handicapping condition. It does not matter if the handicap is caused genetically, intrauterinely, or adventitiously. Parents often feel responsible and cannot find a way to meet the responsibility in a meaningful way.

5. Minimal social support

Our society offers little support or help to parents of handicapped children. While many years of work and billions of dollars have gone into efforts to improve conditions for handicapped children, sufficient emphasis has not been given to helping their most important teachers—their parents. Parents need to learn ways to help their children, to assist in special training when necessary, to provide socialization, and to cope with handicap. They also need psychological support; in effect, they need a community of friends. A parent group could possibly provide such a community.

F. Assisting Children and Families to Utilize Federal and State Services

In many places the establishment of a centralized child-family advocate seems urgent. Third World parents with the best intentions sometimes prevent their child from receiving necessary optimal remedial services. Sometimes the parents refuse to discuss or to approve diagnostic assessments; at other times, parents approve but do not follow through on making or keeping appointments for therapeutic services. For example, like other parents, Pueblo parents do not want handicapped children, but unlike many other parents, the Pueblos deny the presence of handicap. This attitude, in part, derives from a long period with no available useful treatment. The Indian teachers say that there are now many good services for handicapped children, but that it is difficult to convince the parents. The teachers say that the parents should get the information about the handicap and that we have to "let parents know it's not so bad to have handicapped children, that it happens all the time."

Since parents are upset by handicap, it would seem logical that when they recognize a handicapping condition, they tend to overprotect their child. Thus, Boyd, a hydrocephalic child, was never allowed out to play until he came to Head Start. His parents were afraid the other children would hurt him. Conversely, Allie was never let out to play because she was so aggressive that her parents were afraid she would hurt other children. (As an aside, the happy ending is that when Allie came to Head Start and could play with other children, her aggressive behavior stopped).

Here again, it is apparent that Head Start, or some other agency, must play a child advocate role and educate parents regarding handicap and the best methods to accept help for the condition. (It will be very difficult since the Pueblos will not accept Anglo-type interference in their family life.) But, as one talks to the teachers, it does not seem impossible to have a program to serve children and families of handicapped children. A parent at a PAC meeting volunteered that although most parents feel ashamed when a child is handicapped, some parents are ready to be helped. She said parents feel ashamed because they have never been educated in ways to "optimize the child's development and work with their handicap."

With the exception of issues of religious conviction or borderline developmental lags, I believe that parents would approve diagnostic assessments if they understood the nature of the problem and the possible short- and long-term benefits to their child. Many parents are afraid of the effects of labeling their child; others are wary of any institutional intervention; still others have no understanding or information about equipment and training which would ameliorate their child's handicapping condition. Perhaps some federal funds for the handicapped could be obtained to train child-family advocates to carefully establish trust and give assistance and information to parents.

In terms of planning, probably one child-family advocate specialist could be responsible for 30-40 families except in areas where strong cultural differences or long distances would require a smaller family load. Additionally, the child-family advocate would require adequate power to effect recommended services.

Although Head Start is not supposed to be a primary health care agency, the pragmatic fact is that through its auspices many children are being identified and diagnosed and are receiving special services for impairment for the first time in their lives. As pointed out by Zigler (1977), more children are receiving health care from Head Start than from any other single agency. Perhaps it is time to incorporate these realities into funding requests.

SOCIAL AND COGNITIVE INTERVENTION FOR CHILDREN

Across all ethnic groups and all regions, most children appear to be enjoying the time spent in the Head Start Centers, the Home Visits or the Parent-Child Centers. There are surprisingly few tears or tantrums. Modes of play are quite varied and influenced by the structure of the classroom and the outdoor play equipment. When classrooms are divided into activity areas such as homemaking, art, or reading skills, children select and play in groups in these areas. When classroom areas are not structured, children spend more time playing by themselves, regardless of minority group membership. Outside play is also largely determined by the equipment and teachers' activities. If teachers start group games, children play these games; otherwise, they play singly or in small clusters of two or three children. Characteristic of this age, their modal play together is parallel play; that is, they climb jungle gyms together, build individual castles in the sand box or take turns on the slide. Only when a desirable item is in short supply, such as wagons or tricycles, do children characteristically organize group play, so that pulling and riding the wagon or tricycle are shared.

By and large, these children are receiving considerable individual personal attention; most teachers respond to their requests and their moods empathetically. More, they are learning to share and cooperate with peers and adults and thus, enhancing their own social development.

It is the view of some educators that feelings of self esteem and social competence transcend the need for preparation for the academic requirements of kindergarten or first grade. However, this philosophy seems appropriate only in some areas for some children. For example, many of the white Appalachian children lived in isolated areas and had never met any children other than their own siblings. The same social isolation was found among some Navajo children who not only had not met other children, but had never been inside a building with electric lights, flush toilets, and running water. Obviously, the first task for these Appalachian and Navajo children was to learn to feel comfortable in alien surroundings with strange children and adults. On the opposite end of the continuum of social development, I visited a day care preschool in the Northwest where all the parents were students in the college where the preschool was housed. These parents, like many students, met the poverty guidelines of ACYF, so their children could be enrolled in Head Start. But their career trajectory was very different from most Head Start parents. In these classes, the teachers did not worry about chil-

dren's academic preparation because they believed the children were receiving adequate cognitive stimulation at home. Their concern was whether the children felt good about themselves when they were away from home and parents from 8:00 to 5:00—a long day for young children.

However, the situation changes radically when academic standards for kindergarten are established by the public schools. In one Midwest city, there are entrance examinations for all beginning kindergarten children. In some Pueblo Indian kindergartens, children are expected to understand number concepts and names of colors, to use scissors, and to print their names. It seems to me that it is the responsibility of the preschool to help children meet these demands. Again, many children whose primary language is Spanish, an Indian dialect or Black English enter public schools where teachers neither comprehend nor speak languages other than American English. In these cases, the development of social skills in preschool is not as important for the child as being able to make one's self understood by teachers and peers. The inability to speak English has led to the tragic misplacement of thousands of children in classes for retarded children or has utterly prevented them from obtaining all but a rudimentary education. In many states, bilingual teaching is now mandated by law. But in many states, this social change has not yet occurred and children enter schools where they cannot talk to their teachers and their teachers cannot talk to them.

Non-legislative solutions are possible—the children can be taught to speak English before entering public school. Many Head Start programs attempt to do this with varying degrees of success. One Texas migrant preschool, G-, established what is, in my view, a model solution to the language problem.

The parents of the G- Head Start program demanded a change to a more academic program for their children which emphasized learning English. This community also insisted that the Mexican-American traditions and mores be respected and maintained. In my opinion, all of the demands of the G- parents, and more, have been met. The G- program appeared to meet the academic and cultural needs of the children and of the parents. In brief, the program consisted of short intervals of individual teaching followed by equal intervals of free play. This model of teaching prevented children from being disadvantaged when they entered kindergarten. At the same time, their cultural traditions were upheld and the social and emotional needs of young children were met.

My opinion is that Head Start should endeavor to give the preschool child the competencies to function in public school—whatever the competencies are. The range of expectancies for kindergarten children is very wide and ranges from simple self-help, such as ability to toilet unassisted, to fine motor development, such as using scissors, and pre-reading skills. These variations often vary within neighborhood, town, county, state, or region. In the West, one Home Start program has developed a Kindergarten Survival Checklist by talking to kindergarten teachers and observing the kindergarten classrooms. Teachers are not always aware, or would not always admit, that they expect an average child to say "please" and "thank you" or to print his own name. Yet a child who can do these simple tasks often receives more approval than a child who cannot. If the overt and covert requirements of the local kindergarten or first grade can be ascertained and taught, Head Start will be doing children a great service.

INTEGRATION OF HANDICAPPED CHILDREN AND ITS EFFECTS

Since 12 percent of children in Head Start are diagnosed as having handicapping conditions, such general issues as the desirability of integrating handicapped children into regular classrooms must be addressed. There are many education specialists who continue to believe that the special training required by some handicapped children makes segregation desirable. But, data on special education (e.g., Goldstein, et al., 1965, Vacc, 1972) suggest that separate classes have been less effective than integrated classes for mentally retarded and emotionally disturbed children. White (1977) found that older mainstreamed handicapped children are more isolated and are recipients of more negative behaviors than normal children. But, as White points out, the differences are small and, while statistically significant, may not be as important as the advantages of mainstreaming to both handicapped and nonhandicapped children. Further, it is my belief that preschool mainstreaming could help reduce negative effects of integration among older children. Preschool children are comfortable with handicapped children because of their own level of egocentricity, and this, in turn, often reinforces and stabilizes their positive interactions with children with handicapping conditions. Thus, preschool mainstreaming could help to reduce the negative attitudes of older nonhandicapped children. The experiment of integrating all types of handicapped children into regular classrooms appears promising *provided* that suitable cognitive and social education and special services are made available in an integrated setting.

There are some limits to the extent of integration. Although one Handicap Coordinator expressed the fervent belief that "if children can breathe, they can be helped," I cannot agree that the state of our art warrants such optimism. For example, one of the children in the A-B program in the Southwest had cerebral palsy and seizures, was severely mentally retarded, deaf, and visually impaired. He could not walk or talk and was estimated to function at well below the one-year age level. He has never been seen to interact with children and does not play with toys. By contrast, in the Texas Migrant program, another cerebral palsy child has learned to signal his needs, has a favorite friend, and could use a walker.

In general, Head Start Centers cannot be caretakers of children who do not respond to their peers or teachers, either verbally or with some signal. Moreover, if a child does not show minimal gain in some aspect of self-help, motor, social or cognitive development after a six-month intensive trial, a more suitable placement should be found.

I have noted, but not directly addressed, the question of the effects on nonhandicapped children of the presence of handicapped children in the classroom. Under most circumstances, these young children get along remarkably well. The nonhandicapped children accommodate beautifully: if they can play ball, but not have conversation with a handicapped child, then they play ball and don't talk to the child. The process at the three- and four-year-old level is remarkably pragmatic: If a child can share an activity, it is generally shared; if the child can't share an activity, it is of little concern or consequence to the nonhandicapped child. In this stage of development, children are primarily egocentric and as long as their needs are met, they are not really concerned about what happens to others. The limited research available on preschool children (Asher, 1975) supports this view. Role-playing and empathy appear to occur later in development, although the modeling methods used in Cerrito's research (1976) could be tried with preschool children. Friedland et al. (1977) suggest that such experiences promote mutuality and decentration among normal preschool children. In any event, it appears that normal preschool children are not frightened or made anxious by the handicaps of their less fortunate peers.

Are normal children ever hurt by the presence of handicapped children in the classroom? Yes, sometimes when a severely handicapped or disruptive child requires continual one-to-one attention. Under these circumstances, children can be intruded on by the disruptive child or can receive less teacher time and attention than under usual conditions. The handicapped children who fit into this category are a small minority, but very disturbing whenever present. The best solution I have seen to the problem is in the Northwest, where an occupational therapist was an auxiliary teacher on a daily basis. The disruptive handicapped child was helped and contained and the class activities could proceed without continual disruption. A separate resource training room, with a very low pupil teacher ratio, also serves to reduce disproportional amounts of classroom attention required by some handicapped children.

A secondary feature of these auxiliary services to handicapped children is to minimize the development of negative feelings toward handicap. Normal preschool children may not experience prejudice or anxiety about handicap, but they do experience dislike. If a handicapped child ruins their art work, hits them, or has an unpleasant urine odor, they are not going to like that child. Sometimes a teacher can intervene to repair the art work or provide a change of clothing, but the teachers rarely seem to have the time or techniques to do so. For these reasons it would be desirable to provide extra people to work with severely handicapped children.

Are normal children ever helped by having handicapped children in the classroom? The answer depends on whether the question is directed toward short-term or long-term benefits. For short-term benefits, the answer is generally no, with the qualification that this is the fault of the system and not of the children. With the exception of one teacher who fingerspelled and sang the words of one song, I have not seen normal children being given the opportunity to learn the skills or to share the experiences of handicapped children. The gross motor ability required to use crutches or operate a wheelchair, the remarkable tactile discrimination of blind children and deaf children, and the mime ability of children without verbal language are examples of some remarkable abilities of handicapped children. It would be a good learning experience for normal children to try to develop these skills. In point of fact, there are data which suggest that children can learn the alphabet and beginning vocabulary faster using finger-spelling or sign language than using seeing or hearing modalities (e.g., Webster, et al., 1975). (And think of the satisfaction of the handicapped child who receives teacher and peer recognition for his special abilities.)

The data are not yet in for the long-term benefits: However, the specific philosophy in support of integration is that the increased knowledge and understanding of different people reduces prejudice. Strange and foreign behaviors generally are not viewed as likable or desirable when our own standards of performance are exceeded or ignored. Generally, it is only as strange and foreign behaviors become familiar that people are able to experience the pleasures associated with the behaviors. For example, living in a Navajo hogan, migrating 6000 miles every year, and having to live in an Arctic village were foreign and undesirable to me before I undertook this project. I have learned from the people who live in these ways why they prefer to continue and what satisfactions they find in these life-styles. They have shared their views with me and gained my respect and admiration. When one gets to know persons with handicapping conditions, the response can be much the same. What was strange and alien becomes comfortable and satisfying.

There are, of course, reasons other than strangeness or alienation for prejudice toward handicapped persons. The sociological power aspects of nonhandicapped people in relation to handicapped people can scarcely be ignored (Gledman and Roth, 1976). At present, the power supply of preschool children is not much of a problem. In 20 years, this process of integrating handicapped and nonhandicapped preschool children could help to modify the power structure of our society and reduce prejudice toward handicap. In the meantime, it can be hoped that early positive experiences of handicapped children with nonhandicapped children will improve the world of all children.

How do Head Start programs to date handle the problems of integrating children with handicapping conditions? Table 1 summarizes my estimation of services to children in the ten major sites visited. Five variables are listed on a four-point scale for 22 locales. It will be noted that on some visits several Centers have been listed. This did not have to do with population density since two ratings are listed for a Southern state and three for two Southwestern states. Wherever there were widely disparate behaviors within the locale, individual sites were rated. When a range of ratings is given on one variable in one setting, this indicates that there are discrete groups within this setting receiving differential treatment.

I cannot emphasize too strongly that these ratings are based on selected time-limited observations by one person. I know that, like everyone else, I see the world through the processes of my own experience, heredity, and personality. To aid my personal judgment, many random events occurred in each visit which enlarged my understanding or changed my perception of the social and community milieu of these children. I am also aware that many doors were left unopened, sometimes by design of the Head Start staff, sometimes because an illuminating random event did not occur, and sometimes simply because of time limits. I do not apologize for my opinions, but I want the reader to understand their origin.

TABLE 1

Ratings* of Five Variables in the Integration
of Handicapped Children into Head Start

	Identification	Diagnostic Assessment	Social and Cognitive Intervention	Special Services	Parent Involvement
Eastern White Rural:					
County A	1	4	2	1-3	3
Rural Alaska	4	4	4	4	4
Southern Black Rural:					
R—	1	2	1-3	3	4
M—	2	4	4	4	4
Texan Mexican-American					
Urban	4	4	3	2-3	3
Rural	2	4	3	3	4
Eastern Black Urban:					
Day Care A Center	1	4	1	1	1
Day Care B Center	2	4	3	3	3
C	2	1	2-3	2-3	4
D School	3	3	2	4	3
E School	3	4	3	3	4
Southwest Indians:					
Pueblos A-H	3-4	3	3	3	4
Pueblo P	4	4	3	4	4
Navajo	3	1	3	2	2-3
Migrants:					
Head Starts Q, M, K	1	1-2	3	3	4
G—	4	—	1	—	3
Midwestern Urban Black, White, and Mexican-American:					
Public Schools	2	4	3	3	4
Day Care	3	4	2-3	2-3	4
CDC	2	4	1-3	1-3	2-3
L—	3-4	4	3	3	4
Western Polynesian and Multiculture:	2	2	3-4	3	3
Northwestern Urban Black and White:	1	2	1-3	1-2	3-4

*1. Exemplary Program; 2. Good; 3. Average; 4. Poor (Dashes indicate variable not observed)

416   THE PSYCHOSOCIAL DEVELOPMENT OF MINORITY GROUP CHILDREN

CONCLUSIONS

In closing, ACYF services to normal children across minority and majority groups appear to be making available to poverty children better health, social and educational service than has been previously available. Yet children are not always optimally prepared to enter public school.

Integration of handicapped and non-handicapped children could offer beneficial social and learning experiences to both groups of children. Full utilization of this potential is not made. Special services required by handicapped children must be increased to meet the national educational responsibility.

Contrariwise, services to parents in all minority groups are primarily focused on providing them bureaucratic power, vocational assistance and social experience. Very little assistance in problems of child rearing or crisis counseling is available.

There is room for improvement in the ACYF programs, as there is in any large-scale program, but it must be remembered that the program has served and helped millions of children in a comparatively short time. Probably few national programs have done so much in so short a time on such a large scale.

The ACYF model, like any large-scale national program, needs improvement, but I am impressed with the energy and zeal which have been poured into the program nationally and at the local level. The ACYF bureau has made a magnificent effort on behalf of over six million children and promises to help millions more.

REFERENCES

Asher, N. W. An examination of pre-school children's attitudes toward the physically handicapped. Paper presented at Society for Research in Child Development, Denver, 1975.

Birth, H. G. and Gussow, J. D. *Disadvantaged Children: Health, Nutrition and School Failure.* New York: Grune & Stratton, 1970.

Brewer, G. D. and Kakalik, J. *Improving Services to Handicapped Children.* 1974, R-1420/1-HEW.

Bronfenbrenner, U. *Is Early Intervention Effective? A Report on Longitudinal Evaluations of Pre-School Programs.* Volume 2, 1974, DHEW Publication No. (OHD) 74-25.

Cerrito, M. The effects of empathy training on children's attitudes and behaviors toward handicapped peers, 1976. Dissertation completed at the University of Washington in partial fulfillment of the requirements of the Ph.D. degree.

Friedland, E. R., Meisels, S. J., and Hersch, R. G. Piagetian implications of integrating the normal and handicapped preschool child. In: J. Mogary, M. Poulson, P. Levinson, and P. Taylor (Eds.), *Piagetian Theory and Its Implications for the Helping Professions. Emphasis: The Handicapped Child.* Los Angeles, CA: University of Southern California Press, 1977.

Gaines, R. Experiencing perceptually deprived children. *Journal of Learning Disabilities*, 1969, 2, 559-565.

Gaines, R. *Parent Reality Groups: Program and Theory.* 1970. OE C-0-9 143612-4572(019).

Gaines, R. Helping handicapped children: Recommendations for model programs in Head Start Centers. Paper for ACYF, 1979.

Gledman, J. and Roth, W. The grand illusion: Stigma, role expectations and communication. Paper for the White House Conference on Handicapped Children, 1976.

Goffman, E. *Stigma.* Englewood, N.J.: Prentice-Hall, 1963.

Goldstein, H., Moss, J. W., and Jordan, L. J. The efficacy of special class training on the development of mentally retarded children. U.S. Office of Education Coop. Res. Proj. #619, Urband, University of Illinois, 1965.

Mondale, W. Justice for Children. Speech delivered to the U.S. Senate, 1970.

Siller, J., Chipman, A., Ferguson, L. T., and Vann, D. H. *Studies in Reactions to Disability: XI. Attitudes of the Non-Disabled Toward the Physically Disabled.* New York: New York University, School of Education, May, 1967.

Vacc, N. Long-term effects of special class intervention for emotionally disturbed children. *Exceptional Children*, 1972, 39, 15-23.

Webster, C. D., Konstantareas, M. M., and Li, J. Assessing autistic children: Discrimination training and simultaneous communication procedures. Paper presented at Society for Research in Child Development, Denver, 1975.

White, B. N. Classroom interactions and behaviors of mainstreamed special needs children as measured by a new observation technique. Paper given at Society for Research in Child Development, New Orleans, 1977.

Wittreich, W. V., Grace, M., and Radcliffe, K. B., Jr. Three experiments in selective perceptual distortion. In: F. P. Kirpatrick (Ed.), *Explorations in Transactional Psychology.* New York: New York University Press, 1961.

Zigler, E. F. Speaker at the first plenary session of the Child Development and Social Policy Program of the Society for Research in Child Development, New Orleans, 1977.

CHAPTER 25

The Effects of Intelligence and Achievement Testing on Minority Group Children

Eligio R. Padilla, Ph.D.

and Gail E. Wyatt, Ph.D.

The power of intelligence and achievement tests to determine educational opportunities and future occupational roles is unquestionably profound. Though some fine theoretical distinctions have been made between IQ and achievement tests, research has shown that they correlate highly with one another (Bruininks and Feldman, 1970; Johnson and Johnson, 1971; Kennedy, Van de Reit, and White, 1963; Oliver and Barclay, 1967). Moreover, these tests have traditionally been used interchangeably for a variety of purposes by researchers, psychologists and educators. Thus, in this paper the terms achievement and intelligence will be used synonymously.

In the past decade a controversy has resurfaced in psychology regarding racial differences in intelligence. Fortunately,

the scientific, educational, political, economic and moral issues implicit in IQ and achievement testing have come to be seen as too important to leave solely to psychologists and their patrons. In this chapter, the hereditarian as well as the environmental positions on racial differences in IQ will be reviewed. The effect of testing upon minority group children and factors influencing test performance will also be discussed. Alternatives to the use of traditional assessment tools will be presented with a concluding position statement on the status of testing today. However, to adequately understand the controversy that has embroiled psychol-

---

Authorship of this work is listed in an alphabetical order to reflect an equal amount of effort on the part of both the authors.

ogy for almost a decade, the historical development of the testing movement must be considered, along with the philosophical and political ideologies on which it rests. Of greater importance, an historical context is necessary if the adverse effects of intelligence and achievement testing on minority group children are to be fully appreciated.

HISTORY OF INTELLIGENCE TESTING

The Origins of Intelligence Testing

The notion that *other* groups are by nature less intellectually capable is an ancient belief that has persisted to the present day. The Roman orator Cicero advised a friend, "Do not obtain your slaves from Britain because they are so stupid, and so utterly incapable of being taught." It is indeed ironic that the British and their Anglo-American cousins now personify the flower of intellectual development, while people of Latin descent would seem, in two thousand years, to have made rapid progress in reverse!

The specific formulation of this genetic doctrine has varied in sophistication from one period to the next, but its essence remains the same (Thomas and Sillen, 1972). Nature endows certain races with the capacity for abstract thought and the ability to exercise foresight while others are fated to be ruled over (for their own good) because they are creatures of impulse, capable of learning only by rote.

In the 19th century, science and technology were instrumental in raising the concept of racial supremacy from the level of personal belief to that of "objective fact." Adolph Quetelet, a Belgian astronomer and statistician, introduced the concept of the "average man," demonstrating that measurements of the human body tend to be normally distributed (Radford and Burton, 1972). Following Quetelet's lead, Sir Francis Galton argued that psychological as well as physical traits must be normally distributed. Galton collected data on the variability of the species in his anthropometric laboratory and began the business of psychometrics. From this laboratory came two statistical concepts of fundamental importance to psychometrics: regression to the mean, and correlation. The first is essential if the normal distribution is to remain stable over time. The second concept allowed the notion of partial causation to be included in scientific procedures. Nothing contributed more to the typological way of thought of modern psychology than the methods developed by Galton, elaborated upon and perfected by his disciple and biographer, Karl Pearson.

One "type" of special social concern to Galton and Pearson were the Jews. In 1884 Galton wrote: "It strikes me that the Jews are specialized for a parasitical existence upon other nations and that there is need of evidence that they are capable of fulfilling the varied duties of civilized man" (Pearson, 1924). For at least 20 years, beginning in 1908, Pearson collected and analyzed information in order to monitor "the quality of the racial stock immigrating into Great Britain" (Pastore, 1949). Pearson was explicit in his beliefs: "Taken on the average, and regarding both sexes, this alien Jewish population is somewhat inferior physically and mentally to the native population . . ." (Pearson and Moul, 1925). Despite the fact that he failed to find any differences between the Jewish and non-Jewish boys when comparisons were made for the sexes separately, Pearson did, he believed, his scientific and patriotic duty in proclaiming Jewish inferiority (Hirsch, 1970).

Charles Spearman, next in the London line of investigators, proposed the tremendously influential two-factor theory of intelligence. He believed that any intellectual activity must have two kinds of ability underlying it: the first specific to the particular activity and the second common to all activities—general intelligence or *g*. Spearman confidently proclaimed that he had analyzed the nature of *g* and that his analysis had at last provided psychology with a genuinely scientific foundation (Spearman, 1927).

In the work of Sir Cyril Burt, *g* developed into an "innate, general cognitive ability." Burt claimed that he had succeeded in determining the relative contributions of heredity and environment to test performance. His work is considered a cornerstone of the hereditarian position in the nature-nurture controversy which periodically erupts in the social and biological sciences. At about the same time, testing was coming into its own in the United States, when the government gave psychologists an opportunity to apply their techniques to the millions of recruits who were tested, categorized, trained and shipped off to the First World War.

Testing in America

The first usable test of general intelligence was published in 1905, not by Galton or one of the London line, but by a Frenchman, Alfred Binet. He had been commissioned by the French Minister of Public Instruction to develop a test which could identify those students whose academic aptitude was so low as to require special training. Binet, who considered his instrument to be an atheoretical, practical, diagnostic tool, protested against the "brutal pessimism" of those who considered the test score to be a fixed quantity and prescribed corrective courses in "mental orthopedics" for individuals with low scores (Kamin, 1976). The major American importers and translators of Binet's test—Lewis Terman and Maude Merrill at Stanford, Robert Yerkes at Harvard, and Henry Goddard at Vineland, New Jersey—did not subscribe to Binet's position, but rather were in accordance with the London school of thought. Terman, Yerkes and Goddard were also prominent in turn-of-the-century eugenics movements in-

spired by Galton. Like Galton, Terman also had "types" who were of special concern to him. After testing a *pair* of Indian and Mexican children, he wrote:

Their dullness seems to be racial, or at least inherent in the family stocks from which they come. The fact that one meets this type with such frequency among Indians, Mexicans and Negroes suggests quite forcibly that the whole question of racial differences in mental traits will have to be taken up anew . . . here will be discovered enormously significant racial differences . . . which cannot be wiped out by any scheme of mental culture.

Children of this group should be segregated in special classes . . . they cannot master abstractions, but they can often be made efficient workers . . . There is no possibility at present of convincing society that they should not be allowed to reproduce . . . they constitute a grave problem because of their unusually prolific breeding (Terman, 1916).

The concern for social order and rule by an intelligent élite was shared by Yerkes, Goddard and Edward L. Thorndike, among other prominent figures in the history of American psychology. Goddard (1920) argued that, "The disturbing fear is that the masses—the seventy or even eighty-six million—will take matters into their own hands," and that the "four million" of "superior intelligence" must never forsake their responsibility for directing the masses.

Terman also argued that the less intelligent were incapable of social and moral judgment: "All feeble-minded are at least potential criminals. That every feeble-minded woman is a potential prostitute would hardly be disputed by anyone" (Terman, 1917). In completing the symmetry of the argument, Thorndike (1920) found higher moral standards among the more intelligent and was convinced that, "To him that hath a superior intellect is given also on the average a superior character."

Thus, to be labeled as a person of lower intelligence was a serious matter in an era where differences between the poor, the mentally ill, the criminal and the dull were blurred (Kamin, 1976). In many states, all institutions established to house such "degenerates" were administered by a single commissioner of charities and corrections. Prodded by psychologists, many states also passed laws requiring the sterilization of the patient-prisoners in such public institutions prior to their release (Kamin, 1976). Between 1907 and 1927, twenty-one states practiced eugenical sterilization (Karier, 1972).

Intelligence tests were used effectively not only to oppress several thousand "undesirables" in the United States, but to prevent thousands of others from entering the country. Prior to World War I there was no numerical limit or geographical distinction set on European immigration (Kamin, 1976). Throughout the 19th century, the majority of immigrants came from northern and western Europe, but by the turn of the century immigration from southern and eastern Europe had increased dramatically. In 1912, the United States Public Health Service invited Goddard to administer intelligence tests to newly arrived immigrants at Ellis Island. Goddard (1913) reported that his examinations determined that the "great mass of average immigrants" were "feeble-minded," including 87 percent of the Russians, 83 percent of the Jews, 80 percent of the Hungarians and 79 percent of the Italians.

When American involvement in World War I became inevitable, Yerkes, the President of the American Psychological Association, suggested that the major contribution of psychologists to the war effort could be the mass intelligence testing of draftees. Over 2,000,000 were tested under Yerkes' direction, with the assistance of Terman, Goddard and Thorndike. For the first time it was established on a large scale basis that whites scored significantly higher than Afro-Americans. However, the findings of greatest political relevance dealt with the performance of the foreign-born. Latins and Slavs performed poorly, with the Polish not scoring significantly higher than Afro-Americans (National Academy of Sciences, 1921).

After the War, the National Research Council established a Committee of Scientific Problems of Human Migration whose job it was to take the national debate "out of politics," and to place it on "a scientific basis" (Kamin, 1976). Its first product was a book by Carl Brigham (1923) entitled *A Study of American Intelligence*. Brigham showed that immigrants drafted into the Army who had been in the country 16 to 20 years before being tested were as intelligent as native-born Americans, while immigrants who had been in the United States less than five years tested as "feeble-minded." The first group of immigrants were mostly from Great Britain, Scandinavia and Germany, while the more recent arrivals were from southern and eastern Europe. The decline in intelligence among immigrants, Brigham asserted, coincided precisely with the decrease in the amount of "Nordic blood," and the increase in the amount of "Alpine" and "Mediterranean blood" in immigrants. With this contribution behind him, Brigham was hired by the College Entrance Examination Board and developed the Scholastic Aptitude Test.

The political usage of the Army data and Brigham's work was immediate and intense, culminating in the National Origins Quota Act of 1924. This law not only restricted the total number of immigrants, but also assigned quotas to the number of immigrants from each European country. The earlier Census of 1890 was used to further curtail the immigration of the "biologically inferior" from southern Europe. The National Origins Quota Act ultimately led to the death of thousands of Jews in Nazi concentration camps who had been denied entry because the German quota was filled, though other quotas were undersubscribed (Kamin, 1976).

Following the "triumph" of testers who

helped resolve the national debate over immigration on a "scientific basis," the development of intelligence and achievement testing as a national institution was assured. Nevertheless, a challenge arose in the academic world to hereditarian explanations of racial and social class differences in IQ. According to the dogma of radical behaviorism, differences among people are wholly related to formal and informal education. The adoption of a behavioristic belief among academics was stimulated by their horror of events taking place in Europe, where Nazis were utilizing hereditarian arguments to justify genocide. Following the Second World War, environmentalists dominated the nature-nurture debate. During the following decades, research on racial differences in intelligence focused on the effects of the environment on children's intellectual development (Hunt, 1966). Based on this research, federally funded programs, including Head Start and Follow Through, were developed to ameliorate the alleged social, environmental and intellectual deprivation. Though gains in IQ were either small or short-lived, federal funds continued to support a growing number of programs until the hereditarian "backlash," inspired by Arthur Jensen, took place in the late 1960s.

Jensen (1969) argues convincingly that social scientists have not given sufficient attention to the research of geneticists. However, rather than lending support to Jensen's hypotheses and conclusions, a consideration of research in genetics indicates that the hereditarian argument is no better than the environmental position, with neither proving to be adequate. Before touching upon this research, one more set of questions must be answered if the current controversy is to be put into perspective. Testers determine the eligibility of applicants for everything from the military academies to the Peace Corps, universities and the professions. Testers are the traffic cops who control the entry into virtually every profession in modern society—but who polices the police? Who provided financial support for the work of Terman, Yerkes, Goddard and Thorndike? Who permitted testers to assume such vast authority?

The Economic Base of the Testing Movement

Clarence Karier (1972) has perhaps most clearly and succinctly described the actual sources of power which propelled testing to its place of prominence in our society. At the turn of the century, the United States underwent profound social and economic changes as the laissez-faire capitalism of the 19th century was rejected as self-destructive and replaced by a more comprehensive view of enlightened self-interest. Corporate interests recognized that it was to their benefit to work closely with labor and government to deal with the complex issues of industrialization, immigration and urbanization, and to reorganize society for the orderly, efficient production and consumption of goods and services. The corporate liberal state emerged during the Progressive Era with its need for standardized producers and consumers (Wiebe, 1967). Political reformers at all levels of government reorganized public institutions to make administrative and bureaucratic functions more effective (Hays, 1969). In the private sector, new organizations were created to channel corporate wealth toward the support of liberal progressive reform. These philanthropic foundations came to be a major force in political and educational reform. Foundations became so powerful in the policy formation of the corporate liberal state that they were regarded as virtually a fourth branch of government, effectively representing the interests of corporate wealth in the United States.

One of the first beneficiaries of foundation support was the eugenics movement of the early 20th century. The

Eugenics Records Office, supported by the Carnegie Institution of Washington, generated the propaganda needed to gain popular support for their movement. With the collaboration of corporate wealth and the prestige of the scientific establishment, sterlization laws were passed.

After the war, immigration policy became the subject of national debate. Larger manufacturers and labor unions favored restricting immigration. Supported by the Carnegie Foundation of Washington and the Commonwealth Fund, psychologists provided the "scientific" information necessary to justify the National Origins Quota Act which was passed in 1924.

Also after the war, a mass system of public education was developed to serve the manpower needs of the corporate liberal state. Standardizing producers and consumers led some educators to conceptualize schools as factories. The testers, financed by corporate foundations, helped meet the need for "accountability" and "continuous measurement." Thorndike changed the emphasis of his career from assessing the effectiveness of the curriculum to developing the curriculum. Is it any wonder, then, that IQ correlates highly with scholastic success, with essentially the same group of people developing and assessing the curriculum? With the support of the Carnegie Foundation, Thorndike told teachers what to teach, how to teach it, and how to evaluate it (Karier, 1972). Thorndike, Terman, Goddard and others persuaded school officials to standardize the school curriculum with a differentiated track system based on "ability" and the values of the corporate liberal state.

The Educational Testing Service (ETS), with a grant from the Carnegie Foundation, was established in 1947, consolidating a number of independent testing services, such as the College Entrance Examination Board and the Graduate Records Office. The ETS is the modern gatekeeper to the universities and professions. It compiles test scores and, in many cases, determines what students will receive financial aid.

After more than half a century of diligent effort by psychologists, it is clear that they have been highly effective and efficient in serving the interests of society—a society dominated by wealth, power and status. They have played a key role in rationalizing the social class system by creating the illusion of objectivity, while serving the needs of educators to be "scientific" and "accountable" and creating a belief system to convince the poor and "identifiable" minority groups that their lot in life is the work of Mother Nature. The educational system, supposedly designed to meet the needs of the individual, "regardless of race, color, creed" or social class, categorizes and tracks poor and minority children, with remarkable reliability, into occupations appropriate to their socioeconomic background. The tests and their "objectivity" have defused most revolutionary opposition since the disadvantaged are less likely to take violent measures against the social system if they believe their marginal standard of living is attributable to inborn intellectual inferiority. The Russell Sage Foundation released a report which stated—not surprisingly—that the "upper class respondent is more likely to favor use of tests than the lower class respondent." Even more noteworthy, however, is the observation that "the lower class respondent is more likely to see intelligence tests measuring inborn intelligence" (Brim, Neulinger, and Glass, 1965).

The early advocates of testing and their modern counterparts would, in most cases, probably object to being described as servants of power, privilege and status. In discussing the "prestige hierarchy of occupations," Jensen (1969) states: "We have to face it: the assortment of persons into occupational roles is simply not 'fair' in any absolute sense. The best we can hope for is that true merit, given equality of opportunity, will act as the basis for the natural assorting process." But what does it mean to assume "equality of opportunity" and "hope" that "true merit" will somehow lead to "a natural assorting process," given (in this case *undeniably* given) a racist and socially élitist society where wealth, power and educational privilege are so unevenly distributed? The belief that testers are measuring "true merit" is an act of faith predicated on the belief that the "prestige hierarchy of occupations" and the people who occupied those roles and provided the criterion or objective standard upon which the tests are based were in those roles not because of privilege, money, status, power or violence, but because of superior intellect, talent and virtue. On this rather shaky foundation has rested the liberal's faith in the meritocracy which emerged in American education during the twentieth century (Karier, 1972).

THE RESURGENCE OF THE NATURE-NURTURE CONTROVERSY

The Hereditarian Position

In the winter of 1969, the *Harvard Educational Review* published a paper provocatively entitled, "How Much Can We Boost IQ and Scholastic Achievement?" Insignificantly, asserts its author, Arthur Jensen, a professor of educational psychology at the Berkeley campus of the University of California. He argues that compensatory education was doomed to failure from its inception, not because it was poorly funded, planned, administered or executed, but because of innate intellectual deficits among the students for whom these remedial programs were designed.

Jensen's hereditarian argument is based on two observations: Afro-Americans do not perform as well as Whites on standard IQ tests; and compensatory education has failed to reduce these differences. Furthermore, he proposes that these differences in IQ cannot be totally explained by environmental differences such as inferior schooling, poverty, discrimination, etc. His view of the literature and synthesis of existing data lead him to the conclusion that IQ is highly heritable, with most of the variation among individuals arising from genetic rather than environmental sources. Since nature imposes such clear limits, it is impossible to reduce the racial gap in IQ through any educational intervention. He also goes on to suggest that there are qualitative as well as quantitative differences in intelligence and that the best thing that can be done for Afro-American children is to capitalize on their rather limited skills for what they are biologically adapted (Lewontin, 1970). Jensen argues that these children with low IQ scores lack the capacity to acquire the cognitive skills involved with abstract reasoning and problem-solving, which suggests that they should be taught mostly by rote and should not aspire to occupations that call for higher cognitive skills.

The contemporary hereditarian position rests on the assumption that IQ is an index of innate intellectual capacity. According to this argument, it is unimportant that there is no consensus among scientists as to what intelligence "really is." Jensen (1969) states that "the most important thing about intelligence is that we can measure it." Intelligence is thus treated as if it were a metric character, like weight or height, which is measured directly by IQ. However, IQ is not a measure of an individual character like weight; it is actually a measure of rank order or relative standing of test scores in a population. Nevertheless, Jenson proceeds with this assumption to make the argument that intelligence is normally distributed. Apparently Jensen believes that if intelligence were normally distributed, this would demonstrate its biological and genetic status (Lewontin, 1970). In attempting to account for the tenacity with which many investigators cling to this concept, the great French mathematician Henri Poincaré is supposed to have said:

"Everybody believes in the [normal distribution]: the experimenters because they think it can be proved by mathematics, the mathematicians because it has been established by observation" (Layzer, 1973). Genetic theory, however, does not require or even suggest that phenotypic characters be normally distributed (Lewontin, 1970). A normal distribution will usually obtain a number of metric characters such as birth weight in cattle, but it is not the case, on the other hand, for measurements of most kinds of skill or proficiency (Layzer, 1973).

As indicated earlier, Jensen validly emphasized the fact that social scientists have not adequately taken into consideration the research findings in genetics. Jensen's paper relies heavily on his understanding of the concept of heritability. The heritability of a trait or characteristic in a population is an estimate of the proportion of the trait's variation in the population which is due to genetic differences. In other words, heritability is the variation caused by genetic differences divided by the total variance (Block and Dworkin, 1974), but "heritability is a property of populations and not of traits" (Fuller and Thompson, 1960). As a population statistic, like divorce rate or alcohol prevalence, it depends on the genetic and environmental variation present in a given set of persons at a given time. Thus, heritability estimates made in one population can be extrapolated to another population only under very special circumstances. Block and Dworkin (1974) credit Lewontin with nicely illustrating this point: "Consider, for example, the following populations: (A) Jews who live in New York or Miami Beach and (B) people in New York, excluding Blacks. Although the total variance of skin color in A is probably about the same as in B, most of the variance in A is probably due to environmental (sun exposure) differences, while most of the variance in B is probably due to genetic differences. Hence, the heritability of skin color is probably low in A but high in B."

This is but one example demonstrating how a heritability estimate is a far more limited and subtle piece of information than most people, including Jensen, realize (Hirsch, 1970). A review of criticisms by geneticists and physical scientists (Hirsch, 1970; Layzer, 1973; Lewontin, 1970), indicates that Jensen's conceptualization and application of the concept are inadequate and clearly do not provide the scientific basis from which to make generalizations of such broad social significance.

Jensen bases most of his argument on studies involving separated identical twins and adopted children, which are generally accepted as providing the most compelling evidence of the heritability of intelligence. Of the four major studies of separated identical twins, the work of Sir Cyril Burt is repeatedly cited by Jensen as especially clear support for the hereditarian position. Yet it now appears conclusive that Burt's publications contain so many discrepancies that their scientific value must be considered worthless (Kamin, 1976). Kamin's critique of Burt's research was so devastating that Jensen himself has now discounted the bulk of Burt's work on the heritability of intelligence (Jensen, 1974). One critic (Layzer, 1973) argues that existing identical twin studies are so methodologically flawed that one cannot estimate the IQ correlation which would be found between genetically identical children reared in randomly selected environments. The studies of adopted children are equally questionable.

While Jensen's use of the concept of heritability has proven to be inappropriate, it has stimulated geneticists to address the issue of racial differences in IQ, and to correct many of the misconceptions found among social scientists. If one is interested in understanding the development of observable traits, a concept far more important than heritability is the norm of reactions (Hirsch, 1970). The ontogeny of an individual's phenotype (observable outcome of development) has a norm or range of reaction which is not predictable in advance. In most cases the norm of reaction cannot be specified. Nevertheless, it remains an important concept, saving non-geneticists from being misled by standard textbook clichés such as "heredity sets the limits but environment determines the extent of development within those limits." It is impossible to specify the limits set by heredity in the textbook cliché. They are elastic within each person but differ between individuals. Attributing a portion of an individual's intelligence to heredity, another to the environment, and a third to an interaction is an attempt to deny the reality of each genotype's unique norm of reaction. "Interaction is an abstraction of mathematics. The norm of reaction is a developmental reality of biology in plants, animals and people" (Hirsch, 1970).

Jensen's major contention, and the basis for his policy recommendations, is that heritability of IQ is .8. However, even if Jensen is correct in his heritability estimate, it would not have the implications that he draws from it. Jensen errs in assuming an inverse relationship between heritability and the ability to improve through learning. This supposition is based on a belief of the fixity of genetically determined traits. In less enlightened times it was believed that genetic disorders, simply because they were genetic, were incurable. Yet it is now known that many inborn errors of metabolism are indeed curable. Similarly, it has been demonstrated that IQ scores are, in fact, also highly sensitive to variations in relevant developmental conditions.

Skodak and Skeels (1949), in a pioneering study of adopted children and their adoptive and natural parents, reported greater *correlations* of children's IQs with their natural than with their adoptive parents' IQs. These data have often been erroneously understood to mean that the children's *Levels* of intelligence more closely resemble that of their natural parents'. Although the rank order of the chil-

dren's IQs resembled that of their mothers' IQs, the children's IQs were significantly higher. Their IQ scores were distributed, like those of their adoptive parents, around a mean above 100, while their natural mothers' IQs averaged only 85. The children, in fact, averaged 21 IQ points higher than their natural mothers. If the (unstudied) natural fathers' IQs averaged around the population mean of 100, the mean of the children's IQs would be expected to be 94, or 12 points lower than the mean obtained. The unexpected boost in IQ was presumably due to the better social environments provided by the adoptive families.

In Israel, children of European origin have an average IQ of 105 when they are brought up in individual homes. Those brought up in a Kibbutz have an average IQ of 115. In contrast, the mid-Eastern Jewish children brought up in individual homes have an average IQ of only 85. However, when brought up in a Kibbutz, they also have an average IQ of 115. That is, they perform the same as the European children with whom they were matched for education, the occupational level of parents, and the Kibbutz group in which they were raised (Bloom, 1969).

In a study in Milwaukee, Afro-American children whose mothers' IQs were less than 80 were selected as subjects for an intensive intervention program (Heber, 1969). Teaching began soon after the children were born. Over a four-year period Heber and his associates tutored the children for several hours every day and produced an enormous IQ difference between the experimental group (mean IQ = 127) and a control group (mean IQ = 90).

To illustrate the phenotypic changes that can be produced by radically different environments for children with clear genetic anomalies, Rynders (1971) has provided daily intensive tutoring for Down's syndrome infants. At the age of two, these children have average IQs of 85, while control group children, who are enrolled in a variety of other programs, average

68. Untreated children have even lower average IQ scores.

These studies are but four examples of research clearly demonstrating that IQ can be raised remarkably, given adequate resources, commitment, understanding of cultural differences, and intelligence among those planning and implementing intervention programs.

Having considered some of the major flaws in Jensen's argument, it is important to recall that Jensen's paper created such a furor that the *Harvard Educational Review* reprinted it the following year, along with critiques by educational theorists and a population geneticist. It also revived the hackneyed nature-nurture controversy. Most threatened in academic circles were the doctrinaire environmentalists who had been dominant in American psychology since World War II. They preferred to think of racial differences on IQ tests as a consequence of "deprivation" of culture or experience.

ENVIRONMENTAL THEORIES

The social science research which has embellished environmental theories is based upon the idealized norm of American behavior, against which all other behavior is measured. This norm is defined, in other words, as behaviors of the white middle class. Thus, minorities, sometimes with differing languages or dialects, values, attitudes and behavior are considered to be quite different from the norm and thus quite deviant. The application of this ethnocentric model denies the great diversity existing within minority group subcultures and minimizes the similarities that exist between ethnic minorities and whites of comparable social classes. Moreover, the great diversity of the white middle class is also denied, while the norm becomes idealized. Social and personal problems like alcoholism, drug abuse, child abuse, mental illness, divorce, and the "generation gap" are treated as if they

do not exist or are insignificant factors in the lives of the middle class, as if these social problems are limited to those who deviate from the middle class norm. However, as the environmental position gained support of federal agencies, energy was directed toward establishing educational programs for minority group children. The expressed goals of these programs were to "equalize" the probability of entering the main stream of society and finding educational, financial and vocational success.

Several theoretical models have been developed to explain differences in language, behavior and test performance, when minority children are compared to the "norm." The first environmental model to gain support amongst social scientists was that of *cultural deficiency-deprivation and disadvantage*. This model views differences on intelligence and achievement tests as functions of inferior language systems and inadequate stimulation during the preschool years. Afro-American speech has been described as lacking in syntax, expression and structure when compared to standard English (Valentine, 1971). Most social scientists who focus upon language as the origin of deficit are of the opinion that any linguistic system other than standard English is deficient and inferior.

The concepts of language deprivation and critical periods, which often are used in tandem, have also been reevaluated as being oversimplified and misleading. Again, ethnocentrism is implicated when linguistic competence is equated with the development of standard English. The language of poor Mexicans or Afro-Americans may be different, but both follow rules and do not differ significantly in their underlying structures (Houston, 1970). While stressing the need for learning standard English, teachers should not assume that different forms of language preclude intellectual growth and academic achievement. Similarly, there is no evidence for biologically fixed critical periods of cognitive development (Wolff, 1970). While the existing research is inadequate to speak with authority, there is evidence for multiple mental abilities which develop in different ways. Some abilities accelerate with age and others remain more consistent. Differences can be found among individuals and within an individual over time. Rigid adherence to the critical periods concept is scientifically untenable.

The *cultural deficit model* has also been used as a means of explaining low school achievement. When investigators implicitly or explicitly compare ethnic minority behavior to that of the white middle class, Afro-American youngsters are described as coming from homes that are basically "disorganized," with families that are "deteriorating" (Glazer and Moynihan, 1963). Lower class people are said to live more primitively and violently than the middle class (Galdwin, 1967). In education, the minority group child has been described as anti-intellectual (Riessman, 1962), manifesting little intrinsic motivation to learn (Ausubel, 1963), and learning less of what he or she hears (Black, 1965). The emphasis on cognitive understimulation and other alleged psychological deficits is the latest development of scientific racism and part of the pattern of discrimination experienced by minority group people in the United States. "It is bad enough to be poor and to suffer real deprivations of poverty without being saddled with imaginary and irremediable psychological deficits" (Thomas and Sillen, 1972).

Alternative models to cultural deprivation have also been proposed. Among these are the *cultural difference* and *bicultural models*. The cultural difference model varies significantly from the deficit model in that it recognizes the existence of other subcultures. This model views behaviors as an outgrowth of structural and historical constraints unique to minority groups and their assimilation into the mainstream culture. An example of

cultural difference research on the influence of values was conducted by Madsen (1971) with Mexican, Mexican-American and white children. He found Mexican children to be significantly more cooperative, white children to be significantly more competitive, and Mexican-American children to fall in between the two groups. The strongest support for the model of cultural differences as applied to Afro-American behaviors has developed from the research of Baratz and Baratz (1970), and Stewart (1969). Their research demonstrated the distinctiveness of dialect variance of black English in oral performance and in music as well. However, hypotheses derived from this model assume the homogeneity of the Afro-American culture and fail to recognize within-group distinctions in language, group identity, food and clothing preferences, religious beliefs, economics, specific national or regional origin, and ethno-history (Valentine, 1971). Thus, the model of cultural differences recognizes cultural distinctiveness, while it fails to address the great diversity found within minority groups and minimizes similarities between the two groups.

The third model, termed the process of *biculturalism*, describes the extent to which people learn to perform in the mainstream culture according to the "norm," as well as those behaviors which reflect their own ethnic culture. Valentine (1971) describes the situationally determined ability of Afro-Americans to utilize ethnic group behaviors, as well as to exhibit knowledge of white middle class normative behaviors. However, the bicultural model is limited in that it considers only the necessity of minority groups adapting to cultures and languages other than their own. The limitation of the bicultural model is that it fails to recognize that the majority culture could benefit from incorporating certain values, knowledge, and attitudes of minority subcultures. Another criticism of the bicultural model (Simpkins, William, and Gunnings, 1971) has to do with its failure to recognize the independence of many subculture behaviors and values from the white middle-class norm. This is an issue that is an especially sensitive one for some Afro-American social scientists, in light of the resistance that has been met in establishing the existence of the Afro-American culture. In summary, the environmental theories of racial differences in IQ are found to be oversimplifications and are as inadequate as the hereditarian arguments.

Factors Influencing Test Performance

Despite intensive research, there appears to be some controversy about the extent to which the test performance of minority children is negatively influenced. For example, studies have indicated conflicting findings regarding the influence of the *examiner's race*. Many investigators maintain that differences in racial membership negatively affect the examiner-examinee relationship (Anastasi, 1958; Anastasi and Foley, 1949; Barnes, 1969; Blackwood, 1927). Afro-American children have been often found to show suspicion, verbal constriction, strain, unnatural reactions and a façade of stupidity to avoid appearing too bright. Other research (Katz, 1964, 1968) suggests that when a white examiner administers an intelligence test or when there is knowledge that their scores will be compared with white peers, Afro-American subjects tend to become fearful of failure. These subjects may feel victimized and exhibit hostility toward the examiner, which inevitably affects and disrupts the subject's test performance. Testing Afro-American children in the South has also presented special problems for white examiners because children have been found to have an attitude of fear and suspicion that might interfere with their test performance (Klineberg, 1935).

There are also studies which show that the examiner's race does not affect the performance of Afro-Americans or white subjects on individual or group intelligence tests (Caldwell and Knight, 1970; Costello, 1970; Lipsitz, 1969; Miller and Phillips, 1966; Pelosi, 1968). In his review of the literature on the race of the examinee and the examiner, Sattler (1973) stated that there are still too few studies that are methodologically sound enough to make firm generalizations regarding the effect of race on children's performance on intelligence tests.

A second issue related to the race of the examiner-examinee has to do with the *skill of the test administrator*. The examiner-examinee interaction is admittedly an extremely complex one. The examiner can maximize or minimize the child's performance by his/her actions. Similarly, by misinterpreting the child's responses, because of dialect, language or experiential background differences, the examiner can significantly raise or lower the final score.

Mexican-American children have been described in the testing situation as "passive" and unwilling to engage in competition. This kind of stereotype can often bias expectations about the performance of Mexican-American children. This description also ignores the influence of culture upon the child's desire to be competitive (Madsen, 1971).

Other important *motivational factors* include the child's ability to identify success or failure within the testing situation; the ability to perform under stress; and the child's understanding of the testing situation and its importance. The child being tested for gifted class placement can understandably be more motivated to achieve and to overcome anxiety than the child being tested due to underachievement (Padilla and Garza, 1975).

The *language* of the examiner has been found to be a critical factor in test performance. If the examiner is not sensitive to linguistic differences between him/herself and the examinee, these differences will surely have a negative influence on the outcome of the child's performance (Padilla & Garza, 1975).

In studies that have been conducted on Mexican-American children who speak Spanish as their primary language, the white examiner has been found to often have difficulty in communicating with them. Differences inherent in speaking two languages have also been noted. Chavez (1956) noted that there is a different sound that the same letters have in Spanish and English and there are variations in concepts that exist between the two cultures. For example, in Spanish, the word *nose* in some localities is plural, so that a child may say "I hit *them* against the door." The vocabulary of some Spanish-speaking children may be limited, and they may borrow an English phrase or word to complete an expression already begun in Spanish. There is some concern as to how understanding the examiner may be in giving credit for responses which indicate the above variations in grammar and in the use of a second language.

There have been a few studies using black *dialect* with children to observe differences in test performance. Quay (1971) reported that changes in test procedures designed to increase motivation with the use of praise or candy and to facilitate language comprehension with the use of standard English or black dialect did not significantly affect the Stanford-Binet scores of four-year-old children. Interestingly, the speech of the children was predominantly in dialect in both language conditions of the test administration, while comprehension of standard English and dialect was equal. This finding demonstrates the ability of these children to comprehend language communicated in standard English or in dialect—a skill that is seldom found in white children or adults. Contrary to Quay's study, Williams (1970) found that Afro-American children responded more correctly when they were administered standardized tests in dialect. However, it seems unproductive to argue about the benefits of translating tests into Afro-American dialect when the real issue is that the contents of the test items remain unaltered.

What Do Achievement and Intelligence Tests Really Measure?

With a few exceptions that were made starting in the late 1960s, ability tests have been effective and efficient in excluding minority and poor individuals from higher education. Recent developments in the West (Bakke vs. the University of California) suggest that the number of minority students who have been accepted into colleges through special programs may decline drastically in the future. McClelland (1973) raises the issue of the validity of using intelligence and achievement tests as a basis for the acceptance or rejection of potential students, and presents some compelling evidence that should bring the practice to an ignominious end. Supporters of traditional testing repeatedly point out that IQ and achievement scores predict grades in school, but McClelland points out, "The games people are required to play on intelligence tests are similar to the games teachers require in the classroom." That IQ and achievement tests predict grades should, therefore, come as no grand surprise; they are different slices of the same pie. Test scores and grades are used to control access to certain job categories. Are scores and grades related to any other behavior of importance other than getting into college preparatory courses and entering college, graduate or professional schools? Taylor, Smith and Ghiselin (1963) found that better grades in college do not relate in any way to superior on-the-job performance for research scientists. Holland and Richards (1965) and Elton and Shevel (1969) have also shown that no consistent relationship exists between student scores on scholastic achievement tests and their actual accomplishments in science, music, writing, speech, drama, social leadership and the arts.

Alternatives to Traditional Tests

Since intelligence tests have been found to correlate only with school achievement, what then are alternatives to traditional testing which can generate other kinds of information regarding a child's abilities? First, traditional measures and their test construction will be described. A *norm referenced* test is basically a standardized measure which has been administered with standard directions under standard conditions to a sample of examinees who are supposedly representative of the group for whom the test was intended. The purposes of the standardized procedure are to obtain a set of scores which will yield a normal distribution and to gain a set of norms for age, sex and grade of the examinees. In order to obtain the distribution of test scores and consider them "normal," half of the standardization group must have scores above the mean and the other half must have scores below the mean. Items which do not contribute to the normal distribution are discarded.

Until 1972, three of the most widely viewed individual ability tests—the Stanford-Binet (Houghton Mifflin, Revised Form LM, 1960), the Wechsler Intelligence Scale for Children (WISC; Psychological Corporation, Revised, 1974), and the Peabody Picture Vocabulary Test (PPVT; American Guidance Service, 1965)—systematically excluded Afro-Americans and other minority group children from their normative samples. The WISC was standardized on a Caucasian sample in 1949, and the revised form published in 1972 includes a 10 percent sample of Afro-American, Mexican-American and "other" minority children. There is no specific information in the WISC-R manual relating to the number and other demographic information of the minority group children within each ethnic group, so that it is difficult to assume that this 10 percent minority group sample is representative of the number and variety of minority groups in the United States today.

One alternative to the use of norm referenced tests with children who are more fluent in another language (Spanish) than in English is to *translate* the test into that language and to modify credited responses. It is important to note in regard to the WISC that this test was translated into the Spanish used in Puerto Rico. Consequently, some of the items and credited responses are not appropriate for a Mexican-American population whose Spanish vocabulary and cultural experiences are not necessarily the same as those in Puerto Rico. However, this Spanish version of the WISC is still in use today, and the norms used with which to compare and compute the child's performance are those derived from the original white, middle class population of children.

In order to assess the influence of language on the test performance of Spanish-speaking children, Keston and Jimenez (1954) translated Form L of the Stanford-Binet into Spanish and administered Form M in English a week later to bilingual Mexican-American 4th graders. The mean IQ for the English version was 86, while the children's mean IQ on the Spanish version was 72. The authors concluded that the simple translation was not suited for Mexican-American children because their Spanish contained archaisms, contaminations and Anglicisms not found in Puerto Rican Spanish used in the WISC. Other researchers demonstrated that the meanings of words are altered by the translation into Spanish (Chandler and Plakos, 1969; Roca, 1955; Sanchez, 1934). Even so, the translation of the test into Spanish does not appear to resolve the problems the child encounters when introduced to items outside his/her experience.

Educators have been looking for new methods that would prove useful to children speaking different *dialects* than standard English. Efforts have also been made to reconstruct the language of the standardized test in dialect that is fair to the minority group child. Williams and Rivers (1972) showed clearly that test instructions in standard English penalized the Afro-American child. If the language of the test is placed in familiar labels without training or coaching, the child's performance on the test increases significantly. However, little consideration has been given to the problems which dialect differences pose in test construction, standardization procedures, and the comparison of the results with standardized scores derived from non-dialect administration.

Culture-free tests have been developed out of a growing dissatisfaction with the traditional standardized tests' reliance upon verbal and performance skills of the white middle class experience. These tests are theoretically supposed to measure an individual's general abilities (*g*) or "intelligence" without factors such as economics, culture, dialect, or language influencing the test or its score.

There have been a number of culture-free tests developed; the Porteus Mazes, Raven Progressive Matrices, the Davis-Ells Test, and the Cattell Culture-Free Test are a few examples that have been standardized for use with children. The tests rely on perceptual skills and involve neither reading nor reference to culturally-bound pictures, originating from the extensive research of Cattell (1959), Raven (1952) and others.

There are a number of studies measuring the "fairness" of culture-free tests in more accurately assessing the intelligence of minority group children. Higgins and Silvers (1958) administered Form L (primarily verbal) of the Stanford-Binet and the Raven Progressive Matrices (nonverbal) to 7- and 9-year-old Afro-American and white children of lower socioeconomic status. The Binet scores were similar for both groups, but the Afro-American group scored significantly lower on the Matrices. It was concluded that the Binet has less ethnic bias than the Matrices. Stablein, Willey and Thomson (1961) administered the Davis-Ells Test of General Intelligence on problem-solving ability (Davis and Ells, 1953) with other measures to white and Mexican American children in the 2nd through the 5th grade. The authors concluded that the Davis-Ells test was as influenced by cultural factors as were other intelligence and achievement tests.

Another alternative is the *culture-specific test*, intended to accentuate the knowledge and experience of a particular subcultural group. Williams (1970) has developed the Black Intelligence Test of Cultural Homogeneity (BITCH) and Adrian Dove (personal communication) devised the Dove Counterbalanced Intelligence Test to measure the experience of lower socioeconomic Afro-Americans. The tests include words and phrases which are used in the vernacular, and names of people or events familiar to Afro-Americans and their historical experience. However, it would be erroneous to assume that these culture-specific tests were a more accurate assessment of a minority group member's intelligence than the traditional norm-referenced tests. While norm-referenced tests ignore subcultural experiences and values, culture-specific tests assume that Afro-Americans share one culture, one region, one historical background, and are knowledgeable in the same range of Afro-American vernacular. All of these factors influence heavily the experience of the Afro-American and culture-specific tests fail to incorporate all of these important variables.

Budhoff (1969) has developed an alternative referred to as *Learning Potential*

Assessment Devices. These techniques measure the extent to which a subject is a "gainer" or a "non-gainer," after coaching. The learning potential concept defines intelligence as the ability to profit from problem-relevant experience. The focus is on the child's educability and the trainability of the cognitive processes. The learning potential measurement paradigm is an improvement over the one-shot testing model, using a three-stage program: (1) pretest, (2) coaching, and (3) the post-test. The pretest allows the subject to be familiarized with the demands of the task. The coaching session which follows, immediately, provides relevant problem-solving strategies for the reasoning task. The post-test score includes both the child's initial ability and the effects of learning.

Mercer (1971), in a less radical departure from traditional testing, suggests the continued use of traditional, norm-referenced tests, but with several modifications. The score derived through standardized scoring procedures would indicate the probability of success in a regular class in the American public school system as it is presently constituted. The System of Multi-cultural Pluralistic Assessment (SOMPA) was developed by Mercer (1973). The comparison of the child's score with other children of similar sociocultural backgrounds would provide more accurate indications of the potential for learning, with placement in an optimal educational program. The SOMPA includes sociocultural scales, the Adaptive Behavior Inventory, health history inventories, the Wechsler Intelligence Scale for Children—Revised (WISC-R), physical dexterity tasks, the Bender-Gestalt test, measurements of height and weight, visual and auditory activity. This variety of information incorporates aspects of the child's cultural experience and other background, perceptual and health data which are usually not included when standardized tests are used exclusively.

One recommendation towards seeking alternative measures is that we move from norm-referenced tests to *criterion sampling* (McClelland, 1973). McClelland's logic is flawless. Tests which sample scholastic or job proficiency predict proficiency for the designated task. Criterion sampling would require testers to get out of their offices, where they have comfortably played endless pencil-and-paper games, into the real world where actual on-the-job performance would be analyzed. Secondly, tests should reflect changes in what the individual has learned. One good example is the Iowa Test of Basic Skills in which teacher and student know how the student will be tested on spelling, reading and arithmetic, and more importantly, how to prepare for it. Third, for some purposes, it may be desirable to measure competencies in clusters of life outcomes, in order to have tests not become too specific to the criterion involved. Additionally, personality variables such as communication skills, patience, moderate goal setting and ego development would be appropriate to a variety of tasks. Fourth, tests should involve the assessment of operant as well as respondent behavior. McClelland argues that life is much more apt to be characterized by operant responses in that individuals spontaneously react in the absence of a very clearly defined stimulus. Testers generally have used respondent behavior for efficiency to get high test-retest reliability, but at the cost of making the task unnatural. Finally, tests should sample operant thought patterns to obtain maximum generalized ability for various action outcomes. The testing service would thus report to the universities a profile of scholastic and non-scholastic achievements and the number of areas. Tests would be administered periodically during the course of training to give students, teachers and administrators feedback to determine if growth has occurred. Tests would thus provide a genuine service utilized by students and teachers to obtain mutually agreed-upon goals and would become an integral part of the process of education.

In 1969 the Association of Black Psychologists stated their position on testing:

The Association of Black Psychologists call for a moratorium on the repeated abuse and misuse of so-called conventional psychological tests; e.g., the Stanford-Binet Form LM, the Wechsler Series, scholastic aptitude tests, Stanford Achievement Test, Iowa Basic Skills, Graduate Records Examination (GRE), the Miller Analogy Test, and many others . . . The Association of Black Psychologists calls for an immediate moratorium on all testing of Black people until more equitable tests are available.

Other psychologists and educators (Purvin, 1975; Zacharaus, 1975) support the movement to administer no standardized tests until such a time when all children from infancy can be assured the same skills and experience; or until major efforts are made to find other procedures.

A few years later, the Bay Area Association of Black Psychologists published a powerful position statement again calling for a moratorium on the use of group and individual tests of intelligence and scholastic ability. The statement included 14 points requiring the California State Department of Education to follow specific guidelines described to clarify the assessment and policy procedures felt to be necessary for the future placement of Afro-American children in classes for the educationally handicapped (EH), educably mentally retarded (EMR), or other special education programs.

The Association of Black Psychologists fully supports those parents who have chosen to defend their rights by refusing to allow their children and themselves to be subjected to achievement, intelligence, aptitude and performance tests which have been, and are being used to (a) label Black people as uneducable, (b) place Black children in "special" classes in schools, (c) perpetuate inferior education in Blacks, (d) assign Black children to educational tracts [sic], (e) deny Black students higher educational opportunities, and (f) destroy positive growth and development of Black people (Williams, 1970).

The Bay Area Association of Black Psychologists and other groups brought enough pressure to bear upon the schools through legal channels that in 1975 the U.S. District Court ordered verbal and non-verbal IQ tests disapproved for admission to EMR classes for any children until a permanent injunction could be issued stating which tests should be considered "fair" or unbiased. This court action was the result of the famous Larry P. et al. vs. Wilson Riles, State Board of Education, et al. (1972).

Finally, a voice with the educational and political influence necessary to question the 100-year-old credibility of ability tests was heard and the effects have influenced the thinking and behavior of mental health professionals and educators toward all minority group children.

The United States District Court for the Northern District of California ruled in favor of the plaintiffs, including Larry P. The State of California's use of standardized tests to place Black children in educationally deadend, isolated and stigmatizing classes for the educable mentally retarded (EMR) was found to be in violation of Title VI of the Civil Rights Act of 1964, the Rehabilitation Act of 1973 and the Education for All Handicapped Children Act of 1973. The injunction against IQ testing for the placement of black children into EMR was continued.

SUMMARY AND RECOMMENDATIONS

The belief in the intellectual superiority of those controlling economic power in the United States has, in the last two decades, become increasingly methodologically sophisticated. Nevertheless, a careful review of the assumptions, instruments, methods and conclusions demonstrates clearly that the notion of racial supremacy in intellectual ability is no more scientifically valid today than at the time of Cicero—quotients, graphs, normal distributions and standard deviations notwithstanding. Skirmishes between proponents of hereditarian and environmentalist positions have done little to enhance the educational and economic condition of the minority group person in the United States and may, in fact, serve to distract attention from social issues deserving immediate consideration. Teachers in training continue to be exposed to these differing schools of thought, including the point on which there is a consensus—an overwhelming majority of minority students are destined to be inferior students. The hereditarian blames inferior genes; the environmentalist, an inferior home and family environment. The conditions are perfect for a self-fulfilling prophecy, in which teachers' expectations of poor academic performance are conveyed, directly or subtly, to the impressionable students, who are then likely to play the roles designated by authority.

Despite the challenges and consequent changes that may be forced upon it, the testing industry will continue to be a powerful force in allocating roles and legitimizing the status quo. The affluent will continue to resist reforms that could conceivably reduce their privileges; the poor will probably remain too demoralized to protest effectively—the complacency and demoralization, respectively, reinforced by theories attributing economic failure to irremediable genetic or environmental deficiencies (Bane and Jencks, 1976).

The waste of human potential will continue as long as intelligence is defined by the narrow concept of IQ. There are sufficient factors which significantly test performance so as to question not only the validity, but the reliability of intelligence and achievement test scores. The exclusive use of standardized tests reflects acceptance of the white middle class or "normative" behaviors, values and knowledge, and ignores or belittles experiences and values that fall outside of the norms

our society has chosen as the measuring stick. Most unfortunately for all concerned, the greatest disservice is done to those children about whom the mental health professional actually needs additional information—the minority group child whose physical appearance, economic status, language, dialect or experiential background is many times discrepant from that norm.

The focus of this chapter has been to critically evaluate intelligence and achievement testing as it affects minority group children. However, the chapter would be incomplete without certain recommendations which the authors believe must be seriously considered:

1) In the school system, test administration should be the exclusive responsibility of the school psychologist rather than of a teacher or counselor. The school psychologist should have undergone intensive training in the uses and limitations of tests and demonstrate knowledge of assessing sociocultural factors influencing test performance. An understanding of the sociopolitical origins of tests should be an additional requirement. School psychologists are not the only group of professionals who should be required to demonstrate knowledge of these issues. All mental health professionals, including clinical psychologists, who have the responsibility for making decisions about the educational or psychological status of children should be included in this group. Continued effort should be made to increase the number of minority group psychologists who are sensitive to these issues and to raise the consciousness of psychologists presently working in the school system.

2) Currently, investigators conducting research in the schools must obtain formal consent from the students, parents, school principals and boards of education in order to protect subjects' rights. Test administrators, on the other hand, are not so constrained, although their activity is

bound to have short- and long-term negative effects for many of the hundreds of thousands who are tested every year. Prior to test administration, parents have the right to be not only notified that testing may be taking place but also informed of the implications of these scores on the students' future classroom placement, i.e., tracking. This information should be included as part of the information presented by the school to the parent. Again, parents should be given an opportunity to voice an educated consent or disapproval of having their children tested by means of standardized tests.

Finally, of major importance is the direction in which we strongly believe the testing movement must go; it is our belief that traditional testing is scientifically invalid, culturally and economically discriminatory, and politically oppressive. Unless significant modifications are made, the moratorium on the use of intelligence and achievement tests should be supported. The major thrust of the testing movement must be the development of criterion-sampling techniques and the elimination of norm-referenced tests. In order to allow behavioral scientists the necessary time to develop these measures, traditional tests can be used if additional sources of information are considered. The inclusion of adaptive behavior scales and the consideration of sociocultural factors as suggested by Mercer (1971) is the strategy of choice. It must be recognized that this is only a stopgap measure. The ultimate outcome should be the development of tests that measure the individual's ability to meet the criteria of the task.

All people are created equal under the law and must be treated as such from the moral and political point of view (Baratz and Baratz, 1970).

With the adoption of these recommendations, we may yet approximate this ideal.

REFERENCES

Anastasi, A. and Foley, J. P., Jr. *Differential Psychology*. Second edition. New York: Macmillan, 1949.

Anastasi, A. *Differential Psychology*. Third edition. New York: Macmillan, 1958.

Association of Black Psychologists. Official Position on Testing. Meeting, Washington, D.C., 1969.

Ausubel, D. P. A teaching strategy for culturally deprived pupils: Cognitive and motivational considerations. *School Review*, Winter 1963, 71, 454-463.

Bane, M. J. and Jencks, C. Five myths about your IQ. In: N. J. Block and G. Dworkin (Eds.), *The IQ Controversy*. New York: Random House, 1976.

Baratz, S. and Baratz, J. Early childhood intervention: The social science base of institutional racism. *Harvard Educational Review*, 1970, 40, 29-50.

Barnes, E. J. Cultural retardation or shortcomings of assessment techniques. Proceedings of the 47th Annual International Convention, Denver, Colorado, April 1969. Washington, D.C.: Council for Exceptional Children, 1969.

Birch, H. G. and Gussow, J. D. *Disadvantaged Children: Health, Nutrition and School Failure*. New York: Harcourt, Brace & World, 1970.

Black, M. H. Characteristics of the culturally disadvantaged child. *The Reading Teacher*, March 1965, 18, 465-470.

Blackwood, B. A study of testing in relation to anthropology. *Mental Measurements Monographs*, 1927, 4, 1-119.

Block, N. J. and Dworkin, G. IQ, heritability and inequality. *Philosophy and Public Affairs*, 1974, 3, 331-409 and 4, 40-99.

Bloom, B. S. Letter to the editor. *Harvard Educational Review*, 1969, 39, 419-421.

Brigham, C. C. *A Study of American Intelligence*. Princeton: Princeton University Press, 1923.

Brim, O. G., Neulinger, J., and Glass, D. C. *Experiences and Attitudes of American Adults Concerning Standardized Intelligence Tests*. Technical Report No. 1 On the Social Consequences of Testing. New York: Russell Sage Foundation, 1965.

Bruininks, R. H. and Feldman, D. H. Creativity, intelligence, and achievement among disadvantaged children. *Psychology in the Schools*, 1970, 7, 260-264.

Budhoff, M. Learning potential: A supplementary procedures for assessing the ability to reason. *Seminars in Psychiatry*, 1969, 1, 278-290.

Caldwell, M. B. and Knight, D. The effect of Negro and White examiners on Negro intelligence test performance. *Journal of Negro Education*, 1970, 39, 177-179.

Cattell, R. B. *Handbook for the Culture Fair Intelligence Test: A Measure of "G"*. Champaign, IL: Institute for Personality and Ability Testing, 1959.

Chandler, J. T. and Plakos, J. Spanish -speaking pupils classified as educable mentally retarded. *Integrat Education*, 1969, 7, 28-33.

Chavez, S. J. Preserve their language heritage.

Childhood Education, 1956, *33*, 165-185.

Costello, J. Effects of pretesting and examiner characteristics on test performance of young disadvantaged children. Proceedings of the 78th Annual Convention of the American Psychological Association, 1970, *5*, 309-310.

Daniels, J. and Houghton, V. Jensen, Eysenck and the eclipse of the Galton paradigm. In: K. Richardson & D. Spears (Eds.), *Race and Intelligence*. Baltimore: Penguin Books, 1972.

Davis, A. and Ells, K. *Manual for the Davis-Ells Test of General Intelligence on Problem Solving Ability*. Yonkers, N.Y.: World Book, 1953.

Elton, C. F. and Shevel, L. R. *Who is Talented? An Analysis of Achievement*. Research Report No. 31. Iowa City: American College Testing Program, 1969.

Fuller, J. L. and Thompson, W. R. *Behavior Genetics*. New York: John Wiley & Sons, 1960.

Galdwin, T. *Poverty U.S.A.* Boston: Little, Brown, 1967.

Glazer, N. and Moynihan, D. P. *Beyond the Melting Pot: The Negroes, Puerto Ricans, Jews, Italians, and Irish of New York City*. Cambridge, MA: M.I.T. Press & Harvard University Press, 1963.

Goddard, H. H. The Binet tests in relation to immigration. *Journal of Psycho-asthenics*, 1913, *18*, 105-107.

Goddard, H. H. *Human Efficiency and Levels of Intelligence*. Princeton: Princeton University Press, 1920.

Hays, S. P. The politics of reform in municipal government in the progressive era. In: A. B. Callon, Jr. (Ed.), *American Urban History*. New York: Oxford University Press, 1969.

Heber, R. *Rehabilitation of families at risk for mental retardation*. Madison: Regional Rehabilitation Center, University of Wisconsin, 1969.

Higgins, C. and Silvers, C. H. A comparison of Stanford-Binet and colored Raven Progressive Matrices IQ's for children with low socioeconomic status. *Journal of Consulting Psychology*, 1958, *22*, 465-468.

Hirsch, J. Behavior genetic analysis and its biosocial consequences. *Seminars in Psychiatry*, 1970, *2*, 89-105.

Holland, J. L. and Richards, J. M., Jr. Academic and nonacademic accomplishment: Correlated or uncorrelated? (Research Report No. 2.) Iowa City: American College Testing Program, 1965.

Houston, S. H. A reexamination of some assumptions about the language of the disadvantaged child. *Child Development*, 1970, *41*, 947-963.

Hunt, J. McV. The psychological basis for using preschool enrichment as an antidote for cultural deprivation. In: F. Hechinger (Ed.), *Pre-school Enrichment Today*. Garden City, N.Y.: Doubleday, 1966, pp. 25-72.

Hunt, J. McV. Parent and child centers: Their basis in the behavioral and educational sciences. *American Journal of Orthopsychiatry*, 1971, *41*, 13-38.

Jensen, A. R. Kinship correlations reported by Sir Cyril Burt. *Behavior Genetics*, 1974, *4*, 1-28.

Jensen, A. R. How much can we boost IQ and scholastic achievement? *Harvard Educational Review*, 1969, *39*, 1-123.

Johnson, D. L. and Johnson, C. A. Comparison of four intelligence tests used with culturally disadvantaged children. *Psychological Reports*, 1971, *28*, 209-210.

Kamin, L. Heredity, intelligence, politics and psychology. In: N. J. Block and G. Dworkin (Eds.), *The IQ Controversy*. New York: Random House, 1976.

Karier, C. Testing for order and control in the corporate liberal state. *Educational Theory*, 1972, *22*, 154-160.

Katz, I. Review of evidence relating to effects of desegregation on the intellectual performance of Negroes. *American Psychologist*, 1964, *19*, 381-399.

Katz, I. Negro performance in the desegregated school. In: M. Deutsch, et al. (Eds.), *Social Class, Race and Psychological Development*. New York: Holt, Rinehart & Winston, 1968, pp. 254-289.

Kennedy, W. A., Van de Riet, V., and White, J. C., Jr. Use of the Terman-Merrill abbreviated scale on the 1960 Stanford-Binet Form L-M on Negro elementary school children of the southeastern United States. *Journal of Consulting Psychology*, 1963, *27*, 456-457.

Keston, M. J. and Jimenez, C. A study of the performance on English and Spanish editions of the Stanford-Binet Intelligence Test by Spanish American children. *Journal of Genetic Psychology*, 1954, *85*, 262-269.

Klineberg, O. *Race Differences*. New York: Harper, 1935.

Larry, P. v. W. Riles, 343 F. Supplement 1306, 1972.

Layzer, D. A physical scientist looks at the IQ controversy. *Cognition*, 1973, *1*, 265-300, 453-473.

Lewis, O. The culture of poverty. *Scientific American*, 1966, *215*, 19-25.

Lewontin, R. Science and public affairs: Race and intelligence. *Bulletin of the Atomic Scientists*. March and May, 1970, 2-8, 23-25.

Lipsitz, S. Effect of the race of the examiner on results of intelligence test performance of Negro and White children. Unpublished master's thesis, Long Island University, 1969.

McClelland, D. C. Testing for competence rather than "intelligence." *American Psychologist*, 1973, *29*, 107.

Madsen, M. C. Developmental and cross-cultural differences in the cooperative and competitive behavior of young children. *Journal of Cross-Cultural Psychology*, December 1971, *2*, 365-371.

Mercer, J. R. Pluralistic diagnosis in the evaluation of Black and Chicano children: A procedure for taking sociocultural variables into account in clinical assessment. A paper presented at Meetings of the American Psychological Association, Washington, D.C., September, 1971.

Mercer, J. *Labeling the Mentally Retarded*. Los Angeles: University of California Press, 1973.

Miller, J. O. and Phillips, J. A. A preliminary evaluation of the Head Start and other metropolitan Nashville kindergartens. Unpublished manuscript, Demonstration and Research Center for

Early Education, George Peabody College for Teachers, Nashville, 1966.

National Academy of Sciences. R. M. Yerkes (Ed.), *Psychology Examining in the United States Army.* Washington, D.C.: Author, 1921.

Oliver, K. and Barclay, A. Stanford-Binet and Goodenough-Harris test performance of Head Start children. *Psychological Reports*, 1967, *20*, 1175-1179.

Padilla, A. and Garza, B. M. IQ tests: A case of cultural myopia. *The National Elementary Principal*, March/April 1975, *54*, 53-58.

Pastore, N. *The Nature-Nurture Controversy.* New York: King's Crown Press (Columbia University), 1949.

Pearson, K. *The Life, Letters and Labours of Francis Galton. Volume 2, Researches of Middle Life.* Cambridge, MA: Cambridge University Press, 1924.

Pearson, K. and Moul, M. The problem of alien immigration into Great Britain, illustrated by an examination of Russian and Polish Jewish children. *Annals of Eugenics*, 1925, *1*, 5-127.

Pelosi, J. W. A study of the effects of examiner race, sex, and style on test responses of Negro examinees. Doctoral dissertation, Syracuse University. Ann Arbor, Michigan, 1968 (University Microfilms No. 69-8642.)

Purvin, G. The hidden agendas of IQ. *The National Elementary Principal*, 1975, *54*, 44-48.

Quay, L. C. Language dialect, reinforcement, and the intelligence performance of Negro children. *Child Development*, 1971, *42*, 5-15.

Radford, J. and Burton, A. Changing intelligence. In: K. Richardson and D. Spears (Eds.), *Race and Intelligence.* Baltimore: Penguin Books, 1972.

Raven, J. C. *Guide to Using Progressive Matrices.* London: Lewis, 1952.

Riessman, F. *The Culturally Deprived Child.* New York: Harper, 1962.

Roca, P. Problems of adapting intelligence scales from one culture to another. *High School Journal*, 1955, *38*, 124-131.

Ryan, W. *Blaming the Victim.* New York: Pantheon, 1971.

Rynders, J. Personal communication to S. Scarr-Salapatek and cited by author in Unknowns in the IQ equation. *Science*, 1971, *174*, 1223-1228.

Sanchez, G. I. Bilingualism and mental measures. *Journal of Applied Psychology*, 1934, *18*, 765-772.

Sattler, J. M. Intelligence testing of ethnic minority group and culturally disadvantaged children. In: *First Review of Special Education.* Philadelphia: JSE Press, 1973.

Simpkins, G., Williams, R., and Gunnings, T. What a difference a culture makes: A rejoinder to Valentine. *Harvard Educational Review*, 1971, *41*, 535-541.

Skodak, M. and Skeels, H. M. A final follow-up study of one hundred adopted children. *Journal of Genetic Psychology*, 1949, *75*, 85-125.

Spearman, C. *The Abilities of Man.* New York: Macmillan, 1927.

Stablein, J. E., Willey, D. S., and Thomson, C. W. An evaluation of the Davis-Ells (Culture-Fair) test using Spanish and Anglo-American children. *Journal of Educational Sociology*, 1961, *35*, 73-78.

Stewart, W. Historical and structural bases for the recognition of Negro dialect. *School of Languages and Linguistics Monograph Series*, No. 22. Georgetown University, 1969, 239-247.

Taylor, C., Smith, W. R., and Ghiselin, B. The creative and other contributions of one sample of research scientists. In: C. W. Taylor & F. Barron (Eds.), *Scientific Inquiry: Its Recognition and Development.* New York: John Wiley & Sons, 1963.

Terman, L. M. *The Measurement of Intelligence.* Boston: Houghton Mifflin, 1916.

Terman, L. M. Feeble-minded children in public schools in California. *School and Society*, 1917, *5*, 161-165.

Thomas, W. and Sillen, S. *Racism and Psychiatry.* New York: Brunner/Mazel, 1972.

Thorndike, E. L. Intelligence and its uses. *Harper's*, January 1920, 233.

Valentine, C. A. *Culture and Poverty: Critique and Counter-proposals.* Chicago: University of Chicago Press, 1968.

Valentine, C. A. Deficit, difference and bicultural models of Afro-American behavior. *Harvard Educational Review*, 1971, *41*, 137-157.

Wesman, A. G. Intelligence testing. *American Psychologist*, 1968, *23*, 267-274.

Wiebe, R. H. *The Search for Order.* New York: Hill & Wang, 1967.

Williams, R. L. Danger: Testing and dehumanizing Black children. *Clinical Child Psychology Newsletter*, 1970, *9*(1), 5-6.

Williams, R. L. and Rivers, L. W. The use of standard and non-standard English in testing Black children. A paper presented at the Annual Meeting of the American Psychological Association, Honolulu, Hawaii, September 1972.

Wolff, P. H. "Critical periods" in human cognitive development. *Hospital Practice*, 1970, *5*, 77-87.

Zacharaus, J. R. The trouble with IQ tests. *The National Elementary Principal*, 1975, *54*, 23-29.

CHAPTER 26

School Desegregation: The Psychological, Social, and Educational Implications

Gloria Johnson Powell, M.D.

... the office of the school environment is to balance the various elements in the social environment, and to see to it that each individual gets an opportunity to escape from the limitations of the social group in which he was born, and to come into living contact with a broader environment.

(Kluger, 1976, p. 319)

INTRODUCTION

John Dewey, one of the nation's best-known social and educational philosophers, articulated more clearly than anyone of his time "the great shaping effect of the early school years on the lives of Americans, whatever their color" (Kluger, 1976, p. 319). The American public school was the leveler and equalizer of opportunity for so many disparate groups who had sought refuge on America's shores. It was the Americanization process that helped mold and shape the heterogeneity of her immigrants into "one nation with liberty and justice for all." However, there were many who were excluded from the dictates of the American creed as expressed above and denied access to the equality of opportunity for educational and socioeconomic advancement. This process was challenged by the National Association for the Advancement of Colored People (NAACP) and its Legal Defense Fund in the now famous Supreme Court decision of Brown vs. Board of Education.

What was particularly significant psychologically and educationally in the great historical drama that Kluger relates in such a poignant historical fashion is the role of social scientists in shaping that moral-ethical epic process as well as the ultimate decision. Indeed, the premises, theories, and propositions presented by those scholars remain at the crux of the current controversy still raging about school desegregation.

Stephan (1978), in reviewing the testimony of the social scientists as well as the Social Scientists' brief which was attached as an appendix to the legal brief filed by the N.A.A.C.P., summarizes the major thrust of their testimony and opinions:

... It is clear from the testimony of the social scientists in the individual trials that they believed that self-esteem and prejudice affected the school achievement of minority students. These three variables (self-esteem, prejudice, and school achievement) were perceived to be interrelated in a vicious circle (p. 221).

White prejudice was perceived as the cause of segregation and the subsequent low self-esteem and low achievement. Stephan has noted that it was expected that the desegregation of the schools would:

1) increase the self-esteem of Afro-Americans by removing the institutionalized and legal sanction of white racism.
2) increase the self-esteem which would then be associated with increased achievement
3) reduce the racism of both groups through the interracial contact in desegregated schools.

The effects of school desegregation will be discussed in relation to these three effects predicted by the social scientists who participated in the 1954 Supreme Court decision. Because the original five cases involved in the May 17, 1954, decision were those involving Afro-American students, this chapter will confine its discussion to the effects of school desegregation on Afro-American children. The school desegregation decision has had many ramifications for other ethnic minority group children. The omission of the presentation of the effects of school desegre-

gation on other minority group children is not intended to imply that there have been no consequences for these children also. Although the studies are not as numerous as those regarding Afro-American children, the research data are growing (Weinberg, 1977). Hopefully, subsequent editions of this volume will include a detailed review of those issues germane to other minority group children.

THE EFFECTS OF SCHOOL DESEGREGATION ON RACE RELATIONS BETWEEN AFRO-AMERICAN AND WHITE CHILDREN

A Review of Racial Awareness Studies in Young Children

Any discussion of the effects of segregation and desegregation is incomplete without a discussion of the work of Mamie and Kenneth Clark (1939, 1947) which spearheaded, as it were, the social science data that proved to have a powerful effect on the jurists on the Supreme Court. The famous doll test in the Clarks' studies has been repeatedly published since 1939. Afro-American children three to seven years old were given four dolls, two brown and two white. The children then were asked a series of questions:

1) Give me the white doll.
2) Give me the colored doll.
3) Give me the Negro doll.
4) Give me the doll you like to play with or the doll you like best.
5) Give me the doll that is the nice doll.
6) Give me the doll that looks bad.
7) Give me the doll that is a nice color.

The majority of the Afro-American children in all age groups made an out-group identification, which is to say that they preferred the white doll and rejected the brown doll (as reported in Kluger, 1976).

Another equally important historical study which has often been cited as supportive testimony regarding the harmful effect of school desegregation is the Radke and Trager (1950) study of "Children's Perceptions of the Social Roles of Negroes and Whites" in which both Afro-American and white were tested. The protocol consisted of showing the children brown and white cardboard dolls with three kinds of clothing: dress-up clothes, work clothes, and shabby clothes. In addition, there were two kinds of houses: a red brick single family house with a lawn and trees and a shabby multiple family dwelling next to an alley. Fifty-seven percent of the Afro-American children and 89% of the white children favored the white cut-out doll. Sixty percent of the white children dressed the brown dolls in shabbier clothing than they did the white dolls. In addition, 82% of the white children and two-thirds of the Afro-American children had the Afro-American doll live in the tenement.

Frenkel-Brunswick and Havel (1953) published their study on the prejudice towards minority groups among white children, adding to the growing literature on prejudice and its effects on children. The report was one of several aspects of a project dealing with social discrimination in children and their attitudes towards Afro-Americans, Mexicans, Japanese, Jews, and foreigners in general. The findings showed that most children were prejudiced and not tolerant. Most of the children were prejudiced against Afro-American; the highest percentage on the seven-point scale indicated a strong bias against Afro-Americans. Likewise, on the ethnocentrism scores, the majority of the high scores revealed manifest racist attitudes towards Afro-Americans. However, prejudice was admitted more openly against Mexican-American and Jews and less often against Afro-American and Japanese (the study was done in Northern California). Prejudice about Chinese-Americans was not admitted openly at all. The children had the usual stereotypes about Afro-Americans and favored seg-

regation. Interestingly, correlations between the subjects and their parents' prejudice clearly indicated the influence of the family upon the ethnic tolerances or intolerances expressed by the children.

The Stevenson-Stewart study (1958) also expanded on the development of racial awareness in young children. The results showed that the ability of young children three years old to seven years old to discriminate between the races increased with age. White children, however, tended to develop this ability at a younger age than Afro-American children who made fewer in-group choices and gave more negative roles to Afro-American children than whites gave to other whites.

These studies and others by Goodman (1952) and Morland (1958, 1966) clearly indicated that by the 1950s "the mold of racial prejudice, with its fixed social expectations, was set at an appallingly early age" (Kluger 1976, p. 319). Indeed, Goodman (1952) concluded that Afro-American children not yet five years old sensed that they were "marked" and "grow uneasy." The theme was reiterated in the social scientists' statement which was the appendix to the appellant's briefs summarizing the evidence against segregated schools:

As children learn the inferior status to which they are almost always segregated and kept apart from others who are treated with more respect by the society as a whole—they often react with feelings of inferiority and a sense of personal humiliation (Allport et al., 1952, p. 168).

Proshansky and Newton (1974) have summarized succinctly the racial awareness process in children. The age period from three to seven years is the time when the child not only makes self differentiations but also becomes increasingly aware of racial differences. He also begins to learn the social attitudes towards various racial and ethnic groups, including his own. The development of racial identification is an integral part of a minority group child's total development of self. Proshansky and Newton noted that the self-differentiation process occurs in a continuing context of social interactions in which others both distinguish and evaluate the Afro-American child by means of his racial category and label him in affectively-laden terms which refer to his race with negative attitudes. There are two basic processes involved in the development of racial identity. The first one, racial conception, is the process by which the child learns to make racial distinctions at a conceptual level; the second, racial evaluation, is the process by which the child evaluates his own racial group.

The studies on racial identity in preschool Afro-American children to date have indicated that they come to identify themselves in a negative way between the ages of three to five. However, it is important to note that the racial identity process is dependent on the social setting to which the Afro-American child is exposed, as well as on individual differences in temperament, socialization, and cognitive style.

For instance, Clark and Clark (1947) noted that racial awareness among Afro-American children was higher in a biracial setting as compared to a segregated Afro-American setting. In addition, it has been noted that Afro-American children have higher self-esteem in segregated Afro-American schools as compared to desegregated schools (Powell, 1973a; Rosenberg and Simmons, 1972). We shall discuss these studies in greater detail later in this presentation.

Clark (1955) pointed out that the child does not learn about racial differences in an affectless value-free milieu. Research data cited here indicated that there is a direct relationship between problems in the development of the self and the degree to which the child's ethnic or racial group is socially unacceptable and exposed to discrimination and deprivation. The early studies of Seward (1956), Clark and Clark (1947), Goodman (1952), and Radke and

Trager (1950) showed that as the self-awareness of a minority child evolved, it evolved in a race-conscious sociocultural milieu which assigned negative values to the perception of any color other than white. In short, by 1954 "the racial evaluation process of racial awareness in American society (could) be summed up by a childhood ditty:

If you're white, you're all right,
If you're brown, you can hang around,
If you're black, step way back (Powell, 1982a).

Replication of the Clarks' Doll Studies Between 1970 and 1980

The Clark and Clark doll study (1939) has been replicated many times. A selective review in the past ten years of some of those replications will be presented to present a more current status on racial identification and preference among Afro-American children.

Datcher, Savage, and Chechosky (1973) conducted an extension of the Clarks' doll technique. The investigators examined the variables of age, race, sex, type of school, and race of experimenter. The subjects included Afro-American and white suburban children from racially segregated and desegregated schools from kindergarten, third, and fifth grades. The questions used by Clark and Clark (1939, 1947) were asked the students by ten female interviewers, half of whom were Afro-American and half of whom were white. The major findings were:

1) A majority of the Afro-American children preferred the black or Afro-American doll.
2) The majority of the Afro-American children made correct racial identifications.
3) Whether the school was segregated or desegregated did not affect the racial preference of the Afro-American children.

4) The importance of grade was basically insignificant except for Afro-American males who had higher own race preference scores in the higher grades than in the younger grades.
5) The Afro-American preference score was higher with Afro-American experimenters.

The effects of race and cleanliness in racial preferences were explored by Epstein, Krupat, and Obudho (1975) as a replication of the Clarks' study. The investigators were interested in determining if other dimensions outweighed race in eliciting children's preferences for Afro-American and white children. The results indicated that the most desirable situation was the clean child of the subject's own race. The children tended, however, to underestimate the degree of favorability the other race actually displayed.

Fox and Jordan (1973) replicated the Clarks' study (1947) but included American-Chinese children as well as white and Afro-American children from integrated and segregated elementary schools in New York City. The Afro-American children preferred and identified with their own racial group and both Afro-American and white children showed similar own-race response. However, the American-Chinese children showed significantly fewer own-race choices.

The Hrabra (1972) and Hrabra and Grant (1970) doll studies were concerned with the methodologies used in the studies of racial preference among children in the Clarks' (1939, 1947) doll studies. In the 1970 study by Hrabra and Grant which reexamined racial prejudice and identification, the same questions used by the Clarks resulted in findings that both white and Afro-American four- to eight-year-old children preferred dolls representing their own race, a trend that was found among all ages and increased with age. Interestingly, Afro-American children with light skin color were as strong in their preference for the Afro-American

doll as were the more dark-skinned Afro-American children. Although a majority of the children made appropriate identification of the dolls, it was interesting to note that 15% of the light-skinned Afro-American children did not identify themselves correctly when asked to present "the doll" that looks like you.

The 1972 Hrabra study which sought to examine the dual technique as a measure of racial ethnocentrism showed that 26% of the Afro-American youngsters and 28% of the white children picked a doll of the same race for the following questions: 1) Give me the doll you like to play with or the doll you like best; 2) Give me the doll that is the nice doll; and 3) Give me the doll that is a nice color. However, in response to the statement "Give me the doll that looks bad," the children gave the doll of the other race. Among Afro-American subjects this pattern increased with age but not so with the white students. In addition, the results showed that the white subjects with more ethnocentrism did not have Afro-American friends, but the ethnocentric Afro-American subjects had more white friends.

In general, most of the studies done to replicate the Clarks' original doll studies on racial awareness and racial preferences since the early 1970s do not show the prominent out-group identification among Afro-American children noted by the Clarks and others in the 40s and 50s. Although ethnocentrism is present among white and Afro-American children in terms of racial preference, the self-hatred and rejection of their group membership among Afro-American children is clearly not as prominent or pervasive (Obudho, 1977).

Studies on Interraciality and School Desegregation

Stephan (1978) in his review of the effects of school desegregation on prejudice rightly noted that there has been a paucity of interracial contact research concerning the public schools. Indeed, Pettigrew (1975) had noted previously "that the failure of private and public funding agencies to support systematic, widespread, and over time research of the racial desegregation process as it occurred is undoubtedly one of the most tragic setbacks the study of race relations has experienced" (p. 14).

Stephan (1978) found only 10 published studies on the effects of school desegregation on prejudice. The low number of published articles in this area reported by Stephan is very surprising inasmuch as Obudho (1977) has 134 entries in her annotated bibliography of *Black-White Racial Attitudes*. The first two chapters concentrate on studies dealing with children and more than 60 percent of all the entries refer to the effects of segregated and desegregated schooling. Likewise, the author found that the ERIC Clearing House has more than 3,000 references on school desegregation, at least a third of which deal with studies on interracial relationships within desegregated schools. There were three studies of those that Stephan (1978) selected that showed that desegregation reduced prejudice (Silverman and Shaw, 1973; Singer, 1967; and Webster, 1961). However, according to Stephan, the Silverman and Shaw and the Webster studies showed a decrease in prejudice for Afro-American students.

Stephan (1978) includes among those studies that showed negative results of school desecregation on racial attitudes the 1967 study of Dentler and Elkins; the Armor (1972) study of an Afro-American high school in a northern city; the Green and Gerard (1974) study from a western city; and the Stephan (1977) study in a southwestern city.

The three studies that found no difference between racial attitudes in segregated and desegregated schools are listed as 1) Horowitz (1936); 2) Lombardi (1963) and 3) Williams, Best and Boswell (1975).

Among the eight unpublished studies that Stephan reviewed, three showed re-duced prejudice of Afro-Americans towards whites; one indicated reduction of white prejudice towards Afro-Americans; two showed increased prejudice of Afro-Americans towards whites; four showed increased white prejudice towards Afro-Americans, and two showed no effects.

However, a mere head counting of the studies on the effects of school desegregation on interracial relationships ignores the very important variables that convert desegregated schools into truly integrated schools. In so many instances school desegregation is implemented by the cessation of segregation of schools to the letter of the law but not in the full spirit of the law.

Does segregation of children in public schools solely on the basis of race, even though the physical facilities and other "tangible" factors may be equal, deprive the children of the minority group of equal educational opportunities? We believe that it does.... Separate educational facilities are inherently unequal (Brown vs. Board of Education).

So spoke the U.S. Supreme Court but there were many who did not believe and did not want to comply. Indeed, Senator Eastland circulated a pamphlet among southern politicians entitled "Black Monday: The Demise of the Southern Way of Life." The *way* school desegregation is achieved largely determines the quality of interaction among students, teachers, and parents.

One of the most thorough reviews of the effects of school desegregation on interracial relations has been done by Weinberg (1977) in *Minority Students: A Research Appraisal*. In his review of interracial interaction within schools, he reviews 46 studies in detail; his review of studies of the effects of school desegregation on interracial attitudes, and interactions in particular, included 39.

Concerning the 46 studies he reviewed on interraciality or interracial interactions and attitudes among school children, he concluded:

... it may be stated with high confidence that the interracial interaction usually leads to the development of positive racial attitudes. Studies of student disorder in interracial schools suggest strongly that institutional resistance to educational change is the single most abrasive factor in generating disorders (Weinberg, 1977, p. 211).

He also concluded, following his review of 39 studies regarding the effects of actual school desegregation on interracial attitudes and interaction:

In most of the cases, the interracial interaction brought on by desegregation produced positive racial attitudes among blacks and/or whites. . . . Leadership by staff and faculty emerged in many studies as a critical factor. In more recently desegregated schools, where representative numbers of blacks and whites are involved, the importance of student involvement and responsibility for the school's program was found to be vital. . . . In all but a few cases a history of having attended a desegregated school facilitated easier interaction in another desegregated school (Weinberg, 1977, p. 212).

A review and further critique of Weinberg's review of the total of 85 studies revealed many studies that should be highlighted because of their extensiveness and the data generated which help one understand the dynamics of a desegregated school and the important variables that lead to certain results. Weinberg's (1977) review brings to the forefront factors that lead to effective school desegregation, which in turn help achieve integration, as well as those factors which mitigate against the effectiveness of school desegregation and thus hamper the development of integration—a process by which all children feel they are an integral part of the school they attend.

From the Criswell study as early as 1939 comes the observation that the nature of the interpersonal relationships between white and Afro-American children was dependent on the racial mixture of the classroom. If the classroom was pre-dominantly white, the element of choice was broader and the result was more intimate interpersonal relationships with Afro-American children. But if the class was predominantly Afro-American, the choices were narrowed and fewer interracial friendships occurred. Dwyer (1958) on the other hand noted that informal association thrived in either situation.

The Webster (1961) study of a junior high school in Richmond, California, reviewed by Stephan (1978) is worth reviewing again because of factors that were noted to be unfavorable to improved interracial contacts. These included the fact that 1) the beginning of school was complicated by physical aggression; 2) the obvious avoidance of the Afro-American students by white students created feelings of resentment among the Afro-American students; 3) the majority of white students had negative stereotypes about Afro-Americans; and 4) there was no parental support among the white parents for the development of harmonious interracial relationships. In fact, the parents supported the hostile, stereotyped attitudes of their children. Among the conclusions Webster made were that a) interracial contact among students cannot work without adult guidance; b) a broad community program of positive acceptance is the only way that interracial classroom behavior can be positive and productive; and c) six months is too short a time to develop constructive interracial attitudes.

Although insights can be drawn from many of the small cross-sectional studies of interracial relations in desegregated schools, large-scale studies such as the one on the Carver School District in Michigan, a virtually all Afro-American lower-socioeconomic school district which merged with the Oak Park School District, an upper-middle-class white suburb of Detroit, produce some interesting data when studied over time (Gordon, 1965). The academic achievement differences between the two schools were great. On the Iowa

Tests of Basic Skills, the Oak Park 4th graders were at the 94th percentile and the Carver 4th graders were at the ninth. In 1961, the first year of the merger, 95% of the former Carver elementary school students were confident that they could succeed at Oak Park. Four years later, only 72% responded affirmatively. Gordon (1965) concluded "that in view of the objective achievement and social status gulf between the two groups of children," the drop was very modest and reflected a necessary and realistic adjustment by the Afro-American children. Gordon also concluded that "lower class Afro-American students from Carver performed more adequately than is generally true of lower class Afro-American students" (p. 233). Gordon believes that the "high achieving student culture of Oak Park was clearly a factor" (p. 233).

In terms of social interactions between Afro-American and white students, several observations were made:

1) The Afro-American students joined nonacademic school clubs more frequently than white students. This was particularly true of athletics.
2) Many more hostile incidents occurred between Afro-American girls and white girls than between the boys—an observation that has been made frequently in many school desegregation studies.
3) There was much more interracial social contact among boys than girls—another common observation made in school desegregation studies.
4) A Human Relations Club was formed in 1964-65.
5) Many more white students joined the varsity athletics after Afro-American students came to the school.
6) The academic achievement levels of the white students remained high—a consistent finding in school desegregation studies.
7) Close to 50% of the Afro-American students planned to go on to college compared to 27% at an Afro-American Detroit ghetto high school.

A systematic study of school desegregation in the secondary schools of Indianapolis, Indiana is one of the most comprehensive to date (Patchen and Davidson, 1973). The process began during the 1970-71 school year and included eleven schools with student populations ranging from 98.9% white to 99.8% Afro-American. The major finding of this in-depth study of a single school system was that interracial interaction had a positive effect on Afro-American and white students. In all of the 11 schools, Afro-American students reported that they had more favorable opinions of whites since attending high school. White students on eight of the school campuses reported favorable attitudes toward Afro-Americans. About two-fifths of the Afro-American students had not had any unfriendly reactions but less than one-fifth of the white students had.

In examining the issue of physical aggression, it was found that the frequency of open violence in the high schools was far less than thought. The predominantly white schools had fewer episodes than predominantly Afro-American schools and most student fighting was intraracial rather than interracial. Indeed, the rate per 1,000 students was five for the entire group of eleven schools, three for the predominantly white, and 7 for the predominantly Afro-American.

Patchen and Davidson's (1973) observations are interesting in helping to understand the totality of interracial interaction. For instance, they found that one of the major forces that played a role in the racial interaction among the students was the teachers' attitudes. For instance, Afro-American teachers were perceived by Afro-American students as favoring congenial relationships between Afro-American and white students. The data also showed that "as students moved through high school, their interracial attitudes grew more positive," which stresses the importance of understanding race relations in the school "within a broader community framework" and the kinds of influences that schools can have "even when desegregation is initiated under temporarily difficult circumstances" (Patchen and Davidson, 1973, p. 290).

Special recommendations were made regarding programs to integrate the Afro-American girl into the life of the school. The fact that Afro-American girls have more difficulty in establishing themselves in non-segregated schools has been supported by numerous studies (Powell 1973a; Weinberg 1975; Stephan, 1978; Morris, 1971; Hall and Gentry, 1969; Gordon, 1965; Marascuillo and Leven, 1966).

Yet another important finding emerging from the Indianapolis study was the importance of racially heterogeneous classes and random assignment of seating. The racial attitudes of the students were significantly related to group context; differences in socioeconomic status between Afro-American and white students were only a secondary source of interracial problems.

Patchen and Davidson (1973) concluded:

School officials and concerned citizens should strive for a level of racial integration at each school which allows students and teachers of both races to feel that they are an integral part of the school and that their presence and interest are reflected in the school's academic and extracurricular activities (p. 295).

The issue of student disorder has received a great deal of attention in school desegregation. Between 1969 and 1970 the Community Relations Service of the U.S. Department of Justice investigated 140 secondary schools in 52 cities and 17 states encompassing a total of 165,737 students. The major finding of the survey was that more than 50% of the teachers were against the idea of protecting students. Student protests were significantly higher in those schools that the Justice Department identified as having institutional racism, "institutional irrelevancy," and poor communication. Other studies of student disorders in desegregated schools conclude that recently desegregated schools had the highest incidence of violence and that in all of the schools studied there had been no preparation of staff, students or community for desegregation (Bailey, 1971; Havighurst, Smith and Wilder, 1970).

There are still many reports such as the one describing interaction in a desegregated junior high school in Chattanooga where five years later the school has resegregated in every way and where there have been no efforts on the part of the staff to change such patterns (Weinberg, 1977).

However, the degree to which a newly desegregated school becomes resegregated or integrated will depend upon the quality of interracial interactions among the students and between the students and the teachers. The importance of the role of the teacher will be discussed in the next section. However, it is clear that the quality of the social interactions within the school and the degree of interracial conflict had their cyclical effects on academic achievement and self-concept. There are many studies which report on the importance of the interracial relationships and its effects on academic achievement and self-esteem. Gastright and Smith (1972) in a report entitled "Friendly Mixing" indicated that "Afro-American students at a newly integrated junior high school could accept the higher academic standards with help from friendly white students" (Obudho 1977, p. 26). They stress how crucial friendships were to Afro-American students who then did not get discouraged by the racist attitudes of the teachers or by the difficult school work. McPartland's study (1968) of the segregated students in the desegregated schools found that although desegregation at the school level had a positive effect on the academic achievement of the Afro-American students, those who remained in segregated classes within the school received no benefits in regard to academic growth. Most often the resegregation of the newly desegregated school begins with the placement of minority group children in remedial classes which are segregated. Such placements result from ingrained teacher biases about minority group children, lowered expectations, and racist attitudes (Jones, 1973). In order to understand the effects of school desegregation on interracial attitudes and interactions, the role of the classroom teacher as well as the school administrators needs to be understood.

The Role of the Teacher in Mediating the Outcome of Interracial Relationships in the Desegregated School

Weinberg (1977) concludes his review of minority students and fellow students by noting an observation by Morland (1966) which in essence reiterated the fact that "social interaction between (Afro-American) and white in a racist America will become more humanizing when notions of racial superordination and subordination disappear." In reviewing more than a dozen studies of teacher attitudes, he concluded that "this section strongly suggests the widespread existence of teacher avoidance behavior as far as minority children are concerned. These students tend to be viewed by their teachers as less promising and more troublesome" (p. 233).

Based on his review of 20 studies of classroom interactions among teachers in desegregated schools, Weinberg (1977) concluded:

The teacher in the classroom tends predominantly to be skeptical of the capacity of minority (group) children to achieve beyond minimal levels. Frequently, minority (group) children are ignored by teachers and subjected to considerable discouragement. As in the case of teacher attitude studies, . . . it seems logical

to infer—and some of the empirical materials permit such an inference—that negative teacher attitudes lead to actual discrimination. This, however, is not always the case. Numerous instances are recorded of teachers in nonsegregated schools relating in a productive, essentially just way to minority students (p. 231).

Reviews of the effects of teacher-student interaction on the success or failure of the desegregation process clearly indicate that the classroom teacher is the pivot of successful desegregation. Willie's (1973) study of four newly desegregated schools in Syracuse found the role of administrative planning and leadership as well as the cooperation of the classroom teacher to be crucial to the success of school desegregation. Indeed, in two schools where the administrators and teachers had been prepared, "success was prompt, if not instantaneous" (p. 67).

The negative consequences of teacher bias had been particularly highlighted in the Riverside, California, study where it was observed that teachers behaved very differently toward the children of different ethnic groups which then had "considerable consequences for the educational welfare of the students." Indeed, the teacher biases against the minority group children were communicated to the white children which increased their biases against the minority group children (Gerard and Miller, 1975).

Carruthers' (1970) review of school desegregation and racial cleavage from 1954-70 concluded that integration will not in and of itself lead to more positive attitudes and behaviors toward minority group people. The Coleman study (1966) indicated, however, that "white students who first attended integrated schools early in their school career are most likely to value their associations with (Afro-American) students" and that "whites who attended desegregated schools expressed willingness to reside in an interracial neighborhood, to have their children attend desegregated schools, and to have (Afro-American) friends" (p. 307). Similar attitudes are reported for Afro-Americans who attended desegregated schools (Crain, 1972; Weinberg, 1977).

Jones (1973) pinpoints some penetrating questions in the midst of the array of such data:

Evidence on the value of the integrated school for facilitating the achievement of the (Afro-American) student and on influencing verbal attitudes toward (Afro-Americans) in some future activities are impressive. But what of the present? What of the (Afro-American) student's adjustment, his self-concept resulting from constant exposure to racism in teachers, students, and administrators? What evidence exists concerning the effects of school integration on intergroup attitudes and intergroup behavior? And what programs exist in the schools for modifying such attitudes and behaviors? If we are going to talk about integration as an educational goal, then we must have answers to these questions lest we err in developing cognitively able (Afro-American) children at the expense of their social and emotional development (p. 344).

Berkowitz, Carr, and Anderson in Chapter 27 discuss the kinds of programs that can be implemented in the schools to offset the consequences about which Jones (1973) rightly expresses great concern. Other such reports refer to the success of human relations groups, parents, citizen groups, and mental health professionals in mediating the intergroup attitudes and behaviors (National Conference of Christians and Jews, 1977; Forehand and Ragosta 1976; MacLennan 1973).

A critique of the studies of the effects of school desegregation on interracial relationships is incomplete without some basic statement about the quality in a methodological sense of most such studies. Studies of newly implemented programs are often compared with longstanding desegregated programs. As Stephan (1978) has pointed out, "this means that in addition to interethnic contact, many other

changes (in the newly desegregated school), such as the introduction of new curricula and the desegregation of teaching staffs, were occurring at the same time" (p. 224). The effects of these variables are rarely measured. Secondly, different communities implement different plans which are rarely assessed and region of the country is often an important factor in how school desegregation was achieved and the existing attitudes prior to desegregation. It is also important in assessing such studies, according to Stephan, to note if the desegregation was voluntary or mandatory, the ratio of minority group children to white children, racial attitudes of the community, and patterns of residential segregation, as well as the age and SES of the students. Another major methodological concern is the measure of ethnocentrism or racism used in each study. The questions may vary in intimacy level, thus creating a lack of comparability in the data (Stephan, 1978). Differences between cross-sectional, longitudinal and 2 × 2 factorial designs each have their own list of problems—e.g. SES, equivalence of groups studied, the effects of historical events between measurement times, maturation of subjects. Stephan concludes that these kinds of problems often make it difficult to ascertain what factors involved in the desegregation process resulted in the pattern of events observed.

SELF-CONCEPT AND SCHOOL DESEGREGATION

In Weinberg's (1977) summary and critique of studies of the self-concept of Afro-American students, he reviews 34 studies on interraciality. Seventeen of the studies indicated that there was a positive effect on self-concept of Afro-American students; ten studies indicated a negative effect on the self-concept; and seven showed mixed effects. Of the 26 studies on desegregation and self-concept, 12 showed a positive effect, 8 a negative effect and 6 mixed effects. Weinberg (1977) concludes that:

Finally, note should be taken of one implication of the generally constructive effect on interraciality and desegregation in relation to self-concept of black children. Since constructive educational experiences are more often sought out than stumbled upon, it follows that a number of teachers and principals have contributed importantly to positive self-concept outcomes (p. 159).

One must accept Weinberg's optimism with some skepticism, however, for as one reviews the studies there are many difficulties which include:
1) different definitions of self-concept;
2) different aspects of self-perception that are measured;
3) different methods of measuring self-concept;
4) the use of many non-standardized scales;
5) difficulties in sampling techniques;
6) studies of racial attitudes and/or race awareness rather than self-concept.

In the haste to evaluate and justify a sociopolitical process, many studies on school desegregation and self-concept ignore the fact that self-concept is a developmental process. We have noted that the ideas and attitudes which make a "self" aware of its own existence take shape during early childhood and that a child understands or realizes different aspects of himself with varying degrees of understanding at different points in time.

Allport (1963) has described seven aspects of selfhood which together comprise the self as felt and known and enumerates them in a developmental sequence: 1) sense of bodily self; 2) sense of continuing self-identity; 3) self-esteem or pride; 4) the extension of self; 5) the self-image; 6) the self as a rational coper; and 7) the self as appropriate striver. He feels that the first three aspects of self-awareness, namely, bodily self, continuing self-identity, and self-esteem, gradually evolve during the

first three years of life. During the period from four to six years, 4 and 5, the extension of self and self-image, begin to develop. The development of coping strategies and long-range purposes add other dimensions to the sense of selfhood and begin to appear in latency and early adolescence.

It is important to remember that because self-concept is a developmental phenomenon: 1) the process of self-discovery is actively continuous as long as the child is developing or discovering new potentialities, and 2) self-concept development is dependent on certain variables whose absence or presence impedes or enhances self discovery. Self-concept in children, then, is not a static process; rather it is always in state of flux.

It is also important to understand the developmental process of self-concept of children because, depending on the age and developmental stage of the child, one may be measuring the process phenomena rather than a particular social psychological process occurring at that point in time. The younger the child, the more the self-concept process may reflect the family and the primary caretaker. The older the child, the greater the influence of peers and the outside world on the self-concept process. Coopersmith (1967) has noted that in studying the children of preadolescent age the likelihood that family experiences will be an important source of self-esteem is very high. Preadolescent children are more highly dependent upon their parents and are very likely to use the family context with its values to judge their own worth, much more so than adolescents. Coopersmith also noted that preadolescents make little distinction about self-worth in different areas of experience; rather such distinctions are made within the general appraisal of self-worth. For the adolescent, however, there is a push-pull phenomenon in which his self-perception may vary from area to area depending upon his experiences in the outside world. His entire system of self appraisal is in flux; thus, he will be more susceptible to changes in the environment, especially political, social, and cultural changes. In his struggle for independence he will struggle to evaluate and even to incorporate some of the changing values he is encountering. Consequently, the socialization process of the child is crucial in understanding his/her self-concept process. It is difficult, then, to compare self-concept studies of first graders with those of junior high school students, or studies of 5th and 6th graders with college freshmen. In this regard there are few valid studies measuring self-concept of children over time.

From the mid-forties to the mid-sixties there has been a confusing array of studies which have intended to measure the self-concept of Afro-American children. Most of the comparative studies of self-concept of white and Afro-American children done from 1943-1958 reported marked differences between the two groups, with Afro-American children allegedly having severe deficiencies (Dreger and Miller 1960). Subsequent reviews of self-percept studies done from 1959 to 1965 confirmed the earlier reviews of the damaged self-concept of the Afro-American child (Dreger and Miller 1968). The explanations offered for such persistent findings included reasons such as:

Confronted by the constancy of failure brought about by the traditional school's philosophy of instruction and its curriculum content, many children from minority subcultures begin to develop feelings of alienation. . . . The decrease in self confidence accompanying increasing age suggests that the school probably provides few opportunities for nurturing the ego of the child from the educationally deprived home (Keach, Fulton, Gardner, 1967, p. 136).

Another prominent theme in the educational literature includes:

Possession of a stunted, warped self-concept is perhaps the most stubborn and persistent obstacle to self-fulfillment for the minority group

youngster. It is a consequence of being socialized into a stigmatized second class citizen status, of being unquestionably ascribed a variety of inadequacies and inferiorities so persistently that one comes to conceive of himself as being an inadequate and second class order of humanity (Hobart, 1964 p. 184).

Since the late sixties there have been many more studies which indicate that Afro-American children do not always have poor self-concept (Powell, 1973a; Rosenberg and Simmon, 1972). However, it has been more difficult to isolate the variables for positive self-concept among Afro-American children than to identify those variables associated with poor self-concept (Powell and Fuller, 1972; Powell, 1973b). For Afro-American children with adequate self-concept, the variables of middle or upper SES, adequate or above IQ, above average academic achievement, family stability, and high educational attainment of parents are not always highly significant in mediating adequate self-concept (Powell, 1982b). In fact, studies have shown that the variables for positive and negative self-concept are difficult to isolate for white children also, indicating that the self-concept processes (and there are many aspects of self-concept) are more complex than we have understood heretofore (Powell, 1973a, b). Understandably, when we try to examine a very complex developmental process in relation to a very complex sociopolitical and educational process like school desegregation, the variables are even more confounding.

Rosenberg and Simmons (1972), in reporting on their Baltimore study in which Afro-American students in grades 3 to 12 had good self-concept, also reviewed the studies of the late sixties and early seventies refuting the prevailing view of the damaged self-perception of the Afro-American child. Likewise Wylie (1978) reviewed the literature on 53 studies on racial status and self-esteem and concluded that the theory of the damaged self-concept of the Afro-American child "must now prove to be the case for those who still adhere to that theory" (p. 205).

Chapter 4 in this volume presents a substantive review of the literature on the self-concept of Afro-American children with particular emphasis on the positive self-concept of Afro-American children, noting in particular the times of the studies and the ages of the children studied and omitting those on racial awareness and preference. The conclusion reached by this author is that the studies fall into two categories: 1) those that indicate that there is little or no difference in self-concept between white and Afro-American children, and 2) those that show that Afro-American children have higher self-esteem than white children.

In reviewing studies on the effects of school desegregation on self-concept, the results are mixed. Some of the inconsistencies are due to the methodological problems in measuring self-concept, but not entirely. Most studies fail to describe the social milieu of the school, how school desegregation was achieved, how resegregated the desegregated school has become, how integrated the school is, the attitudes of the teachers, classroom interaction between minority group students and white students, and classroom interactions between the teacher and the minority group children. The teacher is a significant other in the child's life; what the teacher thinks and feels about the child may be significant in mediating the child's self-perceptions, depending on the age of the child and other family and psychological variables. As the child enters the world of the school, peer acceptance becomes more important in mediating his self-perception.

The teacher effects on academic achievement, interracial friendships, and self-esteem are dramatically evident in the Riverside study (Gerard and Miller, 1975) in which teacher prejudice was shown to have "considerable consequences for the educational welfare of students" (Weinberg, 1977, p. 234). After the first year of school desegregation, self-esteem

of all three ethnic groups declined. Indeed, in Weinberg's (1977) review of teachers and students in desegregated schools, he concluded:

Yet white and at times (Afro-American) teachers in desegregated schools tend to prefer, if not outright favor, the white child. Even in the absence of blatant racial attitudes, personal cruelty to minority group children lingers in the desegregated school as well as in the segregated school (p. 235).

Do such racist or neglectful patterns of interaction between the classroom teacher and the minority group child affect his self-esteem?

Stephan (1978) in his review of 100 published studies and 10 unpublished studies on the effects of school desegregation and self-concepts tallies the following count:

a) three published studies indicated negative effects on the self-esteem of Afro-American students. (Coleman, et al., 1966; Bachman, 1970; Powell and Fuller, 1970; Powell, 1973a);
b) two unpublished studies showed negative effects (Evans, 1969; French, 1972);
c) seven published studies indicated mixed effects (p. 227)d) eight unpublished studies found mixed effects or no effects (p. 228).

This author's studies on self-concept development of Afro-American children have shown some interesting but perplexing results. (Powell, 1973a, 1973b; Powell, 1982b) To recapitulate the final part of the study which occurred in three Southern cities with *de jure* segregation, the following significant findings were noted:

1) Afro-American students (n = 775) score significantly higher on the Tennessee Self Concept Scale (TSCS) than white students (n = 945) and the significant differences hold true for Afro-American and white boys as well as

for Afro-American and white girls.
2) Afro-American students in segregated schools (n = 437) scored significantly higher than Afro-American students in desegregated schools (n = 311).
3) Afro-American boys in segregated schools (n = 202) scored higher than Afro-American boys in desegregated schools (n = 136), but the differences were not significantly different.
4) Afro-American girls in segregated schools (n = 253) scored significantly higher than Afro-American girls in desegregated schools (n = 184) and the differences were significant at the .001 level.

The data analyses indicated that race and type of school were the most significant factors in determining self-concept among Afro-American junior high school students in these three Southern cities. It seemed possible that the cohesive, self-determining, civil rights activist, Afro-American communities of these three cities with readily identifiable adult models played an important role in the positive self-concept of these Afro-American adolescents, in the segregated schools (Powell and Fuller, 1972). It would also seem, then, that a segregated Afro-American community, even in the midst of the severity of racism and "Jimcrow," played an important role in the maintenance of self-esteem among Afro-American children. The work of Gurin and Epps (1975) may shed light on this phenomenon and will be reviewed later.

The second phase of the study was conducted in cities with *de facto* segregation—Minneapolis, New York City and Los Angeles (Powell, 1982b). The same phenomena of high self-esteem among segregated Afro-American students did not occur among the junior high school students tested in the three cities.

The following significant findings were noted for the northern students:

1) There were no statistically significant differences on the TSCS total positive scores between white (n = 1134) and Afro-American students (n = 1236).
2) Afro-American students in desegregated schools scored higher on the total positive score of the TSCS in all three cities; in New York and Los Angeles the differences were statistically significant (p < 0.01 and 0.02 respectively).

However, a comparison of the southern and northern Afro-American students showed that the southern Afro-American students score significantly higher than the northern Afro-American students (p < 0.001). Indeed, the northern Afro-American students scored lower than the white southern students and even lower than the Afro-American students in desegregated schools in the south. Although the northern Afro-American students scored lower than the TSCS norm group, they scored the same as other junior high school samples (Thompson, 1972). Early adolescence is a particularly difficult life stage with many fluctuations in the self-concept. In addition, self-concept increases with age. Typically, high school and college students and the elderly have higher self-concept than young adolescents. Although the effect of age on the self-concept were seen in the self-concept scores of desegregated Afro-American students in the south as well as in the scores of northern Afro-American and white students, it was not reflected in the self-concept scores of the Afro-American students in segregated southern schools, reflecting that total segregation has a more insulating effect on self-concept than a more racially dissonant environment.

Epps (1980) in his review of the impact of desegregation on self-concept concludes that the research results on the impact of desegregation on the self-esteem of Afro-American children are mixed. The Powell (1973a) and Rosenberg and Simmons (1972) studies indicate that "segregation protects self-esteem, while the impact of desegregation is to lower self-esteem" (p. 235). However, there are sufficient findings to conclude, according to Epps, that Afro-Americans have high self-esteem when compared to whites in spite of the inconsistent findings on the impact of school desegregation. Epps, who is a renowned educational researcher, adds further light to this confusing array of data. He takes particular note of the fact that white and Afro-American students base self-esteem on different attributes. Rosenberg's (1979) review of self-concept development reiterates the same theme. The crux of the issue, then, is what specific aspects of self-concept are affected by segregation and what variables are involved in those effects. Epps (1980) has noted "that academic self-esteem is much more strongly related to school achievement than total self-esteem." Indeed, many studies have noted that academic achievement among white students is more significant to self-esteem than it is among Afro-American students. However, there are numerous studies which show that the quality of the interaction between the teacher and the minority group child and the acceptance or rejection of the minority group child by his white classmates affects his academic achievement (Powell, 1969). The more integrated the school, the more likely that the minority group child will experience an increase in academic achievement; the more hostile and resegregated the school milieu, the less likely academic achievement gains will occur (Weinberg, 1975, 1977). Thus, interracial relationships affect self-concept in a specific way —academic self-concept which may also be additionally influenced by particular attributes or characteristics of each particular individual. It is also important to remember that the effects of school desegregation on self-concept are influenced, as noted in this author's previous chapter, by the degree to which the child's parents, neighborhood or community, same-race peers, white peers, and whites in general, including his teachers, are incorporated

into his self-percept.

It is quite probable that across class as well as racial lines, the significance of common general variables (e.g. academic success, athletic ability, physical appearance, and ability to attain and maintain friends) will vary as contributors to the child's overall level of self-esteem. The significance of the three major sources for self-evaluation—the family, the school, and the peer group—also will vary as contributors to the child's overall level of self-esteem (Epps, 1980, p. 236).

SCHOOL DESEGREGATION AND ACADEMIC ACHIEVEMENT

In an extensive and critical review of studies on academic achievement and school desegregation among Afro-American students, Bradley and Bradley (1977) list the St. John (1975) criteria for valid longitudinal studies as consisting of the following:

1) The transferred and control subjects must be equivalent at the outset of the study in terms of such factors as I.Q, SES, sex and age.
2) Subjects must be randomly assigned or matched on key variables.
3) There must be evidence of retention of the sample.
4) There must be equivalent educational programs in the segregated and desegregated schools.

The review of the desegregation studies done between 1959-1975 was divided according to method of achieving desegregation as well as the number of valid studies per method and included the following valid studies: a) open enrollment (n = 4); b) central school (n = 5); c) school closing (n = 6); d) busing (n = 9); e) experimental (n = 1).

Bradley and Bradley concluded from their critique of the open enrollment studies that all valid studies demonstrated positive effects of school desegregation on Afro-American students' academic achievement both in reading and mathematics. Those valid studies of school desegregation achieved by the establishment of central schools demonstrated an increase in academic achievement scores of Afro-American students, especially in mathematics. The data from those studies in which school closings were the major way of achieving school desegregation indicated that there was no positive relationship between desegregation and academic achievement of Afro-American students. When busing is the method of achieving desegregation, several problems arise. Of all of the studies on school desegregation and academic achievement, the busing studies have the most serious methodological flaws, the most common being failure to fulfill the criteria of subject and school equivalence. The busing study with the least flaws is that of Laird and Weeks (1966) in Philadelphia which reported that the bused subjects had significantly higher reading scores two years later than the controls. However, there were no gains in arithmetic scores.

Weinberg's (1977) review of the academic achievement and school desegregation studies revealed 26 studies that indicated positive outcomes. However, the critique is not done in such a way as to assess whether or not certain critical factors specifically crucial to academic achievement gains were present or absent in the studies. Miller's (1977) critique of Weinberg's review noted many misinterpretations of the studies reviewed.

In Stephan's (1978) review of 15 published and 19 unpublished studies on the effects of school desegregation on the academic achievement of Afro-American students, he found six published studies and four unpublished which showed that desegregation led to academic achievement gains. The remaining studies showed no effects or mixed effects, leading to a final summary "that desegregation led to decreases in achievement in 3% of the studies and let to increases in 29% of the studies" (p. 232). Stephan (1978) concluded that the positive effect of school desegregation on academic achievement "has received somewhat more support" and "that the results for the achievement studies are considerably more valid than those for the studies of prejudice and self-esteem because better measures have been employed and the studies were generally more carefully designed" (p. 232-233).

St. John's (1975) book reviewed all of the research available up to 1974, covering more than 120 published and unpublished studies on academic achievement, self-esteem, and interracial attitudes. Her review of studies on academic achievement and school desegregation indicate that many of those reporting positive effects have many methodological problems that detract from the validity of their findings and those showing few or no academic achievement gains usually lacked an adequate control group. Those studies which were well designed and met St. John's (1975) criteria showed conflicting conclusions regarding the use of school desegregation in mediating academic achievement gains for Afro-American students. Likewise Epps (1980) concludes:

The available evidence suggests that desegregation where accompanied by congenial race relations and acceptance by white peers and teachers, may enhance educational attainment—but the evidence is far from conclusive (p. 239).

In concluding their review of academic achievement of Afro-American students in desegregated schools, Bradley and Bradley (1977) suggest that:

(Afro-American) students' academic performance, then, may be more effectively increased if the situational factors that maximize their classroom motivation may be delineated and replicated within their classrooms in both predominantly (Afro-American) and predominantly white schools (p. 445).

We shall attempt to examine these factors in our concluding sections which will focus on several studies which more clearly and more specifically delineate the factors involved in academic achievement and school desegregation. There are three studies which examine the interlocking or interweaving effects of racial attitudes, self-esteem and academic achievement in mediating positive or negative consequences of school desegregation. They include the longitudinal school desegregation study in Riverside, California (Gerard and Miller, 1975); two studies of Afro-American students from Afro-American high schools (Sowell, 1974, 1976) and colleges (Gurin and Epps, 1975); and Crain and Weisman's (1972) study of Afro-American adults in the north who had attended desegregated schools. Extrapolations from these studies may help tease out the variables which are often lost in assessing the effects of school desegregation.

The Riverside Study

A very vast array of reports of evaluations of the school desegregation process in various school systems across the nation have been reported and cited in the educational, legal, and human relations literature. The number of such reports are too numerous to be reviewed within the confines of this chapter. However, the author has chosen to do a systematic review of the school desegregation study in Riverside, California, largely because the results of that school system's desegregation have received much publicity in the popular media and have been analyzed and reanalyzed often with conflicting reports. It is also, however, one of the few longitudinal, multifaceted, and multivariant analytical studies which attempted to grapple with many of the controversial educational, motivational, psychosocial, and assessment processes of school desegregation.

In Bradley and Bradley's (1977) astute and carefully critiqued analyses of the academic achievement of Afro-American students in desegregated schools, the Riverside study is critiqued among those school systems which achieved desegregation by school closing; however, it is also one of the studies that did not meet the St. John's (1975) criteria for a valid study. Some of the difficulties inherent in the Riverside study are also embedded in many studies on the effectiveness of school desegregation on academic achievement. Bradley and Bradley note that a time-series design is used to examine the academic performance of Afro-American students in kindergarten, second, and third grades. The subjects' mean achievement scores were less than one standard deviation below the district-wide mean in each subject sample at each grade level (Bradley and Bradley, 1977, p. 428). The reviewers go on to note that the t-test comparisons of initial and final mean achievement scores yielded no significant changes in mean achievement for any of the subject samples during the five-year period. Citing Campbell and Stanley's (1963) criticisms of a time-series design, reviewers conclude that the results and conclusions regarding academic achievement and school desegregation from the Riverside study are "untenable."

Additional criticisms of the data from the Riverside study include: a) the inappropriate combination of longitudinal and cross-sectional data, b) the lack of an adequate control group, and c) the validity of subject equivalence, particularly the fact that only 25 percent of the original sample of Afro-American students could be followed through the sixth grade. The single most important criterion considered essential to the validity of any longitudinal study of school desegregation is subject equivalence (St. John, 1975). Consequently, no general conclusions regarding the effects of desegregation upon the achievement of Afro-American students can be made on the basis of the school closing studies, including the Riverside study (Bradley and Bradley, 1977).

The severity of the criticisms of the methodological deficiencies seem well warranted considering this author's review of the study; however, the Riverside study has been touted as the most closely studied and most carefully monitored effects of most of the school desegregation plan of the mid 60s. Indeed, Uslem (1977) described the California study published by Gerard and Miller in 1975 as "the most thorough to date" and "the most long-term, completely documented, and widely noted" study. However, before the study is discarded for its many methodological flaws, a review of some of the data may shed some light on the most serious problems in achieving school desegregation, as well as in evaluating its educational and psychosocial outcomes for children.

In the Spring issue (1978) of the *Research Review of Equal Education* Linsenmeier and Wortman reexamined the Riverside study. As conceptualized by Gerard and Miller (1975), the Riverside study was based on three basic hypotheses which were popular in the mid 1960s in thinking of and conceptualizing the problems of school racial composition and academic achievement initiated by the Equality of Educational Opportunity Survey (E.E.O.S., Coleman et al., 1966). Linsenmeier and Wortman concede that some of these models "seem less plausible in the late 1970s than they did ten or fifteen years ago due to the increased experience with desegregated schooling, a change in social climate, and apparently negative empirical findings from studies like that conducted in Riverside" (p. 4). Their critique, rather than focusing on the methodological deficiencies for "certain ideas which now seem untenable," outlines the three major hypotheses or models and they try to examine the data from Riverside as they relate to these hypotheses. This seems a more profitable form for the reanalysis because it may help us review what we thought we knew, understand what we do not know, and move to other levels of investigations that may be more helpful in formulating studies and programs that have more positive outcomes.

The E.E.O.S. report in 1966 linked the academic achievement of minority group children in desegregated schools to "the lateral transmission of values" (Gerard and Miller, 1975; Coleman, et al., 1966). This hypothesis presumes the following:

1) White children value academic achievement more than minority group children.
2) Once school desegregation occurs, minority group children and white children will interact in a meaningful way and, consequently, minority group children "will be exposed to the achievement-oriented values of their white peers."
3) The exposure of minority group children to such norms will help them value academic achievement like their white peers.
4) Once minority group children increasingly value academic achievement, their own levels of academic achievement will increase; i.e., in methodological testable terminology, "a linear and causal relationship exists between an individual's desire for achievement and the level of achievement which he or she attains" (Linsemeier and Wortman, 1978, p. 4).

According to Linsemeier and Wortman (1978), the second hypothesis of the Riverside study included the theory of normalization of instruction. This theory assumes that there is the tendency of teachers to teach to the average level of the students in the classroom. Consequently, once this occurs, one could expect that the minority group children in the desegregated classroom would perform at a higher academic level because of the exposure to higher performance standards. This second model also assumes that desegregated classrooms will enable minority group children to experience for the first time more advanced curricula as well as higher performance standards and thus help them acquire higher expectations as well as increased motivation to perform better.

The third model from which the Riverside study operated was that beneficial effects will arise from a desegregated school—effects which could be equated with the absence of discrimination and the resulting increase in self-esteem. Indeed, the 1954 Supreme Court decision outlawing school segregation did so on the premise that segregated schools were harmful "to the hearts and minds of (minority group children) in ways never to be undone." The Court assumed and indeed affirmed that cessation of segregated schools would eliminate the feelings of self-inferiority of minority group children and enhance their self-esteem. This third model assumes that once in desegregated schools minority group children will not be regarded as inferior; that the favorable attitudes of white peers and teachers will indeed enhance the minority group child's self-esteem; and that increased self-esteem will cause improved academic achievement.

Within the framework of these three models, Linsenmeier and Wortman (1978) review the Riverside school desegregation data and begin by noting the unique situation in Riverside that initiated school desegregation. There is sufficient data to substantiate the fact that local variables will affect the outcome of school desegregation programs which the Riverside study inherited (St. John, 1973). These variables must be taken into account in order to avoid the problem of the lack of an experimental group.

An essential requirement for establishing the internal validity of any study is to have some information on what would have happened in that particular setting in the absence of the critical treatment. Thus, in order to be able to state with confidence that certain outcomes for school children in Riverside were a consequence of the desegregation of Riverside's schools, we must have some idea of how things would have differed if desegregation had not occurred (Linsenmeier and Wortman, 1978, p. 8).

Some of the problems which caused the lack of experimental control were very simplistic. For instance, scores obtained by school children actually being studied following desegregation were often compared with those obtained by children in the district the year before wide-scale desegregation was introduced, many of whom were not participating in the study. Another occurrence not accounted for in the analysis was that many events besides the implementation of desegregation occurred between the collection of measures from the baseline control group and the collection of measures from the desegregated children one to five years later. For example, a number of new curricula were introduced following the decision to desegregate and the average class size in the elementary schools increased significantly with the introduction of desegregation. Prior to desegregation, minority group children were in much smaller classrooms than they were when they entered desegregated classrooms. Adding further to the lack of control, children were classified according to the average socioeconomic status of students in the schools in which they were enrolled or to the degree of racial bias of their classroom teachers. The investigators had no control over the assignment of students to schools or to classrooms.

There were many problems with the interethnic comparisons. First, only a sample of the white children was studied but nearly the entire population of minority group school children was included. In addition, a greater percentage of white parents than minority group parents declined permission for their children to participate in the study. A greater percentage of white and Afro-Americans were lost by attrition over time than Mexican-Americans and within all three ethnic groups there was a tendency for children with lower achievement test scores to be more likely to leave the study. However, within the two minority groups, children from families higher in socioeconomic status were more likely to leave. Thus, the post-desegregation scores came from children whose average SES scores were slightly lower than the pre-desegregation scores, which in turn may have accounted for depressed scores.

The third area of major methodological difficulty with the study was the incomplete use of data. Not all variables were measured for every school year. No data from parents or teachers were available for the last two years of the study. Variables thought to play key roles in children's reactions to school desegregation were not measured at all during the third and fifth years of the six-year study. By the sixth year, data were being collected only from those children who had been in kindergarten and first grade at the start of the study. The chapter on teachers' attitudes consisted of data from only one year. The chapter on teacher effects combined children from all grade levels together. The study concentrated only on verbal achievement although several studies indicate that school desegregation may affect arithmetic achievement more than verbal or reading achievement. Very little attention was paid to variations among schools.

In the midst of such a confusing array of omissions and lack of organization, what can be said about the improvement of the academic achievement of minority group students in desegregated schools? The most serious deficiency in the extrapolations and conclusions from the Riverside data rests on a very important factor and, indeed, a fallacy common to most of the studies on school desegregation: the dependent measures of academic achievement, in this instance the verbal achievement test scores administered to children in grades 4 through 6 each October and to children in grades 1 through 3 each

May. As in most instances of evaluation of school desegregation programs, the specific tests used were chosen by the state and local boards of education. In Riverside as in many other school districts, the test differed from grade to grade and from year to year. Linsemeier and Wortman (1978) have noted, as have Wyatt and Padilla (Chapter 30), that the norms for these standardized tests were based on predominantly white samples. Because of this factor Linsenmeier and Wortman (1978) concluded that the academic achievement measures, as with most measures used in the Riverside study, were unclear in terms of reliability and validity when used with minority group children.

. . . the best that can be said is that minority group children fared no worse after desegregation than before it. Also, contrary to the fears of some opponents of desegregation, white children apparently performed no worse after desegregation either (p. 12).

An examination of the Riverside model vis-à-vis the improved achievement through the lateral transmission of values theory should be discussed. First of all, the assumption that prior to desegregation minority group children do not value academic achievement is another example of the ethnocentrism of investigators who have no experience with non-white groups. This theory is refuted by Sowell (1974, 1976) and Gurin and Epps (1975) and further on in this chapter. Indeed, the lateral transmission hypothesis would suggest that school desegregation must accomplish a personality transformation of the Afro-American child and when this does not occur, then academic achievement gains do not occur (Maehr, 1974). The grand conclusion, then, could be that each time the Afro-American child becomes a little brighter, he becomes a little whiter. These kinds of poorly conceptualized theories recycle to subsequent defeatist attitudes towards minority group children among teachers. If academic achievement gains are accomplished, they are caused by a "Pygmalion" effect (Rosenthal and Jacobson, 1968) or a Rist effect (Rist, 1975)—that is to say that teachers teach more and try to teach more effectively the greater the number of white children there are in the classroom—the Rist effect—or when there is a greater expectation of white middle-class behavioral patterns among their students—the Pygmalion effect. The lateral transmission hypothesis as an explanation for the academic achievement gains of Afro-American students in desegregated schools is contradictory to the same E.E.O.S. (Coleman et al., 1966) report that the educational aspirations of Afro-American students were equal to or greater than that of white students.

Be that as it may, Gerard and Miller (1975) attempted to use six measures of achievement-relevant motivation, but only two were actually used. Then, too, the two achievement motivation tests used have questionable validity with minority group populations (Linsenmeier and Wortman, 1978).

The second assumption within this lateral transmission model is that because the schools are desegregated minority group children will interact and mimic white students more and thus acquire their values. The Riverside data did show that some interethnic friendships occurred but not to the degree or extent expected. In short, in a large measure the schools remained desegregated and not integrated. It is interesting to note, however, that the children were not asked directly about their interethnic interactions and their views of the significance of it.

Since the various scales used to measure achievement motivation cannot be said to be valid for minority group children, the assumption that the achievement relevant values of their white peers are assumed by the minority group children cannot be validated. And, finally, inasmuch as the achievement test scores had no significant relationship to need for school achievement, the assumption that having high achievement motivation will enable a person to reach higher levels of academic achievement cannot support the lateral transmission hypothesis based on the data of the Riverside study. It cannot go unsaid that a very serious flaw in the Riverside study is that no serious attempt was made to construct measures that were not culture bound. The three ethnic groups in this regard were treated as though they were culturally homogeneous in ways of thinking and behaving and viewing the world. The other underlying culture-bound ethnocentric concept inherent in the protocol was that the only ways of thinking and feeling about motivation, achievement, school aspirations, and interpersonal relationships are those identical to white norms. Some of these theories will be discussed in regard to the work of Gurin and Epps (1975).

Since the Riverside study omitted data about the curriculum used in various schools, little can be said about improved achievement through normalization of instruction. Linsenmeier and Wortman (1978) make note of the fact that "indirect evidence" that performance standards differed in desegregated and minority group schools comes from information on the school grades received by Riverside children before and after the desegregation program was introduced. Following desegregation, grades received by white children gradually improved relative to their achievement test scores. At the same time the grades received by Afro-American and Mexican-American children gradually worsened.

The most significant and important finding of the Riverside study deals with the third model which the study intended to study: improved achievement as a consequence of the absence of discrimination. The assumptions are made that improved achievement among minority group children in desegregated schools is a consequence of the absence of discrimination because school desegregation fosters favorable attitudes on the part of the community and the school and minority group children's perception of their acceptance will enhance their self-perceptions. The data from Riverside were to the contrary. On all three measures of self-esteem minority students did less well before and after desegregation than white students. The assumption that improvement in self-esteem will cause improvement in academic achievement is not borne out by the Riverside study. School desegregation as reported by Powell (1970, 1973a, 1973b) does not remove minority group children from exposure to prejudiced attitudes. Powell's findings (1973a, 1972) showed that the self-esteem of Afro-American children in desegregated schools was significantly lower than those of Afro-American students in segregated schools. Other studies have confirmed these findings (Simmons and Rosenberg, 1972). The Riverside study, like the Rist study (1975), showed that classroom teachers viewed minority children as inferior to whites on those traits most closely linked to classroom performance.

The data from Riverside showed higher scores on the Lambert-Bower self-esteem measures for older Afro-American students and these were associated with increased academic achievement as measured by test scores and grades. However, further review showed that there was no consistent relationship when all grades and ethnic groups were considered. The investigators still conclude that with some justification that it is possible that beneficial effects of self-esteem on academic achievement could result from long-term exposure to desegregated classroom "where desegregation was an established way of life rather than a new and still evolving phenomenon."

The Riverside study has made a significant contribution in helping us examine the variables for positive self-esteem and academic performance for minority group children in school desegregation. However, considering the overwhelming prob-

lems in methodology and data analysis, it cannot be concluded that it is *the study* that proves school desegregation does *not* work. It can only be concluded that the Riverside study highlights certain aspects of school desegregation that need to be investigated more thoroughly and exactly. Based on the Riverside study, this author cannot concur with St. John (1975) about the dismal effects of school desegregation. Rather, it should be concluded that social scientists have had extreme difficulty in developing techniques to investigate and assess the many confounding variables involved in this complex political, educational, social, and emotional process.

The Outcomes of School Desegregation Among Northern Afro-American Adults

The National Opinion Research Center (NORC) survey of northern Afro-American adults was conducted at the request of the U.S. Civil Rights Commission in 1966 to assess the effects of attending a desegregated or segregated school. The survey included 1651 Afro-American men and women between the ages of 21 and 45 years from 25 metropolitan areas of the North. The northern Afro-American respondents are compared to 1326 white respondents from another NORC survey. The data reviewed here are from the Crain and Weisman (1972) book entitled, *Distrimination, Personality and Achievement*. This study is the first study which tries to evaluate the long-term effect of school desegregation after completion of high school and on into adulthood looking particularly at educational and occupational achievement as well as psychological effects and racial attitudes. The data regarding the effects of school desegregation on educational and occupational achievement are particularly germane to the debate over what effects if any school desegregation has on the academic achievement of Afro-American students. They clearly indicate that students who attended desegregated schools in the North during the elementary and high school years scored significantly higher on verbal achievement tests than those who did not attend desegregated schools. Indeed, the investigators note a trend for "respondents from all integrated schools scoring highest, those from mixed schools scoring second, and those from all segregated schools lowest" (p. 158). Family background did not prove to play a significant role in this finding. The data analysis indicated:

1) The association between mother's education and desegregation was too low to explain the academic achievement differences.
2) Afro-American students in the desegregated schools did not come from the highest SES families.
3) Although there was a tendency for students in desegregated schools to come from stable homes, the differences were insignificant and could not have affected the results.

In terms of the effects of school desegregation on educational achievement, subjects from desegregated schools had more education. Indeed, desegregation decreased the drop-out rate by 25%. There was also a tendency for desegregated schooling to lead to higher rates of college attendance—e.g. 32 percent of the men from desegregated schools went to college and 24 percent of those from segregated schools did. The investigators also found that 75 percent of the graduates from desegregated schools were more likely to finish college.

For those subjects who had "a mixed" school experience—segregated elementary school and desegregated high school, or vice versa—their educational attainment was similar to those who had attended desegregated schools throughout their school years. However, analysis of the separate effects of elementary and high school desegregation showed:

1) Desegregated high schools had a more significant effect on high school graduation than desegregated elementary schools.
2) Elementary desegregated schools seemed to be more significant in rates of college attendance.

An additional important finding on educational achievement was that in the North and in the South segregated schools favor the educational attainment of women more than men. However, in northern desegregated schools, men have higher educational attainment than women.

The Crain and Weisman (1972) study also found differences in occupational achievement between northern Afro-Americans from desegregated schools and those from segregated schools: Those from desegregated schools are more likely to be in occupations traditionally closed to Afro-Americans and earn more money. About one-third of Afro-American males from desegregated schools were in traditionally white occupations such as crafts, sales, and the professions and only 20 percent of the males from segregated schools were in such occupations. Particularly interesting was the fact that men from desegregated schools were more likely to be employed in an occupational group with less than a 3 percent Afro-American workforce. The investigators concluded that there was "convincing evidence that (Afro-American) alumni of 'integrated' (or desegregated) schools are in 'integrated' jobs" (p. 162). In addition, Afro-Americans in non-traditional jobs tend to be better educated and have higher incomes than those who are in more traditional jobs. These income differences are not completely explained by education, however.

The interactional and contextual effects of school desegregation explored by Crain and Weisman (1973) present some interesting insights into the actual interpersonal processes of desegregation. In this respect, the contextual effects of school desegregation were such that those Afro-

American adults who had attended desegregated schools were "less likely to be delinquent, less likely to be slow learners, less likely to drop out and more likely to go to college than the average Afro-American adult who attended segregated schools." The investigators attributed these findings to the predominance of white norms, especially regarding rates of dropouts and early marriage. They conceded, however, that the decrease in dropout rates among their desegregated high school graduates was "probably the result of school climate and a black student in a black school with a low dropout rate would probably be almost as likely to graduate as one in an integrated school" (pp. 165-166). The Gurin-Epps (1975) and Sowell (1974, 1976) studies focus on the milieu and school climate as important factors in the achievement of Afro-American students. Crain and Weisman (1972), however, infer that "a favorable school climate" is associated with a predominant middle-class student body. The Gurin-Epps (1975) review of achievement and identity among Afro-American students at Afro-American colleges indicated that family background and middle-class socioeconomic status were not the major variables mediating academic achievement; rather the strongest factor was the college environment which promoted personal collective identity within the context of achievement.

The most important interactional effects of school desegregation were that those Afro-American adults who had attended desegregated schools continued their interactions with whites in adulthood, were less anti-white, lived in integrated neighborhoods, and had more contacts with persons who were better educated, which in turn meant that "having friends who are white college graduates (paid) off in more information about job openings."

Although Crain and Weisman (1972) looked at the psychological effects of school desegregation vis-à-vis self-esteem, their self-esteem measures, in this author's judgment, are questionable in terms of what the investigators actually measured. Their measures of "happiness" and/or psychological well-being are also questionable in terms of their construct validity. Their most important finding, although based somewhat on their measures of self-esteem and happiness, was that "consistent schooling is better than inconsistent school." The negative effects of inconsistency in the child's racial experience were described in terms of marginality or a lack of a clear sense of belonging to either cultural group and culture shock leading to withdrawal and a tendency to cling to one's old culture or identity.

Part of the explanation for this may be that the personality develops over time, with certain phases of one's life being more important than others to the development of certain traits and skills. For example, elementary school integration has an important effect on personality as we have shown, but southern migrant children tend to be unprepared for integration and therefore cannot benefit at this level. Expectations learned in the South are unfulfilled by the integration experience, leaving the individual disoriented (p. 178).

This particular finding may have important relevancy about how the logistics of school desegregation could be worked out. However, the Crain-Weisman (1972) study has the major, but not serious limitation that their sample consisted of high school graduates of the early sixties back to the late thirties (1939 to 1963). The social context, urban environments, and economic conditions within the country have changed considerably since them. Wilson (1980) has explored in depth the changing political-economic structure of the United States and how it will affect the position of Afro-Americans in the 1980s. These changes are having profound effects on the process of school desegregation. Today, there are effects that may not have been as visibly operant from 1939 to 1963 as they will be in the 1980s. Whether the contextual and interactional effects of school desegregation will remain similar to those found in this important study remain to be seen.

The Cultural Context of Achievement and Identity Among Afro-American Students

An important part of the advancement of Afro-Americans in this country has been educational achievement. However, only the educational pathology is known and extensively documented, while the educational success has been relatively ignored and unstudied. Yet educational excellence among Afro-Americans has been achieved often in Afro-American educational settings.

In a well researched and well documented study, Sowell (1974) notes the achievement of Afro-American students from an Afro-American high school in Washington, D.C —"one of the most remarkable black educational success stories: Dunbar High School." For instance, Dunbar students scored the highest in tests given to both Afro-Americans and whites throughout the city. Of the 34 Dunbar students admitted to Amherst College between 1892 and 1954, more than 25 percent were Phi Beta Kappas. Dunbar graduates include: Benjamin Davis, the first Afro-American general; William H. Hastie, the first Afro-American judge; Robert C. Weaver, the first Afro-American cabinet member; Charles Drew, the discoverer of blood plasma; and Edmund W. Brooke, the first Afro-American Senator since Reconstruction. However, as Sowell has noted, the "ignoring" of Dunbar's achievement is most remarkable considering the voluminous outpouring of Afro-American educational pathology.

The Dunbar experience can be contrasted with and supported by the report of the National Scholarship and Service Fund for Afro-American Students which from 1948 to 1963 helped over 9,000 Afro-American students to enroll in interracial colleges situated mostly in the North (NSSFNS, 1963). The record of college success was far above the national average with 5.6 percent having an average of A or A -- 50.3 percent with a B average; 32.4 percent with a C average; and .7 percent with D averages or below (p. 9). Additional material on these students suggests that academic success was associated with social acceptance on the campus (Katz, 1964).

What the Dunbar history shows is the enormous importance of time, tradition, and institutional circumstances in providing the setting in which individual achievement can flourish. If such achievements were wholly or predominantly a matter of personal ability, so many outstanding individuals would not have come from one institution (Sowell, 1974 p. 16).

In another paper entitled "Patterns of Black Excellence," Sowell (1976) studied six of the Afro-American high schools from Bond's (1970) study of Afro-American scholars and professionals and two elementary schools with outstanding records of academic achievement. The high schools were chosen because the alumni had the most doctorates from 1957-1962. The Bond (1970) study of 609 Ph.D.s awarded to Afro-Americans between 1957-1962 showed 5.2 percent of the 360 different high schools attended by these Afro-American scholars had produced 20.8 percent of all the Ph.D.s. Dunbar High School in Washington, D.C. has already been noted as among that group of outstanding high schools. The other schools among the 5.2 percent included Booker T. Washington in Atlanta; St. Paul of the Cross in Atlanta; Frederick Douglass High School in Baltimore; St. Augustine High School in New Orleans; Xavier Preparatory School in New Orleans; and Brooklyn (N.Y.) P.S. 91. Four of the 5.2 percent of the oustanding Afro-American high schools produced a disportionate number of outstanding alumni:

1) McDonough 35 in New Orleans (Wilson Riles)
2) Frederick Douglass in Baltimore (Thurgood Marshall)
3) Dunbar High School in Washington
4) Booker T. Washington in Atlanta (Martin Luther King, Jr.)

The common denominators of these schools were: "1) dedication to education; 2) commitment to children and 3) faith in what it was possible to achieve" (Sowell, 1976 p. 53).

Wilson Riles, who graduated from McDonough 35, in recounting his high school years noted that the school took Afro-American children from economically and culturally limited backgrounds, "giving them both the education and self-confidence to advance later in life." Another prominent graduate of these six schools noted how teachers promoted the idea of self worth of the individual—how they always called the students "Mr." and "Miss," emotionally important titles in a segregated South. Other famous graduates emphasized the importance of the teachers who were counselors, instructors, and role models. Other characteristics that were noted in the schools Sowell (1976) studied were the structured settings, discipline, and respect within these schools; the outstanding characteristics and abilities of the principals; and ability groupings in the same classrooms. In his concluding comments, Sowell (1976) makes a major observation about these outstanding Afro-American schools and their alumni:

. . . the rise of such prominent (Afro-Americans) as those who came from these schools—which is to say, most of the top (Afro-American) pioneers in the history of this country—seems a matter less of innate ability and

more of special social settings in which individual ability developed . . . (p. 57).

Clearly both the milieu of these schools and educational leadership were major factors in the achievement records of these schools and their students.

Many of the pieces missing from the conflicting, inconsistent, and divergent data on academic achievement among Afro-American students can be found in the scholarly, well researched study of Afro-American students at Afro-American colleges in the South by Gurin and Epps (1975)—an area which has been overlooked and neglected by most educational researchers. Gurin and Epps give an in-depth insiders' view of a very critical aspect of self-concept for Afro-American youth. The dichotomy and "tension between individual and collective identity," a process that begins during preadolescence, never really ends for the Afro-American in this society. In examining the educational and occupational aspirations of Afro-American students in Afro-American colleges, Gurin and Epps elucidate the complex process by which these students resolve the *collective* base of their identity as they also strive for individual achievement and personal identity. Although it is not possible to review the entire eight-year study, some of the oustanding findings which contravene the myths about the achievements, aspirations, and motivations of Afro-American students need to be highlighted.

The first issue to be considered is the very term "achievement." According to Gurin and Epps (1975):

Reserving the term achievement only for the accomplishments of the individual misses the important elements of achievement motivation for the personal identities of minority (group) students. Group identification and collective commitments play an important role in identity formation. We foster minority (group) student's ambivalence about achievement if an exclusive press for individualistic mobility cements the fear that individual accomplishments must come at the expense of, or at least from the indifference to, other members of the group (p. 386).

The authors go on to note that typical achievement theory views family and group loyalties as inhibiting achievement because of the inevitable conflict between individual advancement and group or family goals, mores, or customs. Within this particular conceptualization of achievement, competition with others is the co-variable for individual achievement, while collective commitments are seen as negating personal achievement. They refute the theory that competition with others is necessary for the development of achievement motivation, noting that Russian school children develop individual achievement motivation from cooperative, rather than competitive, experiences within the peer group. Indeed, among the 10 colleges studied, those colleges which provided a milieu which fostered students' personal, educational and occupational goals but also "stressed communal and familial themes, especially the idea that success need not depend on the failure of others" (p. 387) were the most effective in enhancing individual achievement and personal expectancies of success among their students.

Gurin and Epps also critique the significance of "a differentiated conception of internal and external control" (p. 391). Performance on standard achievement tests has been highly correlated with internal scores on Internal-External Locus of Control scales, and particularly so for minority group students. Indeed, many intervention strategies have been mounted to increase the sense of internal control which many social scientists feel is the central issue in the attainment of academic achievement for minority group students. Supposedly, those students who have achieved a strong sense of personal

control perform better on traditional achievement tasks and have higher educational and occupational aspirations. The data from the Gurin and Epps study indicated that only some types of internal control carried positive motivational implications. The high achievers in these Afro-American colleges had high external control scores that were significantly associated with several of the traditional achievement indicators when they pertained to the external world—e.g. the role of social and economic factors which determined racial inequities.

Blaming the system was also associated with more effective performance at least among students who felt personally efficacious themselves. These results clearly showed that an external orientation promoted rather than inhibited healthy motivation when it depended on assessing systematic social forces that do realistically structure the achievements of minorities. . . . Students who managed to feel personally efficacious but recognized the critical role of systematic external forces in determining what happens in the lives of (Afro-Americans) also showed they could integrate collective and individual achievements (p. 392).

The third myth about Afro-American students' achievement that the Gurin and Epps data explode is the significance of family background. Instead, educational and occupational aspirations as well as students' expectancies of success were more significant than family background. The greater importance of current environmental resources and opportunities rather than the impact of early family socialization is clearly indicated by both Gurin and Epps (1975) and Sowell (1974, 1976) data.

The fourth crucial finding from the Gurin-Epps study was "the absolute irrelevance of father absence" on academic achievement. Family structure had no relationship to individual achievement as measured by grades, college entrance test scores, achievement tests, job aspirations or career goals, self-confidence about ability, or achievement motives and values. The importance of family status and socialization became more doubtful but the data buttress the importance of environmental opportunities and college socialization.

The study also exploded the myth of the dominance of the Afro-American woman over the Afro-American man, as well as the myth of the dominance of the affluent Afro-American student over the poverty of the Afro-American student. The poor students could not be distinguished from their affluent peers by motivation or academic performance. In short, the results of this study underscore that the interplay of the dynamics of motivation and the attainment of academic achievement for Afro-American students at 10 Afro-American colleges studied over a period of eight years heavily depended on environmental pressures and supports.

The Sowell studies (1974, 1976), the NSSFNS (1963) study and the Gurin and Epps' study (1975) have some commonality with the Afro-American students in segregated schools in the South that the author studied (Powell, 1973; Powell and Fuller, 1972). The expectation of achievement was there, personal and collective identity were stressed. The models for such were everywhere—the teachers who prodded students on because they knew they could do better, as well as the principals who espoused academic excellence and achievement and pride in one's heritage. The models were on the walls of the schools—Frederick Douglass, Marcus Garvey, George Washington Carver, Charles Drew. The message was clear: "They made it and so can you in spite of the adversities." Collective commitment to the group was taught at home and at school. Indeed, in one city all the segregated Afro-American schools were closed for a day because teachers, students, parents, shopkeepers, and community leaders were all at the fairgrounds to help with

The Poor People's March that was coming through their city (Powell, 1973a). The entire Afro-American community was committed to that effort as they has been to the entire Civil Rights Movement. For Afro-American students in Afro-American communities in the South, individual and collective commitment and achievements were stressed; the co-existence of each is so very vital for the total personal identity of the Afro-American student. Indeed, the survival of the Afro-American youth academically and psychologically is dependent upon the merger of these two levels of identity and these two types of achievement—individual and collective.

SUMMARY AND CONCLUSIONS: FROM SCHOOL DESEGREGATION TO SCHOOL INTEGRATION

There are two major processes which are rarely explicitly and methodologically addressed in the many studies attempting to measure the academic achievement in the desegregation of schools. The first and foremost is the distinction between a desegregated and an integrated school. Desegregation merely means the end of segregation of children in schools because of race or ethnic group membership. It means only that children of different races are attending the same school. Desegregation means that there has been legal compliance with the abolishment of separate schools for white and minority group students. Desegregation relates only to the way the *de jure* or *de facto* segregation is logistically accomplished. Desegregation does not deal with what actually goes on within the school after the children have entered the door. It is only the first step, and maybe one of many steps, to equality of educational opportunity. It is only the first step towards school integration.

School integration is a more difficult process to achieve and will be determined by how carefully the first step, school desegregation, is accomplished. School integration and school desegregation are not synonymous. To integrate a school is to *unify* a school—to unify the various aspects of the school into a coordinated, harmonious process whereby all of the students feel they belong to that school and participate equally in all of the programs in the school. With public education in the state that it is in, it may be that there are no integrated schools even in all white schools. It is important, however, that we remain clear about the distinction between the two processes—school desegregation and school integration—so that we may be clearer about which process we are evaluating. The distinction is rarely explicitly defined in most of the school desegregation literature, which largely concerns school desegregation and its outcomes and not school integration. We need to focus, then, on how to change a desegregated school into an integrated school and prevent the resegregation after the initial desegregation has been implemented. Then we can begin to assess more accurately the consequences for children in terms of academic achievement, psychosocial development, and racial attitudes.

In an extensive review of studies on academic achievement and school desegregation, Weinberg (1975) enumerates several factors which lead to academic achievement gains for Afro-American students in desegregated schools:

1) an absence of interracial hostility;
2) acceptance of minority group students by teachers and administrators who are encouraged to attend in-service training programs;
3) the predominance of middle and upper SES students in each classroom;
4) classroom desegregation, especially in elementary schools;
5) absence of rigid ability grouping or tracking;
6) acceptance by the community of the desegregation plan;
7) the involvement of younger children in desegregation.

From the author's conceptualization of the school desegregation to school integration process, Weinberg has outlined some basic processes which are necessary to move from a desegregated school to as nearly as humanly possible an integrated school and prevent the resegregation process.

It is important to discuss the first factor listed among Weinberg's seven needs. Although a review of the literature on the effects of school desegregation/school integration is fraught with many conflicting results and conclusions, one theme does ring out loud and clear: Interracial hostility is a deterrent to the process and interracial harmony and acceptance promote favorable academic and psychological consequences for all children. Chapter 31 by Berkowitz, Anderson, and Carr will be helpful to the school consultant in understanding how to help prevent the hostile interactions among the students and between students and teachers and presents some problem-solving techniques that have been helpful in decreasing hostile interaction.

The importance of the human relations aspects of the school desegregation process has been stressed by many. For instance, Clement et al. (1976) concluded in their review of the desegregation literature that mere "social race mixing alone has little consistent effect on black-white outcomes" (p. 47). Pettigrew et al. (1973), in his review of school desegregation, concluded that where there are negative effects and even no effects, conditions for positive intersocial contact were not well-established in the desegregation setting.

In his summary of principles relevant to successful school desegregation, Miller (1977) outlines "a set of well-accepted social science principles that bear on the design of a successful desegregation program" (note again the word desegregation and not integration). Among the principles for beneficial interracial contact, he lists:

1) Desegregation plans should explicitly implement the conditions of favorable contact.
2) Desegregation plans should minimize the adverse effects of the achievement gap.
3) Use of criterion-referenced testing should be expanded.
4) Multicultural curriculum and programs should be coordinated with interracial contact.
5) Desegregation plans should include programs to increase the multiracial composition of the teaching and administrative staff.
6) Desegregation plans should rely on voluntary action and choice as extensively as possible.
7) Teacher selection and preparation must precede the implementation of desegregation plans.

The second set of principles listed among Weinberg's (1975) factors which mediated academic achievement gains for minority group children in the desegregated-moving-towards-integrated schools are those of classroom desegregation and the absence of rigid ability grouping or tracking.

The Equality of Educational Opportunity Survey (E.E.O.S.) (Coleman et al., 1966) reported that the average Afro-American students' verbal ability scores were one standard deviation below the mean scores of white students and that there was a widening performance level gap at successive grade levels between Afro-American and white students. The most significant finding, however, was that when family background was controlled, other attributes of Afro-American students accounted for far more variation in the verbal ability scores than did any school environment and teacher variable. Indeed, Afro-American students' verbal

ability scores increased as the proportion of white students in the schools increased, leading to the now infamous "lateral transmission of values hypothesis." Thus, the positive relationship between Afro-American students' academic achievement and the proportion of white students in the school was the result of Afro-American students' acquisition of achievement-related values held by whites. However, the reanalysis of the E.E.O.S. data by Cohen et al. (1972) and U.S. Commission on Civil Rights (U.S.C.C.R.) (1967) and McPartland (1968) indicate that, in fact, the increase in academic achievement scores of Afro-American children was the result of the actual numbers of white students in the classroom and not just in the school.

It has already been noted that desegregation plans should explicitly implement the conditions for favorable interracial contact and minimize the adverse effects of the achievement gap (Miller, 1977). However, so very often in a newly desegregated school the Afro-American students are put in the remedial classes, leaving the academic classes entirely white. This process begins the resegregation of the desegregated school which then extends to the social interaction process where whites intermingle only with whites and Afro-Americans interact only with Afro-Americans. No achievement gains are seen in schools with such rigid ability grouping and tracking. The message given is that whites are superior to Afro-Americans, which then serves as a catalyst for the development of interracial hostility. Although numerous studies have indicated that it is the classroom desegregation-to-integration that leads to academic achievement gains for Afro-American students, many schools still insist upon this practice of tracking, sometimes out of fear that the Afro-American students will interfere with the quality of education for white students although numerous studies have indicated that white students do not decline in academic achievement in the desegregation-to-integration process (Coleman et al., 1966; Weinberg, 1975). Sadly enough, the practice often continues in spite of the evidence of the negative effects on the achievement of Afro-American students when teachers believe Afro-American children cannot achieve (Jones, 1973).

Finally and importantly, the third set of Weinberg's (1975) recommendations to promote academic achievement gains for minority group children are that the minority group students need to be accepted by teachers and administrators who have received preparation for the process of desegregation-to-integration and that there be acceptance by the community of the desegregation plan. Such principles as the use of multicultural curricula and criterion-referenced testing, and teacher selection and preparation have also been emphasized as effective means of accomplishing the task of beneficial interracial contact and academic achievement gains (Miller, 1977).

There have been numerous studies which indicate that the classroom teacher is the *crucial* ingredient in classroom integration. Her attitudes toward her children, her teaching skills, her basic understanding and knowledge of the growth and development of children, her willingness to even *learn* about the cultural heritage as well as the developmental process of minority group children are essential to the success of the integrated learning experience. In-service training of teachers is *not* enough. No teacher in the public schools should be able to receive a teacher's credential or license to teach until he/she has been trained in multicultural teaching techniques, has had sufficient course material in the growth and development of children in general and in the psychosocial development of minority group children in particular. School officials, principals and teachers *must* be held accountable for the outcome for children. This author maintains that the decreased learning outcomes for minority group

children in the public schools of this country are iatrogenic. If the process of desegregating the schools has not worked, it is because the public schools have not wanted it to work. In so many instances where minority group children have not succeeded, it is because teachers and school administrators have not wanted them to succeed (Kozol, 1967). They have followed the letter of the law, but not the spirit of the law. A great deal has been said about how to teach minority group children how to learn, a great deal more needs to be said and done about teaching teachers how to teach *all* children effectively and humanely.

Yet the schools cannot stand alone in this difficult political social change process. The community must be accepting of the school desegregation plan. Smith, Downs, and Lachman (1973) discuss in detail techniques for achieving effective desegregation which include: a) curriculum adaptations; b) student adaptations; c) teaching techniques and training; and, most importantly, d) administrative measures and community relations. Unfortunately, the latter often get ensnarled in the political process and the issue of school financing, issues which have not been discussed here but are critical to the desegregation-to-integration process. However, as long as our goal is merely desegregation, there will be no benefits to any children—only the continued psychological, educational, and spiritual annihilation of the minority group children in our nation's public schools. Those who survive the system do so in spite of it.

In conclusion, since 1954 we have moved from *de jure* segregation to *de jure* desegregation, and from *de facto* segregation to uncommited desegregation. Integration of the nation's public schools has not occurred in most instances and is beginning only in a few communities where parents and teachers are dedicated to an integrated learning experience in spite of school boards, administrators, and politicians. Secondly, public school education is a dying institution not because of school desegregation but because we as a nation have not committed our dollars or technology to the education of our youth. In order to survive, the system needs new blood, new technology, better trained teachers who are adequately paid for their services and given the professional status and esteem they need, more appropriate evaluation techniques, and, most important, learning environments that promote not only the intellectual growth of children but the psychological and social enhancement of all children. Finally, schools, teachers, parents, and children cannot do it alone—the Presidency, the Congress, and the courts must also be committed. The kind of educational revolution I am espousing means that our country must be more committed to books than to bombs.

REFERENCES

Allport, G. W. *Pattern and Growth in Personality.* New York: Holt, Rinehart and Winston, 1963.

Allport, F. H. et al. The effects of segregation and the consequence of desegregation: A social science statement. *Minnesota Law Review*, 1952, *37*, 429-440.

Armor, D. J. The evidence on busing. *The Public Interest*, Summer 1972, *28*, 90-126.

Asher, S. R., and Aller, V. J. Racial preference and social comparison processes. *Journal of Social Issues*, 1969, *25*(10), 157-166.

Bachman, M. E. Relationship of ethnicity, socioeconomic status and sex to patterns of mental abilities. Doctoral dissertation, Columbia University, 1970 (Univ. Microfilms Order No. 73-8929), 1970.

Bailey, S. K. *Disruption in Urban Secondary Schools.* Washington, D.C.: National Association of Secondary School Principals, 1971.

Bond, H. M. *The Education of the Negro in the American Social Order.* New York: Octagon Books, 1970.

Bradley, L. A. and Bradley, G. W. The academic achievement of Black students: A critical review. *Journal of Educational Research*, Summer 1977, *47*(3), 399-499.

Campbell, D. T. and Stanley, J. C. *Experimental and Quasiexperimental Designs for Research.* Chicago: Rand McNally, 1963.

Caruthers, M. W. School desegregation and racial cleavage, 1954-1970: A review of the literature. *Journal of Social Issues*, 1970, *26*, 25-47.

Clark, K. B. *Prejudice and Your Child.* Boston: Beacon, 1955.

Clark, K. B. and Clark, M. K. The development of consciousness of self and the emergence of racial identification in Negro pre-school children. *Journal Social Psychology*, 1939, *10*, 591-599.

Clark, K. B. and Clark, M. P. Racial identification and preference in Negro children. In: T. M. Newcomb and E. L. Hartley (Eds.), *Readings in Social Psychology.* New York: Holt, 1947.

Clement, D. C., Eisengart, M., and Wood, J. W. School desegregation and educational inequality—Trends in the literature 1960-1975. In: *The Desegregation Literature—A Critical Appraisal.* Washington, D.C.: DHEW, 1976.

Cohen, D. K., Pettigrew, T. F., and Riley, R. T. Race and the outcomes of schooling: In: F. Mostellen and D. P. Moynihan (Eds.), *On Equality of Educational Opportunity.* New York: Random House, 1972.

Coleman, J. S., Campbell, E. Q., Hobson, C. J., McPartland, J., Mood, A. M., Weinfeld, F. D., and York, R. L. *Equality of Educational Opportunity.* Washington, D.C.: U.S. Government Printing Office, 1966.

Coopersmith, S. *The Antecedents of Self-esteem.* San Francisco: W. H. Freeman, 1967.

Crain, R. L. School integration and academic achievement of Negroes. *Sociology of Education*, 1972, *44*.

Crain, R. L. and Weisman, C. S. *Discrimination, Personality and Achievement: A Survey of Northern Blacks.* New York: Seminar Press, 1972.

Criswell, J. H. A Sociometric Study of Race Cleavage in the Classroom. New York: *Archives of Psychology*, January 1939, *33*(225), 5-82.

Datcher, A. H., Savage, J. E., and Chechosky, S. F. School type, grade, sex, and race of experimenter as determinants of the racial preference and awareness in black and white children. *Journal of Social and Behavioral Sciences*, 1973, *20*, 41-49.

Dentler, R. A. and Elkins, C. Intergroup attitudes, academic performance, and racial composition. In: R. A. Dentler, B. Mackler, and M. E. Warshauer (Eds.), *The Urban R's: Race Relation as the Problem in Urban Education.* New York: Praeger, 1967.

Dreger, R. M. and Miller, K. S. Comparative psychological studies of Negroes and Whites in the United States: *Psychol. Bull.*, 1960, *57*, 361-402.

Dreger, R. M. and Miller, K. S. Comparative psychological studies of Negroes and Whites in the United States: 1959-1965. *Psychol. Bull.* September 1968, *70*(Supplement), 1-58.

Dwyer, R. J. A report on patterns of interaction in desegregated schools. *Journal of Educational Sociology*, March 1958, 253-256.

Epps, E. E. The impact of school desegregation on aspirations, self-concepts and other aspects of personality. In: R. L. Jones (Ed.), *Black Psychology* Second Edition. New York: Harper & Row, 1980.

Epstein, Y. M., Krupat, E., and Obudho, C. E. Clean is beautiful: The effects of race and cleanliness in racial preferences. In: E. Krupat (Ed.), *Readings and Conversations in Social Psychology: Psychology is Social.* Glenview, IL: Scott, Foresman, 1975.

Evans, C. L. The immediate effects of classroom integration on the academic progress, self-concept, and racial attitude of Negro elementary children. Doctoral dissertation, North Texas State University, 1969 (University Microfilms Order No. 70-9127).

Forehand, G. A. and Ragosta, M. *A Handbook for Integrated Schooling*. A Report Prepared under Contract No. OEC-0-6341. U.S. DHEW, July 1976.

Fox, D. J. and Jordan, V. B. Racial preference and identification of Black, American, Chinese, and White children. *Genetic Psychology Monographs*, November 1973, *88*(2), 229-286.

French, J. T. Educational desegregation and selected self-concept factors of lower-class Black children. Doctoral Dissertation, Florida State University, 1972 (University Microfilms Order No. 72,27,914).

Frenkel-Brunswick, E. and Havel, J. Prejudice in the interviews of children: I. Attitudes toward minority groups. *Journal of Genetic Psychology*, 1953, *82*, 91-136.

Gastright, J. and Smith, L. Friendly mixing. *Human Behavior*, 1972, *1*(5), 52.

Gerard, H. B. and Miller, N. (Eds.) *School Desegregation: A Long-term Study*. New York: Plenum Press, 1975.

Glasgow, D. G. *The Black Underclass: Poverty, Unemployment and Entrapment of Ghetto Youth*. San Francisco: Jossey-Bass, 1980.

Goodman, M. A. *Race Awareness in Young Children*. Cambridge, MA: Addison-Wesley Press, 1952.

Gordon, L. The Carver-Oak park merger. *Integrated Education*, June/July, 1965, *3*, 26-32.

Green, J. A. and Gerard, H. B. School desegregation and ethnic attitudes. In: H. Fromkin and J. Sherwood (Eds.), *Integrating the Organization*. New York: Free Press, 1974.

Gregor, A. J. and McPherson, D. A. Racial attitudes among White and Negro Children in a deep South standard metropolitan area. *Journal of Social Psychology*, 1966, *68*, 95-106.

Gurin, P. Social class constraints on the occupational aspirations of students attending some predominately Negro colleges. *Journal of Negro Education*, 1966, *35*, 336-50.

Gurin, P. and Epps, E. Some characteristics of students from poverty backgrounds attending predominantly Negro colleges in the deep South. *Social Forces*, 1966, *45*, 27-40.

Gurin, P. and Epps, E. *Black Consciousness,Identity, and Achievement: A Study of Students in Historically Black Colleges*. New York: John Wiley & Sons, 1975.

Hall, M. W. and Gentry, H. W. Isolation of Negro students in integrated public schools. *Journal of Negro Education*, Spring 1969.

Havighurst, R. J., Smith, F. L., and Wilder, D. E. *Profile of the Large-City High School*. Washington, D.C.: National Association of Secondary School Principals, November, 1970.

Hobart, C. W. Underachievement among minority group students: An analysis and a proposal. *Phylon*, 1964, *24*(2), 184-196.

Horowitz, E. L. Development of attitude toward the Negro. *Archives of Psychology*, 1936, 194, 246-254.

Horwitz, R. Racial aspects of self-identification in nursery school children. *Journal of Psychology*, 1939, *7*, 91-99.

Hrabra, J. The doll technique: A measure of racial ethnocentrism. *Social Forces*, June 1972, *50*(4), 522-527.

Hrabra, J. and Grant, G. Black is beautiful: A reexamination of racial preference and identification. *Journal of Personality and Social Psychology*, 1970, *16*, 398-402.

Jones, R. L. Racism, mental health, and the schools. In: C. V. Willie, R. Kramer, and B. Brown (Eds.), *Racism and Mental Health*. Pittsburgh, PA: University of Pittsburgh Press, 1973.

Katz, I. Review of evidence relating to effects of desegregation on intellectual performance of Negroes. *American Psychologist*, 1964, *19*, 381-399.

Keach, E. T., Fulton, R. F., and Gardner, W. E. (Eds.) *Education and Social Crises: Perspectives on Teaching Disadvantaged Youth*. New York: John Wiley & Sons, 1967.

Kluger, R. *Simple Justice*. New York: Knopf, 1976.

Kozol, J. *Death at an Early Age*. Boston: Houghton Mifflin, 1967.

Laird, M. A. and Weeks, G. J. The effects of busing on achievement in reading and arithmetic in three Philadelphia schools. Philadelphia: Board of Education, Division of Research, 1966.

Linsenmeir, J. A. W. and Wortman, P. M. The Riverside School study of desegregation: A re-examination. *Research Review of Equal Education*, 1978, *2*(2), 3-37.

Lombardi, D. N. Factors affecting changes in attitudes toward Negroes among high school students. *Journal of Negro Education*, 1963, *32*, 129-136.

MacLennan, B. W. Community mental health professionals assist in school desegregation. In: W. L. Claiborn and R. Cohen (Eds.), *School Intervention Volume I*. New York: Behavioral Publications, 1973.

Maehr, M. L. Culture and achievement motivation. *American Psychologist*, 1974, *29*, 887-896.

Marascuillo, L. and Leven, J. R. Inter- and intraracial group differences in the perception of a social situation. Paper presented at annual meeting of American Educational Research Association, 1966.

McPartland, J. The relative influence of school desegregation and of classroom desegregation on the academic achievement of ninth grade Negro students. Interim Report. Baltimore: Center for the Study of Social Organizations of Schools, John Hopkins University, 1968.

Miller, N. Principles relevant to successful school desegregation. Los Angeles: Social Science Research Institute, University of Southern California, August, 1977.

Morland, J. K. Racial recognition by nursery school children in Lynchburg, Virginia. *Social Forces*, 1958, *37*, 132-137.

Morland, J. K. A comparison of race awareness in Northern and Southern Children. *American Journal of Orthopsychiatry*, January 1966, *37*, 132-137.

Morris, W. *Yazoo, Integration in a Deep South Town*.

New York: Harper and Row, 1971.

Moskovitz, J. M. and Wortman, P.M. A Secondary Analysis of the Riverside School Desegregation Study. Draft paper. Evanston, IL: Northwestern University Psychology Department, 1977.

National Conference on Christians and Jews. Desegregation without turmoil: The role of the multi-racial community coalition in preparing for smooth transition, 1977.

National Scholarship and Service Fund for Negro Students: Annual Report 1962-1963. New York: NSSFNS, 1963.

Obudho, C. E. *Black-White Racial Attitudes: An Annotated Bibliography*. Westport, CT: Greenwood Press, Second Edition, 1977.

Patchen, M. and Davison, J. D. (with G. Hoffman on William Brown). *Patterns and Determinants of Inter-Racial Interaction in the Indianapolis High Public Schools*. West Lafayette, Indiana: Department of Sociology and Anthropology, Purdue University, July 1973.

Pettigrew, T. A. Social evaluation theory: Convergences and applications. In: D. Levine (Ed.), *Nebraska Symposium on Motivation*. Lincoln, NB: University of Nebraska Press, 1967, pp. 241-311.

Pettigrew, T. F., Smith, M., Useem, E. L., and Normad, C. Busing: A review of the evidence. *Public Interest*, 1973, *30*, 88-118.

Pettigrew, T. F. Trends in research on racial discrimination. In: T. F. Pettigrew (Ed.), *Racial Discrimination in the United States*. New York: Harper & Row, 1975.

Powell, G. J. Self-concept, academic achievement, and school desegregation. Invited paper presented at the American Education Research Association Annual Meeting. San Francisco, April 1969.

Powell, G. J. *Black Monday's Children: A Study of Psychological Effects of School Desegregation on Southern School Children*. New York: Appleton-Century-Croft, 1973a.

Powell, G. J. The self-concept of white and black children: Some regional variables. In: C. V. Willie, B. Kramer, and B. Brown (Eds.), *Racism and Mental Health*. Pittsburgh, PA: University of Pittsburgh Press, 1973b.

Powell, G. J. The impact of television on the self-concept development of minority group children. In: G. Berry and C. Mitchell-Kernan (Eds.), *Television and the Socialization of the Ethnic Minority Group Child*. New York: Academic Press, 1982a.

Powell, G. J. A six city study of school desegregation and self-concept among Afro-American junior high school students: A preliminary study with implications for mental health. In: B. Bass, G. Wyatt, and G. J. Powell (Eds.), *The Afro-American Family: Assessment, Treatment and Research Issues*. New York: Grune & Stratton, 1982b.

Powell, G. J. and Fuller, M. The Variables for positive self-concept among young Southern black adolescents. *Journal of National Medical Association*, 1972.

Powell, G. J. and Marielle, F. Self-concept and school desegregation. *American Journal of Orthopsychiatry*, 1970, *40*, 303-304.

Proshansky, H. and Newton, P. Colour: The nature and meaning of negro self-identity. In: P. Watson (Ed.), *Psychology and Race*. Chicago: Aldine, 1974.

Purl, M. C. and Dawson, J. A. The achievement of students in primary grades after seven years of desegregation. Riverside, CA: Riverside Unified School District, 1973.

Radke, M. and Trager, H. G. Children's perceptions of the social roles of Negroes and Whites. *Journal of Psychology*, 1950, *29*, 2-33.

Rist, R. C. Student social class and teacher expectation: The self-fulfilling prophecy in ghetto education. In: Challenging the myths: The schools, the Blacks, the poor. *Harvard Educational Review*, 1975, Reprint Series No. 5, 70-111.

Rosenberg, M. *Conceiving The Self*. New York: Basic Books, 1979.

Rosenberg, M. and Simmons, R. G. Black and White self-esteem: The urban school child. *Rose Monograph Series*. Washington, D.C.: American Sociological Association, 1972.

Rosenthal, R. and Jacobson, L. F. *Pygmalion in the Classroom: Teacher Expectations and Pupils Intellectual Development*. New York: Holt, Rinehart & Winston, 1968.

Seward, G. *Psychotherapy and Culture Conflict*. New York: Ronald Press, 1956.

Silverman, I. and Shaw, M. E. Effects of sudden mass school desegregation on interracial interaction and attitudes in one southern city. *Journal of Social Issues*, 1973, *29*, 133-142.

Singer, D. Reading, writing, and race relations. *Trans-Action*, 1967, *4*(7), 27-31.

Smith, A., Downs, A., and Lachman, M. L. *Achieving Effective Desegregation*. Lexington, MA: Lexington Books, 1973.

Sowell, T. Black excellence: The case of Dunbar high school. *The Public Interest*, 1974, *4*(3), 11-18.

Sowell, T. Patterns of black excellence. *The Public Interest*, 1976, *43*, 26-58.

Spurlock, J. Some consequences of racism for children. In: C. V. Willie, B. M. Kramer, and B. Brown (Eds.), *Racism and Mental Health*. Pittsburgh, PA: University of Pittsburgh Press, 1973.

Stephan, W. G. Cognitive differentiation and intergroup perception. *Sociometry*, 1977, *40*, 50-58.

Stephan, W. G. School Desegregation: An evaluation of predictions made in Brown vs. Board of Education. *Psychological Bulletin*, March 1978, *85*(2), 217-238.

Stevenson, H. W. and Stewart, E. C. A developmental study of racial awareness in young children. *Child Development*, 1958, *29*, 399-409.

St. John, N. H. The elementary classroom as a frog pond: Self-concept, sense of control and social context. *Social Forces*, 1971, *49*, 581-595.

St. John, N. H. *School Desegregation: Outcomes for Children*. New York: John Wiley & Sons, 1975.

Thompson, W. Correlates of self-concept. Dede Wallace Center, Monograph VI. Nashville: Counselor Recordings and Test, 1972.

U.S. Commission on Civil Rights. *Racial Isolation in the Public Schools* Volume 1. Washington, D.C.: U.S. Government Printing Office, 1967.

Uslem, E. Review of School Desegregation by H. B. Gerard and N. Miller. *Harvard Educational Review*, 1977, *47*, 71-74.

Webster, S. W. The influence of interracial contact on social acceptance in a newly integrated school. *Journal of Educational Psychology*, 1961, *52*, 292-296.

Weinberg, M. The relationship between school desegregation and academic achievement: A review of the research. *Law and Contemporary Problems*, 1975, *39*, 240-270.

Weinberg, M. *Minority Students: A Research Appraisal*. U.S. DHEW, National Institute of Education. Washington, D.C.: U.S. Government Printing Office, 1977.

Willie, C. V. (with Beker, J.) *Race Mixing in the Public Schools*. New York: Prager, 1973.

Wilson, A. N. *The Developmental Psychology of the Black Child*. New York: Africana Research Publications, 1980.

Williams, J. E., Best, D. L., and Boswell, D. A. The measurement of children's racial attitudes in the early school years. *Child Development*, 1975, *46*, 494-500.

Wylie, R. C. *The Self-Concept: Vol. II. Theory and Research on Selected Topics*. Lincoln, NB: University of Nebraska Press, Revised Edition. 1978.

CHAPTER 27

Attending to the Emotional Needs of Junior High School Students and Staff During Desegregation

Irving H. Berkovitz, M.D.,

Elizabeth Carr, R.N., M.N.

and George Anderson, M.S.W.

Young people in junior high schools (grades 7-9) can benefit from assistance for emotional needs possibly more than any other age group. This is so especially because this age (11-14) involves setting a foundation for future attitudes to learning, peer relating, appreciation of self and others, attending school, and use of violent or peaceful expression of aggression (Miller, 1970; Berkovitz, 1980a). During desegregation, especially the beginning phase, these issues are aggravated for young people because of the uncertainty, new procedures and the time needed for educators to adjust to changes. In addition, if school district leaders and parent groups are open and insistent about their opposition to particular methods of implementing the desegregation, e.g., busing, this can cause confusion and encouragement of oppositional attitudes and possibly behavior problems in some students, as well as in some staff.

In 1978-79 Los Angeles Unified School District began court mandated desegre-

Susan Moan, R.N. helped with consulting and editing. Numerous educators helped with useful comments and corrections. While not all can be mentioned, the integration coordinators—Mitzi Kono and Ken Latzer—deserve special thanks. This consultation would not have been possible without the sanction and the ready acceptance of the Area 4 Assistant Superintendent, Mrs. Eugenia Scott.

gation for grades 4-8. This paper will describe the impact of this desegregation process on the educational-psychosocial environment of a pair of junior high schools (grades 7-8) and the influences contributed by the involvement of mental health consultants from the Los Angeles County Department of Mental Health. Events in the District as a whole will not be detailed or evaluated here. The highlight of the consultants' experience was seen in the school staff's developing sensitivity to the needs of minority students and the improvement of services for the emotional needs of all students.

While the presence and participation of the consultants provided tangible as well as intangible effects on the program and the process of the desegregation effort, the major directions and content were provided by the school staffs, both in the schools and in the district administrative offices.

Mental health consultation to school personnel has been provided to many educators for decades, for better attention to student problems, as well as to system problems and program development (Caplan, 1969; Berlin, 1962; Berkovitz, 1980a). Consultation during desegregation has been less frequent (MacLennan, 1973; Batson and Peters, 1976).

The type of consultative experience to be described here has not been previously reported and undoubtedly is unique due to the individual schools involved and the special history of school consultation in Los Angeles County (Berkovitz and Thomsen, 1973). The special benefits and techniques of mental health consultation to school personnel have been detailed in the articles cited above.

The two junior high schools to be described were racially segregated prior to desegregation. School M, located in Los Angeles proper, was 90% minority, primarily black. School C, located in an affluent section of suburban San Fernando Valley, was 90% Caucasian. These schools

agreed to enter into a pairing in order to comply with the court-ordered desegregation. "White flight" from school C just prior to September, 1978 resulted in the loss of about 500 students. The 100 Caucasian students who remained to be bused from School C resulted in a ratio of 80% minority to white in the 7th and 8th grades at school M. The 350-400 minority students bused from School M resulted in a 60% ratio of minority to white at School C. At both schools 9th graders were not moved. There were 400 primarily black 9th graders at School M and 600 primarily white 9th graders at School C. Hispanics and other minorities averaged 10-20 percent in each school. School C already had 15-20 percent voluntary bused minority students (300).

Mental health consultation takes place primarily with staff members in the expectation that benefits will result for students, as well as staff. In this particular project, consultants had more discussion contact with students than would occur in the usual consultation. However, this contact with students did differ from that of school personnel. With the consultant the contact was only periodic and did not usually relate to academic content. Often it was intended to demonstrate procedures to school personnel. In this presentation, while the major input was to staff, a strong focus will be on the changes evidenced by students. First, we will present the consultative activities with integration coordinators, counseling staff and teachers.

WORKING WITH INTEGRATION COORDINATORS

The mental health consultants worked closely with the principals and assistant principals, but especially with the newly appointed *integration coordinators* at each school. The integration coordinators had primary responsibility for directing the desegregation activities in each school. Each had previously been a teacher in the school. They were receptive to close collaboration with the consultants so that several innovative staff development programs and services were developed to address desegregation needs. For example, one consultant at School C suggested that she, the integration coordinator, and the bus drivers meet to explore that dimension of the students' lives. As a result of this meeting, a rap group was held, facilitated by the consultant, first with the bus drivers alone and then also with selected students who exhibited behavior problems on the bus. Follow up revealed that communication between bus drivers and students dramatically improved to the point that students were no longer receiving bus suspensions.

COUNSELING SERVICES

Prior to desegregation, the emphasis of counseling at school C was educational guidance and class scheduling, which involved extensive paperwork. A counselor's caseload was approximately 500 students. Counselors felt that they did not have enough time to provide the meaningful counseling service needed in a junior high school. For example, there was not sufficient group or individual counseling (prior to desegregation). The head counselor had long wanted the opportunity to develop with her staff expanded counseling services.

School desegregation made this possible through additional funding and staff for counseling services at both schools. Class size was reduced to 27 students. In addition, a counselor's caseload was reduced to 350 pupils. At School C an assistant counselor and additional clerical staff were hired. The head counselor took this opportunity for change and requested program consultation from the mental health consultants.

Prior to desegregation at School M, counselors used the "whole child approach." Essentially, this involved attention to discipline and left less time for counseling of emotional or behavioral problems. Students were referred to the counselors for classroom disturbance, fighting, and management problems in general. With the arrival of the more verbal students from School C, the counseling staff quite naturally found itself spending more time getting to know these students. There was a planned effort to see all the seventh and eighth graders and to let them know of counseling availability. Also, with the reduction in a counselor's caseload, more time was available for counseling. Counselors reported that the students from School C were demanding, articulate, and challenging. Several new programs were developed at both schools:

1) Weekly staffing case conferences for faculty and counselors where individual student problems were presented and discussed.
2) Group counseling was introduced for each grade level. Counselors co-led groups with a social worker from an additional outside agency.
3) Noon-time rap groups for students were instituted.
4) Classroom discussion groups became an expanded feature at both schools. Consultant and counselor(s) would enter a classroom after being invited or after requesting a visit with the teacher of that classroom. Counselors later discussed these classroom experiences with the consultants. Through observation and this follow-up evaluation, they enhanced their skills in working with groups. These discussions with students were primarily unstructured, soliciting reactions from students about the process of the educational experience so far this year, not necessarily related to desegregation, but con-

cerned with that if the students wished to discuss it. Many did.

All of these programs enhanced the communication and relationship between the teachers and counselors at both schools. The classroom discussion groups demonstrated to teachers the value of a counseling type discussion in the classroom. Faculty reported benefit from the staffing conferences where they shared experiences and problem solved around approaches with a troubled child.

TEACHERS

The consultants first met the teachers at the staff development program prior to the opening of the school in the fall of 1978. Two of the consultants each conducted one-hour discussions with a group of 10-15 teachers. Discussion centered around understanding and working with depressed, withdrawn, and angry teenagers. Teachers from School C, with little experience teaching minority students, were interested in the experience of teachers from School M relevant to classroom management, student motivation, and effective teaching approaches. Later reports from these teachers indicated an appreciation and feeling of value regarding this opportunity for discussion.

As the fall semester progressed at School C, teachers complained of difficulty maintaining student attention and work habits. They found that their previously effective teaching methods no longer motivated their students. Teachers reacted in a number of ways. There was an initial increase in frequency of student referrals to the office for such issues as disruptiveness or missing a pencil or book. Some teachers were openly dissatisfied and spoke pessimistically about the entire desegregation effort. A few teachers had difficulty in appreciating the differences in learning patterns for many of the minority stu-

dents. Others did accept that there was a different educational task and made efforts to change their expectations and styles of teaching and discipline. Some faculty reported that the minority students were more respectful and less unruly than they had anticipated, and expressed satisfaction with the desegregation plan. This wide range of responses demonstrates the complexity of the problems confronting teachers and consultants.

At School M, parents from both communities expressed concern about the academic quality of the school, although it had been generally good. They were vociferous in their demands that their children be more academically challenged. At the same time, parents from School C had a long-standing reputation of placing intensive pressure on teachers regarding academic standards and teaching styles. Teachers at School M initially expressed some apprehension in anticipation of pressures from parents of School C. However, as the school year progressed, this apprehension dissolved.

One consultant (G.A.) established a relationship with the teacher of the special class for educationally handicapped students at School M. He consulted around the emotional needs and available resources for these children, as well as assisting with classroom management techniques. Some teachers requested rap/support groups for themselves. This was minimally attended when offered.

STUDENTS

A visitation program was arranged for the prospective seventh and eighth grade students at Schools C and M in the Spring, 1978. There was an opportunity for students to tour the school and meet students who were currently enrolled in the schools they were visiting.

A small group of students from both

schools were involved in a rap group in June, 1978, and reported feeling pleasure at the prospect of visiting and attending a new school in the Fall because they now had friends. They exchanged information about the teachers at each school, course content, activities, and so on. Students looked forward to learning more about each other, for example, dance steps, special customs, etc.

Samples of student reactions were available to the consultants through the various group discussion opportunities previously described. Several students from School C said it was a positive experience to come to a new community and meet people of different races, "We can't just be separate." Others complained, "Why is there busing? Why is there not school improvement?"

Once the busing program began in September, 1978, many students from both schools complained that they were tired from the early rising hours in order to catch the bus. Some students reported that they hated the long bus ride (40-60 min), while other students said it was "O.K." Several students from School C reported difficulty completing homework because of responsibilities at home and tiredness from the early rising. Some of the adolescents felt cut off from their friends who were in the other half of the class not being bused or were now going to private schools.

An issue that concerned students, as well as staff, was the midyear switch which was a planned part of the desegregation program for the two schools. Some students wanted to stay for the entire year rather than changing at midyear. Many teachers and counselors expressed regrets because they were just getting to know their students. On the other hand, some students were happy to spend only one semester away from their neighborhood school.

Through the various groups and classroom discussions, reactions of the stu-

dents regarding desegregation were brought into the open. These groups also provided valuable information regarding individual students' situations. For example, one student described his home life as upsetting because there were many adults living in the home. The teacher appreciated learning of this factor influencing his learning.

In an ongoing therapy group at School M co-led by a consultant (G.A.) and the integration coordinator, ten black adolescents met on a weekly basis for one semester. The themes that emerged were concerns over poor academic achievement, problems with peers, and difficulties at home. Almost all of these students felt that they were in some way defective and expressed fear that they would be unable to perform at school C next semester. The consultant brought these concerns to the attention of the appropriate school staff. This increased understanding of these students. This experience also provided training in interviewing and group counseling techniques for the coordinator.

Other groups were co-led at both schools by school counselors and social workers from a second agency. In one group at School M, several concerns were expressed. The black students in the groups verbalized fears of going to the "white" junior high school in the Valley. They feared stricter academic standards, likelihood of failure, and possible violence toward them from Anglo students. These fears persisted despite the reassurance that they would be with many of the students who were currently in their classes at School M. The white students in the groups from School C also attempted to reassure them, but seemed unsuccessful. At the same time, students of both races talked of difficult family conditions. They were able to see that the kinds of problems they were facing occurred in both races and were universal.

On the last day of the semester, rather than an expected disruption from a previous altercation, what occurred was that students of both races were grieving about leaving School C. Many students cried and expressed feelings of loss. Staff expressed many of the same feelings about ending their association with these students.

END OF SEMESTER ASSEMBLIES

As a way of helping the transition of the students about to be bused, the semester ended with an assembly being conducted at each school. At the assembly, 10-15 students spoke briefly. These assemblies were notable in that it was one of the first times students were able to speak openly of faults, as well as of virtues, of the experience in school. There are few places where this kind of open comment is allowed in the school milieu, especially in the junior high schools. The criticism spoken by the students dealt mainly with the quality of school food and the condition of the playground, but also referred to the general academic program and teaching. Questions and comments from the 7th and 8th grade students became active and energetic. The assemblies did allow for ventilation and correction of some stereotypical distortions such as rumors of violence or prejudice at each school, delayed buses, and other topics. The assemblies were a fascinating experience in expression of student opinion.

SECOND SEMESTER

The new semester began with a new group of 500, mostly black 7th and 8th graders being bused to School C and only 50 to 60 Caucasian students being bused to School M. The consultation activities of the previous semester were somewhat stabilized and took several forms.

At School M weekly noontime case conferences were attended by one or two teachers and occasionally by the counselors concerned with the particular student being discussed. By the end of the semester, more of the counselors were beginning to attend.

At School C, the consultant gave impetus to reestablishing case conferences. She functioned as an expert, providing insights into student behavior. Teachers appreciated hearing each other's experiences and gaining helpful insights.

At School M weekly noontime groups for interested students were conducted by the integration coordinator with a new integration staff person and the consultant (G.A.). It turned out that this particular noontime meeting provided a supportive forum for about 25 of the Caucasian students being bused, as well as for a few black and Hispanic students. Various incidents were discussed. For example, one girl talked about a particular black boy who bothered her by pulling her hair. The discussion helped her decide what to do. Occasionally an encounter with a teacher was talked about and assistance was given in that case as well.

At School C a daily noontime student rap group was attended mostly by Caucasian 9th graders who talked about problems at home or with boyfriends and girlfriends, but less about school-related problems.

There was the continuation of the three counseling groups at each school by the second outside agency. These groups seemed to be primarily for students referred because of academic or emotional problems, but not for more disciplinary issues.

The consultant did not continue to meet with the counseling staff at School C as she had in the first semester. The counseling staff felt that they needed to get back to considering procedural matters which they said had been neglected. The meetings of the previous semester seemed to have prepared the counselors to be more open with each other, expressing feelings and needs. The consultant had been an important catalyst for the reevaluation of services.

SECOND SEMESTER CRISIS

Unfortunateiy, as the semester passed, the Caucasian 9th graders at School C seemed to be becoming increasingly tense. There were incidents of taunting some 7th and 8th grade bused black students. The situation erupted in mid-April and nearly ended in tragedy. That it didn't was possibly testimony to the value of the consultation program, as well as other affective measures.

The events were as follows:

A 9th grade Caucasian boy, who was known as a bully on campus, was involved in a drug purchase. He was "attacked" by two or three black students. Other 9th grade Caucasian students then taunted some of the black students. After lunch, many white and black students would not go back to class. They were milling around and the threat of physical confrontation seemed imminent. Finally students dispersed. A great deal of media coverage occurred the next day when the son of a prominent county official was pushed around by some bused-in students. This incident was reported as "an attack."

A near-emergency situation developed. Special resources were summoned. A worker from the County Human Relations Commission conducted problem-solving discussions in the classrooms with students. He also trained some teachers in this technique. In addition, he helped set up an interracial human relations committee to plan student activities. The consultant at School C (E.C.) was asked to conduct, with the assistance of school personnel, an interracial counseling group meeting with some of the more angry students. With the assistance of the consultant at School M (G.A.), two groups were set up.

Group A (E.C.) consisted of 8-12 of the 7th, 8th, and 9th graders who were con-sidered leaders by the counselors. These were the ones who had most often been referred to the counseling office for disciplinary problems on campus. The composition was one-third Black, one-third Hispanic and one-third Caucasian. For two months this group met weekly. These were the informal leaders among the students who had known of each other but had never sat down to talk to each other. The discussions were frequently heated and were fascinating in the interplay of individual and group dynamics. Especially notable was the learning of verbal expression and understanding as an alternative to physical violence. It so happened that some of the students had been subjected to physical abuse in their families and thus it seemed to encourage their use of physical violence as a solution to tension and threat on campus. In the group discussions, however, they were able to explain to each other the risk of these physical responses. For example, one black boy said, "If that teacher bothers me one more time, I'm going to pop-off and hit him." A formerly overly aggressive Caucasian boy then said, "Don't do that, man. You'll be the one who gets hurt."

The members of the group began to be helpful to each other. When they saw one of them about to get into trouble on campus, they would help each other to avoid fighting. One even began to break up interracial fights on campus. They recommended that there be more groups next year: "If there's a chance to talk, then you don't have to fight." It was interesting to note that for almost all the sessions the three ethnic groups sat separately in segregated groupings. In the last meeting, however, there was a spontaneous mixed seating, which attested to the success of the communication.

It was of significance that this group of boys had not become involved with any of the previously described group discussions that had been available on the campus. Possibly if communication groups had been provided earlier in the first semester for 9th graders at School C, as had been provided for the 9th graders at School M, a forum might have been available for this group to feel more connected with the desegregation process. Or perhaps it did require the eruption of strong angry feelings to give these particular boys the stimulus to enter such group discussion.

At any rate, the corrective experience that these 12 leaders had seemed to have a ripple effect on campus, reaching many others as well. The second group (B), which was started simultaneously, seemed to confine itself more to planning activities and had less heated discussions.

The high point of the year's program took place in June, two weeks before the end of school. Several students from these and other groups (County Human Relations) suggested having a "start-all-over-again" day. Each student and faculty member was assigned to an activity in interracial teams. Activities consisted of dancing, sports, games such as chess, etc. Classes were suspended.

Some of the faculty at School C had been worried that there might be loss of control and a bad outcome to the day. It is true that there was much free energy during the day, but no loss of control or damage occurred. Some Caucasian teachers even commented with new respect to some of their black colleagues about the dancing and other skills of some of the black students who didn't seem to do as well in their academic classes. It was significant, also, that after the special day there were no suspensions of students. The campus seemed calmer, and the semester ended happily two weeks later.

OVERVIEW—GREATER OPENNESS

The keynote of the year's experience seems to have been that for counselors, students, and many, but not all, of the teachers there was a greater degree of openness of emotional expression, espe-

cially of angry and critical feelings, and greater attention to the feelings of the students. It certainly appeared that this helped abort a situation of incipient violence. But it also seemed to enhance a personal, emotional kind of learning for many young people and probably also improved their academic learning.

The 1979-80 school year presented new challenges. There were a number of 9th graders at School C who had been in private schools during 1978-79 to avoid the busing in their 8th grade year. They did not take part in any of the year's learning experience described above. Special discussion groups were necessary, leading to further changes in the school.

There still are many teachers and parents in both schools opposed to a second year of mandatory desegregation. There had been an attempt to remove School C from the previous pairing with School M. However, the Superior Court judge involved ordered a continuation of the pairing.

In 1979-80 the student body at school C has been reduced to 800 students (from 2200) due to further "white flight" and declining enrollment for other reasons. This decline caused the loss of 17 teaching positions and also some of the programs taught by these teachers. The reduction of students and teachers was less at school M than at school C. The number of students bused from school M still numbered about 400, contrasted to about 70 bused from school C. At school C in 1979-80 the 7th grade was 76% minority, the 8th grade was 81%, the 9th grade was 34%. Overall, School C was 62% minority. School M was about 82% minority in 7th and 8th grades. Schoolwide was 89%.

In 1979-80 the district's entire desegregation program was reviewed in the courtroom. The school board was requesting an end to mandatory busing because of the loss of too many white students. In 1981 mandatory busing was discontinued. Some racial mixing continued on a voluntary basis at School C, but not at School

M. The team from the Department of Mental Health continued the consultation but the agenda had to change.

SUMMARY

The desegregation experience in Los Angeles occasioned the rearrangement of educational programs for thousands of children in grades 4-8 in 1978-79. Many desirable and undesirable consequences resulted and continue to reverberate throughout the Los Angeles Unified School District.

The observations described in this paper pertain to the desegregation process influencing young adolescents in the 7th and 8th grades in a pair of junior high schools. Thanks to close collaboration with administrative staffs from the schools' central office and the two schools themselves, mental health consultants from the Los Angeles County Department of Mental Health were granted entry to all sectors of school operation. Two other agencies also provided significant assistance. The consultation service, combined with readiness and need for change spurred by mandated desegregation, resulted in several desirable changes in the mental health climate of these two schools. Notable were the changes within the counseling services, more assistance to troubled students, changes in teaching methods, and provision of more group experiences for students to discuss personal needs, as well as reactions to racial mixing. Negative as well as positive reactions to the changes were voiced by students and faculty members on both campuses. In the second semester, in one school, near tragedy was averted by several timely measures, especially increased classroom discussion groups and a special group for informal student leaders. In the latter group, the learning of verbalizing to avoid physical violence was notable. Quantitative evaluations are as yet unavailable but it seemed that many individual students received a greater opportunity for counseling attention and the improvement of communicative skills, whether about personal school problems or alternatives to violent expression of emotions.

Unfortunately, about 500 primarily Caucasian students avoided desegregation by placement in private schools and tutoring groups. The remaining 1200 7th and 8th graders in both schools received a valuable multicultural experience.

REFERENCES

Batson, R. M. and Peters, L. S. Community crisis intervention and the Boston desegregation effort. A publication of the crisis intervention program of the Boston University School of Medicine, Division of Psychiatry/Solomon Carter Fuller Mental Health Center, Boston, MA, 1976.

Berkovitz, I. H. School interventions: Case management and school mental health consultation. In: G. P. Sholevar, R. M. Benson, and B. J. Blinder (Eds.), *Emotional Disorders in Children and Adolescents.* New York: SP Medical and Scientific Books, 1980a.

Berkovitz, I. H. Improving the relevance of secondary education for adolescent developmental tasks. In: M. Sugar (Ed.), *Responding to Adolescent Needs.* New York: Spectrum, 1980b.

Berkovitz, I. H. and Thomson, M. Mental health consultation and assistance to school personnel of Los Angeles County. Office of the Los Angeles County Superintendent of Schools, Downey, CA: 1973.

Berlin, I. N. Mental health consultation in schools as a means of communicating mental health principles. *Journal of the American Academy of Child Psychiatry,* 1962, *1,* 671-679.

Caplan, G. *The Theory and Practice of Mental Health Consultation.* New York: Basic Books, 1969.

MacLennan, B. W. Community mental health professionals assist in school desegregation. In: W. L. Clairborn and R. Cohen (Eds.), *School Intervention.* New York: Behavioral Publications, 1973.

Miller, D. Adolescents and the high school system. *Community Mental Health Journal,* 1970, *6,* 483-491.

CHAPTER 28

Bilingual Education: Fact or Fancy?

Esther Sinclair, Ph.D.

HISTORICAL CONTEXT

School districts are increasingly compelled to provide bilingual education programs for their non English-speaking and limited English-speaking students. This commitment to bilingual schooling may result from federal or state legislation, community pressure, or court order.

The Bilingual Education Act of 1968, most recently brought bilingual education to the political forefront. This act provided the first federal funds for bilingual education. However, public interest in bilingual education is not only a recent educational concern. The emergence of bilingual education programs in the United States can be traced to pre-1800 when German schools flourished throughout the country. This period also saw the beginning of many French schools in New England and many Scandinavian and some Dutch schools in the Midwest (Kloss,

1966). During the late nineteenth and early twentieth century, parochial schools geared to newly arrived Catholic immigrants from Southern and Eastern Europe were founded. The next major phase of bilingual schooling began in 1963 when Cuban refugees settled in Miami, Florida. The first bilingual public elementary school programs were developed there to meet the needs of the Cuban refugee children (Andersson & Boyer, 1970).

Following 1963, bilingual education programs spread to Texas, California and New Mexico. Title VII of the Elementary and Secondary Education Act of 1965 established a national policy and federal guidelines regarding bilingual education. Essentially, Title VII recognized that large numbers of children of limited English-speaking ability had educational needs which could be met by the use of bilingual methods and techniques; and that, in addition, children of limited English-speaking ability benefited through the fullest utilization of multiple language and cultural resources.

The landmark court case in bilingual education was *Lau* v. *Nichols* in 1974. The representative issue was whether non English-speaking students, who constitute national-origin minority groups, receive an education free from unlawful discrimination when instructed in English, a language they do not understand. The Lau decision raised the nation's consciousness to the need for bilingual education, encouraged additional federal legislation, energized federal enforcement efforts, led to federal funding of nine regional "general assistance Lau centers," aided the passage of state laws mandating bilingual education, and spawned more lawsuits (Teitelbaum & Hiller, 1977).

Lau v. *Nichols* was brought on behalf of Chinese students in the San Francisco Unified School District in 1970. The plaintiffs charged that Chinese-speaking youngsters were entitled to instruction in their native language and that the San Francisco schools had failed to provide special language instruction to certain Chinese-speaking students, in violation of Title VI of the Civil Rights Act of 1964. Relatively few schools received federal monies in 1964, but by 1974 virtually all of the country's school districts received some form of federal aid and fell within the prohibitions of Title VI: "No person in the United States shall, on the ground of race, color or national origin, be excluded from participation in, be denied the benefits of, or be subjected to discrimination under any program or activity receiving Federal financial assistance." Because each school district receiving federal monies must agree to comply with this anti-discrimination statement, Title VI has become an increasingly powerful lever for eradicating discrimination in education.

Teitelbaum and Hiller (1977) further state that the parties in Lau did not dispute the critical fact that 1,790 Chinese students received no services designed to meet their linguistic needs and that these students suffered educationally. What was in question was whether non English-speaking students receive an equal educational opportunity when instructed in a language they cannot understand.

The U.S. Supreme Court ruled that California requires that a student attend school and insists on mastery of English as a requirement of graduation. "Under these state-imposed standards there is no equality of treatment merely by providing students with the same facilities, textbooks, teachers, and curriculum; for the students who do not understand English are effectively foreclosed from any meaningful education." The Supreme Court opinion did not mandate a specific approach to teaching national-origin students with English language deficits. This ruling led the San Francisco Board of Education to approve a modified version of a master-plan prepared by a citizens' task force. The task force set forth procedures to insure that a diagnostic-prescriptive educational plan be developed for each student whose primary language was other than English. The result was that a bilingual, bicultural program was developed for the Chinese, Filipino, and Spanish-language groups in the school district. Responsibility for monitoring implementation of the programs was placed with a community council which was established and administratively supported by the school district.

The impact of the Lau ruling resulted in further lawsuits. Two of these suits are presented here because they had specific implications for bilingual education programs. In 1972, Chicano students challenged the English-only instructional program in the schools of Portales, New Mexico. The court found a violation of the students' constitutional rights to an equal educational opportunity and ordered that bilingual instruction be provided. The instructional format consisted of 60 minutes of bilingual instruction per day for all students in grades one through three. Students in grades four through six received 45 minutes of instruction per day. The plan was significant in that English-dominant Chicano and Anglo students were required to receive some bilingual instruction.

The 1977 *Rios* v. *Read* decision focused on the obligations of school authorities toward their non English-speaking students. English as a Second Language (ESL) programs were evaluated by relating student achievement levels, reading scores, and attendance rates to tenure in the special ESL programs. For the first time, the Court emphasized the importance of bilingual education in the academic and personal growth of the language-disadvantaged child.

It is not enough simply to provide a program for disadvantaged children or even to staff the program with bilingual teachers; rather, the critical question is whether the program is designed to assure as much as is reasonably possible, the language deficient child's growth in the English language. An inadequate program is as harmful to a child who does not speak English as no program at all.

SOCIETAL MODELS

Bilingual education is currently a volatile, political issue in this country. Every system of educational practice is based on certain assumptions about the nature of society. Proponents of bilingual schooling have been labeled as supportive of a culturally and structurally pluralistic view of American society. Opponents of bilingual schooling have frequently been aligned with the Anglo-conformity model of American society.

Mercer (1979) described cultural and structural pluralism as a model of American society constituting numerous ethnic groups in various relationships to the Anglo core culture. Figure 1B describes the complexities of this model. The large circle represents the Anglo core culture, whose domination has existed since colon-

ial times and has been continued through public education and other social institutions. The descendants of most non-Anglo immigrants who arrived during the colonial era have been culturally and structurally absorbed into the Anglo sector of society and are no longer ethnically indentifiable, notably the descendants of most German Protestants, the Scotch Irish, the Swedes, and the Norwegians. There are other groups that are culturally integrated but have maintained sufficient

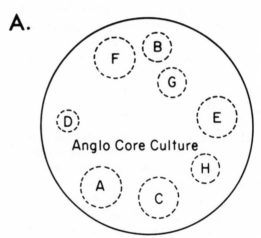

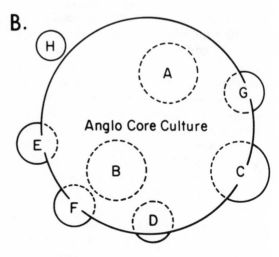

Figure 1. Two Models of American Society. From Mercer, 1979.

structural separatism through religious and communal ties to be ethnically identifiable, groups such as the descendants of the Irish Catholics and the Jews. They are represented by circles A and B. They are drawn with dotted lines to indicate cultural integration associated with structural separatism. Other groups appear to span the boundaries of the core culture. Circles C, D, E, F, and G show some members of the same ethnic group to be of varying sociocultural distance from the core culture. Some members may be recent immigrants who do not speak English and who share none of the values and behaviors of the core culture, while others may be indistinguishable from the core groups except for their surnames. Circle H depicts an ethnic group that has maintained almost complete cultural and structural separatism from the Anglo core culture, groups such as the Amish, the Navajo nation, and the Hutterites.

The ideology of cultural democracy supports public policies that would attempt to develop an American society shaped upon the model of cultural and structural pluralism (Ramirez & Castaneda, 1974). This ideology argues that, in addition to the perpetuation of the Anglo cultural tradition, there should be perpetuation of non-Anglo languages and cultures. Thus, cultural maintenance of non-Anglo traditions would be a function and concern of public education. Such a policy would produce educational options such as a monocultural, monolingual educational experience or a bicultural, bilingual educational experience. The goal of education would be to provide for the development of bicultural, bilingual children who not only could function effectively in the Anglo core culture but also could function linguistically in one or more non-Anglo cultures.

Proponents of cultural pluralism argue that the school should recognize the legitimate right of other languages and cultures in the classroom. The essential and critical argument is that the schooling

experience is enriched for all children if education is conducted bilingually and biculturally.

Mercer (1979) also depicted the Anglo-conformity conception of American society in Figure 1A by a single large circle representing the Anglo tradition. Within the larger circle are smaller circles depicting non-Anglo ethnic groups. The model assumes that the non-Anglo groups have been acculturated to the dominant Anglo culture, although they may remain identifiable because they have maintained some structural separatism. The dotted lines relate to the assumptions that groups are permeable and that cultural homogenization has taken place.

The ideology of Anglicization is to the Anglo-conformity model what the ideology of cultural democracy was to the cultural and structural pluralism model. Anglicization guides the social politics of this model. A central assumption of Anglicization is the desirability of maintaining English institutions, the English language, and English-oriented cultural patterns as dominant and standard in American life. The primary goal of public education is to teach all children the English language and the values and skills needed to perform in Anglo-American institutions. Languages other than English and non-Anglo cultural traditions should not be perpetuated through educational and governmental institutions, although they may be maintained by privately funded schools and organizations. Anglicization provides no educational options. There is a single, monocultural, Anglocentric public educational system for all children.

RATIONALE FOR BILINGUAL EDUCATION

Broadly speaking, there are two functions of bilingual schooling. The first is to provide the student from a different language and culture with the tools necessary to gain entry into mainstream society without having to give up the language and values of the home. The second function is to provide majority group students with an educational experience in another language and culture. Focusing on these two functions of individual and intergroup relations, Andersson and Boyer (1970) presented 10 reasons that explain why an alternative to mainstream education is needed. Their views, summarized in Table 1, are still valid 10 years later.

For the purpose of example and discussion, bilingual education may be viewed as representative of three distinct philosophies. Advocates of bilingual education espouse either a philosophy of cultural separatism, a philosophy of cultural assimilation, or a philosophy of cultural pluralism (Padilla, 1976).

Cultural separatism advocates argue that mainstream American education has failed to meet the needs of culturally different, non English-speaking students. The only viable educational alternative is a totally different educational experience. The argument is that the school has failed the child. Therefore, the ethnic community must take over the educational concerns of its children. In the past, the community group has provided input by recommending curriculum that is highly relevant and identifiable with the culture of the particular ethnic group. Furthermore, they have strongly advised school districts to hire culturally similar teachers from the same ethnic group. The minority community groups have consistently stressed the importance of pride and reinforcement for culture membership.

No mention is made of the Anglo student's educational needs within such a community. Cultural separatists would prefer to exclude Anglo cultural values and traditions from the curriculum. Most frequently, school programs representing this philosophy are found as either after-school tutorial programs or as after-school language and cultural maintenance programs. Regular classroom programs mostly

TABLE 1

Ten Reasons that Necessitate Bilingual Education

1. American schooling has not met the needs of children coming from homes where non-English languages are spoken; a radical improvement is therefore urgently needed.

2. Such improvement must first of all maintain and strengthen the sense of identity of children entering the school from such homes.

3. The self-image and sense of dignity of families that speak other languages must also be preserved and strengthened.

4. The child's mother tongue is not only an essential part of his sense of identity; it is also his best instrument for learning, especially in the early stages.

5. Preliminary evidence indicates that initial learning through a child's non-English home language does not hinder learning in English or other school subjects.

6. Differences among first, second, and foreign languages need to be understood if learning through them is to be sequenced effectively.

7. The best order of the learning of basic skills in a language—whether first or second—needs to be understood and respected if best results are to be obtained; this order is normally (especially for children): listening comprehension, speaking, reading, and writing.

8. Young children have an impressive learning capacity; especially in the case of language learning, the young child learns more easily and better than adolescents or adults, the sound system, the basic structure, and vocabulary of a language.

9. Closely related to bilingualism is biculturalism, which should be an integral part of bilingual instruction.

10. Bilingual education holds the promise of helping to harmonize various ethnic elements in a community into a mutually respectful and creative pluralistic society.

Taken from Andersson and Boyer (1970)

do not exist (Padilla, 1976). In those very few cases where federal monies were initially used to support separatist type programs, the money has been withdrawn owing to the exclusionary enrollment policies of the schools (Appleton, 1973).

The antithesis of cultural separatism is cultural assimilation. Assimilation advocates encourage bilingual schooling to bridge the cultural and language gap between the minority child's home and the school. The child's native language is treated as an ancillary learning vehicle along with English. The native language is used until the child has acquired enough English to participate in an English-only program. Bilingual programs of this type are labelled transitional since they emphasize a change from the native language to the majority language. Transitional programs are "one-way" educational experiences leading the unassimilated minority child toward assimilation with the majority group language and culture. As with the cultural separatist model, no mention is made of the Anglo child.

An example of a school program based on the philosophy of cultural assimilation is the English as a Second Language pullout program. Here, limited English-speaking students and non English-speaking students are removed from their regular classroom program in order to receive special instruction in English language vocabulary and basic grammatical structure. It is not a requirement for the ESL teacher to be fluent, or even, familiar, with the native languages of his/her students.

The curriculum in cultural assimilation programs is usually oriented toward the majority group culture and values. Ethnically different content is frequently expressed in a multicultural social studies unit that may last from one week to six weeks. Within such a unit, the Chinese New Year, Black History week and Mexican Independence Day may be given comparable exposure.

Cultural pluralism advocates stress the importance of a bilingual schooling experience that is a "two-way" learning experience. Students of both the minority and majority group learn basic educational skills and curriculum content in two languages. Classes are ethnically mixed. Ideally, both languages are presented by the same teacher. In this way, the students perceive both languages as receiving parallel exposure and stress. The program encourages students to become proficient speakers in two languages and to feel comfortable in switching between them. Both languages and cultures are equally valued. Yet, it is important to assist the minority group children in the acquisition of the language of the core culture so they will have an equal opportunity to participate fully in the economic and political life of American society, to share in its benefits and responsibilities, and to enjoy its material abundance (Mercer, 1979). Presently, there are few programs in existence which can be labeled culturally pluralistic in ideology and implementation.

CONCLUSIONS AND IMPLICATIONS FOR DESEGREGATION

Establishing a violation of the Lau decision by providing data that a school district is not meeting the needs of non English-speaking and limited English-speaking students is relatively straightforward. Determining what type of bilingual program will best meet these children's needs is not so straightforward. Finding fault with a particular program is a long step away from proposing a proven better alternative. Definitive research, with reliable evaluation indices, is needed to sort out the following evaluation concerns of various bilingual programs: Does bilingual education positively affect a student's self-concept? Does bilingual education hinder academic progress during the course of second language acquisition? Does bilingual education improve achievement?

Heretofore not mentioned, the problem of evaluating the degree of an individual student's bilingualism appears as an extremely important consideration in questions of research and in questions of appropriate school programs. There are numerous variations in definitions of bilingualism ranging from minimal to maximal qualifications of fluency (Bloomfield, 1933; Haugen, 1956; Weinrich, 1953).

Three philosophies of bilingual education have been presented in this chapter. Depending on the philosophical orientation of the program, there are variations in the desired goals and outcomes of a particular program. For example: Which of the two languages will be the language of instruction in a bilingual community? Should classes in both languages be available to students? Will the use of second-language teaching increase competency in the weaker of the two languages?

The legal mandate to desegregate the nation's schools does not necessarily represent obstacles to implementing bilingual programs which are educationally viable. Teitelbaum and Hiller (1977) stated that bilingual education and desegregation need not be headed on a collision course. In fact, the court's power to right unlawful school segregation, a constitutional wrong, may provide the best hope for achieving comprehensive court-mandated bilingual education programs.

Bilingual education advocates characterize their programs as integrative and not segregative. Many of the minority groups that now support bilingual education were themselves victims of segregation. Past segregation of non-Black minority students often was justified on the basis of English language deficits. The limited separation that may accompany the establishment of certain transition-type bilingual programs has neither the same intent nor the same effect as past segregation practices. The critical point that bilingual education programs share with school desegregation is that they both support equal educational opportunities for core culture and minority group students.

REFERENCES

Andersson, T. and Boyer, M. *Bilingual Schooling in the United States.* Volume 1. Washington, D.C.: U.S. Government Printing Office, 1970.

Appleton, S. F. Alternative schools for minority students: The constitution, the Civil Rights Act and the Berkeley experiment. *California Law Review,* 1973, *61,* 26-86.

Bloomfield, L. *Language.* New York: Holt, Rinehart & Winston, 1933.

Haugen, E. *Bilingualism in the Americas: A Bibliography and a Research Guide.* Montgomery: University of Alabama Press, 1956.

Kloss, H. German-American language maintenance efforts. In: J. A. Fishman et al. (Eds.), *Language Loyalty in the United States.* The Hague: Mouton, 1966.

Mercer, J. R. *System of Multicultural Pluralistic Assessment Technical Manual.* New York: The Psychological Corporation, 1979.

Padilla, A. M. Bilingual schools: Gateways to integration or roads to separation. Prepared for the National Institute of Education, Developmental Conference on Policy Problems in Educational Options, Chicago, Illinois, 1976.

Ramirez, M., III and Castaneda, A. *Cultural Democracy, Bicognitive Development, and Education.* New York: Academic Press, 1974.

Teitelbaum, H. and Hiller, R. J. Bilingual education: The legal mandate. *Harvard Educational Review,* 1977, *47*(2), 138-170.

Weinrich, U. *Languages in Contact.* New York: Linguistic Circle of New York, 1953.

CHAPTER 29

Important Issues in the Language Development of the Black Child

Esther Sinclair, Ph.D.

The ability to generate language is a universal genetic endowment of all normal human beings. This inherent linguistic capacity permits the child of any race, creed or color to learn the most complex system of rules a person ever learns (Hetherington and Parke, 1979). Papolia and Olds (1925) were among the first to write that all infants, regardless of cultural or environmental background, in their acquisition of spoken language, follow basically the same rate, sequence or order of pre-linguistic oral behavior. This includes undifferentiated crying, differentiated crying, cooing, chuckling, pre-babbling and babbling, time of onset of using one-word meanings, two-word meanings, and later multi-word sentences.

These universal features seem to indicate a biological basis of language behavior. Lenneberg (1967) argued that human language learning capacity is a correlate or result of maturational processes. Certain stages of language development are interlocked with certain relevant stages of motor development and are not socially determined. Houston (1970) supported Lenneberg by stating that previously considered learned behavior such as language may be innate or biologically determined. One reason for this conclusion is that both the language acquisition process and the structure of language have a number of significant universal features. For instance, it is a universal fact that all children learn language merely by being placed in the environment of the language and that they do not need any special training or conditioning (Chomsky, 1959; Langacker, 1967; Lenneberg, 1967). Language development appears to follow a definite fixed sequence at a relatively constant chronological age.

SOCIOCULTURAL LANGUAGE DEVELOPMENT

The sociolinguists emphasize the part played by environmental and/or social factors in language acquisition and production. This includes the role of imitation and reinforcement in the acquisition of certain speech patterns and habits as well as the role of social class membership, and regional habitation in language behavior. According to Osser (1970), the child must learn the structural rules of his language. These rules refer to when he should speak, when he should remain silent, which linguistic code he should use, and to whom.

It is from the sociolinguistic orientation that the evidence relevant to the black child and his use or nonuse of black English and/or standard English is derived. Interest in black English converged with the social protest movement of the 1960s in a scene of black-white polarization, black demands for social and educational equality, and the nationalist drive for recognition of a black cultural heritage and identity. Black English consists of the totality of language used in the black community. It contains many varieties and differences according to such variables as geography, social class, age, sex, amount of education, etc. Differences emerge as a function of the social situations in which the language is produced. There is, nonetheless, a common core of features across all types of phonology, syntax, vocabulary and surprasegmental aspects. Hunt (1969) felt that neither the cognitive processes nor the cognitive development of the black child was different from that of the white child, particularly in terms of one's capacity to discriminate, recognize, identify and manipulate the features and processes of the world around him. Up to two years of age the cognitive processes of black children and white children do not differ. After two years, children begin to label those events around them with language. Hunt proposed that the labelling or attaching of language to cognitions was different in black and white children because of culturally different environments and backgrounds.

The process of attaching labels to the cognitions was not different—it was the actual labels assigned to the cognitions that were. A child develops language comprehension and language production primarily as a result of the language model he encounters in his environment. His own internal schematic organization and self-instruction are based upon manipulation of those items which he differentially selects from the environment to fit his conceptual scheme (Williams and Rivers, 1975). The black child is in a different labelling environment than the white child. It does not mean that he is deficient in communication skills because he uses different labels nor does it mean that he has less of a language to use.

BRIEF HISTORY OF BLACK DIALECT

Black American dialects are probably the result of a creolized form of English at one time spoken on Southern plantations by black slaves (Bailey, 1966; Dillard, 1972; Stewart, 1967). Creolized plantation English appears to be related to the creolized English spoken by some blacks in Jamaica and other Caribbean islands. This and other observations unleashed a flurry of articles that sought to make dialect of singular importance in understanding the black past and present. A few creolists discovered similarities between present black dialect and certain West African languages. They observed that creole languages developed where economically and militarily stronger European countries made contact with the weaker African tribes. The black Africans borrowed the vocabulary of the European language and inserted it into their grammatical structure. Through the interaction with white speech, the black dialect can no longer be considered true creole dialect (Williams, 1975).

Africans who were captured as slaves and brought to the new world were forced to learn to use some type of English. Dillard (1972), a student of Black English, states:

Many slaves . . . found themselves in a situation in which they had to learn an auxiliary language in a hurry in order to establish communication in the heterogeneous groups in which they were thrown (p. 72).

This mixing of speech of a large number of languages, with no one language predominant, is the perfect condition for the spread of pidgin English, which is in a sense the ultimate in auxiliary languages.

As time passed during the course of the 18th century, the character of pidgin English changed in response to changes in the black population and other social pressures. Among blacks during this time, language behavior differed according to their social-occupational status. The more privileged domestic servants and educated, wealthy, and free blacks spoke a more standardized form of English than did the field hands who used a more creolized English. This situation existed up to the time of the Civil War and until after the war when the dissolution of slavery and the plantation system and the increasing access to education for blacks of all social ranks caused the older creolized English to lose many of its unique characteristics and to assume those of the white oral and written English dialects. Both whites and blacks influenced the language behavior of the other as they continued to interact.

It has been estimated that some 80 percent of blacks speak a "radically nonstandard" English (Wilson, 1978). Thus, present-day black English still features the linguistic remnants of its creole past in addition to the fact that it reflects the current black sociocultural situation. This demands that we conceive it as a dialect in its own right, not as just a distortion of standard English.

LANGUAGE DEFICIT THEORIES

The two major schools of thought that attempt to explain language development in the black child are the language deficit theorists and the language difference theorists. These two groups offer parallel explanations of "appropriate" language development in ghetto children. Briefly, the language difference theorists see the language problem of black ghetto children not as one of linguistic competence, but rather as one of linguistic interference (Bailey, 1967; Dillard, 1967; Labov, 1965; Povich and Baratz, 1967; Stewart, 1965, 1967, 1968). The language deficit theorists view black children as having systematic but underdeveloped language behavior; therefore, their underdeveloped system leads to cognitive deficits (Bereiter, 1965; Bernstein, 1960; Deutsch, 1965; Hess, Shipman, and Jackson, 1965).

Underdeveloped language is generally thought to be due to environmental factors such as limited mother-child verbal interaction, noise in the environment, and sensory-social deprivation. Thus, between the school and the community of the black ghetto children there exists a cultural discontinuity based on two radically different systems of communication. Standard English has been the criterion upon which the language underdevelopment studies rest. Following, is a brief synopsis of the major language deficit theorists and their views on language development in the black child.

Bernstein (1960, 1961) coined the terms restricted code and elaborated code to explain language development. Restricted code is classified as stereotyped, limited and condensed speech patterns which lack the specificity needed for precise conceptualization and differentiation. The restricted code often consists of sentences which are short, simple and unfinished. It is alleged to be a language with implicit meaning, easily understood and commonly shared.

The elaborated code consists of communication that is individualized, where the message is specific for a particular situation, topic or person. It is reported to be more particular, more differentiated, complex and precise. It permits expression of a wide and complex range of thought with discrimination among cognitive and affective content.

Bernstein assumed a direct relationship between overt language form and concept formation. He felt that crude expressions of logical relationships based on simple, concrete sentences were characteristic of lower-class child rearing techniques. For example, the absence of conjunctions such as "if" and "then" as well as the initial subordinate clause "if A . . . then B" rendered the language restricted and deficient in dealing with hypothetical complexities. Numerous opponents to Bernstein's view of language development criticized his assumed relationship between concept formation and speech as a relationship that has never been clearly proved.

Bereiter and Engleman (1966) pointed out that disadvantaged children frequently score 5 to 15 points below average. Since intelligence tests measure, to some extent, the impact of middle-class scholastic and cultural values on intelligence, they are good indicators of cultural, social, and educational deprivation (Bannatyne, 1971). Bereiter and Engleman further said:

Disadvantaged children of preschool age are typically at least a year behind in language development in vocabulary size, sentence length, and use of grammatical structure. Indeed, in practically every aspect of language development that has been evaluated quantitatively, young disadvantaged children have been found to function at the level of average children who are a year or so younger (p. 129).

Bereiter and Engleman (1965) are best known for their input in preschool intervention programs to help aid the language development of minority-group children. They clearly felt that nonstandard English was inferior to standard English and that the black child develops speech and thinking patterns that are at variance with what he needs to learn. The program they developed at the preschool level involved a direct instruction approach calling for regular lessons and lesson plans, opportunities for practice and feedback, corrective procedures, and definite criteria for the children to meet.

LANGUAGE DIFFERENCE THEORIES

This broad school is supported primarily by linguists. Language is examined in terms of a well-ordered, highly-structured system. The assumption is that any verbal system that meets the needs of a community is a language and no better than any other language. All children learn language in the context of their environment. By age 5, the rules of the linguistic system are learned. They see a definite structure to the "errors" of standard English that the black nonstandard speaker makes. His language does not represent a pathology, or a failure to learn the rules of the linguistic system, but rather it represents the fact that he has learned some difficult, equally highly structured, highly complex rules of language behavior.

Baratz (1969, 1970) is perhaps one of the best known researchers among the cultural difference theorists. She examined the failure of urban education to prove effective for ghetto children. She focused on reading achievement and urged the recognition of established black dialect in the educational programs for black children. Her later work (1970) elucidated the central problem of the speaker of black English in confrontation with the dominant standard English-speaking society. It should be obvious from this study that the white child is as linguistically deficient when it comes to dealing with black English as the black child is when it comes to dealing with standard English. As each child is imprinted with the language of his own environment, he becomes less capable of dealing competently with the language used in another. His deficiency has nothing to do with an inherent or learned deficiency in cognitive ability.

In 1969, Baratz reviewed the relative merits of the linguistic studies of the black child and summarized them as representing two major methodological limitations. Firstly, middle-class children had been compared with lower-class children on their performance on typical middle-class tasks or variables. There was control for race and socioeconomic status but no control for black language variations. Secondly, most research comparing linguistic abilities of standard and nonstandard speakers has been contaminated by such use of test materials and scoring procedures in the standard dialect. The situation is equivalent to asking a white child, "How well have you learned the language of your environment?" while asking the black child, "How well have you learned standard English, a language which is not your native tongue?"

Labov's (1968, 1970) major research concerns the relationship between black dialect and standard English. He cast doubt on the deficiency theories by stating that blacks possess a mature and socially efficient language; therefore, a simplistic deficiency hypothesis cannot explain reading difficulties experienced by these children. He asserted that the language ability of the black child can be regarded as an asymmetrical relation; he can comprehend both nonstandard and standard English but can produce only nonstandard English. Thus his scores on the usual imitation tests made in standard English

will be lower than his actual ability to comprehend. He saw a conflict between the spontaneous use of black dialect and the form of speech required in the classroom.

In Labov's (1968) view, the use of nonstandard English adversely affects the acquisition of reading skills requiring the use of standard English in at least two ways. Firstly, there may exist a structural conflict between black English and standard English so that a written or spoken standard English sentence is almost rendered or translated in its nonstandard equivalent. Schools usually demand that standard English be used exclusively and this presents a source of conflict between black values and white middle-class school ideology.

Secondly, Labov sees a functional conflict as being a source of difficulty confronting the users of nonstandard English in attempting to acquire standard sentences. One's language serves, in addition to its communicative function, an identity function. Using standard English exclusively may imply to the black child that he has to repudiate one of the most important things, his language, which identifies him with his family, race, culture, peer group and with himself. The functional conflict boils down to a question of not whether the black child can learn to use fully standard English, but whether he wants to learn to use it.

In summary, the deficit position has its roots in a nativist view of biological predispositions for language development with environmental factors serving as appropriate catalysts (Chomsky, 1965; Lenneberg, 1967; McNeill, 1966). The difference position contends that the language development of ghetto children is merely different, emphasizing sociological factors (Labov, 1966; Stewart, 1965). These two views of language development offer parallel explanations for the failure of "appropriate" language development in ghetto children. The deficit explanation, in its most extreme position, suggests that black children essentially lack any systematized language (Bernstein, 1961) as a consequence of genetic inferiority (Jensen, 1969). The authors supporting the development of a different language in ghetto children emphasize that these children, predominantly black, have learned a well-developed, rule-governed language that not only interferes with middle-class language but also penalizes them unfairly (Baratz, 1968; Labov, 1970). Thus, between the school and the community of the black ghetto child there exists a cultural discontinuity based on two radically different systems of communication.

OTHER MODELS OF LANGUAGE DEVELOPMENT IN THE BLACK CHILD

Ebonics, coined by Williams (1975), consists of the linguistic and paralinguistic features which on a continuum represent the communicative competence of West African, Caribbean, and United States slave descendants of African origin. Ebonics includes the various idioms, patois, argot, idiolects, and social dialects of these people. It is thus the culturally appropriate language of black people and is not to be considered deviant. Acknowledgement of the term ebonics places the focus of the difficulty of black children at the level of the school, the curriculum and the staff. The deficit is not so much within the child as within the school's inability to deal adequately with the child's resources. In this model, emphasis is placed on teacher training and retraining, increasing the teacher's sensitivity and knowledge about the child's culture and resources, fostering curriculum changes, and developing mutual communication between community and the school.

BILINGUAL-BICOGNITIVE RESEARCH

Valentine (1971), an anthropologist, emphasized the existence of two cultures.

Survival for the black child means the acquisition of two languages and two cultures. The model does not require white children to become enculturated into the black lifestyle and is therefore considered racist.

Torrey (1970) studied cross-cultural variations in the social function and significance of language that create barriers to teaching and learning. The functional aspects of language have more serious implications for illiteracy than the structural ones. The functional aspects are closely connected with conditions of life that keep people out of schools and conditions of schools that keep people from learning to read despite ostensible efforts to teach them.

Torrey further states that the attitudes of teachers toward black dialect and the dialect speaker's attitude toward the teacher's language have affected the social relationships of children with schools in such a way as to make education almost impossible. Children in lower grades commonly accept the teacher as a kind of substitute mother. However, teachers often do not accept their students and the black child is likely to become alienated from the teacher and from the culture that the teacher represents. Differences in language and culture become a basis of hostility and rejection of the whole educational process.

In 1973, Frasure and Entwistle studied the effect of two different kinds of language structure, syntactic structure and semantic structure, on the development of children's ability to process verbal information. The presumption was that increasing knowledge of syntax and increasing knowledge of semantics are reflected in improved ability to process sentences with varying amounts of syntactic and semantic content. Most studies of children's language development have concentrated on acquisition of syntax and phonology in the first five years of life. The few studies after age five, have suggested that environmental effects on syntactic development are negligible (Manyuk, 1971). Evidence concerning environmental effects on semantic development over the early school years is indirect and primarily comes from two sources, word associations and vocabulary tests. The amount of data from both sources is so small that generalizations about racial and social class differences in semantic development have not been possible. Although social class and racial differences in children's use of language are often cited, these differences are rarely studied in the developmental context. A fundamental hypothesis that prompted the Frasure and Entwistle study was that semantic development takes longer than syntactic development and occurs later in the life cycle. The data suggest the opposite. Namely, semantic cues facilitate performance somewhat later.

Genshaft and Hirt (1974) worked with black and white children, matched for social class and nonverbal IQ. They were examined in a free-recall situation on vocabulary words and sentences presented in black dialect and standard English. The results indicated that on standard English, black subjects performed significantly worse. These findings were interpreted as support for bilingual language development in black ghetto children, and emphasis was lent to the importance of social class and intelligence when comparing black and white subjects on language tasks.

Gay and Tweney (1976) worked with 72 lower-class black kindergartners, third graders and sixth graders. They were tested for comprehension of stimulus sentences with contrasting grammatical characteristics in black English and standard English. The results indicated that comprehension of both easy and hard contrasts in both black and standard English increased with age in parallel fashion. However, production of black English decreased with age. The results are consistent with previous results suggesting that black children "code switch" although the

effect of semantic constraint on young black English speakers needs to be further investigated.

IMPLICATIONS FOR EDUCATION

The research evidence generally supports the need for some types of structured preschool language intervention to counteract the demonstrated deficiencies of disadvantaged children. Recognition of this need has given impetus to the development of a variety of language programs and the widespread establishment of compensatory preschool centers. According to Bereiter (1965) and Weikart (1969), the most effective preschool intervention programs seem to be those that not only are highly structured in terms of academic orientation but also provide many opportunities for the acquisition of verbal skills through effective participation and repetition.

The introduction of dialect-specific readers into the schools has been resisted by a cross section of the black community, such as middle-class black teachers, the black working class, and the Black Muslims. Ironically, whites found themselves in the position of defining blackness. Many educators were concerned about the possible negative effects of a nonstandard dialect on a speaker's progress in learning to read and write standard English. Williams (1975) feels that the use of dialectal readers in a country that is already divided by race and poverty is to institutionalize a low-prestige dialect in the schools. The proponents of dialectal readers argue that these readers would be used only in the early grades and that the children would then be shifted to standard English readers.

Much attention has been given to the receptive and productive language processes required in the teaching of reading. The hypothesis is that since reading is a receptive process, a reader does not need to be able to speak a dialect in order to read. That is, a speaker of black dialect can learn to read standard written English without becoming a speaker of standard English. However, it seems likely that in order for one to learn to read standard English, one needs receptive control of standard English.

Much discussion has been centered on the materials needed for initial reading instruction. Here the task is to find reading material both in terms of language structure and content that can best enable children to build on the language strengths they bring to school. This argument does not imply that the teaching of standard English is an infringement on the rights of minority cultures. It is necessary that students learn standard English, but there is a difference between emphasizing the development of positive skills which may facilitate a successful adaptation to a particular majority culture versus devaluating a group of people who may not emphasize the development of these particular skills.

REFERENCES

Bailey, B. *Jamaican Creole Syntax*. London: Cambridge University Press, 1966.

Bailey, B. Toward a new perspective in Negro English dialectology. *American Speech*, 1967, *40*, 171-7.

Bannatyne, A. *Language, Reading and Learning Disabilities*. Springfield, IL: Charles C Thomas, 1971.

Baratz, J. C. Language development in the economically disadvantaged child: A perspective. Paper presented at meeting of American Speech and Hearing Association, Washington, March 1968.

Baratz, J. C. A bi-dialectal task for determining language proficiency in economically disadvantaged Negro children. *Child Development*, 1969, *40*, 889-901.

Baratz, J. C. Language and cognitive assessment of Negro children: Assumptions and research needs. *Journal of American Speech and Hearing Association*, 1969, *11*(3), 87-91.

Baratz, J. C. Should Black children learn white dialect? *Journal of American Speech and Hearing Association*, 1970, *12*(9), 415-7.

Baratz, S. S. and Baratz, J. C. Negro ghetto culture and urban education: A cultural solution. *Social Education*, April 1969, 401-4.

Baratz, S. S. and Baratz, J. C. Early childhood intervention: The social science base of institutional racism. *Harvard Educational Review*, 1970, *40*, 29-50.

Bereiter, C. Academic instruction and pre-school children. In: R. Corbin and M. Crosby (Eds.), *Language Program for the Disadvantaged*. Champaign, IL: National Council for English, 1965, pp. 195-203.

Bereiter, C. and Engleman, S. *Teaching Disadvantaged Children in the Pre-School*. Englewood Cliffs, N.J.: Prentice-Hall, 1966.

Bernstein, B. Language and social class. *British Journal of Sociology*. 1960, *11*, 271-6.

Bernstein, B. Social class and linguistic development: A theory of social learning. In: A. H. Halsey, J. Floud, and C. A. Anderson, (Eds.), *Education, Economy, and Society*. New York: Free Press, 1961, pp. 288-314.

Bronfenbrenner, U. and Mahoney, M. A. *Influences on Human Development*. Second edition. New York: Dryden Press, 1975.

Castaneda, A., James, R. L., and Robbins, W. *The Educational Needs of Minority Groups*. Lincoln: Professional Educators Publications, 1974.

Chomsky, N. *Syntactic Structures*. The Hague: Mouton, 1959.

Covington, A. Teachers' attitudes toward black english: Effects on academic achievement. Paper presented at Conference on Cognitive Language Development of the Black Child. St. Louis, January, 1973.

Deutsch, M. The role of social class in language development and cognition. *American Journal of Orthopsychiatry*, 1965, *35*, 24-25.

Dillard, J. L. Negro children's dialect in the inner city. *Florida Foreign Language Reporter*, 1967, *2*, 7-10.

Dillard, J. L. *Black English: Its History and Usage in the U.S.* New York: Random House, 1972.

Edwards, J. and Stern, C. A comparison of three intervention programs with disadvantaged preschool children. *Journal of Special Education*, *4*(2), 205-14.

Ends, R. and Strawbridge, W., (Eds.), *Perspectives on Black America*. Englewood Cliffs, NJ: Prentice-Hall, 1970.

Foreit, K. G. and Donaldson, P. L. Dialect, race, and language proficiency: Another dead heat on the merry-go-round. *Child Development*, 1971, *42*, 1542-74.

Frasure, N. E. and Entwistle, D. R. Semantic and syntactic development in children. *Developmental Psychology*, 1973, *9*(2), 236-45.

Gay, J. and Tweney, R. D. Comprehension and production of standard black english by lower-class black children. *Developmental Psychology*, 1976, *12*(3), 262-8.

Genshaft, J. L. and Hirt, M. Language differences between Black children and white children. *Developmental Psychology*, 1974, *10*(3), 451-6.

Hess, R., Shipman, V., and Jackson, D. Some new dimensions in providing equal educational opportunity. *Journal of Negro Education*, 1965, *34*, 220-31.

Hetherington, E. and Parke, R. *Child Psychology: A Contemporary Viewpoint*. New York: McGraw-Hill, 1979.

Houston, S. H. A Re-examination of some assumptions about the language of the disadvantaged child. *Child Development*, 1970, 4(4).

Hunt, J. M. *The Challenge of Incompetence and Poverty*. Urbana: University of Illinois Press, 1969.

Jensen, A. R. How much can we boost IQ and scholastic achievement? *Harvard Educational Review*, 1969, *39*, 1-123.

Katz, I. The socialization of academic motivation in minority-group children. In: D. Levine (Ed.), *Nebraska Symposium on Motivation*. Lincoln: University of Nebraska Press, 1967.

Labov, W. Stages in the acquisition of standard english. In: *Social Dialects and Language Learning*. Champaign, Illinois: National Council of Teachers of English, 1965, 77-104.

Labov, W. *The Social Stratification of English in New York City*. Washington, D.C.: Center for Applied Linguistics, 1966.

Labov, W. The logic of non-standard English. In: F. Williams, (Ed.), *Language and Poverty: Perspectives on a Theme*. Chicago: Markham, 1970, pp. 153-89.

Labov, W., Cohen, P., Robins, C., and Lewis, J. *A Study of the Non-Standard English of Negro and Puerto Rican Speakers in New York City*. Cooperative Research Project No. 3288, U.S. Office of Education. New York: Columbia University, 1968.

Langacker, K. W. *Language and Its Structure*. New York: Harcourt-Brace, 1967.

Lenneberg, E. H. *Biological Foundations of Language*. New York: John Wiley, 1967.

Loban, W. D. *The Language of Elementary School Children*. Champaign, IL: National Council of Teachers of English, 1963.

Manyuk, P. *The Acquisition and Development of Language*. Englewood Cliffs, N.J.: Prentice-Hall, 1971.

McNeill, D. Developmental Linguistics. In: F. Smith & G. A. Miller, (Eds.), *The Genesis of Language: A Psycholinguistic Approach*. Cambridge: MIT Press, 1966.

McNeill, D. The development of language. In: P. J. Mussen (Ed.), *Carmichael's Manual of Child Psychology*. Volume 1. New York: John Wiley, 1970, pp. 1061-1152.

Murray, F. B. and Pikulski, J. J. (Eds.) *The Acquisition of Reading: Cognitive Linguistic and Perceptual Prerequisites*. Baltimore: University Park Press, 1978.

Osser, H. Biological and social factors in language development. In: F. Williams, (Ed.), *Language and Poverty*. Chicago: Markham, 1970.

Papolia, E. and Olds, S. *A Child's World: Infancy through Adolescence*. New York: McGraw-Hill, 1925.

Povich, E. and Baratz, J. Grammatical constructions of pre-school Negro children. Paper presented at meeting of American Speech and Hearing Association, Chicago, November 1967.

Stevenson, H. W. *Children's Learning*. Englewood Cliffs, N.J.: Prentice-Hall, 1972.

Stewart, W. Sociolinguistic factors in the history of American Negro dialects. *Florida Foreign Language Reporter*, Spring 1967.

Stewart, W. Continuity and change in American Negro dialects. *Florida Foreign Language Reporter*, Spring 1968.

Stewart, W. A. Urban Negro speech: Sociolinguistic factors affecting English teaching. In: R. W. Shuy, (Ed.), *Social Dialects and Language Learning*. Champaign, IL: National Council of Teachers of English, 1965.

Torrey, J. W. Illiteracy in the ghetto. *Harvard Educational Review*, 1970, *40*(2), 253-9.

Valentine, C. Deficit, differences, and bi-cultural models of Afro-American behavior. *Harvard Educational Review*, 1971, *41*(4), 137-57.

Weaver, S. J. Psycholinguistic abilities of culturally disadvantaged children. In: *Early Training Project*. Murfreesboro, TN, 1963.

Weikart, D. P. Comparative study of three pre-school curricula. Presented at the biennial meeting of the Society for Research in Child Development, Santa Monica, March 1969.

Williams, R. L., (Ed.) *Ebonics: The True Language of Black Folks*. St. Louis: The Institute of Black Studies, 1975.

Williams, R. L. and Rivers, L. W. The effects of language on the test performance of Black children. R. L. Williams (Ed.), *Ebonics*. St. Louis: The Institute of Black Studies, 1975.

Wilson, A. N. *The Developmental Psychology of the Black Child*. New York: African Research Publication, 1978.

CHAPTER 30

Educational Policy and Cultural Plurality

Armando M. Rodriquez

INTRODUCTION

As soon as one begins to speak about educational policy relative to any topic, the first problem one faces is determining what is meant by "educational policy" itself. Policy is developed at every level in the educational bureaucracy and it is influenced by all sorts of agencies and groups. It is also no secret that few educational policies or deliberations relate to any other policies or agencies and that most policies are developed to speak to a particular goal or problem in a particular educational setting.

There is very little, if any, agreement within the educational community on the definition or characteristics of an educational policy. In the everyday world of school boards and administrators there is no clear distinction between educational policy and an administrative rule or regulation. If we are going to look at how educational policy has impacted the na-

ture of cultural plurality, we will have to examine "policy" as it occurs on several different levels of the educational structure—from the federal level all the way down to the classroom level. The phrase "down to," by the way, is used intentionally. Without wishing to lay any value on the process, it is also a fact that most policy decisions on the local level of education are *reactive* rather than *proactive*. Federal or state guidelines appear (admittedly with some effort to obtain public reaction) and, generally, it is only then that local school boards and administrators begin to scramble to devise an appropriate "implementation policy" for their schools.

Cultural plurality, on the other hand, would seem to be a rather straightforward concept. In its simplest form, cultural plurality describes a situation in which the language, heritage, values, patterns of thinking and motivation *of more than one culture* are present. Historically, however, we know that there can exist a wide range of relationships between cultures in a so-called culturally pluralistic society. In our country, which certainly is pluralistic, we have seen everything from the melting pot characteristics of the acculturation movement and the paternalistic "compensatory" attitudes of recent years to the newer notions of cultural democracy. This latter philosophy espouses the concept that the home and community socialization experiences of all children, regardless of cultural background, are valuable in their own right. It is the recognition of *cultural democracy* that most accurately describes the intercultural relationships which we would regard as the full evolution of educational policy. But we are getting ahead of ourselves. It is both interesting and instructive to follow the development of multicultural awareness as it occurred on the various levels of our national educational scene.

NATIONAL EDUCATIONAL POLICY: OUT OF THE MELTING POT

From its earliest days of discovery and exploration, America was populated by an unusually diverse group of peoples and cultures. The colonies' settlers came to the new land from widely different racial, ethnic, and religious backgrounds. In later years, statesmen and philosophers argued that the unique American spirit, character, and strength came from the fusion of these disparate groups. The expression "melting pot" came into use to describe the process by which a unique national unity grew out of initial diversity. Like some ferrous alloy, the new "people" was viewed as stronger than any of the individual parts that went into its composition.

This vision of the superiority of the melted product over the ingredients led to two formulations of educational policy along the same lines. The more permissive view was articulated by the noted American educator and philosopher, John

Dewey. Dewey (1899) clearly felt that one's own cultural heritage is acceptable, but he also suggests that when it is merged with others it is even better. Although Dewey's view was certainly not exclusivist it nonetheless carried the latent message that the uniquely American cultural product was a step above the pre-existing cultures.

Another less tolerant viewpoint was characterized, around the turn of the century, by many respected educators whose attitude was that some cultural groups have brought with them traits which are unfit to be infused into the new American character (Itzkoff, 1969). The Anglo-Saxon model was held to be the ideal and all those who were in any way different from that model were encouraged to divest themselves of their objectionable qualities and conform to the model. This attitude reached its fullest expression during the "Americanization" movement of the early 1900s. The newly arriving immigrants were described as "illiterate," "docile," lacking in "self-reliance" and "initiative." They presented problems of "proper housing and living, moral and sanitary conditions, honest and decent government and proper education." These same assumptions were later to underlie the educational policies which would try to "help" culturally different children through compensatory education.

Both the permissive and the restrictive applications to education of the melting pot philosophy seriously affected the right of minority children to remain consonant with their culturally unique socialization processes. The pro-Anglo-Saxon attitude, especially, led to the use of the "family-is-damaging" model in the development of educational programs for non-Anglo-Saxon children. The family influences of ethnic groups were viewed by many educators as counterproductive and, in fact, harmful to the intellectual, social, and emotional growth of minority children. The family was seen as sabotaging the development of life styles and values typical of mainstream American culture. Children were daily confronted with teachers who demanded that each child identify exclusively with these "typical" ideals. And American public school teachers have characteristicly considered it their professional—and, in some cases, patriotic — responsibility to bring minority children into the mainstream.

The cultural exclusionist philosophy which we have been describing has affected national educational policy in three important areas: (a) in the determination of what children ought to learn or experience; (b) in the determination of how they ought to learn; and (c) in the determination of how the teacher should participate in the learning process. We will look at each of these policy determinations in more detail in later sections. However, it is important to get a sense of the classroom impact of these policies before we leave this topic. What children ought to learn or experience refers to decisions relating to curriculum in our schools. An obvious example of cultural exclusionism in curriculum is in the subject area of history. American public schools have developed and taught a very restricted history of the American people. Recognition was given primarily to historical figures and events which embodied the traits and qualities held in esteem by the majority group. The contributions of such groups as Native Americans, Black Americans, Mexican Americans, Asian Americans, women, and the poor were either overlooked entirely or seriously distorted. Even today, the success of the recent book and teleplay *Roots* (Haley, 1977) is, at least in part, attributable to the fact that many people were reading or hearing a different side of the slavery issue *for the first time.*

How children ought to learn brings into the discussion the question of differing learning styles. Recent research would seem to demonstrate that intellectual patterns observed in minority children are manifestations of culturally unique learning styles. The cultural exclusionists, if they recognized these differences at all, choose to ignore them and instead attempted to impose learning styles of their own choosing. As a result, because the dominant culture placed such a high value on competition, for example, the entire educational system was (and, in many instances, still is) competitive. Overlooked was the fact that many minority cultures place a much higher value on cooperative behavior than on competition. As a result, when minority children entered the American school system, they were plunged into a completely contra-culture learning experience.

The final area where cultural exclusionism influenced national educational policy was in the determination of how the teacher should participate in the learning process. This discussion is perhaps the most critical because it speaks to teaching styles (incorporating individual learning styles) and the kind of interpersonal relationship that should exist between teacher and pupil. Again, recent research has shed light on an area which was never even considered by the cultural exclusionists. The concepts of field sensitivity and field independence have provided some interesting insights into the dynamics of interpersonal perceptions between teachers and students. When one considers that most teachers were from the dominant, generally field-independent culture, while most minority children were field-sensitive, it is immediately obvious why these children have so often been misunderstood by their teachers. The notion of field-independence vs. field-sensitivity will be examined later at greater length but even in this brief introduction it becomes apparent that the curriculum, learning styles and teaching styles encouraged by the cultural exclusionists all said quite clearly to the minority child, "The way you and your parents do things is not good, and the only way you will ever achieve success is to abandon your ways and become like us." Is it any wonder that the children were torn. To follow this advice would be to betray their family and community. Not to follow the advice was to risk interminable conflict in school.

The next phase of the move out of the melting pot, on the national scene, occurred in the late 1950s and early 1960s. Almost overnight, social psychologists became enamoured of new research in the area of sensory stimulation and deprivation. Laboratory experiments conducted on animals and later on humans indicated a close relationship between sensory deprivation and impaired learning ability. Puppies, for example, that were raised in isolation or darkness were found to require much longer time than normal puppies to learn to avoid painful encounters with toys which carried an electric shock. It wasn't very long before educational psychologists began to make some interesting comparisons. Everyone knew that minority children were not doing as well in school as majority children. And, of course, there was nothing wrong with what was being taught or how it was being taught. Therefore, the explanation must be with minority children as it was with the poor puppies. "Sensory deprivation" was the explanation for retarded development. Something must have been missing in the home lives of the minority children. If you think this is beginning to sound familiar, you're right. The new movement which could come to be called "Compensatory Education" was only the old cultural exclusionist philosophy clothed in new language (Beck and Saxe, 1965; Gordon and Wilkerson, 1966).

College and university courses began to be introduced into teacher-education curricula with titles such as "Education of the Culturally Disadvantaged" and "Psychology of the Deprived Child." With the help of government funds which were made available to "improve the educational opportunities of impoverished children," scholars began producing books and papers on the harmful effects of "restricted" learning environments. The common assumption was that certain so-

cialization processes (namely, minority cultures, languages, heritages and values) were deficient in providing the kind of experiences required for normal intellectual development (Passow, 1963). Something had to be done to make minority children capable of profiting from educational opportunities. The solution to the deprivation of the children was to counteract the influence of their parents with enriched learning experiences at the preschool and grade school level. Elaborate strategies were devised for neutralizing the harmful socialization processes of culturally different homes. Well-intentioned educators and social psychologists decided that the only hope for the children was to expedite the process of their acculturation. The children must assume, as soon as possible, the language and cultural, motivational, and cognitive learning styles of mainstream America.

Once again the home and real-life experiences of the children were found to be irrelevant and harmful. Once again minority children were being forced to conform to a predetermined mold created for them by those who knew what was "better" for them. Once again, membership in certain ethnic groups was "established" to be a "depriving" experience. In the final analysis, compensatory education, however well meaning, did in fact only reinforce the previous distortions of the cultural exclusionists.

The third phase of the development of national educational policy relative to cultural plurality is occurring now. Such well-known educational leaders as Dr. Alfredo Castañeda at Stanford, Dr. Leslie Herold at California State University, San Bernardino, and Dr. Manuel Ramirez at the University of California, Riverside, have now begun to speak of what they call "cultural democracy" (Ramirez and Castañeda, 1974). They would challenge the assumption that the mission of American schools is to promote and transmit some higher culture and values which just so happen to coincide with the culture and values of the majority culture. It is their belief that it is the right of every American child to remain identified with his own home and community socialization processes. And it follows, therefore, that the school should actively contribute to the positive development and strengthening of these unique socialization experiences as valuable in their own right. Instead of discarding the culture of their homes, the children can use these unique experiences as a basis for exploring Anglo-American middle-class language, heritage, values, pattern of thinking and motivation.

Dr. Ramirez maintains that educational programs which are not based on the unique learning styles of the people they serve do not provide culturally relevant learning environments and are culturally undemocratic. He further suggests that the direct results of practices which make students question the values they have acquired in their homes and neighborhoods are reflected in the school drop-out rates and in the low level of educational attainment of minority children (Ramirez and Castañeda, 1974).

For the first time someone is suggesting that the lack of educational success of minority children is not a result of the fact that they belong to a certain minority group, nor is it a result of the so-called deficient values they have learned from their parents. The problem is not with the children, it is with the prevailing American educational philosophy which denies the right of minority children to be educated in a manner commensurate with their own learning styles. In short, American schools have become institutions of Anglo-American middle class acculturations rather than institutions of education.

The concept of cultural democracy, on the other hand, implies that the individual has a right to maintain a bicultural identity—that is, to retain his identification with his ethnic group while at the same time learning to adopt mainstream American values and life styles. As an educational philosophy, cultural democracy encourages schools to develop curriculum, teaching strategies and instructional methods which are sensitive to the uniqueness which each individual student brings to the classroom. Because cultural democracy focuses on the teacher-pupil relationship (specifically with regard to field sensitive vs. field independent characteristics), it also suggests a greater emphasis on humanism in the educational process (Martinez, 1970).

At this point the reader may be thinking that what we are discussing is merely "multicultural education" and that we already have that in our schools. To be sure, some efforts towards multicultural education have been made in some schools by some teachers. Typically, however, such efforts have emphasized only the most obvious aspects of social, racial and cultural groups which the child must master in order to competently and effectively participate in those groups. Multicultural programs have generally included the introduction of such things as language, holidays, historical figures and some traditions which previously were excluded from the school curriculum.

The type of multicultural program which we would envision would include these curricular objectives but would recognize and use those features of the child's socialization experiences which have shaped his preferred or dominant learning style. Such a program would use the familiar as building blocks to the unfamiliar. The child would be first encouraged to label and understand important features of his own cultural origins and loyalties. His own language, heritage, values and modes of cognition and motivation can then serve as the basis for exploring and developing a familiarity and attachment to alternative expressions of thought, values, and life styles. Democratic cultural pluralism, therefore, implies that the educational goal of all children in America should be that of learning to function competently and effectively in more than one cultural world.

Cultural democracy, as an educational philosophy, is not yet a reality in America. It can only be hoped that adequate funding to promote efforts in a cultural democracy will soon become available in order to produce positive effects on a national scale to equal, and hopefully exceed, the negative effects created, even though unintentionally, by compensatory programs.

We now have some idea of where we have been and where we should be going with respect to national policy regarding cultural plurality. These broad national attitudes we have examined have formed and will continue to form the framework for the bread-and-butter decisions, or policies which are implemented on the state and district levels.

LOCAL EDUCATIONAL POLICY: A LOOK AT THE SOUTHWEST

In February of 1974, the U.S. Commission on Civil Rights (U.S.C.C.R.) completed its report to the President and Congress on the education of Mexican-American children in the Southwest (U.S.C.C.R., 1975). That report, which examined conditions and practices in schools in Arizona, California, Colorado, New Mexico and Texas, documented an educational system which *ignores* the language and culture of Mexican-American students. The Commission specifically studied four areas of education which relate to our discussion of cultural plurality and local educational policy; curriculum, student assignment practices, teacher education, and teacher-pupil interaction.

Curriculum

Curriculum is the "stuff" of education. Although its primary purpose is to provide students with intellectual and social skills, we have already seen that it is also a powerful means of transmitting to children the culture and values of a society.

The critical question, therefore, is how are policy decisions made regarding curriculum. On the state level, in the five Southwestern states, there are three main bodies which regulate the curriculum offered: the legislature, the board of education, and the department of education. Several states also have a fourth body, a textbook selection committee, which impacts the shape of the curriculum. Typically the state legislatures set only broad outlines for the state's curriculum. However, in each case the legislature possesses many more specific powers than are typically used. Only California and Colorado have made any provision for requiring inclusion in the curriculum of the history and contributions of minority peoples. (And these two efforts carry no mechanism to monitor compliance.) Why have the legislatures failed to act to improve equal educational opportunity for all their state's children? The answer is probably because there are so few minority legislators. For example, of a total of 602 legislators in Arizona, California, Colorado, New Mexico and Texas, only 62 are Mexican-American, and more than half of these are in New Mexico.

A similar situation exists when we look at state boards of education. In the educational hierarchy, the state board of education is given the greatest educational policy making authority. State boards are vested with the power to review the educational needs of the students in the state, to adopt and promote policies to meet those needs, to evaluate the services of the educational program, and to set policy concerning general curriculum needs. Again, however, although the power is there, nothing has been done to revamp curricula to include materials which describe models and achievements of cultures other than those of the Anglo-Saxon majority. Of 58 members of the five state boards of education, only 6 are Mexican-American. Minorities are simply grossly underrepresented where decisions are made (U.S.C.C.R., 1972).

Although state departments of education have little direct power to set policy—they are generally the implementation arm of a state educational system—indirectly they can have a tremendous effect on school curriculum. State legislatures and boards of education usually outline the theory behind a course or program but do not specify the method of implementation. Departments of education detail the component of programs, define how the program is to be operated, prescribe the amount of time within the curriculum that a program shall have, and provide specifications to publishers of the texts to be used. Therefore, there is nothing to prevent state departments from setting comprehensive guidelines aimed at providing a culturally democratic learning environment. To date, none of the departments in the Southwest has developed such guidelines. There are 1898 professional staff members in the five state departments of education. Only 110 are Mexican-American. If the Mexican-American student population alone was fairly represented in the state departments, there would be 370 staff members. The only way that the concerns of the culturally diverse populations of our country will ever be heard will be when members of those populations have an equal say in the decisions that affect them.

Four of the states studied by the Civil Rights Commission also had what are called Textbook Committees (U.S.C.C.R., 1971, 1972). All of these are appointed positions. In general, the procedure for selecting textbooks involves writing publishers' specifications for texts, evaluation of materials, and selection and publication of a list of "approved texts." If districts want to receive state aid for textbooks they must choose from the approved list. Although textbook committees could act to insure that minorities are fully and fairly represented in the approved textbooks, by and large they have not done so.

Again, minority representation on these committees was characteristically low. Although Textbook Committees are tremendously important to the whole curriculum definition process, minorities on all states' committees were underrepresented.

When we look at how curriculum decisions are made on the local or district level, we find that districts generally have three curriculum decision-making bodies: the local school board, the school district administrative staff, and the teachers. Without going into great detail, we can summarize by saying that what was found to be the case at the State level is found in microcosm on the local level. Minorities are underrepresented on school boards, on district administrative staffs, and among teachers. As a result, curriculum in the schools in the Southwest is geared to meeting the educational needs of the middle-class Anglo child. Some efforts have been made to develop curriculum which is responsive to the minority child. Generally, however, these are patchwork responses to an exclusion of minority children which pervades the entire curriculum.

Student Assignment Practices

The second area which the Commission studied regarding local education policy in the Southwest was student assignment practices. At first glance, one may question how assignment practices can in any way be construed to be affected by cultural differences. Assignment practices generally involve three common policies: grade retention, ability grouping, and placement of students into classes for the mentally retarded. The practices are ostensibly aimed at providing a learning environment where students can achieve at the level of their ability. Each assignment practice requires evaluations by school officials concerning student abilities. The reason we feel these practices should be discussed here is because under all these policies children are weighed in the balance by the educational system. Many are found wanting. For some reason a disproportionate number of these are minority children.

Using Mexican-American children as examples again, we will look at each of these practices; however, this time, we will not ask *who* is making the decision, but rather *how* the decision is being made.

Grade retention is widely practiced to remedy inadequate academic progress and to aid in the development of students who are judged to be emotionally immature. In the Southwest, Mexican-American children are retained in grades at a rate two to three times greater than Anglo children (Lopez and Padilla, 1978; U.S.C.C.R., 1972, 1975). A few of these children are retained because of "bad grades." The problem is that in the review of the research done by the Commission there was found no reliable data that suggested retention improved the students' academic ability. Generally, students were merely recycled through the same instructional program that was inappropriate for them the first time and which was equally inappropriate—and of even less interest—the second time.

The vast majority of children are retained in grade because school personnel decide they are socially or emotionally immature for their age. Decisions to retain students in grade because of immaturity typically are not made on the basis of objective data but rather on the basis of personal judgments of teachers and principals, none of whom generally has received any specific training for making these decisions. Most principals and teachers are Anglos and tend to have only a superficial understanding of minority cultures. Hence, judgments regarding the emotional and social adjustments of minority children are likely to be based on limited information and distorted perceptions of minority behavior. In fact, there is evidence that Anglos often perceive the culturally

different behavior as "pathological."

A second assignment practice which is decreasing but still very common is ability grouping, whether in the form of *tracking* (assigning students to the same ability group for all academic classes) or *homogenous grouping* (placing students in different ability group classes for academic subjects). Without getting into a discussion of the pros and cons of ability grouping, the question that is relevant to our discussion is how students are assigned to different ability groups. There are two criteria which are most commonly used to place students in ability groups — evaluation of student performance on IQ or standardized achievement tests and recommendations of teachers.

Each of these methods has built-in flaws which result in the fact that throughout the Southwest twice as many Anglos are in *high* ability classes than are Mexican-Americans and twice as many Mexican-Americans are in low ability classes than are Anglos. The percentages become more disparate as the minority percentage in the school declines. In other words, the fewer minority children there are, the more they are regarded as different and the more they are placed in low ability grouping.

The problems with cultural biases in IQ and standardized tests are now well documented. The biases, basically, are of three types. Sometimes the tests refer to things, concepts, or experiences which are not found in minority cultures. Sometimes a minority child may be familiar with the concept but is not familiar with the applications of the concept in the test. Finally, tests which are supposed to measure skills other than reading oftentimes actually measure a child's vocabulary, English language skills, reading speed or comprehension (Mercer, 1974).

When placement is done as a result of teacher recommendations, we are frequently faced again with the situation of the Anglo teacher who does not understand the minority child—his culture, learning style, etc.—and therefore declares the child a failure.

There are two significant negative factors which affect ability grouping in general but which become magnified when one is speaking of minority children. The first is the self-fulfilling prophecy effect. Place a kid in a "dumb" class—and in spite of some rather creative efforts to label the classes, kids still know which are the "dumb" classes or groups and which are the "smart" classes—and both he and the teacher will begin to think of him as "dumb." Minority children already feel at a disadvantage coming into an Anglo-dominated school environment. Add to that the onus of being considered "dumb" and it's no wonder minority children are not turned on by school. A second negative effect results from the fact that most teachers would rather teach high ability groups than low ability groups. This suggests that children in low ability groups are likely to be taught by teachers who are unenthusiastic, dissatisfied with their teaching assignment, and with a low opinion of the children's abilities.

A final assignment practice which disproportionately affects minority children is placement in EMR classes. When a school determines that a child is academically too slow to benefit from the regular school curriculum, it may place that child in a class for the Educable Mentally Retarded (EMR). Unlike ability grouping and grade retention which, at least theoretically, hold out the hope that the students will catch up with their peers, children in EMR classes are told, in effect, that they cannot compete in a regular classroom environment and must remain in special classes. All the states in the Southwest have such classes and it is significant that twice as many minority children—and in some cases three times as many—are placed in these classes than are Anglos. Again the question is how children are evaluated as needing to be placed in EMR classes. And, again, the answer is by IQ and standardized tests and by teacher recommendation.

Although the words "mental retardation" sound as if they refer only to impairment in intellectual functioning, most authorities agree that true mental retardation is *manifested* by impairments in both intellectual function and adaptive behavior. Adaptive behavior is described as the ability to perform day-to-day functions appropriate to one's age group. This has led to the concept of the so-called "Six-Hour Retarded Child" (Mercer, 1973, 1974). Such a child is considered retarded from 9 A.M. to 3 P.M., five days a week, but may be exceptionally adapted to the situation and community in which he spends the rest of his hours.

In summary, we are not necessarily advocating the discontinuance of such practices as grade retention, ability grouping, or EMR classes. We are suggesting, however, that state and local school boards need to give greater attention to *how* these types of assignments are being made. Instruments must be devised which are relevant and valid and teachers and counselors must be trained to observe differences between lack of intellectual ability and mere incompatibility with a given learning style.

Teacher Education

A third area where state and local authorities have a great deal to say regarding "policy" is teacher education. Obviously, if teachers are ever to have the skills we have called for all through this chapter, the first steps will have to occur during the teacher education process. Most teacher education programs are composed of four parts—several years of liberal arts courses, foundation courses which deal with educational principles, methods courses which explore teaching techniques, and a period of supervised practice teaching. What is taught in these four components is generally controlled by the state through the state board of education, by the federal Office of Education through special funding it makes available, and by the staffs of the teacher education institutions themselves. The Commission study discovered that no teacher education institution in the Southwest requires that teacher trainees take Spanish, anthropology, sociology, ethnic studies courses, or any other course which would help prepare the teacher to deal effectively with the culturally different child (U.S.C.C.R., 1975). Furthermore, in the practice teaching component which could allow teaching trainees to experience firsthand the need for some of the unique skills which they should develop in order to work effectively with minority children, the process is again frustrated. Many teaching institutions are located in predominantly Anglo middle-class areas. The institutions generally have agreements with nearby schools to accept teaching trainees, with the result that training takes place in Anglo middle-class schools. The overwhelming majority of student teachers are Anglos and most likely live in Anglo neighborhoods. Teacher training institutions, if they cannot find a training site near their institution, will try to place the trainee in a school near his or her home. Again, the training most likely takes place in an Anglo middle-class neighborhood.

We have now examined the broad philosophical "policies" which have guided American education and we have discussed some of the particular policy areas which are articulated by state and local authorities. In each we have discovered that, intentionally or otherwise, these policies have all had negative effects on minority children primarily because the policies themselves have grown out of a predominantly Anglo-Saxon middle-class mentality. In the final sections of this chapter we will examine what learning and teaching styles are most suited to minority children and we will also discuss the findings of the U.S. Commission on Civil Rights' study of the kind of instructional styles which are actually used in schools in the Southwest.

The Classroom Educational Policy: Where It Happens

The final educational policy level that we want to look at is, in many ways, the most important. When all has been said and done at the other levels of educational policy-making, it is the individual teacher within the four walls of his or her classroom who gives flesh and blood to the educational philosophies. The U.S. Commission on Civil Rights report points out that the heart of the educational process is the interaction between teacher and student (U.S.C.C.R., 1975). It is through this interaction that the school system makes its major impact upon the child. The way the teacher interacts with the student is a major determinant of the quality of education the child receives.

All the notions of cultural plurality which we have discussed so far come to focus in the personal policy decisions which the teacher makes regarding the students in his or her classroom. Before we discuss the findings of a nationwide study of multicultural classroom interaction patterns, let us take a closer look at the concepts of field independence and field sensitivity which we introduced earlier.

Witkin (1967) and his colleagues were among the first to articulate the difference between field independent and field dependent cognitive styles. Ramirez and his associates (Ramirez, Taylor, and Petersen, 1971) found the Witkin (1967) dichotomy to be good but moved away from the valuing by which Witkin established a superiority of field independence over field dependence. Ramirez, in fact, changed field dependence to field sensitivity to balance the two notions. In summary, some of the major research findings regarding the difference between field sensitive and field independent persons are as follows (Figueroa, 1980):

1. Field independent persons perform better than field sensitive persons on tests which involve separating a part from an organized whole or rearranging parts to make a whole.
2. Field independent children tend to be "task centered" in taking tests; field sensitive children tend to glance at the examiner and pay more attention to the social atmosphere of the testing situation.
3. Field sensitive persons appear to be more imaginative in verbally describing social situations. The social environment seems to be more significant for field sensitive persons in other ways. They tend to remember faces and social words better than field independent persons. They are more influenced by expressions of confidence or doubt than are field independent persons.
4. Students and teachers who share a common cognitive style tend to perceive each other more favorably than do students and teachers whose cognitive styles are dissimilar.
5. Field sensitive persons prefer psychotherapists with whom they can establish a personal relationship. Field independent persons, on the other hand, prefer therapists who take a more passive, consultant-like role. Field sensitive and field independent psychotherapists, in turn, tend to prefer the very kinds of client-therapist relationships that field sensitive and field independent persons, respectively, seem to be seeking.

With the differences in mind we can now turn to the observations of the U.S. Commission on Civil Rights regarding teacher-student interaction in the multicultural classroom. The Commission found six areas of interaction in which there was a significant disparity between the treatment Anglo children received and the treatment minority (Mexican-American) children received (U.S.C.C.R., 1975).

The first disparity was in teacher praise and encouragement. Most teachers give very little praise to any of their students, but the average Anglo child received about 36 percent more praise or encouragement than the average minority pupil in the same classroom. When we consider that Anglo children are typically more field independent and less dependent on social rewards and that typically minority children are field sensitive and very dependent on warm, affectionate support, the 36 percent disparity is multiplied manyfold. Another interesting finding regarding teacher praise was that minority teachers gave praise or encouragement to Anglo children 58 percent more often than to minority children!

A second area of disparity was in the acceptance and use of student ideas. One of the most effective means of encouraging students to participate in classroom discussion is through the use of behavior characterized as the "acceptance and use of student ideas." When a teacher makes statements acknowledging or incorporating a student's contribution, the teacher is both commending the child and informing the class that the teacher thinks that this student's contribution is worth listening to. In short, it is a very positive, constructive way of giving praise.

In view of the importance of this type of teacher behavior it is disturbing that the Commission discovered that the average Anglo pupil heard the teacher repeat, or refer to, an idea he or she had expressed about 40 percent more than did the average minority child. This is the exact opposite of what the disparity should be if teaching styles were adjusted to individual children's learning styles. Minority children (and many Anglo children also) need to know that what they say—and thereby they themselves—are valuable in the eyes of the teacher. The personal approval is much more important than gold stars or As.

The category "Positive Teacher Response" represented a composite of acceptance of student feelings, praise and encouragement, and acceptance or use of student ideas. The combined category, therefore, measured the degree of teacher warmth, approval, and encouragement, and, as such, was an indicator of the emotional tone of the teacher-student interactions. As a result of its study, the Commission found that the average Anglo child receives about 40 percent more positive response from the teacher than does the average minority child. When we consider that field sensitive children depend heavily on expressions of approval and confidence, we can see why for many minority children the school classroom is a very cold and uncomfortable atmosphere and why many Anglo teachers are viewed with an uncertainty that often borders on fear.

One of the common criticisms of minority children by insensitive teachers is that they do not speak out in class . . . they just sit there. The Commission decided to look into the amount of encouragement to speak which teachers give minority students. The study showed that the average Anglo student received 21 percent more questions from the teacher than the average minority child. The amount of teacher questioning is important because it indicates the extent to which students are asked or allowed to speak by the teacher. Class participation, an indispensable element of a live learning environment, is typically stimulated by teacher questions. To be sure, not all questioning is positive and there appears to be a fairly reliable relationship between the frequency of asking questions and increased pupil achievement. It is also characteristic of minority children to be more reserved and to refrain from speaking until invited to do so. A teacher who is not aware of this could wait forever for the child to volunteer an answer or make a comment.

The Commission also studied the amount of all non-critical teacher talk that was directed to Anglo and minority children and found that teachers spend 23 percent more time talking to Anglo students than to minority children. It was no surprise,

therefore, that Anglo students spoke out in class 29 percent more often than did minority children. All of these statistics, viewed as a composite, display a classroom pattern in which minority children are not encouraged to become involved participants in the activities of the class to the same extent that Anglo children are. Is it any wonder that minority children "just sit there"?!

If a teacher really wanted to do something to encourage greater involvement by minority children, what should he or she do? How does one create a culturally democratic learning environment? How can teaching style be adjusted to take into account both the field-independent and field-sensitive learner? This is obviously not the place to go into detail in response to these questions. However, it may prove helpful to share two summaries of field-sensitive and field-independent teaching strategies and curriculum. Even a brief examination of these summary categories will reveal some of the marked differences in approach which the two styles take to presenting instructional material to children (Ramirez and Castañeda, 1974).

TEACHING STRATEGIES

Field Sensitive Teaching

1. openly warm and affectionate

2. social rewards used to strengthen personal ties and group spirit

3. lessons prefaced with supportive assurances from teacher and detailed overview of objectives

4. problem solving strategies modeled by teacher who then stresses application of general rules to particular problems

5. students' attention drawn to generalization and global characteristics ("the big picture")

6. curriculum is humanized and adapted to students' personal experiences

Field Independent Teaching

1. formal and serious

2. non-social rewards given in recognition of individual achievement

3. lessons prefaced with factual information and reminders of individual effort

4. solutions to problems often left to imagination of students who use teacher more as a resource person than model

5. students' attention directed to individual elements and ways of combining these to reach conclusions and generalizations

6. curriculum focuses on factual details, often making reference to formulas, graphs and tables

CURRICULUM

Field Sensitive

1. materials readily lend themselves to fantasy, humor and humanization

2. relevant—teacher and students can easily relate personal experiences to curriculum

3. materials "invite" expressions of feelings from both teacher and students

4. design or format of materials is suitable for cooperative efforts and group projects

5. main principles and solutions are easy for teacher to demonstrate and model; materials given to students call for application of principles

Field Independent

1. materials (such as graphs and charts) draw attention almost exclusively to factual details

2. materials have high intrinsic appeal; although irrelevant to personal experience, concepts are sufficiently interesting in and of themselves to sustain student interest

3. materials require a high degree of concentration and methodical attention to subtle details

4. materials are more suitable for individual

effort and competition than for cooperative group work

5. materials stimulate students to search on their own for generalizations and unique solutions

The reason we have discussed field-sensitive vs. field-independent learning and teaching styles at such length is because the policy which the teacher establishes in the classroom regarding how concerned he or she will be about the culturally imbedded learning styles of the children is, in the final analysis, the most important policy decision made within the educational system. All the policies established at the federal, state, and district level are meaningless if the teacher, in his or her daily lessons, chooses to contradict or ignore them.

We have now looked at educational policy decisions regarding cultural plurality as they occur at all levels of American education. We have seen the move from melting-pot cultural exclusionism to the beginning notions of cultural democracy. We have seen the effects of the lack of minority representation on state and district boards in such areas as curriculum development, student assignment policies, and teacher education. Finally, we have seen how teacher policy decisions regarding instructional styles can dramatically affect the ability of minority children to participate in classroom activities and to feel comfortable and positive toward their learning environment. At every level we have found that minority children have not received an equal opportunity. But the picture is not all bad. New efforts to bring the nation's educational system more in line with the principles of cultural democracy hold great promise for all American children.

REFERENCES

Beck, J. M. and Saxe, R. W. (Eds.) *Teaching the Culturally Disadvantaged Pupil.* Springfield, IL: Charles C Thomas, 1965.

Dewey, J. *The Schools and Society*. Chicago: University of Chicago Press, 1899.

Figueroa, R. A. Field dependence, ethnicity, and cognitive styles. *Hispanic Journal of Behavioral Science*, 1980, *2*(1), 10.

Gordon, Edmond W. and A. Wilkerson. *Compensatory Education for the Disadvantaged*. New York: College Entrance Examination Board, 1966.

Haley, A. *Roots*. New York: Dell, 1977.

Itzkoff, W. *Cultural Pluralism and American Education*. Scranton, PA: International Textbook, 1969.

Lopez, R. E. and Padilla, A. M. Civil rights noncompliance letters to schools: A review. *Research Bulletin*, Spanish speaking mental health Research Center, U.C.L.A. Summer 1978, *3*(2), 1-6.

Martinez, A. Literacy through democratization of education. *Harvard Educational Review*, May 1970, *40*, 3-6.

Mercer, J. *Labelling the Mentally Retarded*. Berkeley: University of California Press, 1973.

Mercer, J. R. A policy statement: On assessment procedures and the rights of children. *Harvard Educational Review*, February 1974, *44*, 17-34.

Passow, A. H. *Education in Depressed Areas*. New York: Bureau of Publications, Teacher College, Columbia University, 1963.

Ramirez, M., Taylor, C., and Petersen, B. Mexican-American cultural membership and adjustment to school. *Developmental Psychology*, 1971, *4*, 41.

Ramirez, M. and Castañeda, A. *Cultural Democracy, Bicognitive Development, and Education*. New York: Academic Press, 1974.

U.S. Commission on Civil Rights. *The Unfinished Education*. Report #2, Mexican American Education Study, October 1971.

U.S. Commission on Civil Rights. *The Excluded Student: Educational Practices Affecting Mexican Americans in the Southwest*. Washington, D.C.: U.S. Commission on Civil Rights Mexican American Education Study Report III, May 1972.

U.S. Commission on Civil Rights. *Toward Quality Education for Mexican Americans*. Washington, D.C.: U.S. Commission on Civil Rights, February 1975.

Witkin, H. A. A cognitive-style approach to cross-cultural research. *International Journal of Psychology*, 1967, *2*, 233-250.

PART VI

Research and

Social Policy

Issues

CHAPTER 31

The Juvenile Justice System and Minorities

Armando Morales, D.S.W.,

Yvonne Ferguson, M.D.

and Paul R. Munford, Ph.D.

The "Juvenile Justice System" refers to official structures, agencies and institutions with which juveniles may become involved, including the Juvenile Court, law enforcement agencies, detention facilities, the probation department, correctional institutions and after-care programs. This system is guided by a complex interplay of laws, heritage and current cultural and political forces. Its resultant functions reveal major philosophical and programmatic contradictions. For example, the juvenile court is ostensibly a benevolent setting functioning to help the child; however, children now have to be protected by attorneys in court, given common due process violations. The goal of punishing the child is rarely stated as the philosophical rationale regarding the purpose of the Juvenile Court, yet this seems to be the clear intention of many individuals in the general public and among many judges and law enforcement personnel. In some instances, these intentions are also present in the law. For example, in discussing Juvenile Court Law, the California Welfare and Institutions Code (Section 502a) states that "the purpose of this chapter is . . . to impose on the minor a sense of responsibility for his own acts."

Even a liberal such as Senator Edward Kennedy shares such views regarding what should be a goal of the juvenile justice system. In a 1978 speech to the International Association of Chiefs of Police, he advocated "significant punishment" for juvenile offenders (L.A. Times, 1978b).

Currently, one finds three trends in the

handling of youths in the juvenile criminal justice system: 1) more lenient dispositions—often non-court—of those youngsters (sometimes called status offenders) who commit crimes which, had they been committed by adults, would not have been considered crimes (truants, runaways, incorrigibles); 2) the effort to shift the treatment of status offenders from courts and probation programs to community social agencies; and 3) harsher treatment of juvenile offenders who commit serious crimes. The literature does not make it clear, however, whether or not minority youth are receiving equal treatment in the juvenile justice system as to arrests, diversion opportunities (out-of-court, probation, and institution handling) and punishment. Some authors, such as Sarri and Vinter, would argue that minority youth are *not* receiving equal treatment. For example, a National Assessment of Juvenile Corrections (NAJC) study of 42 randomly selected correctional programs involving 922 youths ranging in age from 8 to 24 revealed that more than half (55 percent) of institutionalized youth were minority (mostly Blacks, 32.2 percent), with whites representing 45 percent. For juvenile delinquents referred to community residential programs, the opposite was found to be true with whites comprising almost 54 percent of those in community programs and minorities 46 percent. This finding is even more dramatic considering that the minority population in the United States is only 15 percent. Sarri and Vinter (1976) therefore concluded that:

... these findings clearly indicate that juvenile correctional programs disproportionately represent minority populations. Overall, however, we have no information showing that minority youth are more delinquent than whites, either in terms of self-reported frequency or in engagement in a variety of delinquent behaviors, or in terms of the offenses for which they were committed.

It would appear that subtle, institu-tional racism dynamics in the juvenile justice system would be one factor to be considered in the over-representation of minority youth. In this respect, minority children are at far greater risk than white children of being permanently emotionally scarred by their experiences with the juvenile justice system. Additionally, the impact of their arrests and court records will handicap them further in future employment in a society with an increasing paucity of job opportunities for inner-city minority youth. Meager employment opportunities will further lock them into a life of continued poverty and possibly also criminality.

This chapter will examine more closely the minority youth experiences in the juvenile justice system in the Los Angeles area where the total minority population reached 51 percent in 1980. These experiences might be shared by minority youth in other parts of the country. Following a few historical comments concerning the juvenile justice system, the components of the system (police, probation, Juvenile Court, and institutions) will be discussed in greater detail.

HISTORICAL OVERVIEW

A review of selected philosophical treatises on children's rights by Worsfold (1974) serves to highlight parallel milestones in the history of the juvenile justice system. In the 17th century, Thomas Hobbes espoused the paternalistic view that children were cared for solely because they were capable of serving their fathers who held absolute authority over their offspring's life and well-being. John Locke later emphasized the element of children's "natural rights" which included freedom from anything which might ever injure or affront them, the safeguard of which rested solely on the benevolence of parents. Still later in the 19th century, John Stuart Mill pronounced society's absolute authority over children, excluding them from any right to free choice because of their inability to decide what is in their own best interest.

Embracing these themes of ideological development, medieval society for all practical purposes regarded children as little adults, as, for example, manifested by their dress and titles, if aristocratic, with many attendant adult responsibilities once they became verbal and motorically developed enough to not require adult supervision. The psychosexual period called adolescence was virtually ignored in order to provide necessary labor to a society which was inching its way out of an agrarian order and to condense life scripts into the much shorter life span of that period. At the turn of this century, the large demand for cheap and free labor necessitated by the Industrial Revolution heralded the era of social reform in regard to the rights of children—particularly children of the poor who were being exploited in factories and incarcerated with adults in almshouses, asylums, and prisons. Juvenile reformatories in the U. S. numbered sixty-five by 1900 (Polier, 1974).

In 1909 the White House convened a Conference on the Care of Dependent Children organized by the leaders of the Settlement House Movement such as social workers Jane Addams and Lillian Wald, and the National Child Labor Committee. This was the first of such conferences held each decade thereafter which brought together concerned professionals, parents, and political agitators for child advocacy. Congress created the Children's Bureau with its focus on infant and maternal mortality and health, funding it a controversial $25,000 (Beck, 1973). As a result of these collective efforts, several states passed statutes establishing juvenile courts in which delinquent children were to be handled separately and differently from adult violators of the law. The practice of placing youth on probation and assigning probation officers was initiated as an alternative to sentencing and dismissal of the case (Kanner, 1972).

These reforms ushered in the child guidance movement of the 1920s, led by Thom in Boston. With the opening of demonstration clinics in several New England cities staffed by interdisciplinary professional teams, the field of psychiatry officially recognized the unique problems and needs of persons under 18 years of age. Gradually, foster home placement organizations and the field of special education arose, providing yet additional services to juvenile courts (Kanner, 1972).

Currently, within the juvenile justice system there is wide variation in policies and practices from state to state and within states. This should not preclude the determination of a set of policy and operational standards which would ultimately permit optimal reintegration of youth into society where guilt is judged. In cases where guilt is not found, such standards should ensure that innocent youth are not traumatized by society's mistakes.

THE POLICE

Juvenile delinquency, crime, violence and police policy and practices have a strong effect on children growing up in minority communities. The Joint Commission on Mental Health of Children (1969) recommended that the nature of this effect and its relationship to mental health be more closely examined. The majority of Hispanic *barrio* and Black ghetto residents resent police surveillance. The feeling is even more intense among minority youth (Wertham and Piliavin, 1975). As soon as a patrolman begins to interrogate these youngsters, they often feel their moral identity is being challenged because of their dress, hair style, skin color and presence in the community itself. Often this is true. It is not uncommon, for example, for police to *believe* it to be a fact that minorities commit more crimes than whites even when actual statistics may reveal the contrary

(Morales, 1975). These stereotypic beliefs will often lead to a greater saturation of police in the minority community. Such saturation will produce a larger number of arrests and no doubt inhibit some kind of criminal activity, but according to criminologist Gilbert Geis (1962), "it is the police activity and not the behavior of the group itself which is conditioning the crime rates for the group as these eventually appear in the printed statistics." This phenomenon leads to what Robert K. Merton called a "self-fulfilling prophecy."

Los Angeles has numerous juvenile gangs, comprised of Hispanics, Blacks, Whites, Asian-Americans. The majority, however, are Hispanic and Black. A major police agency in Los Angeles has developed a "Street Gangs" manual to "assist the field officer in understanding and dealing with the gang phenomenon." It is filled with racist stereotypes of Black and Hispanic youth in terms of clothing, nicknames and lifestyles common in inner-city minority communities. In the 16-page manual, *only one sentence is devoted to Anglo gangs*! The officer is psychologically conditioned to seek out Black and Hispanic youth who conform to the manual's criteria as to who is supposed to be a gang member. The fact is that over 95 percent of minority youth are not gang members, yet may meet the stereotypic criteria in the manual. Furthermore, intentionally or not, the manual in effect is asking officers to ignore white gangs by not providing them with any specific information about white gangs. The following are some instructions in the manual as to an Hispanic gang member's appearance (Street Gangs, 1980):

Watch Cap—The cap ("Beany") is worn by the member primarily in the winter but may be worn in the summer. It is pulled down to cover the ears, with a small roll at the bottom. It is blue in color and made of a knit material.
Bandana—The bandana or "moco rag" is worn just over the forehead and tied in the back.

Hat—The "stingy" brim is favored by the gang member but recently the baseball cap is being utilized.
Shirts—The Pendleton shirt has long been a favorite of the gang member.
T-Shirt—The round or V-neck T-shirt is worn during the summer.
Blue Jeans—also known as "counties," are highly starched, baggy, and rolled in small rolls at the cuff and slit up the side.
Shoes—Shoes may range from tennis shoes to french-toed shoes. If the shoes are leather they will be highly shined.

The manual described the Black gang member's appearance as follows:

Headgear—Black gang members wear "stingy" brims, leather "pork-pies," and floppy-type hats, with jewelry attached. Some will wear handkerchiefs.
Jackets—The bomber- and tanker-type are preferred.
Shirts—The Black gang member likes to wear the black T-shirt rather than the white T-shirt.
Pants—The pants are usually jeans with rolled-up cuffs. Suspenders are commonly worn with the pants.
Shoes—The shoes range from canvas Crocker Sacks to shiny leather shoes.
Miscellaneous—Black gang members may wear earrings and carry a cane or umbrella (walking type). Many carry handkerchiefs, railroad-type (blue or red), hanging from the rear pocket.

With regard to the type of vehicles Black and Hispanic gang members drive, the manual informs officers that they favor Chevrolets of the mid-1960s era, which are "lowered and may have a very small chrome or vinyl covered steering wheel, fur on the dashboard and chrome or mag wheels. (p. 11)" Car clubs in minority communities, therefore, may be perceived by police as being gang-oriented. The manual also familiarizes officers with nicknames gang members have, such as "Angel," "Blackie," "Huero," "Junior," "Pee Wee," "Porky," "Cowboy," "Turkey," and "Mando," the latter being a nickname of one of the authors. Considering that the vast majority of minority youth are not gang members, these very common nicknames would be more prevalent in the general minority population. The manual concludes with the statement that the police are taking a "proactive" rather than a "reactive" stance, and that they are attempting "to identify the gang members before they commit a crime, thus removing the anonymity factor. (p. 15)" Such a policing strategy would not appear to be consistent with a basic American judicial tenet of "innocent until proven guilty."

A proactive rather than a reactive law enforcement stance is not an uncommon police deployment strategy, sometimes referred to as "aggressive preventive patrol." The President's Commission on Law Enforcement and the Administration of Justice found that police spend half of their time on preventive patrol, but that no police chief can obtain even a rough estimate of how much crime is thereby prevented (President's Commission, 1967). Although it might be difficult to measure the crime prevention outcomes of police patrol, it would be possible to measure what James Q. Wilson calls "Police-Invoked Order Maintenance," that is, police-initiated intervention. One of the authors was able to demonstrate this dynamic in operation in contrasting a white and Hispanic community in Los Angeles having comparable general populations, and similar percentage of alcoholics and major crime ratios. Adult Hispanics had a six-to-one greater chance (9,676 to 1,552 arrests) of being arrested for drinking behavior than adult whites. This was due to more police being assigned to the Hispanic community, 375 officers averaging 13.5 officers per square mile, as compared to 151 officers in the white community averaging 3.5 officers per square mile (Morales, 1978). These discriminatory law enforcement practices have mental health implications since the majority of those being arrested (and many placed in jail)

in the Hispanic community were married fathers with an average family of four to six children. In other words, when families are included, the law enforcement behavior was affecting about 48,000 people in one Hispanic community.

The "proactive" patrol, "aggressive preventive patrol," or "police-invoked order maintenance"—all representing police-initiated intervention—also may have negative consequences for minority juveniles. There is no denying that gang violence exists in the inner cities, but often public and police beliefs surpass the actual facts. For example, the major newspaper in Southern California, the *Los Angeles Times*, reported that there had been "160 gang-related deaths in East Los Angeles last year (1979)." East Los Angeles is a predominantly Hispanic community. The statistical facts are that there were only a total of 20 gang-related deaths in East Los Angeles for the year in question (Friendship, 1978).

During the early part of 1979, a gang film about East Los Angeles called "Boulevard Nights" was shown. Based upon the belief that gang members were as dangerous as the press had led people to believe, the L.A. County Sheriff's Department increased its patrol of Whittier Boulevard—a popular social area for Hispanic youth—four times the usual number. The result was that arrests for the weekend quadrupled, with 391 arrests being made, five for assault and the rest for minor offenses such as loitering (L.A. Times, 1979a). This is a clear example of police behavior inflating the crime rate in a specific community.

One may argue that only in some special circumstances, such as the showing of a gang film, will there be a need to increase police-initiated patrol intervention. The point is that the probabilities of a juvenile being arrested by the police is more a function of where that person lives rather than of his or her behavior. Consider the following selected arrests involving juveniles in a lower-class predominantly Hispanic community, and a middle-class predominantly white com-

munity in Los Angeles County (Statistical Summary, 1974-75):

TABLE 1

Community	Sq. Mi.	Population	Annual Juvenile Arrests			
			Grand Theft	Burglary	Petty Theft	Loitering
Predominantly Hispanic	8.36	102,358	13	131	49	483
Predominantly White	9.55	81,630	11	121	208	21

From the above arrests, it is seen that proportionately, because of the smaller white population, there is more crime in the white community for grand theft, burglary, and especially petty theft. These are not police-invoked order maintenance types of offenses since the police became involved *after* the offenses had been committed. However, loitering offenses are police-invoked order maintenance type of offenses as the police are initiating the contact with the juvenile. In other words, because the police believe that minorities generally commit more crime than whites, with their belief reinforced by field deployment and patrol policies which supposedly describe minority gang members in terms of clothing, nicknames and lifestyles, Hispanic youth would appear to be 23 times more likely to be arrested for loitering offenses as compared to whites. Such discriminatory practices, which are supposed to be crime preventive in nature, actually increase crime statistics in the minority community, generate the need for more police manpower based upon an increase in "crime," contribute to a juvenile's arrest record, and prematurely introduce minority youth into the juvenile justice system. As the minority juvenile's arrest record increases, it makes it more difficult for him or her, in comparison to white youngsters, to qualify for more lenient juvenile diversion (away from the

juvenile justice system) processing by police.

Pursuant to Sections 224 (a) (3) and 527 of the Juvenile Justice and Delinquency Prevention Act of 1974, and Sections 301 and 451 of the Omnibus Crime Control Act of 1968 as amended, the purpose of diversion programs is to divert juveniles from involvement with the traditional juvenile justice system at the critical points of penetration, and to determine the significance of providing effective and coordinated services to some of those youth diverted. Various dispositional alternatives may be available to juvenile justice system officials at the various points where a youth is in contact with the system. These alternatives might range from counsel and release by police to participation in a community-based public or private residential program by direction of the juvenile court prior to adjudication. *Diversion* as a concept would appear to hold promise for minority youth who are overrepresented in the juvenile justice system. Police cooperation, however, would be paramount in order for this to become a reality.

In a study of 35 police departments with diversion programs, Klein and his colleagues (1976) found that police motives for diversion are often not what is commonly implied by the term "diversion." Factors which led to referral away from the system included shorter prior arrest records (two priors or less), a preference for younger offenders over older ones, and the officer's estimation that the youth was not likely to be rearrested. "Thus," Klein concluded, "the composite picture of the more referrable offender seems to be of the young, minor offender with little or no record, who is unlikely to be rearrested in any case (page 107-108)."

Klein and colleagues cite the case of one rather large police agency which specifically lists cases for which diversion may not be employed. Cases may *not* be diverted and referred if they involve the following (page 108):

1. felony offenses resulting in death or serious injury;
2. known gang members;
3. more than two prior arrests;
4. offenders already on probation or parole;
5. crimes against police officers, school personnel (teachers, administrators, or any other regular employee), or employees of the recreation department;
6. offenses that disrupt school or recreation department activities or destroy property of school and recreation departments;
7. use or possession of a deadly weapon;
8. offenders judged physically dangerous to the public because of a mental or physical deficiency, disorder, or abnormality;
9. escapees from probation institutions;
10. selected Vehicle Code violations, primarily hit-and-run, auto theft and driving under the influence of or in possession of drugs, liquor, or weapons;
11. a prior arrest with a referral to a treatment agency.

Klein concludes that the dominant trend in diversion has been to ignore the more serious cases while diverting and referring those less in need but more likely to yield positive results, since the less serious cases seldom recidivate. It would also seem that minority youth would have less of a chance to be diverted due to the increased likelihood of their having more than two arrests and being labeled (often erroneously) a gang member.

A recent study revealed that the Los Angeles diversion situation leaves much to be desired and is similar to the findings of Klein and associates. Lipsey and Johnston (1979) report:

Diversion has considerable *potential* for reducing the volume of referrals to probation—law enforcement diversions are equivalent to about 20% of the number of juveniles they refer to probation. The projects of the Regional Diversion Program,* however, do not appear to be receiving a significant number of cases that otherwise would have been sent for probation processing. Instead, most law diversions are made from among those juveniles who otherwise would have received counsel-and-release dispositions (page II).

The authors of the report recommended an increase of diversion referrals of cases involving more serious juvenile offenders. The report did not make it clear, however, the impact diversion programs were having upon minority youth. Rarely, if ever, were minorities mentioned in the 104-page report. If the general conclusion is that the police are diverting those juveniles who otherwise would have received counsel-and-release dispositions anyway, it could also be concluded that the number of minority youth being referred to the probation department, i.e., into the juvenile justice system, remains relatively unchanged.

PROBATION

Juveniles are referred to probation by the police, schools, welfare departments, and parents. The probation department may undertake an investigation of the case and close it at intake, which results in no further action, or file a petition to the Juvenile Court, where a formal pres-

---

*The Los Angeles County Regional Diversion Program is comprised of thirteen projects with a combined annual budget of 4.5 million dollars.

entation is made of information surrounding the alleged offense. This procedure is similar to a criminal petition for an adult. The Court may order detention of the youth in a juvenile institution or, as an alternative, refer the youngster to probation supervision which permits the juvenile to remain in the community. A youngster on probation typically receives supervision and casework services. A deputy probation officer usually provides these services to the extent of his/her training, caseload, and department organization permits. In addition, the deputy probation officer also makes referrals to a variety of educational, health, vocational, social welfare, mental health and legal agencies.

Supervision of the minor is a major function of the deputy probation officer. Since the youth has been declared a ward of the Court for a specified period of time, it is the deputy probation officer's responsibility to supervise the ward to ensure that he or she is following the requirements of probation. The following general conditions are usually applicable to all probationers: regular school attendance or steady employment; maintaining periodic contacts with the deputy probation officer, abiding by curfew regulations, avoiding contacts with other delinquent youths, complying with parental directions and obeying the law. In addition, specific requirements can be stipulated relative to the nature of the offense committed and the history of the probationer. These include financial or other forms of restitution to victims, avoiding specific individuals or situations deleterious to the probationer and seeking and participating in psychotherapeutic treatment or other rehabilitation procedures such as special educational or training programs. Another major task of the deputy probation officer is to provide casework services. These include the provision of individual and group counseling, functioning as a liaison between the home and school, providing parent counseling and making referrals for their probationers to other agencies, institutions and health care providers.

Finally, the deputy probation officer makes periodic reports to the Court on their probationers' adherence to the conditions of probation or commission of new offenses. On these occasions, the officer may recommend the Court to terminate probation, continue probation or commit the youth to an institution. Although the final decision is the Court's, it usually concurs with the probation officer's recommendation.

The projected ethnic composition for Los Angeles County for 1980 was estimated to be 44.4 percent white, 28.8 percent Hispanic, and 21.5 percent Black. Presumably the remaining percentage of 5.3 percent is comprised of Asian-Americans, American Indians and "others" (L.A. Times, 1978a). The total number of juveniles referred to the Los Angeles County Probation Department in 1976 was 54,767. Of these, 23,341 (42.6 percent) were White; 14,154 (25.8 percent) were Hispanic; 15,860 (29 percent) were Black; 94 (.2 percent) were Asian-American; 219 (.4 percent) were American Indian; and 1099 (2 percent) were "other (Probation, 1978)." Since the probation department figures were from 1976, it is apparent that there was an overrepresentation of Hispanics and Blacks in probation referrals and conversely, an underrepresentation of whites, Asian-Americans and American Indians. Table 2 reports the six most frequent offenses for which the various ethnic/racial groups were referred to probation.

From the data presented in Table 2, it is seen that the first three most common offenses for whites and minorities were similar, that is, burglary, petty theft and the possession of marijuana. From the standpoint of dangerousness to others in the remaining offenses, Whites were the most dangerous group as they had committed 41 percent (1053) of all manslaughter offenses, as compared to 31 percent for Blacks and 21 percent for Hispanics. White

TABLE 2

Six Most Frequent Probation Referral Offenses
By Ethnicity and Race

White	#	%	Hispanic	#	%	Black	#	%	Asian-American	#	%	American Indian	#	%
Burglary	(4234)	44	Burglary	(1876)	20	Burglary	(3395)	35	Burglary	(12)	1	Burglary	(31)	.3
Poss. Marij.	(2699)	51	Poss. Marij.	(1052)	20	Petty Theft	(1653)	35	Petty Theft	(9)	-0-	Transient	(15)	1
Petty Theft	(2033)	43	Auto Theft/ Joy Riding	(1045)	32	Poss. Marij.	(1417)	27	Auto Theft/ Joy Riding	(7)	.2	Glue Sniffing	(15)	1
Transient	(1468)	67	Petty Theft	(969)	20	Robbery	(1288)	60	Poss. Marij.	(7)	.1	Battery	(14)	.7
Manslaughter	(1053)	41	Curfew	(814)	33	Auto Theft/ Joy Riding	(966)	29	Manslaughter	(4)	-0-	Petty Theft	(14)	-0-
Drunk	(1030)	50	Drunk	(801)	50	Assault w/ Deadly Wpn	(792)	41	Curfew	(4)	.2	Poss. Marij.	(12)	.2
									Runaway	(4)	-0-	Drunk	(28)	1

juveniles committed 24 homicides, Blacks 60, and Hispanics 41. Since seriousness of offense is an important factor in referring juveniles into the juvenile justice system, one would expect whites to be very well represented in juvenile hall. They are not, as will be seen in the following discussion of minorities detained in Juvenile Hall awaiting a court disposition of their case.

MINORITIES IN JUVENILE HALL DETENTION

A case study program evaluation involves data collection on a unique, uncontrolled population for purposes of recommending improvements in the delivery system for evaluating the effectiveness of service programs (Fink and Kosecoff, 1978). Of such a nature is this case study of a typical, large urban juvenile detention facility for youth awaiting adjudication and placement for the alleged commitment of "602" offenses, that is, offenses which, if committed by adults, would constitute a crime, according to the California Penal Code. The study, undertaken by one of the authors, a child psychiatrist for the Western Center on Law and Poverty, Inc., in Los Angeles, California, was submitted as expert testimony in a 1975 class-action suit, Manney vs. Cabell et al., filed in the United States District Court. The suit was filed on behalf of Dwight Manney and all other male juveniles being held in detention at that time and previously, charging the Central Juvenile Hall administration and Los Angeles County officials with the abridgment of the youths' civil rights. Some of the civil rights in question were those guaranteed by the Eighth Amendment which prohibits "cruel and unusual punishments," including mental and psychological anguish; the right to due process and equal protection of the laws; and rights provided by the First Amendment—freedom of privacy and speech.

Two purposes of the study were to make recommendations for improvements in the existing detention program at the Los Angeles County Probation Department Central Juvenile Hall, hereafter referred to as CJH, and to evaluate its effectiveness from the perspective of its delivery of mental health services. The population consisted of the staff (administrative as well as on-line staff counselors) and male residents, ranging in age from 12 to 17. On-line counselors at CJH are probation officers hired by the Los Angeles County Probation Department through the civil service process. The following means of data collection were used: observations of the physical facility, observation of staff-resident and resident-resident interactions, interviews of staff and residents who were available for questioning, archive review of available documents from CJH and the Los Angeles County Department of Public Social Services, including a review of two hundred medical and behavioral charts of residents. The focus of the study was the evaluation of the psychological milieu at CJH and its effects particularly on the alleged first-time offender.

Although the stated philosophy of CJH, according to administrators, was indeed the optimal reintegration of youthful offenders, in fact it was the "unspoken philosophy" perceived as being operational at CJH which determined policy and practice at the institution. Some of the effects of this philosophy were explored. First there was a presumed "guilt-until-proven-otherwise" attitude which pervaded the administrative and on-line staff thinking throughout the facility. Secondly, approximately 80 to 85 percent of the resident population were Black, with Whites and Hispanic youth making up the remainder. As was seen earlier in this chapter and documented by other investigators, minority youth are more likely to be subjected to discriminatory apprehension practices by police prior to detention, which would account for the ethnically disproportionate ratio observed. These two features of practice taken together might make it difficult for personnel to draw other than the conclusion that minorities must have the upper hand on delinquency. Once a youth reached the facility, the Intake Detention Control (IDC) became the critical point of entry where far-reaching decisions appeared to be made on rather arbitrary bases by non-professionally trained personnel. Not only did personnel in IDC determine whether a juvenile was to be detained, but they also employed unproven criteria for classifying youth according to their "releasibility." Characteristics such as age, size, previous arrests and detention records and family histories, constituted subjective indices for making judgments as to youths' escape risk.

Following processing by IDC, unit assignments appeared to be made on the basis of capricious criteria—in some cases involving ethnicity or race. For example, there was a Spanish-speaking only unit; on others, it was physical size. Once a youth was processed within the system and assigned to a unit, the guiding principle in terms of how staff were to interact with the youth appeared to be related to institutional needs such as behavior control and management of large numbers of boys—this, in direct contradiction to the commitment to rehabilitate and fulfill the role of *parens patriae*. In many instances the CJH system exhibited elements existing primarily to meet the needs of the staff, not of the youth who resided there. This was evident in the restrictive, negatively phrased language of rules. For example, youth were forbidden to talk during meals or mass movements. "Horseplay" was forbidden. Attendance to physiological needs such as the satisfaction of one's thirst or the elimination of one's bladder or bowels was forbidden except at prescribed times.

One of the greatest obstacles to juvenile rehabilitation is seen when no attempt is made to pre-screen counselor applicants who may have personality factors such as violence-proneness, problems with authority, and sadistic tendencies. Under these circumstances, detention centers with such hiring practices may become the stage for some disturbed personnel who may unconsciously trigger acting-out among the juveniles. In this regard the lack of an effective grievance procedure for juvenile residents prevented the discovery of abusive conduct on the part of staff and encouraged the tacit approval of such behavior as a routine part of institutional life. All animals tend to adapt and become sophisticated with experience, and humans are no exception. Unfortunately, it is the newcomer, the first-time alleged offender, who pays the greatest emotional toll in this type of setting. After the initial shock of confinement to a new residential system, he is likely to experience the conflict of succumbing to feared retaliation if he does not conform or of forfeiting some of his identity if he does. In such a youthful population, one would expect to find the usual adolescent turmoil and chaos exacerbated by this type of stressful environment. It would be difficult, if not impossible, for a first offender or innocent juvenile to pass through such an environment emotionally unscathed.

The physical milieu of the facility may be as traumatic as the emotional atmosphere at CJH. The oldest buildings, which were more than fifty years old, were laid out on a campus model set around a main recreation field. There were a total of ten units housed in five buildings on the "602" side, which had a bed capacity of 328. One of these (Unit I) was the infirmary. There was a multidenominational chapel, a school, one dining hall, two basketball courts, a gymnasium, and a baseball diamond. Although the large fields gave the impression of spaciousness, the amount of time spent outside (two 45-minute recreation periods a day) meant that most of the juveniles' day was spent indoors. The interiors of most units were lacking any aesthetic qualities. Dark or dingy colors, with a few exceptions, cast a forlornness throughout the units. In some, paint was peeling, collections of dust could be seen in the corners of the rooms, and the amount of daylight entering through the windows was considerably less than optimal.

The rooms, as they were called, looked like cells. They were small, allowing for a single bed with a non-spring mattress; usually a metal desk with an attached swing-out stool; a wash basin; and in some rooms, a urinal. On unit "EF," there were no urinals in the rooms. Estimated room size was $8' \times 10' \times 6'$. There was a dim ceiling light which appeared to be inadequate for nighttime reading. Each door had a small $1' \times 1\frac{1}{2}'$ window, usually without safety glass but with iron bars on the outside. The only means of communication once the doors were locked was yelling or banging—ironically, the very reasons why some youth were sent to the intensive care unit.*

There was no evidence of any resident individuality or creativity in any of the rooms expressed through the presence of posters or personal items such as pictures or radios. At night when the doors were locked and the lights turned off, the ensuing nine or ten hours of relative sensory deprivation with entrapment would be sufficient to precipitate an acute psychotic episode in a normal sleep-deprived youth such as an anxious first-timer or in an emotionally unstable one. The mechanism of this phenomenon is as follows: With decreased stimulation, conflicts from past experiences begin to surface to the consciousness but have no means for expression, as talking or noise-making at this time was forbidden. Furthermore, this is the time when staff are least available. Most units had only one evening staff member for 40 boys. Indeed, counseling

youth at this most appropriate time, which is statistically when most suicide attempts, hallucinations, disturbing thoughts and dreams occur, would tend to interfere with other duties of the staff such as charting or college "homework." Despite their age and superficial sophistication, these youth *do* experience anxiety about being separated from their families, which tends to be exaggerated and intensified under such conditions (Crewe, 1973).

All units had a day room for approximately every 20 occupants, which had a television, several straight-backed metal chairs, and occasionally a ping-pong table. This was the room where any counseling, outside of one's individual room, usually took place as well, if it occurred at all. It was not possible to find a relatively quiet atmosphere in this or any other room on a unit. No units had any facilities for privacy other than individual residents' rooms. There were no treatment or consultation rooms on the residential units. The lack of privacy in some units even extended to residents' use of the toilet. On Unit "M and N," large glass windows on two sides of the bathroom afforded more than ample opportunity for observation by anyone, an interior design feature which can contribute to paranoid ideation in persons so disposed.

Among some youths interviewed, the physical conditions most disturbing were the cold, unsavory meals which often were not served in sufficient proportions; the cockroaches, which crawled under some of the residents' bodies at night; and the mice which ran around the rooms. A meal cart was observed which contained food overcooked to the extent that its exact nature was indeterminable. Some youths stated the taste of the food was so bad they refused to eat it and drank only the milk.

In summary, this "almshouse" standard of care constituted basically a custodial milieu. The counselor's primary responsibilities consisted of supervising the juveniles in carrying out personal hygiene activities, procuring meals, attending

---

*"ICU" for short was Unit XY which served the dual purpose of providing isolation as punishment and the purported observation of severely disturbed youth such as psychotic or suicidal individuals.

scheduled events and bedding down for the night. Hence, the misnomer of "counselor." Anything which interfered with these responsibilities was considered obstructive and the desire for counseling itself tended to fall into that category if it was not requested at a convenient time or if it was solicited through attention-getting behavior rather than verbally.

The adequacy of the school program was not investigated as it was not felt by the plaintiffs to constitute a civil rights abridgment. During hours which were scheduled as school time (8:30 a.m.-11:30 a.m. and 1:00 p.m.-3:00 p.m.) many youths were observed lying around in their units, some sleeping, others looking bored. When inquiry was made regarding their absence from school, the explanation given was that some were messengers, an élite group of youth who escorted other youth to appointments and performed special duties which conflicted with school attendance several times a week. These youths were therefore being kept out of school for the convenience of the institution. Other youth were awaiting testing, medical appointments or court hearings.

Recreation was theoretically scheduled for 2½ hours per day but an average individual juvenile spent at most two 45-minute sessions in recreational activities. On Unit "XY," one of these sessions was spent indoors. Outside recreation consisted of volleyball, football, baseball and relay races. All recreation was of a competitive nature and in actuality encouraged only the athletically proficient. Thus smaller, less motorically adept youth became socially ostracized and often the target for cruel name-calling and jokes by peers. There were no individualized recreational programs nor was there any opportunity for a youth to participate in recreation at times other than those scheduled. No therapeutic use of recreational facilities, such as the displacement of aggressive impulses onto a punching bag rather than a person, was observed. Recreation time was sometimes withheld

from youth as a disciplinary measure.

Even less individual flexibility was permitted during meal times. In the classic American family setting this is a time of coming together of all the members and sharing of the fruits of parental labor. In some families it may have religious significance as well. It is ideally a relaxed time when events of the day are exchanged by different members of the family and important issues are discussed. No such significance appeared to apply in the dining hall and pantries at CJH. Here again the theme of control was dominant. Serving and eating were accomplished in 30 minutes per shift. Talking was prohibited. Food at best symbolized satisfaction of physiologic hunger but had to be competed for as there was never enough to go around. Frustration during dining, therefore, often was a set-up for fights. One youth stated that handwashing before meals was not allowed. In Unit "XY," youth were even deprived of the non-verbal experience of eating with other youth as they had to eat solitarily in their rooms.

Though counselors reported that youth were permitted many kinds of activities during what "free time" existed between activities, this time was observed to be spent either watching television or just sitting. Juveniles were noted to look bored and lethargic. Few engaged in activities requiring participation by two or more, such as ping pong. Rarely could music be heard on a unit. According to the residents interviewed, "free time" had to accommodate institutional work details. These consisted of garbage collection, serving meals, mopping floors, laundry work, and other maintenance responsibilities. On some units, this free labor formed the foundation of elementary merit systems. In some cases, basic accommodations such as toilet and shower activities had to be earned by performance of these tasks. Refusal to carry out one's work detail could result in an "F" grade or transfer to ICU, both of which carry negative influence in Court disposition hearings. Were it not for the free labor extracted from these youths, the County would have had to hire personnel to perform these maintainance functions.

No occupational therapy program existed at CJH. Not only could leisure time be used constructively through tapping undeveloped avocational talents of youth, but important assessments could be made about the juveniles' perceptual and motor skills by occupational therapists trained to design and execute individualized programs for each of the residents. Job training could be one aspect of such programs.

The above description of daily activities is the operational schema when there are no kinks in the system; but what if a youngster did not want to go to school or do his work detail or get out of bed? In a family or small institutional setting there would be some flexibility in the expectation for performance of various responsibilities. The perception of most staff interviewed was that one or two youths' refusal to comply with institutional expectations for the day would negatively influence every other youth's participation. To avert this end, strict compliance was always demanded rather than seeking an individual's motivation for refusing to comply and in some instances allowing it where appropriate, e.g., illness or emotional upset. Lacking sophisticated behavioral skills, however, staff often resorted to various punitive measures such as those described above in order to enforce rigid adherence to routine.

Personal hygiene activities such as showering and use of the toilet as well as the opportunity for drinking water or moving to or from another location had become highly ritualized and regimented events for the convenience of the staff. If a youth found himself with the urge to urinate after "head call," then he either had to suppress that urge until morning or urinate out of his window. Whenever unit movement was called for, such as in going to the school, the dining hall, or to recreational activities, the residents were

required to do so in a militaristic fashion—marching double-file with hands in their pockets and without talking. Even the terminology employed in such an activity illustrates the point—"movement control." This was felt to be one of the most anti-therapeutic, depersonalizing aspects of the entire milieu. Individuality and creativity, powerful adolescent needs, were extinguished whenever they surfaced, as manifested in the restrictions against individualized dressing, certain hair styles, roughhousing, certain language, and the like (Kahn and Piockowski, 1974). One youth was transferred to ICU because of wearing his clothes in an "unusual manner," namely with his T-shirt sleeves rolled up and his sweatshirt tied around his neck. Another youth was sent to ICU for not combing out his braids before going to school (braids are an acceptable male hairstyle in the Black subculture). Any behavior which deviated from a fantasied norm in the minds of staff—and this differed from person to person—was considered unacceptable and a target for alteration. Consequently, individual expressions of emotional release such as singing, laughing, graffiti-writing, and "horseplay," became punishable behaviors.

Often it was difficult to trace an individual resident's stay at CJH chronologically because of what appeared to be an inordinately large number of transfers between the Los Angeles County detention facility and other outlying facilities. Therefore, an attempt was made to roughly assess an "average" number of transfers for a given period of time for a given youth. An audit of some 75 randomly selected charts revealed transfers ranging on the order of four to six a month for many youths. These transfers were for various reasons—medical evaluations or treatment, disciplinary actions, court hearings, and placements; however, the effect of these moves was to create a sense of instability, a lack of esprit de corps, and a rationalization for not effecting any kind of treatment program. It was argued by some staff that the residents did not remain on a unit long enough to carry out treatment. The time required for these transfers varied but often a resident's whole day was spent in waiting and/or actual travel time. Valuable school and potential treatment time was lost, youth became bored, uncomfortable, and experienced a sense of confusion, lack of time and spatial orientation, and frustration. In addition, valuable staff time was wasted in supervision of these transfers. Such adverse effects, as well as the expense involved, could easily have been prevented by availing each facility of such satellite services as medical facilities and courtrooms.

Transfers to ICU and downgrading (issuing "F" grades) as two forms of discipline have been mentioned; however, the concept of discipline in general deserves discussion. One staff person commented that if he had his way he would make CJH "tougher" so that youth would not want to come back. This philosophy unfortunately has prevailed among some lawmakers, correctional personnel, and society in general for some time. Most staff had very few psychologically sound behavioral skills which they exercised for altering "negative behavior" on the part of juveniles. "Negative behavior," for example, talking after lights went off, was arbitrarily defined and tended to reflect individual staff persons' personal attitudes rather than being based on sound psychological principles. Since staff were outnumbered, they most frequently used the mechanism of verbal threats to elicit compliance. When this failed, as most normal adolescents will eventually challenge threats, then staff sometimes resorted to room restrictions, downgrading or the withdrawal of "privileges." Such practices could be very effective means of shaping behavior if used properly; however, even on the so-called merit or point-system living units which subscribed to behavior modification principles, no consistently

well-planned and practiced behavioral programs were observed. When these more benign strategies failed, some staff, feeling frustrated and impotent, would resort to rather regressed means of control —name-calling (an infraction when used by the juveniles). Some youth even reported instances of physical abuse by staff. These two measures were reported to be frequently exercised by certain staff according to juveniles interviewed. Ultimately a youth might be transferred to ICU (Intensive Care Unit), otherwise known as Unit XY (or to the youth as "lock-up") for rules infractions. A log documenting the reason for each transfer was kept. Behaviorally speaking, most inconsequential behavior, i.e., behavior resulting in no harm to persons or property but primarily attention-seeking in nature, can be reduced in frequency or extinguished altogether by ignoring it; however, many instances of behavior that would fall into this category were dealt with by transferring the youth to ICU. According to staff, disciplinary transfers should have never lasted longer than 24 hours; however, youths reported being there up to a week in some cases.

Unit XY itself merits mention, for being there was by definition restrictive and punitive. It was the maximum security unit, surrounded by a high wall that segregated its residents from the rest of CJH population. It had two wings, an "X" wing for "hard-core" offenders, or youth alleged to have committed serious offenses such as those against persons, and a "Y" wing for disciplinary problem youth from other units or other facilities. As mentioned previously, recreation was more restricted—no intramural activities took place with other units, for XY residents had their own small field which was approximately the length and width of the unit itself. The grass on this field was remarkably unworn. There was no collective eating and the youth attended school on the unit. For having allegedly committed a serious offense, therefore, a youth could be sent directly to XY before his adjudication hearing and be deprived of many of the "relative freedoms" experienced by his peers in other units. Unit XY also served as an observation unit for the more seriously disturbed youth, as was the case of Unit J. In particular, youth who had attempted suicide were sent to XY for "their own protection." Therefore, it might be expected to be the unit with the most psychologically sophisticated personnel and its residents might be expected to receive the most intensive psychiatric care. Unfortunately, this was not the case. Psychiatric treatment for these disturbed youth was not routine, but rather obtained at the discretion of the counselors in this unit who possessed no particular behavioral science skills and who often felt the disturbed behavior was a manifestation of the youth's "just being bad," manipulating, or wanting attention.

There were gross examples of behavioral problems which in adolescents often indicate depression, hyperkinesis, mental retardation and learning disorders, and even psychosis, which did not result in psychiatric referrals. Such problems often required exhaustive use of staff and even resulted in the youth or others being injured as a result of the problem. Some serious disturbances lasted for months or the duration of the youth's stay. Another glaringly overlooked psychiatric disorder was that of drug dependency. In none of such cases reviewed could instances of psychiatric referrals for the drug dependency itself be found although often extensive medical workups had been performed.

Psychiatric consultations reviewed were of varying quality. Most initial consultations appeared to reflect a 30- to 60- minute session spent with the youth. Rarely was this stated. The type of report on the charts was usually a court-ordered report and since court-ordered psychiatric reports need not include all information obtained by a consultant and because they are written for lay persons, it was not always clear just how thorough such evaluations had been. The most glaring variability was in diagnoses. From the reports it was often difficult to determine the basis for a particular diagnosis, with different consultants appearing to employ their own unique criteria rather than universal standards, as found in the American Psychiatric Association Diagnostic and Statistical Manual (DSM III). A most disturbing phenomena, given the present state of the art in psychiatry, was the prediction of violence and the labeling of certain youth as potential murderers by psychiatrists and psychologists. It is generally agreed upon by colleagues in this field that because of infrequent commission of violence, particularly murder, by a given individual, and because murderers fall into many different diagnostic categories, including essentially normal persons, behavioral scientists are not equipped to make such predictions (Sendi and Blomgren, 1975). Furthermore, to do so can be extremely dangerous since, once someone receives the label of potential murderer, a self-fulfilling prophecy is often set in motion. Often mental health professionals unwittingly become tools of social control when they impose subjective definitions of behavior and use arbitrary criteria which ensure certain predictable social consequences (Miller, 1971).

The second phase of treatment is the actual therapy which is usually delivered primarily by psychiatrists, clinical social workers and psychologists. In a setting such as CJH where other staff have more frequent contact with the residents, mental health professionals may prescribe certain therapeutic milieus or interventions which can be carried out by non-mental health personnel. As far as could be determined from the charts, post-evaluation therapy at CHJ consisted of medication. Only rarely did the same therapist see the youth in subsequent follow-up sessions, so that continuity of care for the most part did not exist. Body restraints, a medical tool, were used, as far as could be determined, by non-medical personnel *without* a physician's order.

Family therapy, a modality which is being used with increasing efficacy for adolescents, was recommended in only *one* consultation which was reviewed. Of all the youth interviewed, only one was scheduled to receive this form of therapy, which is no longer conducted at CJH. Where individual therapy was recommended, it often was not clear who would carry it out and whether it was to take place at CJH, in a placement facility, or after release. When intensive individual therapy in an inpatient setting was recommended, it was not effected if Unit III (psychiatric unit) of Los Angeles County-USC Medical Center had no beds available.

Comprehensive psychiatric care should include some form of follow-up or a built-in assessment and maintenance of the efficacy of interventions. This is made difficult at CJH because of the mobility of this population. Often follow-up can be effected by a mere phone call and not necessarily by a medically trained person, although where medication was the intervention a physician should assess its efficacy over time. This phase of treatment becomes extremely important in such a population as the one at CJH where psychiatric intervention was not sought by the youth or family itself. Home visits by the probation officer, social worker, or public health nurse, or calls to placement facilities to ascertain the status of the presenting problem and to insure continuity of care, are critical in this age of cost-effectiveness, dwindling resources and ever-increasing demand for those resources. Without such follow-up, valuable assessment and treatment time and energy may be for naught.

Of the various indirect psychiatric services in a program such as the one at CJH, charting also becomes critical. It assumes systematic, uniform recording of events in an unbiased, objective, scientifically observant fashion by staff on all shifts. Charting must be legible, it must leave nothing to the imagination, and entries should be based on reliable information. Such was not the case in charts which were reviewed.

First, there were two sets of charts for all residents: (1) a medical chart which remained in the infirmary and (2) a behavioral chart which remained on the unit. This was an extremely cumbersome system, although it raised an important issue—that of confidentiality. Ideally, non-medical personnel should not have access to medical records without proper consent; however, there must be some communication between medical personnel and on-line staff who work with the youth daily. To deliver comprehensive medical care, medical personnel should be aware of the day-to-day behaviors of a resident and, conversely, counselors need to be aware of certain medical problems which may affect youths' on-the-unit behavior. The impression formed was that such an exchange of information did not take place in either direction, at least not in any systematic fashion. Evidence in the charts revealed that there was no indication of implementation of many of the psychiatric consultants' recommendations. Similarly, a familiarity with a patient's daily behavior was not conveyed in many of the psychiatric consultations. The apparent lack of training in charting skills by the staff was evidenced by contradictory entries by different staff regarding the same event. For instance, one staff member graded a youth's behavior with an "A" for being exceptional, while another staff member commented on the youth's behavior as "rapidly deteriorating" and deserving an "F." Colloquial expressions were used without explanation. A behavior was described as "a bit loose" without any elaboration. Even pseudo-objective jargon such as "negative behavior" as a reason for being downgraded is not sufficiently defined for someone else to understand its meaning. The negative orientation of many staff towards behavior was reflected in the manner in which entries are phrased: "No problems today," rather than recording positive, healthy examples of behavior. Even forms, which are presumed to be an effort to bring some uniformity to charting, are vague. Such a form was the *Special Incident Report* form under the section "classification of incident," which contained a checklist of various generic types of incidents without requiring further explanation.

The juvenile population at Central Juvenile Hall, by virtue of its age and sex, is at risk for having emotional and psychological problems—many of which have social, familial, and economic components—such as depression, drug abuse, and academic failure, to name but a few (Glueck and Glueck, 1962). Often these problems are related to the nature of the offenses the youths are *alleged* to have committed, as in the example of the commission of burglary to maintain a drug habit. The necessity for comprehensive psychiatric treatment by the most competent practitioners speaks for itself. What was found at CJH was the following situation: the population was one with a high incidence of problems for which some form of treatment exists and *almost one half of detained youths subsequently were released at court detention hearings because their petitions were not sustained (found not guilty)!** The question arose, then, of whether such a facility at CJH was in fact necessary. Certainly, the large number of beds observed at the time were not needed, for many youth should never have been detained in the first place and many whose petitions were sustained had committed the less serious types of crimes—victimless crimes, e.g., curfew violations, or running away from place-

ment, or crimes against property. For this group of offenders, diversion-type community-based programs such as drug rehabilitation programs, individual, group and family programs, employment and job training programs, special education, foster homes and the like are necessary and preferable to institutions to meet the particular needs of the individual youth (Nelson, Wolff and Batalden, 1975).

SOCIAL AND COMMUNITY AND BEHAVIORAL INTERVENTION PROGRAMS

Within the general framework of the casework method, the predominant approach to delinquency has been based on the medical model of treatment which has produced disappointing results (Schwitzgebel, 1972). Traditional psychiatric approaches have had even more dismal results with minority group clients because of the wide acceptance of the hypothesis that "difference equals deficiency." Hence, minority patients have been assessed as more pathological than they actually are. This misperception, as well as preconceived notions regarding their response to certain treatment modalities, has led to referrals to inappropriate services (Mayo, 1974). As a consequence, minority clients have not received even the benefits that are possible from traditional interventions. To remedy these and other shortcomings, alternative approaches to the rehabilitation of delinquents have emerged. Generally, they can be classified under the headings of social and community interventions and behavioral interventions. Both show promise for providing more effective rehabilitation outcomes than the traditional model because they are highly adaptable to the particular needs and values of the ethnic and cultural groups to which they are addressed.

The Crenshaw Community Day Center (CCDC), a social and community inter-

---

*In March, 1976, according to CJH and Los Padrines IDC Monthly Statistics, of 1122 boys accepted for temporary custody, 551 were released.

vention-type program funded by the Los Angeles County Probation Department and the State of California Youth Authority, serves 30 Black adolescents who have been adjudged wards of the Juvenile Court. The youths reside in their own homes and attend classes at the Center which is located in their neighborhood. The offenses which have resulted in their probationary status range from relatively minor delinquent acts such as curfew violations and truancy to more serious offenses such as assault and robbery. Although the degree of delinquent sophistication varies, as well as the socioeconomic status of their families, the youths all share the common problems of school failure resulting from chronic truancy, learning disabilities, and behavioral disorders. The program is located in the facilities of a community YMCA where the youths receive individualized attention to overcome their school learning difficulties and behavioral problems. Once this occurs, they are mainstreamed back into their neighborhood schools.

The program is staffed by Los Angeles County probation officers, Los Angeles City continuation high school teachers, and graduate students and faculty from the Department of Special Education of the University of Southern California. Thus, it draws on a wide range of expertise in education, adolescent development and rehabilitation of juvenile offenders. Through weekly staff meetings, the combined agencies provide input into educational programs and policies and casework problems. Furthermore, the youngsters have daily contact with their probation officer who is a resident member of the Center. Thus a climate of trust and mutual cooperation is fostered between probation officers and probationers.

The academic program centers around the concept of individualized instruction and providing each student the opportunity to learn various subjects at his or her own pace. Upon entering the program, the student is educationally assessed and placed at the appropriate level of difficulty of subject matter which corresponds with that required for a regular high school graduation. The daily school program applies social learning principles in the form of a token economy system. Points are used as reinforcers for school attendance, academic achievement, and appropriate social behavior. Social praise is paired with delivery of these points with the expectation that eventually the youths will function effectively with only social reinforcement. The points, however, are redeemable for free time, snacks, and even money. Thus, for the first time, tangible motivation for achievement and appropriate social interactions are experienced by many youths who have heretofore viewed school as nothing but a series of repeated failures.

Frequent parent conferences are held to apprise parents of their child's progress. The topics discussed include learning problems and other difficulties the youth may have in successfully completing a period of probation. The Center's staff interacts with parents in a style designed to alter their misconceptions of school and probation personnel as nothing more than disciplinarians. A positive experience between the Center staff and parents is generally achieved by reinforcing with praise the progress made by their children. This also helps to promote the parents' increased use of positive statements in the home.

The results of the Crenshaw Community Day Center program have been good. There have been fewer arrests of CCDC students following their enrollment in this program as compared to their pre-enrollment experience. Also, there have been fewer arrests of CCDC minors than similar minors supervised on a regular probation caseload in the same area. School attendance increased for CCDC minors once they entered the program. As a consequence, academic achievement has been educationally significant in that for each month of school attendance the CCDC youths' average improvement in reading was 2.6 months, for spelling, 1.9 months, and for math, 2.2 months.

Another alternative to the medical model has been the application of behaviorally oriented approaches to the youthful probationer. An excellent example of the work in this field is demonstrated by the community-based, family-style treatment home called *Achievement Place* (Phillips, 1968). This is a behavioral-intervention type of program. It was conceptualized and implemented in Lawrence, Kansas for 12- to 16-year-old Anglo and Black youths referred by the Department of Probation as a result of a variety of delinquent acts. The treatment program centers around teaching parents. A married couple is responsible for the administration and delivery of the program which is conducted on a small scale consisting of six to eight youths in a renovated home in a quiet residential community. Therefore, the youths receive considerable individualized attention and treatment in their own environments. The program was also designed to permit the residents' participation in the direction and operation of the home through self government, by means of monitoring each other's behavior and participating in "family conferences." Because of the success of the original Achievement Place, the model has been replicated in different locations throughout the country. One such program was comprised entirely of Mexican-American teenagers in a rural Southern California community.

The program, known as Welcome Home (Liberman et al., 1975) was carried out in a family-style home in Santa Paula, a small agricultural town of 20,000 inhabitants in Southern California. It housed a total of 16 delinquent youths, all of whom were Mexican-American, and a married couple who served as teaching parents. The teaching parents were Mexican-Americans with high school educations, some college, and two years'

experience in counseling young people. In addition to receiving training in behavioral techniques through a variety of workshops and professional consultations, the teaching parents attended an intensive, week-long workshop sponsored by the original Achievement Place program on treatment and administrative aspects of running the home. While operating Welcome Home, they received weekly consultations with a psychologist and also attended weekly meetings led by another behavioral psychologist aimed at teaching simple reinforcement methods to the parents of the delinquent youths.

The boys at Welcome Home were committed by the Juvenile Court and supervised by the County Probation Department while in placement. They ranged in age from 12 to 16 years of age, and seven was the maximum census at any one time. Their delinquent activities ranged from "beyond parental control" to offenses that would have been classified as felonies had they been committed by adults. Generally, the youths were from low-income families with only one parent in the home. Their average stay in Welcome Home was 6 months, with a range of 3 to 15 months.

The behavioral treatment approach used was that of a token economy. The youngsters earned points for appropriate social, self-care and academic behavior and lost points for inappropriate behavior. They received specific instructions from the teaching parents in acquiring behaviors that were absent and in improving those that were deficient. Points were earned or lost on a daily or weekly basis, depending upon progress through the program. The points could be exchanged for privileges such as snacks, television time, allowance, permission to attend special social events, and weekends in their own homes.

A typical day at Welcome Home started at 7:00 a.m. The boys showered, dressed, and cleaned their bedrooms and bathrooms before breakfast. After breakfast, they cleaned up the kitchen and went to school, where they earned points for academic and social performance. After school, they returned home where they had a snack if they had earned that privilege. They then began chores which were usually finished by 4:00 p.m. Until dinner at 6:00 p.m., the boys studied or engaged in activities they had earned. After dinner, a family meeting was held for the purpose of teaching self-governing skills. Grievances were aired, rules infractions reported, appropriate consequences enacted, and individual accomplishments praised and rewarded. Changes in household operations and program policies were also discussed and made. At 10:00 p.m. the boys retired for the evening.

Several objective studies of the effectiveness of various components of the treatment program have been conducted. These involved assessing the effectiveness of methods for changing behaviors in directions thought to be important for the youths' successful adaptation to their home and school environments. Some of the specific behaviors studied were decreasing annoying interruptions of conversations, performing chores, and increasing promptness. Since talking-out inappropriately in class and other social situations is a common problem with delinquent youth, an intervention was designed which fined the boys for interrupting ongoing conversations. It was determined that this approach significantly reduced incidences of inappropriate talking-out. The performance of chores was increased by rewarding the youths for the performance of specified tasks. After an initial phase of using points as rewards, they were gradually discontinued and replaced with warm encouragement and attention from the teaching parents which sufficed to maintain a high level of task completion. A common problem among delinquents is the lack of promptness at school and in meeting family schedules for meals and time home. Therefore, a program was devised in which the boys were fined for being late to dinner or other agreed-upon times. Again, it was found that this method significantly reduced tardiness. In addition to the above specific improvements, the boys at Welcome Home made important gains in their academic records and their successful completion of probation.

The above described social and community interventions and behavioral approaches share some general features. First, they focus far more on concrete observable behaviors than do traditional approaches. Thus, the assessment of the effects of the interventions becomes an ongoing process which permits inappropriate strategies to be discarded while effective ones are maintained. A second feature is that they share organizational structures and modes of delivery that are in full view of the community they serve, thus permitting them to reflect the needs and values of the people they serve. Third, their goals, in addition to effecting more adaptive coping styles for the probationers, also include effecting institutional and community change. Fourth, they deal with problems of living directly in the natural environments of those in which these problems occur. Finally, they use the resources of the community and the talents of nonprofessionals in carrying out the delivery of service.

CONCLUSION

The juvenile justice system was seen as having four interacting components: the police, probation, the Juvenile Court, and placement institutions. Three trends appear to be evolving in the handling of juvenile offenders: more lenient dispositions (out of court) of those who commit very minor crimes, sometimes called status offenders; the effort to divert from the juvenile justice system offenders who might benefit from community-based treatment alternatives; and harsher treatment of juveniles who commit serious crimes. Some surveys have shown that minority juveniles are not receiving equal treatment and that juvenile correctional programs disproportionately represent the minority population.

The police, as "gatekeepers," were seen as having the most influence in determining that juveniles are kept out of, or in, the juvenile justice system. Stereotypic beliefs regarding clothing and lifestyle about minority juveniles, reinforced by field deployment patrol policies, greatly increase the likelihood of those persons being arrested by police. These police-initiated preventive patrol arrests increase minority community crime statistics, generate the need for more police, and prematurely introduce minority youth into the juvenile justice system. It also makes it more difficult for minority youth to qualify for more lenient, diversion processing.

Probation Department referral statistics revealed that there was an overrepresentation of Black and Hispanic youth. These statistics further indicated that, contrary to common belief, white juveniles had their fair share of serious offenses, even surpassing minority groups in the number of manslaughter incidents. However, it was surprising to see that Blacks comprised 85 percent of those minors detained at Juvenile Hall awaiting a court hearing. Hispanics and whites represented the remaining 15 percent of those in detention. It was not specifically clear what forces were at work which caused such a gross overrepresentation of Blacks. This finding supported other evidence in the country showing that minorities are overrepresented in juvenile corrections programs. The answer appears to be related to institutional racism.

The case study of minorities in Juvenile Hall detention demonstrated an almshouse-like standard of care which constituted basically a custodial milieu. Serious behavioral problems, which in adolescents often indicate depression, hyperkinesis, mental retardation, learning disorders,

and even psychosis, did not result in psychiatric referrals. Often this was due to staff not being adequately trained to detect these problems. The policies and procedures of the institution appeared to operate for the convenience of the institution rather than for the biological, social and psychological needs of the juvenile inmates. Perhaps the most tragic finding was that at least half of those juveniles, mostly minority, being subjected to those inhuman conditions were subsequently released by the Court because their petitions were not sustained (found not guilty)!

Social and community and behavioral intervention types of programs were discussed as being particularly helpful to juvenile minority offenders. These programs have also worked well with white youths. Rather than following a medical model focusing on individual, psychological treatment, these programs follow a residential approach *in the community* and reflect the needs and values of the people they serve. They also have the advantage of using available resources in the minority community, and the skills and talents of minority nonprofessionals in carrying out the delivery of services.

REFERENCES

Beck, R. White House conference on children: An historical perspective. *Harvard Educational Review*, 1973, *43*(4), 653-668.

Crewe, H. J. Fears and anxiety in childhood. *Public Health*, 1973, *87*(5), 165-171.

Fink, A. and Kosecoff, J. *An Evaluation Primer.* Washington, D.C.: Capitol Publications, 1978.

Friendship Station Newsletter, Los Angeles, California, 1978, p. 2.

Geis, G. Statistics concerning race and crime. Unpublished paper submitted to the U.S. Commission on Civil Rights, September 13, 1962, p. 6.

Glueck, S. and Glueck, E. *Family Environment and Delinquency.* Boston: Houghton Mifflin, 1962.

Kahn, C. and Piockowski, G. Conditions promoting creativity in group rearing of children. *Psychoanalytic Study of the Child*, 1974, *29*, 231.

Kanner, L. Outline of the history of child psychiatry. In: *Child Psychiatry*, (4th edition). Springfield, IL: Charles C Thomas, 1972.

Klein, M. W., Teilman, K. S., Styles, J. A., Lincoln, S. B., and Labin-Rosensweig, S. The explosion in police diversion programs: Evaluating the structural dimensions of a social fad. In: M. W. Klein (Ed.), *The Juvenile Justice System*. Beverly Hills: Sage Publications, 1976, pp. 107-108.

Liberman, R. P., Ferris, C., Salgado, P., and Salgado, J. Replication of the achievement place model in California. *Journal of Applied Behavior Analysis*, 1975, *8*, 287-299.

Lipsey, M. W. and Johnston, J. E. The impact of juvenile diversion in Los Angeles County. A Report to the Los Angeles County (AB90) Justice System Advisory Group, July, 1979, p. ii.

Los Angeles Times, Monday, February 27, 1978a.

Los Angeles Times, October 8, 1978b.

Los Angeles Times, Calendar, March 18, 1979a, p. 38.

Los Angeles Times, Part I, April 2, 1979b, p. 3.

Mayo, J. A. The significance of sociocultural variables in the psychiatric treatment of black outpatients. *Comprehensive Psychiatry*, 1974, *15*, 471-482(a).

Miller, J. G. Professional dilemmas in corrections. *Seminars in Psychiatry*, 1971, *3*(3), 357-362.

Morales, A. Police deployment theories and the Mexican American. In: J. H. Skolnick and T. C. Grey (Eds.), *Police in America*. Boston: Educational Associates, 1975, pp. 118-125.

Morales, A. Institutional racism in mental health and criminal justice. *Social Casework*, July 1978, *59*(7), 391-392.

Nelson, S. H., Wolff, B., and Batalden, P. B. Manpower training as an alternative to disadvantaged adolescent drug misuse. *American Journal of Public Health*, 1975, *65*, 599-603.

Phillips, E. L. Achievement place: Token reinforcement procedures in a home-style rehabilitation setting for "pre-delinquent" boys. *Journal of Applied Behavior Analysis*, 1968, *1*, 213-223.

Polier, J. W. Myths and realities in search for juvenile justice. *Harvard Educational Review*, 1974, *44*(1), 112-124.

President's Commission on Law Enforcement and Administration of justice. *The Challenge of Crime in a Free Society*. Washington, D.C.: U.S. Government Printing Office, 1967, p. 247.

Probation Automated Intake Data System, Los Angeles County Probation Department, 1978.

Report of the Joint Commission on Mental Health of Children. *Crisis in Child Mental Health: Challenge for the 1970's*. New York: Harper and Row, 1969.

Sarri, R. C. and Vinter, R. D. Justice for whom? Varieties of juvenile correctional approaches. In: M. W. Klein (Ed.), *The Juvenile Justice System*. Beverly Hills: Sage Publications, 1976, p. 180.

Schwitzgebel, R. K. Limitations on the coercive treatment of offenders. *Criminal Law Bulletin*, 1972, *8*, 269-319.

Sendi, I. B. and Blomgren, P. G. A comparative study of predictive criteria in the predisposition of homicidal adolescents. *American Journal of Psychiatry*, 1975, *132*(4), 423-427.

Statistical Summary, Los Angeles County Sheriff's Department, Fiscal year, 1974-75, pp. 80, 97.

Street Gangs. Copy in the possession of the ACLU Foundation of Southern California, 1980, pp. 11, 15. Also see Attorney General George Deukmejian's *Report on Youth Gang Violence in California*. Department of Justice, State of California, June 1981, pp. 21,22,24,25.

Wertham, C. and Piliavin, I. Gang members and the police. In: J. H. Skolnick and T. C. Gray (Eds.), *Police in America*. Boston: Educational Associates, 1975, pp. 155-168.

Worsfold, V. L. A philosophical justification for children's rights. *Harvard Educational Review*, 1974, *44*(1), 142-157.

CHAPTER 32

The Mexican-American Child: A Socioecological Approach to Research

Arturo Romero, Ph.D.

Research interest in Mexican-American children has increased dramatically during the present decade. This interest is evidenced by an expansion in the volume of research articles and by the number of disciplines contributing to this rapidly expanding body of literature. For example, a recently published bibliography (Padilla, Olmedo, Lopez, and Perez, 1978) lists approximately 250 articles on Mexican-American children, 210 of which have been produced since 1970. It is noteworthy that of the total number of research articles, 80 percent are based on empirically oriented data. As for the disciplines themselves, the majority of the articles emanate from the fields of psychology, education, anthropology, and linguistics. Fewer articles derive from the fields of social welfare, psychiatry, and public health. Clearly, researchers are demonstrating an active interest in the problems and overall development of Mexican-

American children.

In spite of these advances, it would be unwise to take too optimistic a view on the current state of the literature since a number of shortcomings can be noted that place limitations on the utility of the research effort. These limitations can be well illustrated by taking a synoptic view of the literature.

- At least 50 percent of the empirical research is based upon cross-cultural com-

Preparation of this paper was supported by Research Grant MH 24854 from the National Institute of Mental Health to the Spanish Speaking Mental Health Research Center, UCLA, Dr. A. M. Padilla, Principal Investigator.

I would like to extend my appreciation to Dr. A. M. Padilla, Director of the SSMHRC, for his careful reading of the initial draft of this paper. Acknowledgment is also due to Drs. Esteban Olmedo and Rene Ruiz for their efforts in reading a later draft of this work. Collectively, the comments, criticisms, and suggestions that were offered made substantial contribution to this paper.

parisons. This practice, while useful, can lead to faulty conclusions. For example, the majority of the studies show a consistent finding that Anglo children score higher, or in some way do better, than Mexican-American children (usually with contrived tasks). However, descriptive statements tell us little or nothing about the basis of these differences.

- There is an almost complete reliance on cross-sectional as opposed to longitudinal research designs. Typically, a cross-sectional method compares two or more groups during the single time period of the investigation. This method is appropriate for describing differences among groups born during different periods, but it does not permit unequivocal explanation regarding developmental processes.
- The studies suffer from inadequate description of Mexican-American subject populations, especially with regard to children's language use, generation, and the type of community in which they reside.
- Many of the studies lack control of important confounding variables such as the child's home language, language fluency in English or Spanish, and socioeconomic status.
- There are many studies conducted in school settings while relatively few studies have been conducted in home or neighborhood settings. These latter settings have an equally powerful (if not greater) impact on children's behavior and development.
- Although, as noted earlier, many disciplines have contributed to the body of literature, much of the work has been encapsulated within particular disciplines (e.g., psychology, sociology, and education). This has resulted in very little cross-fertilization with regard to lines of research and theory between disciplines.
- Finally, with a few notable exceptions, much of the research has been piece-meal and has suffered from a lack of coordination and long-range planning. As a result of this unsystematic approach, this research has contributed little to theoretical formulations; more important, this research has had minimal impact on social policies and programs which affect the Mexican-American child's development.

Based on these delimiting characteristics of the research literature, it is apparent that a more flexible research approach is needed. To be effective and meaningful, such an approach must be able to provide direction and cohesion to a long-term, theoretically oriented, multi- and interdisciplinary research effort. A research effort must be made that combines basic and applied research strategies and directs them toward a common goal of understanding and improving the life of Mexican-American children. As a first step in meeting this challenge, this paper is written with a singular objective: to propose a socioecological approach to research on Mexican-American children.

In order to facilitate discussion leading to the aforementioned objective, this paper will be divided into two major sections. The first section serves as a brief introduction to the socioecological perspective. The purpose is to acquaint the reader with the characteristics and the methodological and conceptual features of the socioecological approach. In addition, this section lists some principles and procedures which begin to define the rudiments of the approach as it will be applied to the study of the Mexican-American child. The second section is devoted to constructing a research framework capable of orienting differently trained researchers to some of the problems of psychosocial development. Here an attempt will be made to place the child within a socioecological context and to identify fruitful avenues for systematic research which can both further our understanding of the child's development and provide data useful in program development for these children.

THE SOCIOECOLOGICAL PERSPECTIVE

In Kuhn's (1962) classical treatise, a paradigm is defined as "the entire constellation of beliefs, values, techniques, and so on shared by the members of a given community" (p. 175). He argues that with a paradigm, a community chooses problems and guides its research. In a very rough way, we can say that a paradigm sets the intellectual boundaries within which scientific inquiry can proceed.

The importance of a socioecological approach can best be appreciated in defining a new paradigm. It makes explicit the assumptions upon which research is based and offers a new conceptual framework from which we can begin systematically to study the Mexican-American child.

Moos and Insel (1974) have described social ecology "as the multidisciplinary study of the impact that physical and social environments have on human beings" (p. 5). More recently, Moos (1976) has elaborated upon a number of characteristics which distinguish this approach from other perspectives. First, the basic unit of study is the individual. The objective is to understand the impact of the environment from the point of view of the individual. Thus, if one is to make accurate predictions about behavior, then it is necessary to have information about both the individual and the environment. Second, physical and social environments must be studied together since neither can be fully understood without the other. Human behavioral outcomes are to a large degree determined by the intricate relationship between physical and social environments. Third, a socioecological approach is concerned mainly with individual adaptation, adjustment, and coping. However, it is understood that assessments of environments must pre-

cede assessments of the environmental impact, so the focus is more on milieu than on the person. Fourth, the approach is oriented toward practical application of research findings. The concern is with organizing environments which maximize human potential. Finally, a socioecological approach has an explicit value orientation. It is dedicated to increasing the amount of control individuals have over their environments.

The socioecological perspective can also be described as having two primary facets. The first facet is methodological; it implies a point of view about the way research is to be done. Research, from a socioecological point of view, employs both observational and experimental methods. Observational methods reveal and discover natural occurrences; they answer the question "What goes on here?" In contrast to this, with experimental methods there is a direct, causal, or instigating relationship between the methods themselves and the phenomena they observe. What experimental methods discover are results of the conditions imposed or created by the investigator. Experiments answer the question: "What goes on here, under the conditions that have been arranged?" (Willems, 1965).

Sells (1966) has indicated a need for both field observation and experimentation, suggesting that the laboratory should serve an auxiliary function to field research stations where particular aspects of phenomena could be observed in natural settings and then tested and replicated under controlled conditions. Barker and his colleagues have strongly emphasized this point of view (Barker, 1960, 1968; Barker and Gump, 1964; Gump, 1975). Further, Sells has suggested that the methodology for many basic psychological problems is interdisciplinary, necessitating greater cooperation between behavioral, biological, and the social sciences. He emphasizes the importance of a multivariate approach to studying aspects of the social environment and indicates that our understanding of behavior will be incomplete until the variance accounted for by environmental variables can be precisely assessed.

The second facet of the socioecological approach has been clearly delineated by Moos (1976). It brings to bear certain conceptual principles about behavior and research upon behavior. He has provided an organizational framework for describing the fundamental ways in which environments may be conceptualized. He proposes six major categories of environmental dimensions that are nonexclusive and mutually interrelated: ecological dimensions, dimensions of organizational structure, personal characteristics of inhabitants, behavior settings, functional or reinforcement properties of environments, and finally, psychosocial characteristics and organizational climate. The value of this approach is that it attempts to consider both the ecological or physical aspects of the environment and the behavioral and social components. A summary description of each dimension along with examples of some of their variables is now presented.

Ecological dimensions refer to the influence of natural (e.g., climate, topography, geography, etc.) and manmade (e.g., architectural and spatial layout) variables on psychological states and social behavior.

Dimensions of organizational structure refer to a formal structure (e.g., family unit, political group, intervention program, etc.) with size (number of people) and shape (numbers of levels of authority). It is also an environment with explicit rules, roles, and responsibilities. Organizations influence the behaviors and attitudes of the people who participate in them. Among the organizational variables typically studied are size of an organization, its membership ratio, and levels of decision-making.

Dimensions of personal characteristics of milieu inhabitants refer to the notion that the character of an environment is

dependent on the nature of its members, and its dominant features are dependent on their typical characteristics. In other words, if we know the kind of people in a group, we can infer the climate that group creates. Examples of personal characteristics of inhabitants include background characteristics (e.g., age, socioeconomic status, etc.), external characteristics (e.g., race, sex, language use, etc.), rural or urban residence, family size, and group/ethnic identity.

Behavior setting dimensions refer to groups of individuals behaving together. A behavior setting is a naturally occurring unit having physical, behavioral, and temporal properties, and it reveals a variety of complex interrelationships. Some examples of behavior settings are elementary schools, classrooms, playgrounds, youth clubs, homes, city council meetings, and other definable settings where behavioral exchange occurs. (See Barker [1968] for a definitive description and more examples.)

Dimensions of functional or reinforcement properties are an outgrowth of social learning theory. It is assumed that the same people behave substantially differently in various social and physical environments. In this view, people's behavior from one setting to another changes because the reinforcement consequences for certain behaviors vary. People learn what to do in different settings through usual learning processes (i.e., classical conditioning, instrumental conditioning, and social modeling). Examples of some of these variables are reinforcement or punishment of aggressiveness in a school setting, structured game versus unstructured group activity, and preference for different types of reinforcement (praise and social approval, money, etc.).

Dimensions of psychosocial characteristics and organizational climate have been broken down into three subcategories: relationship dimensions, personal development or goal orientation dimensions, and system maintenance and change dimensions. These three subcategories combine to provide a systematic analysis and description of the psychosocial characteristics of different types of social environments.

- *Relationship dimensions* assess the extent to which individuals are involved in the environment and the extent to which they tend to support and assist each other. Variables in this category describe the intensity and type of personal relationships among inhabitants of specific social environments (e.g., peer cohesion, staff support, involvement, etc.).
- *Personal development dimensions* assess the opportunity provided by the environment for self-enhancement and the development of self-esteem. These dimensions vary according to the type of environment. For example, variables relevant to a bilingual education program might be the number of bilingual/bicultural staff, use of culturally relevant materials, and bilingual teaching methods. Other dimensions in a school setting might be competition, task orientation, and academic achievement.
- *System maintenance and change dimensions* refer to qualities inherent in social environments. The basic dimensions are order and structure, clarity, and control. An example of some variables is the amount of formal structure in service-oriented institutions (rules, schedules, procedures) and the extent to which those being served influence the organizational structure.

With this brief overview of some of the characteristics and methodological and conceptual features of the approach outlined, the next step is to determine how the approach will be used. The following are some basic principles and procedures to be used in applying the socioecological approach to the study of the psychosocial development of Mexican-American children.

First, psychosocial development is viewed as a complex adaptation by children to different environments comprising their social ecology. These environments fall into three major classes, each with its own unique subsets: the social environment, including the small-scale, face-to-face, interpersonal environment and the large-scale, organizational environments; the physical environment, including the manmade and natural environments; and the symbolic environment, particularly language use in direct communication as well as the symbolic environment found in the mass media such as television, newspapers, books, and other indirect forms of communication (Sundberg, 1977). Furthermore, these environments, taken together, act upon an individual in different, yet related, ways. They may be actively stressful, selective of particular individual characteristics, limiting in their opportunities for personal growth, supportive of ongoing behavior, or challenging in such a way that personal and social growth is facilitated. It is the task of a socioecological approach to conceptualize these mechanisms to promote better understanding of how environments act on the developing Mexican-American child (Moos, 1976).

Second, the Mexican-American child and each of the major environmental classes and their subsets can be conceptualized in terms of one or more of the six fundamental dimensions described by Moos (1976). For example, the Mexican-American child can be described by such personal and behavioral variables as sex, age, language use, and membership in a particular type of community (e.g., barrio, integrated urban area, rural, etc.). In like manner, the child's environment can be described according to variables of physical design, organizational structure, organizational climate, psychosocial characteristics, and so on. For example, a Mexican-American child's preschool can be described according to the staff's language use, physical design, location, ethnic ratio, and other relevant variables.

Third, the methods used in a socioecological approach are aimed at answering two distinct questions: "What goes on here?" and "What goes on here under the conditions that have been arranged?" The first question is the most important one. It is the initial stage that observes and classifies the phenomena constituting the subject matter of the research. For example, the subject matter may be peer networks within a Mexican-American barrio, teacher language use within a school district, or organizational structure of intervention programs. The objective is to secure information that will play a part in later phases of inquiry, such as the formation and validation of hypotheses. The second question follows from the first. Once a hypothesis has been stated in some precise way, an experiment can be designed to test the predicted functional relationship explicitly stated by the hypothesis.

Fourth, although Moos and Insel (1974) describe social ecology as a multidisciplinary study, when applied to the Mexican-American child, social ecology is both multi- and interdisciplinary. Since both research strategies interrelate variables differently (Gallagher, Ramey, Haskins, and Finkelstein, 1976), researchers must select a strategy appropriate to the problem being studied, with questions stated unambiguously and with both dependent and independent variables carefully defined and operationalized.

Fifth, research on psychosocial development of the Mexican-American child should pay special attention to the behavior settings which a child occupies. As explained by Barker (1968), a behavior setting consists of elements from two realms: It has a milieu (spatial enclosure, physical facilities) and a standing pattern of behavior or program (a regime, a set of procedures, a way of doing). There is a pattern to both the milieu and the program; that is, the milieu of the setting and the standing pattern of behavior in the setting are interdependent.

The importance of behavior settings is that they can be empirically classified based on the measured similarities and differences among them. For example, Moos (1976, p. 219) cites a study in which a statistical cluster analysis was used to obtain behavior setting types. This study organized a large number of settings into groups or types in such a way that the settings within each type were as similar as possible to one another in terms of the descriptive variables. Thus, it became possible to describe a small town with 455 settings in terms of 12 distinct types of settings with particular characteristics (e.g., adult settings, government settings, family-oriented settings, etc.). Conceivably, this classification of social settings may provide hypotheses concerning the socialization and the economic, political, and behavior control functions of social settings in the context of an entire community. Likewise, the setting clusters obtained in one community may provide an empirical basis for selecting a stratified sample of settings in new communities with some assurance that the settings selected represent distinctive and important setting types.

Sixth, the child's ecosystem, or community, is considered to be the whole interacting set of physical and living things in a certain area. Communities can be described in terms of behavior settings which are their primary ecological parts. For the psychologist, a community is an area in which the child acquires his behavioral patterns and carries out the major functions of his life. The boundaries of a community are assumed to be permeable and open. Functional interdependencies of its members establish the form and extent of a viable community. In addition, since function is a defining concept, there may be distinctive but overlapping communities (Lehman, 1975).

Finally, implicit in the socioecological orientation is that research be problem-oriented. That is, the research enterprise must be designed to grapple with problem-focused issues. Since coming into vogue, "problem-oriented" research has been given different interpretations and therefore questions have been raised as to whether it should be subsumed under applied research or represent something different (De Bie, 1970; Emery and Trist, 1973). In the present context, however, "problem-oriented" research refers to domain-based inquiry (McWhitney, 1968) where problems are generic rather than specific. As such, this form of inquiry links a group of disciplines to a major sector of social concern. Furthermore, both basic and applied strategies should complement each other, since they contribute simultaneously to the advancement of knowledge and to human betterment. Of course, the predominance of either a basic or an applied strategy will depend upon the domain and prevailing social concerns (McElroy, 1977).

It should also be added that, ideally, the mapping of domains, identification of immediate research problems, and research planning is made in collaboration with working professionals and community members. One of the major obstacles to be overcome is the stereotype of research as an aloof activity that is far removed from the everyday cares of citizens. An effort must be made to create a research process which is more reciprocal and collaborative and which, over time, will generate trust and support among researchers, working professionals, and community members.

With this broad overview of how a socioecological approach can be used, two points of qualification need to be made. First, the intent has not been to present a rigorous, all-inclusive definition of how a socioecological approach can be used to guide research. To provide such a definition would require a consortium of researchers representing the biological, social, and behavioral sciences. Even then, it is doubtful that total agreement could be reached. Instead, the intent has been to point to a new direction and to suggest an approach which can potentially unify the efforts of differently trained researchers.

Second, it should be emphasized that social ecology is still in its infancy. The six broad types of environmental dimensions may or may not have general utility. Nevertheless, even though it is not yet clear how these different levels of environmental descriptions may eventually relate to each other, it is clear that they are directly relevant to the tasks of scientists—to help design physical and social systems that will maximize possibilities for human growth and facilitate effective adaptation and adjustment (Moos and Insel, 1974). Now we can begin to build a research framework that can incorporate a socioecological approach.

CONSTRUCTING A FRAMEWORK FOR RESEARCH

Constructing a research framework from which to begin a systematic study of the child's psychosocial development is no easy task. The best one could hope for would be to produce a large-scale map which, over time, could be supplemented by more detailed maps. It simply is not feasible to present enough information to satisfy the interests of researchers drawn from the variety of disciplines reflected by the socioecological approach. Rather, the purpose of this section is to orient researchers to some of the salient features of the Mexican-American child's psychosocial development. This will be done by outlining some domains of research which can contribute to a better understanding of the environmental forces impinging on the Mexican-American child's development. The goal, of course, is to produce a body of literature that is useful in promoting the child's health and development.

Before entering into the discussion of specific research domains, some preliminary groundwork needs to be done. Considering the numerous interfaces between the disciplines, it is apparent that common points of origin must be established. Essentially, this means that we must identify those variables, settings, and developmental periods most important to understanding the adaptive process(es).

In the previous section, psychosocial development was simply described as children's active adaptation to the social, physical, and symbolic environments comprising their social ecology. Clearly, this is an oversimplification and obscures the underlying interactive process between the child and the surrounding environments. Also, the description fails to acknowledge the interrelated nature of the environments.

In order to reduce the adaptive process to manageable proportions, the child's developmental years will be divided into three transitional periods: infancy, preschool, and school. Each period represents distinct intervals of time when a child's milieu is dominated by the presence of certain systems. These systems have certain discrete properties that are capable of being studied.

The systems model to be employed is a highly general, content-free, conceptual framework within which any number of different substantive theories of social organization can be constructed (Olsen, 1968). The model is not a description of the real world. It is only a way of looking at and thinking about selected aspects of reality. It is like a transparency that can be superimposed on social phenomena to construct a perspective showing the relatedness of those elements that constitute the phenomena.

Here a system will be defined as an organized unit of interacting parts embedded in larger systems of interaction. These interacting parts are to be viewed as largely symbolic, as information processing subsystems (Sundberg, 1977). This notion can be better illustrated by the use of an example.

Imagine a preschool child within a home setting. In this setting, a system can be defined as the organized unit of the child, father, mother, and siblings. Each is a subsystem of the total system. Within this system, we can see the child as an active processor of information being transmitted by other members of the family. Parents transmit information about how the child should behave at the dinner table, in the presence of relatives, strangers, or when playing with siblings or cohorts. Likewise, sibs may transmit information about other playmates, games of interest, TV programs, roles, or other such subject matter. Furthermore, it should be obvious that the family system is enveloped in a much larger suprasystem (e.g., community, society, etc.) which also imparts information to the family members.

It is through these inputs and feedback (the return of information based on reactions of the environment to children's actions) that children regulate or adjust their activities in ways appropriate to the situation. In brief, what children have is an unspoken plan of habits, coping mechanisms, knowledge, problem-solving skills, and role repertoires which are carried by children as potential programs to be used when the situation calls for them. Moreover, it is important to note that only a small part of children's potential is activated at any given time (Sundberg, 1977).

Returning now to the transitional periods mentioned earlier, we can begin to see that each period is characteristically distinct due to the systems, activities, and demands which interplay in the child's development. Figure 1 presents a hypothetical distribution of how an average child might spend a 24-hour day during

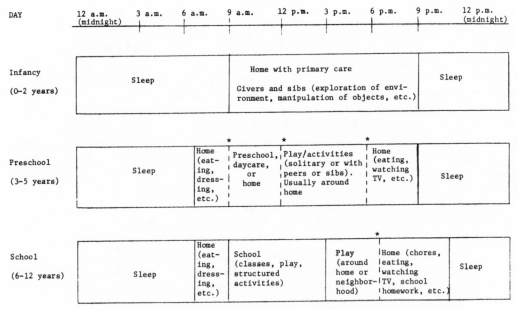

*Indicates potentially unstructured time

Figure 1. Hypothetical distribution of a child's day during three transitional periods of development

the three transitional periods. This is for heuristic purposes only and in no way implies a standard of how children actually spend their day. Also, the age groupings are included only for the sake of illustration and are not meant to serve as criteria for the transitional periods.

As we can see, in the infancy period, the child's development is fairly stable. The infant's interactions are limited to members of the immediate family system, especially the mother. This, however, is not to be interpreted as unidirectional influence since recent evidence shows that infants make significant contributions in shaping the infant-caregiver relationship (Lewis and Rosenblum, 1974). Also, we know that the infant is at least a potentially active information processor and that encounters with human beings and inanimate materials play an important role in determining how active the infant is as an information processor (Yarrow, Rubenstein, and Pederson, 1975).

The preschool period is considerably more complex. It is during this period that the effect of physical, social, and symbolic

environments becomes most clearly apparent. Not only is there remarkable progress in children's motor abilities, language, and cognitive functioning, but there is also a vast change in their personality and motives. In a very real way, this patterning and organization of children's characteristics shaped by the human systems in which children interact comprise the unique way in which they relate and adapt to the surrounding environments. For example, the monolingual Spanish-speaking child attending preschool may be exposed to linguistic and other cultural demands which necessitate adaptation to situations without the comfort of past experience. What the child is learning, in other words, is a coping strategy—a way of dealing with stress.

The last transitional period of school is a time when the Mexican-American child is formally introduced to structured systems. Now, social roles and formalized systems (i.e., teacher/child and peer/child) play an increasing part in shaping abilities, motives, and behavior. Also, it is probably during this period that the child begins to make more use of support systems as an aid in meeting the demands of an increasingly rigid and unyielding structure such as a public school.

Extending this discussion of systems beyond the three transitional periods of development, it becomes possible to make an even finer analysis of the adaptive process. That is, we can begin to describe the environments the child is adapting to. These environments can be subsumed under the general rubric of community.

Because the term carries many meanings, community is an elusive concept. A recent review of the literature on community has concluded that the concept is an evolving one (Meenaghan, 1972). It was suggested that the definition of community depends upon one's perspective and it is useless to try to understand a total community, but the concept can be useful if one begins by selecting issues or problems and then defines community as it is relevant to these particular concerns. For this reason, it is not fruitful to speak of a Mexican-American child's community in general terms. Upon reflection, it is apparent that what may be considered a community for a preschool child is substantially different from that for an adult. Similarly, the community of an infant is substantially different from what may be considered the community of a school-aged child.

In keeping with the general systems model, community will be defined in terms of behavioral settings and networks. Again, a systems model is a valuable heuristic device because it offers a method of describing a community in terms of specific physical locations and social networks that are interrelated and share a common characteristic (e.g., language use). The traditional ways of describing a community (social, economic, religious, and political considerations, etc.) have been productive but have not provided much insight into the interrelatedness of these aspects. The advantage of viewing a community in terms of behavioral settings

and networks is that we have a basis for understanding how the inhabitants of a community are actually or potentially interrelated. For example, we know from the work of Barker and his colleagues (Barker, 1968; Barker and Gump, 1964; Barker and Schoggen, 1973) that behavior settings are naturally occurring units having physical, behavioral, and temporal properties which reveal a variety of complex interrelationships among their parts. By adding the concept of network, we can better describe the interpersonal relationships occurring within a setting as well as the relationships of individuals between settings.

The use of a network as a community descriptor is especially pertinent for Mexican-Americans since they differ from the majority Anglo culture (and also within the Mexican-American culture) along such important socializing variables as family structure, family size, reliance upon extended family (Keefe, Padilla, and Carlos, 1978), language-use patterns (Saville and Troike, 1971), cultural values (Ramirez and Castañeda, 1974), and residence patterns such as *colonia or barrio* vs. integrated neighborhoods (Clark, 1959; Keefe et al., 1978). These variables almost certainly contribute to different functional relationships between behavioral settings in a given community.

Generally speaking, a number of settings and networks can be identified which contribute considerably to psychosocial development. These settings, placed within the context of a community, may be similar or dissimilar to each other depending upon the characteristics of the milieu inhabitants, psychosocial characteristics, reinforcement properties, and so forth. In any case, it is assumed that these settings would elicit particular types of behaviors or actions on the part of the child and that these would be specific to the settings.

A useful way to begin a systematic study of the Mexican-American child is to develop a classification scheme or taxonomy. A taxonomy describes the most im-

TABLE 1

Hypothetical Taxonomy of a Child's
Community/*Colonia* (Urban or Rural)

I. Family setting (within home)
  A. Immediate family network (i.e. parents and sibs)
    1. Size of family, intactness of family, time space between children, parenting roles, etc.
    2. Economic considerations, physical size of home, etc.
  B. Extended family (e.g. grandparents, uncles, aunts, etc.)
    1. Role of extended family in child rearing
  C. Media network (e.g. television, radio, newspaper)
    1. English or Spanish, kinds of programs watched or listened to, etc.
II. Neighborhood/*barrio* setting
  A. Adult network
    1. Extended family living nearby
    2. Immigrants from same locality in Mexico or Southwest
    3. Mixed ethnic groups/similar ethnic group
    4. Work at same place
    5. Housing situation (e.g., housing projects, single family lots, etc.)
  B. Child's peer network
    1. Racially mixed/similar ethnic background
    2. Age of peers, number of same aged peers, etc.
    3. Activity involvement (toys, play area, youth clubs, etc.)
III. Educational setting
  A. Parent-teacher/administrator network
    1. Neighborhood school/out of neighborhood school
    2. Public/private school
    3. Degree of involvement with school (e.g. adult education classes, membership in clubs such as PTA, bilingual programs, etc.)
  B. Child-teacher network
    1. Ethnic similarity and language use
    2. Reinforcement patterns
    3. Teaching style/curriculum
    4. Degree of student involvement in learning process
  C. Child-peer network
    1. Ethnic similarity/dissimilarity
    2. Classroom friendship patterns/

seating
3. Physical characteristics of school (e.g., play yard, classroom design, etc.)
4. Playground activities (organized sports, etc.)

---

portant attributes of the personal and behavioral characteristics of the child and the situation(s) in which the child interacts. For example, Fredericksen (1972) has elaborated upon some empirical procedures for developing situational taxonomies. He suggests that a possible criterion for use in developing a taxonomy of situations is their similarity with regard to the behaviors they elicit. For instance, situations that elicit specific types of behaviors are language communities, school settings, neighborhood playgrounds, and family settings. Theoretically, one could develop a taxonomy for each of these behaviorally defined settings. Table 1 presents a hypothetical taxonomy of some important settings and networks in a child's community and lists some influences which affect the character of the network.

Obviously, this taxonomy does not exhaust the setting or network possibilities which can be found in a child's community. One could also include the parents' involvement (or lack of involvement) in networks corresponding to governmental/institutional, business, health, and religious settings which presumably exert indirect (if not direct) influence on a child's psychosocial development. The purpose here, however, is only to point to those settings and networks that contribute a great deal to the formation of a child's adaptive skill repertoire. Furthermore, the taxonomy provides a systematic framework which lends itself to a social ecological analysis enabling the researcher to determine functional relationships between the various settings and their networks. This is critical if we are to grasp the concept of community and use it to the advantage of the Mexican-American child.

Finally, to assist in the coordination of the various disciplines, a taxonomy is presented identifying the Mexican-American child in Table 2. This taxonomy lists the personal and ecological dimensions which are the most important contributors to variability within the Mexican-American population.

In sum, what has been presented is a first step toward synchronizing the efforts of differently trained researchers working from a socioecological perspective. Clearly, much work of conceptual nature needs to be done. For example, we need a more efficient and systematic method for applying the concept of community toward an understanding of Mexican-American children's development during the different transitional periods. What kinds of settings and networks constitute the community of the Mexican-American infant, preschool, and school-aged child? Which are the important variables that link the setting to the network? And what distinguishes a viable community from one that limits a child's developmental opportunities?

The careful reader will note that no attempt has been made to identify specific adaptive behaviors. With respect to psychology, it appears that adaptive behavior is a relatively unexplored area of study. At any rate, a preliminary framework has been sketched which can assist researchers in planning a long-term research program.

At this point, we can now turn to an examination of each of the three transitional periods mentioned earlier and suggest possible domains of research and specific research problems. For the sake of clarity, the potential areas of research will be presented on two levels. This is done for purposes of exposition and is intended only to demonstrate the broad range of research problems that can be integrated into a socioecological approach. Realistically, distinguishing between basic

TABLE 2

Taxonomy of Mexican-American Child's Personal and Ecological Characteristics

I. Personal
  A. Age/grade
    1. Infants (1-2 years)
    2. Preschool (3-5 years)
    3. School (6-12 years)
  B. Sex
    1. Male
    2. Female
II. External characteristics
  A. Skin color
    1. Light Caucasian
    2. Dark Indian
III. Family background
  A. Family structure
    1. Nuclear
    2. Extended
  B. Socioeconomic level
  C. Parent educational level
    1. Mother
    2. Father
  D. Parent occupation
    1. Mother
    2. Father
  E. Residential stability
    1. Seasonal migrant
    2. Stable/nonmigrant
  F. Generation
    1. Immigrant
    2. Later
IV. Language use
  A. Speaking
    1. Monolingual English
    2. Monolingual Spanish
    3. Bilingual
      a. Spanish dominant
      b. English dominant
  B. Reading
    1. English
    2. Spanich
  C. Writing
    1. English
    2. Spanish
V. Cultural identification
  A. Monocultural
    1. Anglo/dominant culture
    2. Mexican/dominant culture
  B. Bicultural/multicultural
VI. Location of residence
  A. Urban
    1. Integrated neighborhood
    2. *Barrio*/high ethnic density
  B. Rural
    1. Integrated neighborhood
    2. *Barrio*/high ethnic density

and applied research results in a false dichotomy (Kaplan, 1964), especially from a socioecological perspective, since basic research eventually becomes applied in one way or another. Nevertheless, one level of research that will be described is directed toward increasing knowledge of the basic processes traditionally studied in child development. The processes which will be discussed are language development, cognitive development, personality development, and the development of social cognition. By studying these processes we will enhance our understanding of individual adaptation and how it is affected by prevailing social and physical conditions (i.e., behavioral settings and networks). This line of work will be identified as basic research.

The second line of work overlaps considerably with basic research but is broader in scope. The purpose of this research is to develop new skills and approaches to solving problems with direct application to the Mexican-American home, the child's classroom, and other intervention settings. Ideally, the results of this research will aid in the development, implementation, or redesign of an intervention program for the Mexican-American child. This line of work is identified as applied research.

THE INFANT (0-2 YEARS OF AGE)

Basic Research

Unfortunately, serious study of the Mexican-American infant within the home setting has yet to be undertaken, leaving a glaring gap in our store of knowledge. It is generally believed that the setting into which a child is born has as great an influence on development as genetic factors. Each child at birth enters a unique cultural, social, and family setting that helps determine perceptual, cognitive, social, and physical development. Although

it is not clear how the environmental setting influences future development, it is generally believed that child-rearing techniques are the most potent conditioning factors in the life of the child.

In laying the groundwork for basic infant-environment research on the Mexican-American child, a research model similar to that of Yarrow et al. (1975) would be valuable. Their study breaks away from simple characterizations of infant environments as "depriving" or "enriching." Instead, they begin by observing the infant in the natural environment and assess the impact of early experience at a highly differentiated level. They analyze in great detail the environments and the components of functioning of young infants and then look at the relationships between those differentiated dimensions of early experience and the infant's cognitive, motor, and motivational characteristics.

Operationally, these investigators observe mother-infant interaction at home, noting the amount of time the mother spends holding, caressing, and vigorously moving the infant. They also record the frequency of the mother's talking to the infant, distinguishing whether it was in response to the infant's signals or positive vocalizations. Furthermore, these researchers provide a detailed analysis of the usually ignored effect of the inanimate environment—the characteristics of objects within the infant's reach and their complexity and responsiveness (i.e., whether they change shape or make a sound when played with).

In keeping with this research strategy, investigators might well employ ethological methods to study the child-rearing techniques of Mexican-American parents. These methods can be characterized by an emphasis on a preliminary descriptive and observational phase. The advantages of a thorough descriptive phase of an investigation are several. The observational phase of a study establishes what there is to explain in real life occurrences, and it generates new hypotheses at a high rate as it goes along. The hypotheses that result are also likely to be more realistic than hypotheses that result from speculation or traditional theory. Thus, a long observational phase may, in fact, save time on experimental tests of unrealistic hypotheses. An experiment merely chooses between two hypotheses; it does not prove the correctness of either or exclude many of the other possible hypotheses that it was not specifically designed to test. Also, an experiment does not determine whether the tested effects play an important role in the occurrence of the phenomena during real life (Bronfenbrenner and Mahoney, 1974).

Clearly, results from a research model such as that of Yarrow et al. would increase our basic understanding of early environmental influences and would have implications for home intervention strategies. Results from such a study would be an important first step toward developing some theoretical and empirical bases for optimizing the environments of young Mexican-American children. Moreover, such studies should help us gain greater understanding of how particular cultural values, sanctions, and prohibitions interact with maternal and paternal behaviors to influence the child's development. This is especially pertinent for Mexican-American families since so little is known about the roles of the immediate and extended family networks in child-rearing. For example, some questions to consider are: What are Mexican-American parents' belief systems regarding infant care and development? Do behaviors reflect beliefs? Do the beliefs differ cross-generationally? How does the physical environment (housing, family size, etc.) affect the infant-caretaker system? Are infant care responsibilities shared with extended family members or sibs within the immediate family? Also, one might ask questions about the infant's prenatal environment:

What are the mother's nutritional characteristics? Did the mother seek prenatal health care? And which factors of the prenatal environment affect gestational age and development at birth?

Applied Research

There appears to be consensus among most students of infancy that human beings are most malleable during this very early period of life (White, 1971). In a nutshell, the argument is that much of what mediates the impact of formal schooling at age five or six and later has developed or occurred within the home setting long before that time. For instance, early language experiences, intellectual stimulation, and general cultural atmosphere prior to age four are considered important factors in providing a base for subsequent intellectual/academic progress.

While there are very few articles in the scientific literature describing educational programs for the Mexican-American infant, two different approaches have been identified. One involves an organized system of home teaching by trained persons who periodically visit parents and their infants to deliver an extended series of health-related services, including education. A second approach involves bringing infants together on a regular basis in group settings such as a day-care center. Both approaches have relied increasingly upon improving parenting skills and strengthening the family network. There are many variations on this theme, including a varied focus upon the infant or parents as principal recipients of service (Evans, 1975).

In order to develop and implement effective programs for Mexican-American infants and parents, much preliminary work needs to be undertaken. This preliminary work should focus on populations as the unit of observation rather than individuals. In this case, the best method of data collection is the survey.

The survey has been described as the general method that establishes the relation between two or more variables in a population in numerical terms. Surveys rely on the information that can be elicited and collated from existing sources. This includes both records of past events and interviews with members of a population. In its broad sense, the survey can be made to include the secondary analysis of existing data collected from registers of vital statistics, from hospital records, and from censuses (Susser, 1975).

By use of the survey technique, researchers will be able to provide data on the Mexican-American child that are descriptive and explanatory. The descriptive aspect of the survey will quantify the attributes of the Mexican-American infant population and their environments. Essentially, this type of data will provide an understanding of a selected problem, its size, its nature, among whom and where it is to be found, and most importantly, whether a given problem exists. The second function of the survey will be to compare Mexican-American communities differing along specified socioecological dimensions and attempt to account for the variations between them. The thrust of this strategy would be to seek relationships and determine possible causes.

Among the questions deemed most important for Mexican-American infant program development are the following: What are the demographic characteristics of the infant population? What is the incidence of specific types of illnesses, diseases, or forms of mental retardation among this infant population? What is their mortality rate compared to the national average? What kinds of health care delivery systems and support systems (e.g., extended family networks, neighborhood networks, etc.) are utilized by Mexican-American parents and how are infants affected by them? How do variables measuring poverty influence the incidence of premature

birth, developmental disorders, and general infant health?

THE PRESCHOOL CHILD (3-5 YEARS OF AGE)

Basic Research

Language development

Language is undoubtedly the most important symbolic system acquired by the child. It is acquired by exposure to, and interaction with, a community that lives in accord with a particular norm of usage. For the Mexican-American child, who often comes from a bilingual community, language acquisition is even more complex. The Mexican-American child is exposed to two language systems and must learn the mechanical skills of each language. Furthermore, the child must acquire social attitudes, motivations, and corresponding social postures associated with each language.

Obviously, the pervasiveness of the bilingual factor in Mexican-American children's language development suggests a number of possible areas of research. This subsection, however, will focus on only one problem which is of interest to bilingual educators: the degree to which the phonological, morphological, syntactic, and semantic systems of the two language codes overlap.

Research on young second-language learners has shown that their language-acquisition patterns in natural situations are similar in many ways to those of first-language learners (Hatch and Wagner-Gough, 1975; Padilla and Liebman, 1975; Padilla and Lindholm, 1976). In essence, what Padilla and his coworkers have shown is that the notion of language interference, traditionally used to explain disturbances in the bilingual's production or comprehension abilities, is no longer tenable and is in need of reexamination.

A good place to begin to understand the

interaction of two languages is by acknowledging that language is an integrated system of phonology, grammar, and lexicon. Control over the phonology and grammar of a native language is largely unconscious and almost entirely acquired during the preschool years. Thus, we can expect that the perception and production of the native language becomes increasingly fixed and the child may learn to hear all sounds in terms of the phonetics of the native language (Saville and Troike, 1971). For example, Spanish speakers commonly hear English "*ship*" and "*sheep*" as identical because the differences in these vowel sounds are not made in Spanish.

Collecting the kind of data on language structure that is necessary for understanding language interaction requires longitudinal study of children under naturalistic conditions. This includes studying monolingual English and Spanish-speaking children as well as bilingual children. Furthermore, researchers would profit immensely by taking a comparative approach in studying language acquisition and examining bilingual children from other Spanish-speaking groups (e.g., Puerto Rican, Cuban, Latin American countries, etc.) as well as Mexican-American children from different regions of the Southwest. Experimental situations should also be devised to test specific hypotheses about a child's receptive or productive capabilities. Combining the longitudinal and experimental research methods, a comparative framework insures versatility in gathering comprehensive data on the language development of bilingual, or potentially bilingual, Mexican-American children. This, of course, would serve bilingual educators by giving them a basis for predicting language problems and also for preparing to meet these problems. For example, some questions of interest to bilingual educators are: How does the symbolic environment (radio, TV, language community, etc.) influence the child's acquisition of a second language? What are

the strategies employed by Mexican-American children in learning a second language? How does the Spanish used by children born in Mexico and children born in the United States differ? How does their Spanish differ from that of other Spanish-speaking groups? What are the consequences of these differences for the acquisition of one language or two languages simultaneously?

Cognitive development

Cognitive style research has dominated the study of the Mexican-American child's development. None of these studies, however, have explored this development as it occurs during the preschool period. In fact, the studies that have been conducted have focused on children who have already begun attending school (Buriel, 1975; Kagan and Zahn, 1975; Ramirez and Price-Williams, 1974; Canavan, 1969). Moreover, these studies have been directed at only one dimension of the cognitive style construct — field independence/dependence. According to Witkin (1973), field dependents are characterized as strongly oriented toward their social environment and, as a consequence, are distinguished by high levels of social sensitivity and competence. Field independents, in contrast, are presumed to be more task oriented and more focused on the physical environment.

In brief, these studies have found that Mexican-American children have a more field dependent cognitive style than Anglo children. This is generally attributed to the more traditional child-rearing practices of the Mexican culture. These child-rearing practices, which emphasize adherence to convention, respect for authority, and a continued identity with the family, are consistent with the field dependent "socialization" cluster posited by Dyk and Witkin (1965) to explain the development of field dependence in children. Such a socialization cluster is contrary to the usual child-rearing practices of "mainstream" Anglo culture which emphasizes greater assertiveness, autonomy, and a more individualistic sense of self-identity (Ramirez and Castañeda, 1974).

This supposed (or hypothesized) relationship between cognitive style and child-rearing practices, however appealing it may be, is not fully supported by available data. In a recent study, Buriel (1975) focused on cognitive style trends within a generational cross-section of Mexican-American children and compared obtained differences in field independence to a group of completely assimilated Anglo children. His findings indicate that a simple linear model of increasing field independence with successive generations in the United States, as predicted by Ramirez and Castañeda, does not fit the data for Mexican-American children. He speculates that the processes of selective immigration by the parents and the children acculturating more to the life-style of their *barrio* or community have an important influence in the development of children's cognitive style.

In order to understand the antecedents of cognitive style, researchers should focus on studies of socialization paying close attention to the triad of factors suggested by earlier studies—child-rearing, selective immigration, and community acculturation. This proposed research should include other dimensions of cognitive style besides field dependence/independence. For example, other styles which merit examination are reflection/impulsivity, styles of categorization (breadth vs. narrowness), and styles of conceptualization such as analytic, categorical, and functional thematic (Kogan, 1976).

Of course, the preferred method in carrying out this research is to compare different subgroups of Mexican-American children as they progress through the preschool period and into the school-age period. These subgroups would be differentiated according to immigration patterns and the types of communities in which they reside. This research could

also be supplemented by a series of experimental studies designed to elaborate upon correlated variables (such as sex, social class, and language use) that may also contribute to the development of cognitive styles. Some questions to consider in carrying out this research are: Does the child's sex and level of community assimilation interact with measures of cognitive styles? How do cognitive styles affect concept development? What is the relationship of bilingualism to cognitive style development?

Two important reasons can be given for extending and expanding cognitive style research into the preschool period. One reason is the growing body of literature suggesting that cognitive styles share variance with both personality and intelligence indices (Kogan, 1976). Thus, by studying cognitive styles during early development, investigators can shed light on the mechanisms responsible for relationships reported to exist between those domains. The aim is to achieve greater understanding of cognition-personality dynamics in the preschool child.

The second reason, from a strictly developmental perspective, concerns tracking the origin of cognitive styles. The concern is whether cognitive style remains constant from preschool through the life span.

Clearly, cognitive style research can play an important role in furthering our understanding of the adaptive qualities of the Mexican-American child. At the very least, such work will support and help refine the theories that have been proposed regarding bicognitive and bicultural development (Ramirez and Castañeda, 1974). New findings will force researchers to take a new and different look at the developmental processes involved in the MA child's cognitive development.

Personality development

Personality development is an extremely complicated process shaped by a large number of interrelated and continually interacting factors. For Mexican-American preschool children, the most important influences are the effects of cultural factors, unique history of experiences with others, and the situation in which the child is involved (Mussen, 1973).

Considering the generality of these factors, researchers should focus on the socialization process occurring within the immediate and extended family networks. Understanding of this process is crucial since it is the vehicle by which parents and relatives transmit behavior patterns, beliefs, standards, and motives that are valued by the cultural group of which the child is a member. An example of this type of research is the socialization of sex-role behaviors.

The sex-role development of Mexican-American preschool children has yet to receive direct research attention. At present, the available literature can only suggest that there is some validity to the belief that masculine and feminine roles are clearly delineated within the Mexican-American culture (Padilla and Ruiz, 1973). This research is limited in that it does not address itself to the content and the methods used by parents or relatives to transmit pertinent information about sex-role behavior. The importance of obtaining this type of data is underscored by a trend toward sexual equality which is causing many parents, educators, and other professionals involved in child development to reevaluate the notions of what constitutes appropriate male and female behavior. Clearly, this topic of research has many implications for mental health: Are Mexican-American family networks being affected by society's deemphasis of rigid sex roles? How are Mexican-American children being affected by this change? How do Mexican-American parents, relatives, and peers transmit sex-role information? What is the role of the symbolic media in this process?

Current knowledge about sex-role socialization indicates that by age five children are keenly aware of sex-appropriate interests and behavior. Most three-, four-, and five-year-olds prefer toys, objects, and activities (e.g., playing cowboy, dolls, etc.) that are considered appropriate for their own sex (Brown, 1956). An idea of the strong parental pressures that foster sex typing can be found in a study where Anglo parents of three-year-old boys and girls described their child-rearing attitudes and behaviors. The practices used with boys reflected an emphasis on competition, conformity to conventional standards of achievement, control of feelings and emotions, and autonomy. On the other hand, the practices emphasized for girls were cooperation, the development and maintenance of close interpersonal relationships, and dependence on others (Block, 1973).

An appropriate focus of research on the immediate and extended family networks is identification. This is the process which leads the child to adopt integrated patterns of behavior, personal attributes and characteristics, and motives which have been modeled by parents and relatives. Moreover, responses acquired by identification seem to be emitted spontaneously and are, generally, relatively more stable and enduring (Mussen, 1973).

A medium by which this type of research can be conducted is play behavior. Children often exhibit sex-role behavior acquired from parents and other socializing agents during play. In addition, play provides content data which lends itself to many methods of analysis. More important, play occurs only in an atmosphere of familiarity, emotional assurance, and lack of tension and danger (Cazden, 1974). Thus, it offers a special opportunity for researchers to view the Mexican-American child in a relatively "unspoiled" state. Play also offers a glimpse of the child as many other special skills are practiced or developed.

In a study of children's imitative behavior, Whiting (1960) raised questions regarding cultural behavior and focused on the serious purposes of play. Whiting recognized the imitator characteristic of the behavior and was curious as to the relationship of human adaptive processes to the parent culture. The hypothesis of his study was that the games in which children act out social roles and events vary from culture to culture, depending on the models available for imitation. Whiting concluded that a study of the role models most frequently imitated by children in play should yield valuable information about social reality in various cultures. It was suggested that there is a research potential to be realized in exploring the aspects of family and social structures since these are the dominant influences in the child's choice of play activities.

Another interesting aspect of symbolic play during the preschool years is that it allows the child to experiment with life tasks and social roles while teaching rules of behavior. For example, when a young girl plays mother and imagines her doll to be her child, she is reflecting rules of maternal behavior in her actions even though this is not a game with rules formulated in advance. In other words, what children internalize in real life become rules of behavior in their play behavior (Piaget, 1962).

The best research method for studying play behavior is ethological. This is the least obtrusive method of observing children and provides the basic data from which to formulate hypotheses about Mexican-American children's sex-role development.

One possible strategy for employing the ethological method is to select groups of children with different familial characteristics (independent variables) and examine children's play for evidence of culturally distinct roles, specific reinforcement patterns, peer relationships, and verbal interaction with peers or sibs of the same or different sex, with special attention being paid to the content of the play behaviors. Observations could be made sequentially over a short period of time during the pivotal age when sex-role identification is in its most intense state—three to four years of age (Kohlberg, 1969). This descriptive data could be supplemented by parent and relative questionnaires, specially designed questionnaires for the children, and by setting up structured situations in which parent-child or relative-child interactions could be videotaped.

Social cognition

Social cognition is a relatively new area of study and refers to children's representation of others and how they conceptualize others and make correct inferences about their inner psychological states (Shantz, 1975). For the Mexican-American child, this is a particularly important area of study because the way children conceptualize others can have a detrimental or facilitative effect on the kinds of social relationships they form. For example, if the child's conceptual system is not sufficiently accurate, interrelationships are severely affected, making the child less adaptive within the social domain.

A fruitful area in which to begin a study of children's social cognition is in the development of person perception. The major question addressed here is how individuals describe or categorize other people on their actions and what dispositions or traits are attributed to others (Shantz, 1975).

One recent study has yielded preliminary data bearing on person perception by Mexican-American children. This study (Rice, Ruiz, and Padilla, 1974) compared Anglo, black, and Mexican-American preschool children's perceptions of photographs of young Anglo, black, and Mexican-American men. These children were asked questions designed to test their ability to correctly identify three photographs in terms of ethnic or racial membership and to state a preference for one of them. Preschoolers could distinguish between photographs of the Anglo and black males but could not differentiate the Anglo from the Mexican-American. More important, preschool Anglo children preferred photographs of their own group, while black and Mexican-American children did not indicate any preference. It was not until third grade that Mexican-American children displayed a strong preference for their own ethnic group.

This study suggests a relationship between self-concept and person perception. In fact, there are theoretical and empirical bases for asserting that the concept of self is intimately involved in person perception (Mead, 1934). This study also lends some support to the available data (Lively and Bromley, 1973) indicating that preschool children describe others with a strong evaluative orientation based on physical appearance and the child's previous interaction with the other person. Nevertheless, the question of how Mexican-American preschoolers characterize others is still open. We need to begin by investigating the simpler contents and organization of children's ideas about other children within their own family and peer networks. Eventually, we will be able to build up to the study of the more complex and subtle processes underlying person perception in other socially diverse and ethnically imbalanced networks. Some questions of immediate interest are: What are the important variables involved in friendship selection? What is the relationship between self-concept and person perception? How do parents' attitudes influence a child's perception of others?

In order to carry out this process-oriented research, investigators should employ both longitudinal and cross-sectional designs. Longitudinal studies would be valuable in gathering data on preschool children's interactions in everyday situations within family and peer networks. This natural observation would be a satisfactory exploratory procedure for acquiring descriptive data and for isolating key variables which affect the contents and organization of person perception. Cross-sectional designs would be useful in determining changes in person perception as a function of age differences, differences in residential characteristics (e.g., integrated vs. segregated neighborhoods), and other relevant factors involved in social cognition.

Future studies of person perception would profit also from a free-description method of gathering data on the Mexican-American child's perceptions of others. With this method, little attempt is made to manipulate behavior other than designating the stimulus person to be described. This procedure yields large amounts of information and may represent a more valid and productive procedure for person-perception research than the more structured approach referred to earlier in the Rice et al. study. This is readily suggested by studies which show that preschool children's patterning of the contents of their impressions is strongly influenced by the vocabulary and the frames of reference (content categories) used by older children and adults (Livesley and Bromley, 1973).

Applied Research

The relative sophistication of preschool children coupled with the development of comprehensive programming for preschoolers and their parents introduces experimentation as an integral tool of applied research. Experimental methods make it possible to investigate possible cause and effect relationships by exposing experimental groups to treatment conditions and comparing the results to control groups not receiving the treatment (random assignment being essential).

Benefits of experimentation are most clearly evident in the development and subsequent modification of Head Start programs. Following traditional educational practice, most initial programs used the preschool as the site and the teacher as the agent of intervention, and enrolled children beginning at age three. Feedback from experimental studies resulted in modifications in which the parent, not the teacher, has primary involvement and responsibility for instruction. The home replaces or is shared with the preschool as the site of intervention and children under age three are enrolled. These new dimensions, added to traditional approaches, have enriched the understanding of approaches to early educational intervention and have opened new avenues to scientific inquiry (Bronfenbrenner, 1974).

With respect to the Mexican-American preschool child, it is proposed that an applied research program be implemented to study the longitudinal effects of preschool intervention. Specifically, the research would focus on the organizational structure and psychosocial characteristics of Head Start programs (e.g., staff/child ratio, number of bilingual staff members, type of curriculum being used, etc.) and would attempt to assess their effects, experimentally and descriptively, on objective measures of cognitive, language, and social development.

This line of research will prove valuable in several ways. First, it would require facing what has commonly been called the criterion problem, that is, determining specifically what defines a given behavior change and how it can be measured. Second, it would provide insight into the interrelationships between education methods, the children involved, the teacher's skill, and the emotional climate in which learning takes place. Finally, on a more practical level, these kinds of studies would lead to the development of more effective and better designed educational programs for Mexican-American preschool children.

Another series of studies related to this research program would focus on the immediate Mexican-American family network. These studies, more observational in nature, would examine the entire network of family relationships, with emphasis being placed on conceptualizing,

quantifying, and producing information or hypotheses on the mother-child, father-child, husband-wife, and sibling dyads. This research on the family network would provide a basis for examining the hypothesis that intervention in one component of the family system has the potential for changing the previous balance of family relationships. This work is of particular importance since home intervention programs are gaining in popularity (Bronfenbrenner, 1974).

In addition, similar to the preliminary research outlined earlier for the Mexican-American infant, this research program would also include survey techniques to identify other problem areas and to gather demographic information on this subpopulation of children. For example, some questions for which a survey would be useful are: What is the incidence of child abuse and other environment-related problems (e.g., illnesses or disease related to poverty conditions, etc.) that effect a Mexican-American child's development? What is the relationship of the symbolic environment to children's language use, play behavior, and other personal characteristics? What are the prevailing parental attitudes concerning their children's preparation for entering school skills? What kinds of skills do parents feel they should teach their children before entering school?

THE SCHOOL-AGED CHILD (6-12 YEARS OF AGE)

Basic Research

Language development

In the previous section on language development, attention was focused on the developing linguistic systems of bilingual children and how they interact with each other. In this section, research attention is shifted to the functional development of language—that is, how the bilingual child uses language and the conditions under which different languages are used (Mackey, 1972). It appears that with regard to Mexican-American children, this is a virtually unexplored area of study.

Several reasons can be given for undertaking the study of functional language development. For educators, knowledge of the type of language used in a community can be helpful in setting realistic language objectives for children. For instance, as the native language is brought into schools in bilingual communities, the range of concepts and experiences which may be built upon depends in part on the contexts in which that language has been used within the family network at home and the child's peer network within the neighborhood (Guskin, 1976).

Another reason for studying patterns of language use, perhaps more directly pertinent to mental health, is that language choice may well serve as a behavioral index for group preferences (Herman, 1968) and lend insight into the processes of enculturation and acculturation. The latter is particularly important considering the recent trend toward school desegregation and the unknown impact this action will have on cultural (i.e., language) maintenance. Furthermore, an analysis of language choice may shed light on problems of motivation associated with the learning of a new language (Lambert, 1977; Taylor, 1977).

The general problem of functional language development is complex and requires an understanding of the totality of a child's social and symbolic environments. This is a large order and by necessity must include the complement of diverse research methods—naturalistic observation combined with experimental study.

Naturalistic observation, preferably longitudinal in nature, can best be accomplished through the use of a theoretical framework proposed by Fishman (1965, 1967, 1971) for the study of bilingualism. He advanced the notion of the bilingual dominance configuration which describes an individual's bilinguality in terms of language use and proficiency for each of the four language skills (speaking, writing, listening, and reading) across language varieties (i.e., English and Spanish) and across societal domains.

Similar to Barker's concept of setting (1968), Fishman defined a domain as a cluster of social situations which are constrained by a common set of behavior rules. The domains relevant to a given community may vary but they generally include family, neighborhood, religion, and, of course, the school domain. Like Barker, Fishman noted that a domain is more than a context or place. It includes the roles of interlocutors within the domain and the topics these interlocutors are likely to discuss. For instance, within the home domain, the father and child (two interlocutors in a prescribed role relationship) may be talking about the child's school work (topic).

By using this framework, it is possible to perform the very important task of studying the distribution of the Mexican-American child's language use throughout the entire behavioral repertoire. For instance, some questions which may be addressed through the use of the bilingual dominance configuration are: How does the school domain affect language use at home? How do the mass media influence both parents' and child's language use? At what age does the child's peer network begin to have influence on language use (e.g., the use of *Pachuco* argot, code-switching, etc.)? How do regional and generational differences affect the child's language use?

Experimental studies in functional language development can serve to elucidate the role of critical variables involved in language use. For instance, another research topic that warrants attention and has been subjected to experimental study is how a bilingual child's speech style is perceived and evaluated by another peer or adult. Perception by others is important because the feedback received, whether verbal or nonverbal, can affect language attitudes and can alter subsequent language use by the child.

Although speech style evaluation studies have yet to be conducted with preadolescent Mexican-American children, Ryan and Carranza (1975) have explored the evaluative reactions of Anglo, black, and Mexican-American adolescents toward speakers of standard English and Mexican-American-accented English. These three groups of listeners evaluated the personalities of 12 speakers representing four "context-by-accent" categories (English/home, accented English/home, English/school, and accented English/school) and rated them according to semantic differential traits, four status-stressing scales (educated/uneducated, intelligent/ignorant, etc.) and four solidarity-stressing scales (friendly/unfriendly, good/bad, etc.)

The results showed that although standard English speakers received more favorable ratings in every case, the differences were significantly greater in the school context than in the home context and for the status ratings than for the solidarity ratings. Unexpectedly, Anglo and black raters followed the patterns of Mexican-Americans in their overall ratings of the four passages. Thus, even the adolescents who would not associate the accented speech with their own group were more tolerant of deviations from standard English in a home context than in a school context. From these data it appears that a wider range of speech styles is acceptable in an informal setting than in a formal setting.

In another evaluative study, Ryan, Carranza, and Moffie (1974) investigated the relationship between the amount of accentedness heard and the attributed characteristics of the speaker. High correlations were reported between the accentedness ratings and the personality characteristics attributed to the speaker. This finding strongly suggests that small increments in accentedness are associated with gradually less favorable impressions of the speaker.

Clearly, experimentation can offer much to the full understanding of functional language development. Given that critical variables can be isolated and manipulated, experimental study can lead to a finer analysis of the relationship between these variables as demonstrated by the Ryan et al. research on accentedness. For example, using a cross-sectional design, it is possible to manipulate different speech styles and to test their effects on boys and girls from different grade levels and social and cultural backgrounds. This method seems to be an interesting means of tapping the development of stereotype acquisition and also is a good way of assessing subtle changes in social perceptions of stereotypical judgments on the basis of language samples. Other questions to which experimental methods would apply are: What is the relationship between measure of social status and standard and nonstandard forms of language use in various settings? How does the topic of conversation influence the length of utterance, speech rate, and vocal qualities in either of the bilingual speaker's two languages? How do regional or cultural differences among Spanish speakers affect the perceptions and evaluations by Mexican-American children? What are the most important personal characteristics of the person being addressed (age, sex, ethnicity, skin color, etc.) that determine the speech style a Mexican-American child might use? And finally, how do these differences in language use apply to school performance, social relationships, mental health, and so on?

Cognitive development

By and large, psychologists studying the Mexican-American child's cognitive development have tended to focus on what these children can do when presented with tests and laboratory situations. It would not be inaccurate to say that much of this work has been motivated by the consistent finding that Mexican-American children generally score lower on intelligence tests than their Anglo peers (Padilla and Ruiz, 1973). This finding has motivated researchers to propose theoretical formulations to explain how the cognitive development of Mexican-American children differs from that of the Anglo middle-class child.

As suggested in the earlier section on the preschool child's cognitive development, cognitive style research has dominated the field and is currently being applied to the development of educational curricula (Baecher, 1976; Ramirez and Castañeda, 1974). Recognizing that this line of research may soon stimulate the development of a new line of achievement and intelligence tests, it would be wise to critically examine the limitations of cognitive style research.

In most of the laboratory research on cognitive style, a rather static approach has been employed which, instead of viewing cognition as part of a sequence of adaptational efforts and perceived consequences, studies the cognitive activity in itself or for purposes of categorizing the individual (Wachtel, 1972).

One problem with this line of work is that it emphasizes outcome and yields little information on the cognitive processes involved. For example, in assessing cognitive style, researchers usually depend upon a few simple, objective laboratory tests to measure cognitive characteristics. The weakness of this approach is that it may be assessing abilities which may or may not form the basis for a particular personal style. The relation between scores on such tests as the rod and frame or embedded figures and the matters that have traditionally fascinated students of cognition are more complicated and indirect than the literature in this area tends to suggest. This confusion is caused by an empirical and conceptual strategy that implicitly treats children as static structures instead of viewing them as dynam-

ically interacting with and responsive to events.

In an effort to take a more process-oriented approach to the study of the Mexican-American child's cognitive development, researchers must include as its empirical subject matter the growth of intellectual activities such as remembering, thinking, and perceiving as well as using and understanding language. The concern should be with how the Mexican-American child gets, creates, and uses knowledge about the physical and social environments (Ginsburg and Koslowski, 1976). Furthermore, the research program being proposed must distinguish between the products of cognitive development as inferred properties and as observable behaviors that result when individuals face problematic situations and are forced to adapt to them. Research emphasis, of course, will be on the latter.

Implicit in such research is the assumption that cultural and social influences have a powerful effect on the Mexican-American child's competence in certain cognitive skills. Moreover, these influences are mediated by the different problem-solving situations available to the child and how they are interpreted. Thus, the major thrust of the research should be to identify natural problem-solving situations in the environment and observe what these children do in response to these situations.

The most efficient method for initiating research on natural problem-solving abilities is through the use of ethological techniques. As pointed out in earlier sections, ethological methods are best suited for exploratory research and provide the basis for future hypothesis-testing research. These methods involve prolonged observation of individuals in their natural environment and, therefore, are in sharp contrast to the cognitive style data obtained from individuals under controlled conditions within a relatively short time.

One important advantage of this approach is that by observing how Mexican-

American children solve problems in their environment, it will be possible to obtain a better estimate of their adaptive capacity. Once a detailed picture of the adaptive capabilities of a large number of children is obtained, further research will attempt to determine the consistency (or lack of consistency) between the demand characteristics of the child's nonschool environment and the cognitive demands made within the school setting.

Some questions of immediate concern to the ethologically trained observer are: What kinds of problem-solving situations do parents present their children? What kinds of problem situations do children confront within the peer network? What kinds of opportunities does the environment provide children for experimenting with problem-solving skills? How do older children teach younger children problem-solving skills? Under what conditions does cooperative problem-solving occur?

Personality development

It is generally agreed that the sense of "self" refers to the acquired set of feelings and attitudes that a person has toward his/her own appearance, power, and behavior. The concept of self is the core of each personality. In agreement with Mead (1934), Kinch (1963) says, "the individual's conception of himself emerges from social interaction, and in turn, guides or influences the behavior of that individual" (p. 483). Since qualities include attributes and roles, this definition is superior to many others. McCandless and Evans (1973) came to a similar definition of the self-concept as "an individual's awareness of his own characteristics and attributes, and the ways in which he is both like and unlike others" (p. 389).

The development of the Mexican-American child's self-concept is a research topic of vital concern. It is well known that differing opinions and attitudes, which are by-products of unique socialization processes, often play a central role in the for-

mation of a child's personality. When a child is placed in contact with persons of differing values and attitudes, the stage is set for conflict—especially if the Mexican-American child is bilingual and bicultural and entering an environment which is predominately monolingual and monocultural, as in a public school (Padilla and Ruiz, 1973).

Research on the Mexican-American child's self-concept has already begun. Studies by Padilla and his colleagues (Padilla, Rice, and Ruiz, 1973; Rice, Ruiz, and Padilla, 1974) using photograph selection techniques to measure ethnic preference have found that with increasing age these children show a preference for their own ethnicity. The Padilla et al. (1973) study showed that in response to questions related to ethnic identification and selection of friends, Mexican-American male and female children from the second, fourth, and sixth grades selected photographs of a child from their own ethnic group. These results are interpreted as suggesting a positive self-image of the MA child and stand in contrast to another study which found that MA children tend to describe themselves in negative terms (Petersen and Ramirez, 1971).

It should be obvious that the work completed thus far has not addressed itself to the process by which the self-concept develops. The reason for this is that it is difficult to discover at what point in development the sense of self emerges. Although there is an increasing awareness of "me" and "not me," the process through which the individual becomes generally conscious of his/her body, of various abilities, and of ethnic identity is still a matter for investigation. The fundamental difficulty with the self-concept is that we know about it only by inference. This is true for the individual as well as for the observer (Guardo, 1968).

To begin to understand the development of the self-concept of the Mexican-American child, it is instructive to note that consistency or continuity of behavior is largely a result of the self-concept. Although subject to maturation and to environmental influences, modification of the self-concept usually occurs in small steps. Experiences that would radically distort it, such as a child's home language clashing with the dominant "foreign" language of the school, could undermine the self-concept and adversely affect the emerging "self."

In order to gain an appreciation for the role of language in self-concept development, we must look back to the early writings of theorists. The development of the concept of the self in early childhood was analyzed many years ago by Mead (1934), who emphasized the role of language as a means by which children come to conceptualize their own existence in terms of the existence of others. Mead used the terms "I" and "me" to differentiate between the individual and social aspects of the self. In each case, language is considered one of the most important mediating factors in the development of the self-concept. Also, this early writing implied that variation would result from regular exposure of the child to more than one language. Mead assumed, as do most other social theorists, that children are typically exposed to only one language in the family, the community, and the school.

To study the effect of language on self-concept development will require both naturalistic observation and experimental study. Research should initially direct itself toward operationally defining and quantifying the self-concept—what is it and how does it manifest itself? Only after multiple measures of the self-concept have been developed can work proceed. Questions warranting attention are: How does the Mexican-American child adapt linguistically to conflicting social environments? For example, is the child more verbal at home than at school? What is the relationship between language use/preference and specific behaviors indicative of a healthy self-concept? What are the socialization forces which main-

tain positive and negative self-concepts? How do the mass media influence Mexican-American children's self-concept? Does self-concept differ across situations or when tested in either of the bilingual's languages?

Social cognition

The relation between social cognition and interpersonal behavior has been a popular area of research for several decades. Unfortunately, no systematic study of this relation has been made using Mexican-American children. Thus, little is known about how a Mexican-American child's social experiences influence patterns or content of social interaction.

One specific topic of research which presumably taps social development is the process by which children acquire the ability to take the role of another. This process, first described by Mead (1934), is also known by such terms as identification, internalization, and empathic response. The term "role-taking," however, is preferable for a number of reasons. First, it emphasizes the cognitive as well as the affective side of behavior. Second, it involves an organized structural relationship between self and others. Third, it emphasizes that the process involves understanding and relating to all the roles in the society of which one is a part. Finally, it emphasizes that role-taking goes on in all situations involving social interaction and communication, not merely those which arouse empathy or sympathy (Kohlberg, 1976).

Role-taking is a particularly rich area for research since it appears to be a prerequisite for the emergence of many social behaviors. For example, it has been suggested that a variety of prosocial behaviors—cooperation, friendliness, helpfulness, and so forth—emerge and are strengthened by the child's ability to take the role of another (Shantz, 1975). Although these behaviors are influenced by situational variables, role-taking ability affects the ease of shaping, maintaining, and generalizing prosocial behavior. It has also been suggested that certain antisocial behaviors, such as aggression against peers, may be inhibited by the aggressor taking the role of his victim (Feshbach & Feshbach, 1969). Clearly, research on Mexican-American children's role-taking abilities has implications for both educational and clinical practices involving these children.

The expected relation between role-taking abilities and social behavior has stemmed primarily from Piaget's (1967) research. He has proposed a bidirectional causal relation. For example, focusing on the peer network, Piaget argues that peer interaction is a necessary factor for the development of role-taking skills and vice versa. In the first case, Piaget suggests that egocentric functioning is displaced as a result of the child's confrontation with peers who differ in their "wishes, perspectives, needs, and thoughts" (p. 95). Thus, peer interaction in general, and peer conflict in particular, is a necessary condition for role-taking to emerge and stabilize. In the second case, as role-taking abilities emerge, the child can engage in reciprocal social behavior such as cooperation, discussion, and planning.

Selman (1976) has elaborated further on the acquisition of role-taking abilities and has described the process according to successive stages of development. Although Selman has identified five stages of development, only three pertain to the context of the present discussion. In Stage I, social-informational role-taking (about six-eight years of age), the child is unable to maintain his own perspective and simultaneously place himself in the role of others while attempting to judge their actions. Neither can the child judge his actions from another's viewpoint.

In Stage II, self-reflective role-taking (about eight-ten years of age), the child acquires the ability to reflect on the self's behavior and motivation as seen from outside the self, from the other's point of view.

Here the child recognizes that other people can also place themselves in the child's position, so the child is able to anticipate the reactions to his own motives or purposes. The limitation, however, is that the child cannot go beyond the two-person situation and view it from a third-person perspective.

Finally, in Stage III, mutual role-taking (about 10-12 years of age), the child discovers that both self and other consider each other's viewpoint simultaneously and mutually. Both can view themselves from the other's vantage point before deciding how to react. Also, both can consider a situation from the perspective of a third party who can also assume each person's viewpoints and consider the interrelationships.

Based on this stage-related developmental sequence, one could ask many questions relevant to Mexican-American children's social experiences and their influence on role-taking abilities. For example, is Selman's (1976) stage-related developmental process an accurate portrayal of Mexican-American children's role-taking abilities? What conditions affect the development of role-taking abilities (e.g., socioeconomic status, number of peer contacts, language use, etc.)? What kinds of role-taking opportunities are and are not available to Mexican-American children? What is the communicative process underlying the development of role-taking abilities?

Systematic study of Mexican-American children's role-taking abilities might well be modeled after Selman's (1976) research. He began by dividing role-taking content into various concepts. The concepts revolved around two basic categories of social experience noted by Mead (1934): conceptions of the nature of self (e.g., concepts of personality, motives, self-reflection, etc.) and conceptions of the nature of society (e.g., conceptions of roles and relations, the characteristics of "social reality," etc.).

Following the open-ended clinical

method first used by Piaget, Selman engaged the child in "social thought" by posing specially designed dilemmas to different aged children and probing their thinking through specific and open-ended questions. By this, he was able to determine the stage-related characteristics of children's responses and formulate the structural aspects of role-taking stages.

Applied Research

It is well known that no public institution has a greater or more direct influence on future opportunity than the school. With regard to the Mexican-American child, one could argue that the school has failed in its most basic responsibility —providing the opportunity for the student to gain maximal benefit from the educational experience and for developing capabilities to the fullest extent. This has been well documented in a recent series of reports focusing on Mexican-American education in the Southwest (U.S. Commission on Civil Rights, 1971-74).

Applied research can contribute a great deal when directed toward the goal of improving the educational experience of Mexican-American children. The work of Ramirez and Castañeda (1974) illustrates how research can have impact on the development of curricula for bilingual/ bicultural education programs. They emphasize the importance of teachers' accepting and using the bilingual students' cultural and linguistic experiences as bases on which to build better bilingual programs. Specifically, they argue that "bicognitive development" must be nurtured so that Mexican-American children can operate effectively in diverse social and intellectual contexts while at the same time retaining and developing those cognitive abilities transmitted through their home and community experiences.

Applied studies also need to be conducted which examine the influence of the physical school setting and staff on Mex-

ican-American children's education. Research has shown that the location of a school (Gump, 1975) and the way a classroom is organized (Thompson, 1973) can affect students in a positive or negative way. In addition, research has found that disparities exist in the way teachers treat Mexican-Americans and Anglos within the same classroom (U.S. Commission on Civil Rights, Report 5, 1973). This study found that in comparison to Anglo students, Mexican-American pupils receive less encouragement, are asked fewer questions, and less often hear teachers accept or use their ideas. It was also determined that Mexican-American students spoke less during classroom time than Anglo students. Although the relation of physical setting and personnel to academic achievement is unclear (Coleman, 1966), it is safe to assume that these factors exert a pervasive influence on a child's educational experience. Of course, the extent of this influence and its future effects on children's educational attainment are questions open for investigation.

In recent years, the noneducational (i.e., nonacademic) aspects of the school experience have gained increasing recognition. Biber and associates (Biber, 1961; Minuchin, Biber, Shapiro, and Zimiles, 1969) have been vigorous proponents of the position that, as a socializing institution, the school is second in importance only to the family and can have considerable impact on the child's mental health, for either better or worse.

Applied research must play a strategic role in order for schools to function more effectively as an agency for enhancing the future life experiences of Mexican-American children outside of the academic track. This role is much too broad to describe thoroughly in this discussion; however, two examples—social skills curricula development and drug education—will illustrate how applied research can enhance the school's socializing power.

The ability to relate constructively to peers, teachers, and other adults is one of several dimensions of child behavior that is linked to positive, adaptive, coping behavior in the school, as well as in other social environments. When these underlying social skills are mastered early in the educative process, they become incorporated into and developed further in the child's behavioral repertoire during later school years (Erikson, 1959). On the other hand, if the child fails to develop social competencies, a sense of inadequacy or inferiority eventually breeds itself and becomes a permanent part of the self-concept.

Educators have recently become more aware of their responsibility to help the child develop a positive sense of self and an internalized code of behavior. This new perspective has motivated educators and researchers to aim their efforts at constructing elementary school curricula which blend the concepts and skills necessary for successful social adjustment along with the traditional academic skills normally taught in the classroom (Spivak and Shure, 1974). Regretfully, this innovation has yet to be reported in the literature of education within a Mexican-American context. It is probable that social skills are not being systematically taught to Mexican-American children and the conditions under which they can be taught is unknown.

To gain a better understanding of the research task, it is helpful to begin by examining some basic research findings. Based on knowledge derived from studies in social cognition and cognitive development, it is known that children during the early school period (about eight years of age) tend to choose friends from the same neighborhood or classroom who are about the same age (Shantz, 1975). Even at this young age, children tend to choose friends who have the same status as themselves. Also, these primary school children prefer friends of their own sex. Furthermore, the child's interpersonal relationships are based on reciprocity and are rather superficial (Selman, 1976).

During the later elementary school years (8-11 years), the child has begun to acquire concepts involving complex relationships and can begin to have a mental representation of a series of actions. In other words, the child has the capacity to order and relate experiences to an organized whole. This enables the child to deal with information in the present and to relate this information back to past experiences. The skills that begin to emerge during this period are those of organization, planning for problem solving, inhibition of irrelevant behavior, and the beginnings of "genuine cooperation" (Inhelder and Piaget, 1958). Furthermore, Mussen (1973) observes that the friendships that are formed are fairly unstable; interests change easily and "old" friendships are ended and others substituted. By the time the child has reached about 12 years of age, the capacity to form lasting friendships on the basis of meeting others' needs (as well as the child's own) is an indication of the development of social maturity.

Obviously, the primary role of applied research is to determine how well this general scheme of social development fits the developing Mexican-American child. Also, one may ask if there are cultural or social class differences with respect to spatial distancing between interacting children, the use of nonverbal communication channels, resolution of arguments, and friendship selections.

Again, as in other research problems that have been posed, the initial research strategy in answering these questions is direct, natural observation. Once some idea of Mexican-American children's social characteristics is known, curriculum specialists can begin to design curricula, employing materials and activities to enhance the development of social skills.

The second example illustrating the role of applied research in making full use of the school's socializing potential concerns special programming. As envisioned now, these programs are directed primarily at educating children with regard to certain specified topics. The selection of these topics is based on the presence of problem situations within a local community which threaten the child's present or future development. In this case, the topic that will be briefly elaborated on is drug education.

The concept of special programming begins with a needs-assessment approach: applied research to identify specific community problems, to gauge their extent, and to determine their etiology. For example, Padilla et al. (1977), working in four housing projects in East Los Angeles (an area heavily populated by Mexican-Americans), found that Mexican-American adolescents had a higher prevalence of inhalant (e.g., intoxicating aerosols, glue sniffing, etc.) and marijuana use than the national average. The results indicated that these Mexican-American adolescents were 14 times more likely to be abusing inhalants and twice as likely to be using marijuana when compared to a national survey of substance abuse among adolescents. This study also reported that the use of alcohol and other drugs (e.g., hallucinogens, tranquilizers, etc.) by Mexican-American adolescents was comparable to national norms.

What is unique about this example of applied research is that the investigators recruited and trained a number of barrio youth who exemplified the capabilities and maturity necessary for involvement in the research process. These youth were then hired as interviewers to collect the data and encouraged to participate in all stages of the research cycle. The rationale behind this method was that, besides being a rich educational experience for the MA youth, the youth would be better able to gain access to the tightly-knit youth subculture living in the projects. Much like any other subculture, "outsiders," even though from the same ethnic background, are considered intruders in the projects and are highly suspect by the residents. Needless to say, the results of the study and the interest it generated on the part of the young interviewers testifies to the effectiveness of this research strategy.

More to the point, this research is strongly suggestive of a need for school intervention to inform Mexican-American adolescents, especially preadolescents, of the mental and physical damages of substance abuse. It is painful to admit however, that even though millions of dollars have been spent on drug-education programs, the role of the school in the whole scheme of things is still undefined. Also, it appears that school officials, and possibly even classroom teachers, are not adequately informed as to what the drug problem is and what drug education should do. Moreover, school personnel often are not members of the immediate community and do not know the problems of the community.

Although a discussion of the school and the extent of its social responsibility is beyond the scope of this discussion, it is indisputable that applied research can be a powerful tool in orienting program developers to the problems of a community. At the very least, applied research can offer guidance in identifying community problems, and once a program has been developed, applied research can go a step further by pre- and post-testing the program to ascertain its effectiveness. Moreover, the process of research can be exploited to teach children ways of dealing with problems rather than seeking solutions through high-risk, low-gain behavior. Again, it is apparent that much can be learned from the example of Padilla et al. (1977).

Obviously, schools alone cannot solve community problems such as drug abuse. It will take action on the part of society in general beginning with educating parents at home. This responsibility must ultimately be shared by both the public and private sectors of society. Nevertheless, due to its very existence, the school should play a vital role in addressing community problems. Such a role can be developed by making constructive use of the school's socializing potential, especially through the implementation of special programs that are community specific.

SUMMARY

The era of serious research on Mexican-American children has begun. The available literature, however, is not without its limitations. An overview of the empirical research revealed little interaction between the various disciplines, lack of theoretical orientation in many of the studies, and more generally, the absence of a research perspective which consolidates the different environments influencing a child's development.

In view of these limitations, a socioecological approach to research on the Mexican-American child is proposed. As described, the approach is theoretically oriented, positive in its outlook, broad in its conceptual framework, and capable of guiding differently trained researchers working in both basic and applied areas of research. This is illustrated by elaborating on the methodological aspects of a socioecological perspective and by outlining six dimensions which provide a fundamental description of the ways environments may be conceptualized. Further clarification of this approach is provided by listing a number of principles and procedures which began to define a socioecological orientation to research.

Using psychosocial development as a frame of reference, a socioecological approach to research is sketched. Psychosocial development is described as an active adaptation by the child to the surrounding physical, social, and symbolic environments. To better understand this process, the Mexican-American child's developmental years are divided into three transitional periods: infancy, preschool,

and school. This allows a more accurate analysis to be made of the prevailing systems and subsystems which interplay during different periods of development. Greater detail to this form of analysis is provided by the use of a hypothetical taxonomy which classifies the behavior settings and social networks typical of a child's community. The interrelated nature of the behavior settings and networks is emphasized. No attempt is made to further define the concept of community since the concept itself varies according to the transitional period of interest. Finally, another taxonomy is presented listing the personal and ecological dimensions which contribute to variability within the Mexican-American population.

To further illustrate the breadth of the socioecological approach, a number of research problems are suggested. Table 3 summarizes the proposed research on MA children.

In conclusion, it is only fair to reiterate the preliminary nature of this approach to research. Obviously, a great deal of planning and organizing needs to be done before researchers can claim a socioecological perspective. Moreover, lines of communication need to be established between researchers and policy makers and program developers before this approach can legitimately contribute to the future welfare of Mexican-American children. In fact, one might well argue that it is the necessary and vital relationship between policymaker, program developer, and researcher that is the biggest obstacle toward realizing a true socioecological approach to research. Perhaps, once again, we should heed the warning of Kaplan (1964):

The scientist would do well to remember that when science is divorced from policy, the result is not only that science is "set free" but also that policy is thereby thrown on its own resources—which is to say that it is left to be determined by tradition, prejudice, and the preponderance of power (p. 403).

TABLE 3

Summary of Proposed Research on Mexican-American Children

TRANSI-TIONAL PERIODS	RESEARCH	DOMAIN OF RESEARCH	GENERAL RESEARCH PROBLEMS	METHODOLOGY
Infancy	Basic	Infant environment	Child rearing techniques	Descriptive
	Applied	Development of infant education programs	Description of MA infant population	Descriptive
Preschool	Basic	Language development Cognitive development Personality development Social cognition	Bilingual language acquisition Antecedents of cognitive style Sex role socialization Person perception	Descriptive/experimental Correlational Descriptive Descriptive/experimental
	Applied	Preschool intervention programs	Organizational structure and psychosocial characteristics of Head Start programs	Descriptive Experimental Survey
School Age	Basic	Language development Cognitive development Personality development Social cognition	Language function or use Natural problem-solving abilities Self-concept and language Role-taking abilities	Descriptive/Experimental Descriptive Descriptive/Experimental Quasi-Experimental
	Applied	Physical school setting and educational curriculum	Social skills curricula and special development programming	Descriptive/ Experimental/ Evaluative

REFERENCES

Baecher, R. E. Bilingual children and educational cognitive style analysis. In: A. Simoes, Jr. (Ed.), *The Bilingual Child: Research and Analysis of Existing Educational Themes.* New York: Academic Press, 1976.

Baker, R. G. Ecology and motivation. In: M. R. Jones (Ed.), *Nebraska Symposium on Motivation.* Lincoln: University of Nebraska, 1960.

Barker, R. G. *Ecological Psychology.* Stanford, CA: Stanford University Press, 1968.

Barker, R. G. and Gump, P. V. (Eds.), *Big Schools, Small Schools.* Stanford, CA: Stanford University Press, 1964.

Barker, R. G. and Schoggen, P. *Qualities of Community Life.* San Francisco: Jossey-Bass, 1973.

Biber, B. Integration of mental health principles in the school setting. In: G. Caplan (Ed.), *Prevention of Mental Disorders in Children.* New York: Basic Books, 1961.

Block, J. H. Conceptions of sex role: Some cross cultural and longitudinal perspectives. *American Psychologist,* 1973, *28,* 512-529.

Bronfenbrenner, U. Is early intervention effective? In: U. Bronfenbrenner and M. Mahoney (Eds.), *Influences on Human Development.* Hinsdale, IL: The Dryden Press, 1974.

Bronfenbrenner, U. and Mahoney, M. The structure and verification of hypotheses. In: U. Bronfenbrenner and M. Mahoney (Eds.), *Influences on Human Development.* Hinsdale, IL: The Dryden Press, 1974.

Brown, D. G. Sex role preference in young children. *Psychological Monographs,* 1956, *70*(421), 1-19.

Buriel, R. Cognitive styles among three generations of Mexican American children. *Journal of Cross-Cultural Psychology,* 1975, *6*(4), 417-429.

Canavan, D. Field dependence in children as a function of grade, sex, and ethnic group membership. Paper presented at the meeting of the American Psychological Association, Washington, D.C., 1969.

Cazden, C. B. Play and metalinguistic awareness: One dimension of language experience. *Urban Review,* 1974, 7, 28-39.

Clark, M. *Health in the Mexican American Culture.* Berkeley, CA: University of California Press, 1959.

Coleman, J. S. *Equality of Educational Opportunity.* Washington, D.C.: U.S. Department of Health, Education, and Welfare, Office of Education, 1966.

De Bie, P. Problem-focused research. In: *Main Trends of Research in the Social and Human Sciences.* Paris: Mouton/UNESCO, 1970.

Dyk, R. B. and Witkin, H. A. Family experiences related to the development of differentiation in children. *Child Development,* 1965, *30,* 21-55.

Emery, F. E. and Trist, E. L. *Towards a Social Ecology: Contextual Appreciations of the Future in the Present.* London: Plenum, 1973.

Erikson, E. H. Identity and the life cycle. *Psychological Issues,* 1959, *1,* 1-165.

Evans, E. D. *Contemporary Influences in Early Childhood Education.* Second edition. San Francisco: Holt, Rinehart, & Winston, 1975.

Feshbach, N. D. and Feshbach, S. The relationship between empathy and aggression in two age groups. *Developmental Psychology,* 1969, *1,* 102-107.

Fishman, J. A. Who speaks what language to whom and where? *Linguistique, II,* 1965, 67-88.

Fishman, J. A. The breadth and depth of English in the United States. *University Quarterly,* March 1967, 133-140.

Fishman, J. A. The links between micro and macro sociolinguistics in the study of who speaks what language to whom and when. In: D. Hymes and J. J. Gumperz (Eds.), *The Ethnography of Communication: Directions in Sociolinguistics.* New York: Holt, Rinehart, & Winston, 1971.

Fredericksen, N. Toward a taxonomy of situations. *American Psychologist,* 1972, *27,* 114-123.

Gallagher, J. J., Ramey, C. T., Haskins, R., and Finkelstein, N. W. Use of longitudinal research in the study of child development. In: T. D. Fjossen (Ed.), *Intervention Strategies for High Risk Infants and Young Children.* Baltimore: University Park Press, 1976.

Ginsburg, H. and Koslowski, B. Cognitive development. In: M. R. Rosenzweig and L. W. Porter (Eds.), *Annual Review of Psychology.* Volume 27. Palo Alto, CA: Annual Reviews, 1976.

Guardo, C. J. Self revisited: The sense of self-identity. *Journal of Human Psychology,* 1968, *8,* 137-142.

Gump, P. V. Ecological psychology and children. In: E. M. Hetherington (Ed.), *Review of Child Development Research Volume 5.* Chicago: The University of Chicago Press, 1975.

Guskin, J. T. What the child brings and what the school expects: First- and second-language learning and teaching in bilingual-bicultural education. In: A. Simoes, Jr. (Ed.), *The Bilingual Child: Research and Analysis of Existing Educational Themes.* New York: Academic Press, 1976.

Hatch, E. and Wagner-Gough, J. D. Second language acquisition. In: M. Celce-Murcia and L. McIntosh (Eds.), *An Introduction to the Teaching of English as a Second Language.* Second edition: Los Angeles: University of California, 1975.

Herman, S. R. Explorations in the social psychology of language choice. In: J. A. Fishman (Ed.), *Readings in the sociology of language.* The Hague: Mouton, 1968.

Inhelder, B. and Piaget, J. *The Growth of Logical Thinking from Childhood to Adolescence: An Essay on the Construction of Formal Operational Structures.* New York: Basic Books, 1958.

Kagan, S. and Zahn, G. L. Field dependence and the school achievement gap between Anglo American and Mexican American children. *Journal of Educational Psychology,* 1975, *67*(5), 643-650.

Kaplan, A. *The Conduct of Inquiry: Methodology for Behavioral Science.* San Francisco: Chandler, 1964.

Keefe, S., Padilla, A. M., and Carlos, M. L. *Emotional Support Systems in Two Cultures: A Comparison of Mexican Americans and Anglo Americans.* Los

Angeles: Spanish Speaking Mental Health Research Center, UCLA, Occasional Paper No. 7, 1978.

Kinch, J. W. A formalized theory of the self-concept. *American Journal of Sociology*, 1963, *68*, 481-486.

Kogan, N. *Cognitive Styles in Infancy and Early Childhood*. Hillsdale, N.J.: Lawrence Erlbaum, 1976.

Kohlberg, L. Stage and sequence: The cognitive-developmental approach to socialization. In: D. A. Goslin (Ed.), *Handbook of Socialization Theory and Research*. Chicago: Rand McNally, 1969.

Kohlberg, L. Moral stages and moralization: The cognitive-developmental approach. In: T. Lickona (Ed.), *Moral Development and Behavior: Theory, Research, and Social Issues*. New York: Holt, Rinehart & Winston, 1976.

Kuhn, T. S. *The Structure of Scientific Revolution*. Chicago: University of Chicago Press, 1962.

Lambert, W. E. The effects of bilingualism on the individual: Cognitive and sociocultural consequences. In: P. A. Hornby (Ed.), *Bilingualism: Psychological, social and educational implications*. New York: Academic Press, 1977.

Lehman, S. Psychology, ecology and community: A setting for evaluative research. In: E. L. Struening and M. Guttentag (Eds.), *Handbook of Evaluation Research Volume I*. Beverly Hills, CA: Sage, 1975.

Lewis, M. and Rosenblum, L. A. (Eds.), *The Effect of the Infant on its Caregiver*. New York: John Wiley & Sons, 1974.

Livesley, W. J. and Bromley, D. B. *Person Perception in Childhood and Adolescence*. London: Wiley, 1973.

Mackey, W. F. The description of bilingualism. In: J. A. Fishman (Ed.), *Readings in the Sociology of Language*. Third edition. The Hague: Mouton, 1972.

McCandless, B. R. and Evans, E. D. *Children and Youth Psychosocial Development*. Hinsdale, IL: Dryden Press, 1973.

McElroy, W. D. The global age: Roles of basic and applied research. *Science*, 1977, *196*(4287), 267-270.

McWhitney, W. Organizational form, decision modalities and the environment. *Human Relations*, 1968, *21*, 269-281.

Mead, G. H. *Mind, Self and Society from the Standpoint of a Social Behaviorist*. Chicago: University of Chicago Press, 1934.

Meenaghan, T. M. What means "community"? *Social Work*, 1972, *17*(6), 94-98.

Minuchin, P., Biber, B., Shapiro, E., and Zimiles, H. *The Psychological Impact of the School Experience*. New York: Basic Books, 1969.

Moos, R. H. *The Human Context: Environmental Determinants of Behavior*. New York: John Wiley & Sons, 1976.

Moos, R. H. and Insel, P. M. (Eds.) *Issues in Social Ecology: Human Milieus*. Palo Alto, CA: National Press Books, 1974.

Mussen, P. *The Psychological Development of the Child*. Second edition. Englewood Cliffs, N.J.: Prentice-Hall, 1973.

Olsen, M. *The Process of Social Organization*. New York: Holt, Rinehart, & Winston, 1968.

Padilla, A. M. and Liebman, E. Language acquisition in the bilingual child. *The Bilingual Review/La Revista Bilingüe*, 1975, *2*, 34-55.

Padilla, A. M. and Lindholm, K. J. Acquisition of bilingualism: A descriptive analysis of the linguistic structures of Spanish/English speaking children. In: G. Keller (Ed.), *Bilingualism in the Bicentennial and Beyond*. New York: The Bilingual Review/La Revista Bilingüe Press, 1976.

Padilla, A. M., Olmedo, E. L., Lopez, S., and Perez, R. *Hispanic Mental Health Bibliography II*. Los Angeles: Spanish Speaking Mental Health Research Center, UCLA, Monograph No. 6, 1978.

Padilla, A. M. and Ruiz, R. A. *Latino Mental Health: A Review of Literature* (DHEW Publication No. [HSM] 73-9143). Washington, D.C.: U.S. Government Printing Office, 1973.

Padilla, E. R., Padilla, A. M., Ramirez, R., Morales, A., and Olmedo, E. L. *Inhalant Marijuana and Alcohol Abuse Among Barrio Children and Adolescents*. Los Angeles: Spanish Speaking Mental Health Research Center, UCLA, Occasional Paper No. 4, 1977.

Padilla, A. M., Ruiz, R. A., and Rice, A. *Perception of Self and Future Achievement among Children of Different Ethnic Backgrounds*. Unpublished manuscript, 1973.

Petersen, B. and Ramirez, M., III Real-ideal self disparity in Negro and Mexican American children. *Psychology*, 1971, *8*(3), 22-28.

Piaget, J. *Play, Dreams, and Imitation in Childhood*. C. Catteguo & F. M. Hodgson, trans. New York: Norton, 1962.

Piaget, J. *Six Psychological Studies*. New York: Random House, 1967.

Ramirez, M. III and Castañeda, A. *Cultural Democracy, Bicognitive Development and Education*. New York: Academic Press, 1974.

Ramirez, M. and Price-Williams, D. R. Cognitive styles of children of three ethnic groups in the United States. *Journal of Cross-Cultural Psychology*, 1974, *5*(2), 212-219.

Rice, A. S., Ruiz, R. A., and Padilla, A. M. Person perception, self-identity, and ethnic group preference in Anglo, Black, and Chicano pre-school and third grade children. *Journal of Cross-Cultural Psychology*, 1974, *5*(1), 100-108.

Ryan, E. B. and Carranza, M. A. Evaluative reactions of adolescents toward speakers of standard English and Mexican-American accented English. *Journal of Personality and Social Psychology*, 1975, *31*, 855-863.

Ryan, E. M., Carranza, M. A., and Moffie, R. W. *Reactions toward Varying Degrees of Accentedness in the Speech of Spanish-English Bilinguals*. Unpublished manuscript, University of Notre Dame, 1974.

Saville, M. R. and Troike, R. C. *A Handbook of Bilingual Education*. Revised edition. Washington, D.C.: Teachers of English to Speakers of Other Languages, 1971.

Sells, S. B. Ecology and the science of psychology. *Multivariate Behavioral Research*, 1966, *1*, 131-144.

Selman, R. L. Social-cognitive understanding: A guide to educational and clinical practice. In: T. Lickona (Ed.), *Moral Development and Behavior: Theory, Research and Social Issues.* New York: Holt, Rinehart, & Winston, 1976.

Shantz, C. U. The development of social cognition. In: E. M. Hetherington (Ed.), *Review of Child Development Research* Volume 5. Chicago: University of Chicago Press, 1975.

Spivak, G. and Shure, M. B. *Social Adjustment of Young Children.* San Francisco: Jossey-Bass, 1974.

Sundberg, N. D. *Assessment of Persons.* Englewood Cliffs, N.J.: Prentice-Hall, 1977.

Susser, M. Epidemiological models. In: E. L. Struening and M. Guttentag (Eds.), *Handbook of Evaluation and Research* Volume 1. Beverly Hills, CA: Sage Publications, 1975.

Taylor, D. M. Bilingualism and intergroup relations. In: P. A. Hornby (Ed.), *Bilingualism: Psychological, Social and Educational Implications.* New York: Academic Press, 1977.

Thompson, J. A. *Beyond words: Nonverbal Communication in the Classroom.* New York: Citation Press, 1973.

U.S. Commission on Civil Rights. *Mexican American Education Study, Reports 1-6.* Washington, D.C.: U.S. Government Printing Office, 1971-1974.

Wachtel, P. L. Field dependence and psychological differentiation: Reexamination. *Perceptual and Motor Skills,* 1972, *35,* 179-189.

White, B. *Human Infants.* Englewood Cliffs, N.J.: Prentice-Hall, 1971.

Whiting, J. W. M. Resource mediation and learning by identification. In: I. Iscoe and H. Stevenson (Eds.), *Personality Development in Children.* Austin: The University of Texas Press, 1960.

Willems, E. P. An ecological orientation in psychology. *Merrill-Palmer Quarterly of Behavior and Development,* 1965, *11,* 317-343.

Witkin, H. A. *The Role of Cognitive Style in Academic Performance and in Teacher-Student Relations.* Princeton, N.J.: Educational Testing Service, 1973.

Yarrow, L. J., Rubenstein, J. L., and Pederson, F. A. *Infant and Environment: Early Cognitive and Motivational Development.* Washington, D.C.: Hemisphere, 1975.

Epilogue:

Poverty: The Greatest and Severest Handicapping Condition in Childhood

Gloria Johnson Powell, M.D.

and Rodney N. Powell, M.D., M.P.H.

Hopelessness is a home in a fetid ghetto flat where children make morbid sport of chasing cockroaches or dodging rats. There may never be hot water for bathing or a working bathtub to put it in—or any other functioning plumbing. Under these conditions afflictions such as lead poisoning and severe influenza are common . . . Nobody starves, but many people are malnourished on a diet of hotdogs, Twinkies, Fritos, soda pop and whatever can be fished out of the garbage can. Alcoholism abounds; heroin is a favorite route of escape. Another road to fantasy is the T.V. set. On it dances the images of the good life in middle class America, visions that inspire envy and frustrations (American Underclass: Destitute and Desparate in the Land of Plenty. Time Magazine, August 29, 1977, p. 17).

DEFINITIONS OF POVERTY

Wilber (1972) has established a general framework for the measurement and systematic analysis of poverty. He defines poverty as "a result of interrelationships among the resources of a region and their mobilization" (p. 11). According to his definition, "poverty, then, is the lack of resources and/or the inability to employ resources as a means of attaining a goal." The nature of poverty includes the following aspects in Wilber's analysis:

1. Poverty is a multidimensional system with measureable properties.

2. Most poverty properties are continual.
3. Poverty properties of regions differ from those of individuals and families.
4. Determinants of poverty properties include background and intermediate factors (p. 11-12).

Viewing poverty as a consequence of interaction between resources and their mobilization, he describes seven indicators of regional poverty: resource poverty, norm poverty, social class poverty, poverty of information facility and service poverty, economic poverty, and policy poverty. More specifically, Wilber's assumptions of the nature of poverty can be viewed in five important ways. First, as a multidimensional system, poverty is an abstract construction and therefore cannot be quantified or measured; only its characteristics such as income and employment can. Secondly, the dichotomy between the poor and the non-poor is inaccurate in that income distribution operates along a continuum just as other characteristics of poverty do. Thirdly, regional poverty is not merely the sum of individual poverty but is composed of the particular characteristics of poverty of its residents. In addition, the regional poverty indicators can also be viewed as etiological factors which perpetuate poverty. Fourthly and most importantly, poverty is not static and the characteristics of poverty change over time. As such it is part of the life cycle and an integral part of social processes occurring over time. The fifth and final assumption is that determinants and characteristics of poverty should be viewed as a multifactorial model in order to take into account the influence of causes as well as those factors that are antecedent or temporal to certain causes, including the intensity of their effects. In an earlier paper, Wilber (1971) has developed a general systems model of poverty which is preceded by a fuller discussion of the determinants of poverty. His analytical approach, though somewhat esoteric, is useful as we as human service planners anticipate ways in which to min-

imize the effects of poverty and mobilize resources to meet the needs of the poor. This paper will deal with the multifaceted consequences of poverty; the reader is advised to remember Wilber's analytical approach to the subject as a way of perceiving processes of intervention.

Gronbjerg, Street, and Suttles (1978) pay particular attention to the changing concepts and definitions of poverty.

The 'reality' of poverty has continuously been identified, observed, and analyzed. To that extent poverty is social, perhaps even a sociological creation. However, it is crucial to examine in which ways society creates, maintains, and selects the victims of poverty (p. 66).

Miller and Roby (1970) offer a definition of poverty that includes "the absence of income, assets, basic services, self-respect, opportunities for education and social mobility, and participation in many forms of decision making" (in Grønbjerg et al., p. 66). The difficulty with such a definition is that it obscures the identity and number of the poor as well as creating innumerable difficulties in isolating the numerous economic and social factors involved in poverty. Secondly, it creates a circular definition of poverty without taking into account the many poor people who are industrious and are desirous of self-improvement, achievement, and self-respect.

Fuchs (1965) advocates a comparative approach to the definition of poverty—i.e. an income level which is less than one-half of the median income. That is to say those people who are poor are those "who have fallen behind the standards of the society as a whole" (p. 65).

What emerges from the erudite economic discussion of the definition of poverty, whether it be the Hunter's poverty level (1965) or the Joint Economic Committee of Congress poverty level (U.S. Bureau of Census, 1976a), is that poverty usually gets defined in terms of low income and that use of standard income level does not keep pace with the changes in economic conditions.

Neither the definition of poverty in terms of comparative income nor the definition in terms of income share has received any wide endorsement in the United States. This may be for ideological reasons, since such definitions clearly tie the condition of the poor directly to the economic conditions of the rest of society and not just to the individual poor (Grønbjerg et al., 1978, p. 68).

What has occurred as a result has been that each state has established its own definition of poverty which, of course, leads to many inequities.

The Social Security Administration (S.S.A.) definition of poverty established in 1964 is inadequate in several respects but is considered by Grønbjerg et al. (1978) as the most useful for more closely examining the poor. The S.S.A. index gives a range of income cut-off criteria according to such factors as family size, sex of family head, number of children under eighteen years of age, farm-non-farm residence, and a nutritionally adequate food plan or economy plan designed by the Department of Agriculture (U.S. Bureau of Census, 1976b). The annual income level is based on the cost of food × three, based on data that food makes up 33 percent of the total budget for low-income families.

The advantages of the S.S.A. index as enumerated by Grønbjerg et al. (1978) are: 1) the circumstances of the poorest are clearly elucidated by using the most conservative definition of poverty; 2) it allows for adjustment based on variations due to such factors as family size and rural-urban residence; 3) the method used provides more information about the characteristics of the poor.

There has been an overall decline in the number of poor people between 1959 and 1974, 39.5 million to about 24.3 million, with female-headed families increasing from 23 percent in 1969 to 46 percent in 1974 (Grønbjerg et al., 1978). However, it is important to note that this improvement has benefitted *male* heads of households—*mainly white male* heads of households. The "visible poor" remain unchanged, however, and they are "those who are not just poverty-stricken but are also brought to public attention by their race, ethnicity, religion, regional origins or some other public claim that they have a distinctive background" (Grønbjerg et al., 1978).

THE SOCIAL AND ECONOMIC STATUS OF AMERICA'S CHILDREN

The effects of poverty on children begin before birth and can last for life. Babies of poor mothers tend to weigh less and during the first year of life have a death rate two-thirds greater than the nonpoor. The health problems that remain relate to the adverse effects of poverty; the lack of usee of available services and facilities; environmental hazards; and the fact of membership in a minority group (Calhoun, Gorberg and Rackley, 1980 p. 58-59.)

From World War II to the 1970s, the standard of living for all Americans increased steadily, including that for children. However, the distribution of income did not change. Forty-eight percent of all income is received by one-fifth of the nation's families and 4 percent of all income is received by another fifth (Calhoun, Grotberg and Rackley, 1980). The remaining 52 percent of all income is earned by three-fifths of the population. It is well-known that a child's health, education, later employment and earnings are dependent on the economic status of his or her family. Indeed, of children of equal intelligence, those who are from families in the top fifth income stratum are five times more likely to attend college than a bright child from the bottom fifth. In contrast, a child born into a family having an income in the top 10 percent is 27 times more likely to earn a similarly high income as an adult than a child born into a family in the bottom tenth stratum (Calhoun, Grotberg and Rackley, 1980). Clearly, the social and economic environment in which a child is reared is the most

TABLE 1

Children Living in Poverty, 1980

	Number	Rate
In Families	11,114,000	17.9%
Female-headed	5,866,000	50.8%
White	2,813,000	41.6%
Black	2,944,000	64.8%
Hispanic	809,000	65.0%
Other (including two-parent)	5,248,000	10.4%
By Race = Ethnicity		
White	6,817,000	13.4%
Black	3,906,000	42.1%
Hispanic	1,718,000	33.0%
By Age		
Under 18	11,114,000	17.9%
Under 15	9,755,000	19.1%
Under 6	3,986,000	20,3%

Source: U.S. Department of Commerce, Bureau of the Census, *Current Population Reports,* Series p-60, No. 127, "Money Income and Poverty Status of Families and Persons in the United States: 1980 (Advance Data fromm the March, 1981 Current Population Survey)" (August, 1981), Tables 16 and 18.

TABLE 2

Percent of Children, by Age, Race, and Family Income, with Mothers in the Labor Force, 1980

Race/Family Income	Age of Children			
	Under 6	6-13	14-17	Total Under 18
All Races				
<$7,000	30.3%	40.6%	34.8%	37.8%
$7,000-$10,000	30.3%	53.5%	49.3%	47.8%
$10,000-$15,000	41.7%	54.5%	57.7%	50.7%
$15,000-$20,000	45.6%	54.5%	60.4%	52.6%
$20,000-$25,000	45.0%	59.3%	61.6%	55.2%
$25,000-$35,000	51.0%	63.4%	66.7%	61.3%
$35,000+	47.6%	58.2%	64.5%	58.9%
Total	43.0%	55.7%	59.3%	52.8%
White				
<$7,000	28.5%	40.5%	33.6%	34.8%
$7,000-$10,000	36.2%	49.0%	47.4%	44.1%
$10,000-$15,000	39.8%	52.4%	57.9%	48.9%
$15,000-$20,000	44.0%	52.8%	59.3%	50.9%
$20,000-$25,000	43.6%	57.4%	61.1%	53.8%
$25,000-$35,000	48.6%	62.0%	65.9%	59.8%
$35,000+	44.6%	56.3%	63.7%	57.2%
Total	41.7%	54.7%	59.8%	52.0%
Black				
<$7,000	34.3%	41.4%	36.3%	37.9%
$7,000-$10,000	55.1%	66.5%	53.8%	60.0%
$10,000-$15,000	55.8%	65.2%	57.6%	60.7%
$15,000-$20,000	62.0%	69.6%	66.7%	66.7%
$20,000-$25,000	59.7%	73.7%	66.2%	68.0%
$25,000-$35,000	82.1%	81.5%	78.3%	80.8%
$35,000+	89.6%	97.0%	75.2%	88.5%
Total	51.4%	61.8%	56.2%	57.4%

Source: U.S. Department of Labor, Bureau of Labor Statistics, unpublished data from the March, 1980 Current Population Survey.

important predictor of a successful child-hood and future life. Given these basic assumptions and data, what is the current status of America's children?

The issues of health and mental health problems have been addressed in numerous chapters in this book. The basic facts of the effects of poverty on health and mental health are well known. What needs to be addressed is the coordination of services in meeting the needs of children and youth. However, John Mudd (1980) of the Children's Defense Fund has stated the real crux of the problem:

But the fundamental governmental issues affecting children in the 1980's still remain questions of public policy and budgetary resources, not administrative coordination (page 1).

Since 1909, at the time of the first White House Conference on Children and Youth, and each succeeding decade of the Twentieth Century, the United States has held a great national conference devoted to its children, their circumstances and their prospects. The origin or the stated goals and objectives of these conferences should not be impugned since they have made substantial contributions to the well-being of many children of America. However, since 1909, every ten years, the White House Conferences have repeated the same urgency, the same recommendations, put in the jargon of time, followed by almost the same inaction, the magical thinking, that somehow America's great strength, its children, free of handicapping conditions, will emerge, resplendant in the American dream.

The 1909 Conference was a protest against the use of institutional care for dependent and neglected children. The establishment of the Children's Bureau followed this and in 1919 another White House Conference was held on Child Welfare Standards. The 1930 White House Conference produced perhaps the most comprehensive statement on the biological, psychological and social needs of chil-

dren and is referred to as the Children's Charter. The 1939 White House Conference contained further refinement and development of previous recommendations. The Mid-Century White House Conference focused its attention on healthy personality development in the American child and the 1960 "Golden Anniversary" White House Conference on Children and Youth established as its goal, "to promote opportunities for children and youth to realize their full potential for a creative life in freedom and dignity." These lofty goals were followed by a dreary litany of hope, disillusionment, frustration, and finally despair because, unfortunately, the White House Conference on Children and Youth has been purely that, "white."

All of the gains, all of the benefits, may quantitatively and qualitatively be placed in perspective when one looks at what has happened to the infant mortality rate in the United States during this century. Granted there has been a significant drop in infant mortality rate for all people from the beginning of the century to its current rate today. Nevertheless, one cannot dismiss the fact that the mortality rate for the non-white infant is *triple* that for the white infant. One cannot dismiss the fact that the maternal mortality rate is *four times higher* for the non-white mother than for the white mother. One cannot dismiss the fact that the combined perinatal and maternal mortality rates have actually *increased* for the non-white population relative to the white population.

Looking at an array of the five leading causes of death at ages one to fourteen years—accidents, congenital malformations, malignant diseases, influenza and pneumonia, gastroenteritis for the ages one to four and adding nephritis and nephrosis and rheumatic fever and rheumatic heart disease for the age group 5 to 14—it is clear that over the last 40 to 50 years the overall mortality rate has decreased. The rate remains, however, consistently higher (and often as much as doubled) for non-whites than whites at all ages and for all four decades. Accidental deaths remain the major cause of mortality throughout childhood. The shift away from infectious disease as the leading cause of mortality is most significant in the white population. Infectious disease still play a major role in non-white deaths for all ages. In general, the pattern of leading causes of death among non-white children tends to resemble the pattern among white children at least ten years earlier. The fact is that, whatever emphasis we have placed on prevention in the past several decades, it has had greater effect on the more affluent families, that is, on white families.

From all the available infant health data, the U.S. can provide infant care comparable in quality to other countries. The data more than suggest that further improvement in our national ranking (presently twelfth in the world) will depend on creating a favorable prenatal and infant care environment for the low income non-white population. The increased perinatal mortality and increased rates of prematurity for non-whites as compared to whites in the United States are supportive evidence for this thesis. With the higher level of perinatal mortality goes a higher degree of morbidity. It can be safely assumed that the long-term effects of perinatal morbidity, though not precisely documented, mete out a considerable toll in human potential on the survivors. Indeed, it has been noted by many investigators that the non-white infant falls prey to an excessive continuum of risks, reflected at its extremes by perinatal, neonatal and infant death and in the survivors by reduced functional potential.

Much data have been presented which indicate clearly that epidemiologically and etiologically the most handicapping disabling condition in childhood is poverty itself. Those at greatest risks are the non-white, namely, the central city ghetto dweller, the rural dweller, large families, families with one parent, and families headed by a parent of low educational achievement.

What other health conditions have a target population of more than 15 million children? What other conditions have untold, unmeasured and probably unmeasurable devastating consequences in human development? How much energy and how much talent have been devoted to dealing with the pathogenesis, treatment and prevention of this rampant, handicapping, disabling condition of childhood? How many more conferences must occur before substantive change in the status quo is made? The burgeoning process of urbanization; the growing deficit of human resources; the widening gap between the haves and have nots; the air, water and soil pollution by noxious waste in our technocratic industrial society; deteriorating housing and sanitation; the mass communication media phenomena that heighten the reality of war, racism, and want; the despair turned to anger of America's poor, of American's deprived and exploited inner-city dwellers—all these forces are exploding in the face of the protocol of conferences and meetings. Our society is in crisis!

It is not the intention of this paper to deliver a harangue on all the social ills in an affluent society that permits its most obvious and devastating, handicapping, and disabling condition to run rampant in the nation. By any standards such as the biological, psychological and social well-being of children in this country, poverty emerges as the greatest handicapping condition of any named in this book. It is not that this society and its leaders have lacked facts about the handicapping conditions of poverty. Any experienced human service provider could give a list from 1 to 10 in order of priority of those things which would eliminate poverty as the most handicapping, disabling condition in childhood. Read again the platitudinous statements of the first White House Conference in 1909, or the closing statements of the White House Conference in 1970. Review again the scheme for the redefinition and reformulation of Title XIX, Medi-Cal Funds into a comprehensive health care system with an emphasis on disease prevention and health maintenance rather than just episodic disease treatment. Describe again the components of outreach which characterize primary or ambulatory neighborhood based care centers or the need to redistribute our health manpower. Reiterate the need to engage in the development of new types of health manpower and greater output of the existing types of health manpower. What about the need for new legislation to meet the growing demand for better housing or the essential components of a guaranteed annual income program sufficient to afford families an existence not on the poverty level? What about a program as simple as one to increase the availability of food stamps and the distribution of surplus food commodities? Does a description of the ecology crisis need to be repeated? Does the failure of the passage of the Child Health Assurance (CHAP) legislation need to be mentioned?

The glaring discrepancy between our knowledge of the conditions of poverty and our will to eliminate it has produced perhaps the major crisis in our society—the disillusionment of the young, not just the 15 million of our young under the age of 25 who are poor, and not the millions of those who are of minority group background, but perhaps the greatest bulk of our 50 million young people who are lost because of the hypocrisy between what we say we are and what should be done, and what we actually are and what we actually do. If we lose our commitment to our professed ideals and if we continue to try to live on platitudes, America's greatest potential, its children and youth, will be lost to it and America will then be lost. Our society has lived too long on its rhetoric, too long on its platitudes, too long on its promises and they have fallen far too

short of the stated and professed ideals. We have lived too long on the promises of White House Conferences. The White House Conference on Children and Youth are laudable in their ideals; they are short on action and accomplishment, particularly for the non-white.

The deficit is in our capacity to face the reality and the deficit is in our will to change the reality of poverty—to change the reality of the most handicapping, disabling condition in childhood with its deplorable, handicapping effects on the 6 million non-white children in the United States of America and equally devastating disabling effects on another 9 million white children in America. If the plight of 15 million children and their progeny is not enough to generate a will to act, what is there to say? The greatest health problem of our time, the most disabling condition of childhood, and the most significant health problem for all ages is poverty itself. The etiology and pathogenesis of poverty have their roots in this country's capacity to delude itself into thinking that all is well and that we are doing everything possible.

All the past conferences and all the future conferences, all the past recommendations and all the future recommendations, can be reduced to one word — *will*. If we will to change it, perhaps something can be done. If our society does not have the will, then the will of the youth, of the 50 million people in this country below the age of 25, will either give in totally to the disillusionment and hypocrisy or, out of the ashes of the society that we have given to them, perhaps they will have the will to build one without poverty.

CONCLUSION: POVERTY, SOCIAL POLICY, AND SOCIAL CHANGE

The neo-conservatives would have us believe that inequality is no longer a serious problem. They would argue that inequality is decreasing through "the natural workings of the economy" or "through the transfer payments of the welfare state" (Steinfels, 1979). In fact they would try to convince us that "inequality is on the whole a good thing because it induces incentives to succeed" (Grubb and Lazerson, 1980, p. 410) The theme of DeLone's (1979) book *Small Futures* argues instead that reforms to improve the worst in this capitalist system have not altered the basic structure of inequality. The major thrust of his argument is that it is not feasible to achieve real equality of opportunity in an inegalitarian society. Grubb and Lazerson (1980) contend that De-Lone's book is "a major indictment of American policy toward families and children" which is currently embodied in the neo-conservative movement to eliminate government from private lives by destroying social welfare programs.

Grønbjerg et al. (1978) have noted that although there may be fewer poor people in America today, their poverty is more desperate. Indeed, the poor have become poorer in all categories. Concurring with such data, de Lone (1979) concludes that it is a "penalty to be born poor" in America. Likewise, "it is a compounding penalty to be born to parents with little education" but "all these penalties are increased still more for children in racial minorities" (p. 4).

That is why this book needed to be written.

REFERENCES

The American underclass: Destitute and desperate in the land of plenty. *Time Magazine*, August 29, 1977, 14-27.

Calhoun, J. A., Grotberg, E. H., and Rackley, W. R. *The Status of Children, Youth and Families, 1979*. DHHS Publication No. (OHDS.) 80-30274.

U.S. Department of Health and Human Services. Washington, D.C.: U.S. Government Printing Offices, 1980.

De Lone, R. H. (for the Carnegie Council on Children). *Small Futures: Children, Inequality, and the Limits of Liberal Reform*. New York: Harcourt, Brace, Jovanovich, 1979.

Fuchs, V. Toward a theory of poverty. In: Task Force on Economic Growth and Opportunity. Washington, D.C.: U.S. Chamber of Commerce, 1965.

Grønbjerg, K., Street, D., and Suttles, G. D. *Poverty and Social Change*. Chicago: University of Chicago Press, 1978.

Grubb, W. and Lazerson, M. Children, the state, and the limits of liberalism: An essay review of small futures: Children, inequality, and the limits of liberal reform by Richard H. de Lone. *Harvard Educational Review*, August 1980, *50*, 3, 407-414.

Hunter, R. *Poverty: Social Consequences in the Progressive Era*. New York: Harper & Row, 1965.

Jencks, C. Making it: Can the odds be evened? *Psychology Today*, July 1979, 35-39.

Miller, S. M. and Roby, P. *The Future of Inequality*. New York: Basic Books, 1970.

Mudd, J. Services coordination and children. Paper prepared by Children's Defense Fund for the National Academy of Public Administration and Council of State Government. Washington, D.C.: Children's Defense Fund, 1980.

Steinfels, P. *The Neo-Conservatives: The Men Who Are Changing American Politics*. New York: Simon and Schuster, 1979.

United States Bureau of Census. *Current Population Reports Series: Money, Income in 1974 of Families and Persons in the United States*. P-60, No. 101. Washington, D.C.: U.S. Government Printing Office, 1976a.

United States Bureau of Census. *Current Population Reports: Money, Income, and Poverty Status of Families and Persons in the United States 1975 and 1974 Revisions*. Series P-60, No. 103. Advance report. Washington, D.C.: U.S. Government Printing Office, 1976b.

U.S. Bureau of Census. *Special Studies P-23, No. 75*. 1978.

U.S. Bureau of Census. *Characteristics of the Population Below the Poverty Level*. 1977 Series P-60 No. 119. March, 1979a.

U.S. Bureau of Census. *Money, Income in 1977 of Families and Persons in the U.S. Series P-60, No. 118*. March 1979b.

Wilber, G. L. Determinants of poverty. In: G. L. Wilber (Ed.), *Anticipating the Poverties of the Poor*. Lexington, Kentucky: University of Kentucky Social Welfare Research Institute, Monograph No. 1, 1971.

Wilber, G. L. *Systematic Indications of Regional Poverty*. Lexington, KY: Social Welfare Research Institute, University of Kentucky. Reprint No. 2, July, 1972.

Name Index

581

Subject Index

589